Historical Roots of Contemporary Psychology

Under the Editorship of Gardner Murphy
and Wayne Holtzman

HISTORICAL ROOTS OF CONTEMPORARY PSYCHOLOGY

EDITED BY *Benjamin B. Wolman*
Long Island University and The Institute of Applied Psychoanalysis

HARPER & ROW, PUBLISHERS
NEW YORK · EVANSTON · LONDON

Historical Roots of Contemporary Psychology
Copyright © 1968 by Benjamin B. Wolman

The chapter, "Beyond Vitalism and Mechanism: Freud's Concept of Psychic Energy," copyright © 1967 by Robert R. Holt.

Library of Congress Catalog Card Number: 68-10810

CONTENTS

THE STUDY OF THE HISTORY of psychology is not an easy task. Psychology as a science is a comparatively young discipline, while writing about man and his life goes back as far as written history can go. Men have been always concerned with themselves, and there has hardly been any worthwhile thinker who would not dwell on the nature of human nature. This kind of reflection on human nature was usually a part of the traditional philosophy. Rationalists and empiricists, idealists and materialists analyzed human thought and action, and discussed *ex cathedra* the issues of mind and body, feeling and reasoning, and the overall nature of human nature.

Contemporary psychology shies away from these discussions. Psychology could have never become a reliable science by taking sides in the philosophical disputes of the past. Modern psychology is definitely committed to the search for empirical evidence, yet the awareness of trials and errors of the past and of their impact on psychology may add a good deal of clarity, depth, and precision to the contemporary psychological research and theory formation.

Certainly contemporary psychology is centuries apart from its nineteenth-century inception. Contemporary psychology is more sophisticated, more refined in the analysis of concepts, and more precise in methods of research, than the psychologies of the past. However, as Boring put it in his classic work *A History of Experimental Psychology*, "A psychological sophistication that contains no component of historical orientation seems to me to be no sophistication at all" (Boring, 1950, p. 9).

No science can ignore its past. Modern psychology has to be viewed in its historical development, in its interdependence with other disciplines, and in its philosophical origins. Several problems that perplex contemporary psychologists are rooted in past experiences, and the understanding of the origins of a controversy can substantially contribute to its resolution.

I planned this volume in a way similar to the one I used writing my book on *Contemporary Theories and Systems in Psychology*, following three main currents in psychological thought: (1) associationism, animal psychology, and conditioning; (2) critical philosophy, personalistic and cultural currents; and (3) studies of unconscious and psychoanalysis.

I did not intend to cover the entire ground; perhaps future volumes will do it. In the present volume, I chose a few significant ideas and systems, and have invited most-competent men to write on them.

The present volume deals chiefly with the nineteenth-century psychology with some incursions into the antecedent century. It is a series of essays especially written for this volume. No effort was made to secure uniformity in presentation. Some authors preferred to give an overall description, while others concentrated on a certain aspect or part of a system.

The main purpose of this volume is to point to the tremendous wealth of ideas and facts brought together by the forerunners of contemporary psychology. The authors of the volume dig into the past, searching for roots. They go beyond the textbook mentality; they bring new ideas and reveal unknown facts and interpretations.

From the start of the work on this collective volume, I have enjoyed the benefit of advice of a most competent scholar and thinker, Professor Gordon W. Allport.

I have consulted several colleagues in planning this volume. I am especially indebted to Professors Ross Harrison and Virginia Stout Sexton, who read several chapters of the book and did not spare their constructive criticism. Professors Gardner Murphy and Wayne Holtzman read the entire manuscript and greatly contributed to its improvement. Miss Sylviane Apel offered invaluable aid in planning and editing the book. In the last stage of work, I was assisted by Mrs. Sondra Gerber, Miss Barbara Gottlieb, Mr. Ronald Krate, and Mr. John Mete. The editorial staff of Harper & Row, has been, as usual, cordial and efficient. Thus, I must say, what is good in this book belongs to my colleagues and friends, but the errors definitely belong to myself.

B. B. W.

PART ONE

ASSOCIATION, ANIMAL PSYCHOLOGY, AND CONDITIONING

INTRODUCTORY NOTE

Chapter 1, History of Psychology in Perspective, sets the stage for the entire volume. It stresses two points. First, the necessity for a cultural-historical perspective; secondly, the need for a biographical approach. Psychology, as man's study of himself, has always been influenced by other sciences, especially neurology and physiology, religion, philosophy, and the arts.

All other chapters of Part One deal with associationism, animal psychology, and conditioning. Chapter 2 describes Some Early Associationists: Locke, Hume, Hartley, Reid, Brown, James Mill, Bain.

Chapter 3 analyzes the Historical Role of Johann Friedrich Herbart and his struggle against idealistic philosophy. Herbart's materialistic associationism was instrumental in paving the road for an objective psychology, but the true forerunners were animal psychologists. Chapter 4 describes Some Historical Roots of Present Day Animal Psychology, from the ancient origins through the nineteenth century, emphasizing the role that Yerkes played in the development of this branch of psychology. Chapter 5 analyzes the pioneering work of Sechenov, the father of Russian physiology, who prepared the ground work for the works of Pavlov and Bekhterev. Chapter 6 describes the work of William McDougall, who introduced the teleologic, purposivistic point of view. The mechanistic point of view, and the theory of conditioning, represented by Ivan P. Pavlov is analyzed in Chapter 7.

CHAPTER 1

HISTORY OF
PSYCHOLOGY IN PERSPECTIVE

Benjamin B. Wolman

Men and Nature

ONE CAN distinguish two consecutive phases in the history of the earliest Greek philosophy. The first phase includes the Milesians, Pythagoreans, Eleatics, and Atomists; the second, the Sophists, Socrates, the Megareans, Cynics, and Cyrenaics. The philosophers of the first group were mostly concerned with the universe, the philosophers of the second group with man. Plato and Aristotle dealt with both.

The necessity to deal with both man and the universe simultaneously was self evident to the two giants of Greek philosophy. However, it does not seem obvious to modern psychologists.

Early Christianity deepened the gulf between mind and body and man and nature. The Renaissance built bridges between the two sets of concepts. Da Vinci believed in the "identity between the microcosm of man and the macrocosm of nature," in contradistinction to the medieval ideas of man being separated from nature. The belief in the unity of nature and man, which was deeply rooted in the classic tradition and in Ecclesiates's comparison of man to animal, again came to the fore in Charles Darwin's great discovery. Man was no longer apart from nature. The human species was viewed by Darwin as a high point in the universal process of evolution, mutation, and adjustment.

Civilization is the way species live. Birds build nests; beavers build dams. Primitive men lived in caves; modern men live in skyscrapers. Culture and nature are not antinomies. Human history is but a fraction of natural history; it is a natural history of a certain biological species. Thus, the study of human behavior, called psychology, is a branch of the overall study of life processes, called biology. And the history of psychology is the story of what a certain species, called *homo sapiens,* knew and thought of himself.

Being a part and parcel of nature, man must not forget that his own behavior is but a fraction of the universal processes. Human behavior may be a higher level biological process; it cannot, however, be exempt of laws of nature.

3

Times and Men

The history of psychology is not just a history of a certain science, such as the history of chemistry or the history of botany are. For better or worse, all history of science is a history of how certain human beings went about the discovery of scientific truth in various branches of science, how they observed, reasoned, abstracted, tried, and erred. But all of these actions belong to psychology, for all of them deal with certain actions, namely the cognitive ones. Thus, all history of science is sort of an applied psychology, and the history of psychology is the history of what certain scientists had to say about themselves and others.

To make matters more involved, logic and scientific methods are inseparably interlocked with the psychology of the cognitive processes. Not all thinking is rational. Whenever scientists tried to establish objective rules for their conduct in laboratories, observatories, study rooms and lecture halls, they themselves have established these rules.

There is no reason to ascribe superhuman, divine, and infallible intellectual powers to a Descartes, Spinoza, Locke, Newton, Boyle, Darwin, Pavlov, or Einstein; all were members of the *homo sapiens* species, and were driven by curiosity and ambition, vanity and altruism, self-confidence and fear, and many other human motives. None of them lived in a vacuum. All of them were brought up within a certain cultural system, studied certain subjects, and were faced with problems presented by their ancestors and contemporaries.

Here is an example of this interlocking chain of factors. Descartes was concerned with the separation of physics from theology, for this was the burning problem at the times of religious wars and beginnings of scientific inquiry. Whether Descartes was afraid to express his true feelings in religious matters is still a controversial issue. But Descartes' times were certainly not too conducive to an outright rejection of religion, nor to an uncritical theological interpretation of the universe. A hundred years later, the Encyclopedists interpreted the world without resorting to religious concepts. But 100 years before Descartes's time no one could have known what Descartes learned from Harvey on the nature of living organisms.

Descartes had to split the world into matter ruled by mechanical laws of physics of his time and mind ruled by the traditional soul. Descartes's dualism of mind and body bears witness to the split between science and religion at that time.

When John Locke embarked on a sensualistic theory of mind, he had to face some Cartesian problems. I can imagine the reader frowning at my ascribing to this outstanding sensualist and empiricist certain rationalistic tendencies. But introspection was Descartes's method: Cogito, ergo sum! "I think, therefore I am" was Descartes's credo. Thus, introspection became the cornerstone of the new empiricism. Certainly Locke was opposed to "innate ideas" as developed by Descartes, Spinoza, or anyone of the "scholastic men," as Locke named them. According to Locke, human mind at birth was a *tabula rasa*. Yet, in his criticism of Descartes, Locke could never overcome

Descartes' rationalism; thus Locke's empiricism was more programmatic than factual. Furthermore, Locke's system was an empiricism only insofar as it was opposed to the rationalist tradition of erecting metaphysical structure unrelated to sensory data. Locke was a protagonist of Spinoza, as Hume was a protagonist of Descartes.

LOCKE AND HUME

The heritage of introspection perplexed both Locke and Hume. Both Locke and Hume dealt with their *own* perceptions of the world. Being empirically minded, they had to admit that they had had no evidence as to whether these perceptions truly represented the world as it was. Locke's world was composed of sensations and reflections. Sensations are observations of external objects; reflections are observations of oneself of the "internal operations of our minds" (1894, Vol. I, pp. i, 2). Hume questioned whether causation was a real happening or our supposition. Hume put all trust in the witness of our sensory apparatus and in nothing else. Our senses notice that one event follows another, but "there is not, in any single particular instance of cause and effect, anything which can suggest the idea of power or necessary connection" (1896, Vol. III, pp. ii, 1).

Apparently, the problems described by Locke and Hume were *psychological* problems. One may ask whether other men, besides Mr. Locke and Mr. Hume saw the world the way these two men did. In fact, Locke and Hume have assumed that their way of perception was the general way. Their ideas about how one sees the world became *the* psychological system of their times.

Needless to say, neither Locke nor Hume could have seen things the way twentieth-century psychologists see it. The method they used was the only available method at that time—the method of introspection. Yet, these psychological systems have not developed merely as a product of introspectionistic observations of these two thinkers. These two psychological systems were honest efforts to answer the problems posed by Descartes and Harvey—and the Thomistic epistemology and Aristotelian logic. The first steps toward an empirical psychology were paved with dead bodies of obsolete ideas and live bodies of new scientific discoveries.

FREUD AND ADLER

Consider the Freud-Adler controversy. There cannot be any any doubt as to Freud's impact on Adler's *clinical* work. But, as far as their basic philosophies and their views on man's place in the universe, Freud's and Adler's outlooks have been diametrically opposed.

Biographers of Freud and Adler argue whether Adler was Freud's disciple. The argument seems to be of special importance to Adler's followers and disciples, who are anxious to prove that Adler was an independent thinker (Ansbacher, 1956).

From the point of view of history of civilization this aspect of the Freud-Adler controversy seems to be of lesser import. Perhaps Jones (1953) was too partisan, too close, and too involved to be objective, but there is no doubt that Adler was a member of the Viennese Psychoanalytic Society composed of Freud's disciples, and Adler's early work bears an undisputable witness to Freud's impact (cf. Adler, 1931; Freud, 1924; Nunberg & Federn, 1962; Wolman, 1965a).

Yet, in regard to their basic philosophies, Freud and Adler represent two distinct cultural traditions. Freud's main principles can be defined as reductionism, biological concept of humanity, and deterministic philosophy. Freud's orientation stems from his academic years (Bernfeld, 1950; Glicklhorn, 1960; Spehlman, 1953). Freud's theoretical concepts are rooted in and modeled after the neurological and neuroanatomical concepts of the second half of the nineteenth century (Pribram, 1962; Wolman, 1960).

The term "reductionism" can be used in a methodological or theoretical sense. In methodological sense, reductionism means application of research methods of a certain scientific discipline to another, the one to be reduced. For instance, the use of neurological research methods in psychology is methodological reductionism. K. Lewin and B. F. Skinner have been strongly opposed to such a reductionism. Freud, however, was a methodological reductionist.

Theoretical reductionism deals with reducing of the concepts of the to-be-reduced science to concepts of another science. One can distinguish three types of theoretical reductionism: (1) radical, (2) hoped-for, and (3) logical reductionism (Wolman, 1965b). Freud hoped that "the future may teach us how to exercise a direct influence, by means of particular chemical substances, upon the amount of energy and their distribution in the apparatus of mind" (Freud, 1949, p. 79). Thus, his reductionism was of the "hoped-for" type (cf. Holt, 1965).

Freud saw man as a part of nature, as a product of evolutionary processes in a truly Darwinian sense. Freud saw human behavior in a deterministic continuum of causes and effects. To safeguard this continuum, Freud interpolated biological data with "fresh hypotheses" and "fresh concepts" of a psychogenic nature (Freud, 1949, p. 36). Freud's psychogenic concepts are derivatives of his neurophysiological ideas. Freud never excluded man from nature or psychology from biology.

Adler's starting point of view was separation of man from nature. It was not merely a difference in emphasis. Just as Freud's way of thinking reflected the tradition of the French Encyclopedists, Auguste Comte, Charles Darwin, and Herbert Spencer, Adler's system was a continuation of vitalism and neo-idealism. It was Immanuel Kant who counterposed man, the perceiving subject, to universe, that is the perceived object. It was Kant who counterposed "the starry heavens above" to man, to the "moral law within." To quote Brett, Kant "perpetuated the rigid distinction between the outer and the inner with its accompanying assumptions both that there is a radical difference between what we know of our own minds and what others know of them, and that overt behavior alone can be scientifically described" (1951, p. 508).

The Baden-Heidelberg school of neo-Kantians, headed by Heinrich Rickert (1863–1936), Wilhelm Windelband (1848–1915), and Ernst Troeltsch (1865–1923) distinguished between natural and cultural sciences. Adler was profoundly influenced by their way of thinking, and was strongly attracted by Vaihinger's (1925) *Als-ob* (as if) philosophy. One may say that Karen

Horney and Erich Fromm in philosophies that have counterposed man to nature are more Adlerian than Freudian. Yet, despite the deep philosophical differences, all neoanalytical schools did not go too far away from Freud's therapeutic technique (Wolman, 1967).

Freud's psychology belongs to *Naturwissenschaften*, Adler's to *Kulturwissenschaften*. To Freud, man is a biological species. To Adler, man is endowed with creative power and transcends nature. To Freud, heredity and environment determine the fate of all living creatures; to Adler, "not heredity and not environment are determining factors. Both are giving only the frame and the influences which are answered by the individual in regard to his styled creative power" (Ansbacher, 1956, front page).

According to Adler, the individual is not merely a case or an example of a biological species. "Each individual manifests himself always as unique, whether it is in thinking, feeling, speaking, or acting . . . when two people do the same, it is not the same, . . . when two think, feel, or want the same, there are differences" (1933, p. 59).

Both Freud and Adler tried to solve problems transmitted to them by nineteenth century philosophies. Freud's approach was mechanistic-deterministic; Adler's approach was vitalistic-purposivistic.

To discuss the history of psychology or of any other scientific discipline in an isolated manner would be tantamount to presentation of a branch of human civilization outside its true context. Even poets have been indebted to science. Consider John Milton's *Paradise Lost* (VIII, 122–130).

> What if the sun
> Be center to the world, and other stars,
> By his attractive virtue and their own
> Incited, dance about his various rounds?
> Their wandring course now high, now low, then high,
> Progressive, retrograde, or standing still,
> In six than seest, but what if sloquth to these
> The Planet Earth, so steadfast through she seek,
> In sensibly three different motions move?

Psychologists do not live in a vacuum. They are born in definite times and definite places. They are brought up in definite cultural settings, and are exposed in their lifetime to a variety of sociocultural factors. They attend school and college, listen to poetry and drama. They are, as men and scientists, actors and witnesses in the chain of historical and cultural-historical events.

Biographic Elements

Can history be truthful without biography? Is history a mere collection of one *Zeitgeist* after another, with human lives filling the empty spaces? Must history renounce its factual wealth to fit the philosophy of a Hegel, Marx, Spengler, or Toynbee? Must it be robbed of color, of personality, of individual happenings, of living matter, and become a fossilized science?

No scientist could or, as a matter of fact, did ever live in a scientific vacuum tube. All scientists, including those concerned with nature of the human nature, have listened to fables, tales, and myths; attended schools or had private tutors; were loved or hated by parents, spouses, relatives, peers, and neighbors; and witnessed birth, growth, decay, and death. Even the most objective, mathematized, quantified, and brainwashed brains have been motivated by love and hate, fear and courage, hope and despair.

Being human, psychologists communicated with other human beings. They talked and were talked to. All of them have had their little ambitions and great plans. Some psychologists were warm, outgoing, humane individuals, whereas others were pompous, dogmatic, and rigid individuals.

Psychological systems did not grow in a sterilized scientific glass tube. Pavlov did not like Bekhterev. McDougall did not harbor great love for Watson. Freud did not care for Adler. Jung did not like Freud. And Freud was sensitive about his Jewishness. Skinner, besides the Skinner box, created *Walden Two*. Pavlov, McDougall, Freud, and Hull had their heroes whose work they worshipped, sometimes emulated, sometimes criticized, and eventually opposed and denied. The controversy between Külpe and Wundt was not merely related to differences in their experimental methods. Nor was the Watson versus McDougall controversy void of human elements. Titchener's method was, to a great extent, representative of his personality and behavioral patterns. So was Watson's radical, and (before the economic depression) hyperoptimistic behavioristic theory.

The psychological theories of C. L. Hull and of B. F. Skinner are, to a certain extent, a continuation of the works of Pavlov, Thorndike, and Watson. Hull's system is a deductive, Skinner's an inductive brand of behaviorism, and both introduced definite refinements in research method and theory formation.

Both systems have been developed under the aegis of the logical positivism. This philosophy, though by no means a uniform body of reasoning, was a new brand of positivism, as initiated by Hume, Comte, and Mach.

The differences between Hull's and Skinner's neobehavioristic systems are breathtaking. A future biographer will still have to explain why Hull left hypnosis and became interested in mathematical learning theory; why the learning theorist, Hilgard became interested in hypnosis; and now the B. F. Skinner of *Walden Two* was the Skinner of the "Skinner box" and of operant conditioning.

Freud has used his own personality, as it were, for a most magnificent self-vivisection. Freud analyzed his own dreams, childhood memories, infantile wishes and impulses. Psychoanalysis has started as a psychoanalytic study of one human being.

Freud was certainly not the only one to experience mental anguish and turmoil, but it took moral courage and intellectual genius to lay bare the foundations of human nature. Certain elements are common to all humanity: an analysis of one drop of water discovers the chemical composition of all water. Yet, the history of psychoanalytic discoveries would have certainly been different, if the discoverer were someone else, and not Sigmund Freud. James's theory has carried much of James's personality. The theories of Watson, McDougall, and Freud are closely related to the way a certain Watson, McDougall, and Freud felt, thought, and acted.

To write a history of psychology one must write what certain men thought of men. These thoughts, sometimes based on fact, but often reflecting human bias, are called psychology. Some psychologists call their work "pure science." Some confine their scientific curiosity to what can be seen and experimented, others are driven by the insatiable desire to penetrate beyond the surface of overt behavior. The differences between the various psychological schools are themselves a fascinating psychological problem. Be that as it is, the history of psychology is making its first steps. To become what it should be, it has to include the history of sciences, humanities, arts, and all human civilization and, at the same time, never omit the individual scholar, his life, and his personality.

A history of psychology that deals with psychology only, tells an incomplete and truncated story, for psychology has always been interrelated with philosophy, mathematics, and natural sciences. The history of psychology should be viewed in the perspective of the history of civilization with special emphasis on the history of philosophy and science. The cultural-historical continuity will appear to the searching eye in an utmost convincing manner, for each particular scientific issue has always been a link in the chain of human thought and a part in the continuum of human thought. Every single research worker lived in a certain epoch, was influenced by its cultural heritage, and inevitably turned to seek answers to the problems posed by his contemporaries or forerunners. History is not an experimental science, but it seems highly improbable that Einstein's relativity theories could have come into being unless stimulated by the problems posed by Maxwell, Mach, Hertz, and many others.

REFERENCES

ADLER, A. Individual psychologie. In E. Saupe (Ed.). *Einführung in die neuere Psychologie.* 5th ed. Osterwieck-Harz; Zickfeldt, 1931. Pp. 399–407.

ADLER, A. *Der Sinn des Lebens.* Vienna: R. Passer, 1933.

ANSBACHER, H. L., & ROWENA, R. *The individual psychology of Alfred Adler.* New York: Basic Books, 1956.

BERNFELD, S. Freud's scientific beginnings. In *The Yearbook of Psychoanalysis.* 1950b.

BORING, E. G. *A history of experimental psychology.* 2nd ed. New York: Appleton-Century-Crofts, 1950.

BRETT, G. S. In R. S. Peters (Ed.) *History of psychology.* London: Allen & Unwin, 1953.

FOX BOURNE, H. R. *The life of John Locke.* New York: Harper, 1876. 2 vols.

FREUD, S. *An outline of psychoanalysis.* New York: Norton, 1949.

FREUD, S. History of psychoanalytic movement. In *Collected Papers.* Vol. I. London: Hogarth Press, 1924.

CLICKLHORN, J. & R. *Sigmund Freud's akademische Laufbahn im Lichte der Dokumente.* München: Urban & Schwarzenberg, 1960.

HOLT, R. R. A review of some of Freud's biological assumptions and their influence on his theories. In N. S. Greenfield and W. C. Lewis (Eds.), *Psychoanalysis and current biological thought.* Madison: University of Wisconsin Press, 1965.

HUME, D. *A treatise of human nature.* Oxford: Clarendon Press, 1896.

HUME, D. *An inquiry concerning the human understanding* Oxford: Clarendon Press, 1894.

JONES, E. *The life and work of Sigmund Freud.* New York: Basic Books, 1953. 3 vols.

NUNBERG, H., & FEDERN, E. (Eds.) *Minutes of the Vienna Psychoanalytic Society.* Vol. I. New York: International Universities Press, 1962.

PRIBRAM, K. H. *The neuropsychology of Sigmund Freud.* In A. J. Bachrach (Ed.), *Experimental foundations of clinical psychology.* New York: Basic Books, 1962.

SPEHLMANN, R. *Sigmund Freud's neurologische Schriften.* Berlin: Springer, 1953.

VAIHINGER, H. *The philosophy of "As If"; a system of theoretical, practical, and religious fictions of mankind.* New York: Harcourt, Brace, 1925.

WOLMAN, B. B. *Contemporary theories and systems in psychology.* New York: Harper & Row, 1960.

WOLMAN, B. B. Review (of H. Nunberg and E. Federn [Eds.], *Minutes of the Vienna Psychoanalytic Society*), *Amer. J. Psychother.*, 1965a, 19, 326-329.

WOLMAN, B. B. Principles of monistic transitionism. In B. B. Wolman and E. Nagel (Eds.), *Scientific psychology: Principles and approaches.* New York: Basic Books, 1965b.

WOLMAN, B. B. The common rationale of the diverse psychoanalytic techniques. In B. B. Wolman (Ed.), *Psychoanalytic techniques: A handbook for the practicing psychoanalyst.* New York: Basic Books, 1967.

CHAPTER 2

SOME EARLY ASSOCIATIONISTS

James Drever

IT IS necessary to start with a distinction. Associationism has been defined (Drever, 1952) as a psychological theory which takes association to be the fundamental principle of mental life, in terms of which even the higher thought processes are to be explained. Such a theory is different from any view or system in which contingencies of time, circumstance, and motive, though they are held to modify behavior, do not provide the only type of explanation, to which all others must be reduced. Keeping this distinction in mind, it is possible to reject associationism without calling in question the fact that associative learning does occur.

Historically associationism has been linked with the empiricist tradition in British philosophy, and to a lesser extent with the sensationism of Condillac (1754) in France. It has often presented itself in a context of protest against speculation and dogmatism: in this sense it has seemed to be a "scientific" theory. Yet there are good historical grounds for holding associationism itself to be in some degree speculative, and at one time or another it has certainly been dogmatic. The aim of this paper is to explore the discrepancies between prevalent beliefs about the origins of associationism and such facts as can be gleaned from a study of a limited number of source documents.

John Locke

The first of these is John Locke's *Essay concerning Human Understanding*, published in 1690 (1894). Associative learning has been discussed or taken for granted by many philosophers from Hobbes (1651) back to Aristotle. But the empirical succession in Britain through Hartley (1749), Hume (1738), and the Mills (J. S. Mill, 1869; J. S. Mill, 1869), as well as its counterpart in France, owed so much to Locke that his work forms a natural starting point, and to go back beyond it would be of merely antiquarian interest. Locke's *Essay* belongs to the literature of protest. He described himself as "an underlabourer clearing the ground a little, and removing some of the rubbish that lies in the way of knowledge; which certainly had been very much more advanced in the world, if the endeavours of ingenious and industrious men had not been much cumbered with the learned but frivolous use of uncouth, affected, or unintelligible terms." His protest was against the scholasticism which had plagued his Oxford studies more than thirty years previously. His "ingenious and industrious men" were such scientists as Boyle, Huygens, and "the incomparable Mr. Newton."

As a first step Locke was at pains to deprive certain widely held beliefs of the support they had through being considered "natural" or "universal" or "innate." This brought him into apparent conflict with Descartes, from whom in other ways he had learned so much. There was a misunderstanding over what was meant by the term "innate." As Shaftesbury pointed out, "*Innate* is a word Mr. Locke poorly plays upon; the right word, though less used, is *connatural*. For what has birth or the progress of the foetus out of the womb to do in this case?" (Fraser, 1894). What really troubled Locke was the claim that logical reasoning, proceeding by "clear and distinct ideas" could arrive at truth independently of experience, and futhermore that "good sense," or the capacity to think in this way, was "of all things the most equally distributed" (Descartes, 1637). Here it seemed was a door left wide open to dogmatism. After arguing in the first book of the *Essay* that there are no discoverable innate ideas, Locke went on to the eloquent statement of his empiricism in the well-known opening chapters of Book II.

Whence comes [the mind] by that vast store, which the busy and boundless fancy of man has painted on it with an almost endless variety? Whence has it all the materials of reason and knowledge? To this I answer, in one word, from EXPERIENCE; in that all our knowledge is founded, and from that it ultimately derives itself. Our observation, employed either about external sensible objects, or about the internal operations of our minds, perceived and reflected on by ourselves, is that which supplies our understandings with all the materials of thinking. These two are the fountains of knowledge, from whence all the ideas we have, or can naturally have, do spring.

This attack upon rationalism and defence of empiricism, is all too often equated with the emergence of a scientific attitude in place of speculation and dogmatism. But it was nothing of the sort. Descartes was the scientist, like Galileo, whom he understood and accepted. He was moreover a scientist whose experimental work had ranged widely in physiology, and embryology, as well as in physics. Locke, despite his medical training, was not really a scientist; and, although he admired Newton, he could not follow close-knit mathematical reasoning, a weakness which he shared with other well-known empiricists, for example, Hume and Hartley. His attempt to derive all knowledge from experience in the sweeping Lockeian fashion must not be applauded too uncritically. In fact, as we shall see, Locke himself was not consistent in his rejection of rationalism.

Locke's empirical approach was not so important for his psychological theories as was the elementarism to which he thought it led. The "simple ideas of sensation" were made the basis material of much of our knowledge. "Though the qualities that affect our senses are, in the things themselves, so united and blended that there is no separation, no distance between them; yet it is plain the ideas they produce in the mind enter by the senses simple and unmixed." This notion of composition from simple parts was typical of much seventeenth- and eighteenth-century thinking, and might perhaps be related to the growth of chemistry over the same period. What we miss is the biological idea of growth and development. We miss it in Locke, and we miss it in associationism right up to the present day.

But Locke himself did not compound his simple ideas by means of associative bonds. When he came to talk of complex ideas he claimed that "The acts of the mind wherein it exerts its power over its simple ideas, are briefly these three: (1) Combining several simple ideas into one compound one; and thus all complex ideas are made. (2) The second is bringing two ideas, whether simple or complex, together, and setting them by one another, so as to take a view of them at once, without uniting them into one; by which it gets all its ideas of relations. (3) The third is separating them from all other ideas that acompany them in their real existence; this is called abstraction; and thus all its general ideas are made." Association only came to Locke as an afterthought, and a short chapter on "Association of Ideas" was inserted in the fourth edition of the *Essay*. The aim of this chapter was to take account of the fact that although our minds normally proceed by combining, comparing, and relating, and so gain knowledge, they are sometimes influenced by accidents of time and circumstance.

Some of our ideas have a natural correspondence and connexion with one another; it is the excellency of our reason to trace these, and hold them together in that union and correspondence which is founded in their peculiar beings. Besides this, there is another connexion of ideas wholly owing to chance or custom. Ideas that in themselves are not all of kin, come to be so united in some men's minds, and the one no sooner at any time comes into the understanding, but its associate appears with it; and if they are more than two which are thus united, the whole gang, always inseparable, show themselves together.

It would be easy to claim on the basis of this and similar passages, that for Locke the association of ideas was an occasional weakness of our minds rather than the basic way in which they become organized, but this would make him too consistent. Elsewhere, he uses the notion of "habit" or "custom" without analyzing it, in connection with the compounding of simple ideas. It is abundantly clear, however, that although associationism may be traced back to the pages of the *Essay concerning Human Understanding*, Locke himself was not an associationist.

David Hume

Hume and Hartley do not seem to have influenced one another at all. Hume's *Treatise of Human Nature* in 1738 antedated Hartley's *Observations on Man* by ten years, but the two books have independent roots in Locke and Newton, while each author had a moral philosopher in addition, to whom he owed much, Hutcheson (1726) in Hume's case and Gay (1749) in Hartley's. J. S. Mill in the introduction to the 1869 edition of his father's *Analysis of the Phenomena of the Human Mind* called Hartley "the man of genius who first clearly discerned that [association of ideas] is the key to the explanation of the more complex mental phenomena," and went on to complain that it was a "disadvantage to Hartley's theory, that its publication so nearly coincided with the commencement of the reaction against the experience psychology provoked by the hardy scepticism of Hume." Without accepting J. S. Mill's evaluation of the two philosophers, his testimony justifies us in treating Hume as a minor figure in this context. He was to some extent an associationist, and he was a great philosopher, but his greatness and his associationism did not have much to do with one another. Hartley was not a great philosopher, but he was the first man to whom the term associationist can be applied without qualification.

But Hume cannot be left out of the picture entirely. His influence in his native land or across the Border may at first have been slight, but it was *"die Erinnerung des* David Hume" (Smith, 1941) which roused Kant from his "dogmatic slumber,"[1] and so played a part in the more sophisticated analysis of human knowledge to which the *Critique of Pure Reason* (Kant, 1929) gave rise.

Hume took from Newton (1729) what he called his "experimental method," and from Locke the notion of simple ideas, or "impressions," as Hume called them, arising in a mind whose role in the first instance was merely receptive. Newton has described his method "As in Mathematics so in Natural Philosophy, the invesigation of difficult things by the method of analysis, ought ever to precede the method of composition. This analysis consists in making experiments and observations, and in drawing general conclusions from them, and admitting of no objections against the conclusions, but such as are taken from experiments or other certain truths" (Newton, 1729). In following this line Hume reveals how little he realized what is meant by experiment. Moral philosophy has, indeed, this peculiar disadvantage, which is not found in natural, that in collecting its experiments, it cannot make them purposely, with premeditation. . . . We must therefore glean up our experiments in this science from a cautious observation of human life, and take them as they appear in the common course of the world, by men's behaviour in company, in affairs, and in their pleasures. Where experiments of this kind are judiciously collected and compared, we may hope to establish on them a science which will not be inferior in certainty, and will be much superior in utility to any other of human comprehension. Newton undoubtedly left himself open to this kind of misunderstanding when he wrote about his work, when for instance he said that "geometry is founded on mechanical practice, and is nothing but that part of universal mechanics which accurately proposes and demonstrates the art of measuring" (1729). But one who could understand what Newton was doing, could hardly have fallen into Hume's error.

Looking ahead for a moment at Hartley we find him taking almost the same line, with greater awareness perhaps of its inadequacy.

The proper method of philosophizing seems to be to discover and establish the general laws of action, affecting the subject under consideration, from select, well-defined, and well-attested phaenomena, and then to explain and predict the other phaenomena by these laws. This is the method of analysis and synthesis recommended and followed by Sir Isaac Newton.

I shall not be able to execute with any accuracy what the reader might expect of this kind, in respect of the doctrines of *vibration* and *association*, and their

---

[1] Mainly as expounded in an *Essay on the Nature and Immutability of Truth* by an inferior Scottish philosopher, "that bigotted, silly Fellow Beattie" (1770) who fortunately quoted Hume, though he did not understand him (Smith, 1941).

general laws, on account of the great intricacy, extensiveness and novelty of the subject. However, I will attempt a sketch in the best manner I can, for the service of future inquirers. (Hartley, 1749)

It would not be unfair to say of both Hume and Hartley that they were emulators of Newton, but that they failed, if not to understand his method, at least to apply it to their own subject matter. The case is different when we turn to their use of Locke. His views constituted the frame of reference within which both men worked. In particular, the sensory elementarism of Book II of the *Essay concerning Human Understanding* was never called in question. Indeed in the hands of Locke's successors it lost the qualifications and inconsistencies with which his candid and more genuinely empirical mind had hedged it around. Hume's psychological elements were the "impressions" arising spontaneously in consciousness, and their paler copies the "ideas." Impressions are linked to ideas and ideas to one another by the "gentle force" of association, conceived as somehow analogous to gravity: "a kind of ATTRACTION, which in the mental world will be found to have as extraordinary effects as in the natural, and to shew itself in as many and as various forms."

There are difficulties in presenting Hume's account of association briefly, because it is not always clear. He put forward a threefold classification. "The qualities from which this association arises, and by which the mind is after this manner conveyed from one idea to another, are three, viz. RESEMBLANCE, CONTIGUITY in time or place, and CAUSE and EFFECT. I believe it will not be very necessary to prove that these qualities produce an association among ideas, and upon the appearance of one idea naturally introduce another." Notice that where Hume says "it will not be very necessary to prove" he is assuming the existence of such abundant empirical evidence as to make even his kind of "experiment" superfluous. The psychological difficulty lies elsewhere, however, and arises out of the fact that Hume regarded all three relations as "natural," that is operating spontaneously without the need to envisage some sort of activity on the part of the perceiving mind. Locke, it will be remembered, pointed out that "some of our ideas have a natural correspondence and connection with one another," and went on to say "It is the excellency of our reason to trace these and hold them together." Hume could not follow this line, though not for empirical reasons, nor did he want to take the obvious way out and reduce all three to contiguity. He had a use for his threefold division elsewhere in his argument. Thus it is not too much to say that in at least one of its early manifestations associationism appeared as a theory advanced without solid factual evidence, and stated in terms which were psychologically indefensible.

David Hartley

The full title of Hartley's major work, *Observations on Man, his Frame, his Duty, and his Expectations,* obscures the fact that this was a much less ambitious undertaking than that of Hume. While Part II raises theological and ethical issues, Part I, with which we are concerned, is more a psychological than a philosophical work. It has the subtitle "OBSERVATIONS on the Frame of the HUMAN BODY and MIND and on their mutual Connexions and Influence." Though Hobbes had postulated a material basis for the association of ideas, Hartley, like Locke, a physician by training, gave an explicitly physiological formulation for the associative process. His medicine was not the source of his ideas, however, but Sir Isaac Newton, who could on occasion turn aside from brilliantly devised experiments and theoretical deductions to speculate casually on other matters (Newton, 1730). So in Book III Part 1 of the *Opticks* (4th edition) we find the following passage:

Query 23. Is not vision performed chiefly by the vibrations of this medium (aether), excited in the bottom of the eye by the rays of light, and propagated through the solid, pellucid and uniform capillamenta of the optick nerves into the place of sensation? And is not hearing performed either by the vibrations of this or some other medium, excited in the auditory nerves by the tremors of the air, and propagated through the solid, pellucid and uniform capillamenta of those nerves into the place of sensation? And so of the other senses.

Query 24. Is not animal motion performed by the vibrations of this medium, excited in the brain by the power of the will, and propagated from thence through the solid, pellucid and uniform capillamenta of the nerves onto the muscles, for contracting and dilating them? I suppose that the capillamenta of the nerves are each of them solid and uniform, that the vibrating motion of the aethereal medium may be propagated along them from one end to the other uniformly, and without interruption: for obstructions in the nerves create palsies. And that they may be sufficiently uniform, I supposed them to be pellucid when viewed singly, though the reflections in their cylindrical surfaces may make the whole nerve (composed of many capillamenta) appear opake and white. (Newton, 1730)

This passage has been quoted at length for two reasons. First of all because it gives the source of Hartley's physiological ideas, which are often regarded as his own, and not to be taken seriously. Secondly it illustrates a rather pervasive feature of associationism, namely, that explicitly or implicitly it tends to assume a physiology. Sometimes, as in this case, the processes assumed are speculative, sometimes, as Hebb (1949) has pointed out, they are old fashioned. Commonly they are both.

Hartley's version of Newton's theory ran as follows: "External objects impressed upon the senses occasion, first in the nerves on which they are impressed, and then in the brain, vibrations of the small, and, as one may say, infinitesmal, medullary particles. These vibrations are motions backwards and forwards of the small particles; of the same kind with the oscillations of pendulums, and the tremblings of the particles of sounding bodies."

Linked with these vibrations in an unspecified way, for Hartley was a parallelist, are sensations in the mind. These form the basic mental units: they are elementary as Locke described them; but there is no additional inner source corresponding to the "ideas of reflection" in the *Essay*. The vibrations of the brain substance do not die away immediately, their external stimulus is removed. Newton had already called attention to a certain inertia, whereby a whirling piece of coal is seen as a circle of light. Hartley quoted Newton and went a step further. Proposition 9 [2] states that sensory vibrations, by being often repeated, beget, in the medullary substance of the brain, a disposition to diminutive vibrations. These are like the original ones in every way except

[2] Warren (1921) says of Hartley's *Observations* that it had a literary form suggestive of Spinoza. Newton was in fact the model.

strength, "and differ only in being more feeble." Similarly sensations, according to Proposition 8, "by being often repeated leave certain vestiges, types, or images of themselves which may be called, simple ideas of sensation." Notice here that the word idea is no longer used in Locke's sense but in Hume's, in spite of the fact that "simple ideas of sensation" is a phrase often met in Book II of the *Essay*. Propositions 8 and 9 lead up to Proposition 10, which states that "Any sensations, A, B, C, etc., by being associated with one another a sufficient number of times, gets such a power over the corresponding ideas *a, b, c*, etc., that any one of the sensations A, when impressed alone, shall be able to excite in the mind *b, c*, etc., the ideas of the rest." Expanding this in the succeeding paragraphs, "Sensations may be said to be associated together, when their impressions are either made precisely at the same instant of time, or in the contiguous successive instants. We may therefore distinguish association into two sorts, the synchonous and the successive." The distinction between the two sorts of association is not of great importance here. Indeed other theories would tend to group both under the single head "contiguity." The need for such contiguity arises out of the physiological side of Hartley's argument. If we have to think about vibrations as well as sensations then they cannot act on one another when separated in time. To suggest the contrary would be to postulate what Newton called "occult qualities." Hartley seems to go further than he need in regarding the order of association as compelling. "It is to be observed that in successive associations, the power of raising the ideas is only exerted according to the order in which the association is made. Thus, if the impressions A, B, C, be always made in the order of the alphabet, B impressed alone will not raise *a*, but *c* only."

In Proposition 11, however, where the physiological side of the process is being considered, the position is analyzed in a remarkably modern way. To begin with, Hartley states almost precisely Hull's (1943) Second Postulate relating to afferent neural interaction.

Let A and B be two vibrations, associated synchronically. Now it is evident, that the vibration A will, by endeavouring to diffuse itself into those parts of the medullary substance which are affected primarily by the vibration B, in some measure modify and change B, so as to make B a little different from what it would be, if impressed alone. For the same reason the Vibration A *will be a* little affected, even if in its primary seat, by the endeavour of B to diffuse itself all over the medullary substance. (Hartley, 1749, I, Ch. 1).

He then goes on to explain the difficulty of "backward conditioning" making use of another Hullian postulate the perseverative "stimulus trace" which he has already described.

If A and B be vibrations impressed successively, then will the latter part of A, viz. that part which, according to the Third and Fourth Propositions, remains after the impression of the object ceases, be modified and altered by B, at the same time that it will a little modify and alter it, till at last it be quite overpowered by it, and end in it. It follows therefore, by a like method of reasoning, that the successive impressions of A and B, sufficiently repeated, will so alter the medullary substance, as that when A is impressed alone, its latter part shall not be such as the sole impression of A requires, but lean toward B, and end in *b* at last. But B will not excite *a* in retrograde order, since, by supposition, the latter part of B was not modified and altered by A. (Hartley, *ibid.*)

It is possible to discover several other ideas in Hartley which sound oddly up-to-date in his discussion of the motor side, though the term "vigilance" which he introduces aptly in a reference to muscle-tone probably meant no more than wakefulness. But for our present purposes there is only one further point that need concern us, namely, the claim made explicitly in Proposition 5 that "Simple ideas will run into complex ones, by means of association." This may be contrasted with Locke's claim that the mind makes its complex ideas by its natural activities of combining, comparing, and abstracting. Herein lies the crucial difference between an associationist, on the one hand, and on the other someone who was an empiricist, an elementarist, a believer in association as a psychological phenomenon, but not an associationist, in that he ascribed the basic logical structuring of perception and cognition to other processes. We shall return to this question at a later stage.

Though they were in many ways original, Hartley did not claim for his views any important departure from existing beliefs.

> The influence of association over our ideas, opinions, and affections, is so great and obvious, as scarce to have escaped the notice of any writer who has treated of these, though the word 'association,' in the particular sense here affixed to it, was first brought into use by Mr. Locke. But all that has been delivered by the ancients and moderns, concerning the powers of habit, custom, example, education, authority, party-prejudice, the manner of learning the manual and liberal arts, etc. goes upon this doctrine as its foundation, and may be considered as the detail of it, in various circumstances.

But the doctrine which Hartley wanted to make the foundation of so much else was, as a consideration of its sources clearly shows, not itself logically founded. On the one hand we find an uncritical acceptance of some ingenious speculations by Newton with no test of their relevance to physiology. To this is added a psychological elementarism which Locke had introduced into philosophy from empirical motives rather than upon empirical evidence. Finally there is this confident reference to "all that has been delivered by the ancients and moderns." Hartley quite fails to realize that it is the association of ideas that is a "well-attested pheanomenon," not associationism. Yet his was a very considerable theory, the successors of which have not advanced much further, in some directions at least. The high opinion in which it was held by so many able thinkers in the eighteenth and early nineteenth centuries was not without justification.

Thomas Reid

Not all, however, were convinced. In particular there arose in Scotland the so-called "common-sense" school whose views challenged both those of their compatriot Hume and those of Hartley. Though influential, its members were uneven in quality, with "a taste for the small facts," as Ribot (1873) put it, and a tendency to edify rather than enlighten. Yet in respect of both associationism and elementarism they had some shrewd things to say. In Dugald Stewart's *Account of the Life and Writings of Thomas Reid*, contained in Hamilton's edition of Reid's works (1863), we find this paragraph "The circumstance which peculiarly characterises the inductive science of mind is, that it professes to abstain from all speculations concerning its nature and essence; confining the attention entirely to phenomena for which we have the evidence of consciousness, and to the laws by which these phenomena are regulated. In this respect, it differs equally, in its scope, from the pneumatological discussions of the schools, and from the no less visionary theories so loudly vaunted by the physiological metaphysicians of more modern times" (Reid, 1764; also 1863). This passage is interesting for several reasons. Though Reid himself directed his attack mainly upon Hume; Stewart, in the last sentence, has Hartley in mind, and it seems that the two formulations of associationism, though very different, were thought of together. On the other hand, James Mill, who was a pupil of Stewart at Edinburgh, sharply distinguished between Hume and Hartley, and thought the latter much the more important of the two. It may be that by James Mill's time the "physiological metaphysics" had become less prominent. Joseph Priestley's (1775) edition of *Hartley's Observations on Man* omitted most of the physiological sections, and James Mill's teacher said that they seem "after all the support and illustration which they have received from the ingenuity of Hartley, of Priestley, and of Darwin (1792) to be equally unscientific in the design, and uninteresting in the execution; destitute at once of the sober charms of Truth, and of those imposing attractions, which Fancy, when united to Taste, can lend to fiction (Stewart, 1816). The part of Hartley's work which was later adopted and elaborated was on the whole confined to his psychology and its applications.

To return North of the Border, and in particular to the work of Reid, we find an essentially empirical contribution in his "natural realism." We start not with simple impressions which we must somehow combine, but in a real world of which we are aware. Consciousness of sensation is thus not the original condition of the mind; it is rather, in Reid's words, a kind of "abstract contemplation," attainable only by those who "with some pain and practice, can analyse a natural and original judgment." One is reminded here of Titchener's (1929) view that introspection is a skill, and sensation a construct specified by its attributes. Reid, however, is concerned to give an empirical account of the situation as best he can. "Perhaps a child in the womb," he admits, "or for some short period of its existence is a merely sentient being." This is a matter of history or speculation, and carries with it no epistemological implications. Mere sentience, in this account, may possibly precede perceptual awareness of an external world, but it is the latter from which we must start as our empirical datum.

One of the more difficult tasks is to distinguish between what is in fact given and what only seems so through habit, lore, and expectation. Simple sensations are no more given than chemical elements, yet to many philosophers from the end of the seventeenth century until the middle of the nineteenth they were taken for granted. It was realized, of course, that in our day-to-day experience they are found in clusters or in compounds, as Tucker (1768) and Priestley (1775) pointed out; but their existential status was never called in question. Sensations were both reached through analysis and yet somehow immediately presented too, so that they lived a curious double life at the beginning and end of psychological enquiry. The position is well illustrated by an episode recorded in the second edition of Locke's *Essay*.

On March 2nd, 1863 the "learned and worthy" Mr. Molyneux, "a thinking gentleman from Dublin," wrote to Locke as follows:

Suppose a man born blind, and now adult, and taught by his touch to distinguish between a cube and a sphere of the same metal and highly of the same bigness, so as to tell when he felt one and the other, which is the cube and what the sphere. Suppose then the cube and the sphere placed on a table, and the blind man to be made to see, *quaere,* Whether by his sight, before he touched them, he could not distinguish and tell which is the globe and which is the cube. To which the acute and judicious proposer answers: "Not." For though he has obtained the experience of how a globe, how a cube, affects his touch; yet he has not attained the experience that what affects his touch so or so, must affect his sight so or so: or that a protuberant angle in the cube, that pressed his hand unequally, shall appear to his eye as it does in the cube.

In quoting this letter Locke agreed entirely with Molyneux that the blind man, at first sight, "would not be able with certainty to say which was the globe, which the cube, *whilst he only saw them.*" This last phrase is one which a consistent elementarist should not have used in the present context. Instead he ought to have said that in the beginning there could be no object perception at all; that is, that visually the globe and the cube would not exist. But Locke prized candor above consistency, and we are all in his debt for the insights to which his lapses give rise. Here we find him taking for granted that there would be visual objects as soon as there was vision, and this on the whole is what von Senden (1960) and others seem to have found. The trouble is that neither Locke, nor the associationists who followed him, ever worked out the implications of this important empirical fact.

It is interesting to note that Molyneux, who was a tutor at Trinity College, later had Berkeley as his pupil. The presence of some of his ideas in *An Essay toward a New Theory of Vision* is unmistakable (Berkeley, 1709). Berkeley himself only contributed indirectly to the rise of associationism. His claim that apparently immediate perceptual experience may depend on past learning could have been exploited more fully than it was.

There would seem to be a case for teasing out two of the tangled strands in Locke's thinking, and suggesting that one of them can be traced forward into the thinking of the Scottish "common-sense" philosophers, and the other into the elementarism and associationism which is our main concern. The former alone is genuinely empirical. The latter starts with a curious mixture of analogy and assumption, and at no stage offers data in support of its claims.

The "Common-Sense" School

The "common-sense" school accepted associative learning without, for the most part, being associationists. Incidentally the term "common-sense" had a technical meaning which was still partly present in this usage. In scholastic debating an appeal to common sense was a way out of some absurd position to which logic seemed to lead. It was an illegitimate way out.

To this tribunal a professed dialectician was not permitted to resort; he was obliged to answer in form; and if unable to find a solution according to the rules of his art, his defeat was certain. Even at this day, an Irish tutor who should harass a Professor of Salamanca with similar subtleties, and should receive no other answer but this, —*common sense and the general consent of mankind sufficiently shew that your inferences are false,* would gain the victory; his antagonist, having declined to defend himself with those logical weapons with which the assault had been made. (Bayle, 1734)

The rules of the scholastic game would have saved us a parade of prejudice and lore from the lesser Scots, but Reid, Stewart, and Brown (1820) made a distinctive contribution. Stewart was not an originator, but he wrote gracefully and was widely read in England and in France as well as in Scotland. As has been mentioned he taught James Mill, who recalled his lectures with "delight," and Thomas Brown, who used the word "delight" in a similar context. Brown was more nearly an associationist than any other of the Scottish school. Brown followed Stewart at Edinburgh, and was followed by him, for Brown died early. Brown had taken over his father-in-law's courses, succeeding all too well in sparing the older man at his own expense.

Thomas Brown

Brown was born in 1778 and by the age of 18 was already embarked upon a voluminous correspondence with Erasmus Darwin, the first volume of whose *Zoomania* had appeared in 1792. He was a penetrating but disarming critic. "January 21, 1797. Sir, — I am sorry that our mutual objections should still fail to produce conviction. There is a delusion in intellectual optics, by which our own arguments are magnified, while those of our antagonists are diminished and confused, and mine may perhaps appear to me of consequence merely as being mine." Darwin took him seriously but they remained mutually unconvinced. Brown, though himself a Scot, felt it necessary to preface his unfinished *Sketch of a System of the Philosophy of the Human Mind* with these remarks.

The great defect of the system of philosophy of the mind, which has been generally prevalent in the northern part of the Island, so as to distinguish it as the seat of a particular school of metaphysics, seems to me to be a redundancy of divisions, arising partly indeed from imperfect analysis of the complex phenomena of thought which a nicer observation might have shewn to be in their elements the same, but still more from indistinct notions attached to the words *faculty* or *power* of the mind, and to the processes that are termed *operations* or *acts* of these powers. (Brown, 1820)

Yet in so criticizing his compatriots, Brown did not move across into the associationist camp. In particular, he was not an elementarist, but retained the more concrete and immediate starting point of the Scottish school. "In the philosophy of mind, as often as we speak of the analysis of complex feelings, it must never be forgotten, that the analysis of which we speak is virtual, not real, —that it has not for its object what is truly compounded of parts." "Feeling" here is a rather general term for mental content, rather like "idea" in Locke. Brown also attacked

. . . the system of Condillac and other French metaphysicians his followers, who consider all our feelings, in our internal processes of thought and emotion, as mere *Sensations* variously *transformed*. What the nature of the transformation is, by which the affections of sense become reasonings and desires, they have not thought it necessary to explain very clearly; contenting themselves with the mere fact of the priority of our sensations to all our other feelings, as if priority and succession were enough to constitute identity,—or repeating the unsupported assertion in many new forms, and application, as if mere frequency of asserting a proposition were itself a proof of its justness,—or occasionally calling in the aid of authority, and professing to consider themselves as followers of Locke, in a doctrine which is wholly unsanctioned by the very different views of that great philosopher. (Brown, 1820)

In the next paragraph Brown explicitly compares Reid and Condillac as equally erroneous but in opposite ways.

In place of the alternatives which he had rejected Brown seems to have advocated, in the manner of Locke, a mixed economy, but he was very tentative in what he had to say about it. He distinguished four kinds of mental content; sensations, emotions, conceptions, and feelings of relation. The first two of these need not detain us. "Conceptions" meant, not concepts, or not only concepts, but primarily images or "faint copies" as Hume would have said, arising in the absence of external stimulation. The "feelings of relation" present some difficulty. First of all "feelings" in Brown, as we have pointed out, like "ideas" in Locke, were rather general terms for mental content. Here, however, we seem to have something more in the nature of a construct, a "determining tendency" as Ach (1905) would have said. Sequences in the mind are not merely the result of contiguity; we can actively modify the order and arrangement in terms of other relations in order to solve problems, achieve goals, and so on. In other words, Brown is restating Locke's distinction between the "natural correspondence and connection" of ideas and that which is wholly owing to chance or custom."

Brown was not happy with the word "association," which he felt to have explanatory implications going beyond the data. Instead he recommends "suggestion," meaning by it to express "nothing more than is actually observed by us, in the readiness of certain feelings to arise after certain other feelings." To take account of the two kinds of suggestion mentioned in the preceding paragraph, he distinguishes between simple suggestion, where the sequences are determined by the temporal contiguities of the situation in which they first occurred and relative suggestion, where the links are dependent upon the activities and interests of the perceiver, as well as upon "natural correspondence and connection." So we have resemblance and contrast as well as proximity, and a reference to the importance of emotional factors. There is also a reference to "differences that are constitutional in the individual" and that continue, during the whole course of life, to give a peculiar direction to the suggesting principle. "Such are the differences of Genius, or of Temper, or Disposition."

It is unfortunate that the incomplete fragment entitled "The Physiology of the Mind" is little more than a set of notes towards the already tentatively entitled *Sketch of a System of the Human Mind*. During his last illness Brown set down as much as he could for the benefit of his students. His death at the age of 42 prevented the expansion and revision of what might have become a considerable contribution to empirical psychology.

James Mill

It is impossible to determine with assurance why it was that James Mill, a pupil of Stewart, and an admirer, with some reservations, of Brown, should nonetheless have given his philosophical allegiance to Hartley. There is only the bald statement by John Stuart Mill that "at an early period of Mr. Mill's philosophical life Hartley's work had taken a strong hold on his mind, and in the maturity of his powers he formed and executed the purpose of following up Hartley's leading thought, and completing what that thinker had begun (J. S. Mill, 1869). It is likely that associationism appealed in part at least because it could be combined more easily than could any alternative theory with the ethical and political views which were so important to the older Mill and his friends. Certainly he discovered nothing new in the way of data to make Hartley's starting point more plausible, and in the main his efforts were directed towards extending and elaborating a theory whose essential truth was taken for granted. Hence arose the carefree dogmatism with which he dismissed the kind of evidence which seems to be found in immediate experience.

Ideas . . . which have been so often conjoined, that whenever one exists in the mind, the others immediately exist along with it, seem to run into one another, to coalesce, as it were, and out of many to form one idea, however in reality complex, appears to be no less simple, than any one of those of which it is compounded." (J. Mill, 1829)

"The word gold, for example, or the word iron, appears to express as simple an idea as th word colour, or the word sound. Yet it is immediately seen that the idea of each of these metals is made up of the separate ideas of several sensations; colour, hardness extension, weight. Those ideas, however, present themselves in such intimate union, that they are constantly spoken of as one, not many. (Ibid.)

The phrase "Yet it is immediately seen" in the passage corresponds to "All that has been delivered by the ancients and moderns" in Hartley. It is an appeal to an assumption so pervasive that it can be used to controvert the very data which should make it suspect.

James Mill's pages are full of examples in which elementarism and associationism are pushed to their logical and often absurd conclusions. These have been propped and qualified by J. S. Mill, Bain, and others, in the footnotes to the edition of the *Analysis* published in 1869, and there is no need to quote the excesses of a theory in suggesting its basic weakness. Two illustrations are necessary, however, the one to show how great an explanatory function was given to association in accounting for cognitive processes, the other to indicate that even James Mill's elementarism had its limits.

Arithmetic, for Mill was dependent upon association. He wrote:

All men, whose practice is not great, find the addition of a long column of numbers, tedious, and the accuracy of the operation by no means certain. Till a man has had considerable practice, there are few acts of the mind more toilsome. The reason is, that the name sof the numbers, which correspond to the different steps, do not readily occur; that is, are not strongly associated with the names which precede them. Thus, 7 added to 5, make twelve; but the antecedent, 7 added to 5, is not strongly associated with the consequent 12, in the mind of the learner, and he has to wait and search till the name occurs. Thus, again, 12 and 7 make 19; 19 and 8 make 27, and so on to any amount; but if the practice of the performer has been small, the association in each instance is imperfect, and the process irksome and slow. Practice, however; that is frequency of repetition; makes the association between each of these antecedents and its proper consequent so perfect, that no sooner is the one conceived than the other is conceived, and an expert arithmetician can tell the amount of a long column of figures with a rapidity which seems almost miraculous to the man whose faculty of numeration is of the ordinary standard. (J. Mill, 1829)

There is so much confusion as well as special pleading in this passage that quotation without criticism is almost enough. The difference between the arithmetician and the practiced arithmetician is made to explain arithmetic in general, and yet enough is said, for example "wait and search," to suggest that association by itself is not enough.

The fact that a great deal beyond association is simply taken for granted comes out even more clearly a few paragraphs later, when an analysis is given of the term "weights." It involves resistance which is itself compounded of "the feeling attendant upon the contraction of muscles; and the feeling, or feelings, denominated Will." But weight is more than resistance since it is resistance only in a particular direction, and as soon as we have direction we have the "ideas of extension and of place and motion, some of the most complicated phenomena of the human mind." These residual forms of organization are prevalent in the thinking of associationists, though they are not always admitted. James Mill does not have much more to say about space, but his son made a very revealing admission about time. In a letter written in 1834 (J. Mill, 1869) he said, "I know not that anyone can analyse or explain succession and coexistence, when reduced to their simplest forms. The theory of association presupposes them both, and divides association into synchronous and successive. We must, I think, rank them as ultimate laws of our minds, or (what is the same thing in other words) of the phenomena of nature." Considerations like these still haunt the genuinely empirical student of human learning. "Certainly," said Bruner (1957), "Hebb is correct in asserting, like Immanuel Kant, that certain primitive unities and identities within perception must be innate or autochthonous and not learned." Yet John Stuart Mill criticises Brown's "relative suggestion" as a mere verbal generalization, and dismissed his psychology as "no outcome of Hartley's" to be classed as "an original but feebler effort in a somewhat similar direction."

Thus were the cognitive activities and structures pointed to by Locke and again by some of his successors, gradually eroded by confident reiteration of the associationist point of view, which advanced no data in support of its claims, and had to admit at the level of presupposition what it was concerned to deny elsewhere.

It may be felt by some that this critical analysis of an old doctrine has no contemporary relevance. Yet Hartley stated the Hullian postulate of afferent neural interaction, and said something very modern about the "perseverative stimulus trace." James Mill took both of these for granted, and by borrowing a little from Brown to supplement Hartley produced something that might just as well have been written around 1940. This was the claim that "there are degrees in association. One association, we say, is stronger than another: First, when it is more permanent than another: Secondly, when it is performed with more certainty: Thirdly, when it is performed with more facility." (Brown, 1820). In this context "certainty" means "correctness," and "facility" means "speed." If we move forward in time a hundred years or so, we find Hull similarly claiming that association admits of degrees, or, what amounts to the same thing, that there are differences in habit strength. In attempting to measure these differences it is suggested that we can use First: Resistance to experimental extinction (permanence), Secondly: *Percent* of correct reaction evocation (certainty), Thirdly: Reaction latency (facility). Hull did not stop there, but such additional criteria as, for example, amplitude of reaction, do not add anything significant. Turing to what Mill calls the "causes of strength in association" the resemblance is a little less striking, but mainly because of a difference in language. Both are agreed that frequency of association is fundamental, but so have all the other writers who have discussed associative learning. Mill's other cause is what he calls "the vividness of the associated feelings." This confused notion seems to combine stimulus intensity with drive strength and most nearly approximates to what we might call nowadays degree of arousal. Thus, although imperfectly stated, not all of Mill's ideas are out of date.

Alexander Bain

Though we must move back to Scotland for the writer who is generally regarded as the last representative of the first phase of associationism, we find in Bain (1855, 1859) more of the Mills than of Reid or Brown. This is no accident: Bain was born and educated in Aberdeen, and later went back as professor of logic there, but during his early adult life he was for a time a Londoner. At this period he belonged to the lively intellectual circle which included J. S. Mill, and later he helped with the annotation of the 1869 edition of James Mill's *Analysis of the Phenomena of the Human Mind*. But although the Scottish point of view is not conspicuous it is present, and Ribot claims that "The most illustrious representatives of the Scotch school, could they return to the world, would not disown their successor."

Hearnshaw (1964) suggests that Bain may be looked upon as a link between the older associationism and the new beginning made in America by Thorndike (1913). There is a resemblance certainly, and although Bain himself did not experiment he expressed himself more than once in favor of an experimental approach in psychology. More important perhaps is the evidence that Bain's texts *The Senses and the Intellect*, and *The Emotions and the Will*, both published during the 1850s, were widely used on both sides of the Atlantic. They met with less philosophical and theological hostility in America than they did at home, and, until William James's (1890) incomparable *Principles of Psychology* appeared (in 1890) Bain's rather stodgy but thoughtful volumes constituted for many their first acquaintance with psychology.

It was psychology rather than mental philosophy by this time, including as it did some physiology. Bain had a great deal more relevant data from this field at his disposal, especially the work of Flourens (1824) and Bell (1869), and his physiological theorizing was far removed from the speculations of Descartes and Hartley. But he was not a physiologist, was ignorant of important contemporary German research, and depended rather too much upon a medical textbook, Carpenter's *Principles of Human Physiology* (1853), the 4th edition of which appeared in 1853. The central nervous system described in this work operates at different levels of complexity but in the same basic way "An impression is made upon the peripheral extremities of the afferent nerves; and this impression, or rather, the change induced by it in the condition of the nerve fibre, is transmitted by the nerve trunk to the central ganglion. In this ganglion, the influence transmitted . . . excites a reaction change, the occurrence of which is indicated by the transmission along the efferent nerves of an influence, which being distributed to muscular substance excites its contraction." To which Bain adds the well-known analogy "A system of telegraph wires might represent exactly what takes place in the brain." There is not much more in Hull's statement nearly a century later: "The condition of organismic need and the status of the environment evoke from specialized receptors neural impulses which are brought to bear jointly on the motor organs by the central ganglia of the nervous system acting as an automatic switchboard.

But whether we can call Bain an associationist is open to doubt. He regarded association by contiguity and similarity as an important part of our mental life, but he said in as many words that no enumeration of the laws of association can account for all cognitive processes. He had something of Locke's candor and consequent inconsistency, and in his latter years, when the enthusiasm of his London period had subsided, we find him rejecting the extreme position of Hartley and the elder Mill in favor of a view in which such concepts as discrimination and attention play a basic part. He was modern in other ways too. He shifted away from physical/chemical kind of thinking, oddly combined with introspection, which characterized much of the older work towards a descriptive natural history, in which a study of behavior from the outside is recommended. He had some interesting views, too, about the secondary status of cognitive processes and the primacy of action, which are essentially Darwinian. If psychologists in Britain had continued to improve upon Bain as he had improved upon his predecessors, there might have been an earlier development of experimental work. But Bain was assailed by Ward (1885) in his article on *Psychology* in the 9th edition of the *Encyclopedia Britannica* (which appeared in 1885). A sophisticated post-Kantian analysis was directed against associationism, and Bain, perhaps mistakenly, acted as champion of the older view. Ward and his colleagues were victorious, but some mistook a legitimate victory over associationism to be in fact a victory over the view that there can be a science of human behavior. Acute armchair analysis, owing a little perhaps to the "common-sense" school but much more to German philosophy, held experiment at bay.

Yet experiment, when it did come, was purged of some old simplicities, as it was in Germany and France. In the States and in Russia the appeal of objective data and the strict control made possible by animal experiment have given associationism a new lease of life. But qualifications and refinements are multiplying there too. What is most striking, as we look back over this early history, is the resemblance between the "ancients" and the "moderns," and the relative prominence of assumption over data. Associationism has been our only really general theory since we began to think about human behavior. It may be that in this complicated field we have stumbled upon the right answer at our first attempt, that somehow or another we already find ourselves in the alley leading to the food-box with only minor obstacles to surmount. The likelihood seems small, for the maze must be large. Alternatively we may have been scrabbling for a century or two at the rather ill-defined end of a *cul-de-sac* whose entrance was rendered attractive in the eighteenth century by the rapid growth of classical physics, and, above all, chemistry. History would support the latter alternative.

REFERENCES

ACH, N. *Über die Willenstätigkeit und das Denken.* Göttingen: Vandenhoeck & Ruprecht, 1905.

BAIN, A. *The senses and the intellect.* London: Parker, 1855.

BAIN, A. *The emotions and the will.* London: Parker, 1859.

BAYLE, P. *Dictionary. Chrysippus.* London: Strahan, 1734.

BEATTIE, J. *Essay on the nature and immutability of truth.* Edinburgh: Rincaid & Bell, 1770.

BELL, C. *Idea of a new anatomy of the brain* (1811). Reprinted in *J. Anat. Physiol.* 1869, 3, 147–182.

BERKELEY, G. *An essay toward a new theory of vision.* Dublin: Jeremy Pepyat, 1709.

BROWN, T. *Account of the life and writings of Thomas Brown, M.D. with sketch of a system of the philosophy of the human mind.* Edinburgh: Bell & Bradfute, 1820.

BRUNER, J. S. On perceptual readiness. *Psychol. Rev.,* 1957, 64, 123-152.

CARPENTER, W. B. *Principles of human physiology.* 4th ed. London: John Churchill, 1853.

CONDILLAC, E. B. DE. *Traité des sensations.* Paris: Bureaîne, 1754.

DARWIN, E. *Zoonomia.* Vol. 1. London: Johnson, 1792.

DESCARTES, R. *Discours sur la methode.* Leyden: J. Maire, 1637.

DREVER, J. *Dictionary of psychology.* London: Penguin, 1952.

FLOURENS, M. J. P. *Recherches expérimentales sur les propriétés et les fonctions du systeme merveux dans les animaux vértebrés.* Paris: 1824.

FRASER, A. C. *Prolegomena* to Locke's *Essay concerning human understanding.* Oxford: Clarendon, 1894.

GAY, J. *Dissertation on the fundamental principle of virtue.* In W. King, *Origin of evil.* London: 1749.

HAMILTON, W. (Ed.) *The works of Thomas Reid, D.D.* 6th ed. Edinburgh: Longmans, 1863.

HARTLEY, D. *Observations on man.* London: Eyres, 1749.

HEARNSHAW, L. S. *A short history of British psychology.* London: Methuen, 1964.

HEBB, D. O. *Organization of behavior.* New York: Wiley, 1949.

HOBBES, T. *Leviathan.* London: Andrew Crooke, 1651.

HULL, C. L. *Principles of behavior.* New York: Appleton-Century, 1943.

HUME, D. *Treatise of human nature.* Edinburgh: 1738.

HUTCHESON, F. *An inquiry into the original of our ideas of beauty and virtue.* 2nd ed. London: J. Darby, 1726.

JAMES, W. *Principles of psychology.* New York: Holt, 1890. 2 vols.

KANT, I. *Critique of pure reason.* Trans. by N. Kemp Smith. London: Macmillan, 1929.

LOCKE, J. *Essay concerning human understanding.* A. C. Fraser (Ed.) Oxford: Clarendon, 1894. 2 vols.

MILL, J. *Analysis of the phenomena of the human mind.* London: Longmans, 1869.

MILL, J. S. Introduction to J. Mill. *Analysis of the human mind.* London: Longmans, 1869.

MILL, J. S. *The earlier letters of John Stuart Mill 1812–1848.* Volumes 12 & 13 of *Collected Works.* University of Toronto Press, 1963.

NEWTON, I. *The mathematical principles of natural philosophy.* Trans. by A. Motte. London: 1729. 2 vols.

NEWTON, I. *Opticks.* 4th ed. London: 1730.

PRIESTLEY, J. *Hartley's observations on man.* London: Johnson, 1775.

REID, T. *Inquiry into the human mind on the principles of common sense.* Edinburgh: Hamilton, 1764.

REID, T. *The works of Thomas Reid, D.D.* Edinburgh: Longmans, 1863.

RIBOT, T. *English psychology.* Trans. by Hartley et al. London: H. S. King, 1873.

SENDEN, M. VON. *Space and sight.* Trans. by P. Heath. London: Methuen, 1960.

SHAFTESBURY, 3rd Earl of. In A. C. Fraser, *Prolegomena* to Locke's *Essay concerning human understanding.* Oxford: Clarendon, 1894.

SMITH, N. K. *The philosophy of David Hume.* London: Macmillan, 1941.

STEWART, D. *Account of the life and writings of Thomas Reid, D.D.* In W. Hamilton, *The Works of Thomas Reid, D.D.* 6th ed. Edinburgh: Longmans, 1863.

STEWART, D. *Philosophical essays.* 2nd ed. Edinburgh: 1816.

THORNDIKE, E. L. *Educational psychology.* Vol. 2. *The psychology of learning.* New York: Teacher's College, 1913.

TITCHENER, E. B. *Systematic psychology: prolegomena.* New York: Macmillan 1929.

TUCKER, A. *The light of nature pursued.* London: T. Jones, 1768.

WARD, J. Psychology. *In Encyclopedia Britannica.* Cambridge: 1885.

WARREN, H. C. *A History of the Association Psychology.* Baltimore: Scribner, 1921.

CHAPTER 3

THE HISTORICAL ROLE OF
JOHANN FRIEDRICH HERBART

Benjamin B. Wolman

Between Two Worlds

THE STORY of J. F. Herbart's psychological system and its impact on the development of psychology is one of the striking paradoxes in the history of science. Herbart was neither a great and original thinker, nor a path-breaking research worker. His voluminous work reflects his lifelong oscillation between Kant's idealistic philosophy which he never fully abandoned, and the Anglo-French empiricism whose tenets he never fully accepted. Herbart's work was a rather unsuccessful effort to withstand the ebb of German idealism and to set the clock back to the times of the French Encyclopedists. Neither task was wholeheartedly undertaken, nor successfully completed.

Herbart was not what he believed himself to be. All his life he tried to prove how wrong Kant was; but his rebellion against Kant was not convincing, not even to Herbart himself. All his life Herbart paid lip service to empiricism but he simultaneously raised objections regarding experimentation. Needless to say, Herbart neither conducted nor participated in any empirical research. He accused his contemporaries of "being drunk" with idealism, yet his own hazy metaphysical system was somewhat less than sober. Though Herbart had full intentions of starting a new empirical psychology, he lacked the courage of a Freud or a Watson. Thus Herbart was not a pathfinder nor the first to develop empirical science. His was the last great metaphysical system in psychology.

Herbart was born at Oldenburg, Germany, on May 4, 1776. He studied at the University of Jena, was a private tutor in Switzerland and, in 1802, was appointed Privatdozent at the University of Göttingen. In the years 1809–1833 Herbart occupied Kant's chair in Königsberg. In 1833 he returned to Göttingen, where he died in 1841. He barely saw the world outside his study and the classrooms. He refused to get involved in the storms of his times or even to acknowledge them. His world was the world of books, and only books.

Kant's great disciples, Fichte, Schelling, and Hegel dominated the German universities at that time. Herbart studied philosophy at the University of Jena under Fichte. He felt indebted to Fichte for, as he wrote, Fichte "had taught him to think logically." But, because he had learned to think logically, Herbart explained, he could not agree with Fichte. As a university student he wrote a paper critical of Schelling.

"'These philosophers,'" wrote Herbart about Kant and the Kantians, "wanted to join with poets; each one of them desired to have his own poetry." Herbart complained about the decline of intellectual acuity and philosophical courage. He hoped that a day would come when this philosophy that imitated poetry would entirely disappear.

Herbart's voice was a lonely voice of dissent in the upsurge of idealism and romanticism. He accused contemporary German philosophy of being a product of fantasy, exultation, and romanticism. As mentioned before, he often compared himself to a lonely, sober man in a company of drunkards.

Scientists and thinkers live in a spatial-temporal field. The problems they try to solve are, in most cases, presented to them by their predecessors and contemporaries. Kant tried to solve the problems left by Spinoza and Hume, Wolff and Locke. Freud struggled with problems posed by Charcot and Bernheim. Einstein picked up where Faraday, Maxwell, and Hertz left off.

No scientist has ever lived in an intellectual vacuum, but few were more dependent on another thinker as Johann Friedrich Herbart was dependent on Immanuel Kant. Alfred Adler and Carl Gustav Jung were deeply indebted to Sigmund Freud, but gradually they had developed their own independent systems.

Herbart could never break the spell of German idealism. All his life he fought against Kant and Kantians; but like a defiant child who cannot leave his mother, he went back and forth, arguing and criticizing, proving and disproving, yet never breaking loose, never completely cutting off the umbilical cord that had tied him to Kant.

One cannot fully evaluate Herbart's contribution to psychology outside the historical perspective and the context of his times. The Aristotelian type of scholasticism was the underlying system, and all other psychologies were struggling to modify or to overcome its main tenets. The soul was believed to be immortal, the body perishable. Psychology was the study of the soul. The soul was divided into distinct parts that performed distinct functions. Hence the theory of mental faculties, such as thought, sensation, and conation, with conation being divided into desire, feeling and will. The question was not whether mental faculties existed but how many of them.

The Renaissance brought about an increased interest in the human organism. The soul became located in and related to brain. Harvey's study influenced Descartes who relegated all mental activities to the organism, leaving to the soul the function of thought (cogitare). Descartes, however, has left intact the idea of soul and God, and his philosophy deepened the gulf between mind and body.

It was John Locke who attacked "scholastic" men and their ideas, but even the empirically minded Locke postulated two distinct substances of mind and body. The idea of a "substance," whether material or spiritual, was rejected by David Hume, who wrote that the self is "but a bundle or collection of different perceptions" (Hume, 1896, I. IV, 6).

It took the daring of the French Enyclopedists to declare that man was a machine (De La Mettrie [1709–1751]) and reject the "hypothesis" of God and an immortal soul (Holbach and Laplace). Hartley [1704–1757] related mental processes to brain vibrations. While British and French philosophers made strides toward a monistic point of view, psychological problems were omitted by them rather than solved; and a great many thinkers, mostly German, continued the old tradition. Malebranche, Berkeley, Leibniz, and Wolff represented the opposition to the ideas of the Encyclopedists and Toland, to Hartley's materialistic associationism and Priestley's materialism. Christian Wolff (1679–1754) accepted Cartesian dualism and further developed the faculty psychology. According to Wolff, there are two basic faculties of the soul, the cognitive and the conative. Cognition and conation can be further divided into low and high faculties. (Wolff, 1732, 1734.) Faculty was believed to be a bare possibility to act (*nuda agendi possibilitas*) but at the same time it was a disposition or a prerequisite for any action of the soul.

Wolff's bipartite system was modified by N. Tetens (1736–1805). Tetens suggested a division of the soul into three faculties, namely cognition, feeling, and will.

Kant accepted Tetens' tripartite division. Fries [1773–1843] further developed the faculty psychology by adding three stages in the development of the three faculties, namely sense, habit, and understanding. Hegel's [1770–1831] system was also based on Kant and faculty psychology (cf. the chapter on Kant).

Viewed against this background, Herbart's system represents a definite rebellion against both idealism and faculty psychology, and a genuine though awkward attempt to reconcile metaphysics with associationism, materialism, and empiricism. Herbart's theory is a peculiar brand of associationism. For, in opposition to Kantian idealism, Herbart professed to join the British and French empirical scientists. "Forces are the true causes and effects of motions," wrote Isaac Newton [1642–1727] in his *Principia*. Herbart's system was similar, consisting of matter and energy, and associations of forces.

Herbart was impressed by Newton's mechanistic picture of the world. Physics was at that time mechanistic, deterministic, molecular, and Newtonian. All natural sciences were empirical and were dominated by the mechanistic and materialistic theories of Laplace, Herschel, Galvani, Lavoisier, Priestley, Linné, Bichat, and von Humboldt. While science was permeated with statics and mechanics, philosophy was full of Kantian speculation about the transcendent mind that viewed the world in the light of its preconceived, *a priori* set categories.

Herbart's system was a cumbersome compromise between the two worlds. It is, indeed, "a remarkable document of the philosophical fermentation in Germany," wrote F. A. Lange in 1876. "It is 'more striking' that so enlightened a mind [Herbart], with a genuinely philosophical tendency to practical life, could lose himself in the laborious and thankless task of working out a whole system of mental statics and mechanics from his principle, without having any voucher whatever in experience for its truth" (Lange, 1925, vol. 3, p. 163).

Herbart failed to set up a scientific system without metaphysics, nor could he develop a metaphysical system without some allegiance to science. He did not possess Newton's sense for reality nor Kant's keenness for speculation.

Herbart was neither an empiricist nor a rationalist, though he tried, in vain, to be both.

Philosophical Principles

Herbart believed that the three "laws of thought," namely the principles of identity, contradiction, and excluded middle were the only valid principles of logic (Herbart, 1813, vol. 1, pp. 72 ff.). Things cannot contradict themselves; if something is A, it cannot not be A. Any proposition must be either true or false; it cannot be both. Real things cannot be self-contradictory.

There is no knowledge outside of experience, yet experience may bring contradictory concepts. Logic and ontology are two different disciplines. The first deals with the laws of thinking, the latter with laws of nature. Herbart was opposed to Hegel's dialectical logic and even more to Hegel's assumption that the laws of dialectic logic were the laws of nature. The laws of logic, wrote Herbart, "are applicable to what is not and to what may be merely thought of. One may think logically even on things that cannot exist, but thinking does not make things exist" (Herbart, 1872–1912, vol. 12, p. 259).

Kant's critical idealism dictated laws to nature. Wrote Kant: "Hitherto it has been assumed that all our knowledge must conform to objects. But all attempts to extend our knowledge of objects by establishing something in regard to them *a priori*, by means of concepts, have on this assumption ended in failure. We must therefore make trial whether we may not have more success in the tasks of metaphysics, if we suppose that objects must conform to our knowledge" (Kant, 1929, pt. XII).

Herbart called himself a "Kantian of 1828" for he shared with Kant an opposition to speculative theology, scholasticism, and metaphysics (cf. Zimmerman, 1877, pp. 101 ff.). Moreover, Herbart has accepted Kant's distinction between the unknowable things-in-themselves and phenomena. In a sharp disagreement with Kant, Herbart maintained that phenomena were a product of things in-themselves, thus contradicting Kant on the two critical issues of epistemology and causation. To Kant, one's consciousness of oneself, the "pure original unchangeable consciousness," named *transcendental apperception*, was the source of all knowledge. The things-in-themselves are unknowable, except to one's self, the transcendental unity of all perceptions that prescribes laws to the observable phenomena. "All possible perception is thus dependent upon syntheses of apprehension. . . . All possible perceptions . . . must, so far as their connection is concerned, be subject to the categories." Thus, true knowledge is one's own knowledge, the knowledge of our own categories (Kant, 1929).

Herbart replied in an unequivocal way: "Critique of knowledge will never yield the true knowledge. We have no choice but to turn toward the things themselves or, indeed, our ideas of things, for, knowledge deals with ideas only. . . . Then our ideas have to be critically analyzed" (Herbart, 1828–1829, vol. I).

Obviously, Kant's analysis of the analyzing mind did not appeal to Herbart. The human mind must be turned realistically toward the outer world. Experience is the only source of knowledge, said Herbart, thus refuting Kant's critical idealism.

Yet even this refutation was halfhearted. Although, according to Herbart, experience was the only source of knowledge, this knowledge was not immediate. One has to distinguish between the *Sein* (being) of a thing and its *Schein* (appearance). The being of a thing is inaccessible to knowledge, but there cannot be an appearance without being. The appearance of things bears witness to their existence and is their causal product.

Kant maintained that things-in-themselves, cannot be reached by "experience," i.e. by sensory apparatus. What men perceive are phenomena or appearances as they are shaped by the perceiving mind and its space, time, and other *a priori* set categories. Herbart's phenomena were *causally determined products* of true things. Causation was a mental category to Kant, but it was a real thing to Herbart. Kant prescribed to the universe the logical order of the human mind and made knowledge dependent upon the a priori set forms of cognition. Herbart was a *determinist* and an *epistemological realist*.

According to Herbart, though the world is a world of things-in-themselves, the things-in-themselves are perceivable. All *Schein* (appearance of a thing) implies its *Sein* (being, existence), wrote Herbart in 1808 (*Hauptpunkte der Metaphysik*, p. 20). The existing things are called by Herbart *Reals (die Reale)* or units of reality. Herbart's universe was a manifold of *Reals* highly resembling Leibniz's monads.

S. Maimon introduced a causal interpretation of phenomena in another way (Maimon, 1790. Maimon also preceded Herbart in the classification and simplification of logical propositions. Herbart's system was however not a replica of Maimon nor a revival of Leibniz's monadology. It has revived the ancient Greek Eleatic system of the universe where things did not change. Each *Real* is what it is, and all activity is caused by interaction between the *Reals* that resist change. Thus, as Lotze (1882) has pointed out, Herbart has accepted the "uncomfortable assumption of their (the *Reals'*) eternal existence even before the earthly life." For, Herbart maintained, the true reality does not change forever. There are no true actions in the manifold of the *Reals* (Herbart, 1828, § 235).

This was what Herbart believed: Things are unchangeable in the sense of their being what they *are (Sein)*; things change only in relation to one another, in experience, as they *appear* to be (*Schein*). Herbart believed that he had solved the two dichotomies of "thing-in-itself, versus phenomena" and the "being versus change" by assuming that things and being are eternal, and change is an appearance created by interaction between the unchangeable units of the universe. Activity is not *Sein*; it is merely a *Schein*.

The true feature of the *Reals* is unkown, thus it is impossible to determine whether they are material or spiritual. Hence monism is the logical conclusion: the world is one, composed of innumerable units. The only thing we know about these units, is that they are forever the same *Reals*, unchangeable and resisting changes.

The reaction of the *Reals* to external pressure is self-preservation (*Selbsterhaltung*). The *Selbsterhaltung* is however a part of doing and not of being, thus it belongs to the realm of *Schein*. Obviously Herbart ascribed to the physical world the ability to resist destruction (cf. Drobisch, 1876, p. 20). Apparently, Herbart's self-preservation (*Selbsterhaltung*) echoed Newton's Third Law: "Every body continues in its state of rest or of uniform rectilinear motion unless compelled to change its state by the action of forces." The *Reals* are at rest unless disturbed by forces acting from without.

It was indeed a strange universe created in the quiet study of a philosopher who believed himself to be an empiricist. This universe was a collection of particles. Each of them, called a *"Real"* (*das Reale*), seeks to remain in a state of rest, opposing any change. The true state of the universe is the continuity and preservation of the *Reals*, and their opposition to any changes from the outside. But since the *Reals* collide and conflict with one another, forces are brought into being and mutual pressures are created so that each one struggles for its preservation. Everything that appears to us as a change in the world is merely a self-defensive tactic on the part of the *Real* against extraneous disturbances. There are indeed no true changes in the world. The *Real*, the simplest quantitative unit, always remains the same, even when its reactions to various forces gives us the impression of change. The case of water illustrates this point: water may be turned into ice or steam but in the end, it is still water.

Thus the world remains a collection of simple stagnant units, each possessing a distinct quality, existing irrespective of time and space. We cannot know them directly, but only through their mutual relationships, their associations, combinations, and configurations. Our knowledge about them depends upon the circumstances in which they are found. Just as different musical notes are distinguished by their relation to each other (tertia or quinta), so the *Reals* appear to us in different forms despite the fact that each of them is always and forever the same.

Herbart's picture of the world comes close to the atomistic-mechanistic doctrines. There is no room there for teleology, vitalism or spiritual forces. Iron-clad laws rule there: the laws of causality exercise absolute control over the universe.

Herbart has developed a metaphysical system based on the mechanistic doctrines of the physics of his time, coated in Newton's language. In this manner, metaphysics and science were blended by Herbart into a mechanistic deterministic metaphysical system. Even organic and mental life were included in this system and interpreted by the same mechanical forces of disturbance and self-preservation.

It is, indeed, a psychological puzzle: How could this keen thinker build such an imaginary metaphysical structure? Why didn't he follow the French Encyclopedists, keeping away from the philosophical speculations he despised? Why did he seek metaphysical explanations outside the realm of physics, chemistry, and biology?

Herbart's Psychology: the "Real"

Herbart's main work in psychology, written over a period of years and published in 1824–1825 was the *Psychologie als Wissenschaft neugegründet auf Erfahrung, Metaphysik und Mathematik* [*Psychology as a science based on experience, metaphysics, and mathematics*]. One can easly understand Herbart's love for mathematics and his insistence on being empirical. But why metaphysics?

Herbart's distinction between *being* and *appearance* also included psychology. This soul is a *Real*, a Kantian thing-in-itself, a being, thus inaccessible to direct, empirical cognition. Its actions, associations, and interactions are appearances and, therefore observable. Here again Herbart followed the Kantian split. Psychology as a science of the *Real* or the thing-in-itself called "soul" that is inaccessible to direct and empirical cognition, must stay metaphysical. Psychology as a science of actions, changes, behavior, and other appearances is empirical and mathematical.

Herbart severely criticized Kant's idea of self-observation, by questioning who observes the mind that observes oneself? In his criticism of Kant Herbart went farther than Fries [1773–1843]. The soul, as a *Real*, cannot be directly observed, not even from within. But its *doings*, the mental phenomena, are observable, some from within, some from without.

"The soul," wrote Herbart, "is not a *tabula rasa* in the sense as to be open to any alien impressions to shape it. The soul cannot also be a substance in Leibniz's meaning, for it has no original activity. The soul originally has no ideas, emotions, or desires. It has no knowledge of itself nor of other objects. It possesses no categories of thought and intuition, nor faculties of will and action. The soul has originally no predispositions whatever."

The simple nature of the soul is wholly unknown and must remain unknown. Thus it cannot serve as a subject matter either for speculative or empirical psychology" (Herbart, 1816, Pt. 3, pp. 152–153).

The only force of the soul is inertia (*vis inertiae*) or resistance to change. This force is activated in the reactions of the soul to disturbing factors. Accordingly, psychology is the study of these reactions or resistances, of their statics and dynamics. These reactions of the soul are the same as the reactions of any other *Real*: *self-preservations (Selbsterhaltungen)*. The *Selbsterhaltungen* of the soul are the best known reactions of any *Real* to outer stimuli. These self-preservations of the soul are called by Herbart *Vorstellungen*, translated as *presentations* or *ideas*. Ideas do not come from without; they are mere reactions of the soul to external stimuli. Every soul is originally at peace, as are all other unchangeable and unperturbed units of the world. Ideas are the defenses of this particular *Real*.

The totality of the changeable, fluctuating self-preservations or ideas is what is known as conscious or consciousness (*Bewusstsein*). Ideas come and go, emerge or submerge. When they reach the summit of the soul, they become *conscious*. When they stride back and submerge, they are *unconscious*.

It is important to stress that these reactions or ideas are not the soul itself but its appearances. They are not *Sein* but *Schein*. Thus they do not belong to metaphysics but to empirical science, and empirical science must be based on experience and mathematics.

Experience is the second principle of Herbart's psychology. Scientific data are derived from systematic observation and experience. In this respect there is no difference between psychology and the natural sciences. Psychology starts with simple elements and progresses to the complex ones. Psychology investigates the reactions of the soul, and uses the same methods of research as all other sciences do, namely, observation, generalization, and quantification.

Herbart operates with simple, psychological elements, that might be called "psychic atoms," and builds the whole story by *association of elements*, just as physics and chemistry build their universe by combinations of atoms. Herbart's atomistic, mechanistic, and associationistic psychology can be deduced from four postulates: (1) psycho-physical monism, (2) conservation of energy, (3) determinism, and (4) inertia.

Herbart was an associationist, although he did not subscribe to any particular laws of association. Although the soul is a finite entity, it has no innate ideas, feelings, or desires, and certainly not the Kantian a priori forms of cognition. The stimuli coming *from without* determine the reactions of the soul.

The soul, at first is *absolutely passive*, but is *forced* to protect itself against the disturbing factors by forming ideas. Not all ideas (reactions of the soul) are alike. There are great differences among them depending upon the external nature of the stimuli and upon the specific quality of the reacting soul.

The soul, being a *Real*, is in touch not only with the external world, but also with all the other *Reals* that the body is composed of. These reactions of the soul to the other *Reals* of the same organism create the general feeling or feeling-of-life or organic feeling (*Gemeingefühl, Lebensgefühl*). This feeling is the basis of our moods, of our feelings of hunger and fatigue, and is also related to the processes of breathing, digestion, and reproduction. The *organic feeling* represents the lower level of consciousness. It is the reaction of the soul to stimuli coming from without, from the body. *Sensory consciousness* is the higher level reaction to stimuli coming from without.

STATICS AND DYNAMICS

In Herbart's system, the defensive discharges of energy are called ideas. Accordingly, ideas (*Vorstellungen*, representations) *are* units of energy discharged by the *Real* in its resistance to change. One cannot understand Herbart without the basic equation: the action of *Selbsterhaltung* (self-preservation) equals *Vorstellung* (idea).

Ideas viewed as units of energy can merge, combine, or inhibit one another. This Newtonian presentation of sheer physical forces was subordinated in Herbart's system to the content of the ideas. Similar ideas, fuse, like tones blending into a melody. Fusion (*Verschmelzung*) is a mathematical sum of similar ideas. There is, however, a limit to the size of the sum; and the fused idea may contain less energy than its components. The new idea, is, however, always brighter and closer to the summit of the consciousness than its component ideas. When different, disparate ideas that pertain to the same object, joint together, they form a *complex unit (Komplikation)*. For instance, the smell, sight, and taste of a loaf of bread together form such a complex idea.

Conflicting ideas inhibit each other. In this process of mutual inhibition (*Hemmung*) the stronger idea loses less energy than the weaker one. The inhibited idea is pushed down. It may end up above, on, or below the threshold of consciousness. If it is repressed (*verdrängt*) below the threshold, it becomes obscure, dark, and unintelligible.

Ideas, as dynamic units, are rarely in a static position. If an equilibrium is reached, the idea has reached its *static threshold (statische Schwelle)*. In most cases the equilibrium reached is merely temporary. The idea, being in its *dynamic threshold* (*dynamische Schwelle*) must change its position to attain equilibrium.

Ideas move up and down. Each idea struggles and strives to reach the peak of the consciousness. The higher the point reached by the idea, the brighter it becomes. Clarity and lucidity of ideas depends on the dynamic interplay of ideational forces. Ascending and dominant ideas are bright and radiant, descending ideas are diffuse and obscure.

The rise of ideas above the threshold of consciousness is recall. Repressed ideas are forgotten ideas. However, according to the law of conservation of energy, no repression and, resultingly, no forgetting can be complete. The repressed ideas struggle for readmission into consciousness and fight their way through against the opposition of the inhibiting ideas.

Every new idea, whether it is a reaction of the soul to an outer stimulus or a reappearance in the consciousness of a hitherto weak and repressed idea, must be accepted by the body of existing ideas that occupy, as it were, the peak of the consciousness. Herbart called this acceptance or absorption of a new or returning idea *apperception*.

Thus, Herbart's was a peculiar type of associationism. The newcoming (from without) or the coming-back (from the unconscious) idea does not just associate with other ideas. It must be welcomed and accepted by the already existing groupings of ideas. These groupings, called *apperceptive masses*, are comparatively steady bodies of ideas whose content is related to the new idea.

Apperception is related to attention, for it puts the new or newly appearing idea in the focus of one's consciousness. Attention is the viewing of the new idea in the light of the already established ideas. The old ideas have to "apperceive" the newcomer and make it part of the consciousness.

Herbart's concept of consciousness hardly corresponds to Kant's "*Bewusstsein.*" Herbart's *Bewusstsein* is not a closed entity; it is a totality of *Vorstellungen*, a sum of ideas. T. Ribot was certainly right when he wrote of Herbart's consciousness, "*Moi ou la conscience nést que la somme des représentations actuelles. Bref, elle est un effet et non une cause, un résultat et non un fait primitif*" [The self of the consciousness is not a sum of present ideas. Briefly, it is a result and not a cause, a product and not a primitive fact] (Ribot, 1879, p. 24).

Herbart's concept of me, the self or the ego, represents the focus of all the apperceptive masses and a product of the struggle between ideas. It is a continuum rather than a firm point, a flow of consciousness rather than a steady center. Herbart's "*Ich*" (ego) must not be confused with the concept of soul (*Seele*). The soul, being a *Real*, is an unchangeable, metaphysical, unknowable entity. The ego is as empirical a term as Herbart's empiricism permits. It is the intersection of apperceptive masses and the unifying link in the continuous change of mental processes.

Herbart's Mathematics

Herbart's efforts to develop a scientific metaphysical theory needed the assistance of a system developed by a man who dreamed of an universal encycsistance of all sciences. Wrote Leibniz: "The characteristic which I envision requires only a new kind of Encyclopedia. The Encyclopedia will combine logic and knowledge" (Couturat, 1901, p. 79). This Encyclopedia will be a logically organized system of sciences. "Wisdom," wrote Leibniz, "is a perfect knowledge of the principles of all the sciences and of the art of applying them" (Leibniz, 1951, p. 77). "If this Encyclopedia were made in the way I wish, we could furnish the means of finding always the consequences of fundamental truth or of given facts through a manner of calculation as exact and as simple as that of Arithmetic and Algebra" (p. 40). Leibniz believed that mathematics could solve all scientific problems: "For all inquiries which depend on reasoning would be performed by the transposition of characters and by a kind of calculus, which would immediately facilitate the discovery of beautiful results" (p. 15). This belief was wholeheartedly shared by Herbart. Herbart believed that one could calculate the number of inhibited ideas that would become repressed when two ideas conflict. The unrepressed remainder that appears in full clarity can also be accounted. The amount of inhibition repressed shows the force of the conflict between opposing ideas and can be measured by the amount repressed from both sides. It is also possible to calculate the amount of inhibition for each of the ideas. This amount is called the "ratio of inhibition" (*Hemmungsverhältniss*). This ratio indicates how the total inhibition was divided between the dominant and submissive ideas. One might find the amount of the force of each idea, the time it spends in our consciousness, and the complex relationship of repression formed when many ideas clash. The phenomenon of forgetting could then be interpreted as a product of mutual repression and related to the ratio of the forces of the ideas. One could also figure out the strength of the repressed ideas or their parts, and state in mathematical formulae their striving to return to consciousness. This process is closely related to the ratio of the forces of the dominant and submissive ideas. As a result of the struggle between ideas the dominant group may also weaken, thus enabling the inhibited idea to return to consciousness in full clarity.

Herbart elaborated algebraic formulae expressing the ratio between the forces, the laws governing their formation within the soul, and the various connections between ideas and their associations and preservation in the unconscious. Preservation of ideas in the unconscious is the basis of memory. In Herbart's hands, associationist psychology turned into a mechanistic-mathematical system that has explained mental life in a physical fashion.

Herbart followed in the footsteps of Newton's physico-mathematical world and forced psychology into a complete surrender to mathematical physics. For example, the sum of inhibition of ideas is S. After a time interval t, the inhibited quantity is σ. Thus $(S - \sigma)dt = d\sigma$. Hence, in integral calculus

$$t = \log. \frac{\text{const.}}{S - \sigma}$$

Furthermore, if the time $t = 0$, the inhibited quantity becomes $\sigma = 0$. Then, the sum of inhibition S = constant. Thus, figures Herbart,

$$\sigma = S (1 - e^{-t})$$

In the case of two ideas that are equally intense and opposite to one another, the intensity of each of them will be reduced by half. If two unequal and opposite ideas inhibit one another and the idea A is bigger than idea B, the sum of inhibition is inversely related to their strength. Thus the strength of A will be inhibited by $\dfrac{a^2 + ab - b^2}{a + b}$ and the strength of B is inhibited by $\dfrac{b^2}{a + b}$. In case $b - ab/a + b = 0$ the intensity of idea B will become zero, and idea B will disappear below the threshold of consciousness (Herbart, 1824–1825, p. 41).

Herbart, though believing himself to be an empiricist, sacrificed empirical data to his great love for mathematics. On this point Herbart was a faithful follower of the Leibniz-Kant tradition.

Emotions and Desires

Herbart rejected the idea of man as a rational being as taught by Descartes, Leibniz, Wolff, and Kant. In a way, he went back to Aristotle and viewed mental functions in a continuum of degrees. The lower-level ideas are imagination and memory. The lower-level emotions are pain and pleasure, and the lower-level desires are instincts and appetites. The high-level ideas are understanding and judgment; the higher feelings are ethical and esthetic; and the higher desires are passions and will. Men share with animals low ideas, emotions, and desires. The higher ideas, emotions, and desires belong to men only.

There was no room in Herbart's system for emotions and desires independent of ideas. *Gemüt* (mood) is not *Geist* (mind). However, "*Gemüt hat seinen Sitz im Geist, oder Fühlen und Begehren sind zunächst Zustände der Vorstellungen, und zwar grosserntoils wandelbare Zustände der letzteren* (Herbart, 1816, p. 33). In English translation: "Mood has its seat in mind, or feeling and desiring are states of ideas, and mostly changeable states."

Emotions and desires are reactions of the soul to the dynamics of ideas. When an idea breaks through and arrives at the summit with great intensity, it brightens the entire consciousness. The abundance of energy results in victory of the ascending idea and gives the feeling of pleasure. A failure of an idea to overcome the inhibiting forces creates the feeling of displeasure.

The sudden darkening or brightening of consciousness caused by ideas gives rise to powerful affects. Thus, for instance, a strong feeling of joy will affect and brighten all the ideas that occupy our consciousness at the moment. Emotional life is determined by the mutual relationships between ideas and the result of the circumstances created by the repression or the bursting forth of ideas into consciousness.

A desire is merely the rise of an idea over its obstacles. *Will* is formed when the awareness that the goal of the striving idea can be realized is added to a desire and a proper action thereby becomes feasible. All experiences of the will are determined by ideas. "The will takes its root in the circle of thought," says Herbart. Character is a term that indicates the degree of perseverance and stability in decisions and actions resulting from the pattern of ideas, typical for a certain individual.

Educational Psychology

Ideas that appear with extra brightness arouse in us the desire to know them better. These are the ideas that prevail over opposing ideas and inhibit them. Bright ideas evoke interest. Interest is longing for knowledge and it must be stimulated by education.

How should this be done? Interest is related to the process of attention. We can distinguish two types of attention: (a) spontaneous, appearing without effort and (b) deliberate, one that requires conscious effort. The source of spontaneous attention is the true, direct interest, whereas attention resulting from effort is obtained by indirect means, such as commands and threats. Deliberate attention is not fruitful and does not bring much educational benefit, and strained effort may sometimes cause unpleasant feelings. Spontaneous attention, on the other hand, brings mental alertness. This attention originates in strong ideas that come from outside and provoke it.

Aside from this spontaneous attention, which is a preliminary attention, there is a higher level of spontaneous attention, connected with the processes of apperception. This type of attention comes after one has acquired a certain number of ideas. When a new idea appears, a battle breaks out among the existing ideas for a place above the threshold of consciousness. In this battle, certain elements of the old ideas attach themselves to similar elements among the new images. This is the process of apperception where new patterns of ideas are formed.

One may distinguish two stages in apperception: at first the initiative is in the hands of the new ideas that penetrate consciousness and attract similar images submerged in the unconscious. Afterwards the old ideas established in the consciousness take the initiative, and absorb and adjust the new idea. The entire process is one of merger on the part of two ideas or two patterns of ideas. If this merger succeeds without too much trouble, we get a pleasant feeling. This feeling strengthens our effort to preserve the gains of this process and to repeat it, thus creating a desire for apperception of new ideas. Apperception arouses interest.

The task of education is to arouse this interest. The pupil will find nothing too difficult to comprehend, provided the material offered to him is related to ideas already existing in his consciousness. The teacher is expected to make the apperception process easier by making learning pleasant.

Herbart differentiated three types of interest:

1. *Empirical interest,* aimed at isolated elements in the material or spiritual world.
2. *Speculative interest,* directed at law and order in the world.
3. *Esthetic interest,* directed at feelings of beauty and harmony.

The three types of interest correspond to three types of cognition and the three branches of philosophy: (1) longing for knowledge—metaphysics; (2) abstract thinking—logic; and (3) esthetic taste—esthetics.

Interest may be based on feeling as well as on cognition. The emotional interest can be divided into three types: (1) sympathetic interest in the individual, (2) social interest, and (3) religious interest. There exists then a parallel between the three types of cognitive interest and the three kinds of affective interest. The first type is related to the individual, both in cognition and in feeling. The second type is directed towards the group. The third is related neither to the individual nor to the group, but to absolute values, esthetic and religious. At their summit, esthetic knowledge and religious feeling join together into ethics. On the highest level, intellectual interest is close to emotional interest, and they fuse together in morality.

The function of the educator is to bring the pupil to this moral harmony, which is included in *many-sided interest*, comprising all six types of interest together. The teacher must arouse in his pupils interest on all levels and in all directions and bring it to the summit. The teacher should arouse empirical interest by means of observation, speculative interest by means of comparison and explanation of the regularity in nature in general, esthetic interest through emphasis on beauty and harmony in the universe, and interest in friendship between individuals by bringing the object of study close to the life of the persons.

Absorption (Vertiefung) and *reflection (Besinnung)* are the two stages of apperception. At first we concentrate upon the object of cognition and exclude irrelevent elements. This absorption can be compared to breathing and to deep inhalation. Then we exhale and allow the ideas repressed during absorption to reappear in consciousness. This is reflection. These two actions complement each other and together make up the desired cognitive process of absorption.

The absorptive process is subdivided into two further stages, intermediate between the beginning and the end of the process. The first stage of absorption is the repression of the present content of consciousness in order to make room for the new images. The content offered for cognition must be isolated from the other images to which it is connected in order to see it well and with maximum possible clarity. It is therefore called *clearness (Klarheit)*.

After we get to know the isolated idea clearly, we attempt to establish connections between it and the other ideas of that group. This is the second, the active stage in absorption, called *association*. After we already know both the elements and their mutual connections, we have to combine what we learned with our total intellectual system. With this begins the first stage of reflection, the passive stage, called *system*. Then we have to draw conclusions from the acquired knowledge and apply it. This is the active stage in reflection, called *method*.

Herbart's Historical Role

Though it may seem strange, Herbart's ideas were much ahead of contemporary German psychology. Ribot rightly ascribed this fact to the influence of Locke's associationism: *"J'incline a croire, pourtant, qu'elles avaient été suggerées à Herbart moins par ses propres réflexions que par la lecture de Locke"* (1879, p. 4).

Herbart's criticism of the old faculty psychology was indeed remarkable. Herbart refuted the idea of a psychological system derived from mere abstraction and classification of logical concepts. Consider memory. There is the empirical fact of memorizing, but there is not much reason to assume that a logical class of facts is a separate psychological faculty. Nor is there any reason to subdivide this "faculty" or "power" of memorizing into sub-faculties of verbal, numerical, personal, or visual memories.

Herbart was also opposed to the alleged connection between the psychological "powers" or "faculties" and actual experiences. There is no reason to assume that the "power to reason" results in actual reasoning. Actual reasoning does not necessarily result from the fact that such a faculty of reasoning exists. At best, the reasoning faculty indicates a potentiality, a disposition for a certain action. Herbart maintained that no action could start without an external stimulus.

Herbart's idea of *Selbsterhaltungen* has had a profound impact on psychology. Since Herbart, most psychologists have described mental phenomena as reactions of the organism aimed at the restoration of the initial equilibrium. This idea has been incorporated in the psychophysical parallelism, structuralism, functionalism, organismic theories, conditioning, and psychoanalysis (Wolman, 1960).

I would venture to credit Herbart with the spiritual fatherhood of the S-R psychology. It was Herbart who maintained that *all* mental processes are mere reactions (*Selbsterhaltungen,* self-preservations) of the soul against disturbances (stimuli) coming from without. Obviously Herbart's self-preservations and the stimulus-response psychology are replicas of Newton's law of inertia.

Herbart's distinction between actual mental experiences and dispositions toward such experiences became an integral part of nineteenth-century psychology. This aspect of Herbart's psychology has been emphasized by Lindner (1872), who abandoned Herbart's mathematics and metaphysics. Brentano, Husserl, and the entire phenomenological school are profoundly indebted to Herbart.

Herbart's "energetic" theory has had a considerable influence on Freud's thinking. According to Herbart, every idea is identical with a self-preservation act of the soul and a self-preservation act involves discharge of energy. Since energy is imperishable (The Law of Preservation of Energy), no idea can completely disappear. An idea inhibited by another idea does not perish; since it has lost some energy, it sinks below the "threshold of consciousness" (*Schwelle des Bewusstsein*). This is the process of repression (*Verderängung*). The reappearance of repressed ideas meets with "resistance" (*Weiderstand*) offered by the already established "masses of ideas" (*Vorstellungmassen*). Herbart's style, language, and conceptualization have certainly influenced Freud's thinking (Glicklhorn, 1960). Freud learned associationism from Herbart (Wolman, 1967).

Furthermore, Herbart has distinguished between the *Gemeingefühl,* that represents the inner feelings, and the *Bewusstsein,* that represents the soul's contact with the outer world. The correspondence of the former to Freud's id and the latter to the ego is apparent. Moreover, Freud's "memory traces" in the preconscious are almost a replica of Herbart's theory of unconscious serving as a sort of storage room or treasury for ideas (cf. Freud, 1949a).

Freud did not accept Herbart's notion that ideas are forces. Instead, he introduced the concept of cathexis or charge. Ideas can be libido cathected, that is loaded, charged with emotional energy. Freud, however, adapted, after Herbart, the Newtonian idea of conservation of energy applied to mental processes (Freud, 1949b).

Ernest Jones (1953, vol. 1, p. 374) believed that Freud became acquainted with Herbart's psychology in his gymnasium years. Andersson (1962, p. 9 ff.) corroborated this statement, and stressed the impact of Lindner's (1872) textbook. Dorer (1932) maintained that Meynert was instrumental in acquainting Freud with Herbart's ideas. A further discussion of this problem transgresses the scope of the present essay (cf. also Karpinska, 1914).

Not only admirers but some adversaries did not break away from Herbart. Consider the case of Wilhelm Wundt, the man who founded the first psychological laboratory and wrote a textbook of physiological psychology (cf. chapter on Wundt in this volume). Wrote Wundt: "*Der Eintritt einer Vorstellung in das inner Blickfeld wollen wir die Perzeption, ihren Eintritt in den Blickpunkt die Apperzeption nennen*" [We shall call perception the entrance of an idea into the inner field of vision; we shall call apperception its entrance in the point of vision] (1880, vol. 2, p. 206). Thus also Wundt accepted Herbart's concept of apperception as a sort of focalization of new ideas and their acceptance by the already existing sets.

Practically all neurological and psychological research workers in the second part of the nineteenth century were influenced by Herbart to a lesser or a larger extent. The works of Helmholtz, Fechner, Weber, Exner, Ziehen and others operated with concepts borrowed from Herbart's *Lehrbuch zur Psychologie*. For, strangely enough, Herbart has advocated monism, determinism, stimulus-response arc, unconscious, quantification, and empiricism. Though he was often wrong, the ideas he introduced made other men think and reintroduce them years later in a more rational and a more empirical manner. The man who erred so much, pointed the way to many useful ideas!

Herbart's theory dominated the teaching of psychology for decades. The works of Exner (1894), Flügel (1912), Drobisch (1842, 1876), Lazarus (1883), Lindner (1872), Lipps (1883), Nahlowsky (1902), Rein (1897), Strümpell (1884), Volkmar (1884–1885), Ziehen (1900) are an incomplete list of studies that continued or modified Herbart's theories.

F. A. Lange wrote in 1865: "There are a number of sensible and excellent people who quite seriously believe that Herbart with his differential equations has as thoroughly mastered the world of ideas, as Kopernikus and Kepler the world of the planets. This is indeed as thorough an illusion as phrenology, and as to psychology as a natural science, so much mischief has been worked by this pretty name that we might easily run the risk of pouring away bath and child together" (Lange, 1925, III, p. 162).

There is no doubt that this brilliant mind produced the most cumbersome and, at the same time, the most influential psychological theory. It was influential because it carried the promise of determinism, monism, and empiricism and included the idea of unconscious. Herbart's theory was more a promise than a fulfillment. It was a dream of empiricism and a reality of metaphysics. Herbart never was what he thought himself to be. He believed he had had the courage to stand alone against romanticism, mysticism, and idealism. He hoped that his work would be similar to that of David Hume, of empirical data and their calculus. This dream never came true.

Herbart lacked the courage of conviction. Herbart was not cut out to be a Galileo, a Spinoza, a Freud, or an Einstein. He never had the courage to stand alone. In 1837 Herbart was Dean of the Philosophical Faculty at the University of Göttingen. Seven professors refused to sign an Oath of Allegiance forced upon the faculty by the dictatorial king. Herbart did not join his colleagues, as would be generally expected from a man of his stature.

Herbart was a hard-working and profoundly thinking man. His mind was logical, his eye penetrating. But he could not break the chains of conformity. Herbart's life and works were an unfortunate product of his halfhearted effort to be what he never could become.

REFERENCES

ADAMS, J. *The Herbartian psychology applied to education.* Boston: Heath, 1910.

ANDERSSON, O. *Studies in the prehitsory of psychoanalysis.* Norstedts: Svenska Bokförlaget, 1962.

COUTURAT, L. *La logique de Leibniz d'apres des documents inedits.* Paris: F. Alcan, 1901.

DESSOIR, M. *Geschichte der neueren deutschen Psychologie.* 2nd ed. Berlin: Duncker, 1897.

DORER, MARIA. *Historsche Grundlagen der Psychoanalyse.* Leipzig: Meiner, 1932.

DROBISCH, M. W. *Empirische Psychologie nach naturwissenschafftlicher Methode.* Hamburg and Leipzig: Voss, 1842.

DROBISCH, M. W. *Über die Festbildung der Philosophie durch Herbart.* Hamburg and Leipzig: Voss, 1876.

EXNER, S. *Entwurf zu einer physiologischen Erklärung der psychischen Erscheinungen.* Leipzig: 1894.

FLUGEL, O. *Herbart's Lehren und Leben.* 2nd ed. Leipzig: Teubner, 1912.

FREUD, S. *A general introduction to psychoanalysis.* New York: Perma Giants, 1949a.

FREUD, S. *An outline of psychoanalysis.* New York: Norton. 1949b.

FRIES, J. F. *Neue oder psychologische Kritik der Vernunft.* 1807.

GLICKLHORN, J. R. *Sigmund Freud's akademische Laufbahn im Lichte der Dokumente.* München: Urban und Schwarzenberg, 1960.

HERBART, J. F. *Pestalozzi's Idee eines ABC der Anschaung untersucht und wissenschaмich ausgeführt.* Göttingen: Rőwer, 1802.

HERBART, J. F. *Allgemeine Pädagogik aus dem Zwecke der Erziehung abgeleitet.* Göttingen: Röwer, 1806.

HERBART, J. F. *Allgemeine praktische Philosophie.* Göttingen: Bankwerts, 1808.

HERBART, J. F. *Lehrbuch zur Einleitung in die Philosophie.* Königsberg: Unzer, 1813. 2 vols.

HERBART, J. F. *Lehrbuch zur Psychologie.* Hamburg: Voss, 1816.

HERBART, J. F. *Psychologie als Wissenschaft neugegründet auf Erfahrung. Metaphysik und Mathematik.* 1824–1825.

HERBART, J. F. *Allgemeine Metaphysik.* Königsberg. W. Unzer, 1828–1829. 2 vols.

HERBART, J. F. *Psychologische Untersuchungen.* Dieterich. 1839–1840.

HERBART, J. F. *Pädagogische Schiften.* Leipzig: Willman, 1880. 2 vol.

HERBART, J. F. *Sämtliche Werke.* Langensalza: Kehrbach, 1887–1912. 19 vols.

HERBART, J. F. *A textbook in psychology; an attempt to found the science of psycvhology on experience, metaphysics and mathematics.* Trans. by Margaret K. Smith, New York: Appleton, 1891.

HERBART, J. F. *Sämtliche Werke.* Hamburg and Leipzig: Hartenstein, 1883-1893. 13 vols.

HERBART, J. F. *The application of psychology to the science of education.* London: Sonnenschein, 1898.

HUME, D. A *treatise on human nature.* L. A. Selby-Bigge (Ed.) Oxford: Clarendon Press, 1896.

JONES, E. *The life and work of Sigmund Freud.* New York: Basic Books, 1953.

KANT, I. *Critique of pure reason.* Trans. by N. Kemp Smith London: Macmillan. 1,929.

KARPINSKA, LUISE V. Über die psychologischen grundlagen *des Freudismus. Intern. Ztschr. Psychoanalyse,* 1914, 2, 305.

LANGE, F. A. *The history of materialism.* Trans. by E. C. Thomas. London: Routledge & Kegan Paul, 1925.

LAZARUS, M. *Das Leben der Seele in Monographien über seine Erscheinungen und Gesetze.* Berlin: Ferd Duemmler, 1883. 2 vols.

LEIBNIZ, G. W. *Selections.* P. P. Wiener (Ed.) New York: Scribner, 1951.

LINDNER, G. A. *Lehrbuch der empirischen Psychologie als inductive Wissenschaft.* (Dritte Aufflage) Wien: 1872.

LINDNER, G. A. *Enzyklopedisches Handbuch der Erziehungskunde.* Wien: 1884.

LIPPS, T. *Grundtatsachen des Seelenlebens.* Bonn: F. Cohen, 1883.

LOTZE, R. H. *Geschichte der deutschen Philosophie seit Kant.* Leipzig: Hirzel, 1882.

MAIMON, S. *Versuch über die Transzedentalphilosophie.* 1790.

NAHLOWSKY, J. W. *Das Gefühlsleben in seinen wesentlichsten Erscheinugen und Beziehungen.* Herausgegeben von Chr. Ufer. Leipzig: Veit, 1902.

NATORP, P. G. *Gesammelte Aufsätze zur Sozialpädagogik.* Stuttgart: Frommann, 1922.

NEWTON, I. *Principia.* Trans. and Ed. by Andrew Motte-Cajori. London: H. S. Symonds, 1803fl. (First pub. 1687.) 3 vols.

REIN, W. *Enzyklopädisches Handbuch der Pädagogik.* Langensalza. Beyer, 1897.

RIBOT, T. A. *La psychologie allemande contemporaine.* Paris: 1879. (*German psychology of today.* Trans. from 2nd French ed. by James Mark Baldwin. New York: Scribner's, 1886.)

SALLWUCK, E. *Handel und Wandel der pädagogischen Schule Herbarts.* 1885.

STRÜMPELL, L. *Grundriss der Psychologie.* Leipzig: 1884.

TETENS, J. N. *Philosophische Versusche über die menschliche Natur und ihre Entwickelung.* Leipzig: 1777.

VOLKMANN VON VOLKMAR, W. *Lehrbuch der Psychologie.* 1884–1885. 2 vols.

WEISS, G. *Herbart und seine Schule.* Geschichle der Philosophe in Einzeldarstelungen. München: Reinhardt, 1908.

WOLFF, C. *Psychologia empirica.* 1732.

WOLFF, C. *Psychologia rationalis.* 1734.

WOLMAN, B. B. Johann Friedrich Herbart, 1776–1841. (Hebrew) *Hachinuch Quarterly.* 1942, 15, 1–23.

WOLMAN, B. B. *Contemporary theories and systems in psychology.* New York: Harper & Row, 1960.

WOLMAN, B. B. Herbart and his school. (Hebrew) *Educational Encyclopedia.* 1964, 3, 545–556.

WOLMAN, B. B. *The unconscious mind: The meaning of Freudian psychology.* Englewood Cliffs, N. J., Prentice-Hall, 1967.

WUNDT, W. *Grundzüge der physiologischen Psychologie.* Leipzig: Engelmann, 1880. 2 vols.

ZELLER, E. *Geschicte der deutschen Philosophie seit Leibniz.* 2nd ed. München: Oldenbourg, 1875.

ZIEHEN, T. *Das Verhältnis der Herbartschen Psychologie zur physiologisch-experimentellen Psychologie.* Berlin: Reuther & Reichard, 1900.

ZIMMER, H. *Führer durch die deutsche Herbart Literatur.* Langensalza; Beltz, 1910.

ZIMMERMAN, R. *Perioden in Hebart's philosophischen Geistesgang. Sitzungsb. d. philos.-histor. Klesse d. Kaiserlichen Akademie d. Wissenschaften,* Band 83. Wien, 1876.

ZIMMERMAN, R. *Ungedrückte Briefe von und an Herbart.* Vienna: Braümuller, 1877.

CHAPTER 4

SOME HISTORICAL ROOTS OF PRESENT-DAY ANIMAL PSYCHOLOGY

Leonard Carmichael

The Forerunners

THIS CHAPTER is not in any sense intended as a full history of animal or comparative psychology. The present author would very much like, at some time, to write such a history, but here he can merely discuss some aspects of the past study of animals that seem relevant in understanding the present healthy and active state of the scientific study of the behavior of infrahuman organisms. In a summary statement of this sort, it is inevitable that some topics be merely mentioned and others omitted altogether. Near the end of the chapter the work done at the Yerkes Laboratories of Primate Biology is discussed in somewhat greater detail to give the reader one good example of the constructive results that can be secured by a serious and consistent scientific attack on the study of the psychobiology of one group of animals when carried on through a long period of years.

One who wishes to see the history of animal psychology in the setting of the general history of psychology should consult E. G. Boring (1950), G. Murphy (1929), E. A. Esper (1964), R. I. Watson (1960, 1963), B. B. Wolman (1960) and other publications which deal with the development of psychology as a total organized science.

The names of scientific workers given in this chapter are presented as examples of those who have made contributions in specific areas of the study of animal behavior and in many instances other names might have been substituted with equal appropriateness. In general, also, full lists of publications of the authors cited are not given. In many cases, the references that are presented will be found to cite at least some of each author's earlier publications.

Some of the paragraphs of this chapter should indeed be thought of merely as annotations for a bibliography that may help a student who wishes to know how to begin more intensive study of a specific topic.

What animals do has always been interesting to human beings. The remains of very early man are sometimes found in association with the bones of animals, broken so that the marrow could be eaten. These animals had almost certainly been eaten by human scavengers or hunters. Thus, even before fire was used, men must have been concerned, as they developed skill in the chase, with the way different wild animals act when they are sought for as food. The fact that virtually all domestication of animals took place in prehistoric times also attests early man's concern with animal behavior and with what mammals and birds can do for man.

There are references to the behavior of animals in Biblical literature and in ancient Indian and Chinese writings. The Egyptians wrote on this subject as did the early Greeks and the Greeks of the Golden Age (Lange, 1925). Anaximander, who lived between about 611 and 547 B.C. observed animals well and suggested that man had evolved from an aquatic vertebrate (Esper, 1964). The idea that well-adapted biological forms survive was foreshadowed in the writings of Empedocles [ca. 495–435 B.C.] (see Herbert, 1919).

Aristotle [384–322 B.C.] was deeply interested in animals and animal behavior and wrote extensively on this subject (Ross, 1908–1931). He treated especially of the generation of animals, the locomotion and movements of animals and the anatomy of animals. He is said to have described, in all, some 500 different species.

Virgil [70–19 B.C.] wrote charmingly on bees and on the life of the hive (Virgil, 1940). Lucretius [ca. 99–55 B.C.] composed a didactic and materialistic poem on nature (Lange, 1925). He presents many observations on animal behavior such as the different sounds that animals make in fear, pain, and joy.

Galen [ca. 200–130 B.C.] sometimes spoken of as the last great biologist of antiquity, was very much interested in animal behavior and in the relationship between the anatomy of animals and their responses (Sarton, 1954).

From the death of Galen to about 1500, many lasting contributions to human psychology were made by such great men as Saint Augustine and Saint Thomas Acquinas, but these scholars, in their concern with the mind, tended to be more interested in the symbolism of angels with white robes than with the behavior of rodents with white pelts.

René Descartes [1596–1650] however, opens up a point of view of great importance for our subject (Adam & Tannery, 1897–1913). He is known for his position that contrasts the mental life of human beings and that of animals. He recognized man as a thinking and rational being but he described animals as automata. They act "by springs like a clock." An interesting modern essay could be written on this view of Descartes that animals are like machines that have sense organs. In some ways this position may not be far different from a mere acceptance of the fact that only human beings are in a position to report directly by introspection on conscious experiences.

The rise of modern behavioristic psychology has put the Cartesian point of view in a different and more favorable light than was true of the criticism of this position by some nineteenth-century philosophers. Many modern psychologists dispense with the concept of consciousness in explaining human as well as animal behavior (for a contrary view see Eccles, 1966). Such students also do not deny that infrahuman animals show behavior which may be described as "reasoning."

The English and continental philosophers of the seventeenth and eighteenth centuries not infrequently referred to animal behavior in illustrating points in their writings. Bernard de Mandeville [1670–1733] in his famous *The Fable of the Bees* (1714) even used a fanciful reference to insect behavior as the basis for a bitter and witty satire on human motives and human ethics.

The scientific study of animal behavior has one of its main roots in the work of the early physiologists. Much important scientific knowledge of animal behavior has, indeed in every period, been secured by research workers who were primarily interested in the general function of the brain or some other organ system. Some psychologists have attempted to distinguish between behavior as the word is used by physiologists and by psychologists. To the present author this attempted distinction is not especially useful, for both the physiologist and the psychologist are concerned with the observation or measurement of what an organism does in a specific environment. If one uses the squirrel monkey in an investigation of the limbic system the behavior that is noted adds not only to our knowledge of the brain but also to our understanding of the responses of the monkey.

Vesalius [1514–1564] was interested in the anatomical structures and the responses that these structures made possible in animals (Foster, 1901). The great William Harvey [1578–1657] well known for his discovery of the circulation of the blood, made interesting observations on animals and especially on the very early behavior of unborn animals (Spencer, 1921). The understanding of the functions of every organ system of man has been advanced by experiments on animals. This is notably true of the study of the functions of the peripheral and central nervous systems. Robert Whytt [1714–1766] by experiments on animals, proved that the central nervous system was essential for reflex action (Carmichael, 1927a). Sir Charles Bell [1774–1842], to take but one more example, established the anatomical distinction between the sensory and motor roots of the spinal cord by animal experimentation and by observing animal behavior (Carmichael, 1926). The development of knowledge about the brain in relation to behavior was advanced by such men as M. J. P. Flourens [1794–1867] (1824) who studied the responses of operated animals. In more recent days this basic approach to the understanding of behavior through animal experimentation has been carried on most effectively by Sir Charles Sherrington (1906) and Birkenhead (1958) and his school. In America, to name but one investigator, J. F. Fulton (1926) carried on this approach to an understanding of the mechanism of response. A book could be written merely to summarize the work of physiologists who have contributed, by experiment, not only to the understanding of the function of cells and organs but also to the explanation of the basis of the behavior of the total organism. In this connection, it may be pointed out that a knowledge of neuroanatomy and neurophysiology is of assistance in understanding behavior. It can be said, with equal propriety, that the measurement and recording of behavior itself, is one of the essential techniques or methods of experimental physiology and especially of neurology. An example may illustrate this point. The concept, or as it really is, the logical construct, called the synapse, depends in part on an accurate measurement of responses to stimuli under controlled conditions.

Beginning of Modern Animal Psychology

It is customary to assert, in spite of the facts just given, that the real beginning of modern scientific animal psychology, as such, was the work of the great nineteenth-century evolutionary biologists. C. R. Darwin [1809–1882] himself, in many places, made accurate observations on animal behavior. In such books, as *The Origin of Species* (1859), *The Descent of Man* (1874), and *The Expression of Emotions in Man and Animals* (1872), he presented many clear observations on animal behavior and on the evolution of mental processes. This work was not without its predecessors, however. Semipopular books had discussed the behavior of animals before the rise of evolutionary biology. J. Rennie (1838), for example, wrote a book, *The Menageries, The Natural History of Monkeys, Opossums and Lemurs* in which are recorded many acute observations on animal behavior. Similarly, Erasmus Darwin [1731–1802] in his curious book, *Zoonomia* (1796), discusses organic life in an evolutionary way.

Among the nineteenth-century evolutionists, H. Spencer, in his *The Principles of Biology* (1898), and in other works, makes contributions to the understanding of animal behavior. G. J. Romanes, in his books such as *Mental Evolution in Animals* (1885), discusses the mental processes of lower organisms. Later research has not fully substantiated all of his assertions but the problems raised by him have been continuously recognized as important since his time.

One of the greatest contributors to the evolutionary understanding of animal behavior was C. Lloyd Morgan (1900, 1901). This biologist and philosopher discusses in influential publications the problem of the emergence of more and more complex and adaptive capacities as organisms develop in the evolutionary scale. This writer, indeed, still has much to teach every modern student of behavior. His emphasis on the fact that new levels of adaptive response are not necessarily a mere adding together of simpler processes, is a hard but necessary lesson that must be learned by each new comparative psychologist. He is also justly famous for the promulgation of what has been called "Lloyd-Morgan's Canon." He says in his *Introduction to Comparative Psychology* (1901): "In no case may we interpret an action as the outcome of the exercise of a higher psychical faculty, if it can be interpreted as the outcome of the exercise of one which stands lower in the psychological scale." This position continues, down to the present day, to exercise a salutary effect upon the scientific study of animal behavior.

The need for this view is especially important in showing the error of what is called "vitalism" in explaining behavior. H. Driesch (1903), often thought of as the most typical of vitalists, tried to defend the view that nonobservable or nonmeasurable psychic forces or "entelechies" had to be assumed to explain behavior. To some extent, this same nonscientific position was defended by W. McDougall (1926). He was, in many ways, an able student of behavior, but in the opinion of most of his critics he was too willing to give up the established hypotheses and methods of science for what seems to be a purely verbal, or indeed, an almost animistic rather than a general naturalistic view of the animal world. The work of H. Bergson (1907) on creative evolution discusses animal behavior with a similar dependence upon what he considered to be a nonmechanistic vital force.

William James, the outstanding psychologist of his period, in his great *Principles of Psychology* (1890), makes many references, especially in his justly famous chapter on Instinct, to animal behavior. In the *Principles*, James quotes at length from the work of D. A. Spalding. This naturalistic English observer is certainly to be considered as one of the earliest experimental students of behavior and indeed, must be thought of as a member, or as a founder, of what is today called the *ethological school* of behavioral scientists to which reference is made later in this chapter.

James quotes in full the following sentences from a paper of Spalding's which deals with what we now call "imprinting."

[If a chick is born in the absence of the hen, it] will follow any moving object. And, when guided by sight alone, they seem to have no more disposition to follow a hen than to follow a duck or a human being. Unreflecting lookers-on, when they saw chickens a day old running after me, [says Mr. Spalding] and older ones following me for miles, and answering to my whistle, imagined that I must have some occult power over the creatures: whereas I had simply allowed them to follow me from the first. There is the instinct to follow; and the ear, prior to experience, attaches them to the right object. (Spalding, 1873)

William Preyer's book *Spezielle Physiologie des Embryo* (1885), records significant observations on the very early development of the behavior of animals. He also approached the problem of human ontogenetic psychology from a similar comparative point of view in his book *Die Seele Des Kindes* (1882). Karl Groos, in his books *Die Spiele des Tieren* (1896) and *Die Spiele der Menschen* (1899), also used what we today would call a comparative approach to psychology. It must be admitted, however, that at times the Darwinian enthusiasm of Groos led him to accept stories about animals that today seem questionable. In fact, a somewhat naive reliance on hearsay evidence about animal capacity has led some critics to speak of many of the early evolutionary animal psychologists as belonging to the "anecdotal school" of animal psychology.

E. L. Thorndike was one of the earliest and most insightful of what may be called the modern experimental students of animal capacity. As a record of his own early experimentation in this field, he wrote a famous monograph, *Animal Intelligence* (1898). This study, which dealt with cats in puzzle boxes may be considered to have started a new approach to the study of learning in animals in controlled situations. The basic importance of this study has been attested by much later work such as that of E. R. Guthrie and G. P. Horton (1946). L. T. Hobhouse (1915), in England, also developed some quite similar experiments to those of Thorndike but his work was based on a different theoretical point of view.

G. Stanley Hall (1904), another famous American psychologist of the late nineteenth and early twentieth century put much emphasis in his work with students at Clark University, on the so-called biogenetic law of E. Haeckel (1906). This theoretical position led many of Hall's students to a consideration of animal behavior because, according to this theory, each human individual passes through stages in ontogenetic development that are parallel to phylogeny, that is, the development of animals in the evolutionary scale. The present author has elsewhere discussed this point of view in some detail (Carmichael, 1956).

T. W. F. Mills (1898), in a somewhat naturalistic rather than experimental spirit, discusses the gradual growth of intelligence and adaptive behavior in animals such as cats and dogs.

W. S. Small's important investigation at Clark University published as "Notes on the psychic development of the young white rat" (1899), is especially significant for American animal psychology. This research study used a maze in a quantitative investigation of learning with the ubiquitous animal of so much later American comparative psychology, the white rat.

J. B. Watson, famous for his later pronouncements on human objective or behavioristic psychology, studied the relationship between the developmental growth of the nervous system, and especially its myelinization, and the growth of learning ability of the white rat (Watson, 1903). Later, Watson published an influential book, *Behavior: An Introduction to Comparative Psychology* (1914), which is dedicated to J. R. Angell and H. H. Donaldson. Angell was one of the founders of the so-called American Functional School of Psychology which was generally characterized by an interest in animal behavior. H. H. Donaldson was a neurologist and student of behavior who did much to introduce the white rat as a laboratory research animal.

J. Allen wrote "The Associative Processes of the Guinea-Pig" (1904). This research, in many ways similar to Watson's early paper just noted, attempts to correlate neural development and growth of observable behavior in young animals. In this paper, the interesting discovery is reported, that the guinea pig is born with so nearly an adult nervous system that its psychological capacities have reached almost adult level by the first postnatal day.

Contemporary Research

Many other American biologically oriented psychologists or psychologically interested biologists contributed in a significant way to the study of animal behavior during the early years of the present century. Among these may be mentioned E. B. Holt. This mechanistically minded psychologist, in collaboration with Lee, wrote on tropisms (Holt & Lee, 1901). Much later, his *Animal Drive and Learning Process* (1931) developed a number of interesting theoretical positions relevant to comparative psychology.

H. Carr (1917) and W. S. Hunter (1913) made very important contributions to the experimental study of animal behavior and to the comparative capacities of various animals. Hunter, in his studies on the delayed reaction in animals and children and on many other topics advanced fruitful areas of study in quantitative comparative psychology. He made special advances in our understanding of the nature of animal learning, to the sensory control of the maze habit in the white rat, to the significance of the double alternation problem, and to other related topics. W. R. Miles (1930) also contributed to the development of an understanding of learning in the rat in many ways, especially by his use of elevated mazes.

Basic work was done by W. B. Cannon (1932) on hunger, thirst, and emotion in animals. P. Bard (1940) also made special contributions to this area of study and especially to the neurohumoral basis of emotion in animals and men.

The distinguished investigations of N. E. Miller (1951) on brain mechanisms and other physiological processes important in the understanding of animal motivation, and especially hunger and thirst, deserve special attention. F. A. Beach (1958), also in a series of brilliant studies, has investigated the neural and chemical regulation of behavior with special reference to mating behavior in rats, cats, and other mammals. This is an area of study in which C. P. Stone (1934) earlier had made very important contributions.

Modern electronics is used extensively in comparative psychology. It may indeed be said that the development of certain areas of scientific animal psychology is chronologically related to a series of advances that have been made in the last thirty years in instrumentation in the electronic field. These techniques are used in the study of sensory processes, in the direct stimulation of the peripheral and central nervous system, and in the recording of neural activity and of muscle responses. The present status of this work is far too extensive to be summarized in these pages but a few examples may be given to suggest the interesting history of present-day research with such equipment. E. G. Wever and C. W. Bray (1930) in a series of papers, have studied the electrophysiology of hearing in the cat, guinea pig, rabbit, rat, and other animals. A. F. Rawdon-Smith, L. Carmichael, and B. Wellman (1938) recorded the electrical responses of the fetal guinea pig's ear and compared the appearance of the measurable electrical responses of the ear with observed behavioral responses to airborne auditory stimuli.

R. Granit (1933), H. K. Hartline (1938), and many others have studied the vision of a number of animals with electronic devices, especially by the recording of retinal action potentials.

A number of the present writer's students, including K. U. Smith, J. Warkentin, and W. E. Kappauf, developed techniques for the production and recording of optokinetic nystagmus and other unlearned visually controlled reactions as a means of studying visual capacity in relation to brain mechanisms in various animals (Smith, 1934, 1937). This work was complementary to studies of the visual and other mechanisms of mammals based on learning techniques by students and colleagues of the present writer, including also K. U. Smith as well as J. L. Kennedy, L. C. Mead, W. E. Kappauf, C. T. Morgan, P. M. Fitts, and C. S. Bridgman. A number of these investigations were concerned with visual form discrimination, movement discrimination, and the discrimination of various wave lengths of light (Smith, 1937). C. Pfaffman (1951), using electrophysiological and other techniques, has studied the comparative olfactory and gustatory mechanisms of a number of organisms.

The electrical stimulation of the brain by implanted electrodes has produced some very important information about the relationship between the central nervous system and observable response. J. A. Olds (1958) has shown that electrodes, properly implanted in the hypothalamus, can be so arranged that an animal can stimulate its own brain by pressing a bar. When the electrodes are in the proper place, an effect similar to that of giving a food reward to a hungry animal can be elicited by self-initiated electrical stimulation. H. W. Magoun (1948) and his associates have shown the large role played by the reticular mechanism of the brain in behavior. H. H. Jasper and others (1958) have evaluated the nature and importance of this system.

P. D. MacLean (1959) and his associates, working with the squirrel monkey, have demonstrated the great importance of the limbic system of the brain in determining reproductive and other behavior. M. Carmichael and P. D. MacLean (1961) have published on the special advantages of the squirrel monkey as a subject in brain research of this sort.

Another continuing and significant trend in animal psychology has been the study of the behavior of insects. This began in antiquity as we have noted. A complete treatment of the history of comparative psychology would give detailed consideration to the study of insects and related organisms by J. H. Fabre (1886–1907), A. Forel (1904), Sir John Lubbock (1888), E. Wasmann (1897), G. W. and E. G. Peckham (1887), and many others. Later students of the biological study of the behavior of social insects give special weight to the remarkable contributions of one of the greatest of comparative students of behavior, K. von Frisch (1950) and his students. Von Frisch has shown, to take but a single example, that complex information about the distance of nectar from a hive can be communicated by bees in special patterns of behavior called dances.

The American biologist W. M. Wheeler (1910) also made truly notable contributions to the understanding of the whole repertoire of behavior and especially to communication between ants. T. C. Schneirla (1933) has applied techniques formerly used mainly in mammalian psychology in a series of brilliant analyses of the behavior of ants especially in connection with their learning ability, their mechanisms of orientation, and their general field behavior. Many gifted investigators in Germany and in other parts of the world today carry on studies with those social insects, including termites.

At the present time in Germany, England, Italy, Japan, France, Russia, Yugoslavia, and many other countries, great attention is being given by zoologists, and by a few psychologists, to the study of orientating behavior. Following the early work on insect behavior just noted, much research is now being done, for example on insect audition. In America, K. Roeder (1963, 1965), a most insightful student of insect behavior and of the electrophysiology of the insect nervous system, has recently made especially important discoveries concerning the responses of moths to sounds pitched too high for human hearing. He has been able to show that these insects can avoid bats by responding quickly and adaptively to the supersonic signals produced by these flying mammal predators. The neuromechanisms that make this possible are described by Roeder.

A great deal of important recent research has been done on animal orientation. Much of this work is a logical development of the early investigations mentioned below in discussing early work on tropisms. In these modern studies, the role of the proprioceptors and indeed, of all receptor mechanisms, are specifically analyzed. V. B. Dröscher (1965) has summarized much of this work in a delightful semipopular book recently translated from German into English.

Learning in many invertebrates, such as worms and cephalopods, has been studied in relation to the locus of habit in the central nervous system (see Wells, 1962). In the octopus, for example, B. B. Boycott (1965) has shown that there are different neural mechanisms for what may be termed long-term and short-term memories. Some very interesting studies on learning in planaria have also been carried out (Ratner & Denny, 1964). S. C. Ratner and K. R. Muller (1964) have studied classical conditioning in earthworms, thus carrying further much previous work that goes back to a study done by R. M. Yerkes (1912).

The experimental and quantitative investigation of learning, as has been noted in a number of places in this chapter, has indeed been one of the most important areas of study for more than sixty years in comparative psychology. A full history and analysis of this work would require many volumes. M. E. Bitterman (1960) has presented an excellent critical analysis of this problem. N. L. Munn (1950) gives a bibliography and summary of what is numerically the all-important work in this field which has used the white rat as a subject up to 1950. So many of these studies have used the maze as an experimental learning problem that at times scientific comparative psychology has almost seemed, to some not too friendly critics, to be only an investigation of the white rat in the maze. Many of these studies have indeed contributed scientific knowledge of great general importance but it is well always to remind psychologists, who specialize in other areas of psychological investigation, that the record of what rats do in mazes is only a limited part of modern scientific comparative psychology.

So-called homing behavior and migratory behavior have been studied in fish, such as salmon, in eels, in birds, and in mammals. E. G. F. Sauer (1958) in Germany seems to have demonstrated that night bird migrants navigate by the stars. Some of this work has been done in the field and also in an experimental setup in the Bremen Planetarium. J. D. Carthy (1956), G. V. T. Matthews (1955), and others have contributed to the solution of this complex and theoretically interesting problem.

The concept of an internal clock and even of an internal compass has been proposed in explaining certain aspects of migratory and orientating behavior. An important book on the internal clock by one of America's most distinguished and original students of animal behavior, C. P. Richter (1965), has just been published. This is one of the most promising areas of modern comparative psychology because it opens up previously unexpected relationships between life and physical and chemical processes. Richter (1941) had earlier shown how important an understanding of the total internal environment is in explaining overt behavior.

J. P. Scott and J. L. Fuller (1965), at the Jackson Memorial Laboratory at Bar Harbor, Maine, have given more than twenty years of detailed study to the behavior and to the inheritance of behavior in dogs. Preliminary work in the field had been done by C. R. Stockard (1941). These studies deal especially with the relative importance of heredity and environment in determining what may be called the personality and the social behavior of different breeds of dogs, especially in genetic crosses. Both of these investigators are primarily zoologists with special knowledge of modern genetics and molecular biology. Great care has therefore been taken in these studies not to use the word "heredity" loosely as in the old days was all too common in the study of behavior. One very interesting conclusion that has come from this long series of investigations is that real hereditary factors which result from the cross breeding of dogs of one stock with those of another are more clearly seen in the behavior of adults of each group than in the behavior of the same animals as puppies. This is true when all the animals compared have been given identical training and environmental experiences as puppies. Here we see a demonstration of the effect of the maturation of inborn characteristics of behavior long after learning has modified much other behavior in the same organisms. This is a view which until very recently has been resisted in the study of human development by many psychologists and psychiatrists who have tried to explain much that individual animals and human beings do by "infantile experiences" and other mechanisms of learning.

The publications of R. C. Tryon (1940) and his associates have also recorded real advances in understanding genetic differences in the learning of specific mazes by rats. These studies have thrown light on the differential psychological capacities of groups of rats that have been selected through a long series of generations, on the basis of the capacities that they show in standard maze-learning conditions. This newly recognized importance of heredity in animal psychology is referred to again later in this chapter in connection with the discoveries of ethology and the study of prenatal behavior.

One of the persistent tendencies in comparative psychology has been an effort to describe the behavior of organisms in purely objective terms without attributing to all animals or at least to animals below man, conscious processes that can never be directly known. Mention has already been made of the early and, for the time, dramatic approach to this problem by Descartes. In 1888 Jacques Loeb, a distinguished comparative physiologist, began a series of publications on the forced or tropistic behavior of animals (1900). Tropism (or its approximate synonym, "taxis") is a name for an automatic or forced movement of an organism (without any "will," "wish," or "desire" of its own) toward or away from a stimulus energy. Tropistic responses depend on the makeup of the organism and the character and intensity of the stimulus acting upon it. Plants, as well as animals, show tropistic reactions. In passing, it may be noted in considering comparative psychology that something that may be called a psychology of bacteria and of plants has been developed (see Clements, 1935).

The objective, tropistic way of describing behavior was early seen to be especially appropriate in describing responses in connection with the experimental study of simple organisms and in the study of the physiology of the nervous system. A famous proposal for the exclusive use of objective terms in such work was set forth in a paper by three European scientists: T. Beer, A. Bethe, and J. von Uexküll (1899). The physiologist M. Verworn (1899) also made very important contributions to the objective study of behavior.

The study of tropisms continues to be an important field of investigation in the analysis of animal behavior. Now and in the past, it has had its ardent supporters and its vigorous critics. A distinguished student of the nervous system of vertebrates, invertebrates, and of the senses of animals, G. H. Parker (1919) of Harvard, did much in America to advance this point of view. The present writer did some of his earliest research on the amazing and machine-like reactions of the mealworm to the energy of light as a result of a problem suggested by Parker (see Balfour & Carmichael, 1928).

H. S. Jennings (1904), still correctly considered to be a foremost authority on the study of the behavior of the lower organisms, began his work at about the turn of the century. Jennings gives a complete biological description of behavior in such organisms as amoeba and paramecium. His classic book did much to correct the oversimplification of some early ultramechanical theories of response. For an earlier approach to this problem see A. Binet (1889).

S. O. Mast (1911), in an elaborate series of publications which began at about the same time as those of Jennings, urged that a too simplified understanding of the role of tropisms in behavior is not satisfactory in understanding the response of even the lowest organisms to light or to other forms of energy.

Many publications, besides those already noted, have been brought together in systematic form in an effort to give coherence to the field of comparative psychology. The work of G. Kafka (1922) may be mentioned in this connection. J. B. Watson's important, *Behavior: An Introduction to Comparative Psychology* (1914), has already been cited. In 1908 a book appeared in this field which has had broad and continuing influence. This intellectually distinguished and comprehensive work by M. F. Washburn (1926) discusses all the major aspects of the animal psychology of its period. It is basically written from its author's point of view which emphasizes the fact, in her words: "Knowledge regarding the animal mind like knowledge of human minds other than our own, must come by way of inference from behavior."

Increasingly, however, in recent decades, psychologists and biologists alike have moved away even from such indirect, mentalistic explanations of response and have more and more limited themselves to a fully objective and measurable description of behavior. As noted above there is another side to this question as shown in the papers recently edited by Sir John Eccles (1966). Today almost all animal psychology is directly concerned with behavior itself as a datum and not with behavior as an expression of some unknown "conscious" and least of all "unconscious" process.

W. J. Crozier (1929) may be taken as typical of one important tendency in this objective study of behavior. He made a great many quantitative observations on the nature of animal responses. In a series of papers, for example, he offered a mathematical description of the geotropic orientation, on an inclined plane, of mammals such as rats. Crozier's point of view continues to be very influential and is closely related to much current scientific biological study of orienting behavior, especially in Europe.

In speaking of general works on animal psychology, attention should be given to N. R. F. Maier, and T. C. Schneirla, *Principles of Animal Psychology* (1935), and to a notable three-volume publication, *Comparative Psychology*, prepared under the authorship of C. J. Warden, T. N. Jenkins, and L. H. Warner (1935–1940). These books deal with principles and methods, and with the behavior of invertebrates and vertebrates. The separate volumes of *Comparative Psychology* were published from 1935 to 1940. This work provides a valuable assessment of experimental studies on animal behavior up to the time of its issue. In this connection, mention should again be made of the *Handbook of Psychological Research on the Rat: An Introduction to Animal Psychology* by Norman Munn (1950). This is a truly distinguished and painstakingly written book. It has a bibliography of well over 2,500 titles, all of which are relevant to an understanding of the psychological study of the white rat. This same experimental student of animal behavior has recently published a new edition of his book on real comparative psychology, *The Evolution and Growth of Human Behavior* (Munn, 1965), which considers the development of behavior in the animal kingdom and the growth of behavior in the individual. F. A. Moss (1934) earlier edited a book on comparative psychology which contained chapters by many important animal psychologists and especially by C. P. Stone. S. C. Ratner and M. R. Denny (1964) have similarly edited a valuable book, *Comparative Psychology: Research in Animal Behavior* in which the work of many present-day investigators is clearly presented. *Behavior and Evolution*, edited by A. Roe and G. G. Simpson (1958), is also important in this connection. (See also Scott, 1958; Scott & Fuller, 1965.)

Conditioning

Russian physiologists such as V. M. Bekhterev (1928) and the great I. P. Pavlov (1928) have, of course, in their investigations of conditioned reflexes played a role of first importance in the development of comparative psychology throughout the world. This subject is treated in another chapter of the present book. It may be emphasized here that no other single influence has probably been as significant in the study of how behavior can be changed under controlled conditions as has this work on conditioning. Research on conditioned responses has also made possible basic advances in knowledge about certain physiological functions of animals such as their sensory capacities. H. S. Liddell (1934) has carried out significant studies on the conditioning of rabbits, goats, sheep, and pigs. Recently very interesting work on learning in planaria has been conducted (see Thompson & McConnell, 1955).

R. M. Yerkes and S. Morgulis (1909) were among the first in America to point out the significance of the conditioned reflex for comparative psychology.

Many important recent advances in general psychological and behavior theory are rooted in the work of Pavlov and his school. This study which has come to be called "classical conditioning" has done much to advance our modern view of how behavior can be modified. C. L. Hull (1943), for example, in part by his own and his student's use of animal subjects, developed a comprehensive system of psychology on this basis. Similarly, as a reaction, at least in part, against a too strict Pavlovian interpretation of all learning, E. C. Tolman (1932) elaborated an influential system of psychology which avoids vitalism but has been called "purposive behaviorism." This conceptual formulation was based by Tolman and his students on animal as well as human experiments. Many other able psychologists have worked on what may be called the "higher thought processes" as demonstrated in the behavior of mammals. The work of N. R. F. Maier (1937) on reasoning in rats is typical of this trend. (See also Honzik & Tolman, 1936; Krechevisky, 1935).

Besides studies inspired by classical conditioning, what is called *instrumental* or *operant conditioning* has also proved to be of great importance in the laboratory study of animal and human psychology. In conditioning of this type, what the animal itself does leads to a reward such as the securing of a bit of food when the organism is in a state of hunger. Reactions of this sort lead to subsequent responses which would not have been made except for the previously rewarded responses. B. F. Skinner (1938, 1953) and his associates and students have developed a school of animal and human psychology in America based on the elaboration of the concept of operant conditioning. In describing this work, Skinner says: "In operant conditioning we 'strengthened' an operant in the sense of making a response more probable or in actual fact more frequent."

The techniques developed by these investigators have yielded results of theoretical importance and also have demonstrated themselves to be of practical value to those who train animals for theatrical or marina acts. Pharmacologists who wish to test the effectiveness of various drugs also have found this technique of great value. The use of animals in drug studies is indeed one of the greatest applied fields of modern comparative psychology. The importance of using infrahuman primates in early tests of space flight may be mentioned here.

A division of the American Psychological Association has been formed, with the title, *The Division of Experimental Analysis of Behavior*. This division is made up of scientists who are interested in both animal and human psychology and especially in the approaches to the study of behavior made possible by techniques such as those devised by Skinner and his associates. Many different animal species have been investigated by these students. Special emphasis, however, has been given to the study of the white rat and the pigeon. A new terminology and a series of principles that are related to the giving of rewards or what are called *schedules of reinforcement* have been developed by these workers (see Ferster & Skinner, 1957). History already suggests that this use of operant conditioning techniques is certainly one of the new dynamic tendencies of modern psychology that seems bound to continue to guarantee fruitful advances in the truly scientific animal psychology of the future.

Ethology

The name *ethology* is now given to another well-recognized school of students of animal behavior. Most ethologists are basically trained in zoology and in general their studies are on the behavior of animals in their natural habitats. Modern ethologists use all convenient means to make observations accurate and complete. In their publications, members of this school have developed a number of new scientific terms or constructs which they find convenient in summarizing their observations. One of these is *species-specific behavior*. This phrase is employed to characterize the unlearned reactions of specific animal groups. Another concept used by members of this school is *imprinting*. This name is given to what seems to be a special kind of learning, ordinarily seen very early in life, is very rapidly acquired, and also has been shown to be very resistant to extinction or forgetting. In general, ethologists are interested in the total movements of intact animals and in behavior that characterizes an animal which is not the result of specific learning by the individual under study. In this connection, it may be noted that some ethologists are interested in the hypothesis of consciousness of animals. Thorpe (1966) says, ". . . we have powerful reasons for concluding that consciousness at one grade or another is a widespread feature of animal life."

Much of the early work of this group was done on fish and on the stickle-back in particular, as well as various species of birds. N. Tinbergen's book, *The Study of Instinct* (1951), was an early and influential ethological publication. K. Lorenz, another eminent member of the school, in publications such as, "The Comparative Method in Studying Innate Behavior Patterns" (1950), has contributed much to this approach to modern behavior study. W. H. Thorpe has written importantly in this field. His book, *Learning and Instinct in Animals* (1956), has deservedly been widely quoted. This volume demonstrates the great advances that have been made in the field which was well summarized a generation ago by J. Drever (1917). (See also Thorpe & Zangwill, 1961.)

Under the editorship of C. H. Schiller, an important book, *Instinctive Behavior: The Development of a Modern Concept*, with an introduction by K. S. Lashley, appeared containing chapters by Lorenz on companionship in bird life, the nature of instinctive behavior, taxis and instinct, and in general on the comparative study of behavior (Schiller, 1957). The chapter on taxis and instinct was jointly written by Lorenz and Tinbergen. There is also a chapter, by Tinbergen and Kuenen, on feeding behavior in young thrushes. A most important chapter in this book "Innate Motor Action as a Basis for Learning," was written by Paul H. Schiller. He was a European trained ethologist and animal psychologist who, at the time of his sudden death, was a member of the staff of the Yerkes Laboratories at Orange Park, Florida. He made especially important contributions to what may be called quantitative psychobiology because he combined the modern ethological point of view with a clear understanding of the more quantitative American approach to animal psychology.

One interesting point of emphasis of ethologists is that species of animals in their behavior show responses that are important in taxonomy, that is in defining the group to which they belong. More and more, behavior is taking its place with the older criteria of systematic biology which emphasized skeletal makeup and coat or feather color. This is a most important contribution and will certainly continue in the future to give new insights to many of the old static procedures of systematic zoology in which dry museum specimens were almost exclusively relied upon.

The study of communication and vocalization in animals has a long history. The comparison of sounds made by various mammals with the very early growth of vocalization in the human infant is interesting in a truly comparative psychology (Carmichael, 1964).

Some of the early development of the concepts of present day ethology were made before the term ethology itself was coined. In America, the work of C. O. Whitman, as seen in his treatise on *Animal Behavior* (1898), and of W. Craig (1908), in his insightful studies of birds and organisms is now acknowledged by leading modern ethologists as examples of this type of study. The present author owes a deep debt of gratitude to Craig with whom he studied at Harvard. The pioneer work of Spalding (1873), as noted above, is most interesting in this connection.

Down through the years the study of the behavior of birds has added many new and important concepts to comparative psychology in general. E. A. Armstrong in an excellent book, *Bird Display and Behavior* (1965), offers a fine introduction to this field.

E. H. Hess (1962), working in America, has subjected a number of ethological concepts to close scrutiny and has also contributed by objective techniques to our understanding of such processes as space perception in chicks. Sir Julian Huxley has recently written a very valuable critique, *Ethology Elucidated* (1964). In this he says of Lorenz, "By his demonstration of the universal existence and importance of endogenous behavior patterns he has, as he once remarked in conversation, 'taken the stink out of instinct' and has disposed of the claims of the Pavlovians and the behaviorists that all useful behavior is learned behavior, and that all learning is only a matter of conditioning." To this the present author says, "Amen."

Prenatal Life

This history of comparative psychology must also consider the development of knowledge concerning the behavior of animals before birth or hatching, that is, during active fetal life. Similarly, a history of the now much-neglected study of the activities of immature animals immediately after birth deserves notice. Ruth M. Cruikshank (Bussey) has well summarized much of the literature on animal infancy (1954). This field of study is of great importance at the present time because of the understanding developed in this decade about the chemical basis of heredity. The role of DNA in ontogenetic development and the knowledge of the coding of genetic information that has recently been discovered open new vistas of understanding of the timing of the development of the specific neural and other structures on which inborn behavior acts depend. Modern molecular biology is, thus, for the first time providing a key that bids fair to explain the patterning of growth and the time sequences of the appearance of inherited modes of behavior even in adult life. It must be emphasized that this new knowledge makes it clear that behavior changes due to heredity continue in the organism long after behavior changes resulting from learning have also begun. A whole new and important subscience, behavior genetics, is now making many important discoveries and bids fair to help in the solution of some of the most puzzling and persistent problems of comparative psychology. J. L. Fuller and W. R. Thompson (1960) have prepared an excellent introduction to this field. W. J. Burdette (1963) has also recently brought together a series of important contributions that bear on this subject.

In the history of the study of prenatal behavior in mammals and man attention has properly been given to the so-called ontogenetic zero, that is, the point where receptor neuromuscular responses first begin, and to the growth of responses beyond that point and up to the time of birth, and indeed in early postnatal maturation. The present author has summarized, in some detail, and given a bibliography up to 1954, of many investigations in this field on various species of fetal animals (Carmichael, 1954). (See also Needham, 1931.)

Reference has been made above to the fact that the guinea pig is born in an almost adult state, behaviorally speaking. The gradual development of capacity in this organism's fetal life has been studied by the present writer as a basis for a better understanding of the growth of species-specific behavior in a mammal that is born, as noted above, with almost adult behavioral capacity (Carmichael, 1934).

The fact that organisms are born with very varying degrees of behavioral capacity is illustrated by the comparison of the effective behavior of the new-born guinea pig as compared, for example, with the opossum, which is born in many ways as a midterm fetus. The amazingly effective behavior of an animal such the wildebeast (gnu) or the giraffe at birth is interesting in this connection (Carmichael, 1957b). The ungulates, in general, have in the wild state, a pattern of life which makes what may be called a precocity of behavioral maturation at birth of life saving importance to the young of such species in the wild. The study of the behavior of birds before hatching is also significant in this connection as seen in the works of the distinguished comparative psychologist Z. Y. Kuo (1938). For many years those interested in the development of behavior have studied salamanders because their patterns of response are clearly identifiable at various stages and these reactions can be related to the growth of the nervous system. The work of G. E. Coghill (1929) has been most important in this field. It may also be noted that the present writer used the salmaander in a series of studies in which morphological growth and the effect or noneffect of exercise during development was studied. Some salamanders were allowed to develop in an anaesthetic solution in which morphological growth was normal but in which no behavior occurred. The responses of salamanders immediately after coming out of the anaesthetized condition were compared with organisms that had been normally active during the whole period of growth. The results of these experiments demonstrated that the behavior in question seemed to be genetically determined and not at all the result of environmentally determined practice. The animals that had grown without any overt behavior responded normally as soon as they came out of the anaesthetic (Carmichael, 1927a).

Robert M. Yerkes

In a review of the history of animal psychology, it may not be inappropriate to discuss in a little greater detail one of many important programs in this field that has done much to establish the present secure status of comparative psychology as a science. Robert M. Yerkes may be taken as an example of one of the outstanding leaders who has created the modern patterns of this field. Yerkes did much for comparative psychology in general but his greatest contribution was in developing the modern psychobiology of the infrahuman primates.

The programs that he and his associates developed for research with these mammals established a model and may well be used for a comprehensive study of the full repertoire of behavior of other animal species in the future.

Yerkes was born in 1879 and died in 1956 (Carmichael, 1957a). While still a graduate student at Harvard, he became convinced that what was needed to unlock the complex problems inherent in understanding normal and abnormal human and animal mental life, was a research institute for the comparative study of mammals and man which would give its main attention to the great apes. From that time on, for more than half a century, often after overcoming great difficulties, he transformed this dream into an effective reality. In doing this, he planned and raised the money necessary to establish what was first known as the Yale Laboratories of Primate Biology, later renamed in his honor "The Yerkes Laboratories." The importance of his original idea for a primate center is attested by the fact that the United States Congress has in the last few years appropriated $14.5 million for the capital development of seven primate research centers in this country. These centers have been established in association with the University of Oregon, the University of Washington, the University of Wisconsin, Emory University, Tulane University, and Harvard University. A National Center for Primate Biology has also been provided at the University of California. The Federal government is also giving financial support for the research programs at these centers. This present great national effort to secure scientific knowledge about primates clearly developed out of the success of the research center which Yerkes created first at New Haven and later at Orange Park, Florida.

After Yerkes took his doctor's degree at Harvard, he remained at that institution for twenty scientifically significant years. During this period he did much to organize the present-day general American conceptual framework for scientific animal psychology. In 1917 he accepted an invitation to go to the University of Minnesota to carry on in a new and enlarged way, the work that he had brought into being at Harvard. This plan was interrupted by the First World War. Yerkes saw the demands of war work and took upon himself much of the organization of professional colleagues to make a reality of a great program for the psychological examining of soldiers in the United States Army.

In 1924 Yerkes returned to academic work as a professor in the new Institute of Psychology at Yale. From this time on, his research and publications were more and more focused on the development of his great idea of a comprehensive research center for the comparative study of the behavior of primates. In 1929, with the collaboration of his wife, Ada W. Yerkes, he published a monumental volume in this field: *The Great Apes: A Study of Anthropoid Life* (1929). This work has some 650 pages and adequately shows, for the first time, the scientific importance of comparative studies of these mammals which are anatomically, physiologically, and in terms of behavior, most like man.

W. Köhler (1917), famous as one of the founders of Gestalt psychology, published a study of the intelligence of the chimpanzee which has had far-reaching effects because of its emphasis on the role of insight in learning. A distinguished Russian scientist, N. Kohts (1923), has also devoted many years to important chimpanzee research.

The Rockefeller Foundation and Yale University in 1930 jointly provided Yerkes with the funds that allowed the construction of basic buildings for the laboratory at Orange Park, Florida. This unique and historically important center for the study of the great apes has been, from that time on, one of the model laboratories for animal psychology in the world. The geographical location of this facility on Florida's St. John's River, not far from the city of Jacksonville, was based on a careful study made by Yerkes of climate and other relevant environmental factors. A list of the names of the scientists who have worked and been trained at this station and a study of the more than 400 research papers issued from the Orange Park Laboratories show the significance of the work that has been done there.

The book, *The Great Apes*, mentioned above and a later volume, *Chimpanzees: A Laboratory Colony* (Yerkes, 1943), summarize Yerkes's psychobiological point of view. The modern student may wish to consider as a current supplement to these books a two-volume compilation by J. Buettner-Janusch (1963–1964) which deals with the evolutionary and genetic biology of primates.

Yerkes, at all times, stressed the importance of understanding the anatomy, the physiology, and especially the neurology that underlies the behavior of animals which are to be psychologically studied.

Yerkes was succeeded in the directorship of the Orange Park Laboratories by the already world-famous psychologist and neurologist, K. S. Lashley. Lashley was born in 1890 and died in 1958 (Carmichael, 1959). He was already known for his pioneer research on such problems as quantitative relationships between measured brain mass and measured learning ability when he took over the directorship of the Yerkes Laboratories in 1942. Lashley's life work was largely directed toward the development of new techniques for the training of mammals and the study of the effect of the removal of specific amounts of brain tissue on the measured responses of experimentally trained animals. His work clearly demonstrated the equipotentiality of much brain tissue in determining the behavior of the total organism and in making possible the process of learning. The error of the view that every psychological function necessarily has a specific and unchanging anatomical cortical locus was clearly demonstrated by this work. Lashley's research on brain mechanisms basic to specific sensory modalities, and on the cortical structures underlying motor responses also advanced the world's general knowledge of specific neurological structures and functioning even in man.

Lashley received his Ph.D. degree at Johns Hopkins University and as a young man he was a collaborator of the biologist H. S. Jennings whose distinguished work on the behavior of lower organisms has already been mentioned. He was a close friend and collaborator of J. B. Watson whose work on animal psychology as well as on a behavioristic point of view for all psychology has also been noted above. Lashley also was an associate and collaborator of S. I. Franz (1934) whose insightful studies of what can be called the neurology of learning were in part based on experiments with rats. Lashley served on the faculties of Minnesota, Chicago, and Harvard. He continued to be in active charge of the Yerkes Laboratories until 1955. His book *Brain Mechanisms and Intelligence* (1929) is based on his original experiments with animals. He also wrote some 100 monographs and major papers dealing with experimental psychology, neurology, and the biology of behavior.

R. W. Sperry (1951), to mention but one of many workers, in his current studies on brain and behavior, especially in relation to bilateral functions, deals in a brilliant way with problems that were also basic in the work of Lashley. The research of J. Paillard of the Institut de Neurophysiologie et Psychophysiologie of Marseille, France, should also be noted here.

H. Klüver, one of Lashley's closest scientific colleagues, has summarized some important experiments in a book, *Behavior Mechanisms in Monkeys* (1933). Klüver is also the author of many other original studies in comparative psychology. In general, it can be said that Klüver has done much to create a modern truly scientific experimental primate, and indeed general, comparative psychology.

After Lashley's retirement, the directorship of the Yerkes Laboratories was assumed by H. W. Nissen who was born in 1901 and died in 1958 (see, Carmichael, 1965). No man, at least in the non-Communist world, with the exception of Yerkes himself, has ever had so long and so intimate a scientific association with the study of the chimpanzee as did Nissen.

As a young man, he studied this great primate in its wild habitat in Africa (Nissen, 1931) and he also spent all the rest of his life in the skillful care and the scientific study of laboratory chimpanzees.

For more than a quarter of a century at the Orange Park Laboratories, Nissen and his scientific colleagues developed many of the projects that made that center famous. Personally, he was especially interested in the behavior of the chimpanzee but he also concerned himself with those aspects of medicine that are related to the health of the higher apes. He was a master of the special physiology, neurology, and endocrinology of the great apes.

Nissen owed much of his early interest in animal psychology to the influence and inspiration of C. J. Warden whose three-volume work on animal psychology has been mentioned above. Even as a student, Warden noted that Nissen devoted many hours to the close and continuous watching of the animals which he and other students used in scientific laboratory work. A basic willingness for long continued observation of what animals really do in as normal as possible an environment, characterizes, it seems to the present writer, all the truly great students of behavior. There is no shortcut guide to learning what mammals are like or how they solve their problems of daily living except by tireless long continued observation.

In 1941, following the retirement of Yerkes as Director of the Orange Park Laboratories, Nissen became assistant Director and in 1955, upon the retirement of Lashley as Director, he was named director of the Yerkes Laboratories. Nissen can be described as an expert on the infancy, youth, general behavior, reproductive cycles, diseases, diet, general and medical, dental and surgical care of chimpanzees.

Anyone who is interested in a modern assessment of the role of animal psychology cannot do better than to turn to Nissen's chapter, "Phylogenetic Comparison" in the *Handbook of Experimental Psychology* edited by S. S. Stevens (Nissen, 1951). This chapter presents not only a summary of Nissen's own research but also offers a balanced, modern point of view toward the total study of animal psychology. Nissen was especially attracted, in his later years, to the ethological point of view in the study of behaviour which has been discussed above. He looked at the assumptions of this school with eyes trained in quantitative, American psychobiological investigations, but also with a deep sympathy for all students who advocate the study of animals as they really live in their own natural habitats. He was thus a friendly critic as well as an advocate of the conceptual system of ethology. Many other psychologists were indebted to Nissen. D. O. Hebb, for example, whose influential book, *The Organization of Behavior* (1949), deals with many problems basic in animal psychology speaks with special appreciation of Nissen's contributions to his point of view.

Among the many other scientists who have done research with Yerkes, Lashley, or Nissen may be mentioned Kenneth W. Spence (1939), a distinguished comparative psychologist and student of learning and A. H. Riesen (1947), who studied the psychological and anatomical development of the chimpanzee with special reference to the effect of restricted environments. E. F. Kinder has worked on an elaborate time-sampling study of the growth of behavior in young chimpanzees with Riesen (Riesen & Kinder, 1952). Others such as O. L. Tinklepaugh, G. Finch, M. P. Crawford, C. F. Jacobsen, V. Nowlis, S. D. S. Spragg, J. H. Elder, and W. C. Young were active and productive members of this group. W. C. Young (1951) has not only worked on primates but on the anatomy and physiology of reproductive mechanisms in other mammals as well

Nissen was succeeded by A. J. Riopelle as Director of the Yerkes Laboratories. A. J. Riopelle, a distinguished student of primate behavior, primate sensory processes, and brain function, moved from Orange Park in 1962 to become Director of the Delta Regional Primate Research Center at Tulane University (Riopelle, 1960, 1963; Carmichael & Riopelle, 1964). He was succeeded by the present Director of the Laboratory, G. H. Bourne (1942), who superintended the physical move of the Yerkes laboratories from Florida to a large and especially adequate research center not far from Emory University in Atlanta, Georgia.

It is impossible here to mention all the research topics dealing with the life of the chimpanzees that have been carried out at Orange Park in such a successful way over the years. Among the subjects given special attention, however, are the following: factors influencing delayed response; the effect of frontal lobe and other brain lesions (see Jacobson, 1931), especially on specific habit systems; the nature of discrimination learning; prelinguistic sign behavior; reward expectancy; the role of visual, auditory, and other receptors in determining behavior; the discrimination behavior of young animals compared with human beings; conditioned reflexes; the social behavior of primates; capacity to deal with abstractions; the nature of drives and motivation; individual differences in behavior; a comparison of problem solving by monkeys of various species and chimpanzees; the effect of schedules of reinforcement on chimpanzee learning; and above all, the general social behavior of young and adult chimpanzees.

The topics just given present a far from complete picture of the range and scope of studies carried out at Orange Park and now being further developed in the new primate centers of America. These topics may suggest to the reader the importance of laboratory animal psychology and especially the laboratory study of primates as a means of advancing an understanding of the behavior of the great apes and therefore, a knowledge as Yerkes clearly saw, of scientific psychology in general.

It has been noted that Nissen studied chimpanzees in the wild. Necessarily, this work was preliminary. C. R. Carpenter (1964) did much to make field studies of primates scientific and by his studies of howler monkeys has demonstrated the importance of *territoriality* in primate social life. This important concept of territoriality was demonstrated in bird life by Howard (1920). (See also, Ardrey, 1966.)

Recently, Jane Goodall (1963) and her husband (Baron Hugo van Lawick) have made a most detailed study of chimpanzees in their natural habitat at Gombe Stream in Tanzania, East Africa. The present writer has had the privilege of observing wild chimpanzees in this area as a guest of these resident investigators. Goodall's work has already required almost five years of continuous observation. The studies made at Gombe Stream constitute a basic contribution to the understanding of the adaptive life of chimpanzees as they live in their natural surroundings. This amazingly painstaking observational work has demonstrated the fact, for example, that chimpanzees make what can properly be called tools for special purposes such as termite "fishing." These field studies have also thrown light on the types of food used by chimpanzees, sex behavior, maternal activities, dominance, and the general social psychology of the chimpanzee.

All in all, this cumulative work on laboratory and field studies of chimpanzees in the last half century demonstrates how years devoted to study of a specific animal can pay rich dividends in making a true and relatively complete comparative psychology possible. In considering the fruitfulness of field studies of primates, special references should be made to the elaborate research of recent years by Japanese scientists on Japanese monkeys (Kawamura, 1956). Similarly, the research of S. L. Washburn and I. DeVore (1961) and their associates on baboons deserves special notice. H. J. Coolidge (1933), J. T. Emlen (1960), and G. B. Schaller (1963) have made great advances in our knowledge of the gorilla. The latter investigator's work is especially important in presenting a report of the behavior of the wild gorilla in a setting of modern scientific ecology.

H. F. Harlow (1958) has for many years been an insightful and original student of primates. He is now Director of the Regional Primate Center mentioned above at the University of Wisconsin. Harlow is recognized as an original and able student of problems related to motivation, learning and mother-child interaction in primates. His research and the work of his students can be said to have opened up a whole new series of fields of investigation in animal psychology that are today being most profitably investigated. H. L. Rheingold (1963) has recently brought together a most important series of papers on maternal behavior in mammals.

Many field studies of mammals below the primates have been carried on in recent years. J. A. King (1959) has studied the social psychology of the prairie dog and the activities of deermice in their natural ecological setting. He has also investigated the effect of early handling on wild animals. W. N. Kellogg is well known for his early and brilliant pioneer work on rearing an infant chimpanzee with a human child (Kellogg, 1933). For another study of this interesting topic, see K. J. Hayes and C. Hayes (1951). More recently Kellogg (1958) has made special advances in our knowledge of the behavior of the porpoise. J. C. Lilly (1961) and his associates have studied conditioning and communication in this same interesting and intelligent marine animal which is notable for its large and complex brain and its ability to learn and to communicate.

A Look Toward the Future

A cynic has said that historians back into the future with their eyes fixed on the past. In certain ways this is true. If this aphorism is correct, it may be said with assurance that the field of animal or comparative psychology can be considered to be in good intellectual health. What has been written in this chapter shows that the study of animal behavior has had a long and significant past. Clearly, this field or section of modern scientific psychology is closely related to the other biological sciences and is also in many ways basic to human psychology (Carmichael, 1956, 1963). As has been pointed out, many of the advances made in this area of study have been carried on, not only by psychologists but also by medical scientists, physiologists, neurologists, and anthropologists. Above all, zoologists who are interested in behavior are among the modern leaders in research in this field.

To put this in another way, animal or comparative psychology has always been, and is today, a model interdisciplinary field. Through the years and especially since the time of Darwin, facts have been gradually accumulated and tested to establish the broad factual and theoretical basis of this science. In this way a solid structure of established knowledge has been developed which is independent of the allegiance of its individual scientific workers to a professional field such as psychology, physiology, ethology, or any other subsection of biological science.

Virtually, all serious modern scientific students of animals take the point of view that the organisms they study are objects in nature. A starfish is to be understood in the same objective way as a star. These living objects are to be investigated by the use of the established measurements and the conceptual tools of the other physical, chemical, and biological sciences. Thus, the history of work in this field, as is true of the history of any other science, such as geology or organic chemistry, recounts the past and established advances on which future scientific work can be based with assurance.

The sure, progressive, cumulative scientific continuity of animal or comparative psychology sets this area of the study of mental life apart from some other and more speculative branches of psychology. There are still areas of psychology in which constructs of a prescientific age, some even with tell-tale mythological names, are solemnly reified and then talked of as "things." Only in a most involved way, can such constructs be dealt with scientifically. But in animal psychology, save for a few peripheral, vitalistic writers referred to above, the steady advance of knowledge and theory has been very little hindered by bickerings between so-called "schools" as has been true, unfortunately, in much human psychology and in psychoanalysis. As noted above, modern students of the behavior of animals except for some ethologists (Thorpe, 1966) have not felt it necessary to struggle with concepts such as "consciousness" or "the unconscious" which historically have produced much difficulty in traditional theory formulation in normal and abnormal psychology.

In other words, as the history of the scientific study of animal psychology, to use the figure suggested above, backs into the future, one can be sure of real and continuing progress. By the use of more and more modern techniques such as those of present-day molecular biology and by employing better and better electronic and other devices in experimental work, this solid and well-grounded science may confidently be expected to continue to make new discoveries and to establish new and verifiable theoretical constructs. Important discoveries can certainly be expected in this field in the years immediately ahead. This evolving knowledge of systematic comparative psychology will be important for its own sake and in advancing an objective understanding of animals. These novel facts and theories about infrahuman behavior will have applied value in providing an increasingly solid basis for a better understanding of many important aspects of normal and abnormal human mental life.

REFERENCES

ADAM, C., & TANNERY, P. (Eds.) (1897–1913) *Oeuvres de Descartes.* Paris: Cerf.

ALLEN, J. (1904) The associative processes of the guinea pig. *J. comp. Neur. Psychol.*, 14, 293–359.

ARDREY, R. (1966) *The territorial imperative.* New York: Atheneum.

ARMSTRONG, E. A. (1965) *Bird display and behavior.* New York: Dover.

BALFOUR, C. E., & CARMICHAEL, L. (1928) The light reactions of the meal worm (*Tenebrio molitor Linn.*). *Amer. J. Psychol.*, 40, 576–584.

BARD, P. (1940) *The hypothalamus and central levels of autonomic function.* Baltimore: Williams & Wilkins.

BEACH, F. A. (1958) Neural and chemical regulation of behavior. In H. Harlow and C. N. Woolsey (Eds.), *Biological and biochemical basis of behavior.* Madison: University of Wisconsin Press. Pp. 263–284.

BEER, T., BETHE, A. & VON UEXKÜLL, J. (1899) Vorschlage zur einer abjektivi-render Nomenclature in der Physiologie des Nervensystems. *Bio. cent.*, 19, 517–521.

BEKHTEREV, V. M. (1928) *General principles of human reflexology: An introduction to the objective study of personality.* 4th ed. (trans. from Russian). London: Jarrolds.

BERGSON, H. (1907) *Creative evolution.* Trans. by A. Mitchell. New York: Holt, 1911.

BINET, A. (1889) *The psychic life of micro-organisms: A study in experimental psychology.* Chicago: Open Court.

BIRKENHEAD, LORD COHEN OF. (1958) *Sherrington: physiologist,* philosopher and poet. Springfield: Thomas.

BITTERMAN, M. E. (1960) Toward a comparative psychology of learning. *Amer. Psychologist*, 15, 704–712.

BORING, E. C. (1929) *A history of experimental psychology.* 2nd ed. New York: Appleton, 1950.

BOURNE, G. H. (1942) *Cytology and cell physiology.* Oxford: Clarendon.

BOYCOTT, B. B. (1965) Learning in the octopus. *Scientific Amer.*, 212, 42–50.

BUETTNER-JANUSCH, J. (1963–1964) *Evolutionary and genetic biology of primates.* New York: Academic Press. 2 vols.

BURDETTE, W. J. (1963) *Methodology in mammalian genetics.* San Francisco: Holden Day.

CANNON, W. B. (1932) *The wisdom of the body.* New York: Norton.

CARMICHAEL, L. (1926) Sir Charles Bell: A contribution to the history of physiological psychology. *Psychol. Rev.*, 33, 188–217.

CARMICHAEL, L. (1927)a A further study of the development of behavior in vertebrates experimentally removed from the influence of external stimulation. *Psychol. Rev., 34,* 34–47.

CARMICHAEL, L. (1927b) Robert Whytt: A contribution to the history of physiological psychology. *Psychol. Rev. 34,* 34–47.

CARMICHAEL, L. (1934) An experimental study in the prenatal guinea-pig, of the origin and development of reflexes and patterns of behavior in relation to the stimulation of specific receptor areas during the period of active fetal life. *Genet. Psychol. Monogr. 16,* 341–491.

CARMICHAEL, L. (1954) The onset and early development of behavior. In L. Carmichael, (Ed.), *Manual of child psychology.* 2nd ed. New York: Wiley. Pp. 60–185.

CARMICHAEL, L. (1956) *The making of the modern mind.* (Rockwell Lectures, Rice Institute) Houston: Elsevier.

CARMICHAEL, L. (1957a) Robert Mearns Yerkes, 1876–1956. *Psychol. Rev., 64,* 1–7.

CARMICHAEL, L. (1957b) *Basic psychology.* New York: Random House.

CARMICHAEL, L. (1959) Karl Spencer Lashley, experimental psychologist. *Science,* 129, 1410–1412.

CARMICHAEL, L. (1963) Psychology of animal behavior. *Amer. Psychologist, 18,* 112–113.

CARMICHAEL, L. (1964) The early growth of language capacity in the individual. In E. H. Lenneberg (Ed.), *New directions in the study of language.* Cambridge: M.I.T. Press. Pp. 1–22.

CARMICHAEL, L. (1965 Henry Wieghorst Nissen. *National Academy of Sciences of the United States of America Biographical Memoirs, 38.* New York: Columbia University Press.

CARMICHAEL, L. & RIOPELLE, A. J. (1964) Primate biology. *Science,* 146, 1078–1080.

CARMICHAEL, M. & MacLEAN, P. D. (1961) Use of the squirrel monkey for brain research with description of restraining chair. EEG *Clin. Neurphysiol., 13,* 128–129.

CARPENTER, C. R. (1964) *Naturalistic behavior of nonhuman primates.* State College: Pennsylvania State University Press.

CARR, H. (1917) Maze studies with the white rat: I. Normal animals; II. Blind animals; III. Anosomic animals. *J. annim. Behav.,* 7, 259–306.

CARTHY, J. D. (1956) *Animal navigation: how animals find their way about.* London: G. Allen and Unwin.

CLEMENTS, F. E. (1935) Social origins and processes among plants. In C. Murchison (Ed.), *A handbook of social psychology.* London: Oxford University. Press.

COGHILL, G. E. (1929) *Anatomy and the problem of behavior.* London: Cambridge University Press.

COOLIDGE, H. J., Jr. (1933) *Pan paniscus,* pigmy chimpanzee from south of the Congo River. *Amer. J. physiol. Anthrop., 18,* 1–57.

CRAIG, W. (1908) The voices of pigeons regarded as a means of social control. *Amer. J. Sociol.,* 14, 86–100.

CROZIER, W. J. (1929) The study of living organisms. In C. Murchison (Ed.), *Foundations of experimental psychology.* Worcester: Clark University Press. Pp. 45–127.

CRUIKSHANK, R. M. (1954) Animal infancy. In L. Carmichael (Ed.), *Manual of child psychology.* 2nd ed. New York: Wiley. Pp. 186–214.

DARWIN, C. R. (1859) *The origin of species by means of natural selection.* 6th ed. New York: Appleton, 1872.

DARWIN, C. R. (1872) *Expression of emotions in man and animals.* New York: Appleton.

DARWIN, C. R. (1874) *Descent of man and selection in relation to sex.* Ohio: Werner.

DARWIN, E. (1796) *Zoonomia: or the laws of organic life.* New York: Swords.

DREVER, J. (1917) *Instinct in man: A contribution to the psychology of education.* 2nd ed. Cambridge: University Press.

DRIESCH, H. (1903) *Die "Seele" als elementarer Naturfaktor.* London: Black, 1908. 2 vols.

DROSCHER, V. B. (1965) *The mysterious senses of animals.* New York: Dutton.

ECCLES, J. C. (1966) *Brain and conscious experience.* New York: Springer-Verlag.

EMLEN, J. T. (1960) Current field studies of the mountain gorilla. *S. Afr. J. Sci.,* 56, 88–89.

ESPER, E. A. (1964) *A history of psychology.* Philadelphia: Saunders.

FABRE, J. H. (1886–1907) *Souvenirs entomologiques.* Paris: Delagrave. 10 vols.

FERSTER, C. B., & SKINNER, B. F. (1957) *Schedules of reinforcement.* New York: Appleton-Century-Crofts.

FLOURENS, M. J. P. (1824) *Recherches expérimentales sur les propriétes et les fonctions du système nerveux dans les animaux vertèbres.* Paris: Crevot.

FOREL, A. (1904) *Ants and some other insects: An inquiry into the psychic powers of these animals with an appendix on the peculiarities of their olfactory sense.* Trans. by W. M. Wheeler. Chicago: Open Court.

FOSTER, SIR M. (1901) *Lectures on the history of physiology during the sixteenth, seventeenth and eighteenth centuries.* Cambridge: University Press.

FRANZ, S. I. (1934) The neurology of learning. In F. A. Moss (Ed.), *Comparative psychology.* New York: Prentice Hall. Pp. 219–245.

FRISCH, K. VON. (1950) *Bees: Their vision, chemical senses and language.* Ithaca: Cornell University Press.

FULLER, J. L., & Thompson, W. R. (1960) *Behavior genetics.* New York: Wiley.

FULTON, J. F. (1926) *Muscular contraction and the reflex control of movement.* Baltimore: Williams & Wilkins.

GOODALL, JANE. (1963) My life among wild chimpanzees. *National Geographic Magazine,* 124, 272–308.

GRANIT, R. (1933) The components of the retinal action potentials in mammals and their relation to the discharge in the optic nerve. *J. physiol.,* 77, 207–239.

GROOS, K. 1896 *Die Spiele der Tiere.* E. L. Baldwin (Trans.), *The play of animals.* New York: Appleton, 1915.

GROOS, K. (1899) *Die Spiele der Menschen.* Jena: G. Fisher.

GUTHRIE, E. R., & HORTON, G. P. (1946) *Cats in a puzzle box.* New York: Rinehart.

HAECKEL, E. (1906) *The evolution of man.* Ohio: Werner.

HALL, G. S. (1904) *Adolescence. Its psychology and its relation to physiology.* New York: Appleton. 2 vols.

HARLOW, H., & WOOLSEY, C. N. (Eds.) (1958) *Biological and biochemical basis of behavior.* Madison: University of Wisconsin Press.

HARTLINE, H. K. (1938) The response of single optic nerve fibers of the vertebrate eye to illumination of the retina. *Amer. J. Physiol.,* 121, 400–415.

HAYES, K. J., & HAYES, C. (1951) The intellectual development of a home-raised chimpanzee. *Proc. Amer. phil. Soc.,* 95, 105–109.

HEBB, D. O. (1949) *The organization of behavior: a neuropsychological theory.* New York: Wiley.

HERBERT, S. (1919) *The first principles of evolution.* London: Black.

HESS, E. H. (1962) Ethology, an approach toward the complete analysis of behavior. In R. Brown, E. Galanter, E. H. Hess, and G. Mandler (Eds.), *New directions in psychology*. New York: Holt, Rinehart & Winston.

HOBHOUSE, L. T. (1915) *Mind in evolution*. 2nd ed. London: Macmillan.

HOLT, E. B. (1931) *Animal drive and the learning process*. New York: Holt.

HOLT, E. B., & LEE, F. S. (1901) The theory of phototactic response. *Amer. J. Physiol.*, 4, 460–481.

HONZIK, E. H., & TOLMAN, E. C. (1936) The perception of relations in the rat. *J. comp. Psychol.*, 22, 287–318.

HOWARD, E. (1920) *Territory in bird life*. New York: Atheneum, 1964.

HULL, C. L. (1943) *Principles of behavior: An introduction to behavior theory*. New York: Appleton-Century.

HUNTER, W. S. (1913) The delayed reaction in animals and children. *Behav. Mongr.*, 2 (6), 1–86.

HUXLEY, SIR J. (1964) Ethology elucidated. *The graduate journal, University of Texas*, 6, 395–430.

JACOBSEN, C. F. (1931) A study of cerebral function in learning: the frontal lobes. *J. comp. Neurol.*, 52, 271–340.

JAMES, W. (1890) *The principles of psychology*. New York: Holt. 2 vols.

JASPER, H. H., et al. (1958) *Reticular formation of the brain*. New York: Little, Brown.

JENNINGS, H. S. (1904) *Contributions to the study of the behavior of the lower organisms*. Washington: Carnegie Institution of Washington, Publication No. 16.

KAFKA, G. (Ed.) (1922) Tierpsychologie. In *Handbuch der vergleichenden Psychologie*. Munchen: Reinhardt. 3 vols.

KAWAMURA, S. K. (1956) Social organization of a natural group of Japanese macaque. *Japan J. Ecol.*, 6, 45–50.

KELLOGG, W. N. (1933) *The ape and the child*. New York: McGraw-Hill.

KELLOGG, W. N. (1958) Echo ranging in the porpoise. *Science*, 128, 982–988.

KING, J. A. (1959) The social behavior of prairie dogs. *Scientific Amer.*, 101, 128–140.

KLUVER, H. (1933) *Behavior mechanisms in monkeys*. Chicago: University of Chicago Press.

KÖHLER, W. (1917) *The mentality of apes*. (2nd rev. ed. trans. by E. Wenter. New York: Harcourt, Brace, 1925.

KOHTS, N. (1923) *Untersuchungen über die Erkenntnisfahigkieten des Schimpansen*. (In Russian with German summary.) Moscow: Museum Darwinianum.

KRECHEVISKY, I. (1935). Brain mechanisms and "hypothese." *J. comp. Psychol.*, 19, 425–462.

KUO, Z. Y. (1938) Ontogeny of embryonic behavior in aves: II. Stages in the development of physiological activities in the chick embryo. *Amer. J. Psychol.*, 51, 361–378.

LANGE, F. A. (1925) *The history of materialism*. Trans. by E. C. Thomas. New York: Harcourt, Brace.

LASHLEY, K. S. (1929) *Brain mechanisms and intelligence*. Chicago: University of Chicago Press.

LIDDELL, H. S. (1934) The conditioned reflex. In F. A. Moss (Ed.), *Comparative psychology*. Baltimore: Johns Hopkins Press. Pp. 247–296.

LILLY, J. C. (1961) *Man and dolphin*. New York: Doubleday.

LOEB, J. (1900) *Comparative physiology of the brain and comparative psychology*. New York: Putnam.

LORENZ, K. (1950) The comparative method in studying innate behavior patterns. In *Symposium, Soc. for Exp. Biol.*, IV. Cambridge: University Press.

LUBBOCK, J. A. (1888) On the senses, instincts and intelligence of animals with special reference to insects. New York: Appleton.

MacLEAN, P. D. (1959) The limbic system with respect to two basic life principles. In Conference on the Central Nervous Systems and Behavior, Transactions Macy Foundation. Pp. 31–118.

MAGOUN, H. W. (1948) Spasticity, the stretch reflex and extrapyramidal systems. Springfield: Thomas.

MAIER, N. R. F. (1937) Reasoning in rats and human beings. Psychol. Rev., 44, 365–378.

MAIER, N. R. F., & SCHNEIRLA, T. C. (1935) Principles of animal psychology. New York: Dover.

MANDEVILLE, B. DE. (1714) The fable of the bees. F. B. Kaye (Ed.) Oxford: Clarendon, 1924. 2 vols.

MAST, S. O. (1911) Light and the behavior of organisms. New York: Wiley.

MATTHEWS, G. V. T. (1955) Bird navigation. Cambridge: University Press.

McDOUGALL, W. (1926) Outline of psychology. New York: Scribner.

MILES, W. R. (1930) The comparative learning of rats on elevated and alley mazes of the same pattern. J. comp. Psychol., 10, 237–261.

MILLER, N. E. (1951) Learnable drives and rewards. In S. S. Stevens (Ed.), Handbook of experimental psychology. New York: Wiley. Pp. 435–472.

MILLS, T. W. F. (1898) The nature and development of animal intelligence. London: Unwin.

MORGAN, C. L. (1900) Animal behavior. London: Arnold.

MORGAN, C. L. (1901) Introduction to comparative psychology. New York: Scribner.

MOSS, F. A. (Ed.) (1934) Comparative psychology. New York: Prentice-Hall.

MUNN, N. L. (1950) Handbook of psychological research on the rat. An introduction to animal psychology. Boston: Houghton Mifflin.

MUNN, N. L. (1965) The evolution and growth of human behavior. 2nd ed. Boston: Houghton Mifflin.

MURPHY, G. (1929) An historical introdutcion to modern psychology. New York: Harcourt, Brace.

NEEDHAM, J. (1931) Chemical embryology. Cambridge: University Press. 3 vols.

NISSEN, H. W. (1931) A field study of the chimpanzee: observations of chimpanzee behavior and environment in Western French Guinea. Comp. psychol. Monogr., 8, 1–105.

NISSEN, H. W. (1951) Phylogenetic comparison. In S. S. Stevens (Ed.), Handbook of experimental psychology. New York: Wiley. Pp. 347–386.

OLDS, J. (1958) Effects on hunger and male sex hormones on self stimulation of the brain. J. comp. Psychol. Physiol., 51, 320–324.

PARKER, G. H. (1919) The elementary nervous system. London: Lippincott.

PAVLOV, I. P. (1928) Lectures on conditioned reflexes. English trans. with biographical sketch by W. H. Gnatt. New York: International Publishers.

PECKHAM, G. W. & PECKHAM, E. G. (1887) Some observations on the mental powers of spiders. J. Morph., 1, 383–419.

PFAFFMAN, C. (1951) Taste and smell. In S. S. Stevens (Ed.), Handbook of experimental psychology. New York: Wiley. Pp. 1143–1171.

PREYER, W. (1882) Die Seele des Kindes. 5th ed. Leipzig: T. Grieben, 1900.

PREYER, W. (1885) Spezielle Physiologie des Embryo. Trans. by G. E. Coghill and W. K. Legner, Embryonic motility and sensitivity. Monograph of the Society for Research in Child Development, National Research Council, 1937.

RATNER, S. C. & DENNY, M. R. (1964) Comparative psychology: research in animal behavior. Illinois: Dorsey Press.

RATNER, S. C. & MULLER, K. R. (1964) Classical conditioning in earthworms. In S. C. Ratner, and M. R. Denny, (Eds.), *Comparative psychology*. Illinois: Dorsey Press.

RAWDON-SMITH A. F., CARMICHAEL, L. & WELLMAN, B. (1938) Electrical responses from the cochlea of the fetal guinea pig. *J. exper. Psychol.*, 23, 531–535.

RENNIE, J. (1838) The menageries: the natural history of monkeys, opossums and lemurs. In *The Library of Entertaining Knowledge*. London.

RHEINGOLD, H. L. (1963) *Maternal behavior in mammals*. New York: Wiley.

RICHTER, C. P. (1941) The internal enviornment and behavior. *Amer. J. psychiat*, 97, 878–893.

RICHTER, C. P. (1965) *Biological clocks in medicine and psychiatry*. Springfield: Thomas.

RIESEN, A. H. (1947) The development of visual perception in man and chimpanzee. *Science*, 106, 107–108.

RIESEN, A. H., and KINDER, E. F. (1952) *The postural development of infant chimpanzees*. New Haven: Yale University Press.

RIOPELLE, A. J. (1960) Observational learning of a position habit by monkeys. *J. comp. physiol. Psychol.*, 53, 426–428.

RIOPELLE, A. J. (1963) Growth and behavioral changes in chimpanzees. *Ztschr. f. Morphol. u. Anthropol.*, 53, 53–61.

ROE, A., & SIMPSON, G. G. (Eds.) (1958) *Behavior and Evolution*. New Haven: Yale University Press.

ROEDER, K. D. (1963) *Nerve cells and insect behavior*. Cambridge: Harvard University Press.

ROEDER, K. D. (1965) Moths and ultrasound. *Scientific Amer.*, 212, 94–102.

ROMANES, G. J. (1885) *Mental evolution in animals*. New York: Appleton.

Ross, W. D. (Ed.) (1908–1931) *The works of Aristotle*. (trans. into English) Clarendon: Oxford University Press. 11 vols.

SARTON, G. (1954) *Galen of Pergamon*. Lawrence: University of Kansas Press.

SAUER, E. G. F. (1958) Celestial navigation by birds. *Scientific Amer.*, 199, 42–47.

SCHILLER, G. B. (1963) *The mountain gorilla*. Chicago: University of Chicago Press.

SCHILLER, C. H. (Trans. and Ed.) (1957)*Instinctive behavior: the development of a modern concept*. New York: International Universities Press. (With an introduction by K. S. Lashley.)

SCHNEIRLA, T. C. (1933) The process and mechanism of ant learning: the combination-problem and the successive-presentation problem. *J. comp. Psychol.*, 17, 303–328.

SCOTT, J. P. (1958) *Animal behavior*. Chicago: University of Chicago Press.

SCOTT, J. P., & FULLER, J. L. (1965) *Genetics and the social behavior of dogs*. Chicago: University of Chicago Press.

SHERRINGTON, C. S. (1906) *The integrative action of the nervous system*. New Haven: Yale University Press.

SKINNER, B. F. (1938) *The behavior of organisms: an experimental analysis*. New York: Appleton-Century.

SKINNER, B. F. (1953) *Science and human behavior*. New York: Macmillan.

SMALL, W. S. (1899) Notes on the psychic development of the young white rat. *Amer. J. Psychol.*, 11, 80–100.

SMITH, K. U. (1934) Visual discrimination in the cat: II, a further study of the capacity of the cat for visual figure discrimination. *J. genet. Psychol.*, 45, 336–357.

SMITH, K. U. (1937) The post-operative effects of removal of the striate cortex upon certain unlearned visually controlled reactions in the cat. *J. genet. Psychol.*, 50, 137–156.

SPALDING, D. A., (1873) Instinct with original observations on young animals. *Macmillan's Magazine*, 27, 282–293.

SPENCE, K. W. (1939) The solution of multiple choice problems by chimpanzees. *Comp. psychol. Monogr.*, 15, 1–54.

SPENCER, H. (1898) *The principles of biology.* 2nd ed. New York: Appleton.

SPENCER, H. R. (1921) *William Harvey, Obstetric physician and gynaecologist* (being the Harveian oration delivered at the Royal College of Physicians). London: Harrison.

SPERRY, R. W. (1951) Mechanisms of neural maturation. In S. S. Stevens (Ed.), *Handbook of experimental psychology.* New York: Wiley. Pp. 236–280.

STOCKARD, C. R. (1941) The genetic and endocrine basis for differences in form and behavior. *Am. Anat. Memoir* No. 19. Philadelphia: Wistar Institute.

STONE, C. P. (1934) Maturation and instinctive functions. In F. A. Moss (Ed.), *Comparative psychology.* New York: Prentice-Hall. Pp. 37–72.

THOMPSON, R., and McCONNELL, J. (1955) Classical conditioning in the planaria, *Dugesia dorotocephala. J. comp. Psychol.*, 48, 65–68.

THORNDIKE, E. L. (1898) Animal intelligence. *Psychol. Rev.*, Monogr. Suppl., 2 (4).

THORPE, W. H. (1956) *Learning and instinct in animals.* London: Methuen.

THORPE, W. H. (1966) Ethology and consciousness. In Sir John C. Eccles (Ed.), *Brain and conscious experience.* New York: Springer-Verlag.

THORPE, W. H. & ZANGILL, O. L. (1961) *Current problems in animal behavior.* Cambridge: University Press.

TINBERGEN, N. (1951) *The study of instinct.* Oxford: Clarendon.

TOLMAN, E. C. (1932) *Purposive behavior in animals and men.* London: Century.

TRYON, R. C. (1940) Genetic differences in maze learning ability in rats. *Year-book Nat. Soc. Stud. Education*, 39, 111–119.

VERWORN, M. (1899) *General physiology.* New York: Macmillan.

VIRGIL. (1940) *Georgics.* Trans. by C. D. Lewis. London: Jonathan Cape.

WARDEN, C. J., JENKINS, T. N., & WARNER, L. H. *Comparative psychology: a comprehensive treatise.* (Principles and methods, 1935; Vertebrates, 1936; Plants and invertebrates, 1940.) New York: Ronald.

WASHBURN, M. F. (1926) (1st ed., 1908; 2nd ed., 1917.) *The animal minds A textbook of comparative psychology.* 3rd ed. New York: Macmillan, 1926.

WASHBURN, S. L. & DEVORE, L. (1961) The social life of baboons. *Scientific Amer.*, 204, 62–71.

WASMANN, E. (1897) *Vergleichende studien uber d. seelen leben der Ameisen under der hoheren Tiere.* Freiburg: Herder.

WATSON, J. B. (1903) *Animal education: the psychical development of the white rat.* Chicago: University of Chicago Press.

WATSON, J. B. (1914) *Behavior: An introduction to comparative psychology.* New York: Holt.

WATSON, R. I. (1960) The history of psychology: A neglected area. *Amer. Psychologist.*, 15, 251–255.

WATSON, R. I. (1963) *The great psychologists.* Philadelphia: Lippincott.

WELLS, M. J. (1962) *Brain and behavior in cephalopods.* Stanford: Stanford University Press.

WEVER, E. G., & BRAY, C. W. (1930) The nature of acoustic response: the relation between sound frequency and frequency of impulses in the auditory nerve. *J. exper. Psychol.*, 13, 373–387.

WHEELER, W. M. (1910) *Ants, their structure, development and behavior.* 2nd ed. New York: Columbia University Press, 1926.

WHITMAN, C. O. (1898) *Animal behavior.* Biol. lectures. Marine Biol. Lab., Woods Hole, Mass.

WOLMAN, B. B. *Contemporary theories and systems in psychology.* New York: Harper & Row, 1960.

YERKES, R. M. (1912) The Intelligence of earthworms. *J. anim. Behav.,* 2, 332–352.

YERKES, R. M. (1943) *Chimpanzees, a laboratory colony.* New Haven: Yale University Press.

YERKES, R. M., & MORGULIS, S. (1909) The method of Pavlov in animal psychology. *Psychol. Bull.,* 6, 257–273.

YERKES, R. M., and YERKES, A. W. (1929) *The great apes: A study of anthropoid life.* New Haven: Yale University Press.

YOUNG, W. C. (1951) Internal secretions and behavior. C. P. Stone (Ed.), *Comparative psychology.* 3rd ed. Englewood Cliffs, N. J.: Prentice-Hall.

CHAPTER 5

I. M. SECHENOV—THE FOUNDER OF OBJECTIVE PSYCHOLOGY[1]

Michael G. Yaroshevski

DURING the latter half of the nineteenth century, when psychology was beginning to lay claim to independence both from philosophy and physiology, a new doctrine was founded in Russia, setting what was essentially a new trend in psychological thought. The author of this doctrine was I. M. Sechenov [1829–1905].

Pavlov called Sechenov "the father of Russian physiology." We can add to this that he was also the founder of objective psychology, based on the deterministic interpretation of the mental regulation of behavior.

The name of Sechenov was known in the last century outside Russia on account of his discoveries in the field of neurophysiology, and above all, for his discovery of the inhibitory influences of the higher nervous centers on the muscular apparatus of behavior. This discovery quickly gave rise to heated discussions among physiologists. Since that time the concept of central inhibition has always been associated with the name of Sechenov. The discussion on this physiological phenomenon apparently subsided. However, as we shall mention later, the roots of dissension extended much deeper into the region of the most crucial questions of determination of the adaptive activity of living beings.

The Western reader was able to learn of Sechenov's psychological doctrine in the early 1880s from the French translation of a number of articles written by Sechenov and combined under the title of *Études psychologiques* (1884). This book was sympathetically received by the French scientific press.

Although this book is a psychological work, its author is regarded purely as a physiologist. So far as the Russian intelligentsia is concerned, Sechenov appeared to them as an outstanding psychologist. His famous pupil N. E. Vvedenskii, for example, wrote about him: "He was, in our country, one of the most capable advocates and pioneers of psychology as an experimental science, compelled by necessity to come down from the heights of speculation and to establish an intimate association with other sciences and, above all, with physiology."

Although nobody in the West regarded Sechenov as a psychologist, this

[1] Translated from Russian by Basil Haigh.

does not mean that his ideas failed to influence European and American psychological science. However, this influence was transmitted through others, especially Bekhterev and Pavlov.

The Western reader knew Sechenov as a physiologist but has no information concerning Sechenov's contribution to the world's psychological thought. Nor will his name be found in the history of psychological investigation.

The picture has begun to change gradually only during the last fifteen years or so. In the second edition of his *History of Experimental Psychology*, Boring (1950) included a paragraph entitled *Objective Psychology*, in which he writes: "The most important self-conscious school of objectivism has been the Russian, which began with the work of Sechenov. . . ." It was Sechenov who became the Russian pioneer of reflexology and "we must, moreover, remember that he was far ahead of western European thought on this matter."

Although, as we shall show below, Boring's evaluation requires a serious correction, it gives a valuable indication of Sechenov's priority in the development of the new system of psychological concepts, of a new explanatory model of behavior.

This model was not just a reproduction of the Cartesian. It was not behavioristic in the narrow meaning which has become attached to this term. The essence of Sechenov's theory was not the denial of mental phenomena, but the causal explanation of their true function.[2] At the same time, it must be emphasized that Pavlov's theory of conditioned reflexes, which is well known in the West, cannot be regarded as a simple concretization or reduplication of Sechenov's thoughts and accomplishments, although, of course, there is no doubt about the intimate ideological connection between these two Titans of Russian scientific thought.

We shall try to describes briefly what is novel in Sechenov's teaching, for it is natural that only by the careful study of the actual writings of this great Russian thinker and naturalist will a deeper understanding of his theories be attained.

The Cultural-Historical Background

Sechenov formulated his system of opinions at a crucial epoch for Russian society. Russia had changed over to the path of capitalism. Economic development had destroyed the foundations of serfdom. Tsarism was forced to move towards reforms and, in face of the mounting tide of peasant revolution, to abolish serfdom. At the beginning of the 1860s the ideological and philosophical conflict, reflecting the exacerbation of social and political differences, reached its climax.

The revolutionary democrats—the "Chernyshevskii Party"—were the holders of advanced ideas, the advocates of the cherished hopes of the oppressed population. This party, which attracted all that was good and worthwhile in Russian society, was opposed by the ideological forces of autocracy. This political division was matched by a philosophical. The Revolutionary Demo-

---

[2] Wolman (1960, p. 194) wrote: "Starting with I. M. Sechenov, Russian physiologists and neurophysiologists embarked upon most fruitful research in physiology of the nervous system and its relationship to behavior."

crats campaigned for a New Russia under the banner of materialism, while their opponents preached an idealistic doctrine. Materialism bound itself closely to natural science that at this time has made major advances in the deterministic explanation of life and consciousness. A real revolution was taking place in biology. Vitalistic concepts were expunged from science as a result of brilliant advances along the road of the experimental and physico-chemical explanation of vital phenomena. The idea of evolution was born. Darwin's theory set out on its victorious path.

The Russian materialists, who supported all these progressive movements in the world of science, were against any form of compromise with the opposing doctrine. They created a philosophical atmosphere in which Russian natural science, made famous by the names of Sechenov, Mendeleev, Timiryazev, Mechnikov, Pavlov, and many others, could flourish. Not only did Sechenov infuse new philosophical ideas, applying them to the solution of concrete philosophical and psychological problems, but he also was an apostle of the younger generation. His psychological theory was created, not in the calm of the consulting room or laboratory, but in hard and unending ideological skirmishes with the opponents of materialism. Sechenov's battle cry was not to be heard in treatises written for a narrow group of specialists or among the scientific elite, but in arguments in the newspapers, and in lectures for students and workers.

Not surprisingly, this battle cry, heralding the victory of the new method of understanding human mental activity, met with persecution by the police and the censor, resulting in legal proceedings and interdiction. By the strength of social circumstances, Sechenov's reflex theory was transformed into a subversive political doctrine.

The author of this theory was not closely associated with the organization of the revolutionary underground movement. At the same time, neither the devotees of autocracy nor its opponents were left with any shadow of doubt regarding the true ideological meaning of Sechenov's schemes and conclusions.

His book *Reflexes of the Brain* (1863) gave Sechenov the reputation of arbiter of the minds of the younger generation. Although intended for Chernyshevskii's journal "Sovremennik," it was in fact published in another, more strictly medical work which quickly became a bibliographic rarity.

Sechenev was acclaimed throughout Russia and he secured a permanent place in the memory of the Russian people.

Sechenov's Life

It is time to give a short biography of Ivan Mikhailovich Sechenov. His father was a small landowner and his mother a simple peasant woman. He graduated at the St. Petersburg School of Military Engineering, where, incidentally, another genius of Russian culture was a pupil at almost the same time—F. M. Dostoevskii. The young engineer had little enthusiasm for military service. Motivated by high humanistic ideals, he joined the medical faculty of Moscow University, and after graduating, he went to Germany where he worked in laboratories in which the new physiology was being created. He attended lectures by Johannes Müller; conducted experiments under the supervision of Helmholtz and Dubois-Reymond; and collaborated with Carl Ludwig, whose close friend he remained throughout the rest of his life.

On his return to Russia he defended his doctorate dissertation: *Material for the Future Physiology of Alcoholic Intoxication* (1860) and lectured on electrophysiology. He again went abroad, this time to Paris, to work in Claude Bernard's laboratory. In experiments on the frog's brain, he discovered "central inhibition" and, on returning to Russia, he published his *Reflexes of the Brain*. The subsequent activity of the "father of Russian physiology" was marked by a number of brilliant investigations and discoveries in the field of neuromuscular physiology, the physiology of the sense organs and of the higher nervous centers, and also the physical chemistry of the blood gases and salt solutions. However, because of the purpose of this chapter, we shall discuss only Sechenov's most important work in the field of psychology, and we shall mention purely physiological problems only to the extent that they are necessary for this purpose.

The Concept of Reflex

Sechenov's psychological theory did not develop in an ideological vacuum or away from the main line of the world of science. On the contrary, it was directly associated with the general course of development of science. Four main sources of Sechenov's teachings may easily be distinguished, namely the reflex concept, the psychophysiology of the sense organs, the theory of evolution, and the doctrine of associationism. The history of all these trends is replete with events and conflicts, all adequately described in the literature.

When referring the reader to the appropriate sources, we would at the same time direct his attention to the fact that these trends, with all their variety, have a common methodological basis, the most important factor in which, until approximately the middle of last century, was mechanistic determinism.

In its ontological nature the mental phenomenon is a derivative of the material conditions of life. For this reason any truly scientific test of the deterministic interpretation of mental phenomena must allow transgression of the limits of mental phenomena. The starting point and the crux of the deterministic investigation of physiological and mental phenomena is the *concept of reflex*, reflecting the interaction and interconnection of the organism with the material world, and the causal relationship between the activity of the former and the factors of the latter.

By its very origin, this concept was psychophysiological, combining organic processes with acts containing a mental relationship. The decisive factor was the deduction of this relationship from the interaction between material bodies. In this way a point was reached that remained unvarying for any subsequent deterministic theory of mental activity. This point could be reached initially only on the basis of concepts reflecting the simplest type of material interaction. The ability to foretell consistently the behavior of physical systems, acquired as a result of the categories of the new mechanics, inspired a similar approach to human behavior. Its obvious qualitative properties, such as, for example, the regulation of movement by a sensory image or the ability to learn, were also deduced from mechanical causes; and for those who thought deterministically, at that time there was no other way.

Under the influence of, and in the image of the mechanical picture of the world, were born the theory of the reflex, the so-called "causal" theory of perception and the doctrine of associationism. The founder of all these movements was Descartes. To him, also, is due the introspective concept of consciousness—the perpetual stronghold of indeterminism in psychology. The power of self-regulation and self-control, characteristic of the higher forms of human behavior, was converted into the primary fact of mental activity, which can explain everything, but which itself requires no explanation. In this way two opposite poles were formed: the organism, controllable by the general laws of nature, in interaction of a mechanical order with other bodies, and the consciousness standing above nature. Natural scientific thought until the middle of the nineteenth century moved between these two poles.

Admittedly, at the time when mechanistic determinism was dominant, ideas were formed which undermined it, such as, for example, Glisson's theories of irritability, the concept of sensation in Haller's physiological school, Unzer's idea of the "vis nervosa," Prochaska's biological theory of the reflex, Bell's hypothesis of the "nervous circle" and so on. These breaches in the mechanical picture of neuropsychic activity prepared the ground for the new deterministic system of views. In the 1840s the mechanistic school was greatly strengthened by the remarkable progress in physics and chemistry, which rid the physiological investigation of living functions of its vitalism. Consciousness, however, remained outside the sphere of physicochemical explanation of organic processes. As before, it was regarded as belonging to another side of nature. However, since thought does not arise in itself but in reality, it must inevitably reveal itself, and the deeper the penetration of reality the more marked the imperfection of the initial deterministic schemes. The conflict between mechanistic determinism and the progress of biology determined the development of scientific ideas of behavior over a period of two centuries—from Descartes to Darwin.

The New Determinism

The mechanistic-deterministic approach to mental phenomenon had shot its bolt. One clear sign of its methodological powerlessness was the philosophical expression which it was given in the "vulgar" materialism of Büchner, Vogt, and Moleschott; and another was the crises which it engendered in the theories of reflexes, the sense organs, and associations. The new epoch in the development of scientific knowledge demanded a fundamentally new deterministic model, which sprang up against the strong opposition of idealism in various branches of psychophysiology.

Why is it that this model was created for the first time in Russia and not in some other country? There were quite definite social and historical reasons why this should be so. The deterministic, materialistic conception of the mind was developed in Russia by people who, in the service of revolution, sought to create a personality capable of opposing the existing order and of destroying it. A unique antinomy arose: While remaining loyal to the deterministic ideal, it was essential to explain the active character of behavior within the framework of the categories of natural-scientific intelligence.

The postulate of the irrevocable dependence of phenomena on productive, material causes had to be extended to the conscious, voluntary control of actions characteristic of man. It was, of course, these gaps in the natural-scientific knowledge of this method of control which provided the gnosiological basis of the concept of "free will," the stronghold of the idealistic doctrine. A mere 30 years before *Reflexes of the Brain*, the truly physiological concept of the reflex was born, as applied to the causal explanation of a limited category of neurosomatic acts. The distinguishing feature of these acts was recognized to be their strictly automatic machine-like character: under the action of an external stimulus a nervous mechanism is formed, the "input" of which lies at the periphery of the organism, the central element in the spinal cord, and the "output" in the muscular system. A definite group of muscular movements was given an exhaustively deterministic definition. To people with a natural-scientific turn of mind, the concept of the reflex was at once seen as an important acquisition, enabling (even if on a limited scale) the causal factors of nervous activity to be understood and allowing the rejection of a mental principle, incapable of further analysis (spirits, feelings, etc.) as the force of the motor activity of the organism. This explains why the theory of the reflex, as described in the second edition of Johannes Müller's *Textbook of Physiology* and in a series of publications by Marshall Hall, arouses great enthusiasm among naturalists and physicians. The word "reflex" became firmly established as a truly physiological term applicable only to neuromuscular phenomena which were by nature "apsychic." Since the 1830s the concept of the reflex has acquired a purely *physiological* status, whereas during the preceding two centuries it was *psychophysiological*. This was its meaning to Descartes, the physicist, who regarded not only movement, but also sensation, learning, and feeling as products of the work of the nervous machine.

Descartes's outlook was in some ways opposed to the aspirations of the "reflexologists" of the 1830s and 1840s. They attempted to distinguish reflex actions as strictly as possible from those in which the mind was involved, whereas the Cartesian plan envisaged reproduction of the widest possible range of mental phenomena by means of mechanical devices. Admittedly, Descartes maintained that human behavior included certain signs which could not in principle be reproduced in this manner, but his followers a century later evolved a program expressed by the equation: "man equals machine." It must be remembered here that the machine, in the image of which, according to La Mettrie, man is constructed, possesses the ability to feel and its functions must be regarded as psychophysiological. On the basis of Newtonian physics, Hartley developed his reflex scheme, which he used to explain the correlation between mental and nervous processes (understood as physical vibration), and the impossibility of the first without the second. According to Prochaska, like his predecessors in the development of the reflex concept, the reflection of external impressions in the motor sphere is brought about by areas of the central nervous system capable of sensation (the sensorium). The association between sensation and movement was thus universally accepted as indispensable. It was Marshall Hall who broke this association. Like the biologists at the end of the nineteenth century, who required a terminology for the description of behavior which would exclude any allusion to the mind, he insisted in the case of the reflex in calling the sensory nerve pathway "excitomotor" (an innovation which took root in the physiological literature). The incompatability between the reflex act and the activity of the mind was strengthened terminologically. Bearing in mind the vagueness and the idealistic "overlay" of the psychological concepts of that time, Hall's doctrine must be recognized as an important advance towards the establishment of determinism in neurophysiology, although the object of the latter was a half-and-half organism, divided into two levels, belonging to different orders of existence. Very soon, however, progressive biologists and physicians attacked this model from different sides. In 1844, Prochaska's follower, Dr. Laycock, in a communication to the Royal Society, reported the need for extending the principle of the reflex to the activity of the brain. Laycock's successor Dr. Carpenter put forward the theory of "unconscious cerebration." Ten years later the conclusion that the brain, included in the "axis of reflection," is a reflex apparatus like the spinal cord, became generally accepted.

Like the other physiologists of that epoch, before the publication of his Reflexes. Sechenov was involved in discussions on the determination of nervous activity. He recalls how, in du Bois-Reymond's laboratory, he was able "to perform experiments with muscle and nerves of the frog and to repeat, at the wish of the Professor (du Bois-Reymond), the recently published experiments of Pflüger on the spinal reflexes in the eel." Pflüger's important experiments on the spinal frog were definitely idealistic and theoretical in conception: they were intended to overthrow the reflex doctrine which at that time was dominant. Pflüger decisively rejected the views, based on experiments on decapitated animals, that the spinal cord was a reflex automatic system, and the brain the seat of consciousness.

The concept of the reflex as a mechanical reaction was applicable only to those neuromuscular acts which bore no relation to the adaptive character of behavior.

However, according to Pflüger, besides the laws of the reflex there are laws of another order, expressed as sensory functions, to which are subordinated both the spinal cord and the brain, and which determine the purposive activity of both decapitated and normal animals. The purposes of adaptation cannot be realized without sensory function. Pflüger's work aroused long experimental and theoretical discussion, centered around the problem of the determinants of purposive behavior (the irreproachability of Pflüger's experiments has been universally acclaimed). Pflüger, the natural-historical materialist, aroused the opposition of the extreme idealist Lotze. As Fearing rightly concluded, the argument which went on between these two men opened a new era in the evolution of the reflex theory. The "classical" theory of the reflex as a motor reaction, rigidly determined by the anatomical connections between nerves, was shaken to its roots.

The controversy between Pflüger and Lotze paved the way for Sechenov's solution of the problem of the reflex nature of behavior. This solution was not an eclectic combination of the indeterministic idea of consciousness, created under the influence of introspectionism, with the deterministic idea of the reflex as an act of a mechanistic order. This type of solution, of course, was one of the possible ways out of the difficulty (a way also adopted by Lewis, Schiff, and many others), but Sechenov transformed both the concept of mental (feeling) and the concept of the reflex, supporting himself on the deterministic framework of the latter. Hence, he returned to the traditional idea of two centuries previously, according to which the reflex was re-garded as a psychophysiological category, and its basic terms were sensation and movement. However, Sechenov's interpretation had a different ideo-logical and scientific background, embodying a new level of deterministic methodology.

Having adopted the general methodological outlook of deterministic nat-ural science, Sechenov defended the idea of the machine-like character of the working of the brain. He emphasized that "all external manifestations of brain activity may be reduced to muscular movement" and expressed the hope that "the time must eventually come when people will be able to analyze the external manifestations of brain activity just as easily as the physicist can now analyze musical accord or the phenomena associated with freely falling body" (*Selected Philosophical and Psychological Works*, 1935, p. 72). From the nature of these expressions, Sechenov's position could be interpreted as purely mechanistic.

However, such a conclusion would be premature, if not frankly tendentious, for a closer examination shows that Sechenov universally regarded sensation as the regulator of muscular reactions, and he interpreted the reflex itself as an act consisting of sensation and movement. Bearing in mind that sensation, starting with its simplest manifestations, represents a sphere of mental activity (relegated by idealism to the other side of nature, to a special world, apparently accessible only to introspection), it is easy to understand the truly revolutionary meaning of Sechenov's conversion of sensation into a target suitable for objective scientific investigation, such as the movement of a muscle. Moreover, since the latter is determined by sensation, Sechenov's prognosis, that in the future the scope of accurate physicomathematical analy-sis would extend to the whole field of external manifestations of brain activity, included the potential thought that this analysis must inevitably embrace also the whole totality of sensory factors determining the formula of the muscular reaction.

However, in order to introduce sensation into a material system without making the work of that system subjective, it had to be described in funda-mentally different terms from those used by introspectionism. It had to be defined within a system of objective coordinates and signs, based preliminarily on its real function in behavior, and only after that, on how it appeared in consciousness. When, in the course of subsequent investigations, Sechenov continued the line of objective analysis of the sensory regulation of behavior he began in his book *Reflexes of the Brain*, he identified two constituent signs of sensation: discrimination and direction. "Sensation, whenever and wher-ever it occurs, has only two general signs: it is the tool by which the condi-tions of an action are discriminated and the director of actions suited to these conditions (i.e., purposive or adaptive)" (1942, p. 416). Whereas initially Sechenov compared the mechanism of the brain to a clock, he subse-quently took as his example of a machine an automatic device in which there were "regulators, replacing the machine operator's hand and leading to purposive activity, in common parlance automatically, but in fact, under the influence of the changing conditions in working of the machine. The best known example of such a regulator is the safety valve in Watt's steam engine" (*The Physiology of Nerve Centers*, 1952, p. 26).

In technology automatic regulators replace the "intelligently controlled hand." Why, therefore, cannot the nervous system, because of its own organization, carry out something which has been ascribed to the action of the consciousness, or intellect, lying outside its limits? "In the animal, as a self-acting machine, the regulators can evidently only be automatic, i.e. they may be put into operation by the changed conditions in the state or running of the machine . . . hence, it is easy to understand that the operation of the regulators must satisfy the following two basic conditions: the apparatus must be sensitive to any disturbance of the correct state or running of the machine and must direct the activity of the working organs to remove the resulting inconveniences for the organism. This is how the nervous regulators are constructed. The first condition is represented in their activity by the "signal" part of their apparatus, providing the various degrees and forms of sensation, while the second is satisfied by the devices coordinating the activity of the working organs" (ibid.). According to this point of view, the reflex, in the special meaning of the term, is a special case of the universal principle of the *harmony of movement with the executive, signal role of sensation.*

Having overthrown the traditional interpretation of sensation, Sechenov broadened its contact with other forms of self-regulation and proposed that it should be treated as a signal, thereby putting into words the concept which was subsequently to become of crucial importance in cybernetics. "The receiving surface is often called sensory and the same name has been applied to its nerve, however, this name is unsuitable, for stimulation of these surfaces is not always accompanied by a conscious sensation. A more suitable name would be the signal surface, and its nerve would be the signal conductor" (ibid., p. 49). This introduction of the principle of self-regulation into the reflex scheme by Sechenov was a brilliant innovation. Such a principle was foreign to all previous reflex theories.

Since the time of Descartes the reflex had been regarded as a reflected movement—the result of reflection of nervous impulses passing along afferent channels from the brain to the muscles (something similar to the reflection of a beam of light from a surface; the very etymology of the word "reflex" perpetuated the analogy between nervous and optical "reflection").

The reflex is machine-like, it is produced by a nervous machine, but in all pre-Sechenov models of the reflex, it is a machine working without information. To produce its reflex act it did not require information concerning the properties of the external environment, the changing conditions of behavior, just as this information is not required by the beam of light reflected by a surface.

With progress in biology, the idea of the reflex as a "blind" motor act, predetermined by a rigid connection between nervous pathways and independent of what is taking place in the external and internal environment, was subjected to intensive criticism. The criticisms made by Pflüger showed that the natural-scientific interpretations of the mechanisms of behavior do not exclude, but rather assume, the participation of mental components, denoted by the term "sensory functions," in their operation.

Sechenov returned time and time again to the argument between Pflüger and the mechanistic school and invariably took the side of the former. In his general treatise entitled *The Physiology of Nerve Centers* (1891) he states the following.

"With advances in knowledge, Pflüger's view is now even more justified than at the time when he originally expressed it" (1952, p. 115). The view in question was that "a type of consciousness (unconscious sensation) lies at the basis of the purposiveness of reflexes" (*ibid.*). Although adopting this view, Sechenov gave it his own interpretation, marking a considerable step forward along the road of scientific analysis of the purposiveness of reflexes. According to Pflüger, sensory functions ("spinal consciousness") were final concepts, incapable of further analysis or explanation. Sechenov, on the other hand, preferred to regard them as "nothing more than the quality of separateness of the concordant halves of the reflex discharge, signal and motor . . ." and he went on to say that "spinal consciousness is tuned to the activity of the signal part" (*ibid.*).

Following Pflüger, Sechenov asserted that sensory factors must take part in even the simplest purposive movement, such as that observed, for example, in the spinal frog, but these sensory factors do not imply a more closely indefinable instinctive impulse (a feeling of self-preservation, etc.), but factors enabling the condition of the motor reaction to be distinguished and the reaction itself to be suitably corrected. The fact, long recognized by naturalists, that goal-directedness is a characteristic of the behavior of living beings, which preserve their integrity by reacting selectively to external influences, served as a foundation stone for theories according to which the deterministic characteristic of nervous activity is composed entirely of two factors: (1) external stimulation, and (2) an internal, predetermined construction.

According to Sechenov, the hypothesis of the determining role of external influences may also be applied firmly to self-regulating systems. These influences, however, direct behavior not by a series of mechanical jogs, but by a series of signals. The external influences must be converted into sensations before they can become a force governing motor activity and muscular work. This activity, in turn, modifies the objective conditions in which the action is performed, and in order to maintain goal-directedness, an influx of information about the changes taking place must be provided. According to Sechenov, this general principle is also applicable to the goal-directed reaction of the decapitated vertebrate, in which the role of "detectors" is played by the skin and muscles. "The point of origin of the sensory factors determining the direction of a reflex movement must be the skin and muscles, and every change in the position of the latter must modify the character of unconscious sensation, influencing the direction of the reflex" (*Physiology of the Nervous System*, p. 213).

From this conclusion, of great theoretical importance, was born the idea of the feedback, the cyclic control of movement, which underwent further development in Sechenov's description of the ability of animals to move in space and to carry out locomotor activity. Sechenov considered that the determining principles of this activity lay in muscle sensation. The muscle performed a dual function: as a working organ and as an organ transmitting information regarding the conditions of action.

In this manner Sechenov developed a new explanatory scheme—deterministic, but not mechanistic—for application to the interpretation of behavior (remaining reflex in nature). At the present time the term "determinism" has acquired a wider meaning. When applied to any phenomenon, it implies that it is consistently determined by the interaction of material factors. Previously, for centuries, the word determinism implied an alternative to the concept of "free will." These alternatives were expressed as follows: Are human actions determined by man himself or by external forces? This dependence on external factors was opposed by self-regulation, which was regarded as the despatch of controlling impulses from the unique sphere of the will and consciousness into a material system, foreign to this sphere, which required to be controlled.

Determinism implied the denial of self-regulation. Self-regulation was equivalent to indeterminism. Sechenov for the first time gave a deterministic interpretation of self-regulation.

We must stress again and again the fundamentally new approach to sensation (in the case we are considering—muscular). Sechenov was not interested in the sign of survivability, awareness, or subjective sensation.

What type of awareness can be conceived in respect of the spinal frog, the behavior of which has occupied a central point in the reflex theory throughout its history. Nevertheless, the reactions of this spinal frog, recorded so objectively, are controlled mentally.

It has been discovered that, without regard to the hypotheses of consciousness as a special and mysterious internal factor, but in relation to the objective structure of external reactions alone, we can confidently decide whether the mind is concerned in these reactions and, if so, in what form.

Is it not clear that such an approach implied in fact a complete revolution in the views on the nature of mental activity?

As a result of this refusal to presume the direct awareness of mental phenomena, and the decision to approach them objectively, it was possible to compare the mental act with the physiological, and to model the first in the image of the second.

Biological Purposes

The concept of the reflex had long been used in neurophysiology as a model for the strict deterministic analysis of individual manifestations of vital activity; but it was applied to the simplest, so-called involuntary movements. Sechenov was able to initiate the extension of this concept (after first transforming it) to voluntary movements, i.e., those including what was usually called consciousness and will.

He regarded the main purpose of his book *Reflexes of the Brain* to explain "the activity of a person with an ideally strong will . . . activity constituting the highest type of arbitrariness," by means of a nervous scheme effective in the case of involuntary movements. If the ideas of the reflex theory can provide an exhaustive explanation of the behavior of the most advanced mental type, "how much more must they apply to less advanced types."

As previously mentioned, the development of these views on will in Chernyshevskii's "Sovremennik" did not mean the exclusion of the mind or consciousness from the sequence of cause and effect. It was not the denial of will, but the discovery that it obeyed extremely strict laws that constituted the pathos of materialism, the enemies of which attempted to identify the thesis of the determinism of human actions with the idea, foreign to the

Revolutionary Democrats, of the predeterminism of behavior by physico-chemical and physiological causes.

When presenting his theory, Sechenov expressed the hope "that the very difficulty of the task will incline the reader to be lenient towards this first attempt to bring the phenomena of voluntary movements into line with the machine-like activity of the comparatively simple mechanism." In fact, this was the first attempt in the history of science to deduce the structure of voluntary movements, without denying their specific features, from the basic principles of the reflex theory. However, the mechanism whose working principles were used to explain the most complex act of human conscious behavior is by no means as simple as might appear to one who thought in traditional physiological categories, but who saw nothing in reflex movement other than a transfer of excitation from an afferent nerve to an efferent, and nothing in a nervous phenomenon other than a displacement of molecules. When Sechenov spoke of a "machine" what he implied was, as we shall show below, not so much a synonym as a broad term embracing all forms of regular relationships, by means of which he endeavored to strengthen the idea that physiological and mental phenomena, like physical phenomena, are subject to inexorable laws of causation.

When he asserted that the idea of "the brain as a machine is a godsend for every naturalist," besides implying a regular relationship between the external agent, the internal mechanism, and the final result, Sechenov also introduced the notion of the objective awareness of this relationship. The presence of a strict causal link between the external influence, the brain analyzing this influence, and the response reaction of the organism enables the internal mechanism to be defined in accordance with external manifestations. Sechenov was in no doubt of the difficulty of solving such problems "in view of the nature of the machine which constitutes the brain, probably the most curious machine in the world," but from his point of view the difficulty was a technical one, and not one of principle.

A closer examination shows that the brain "machine," as envisaged by Sechenov, possesses properties which are not found in the world of mechanics. In the structure of the reflex, as it was imagined before the time of Sechenov, the nervous center played the role of an indifferent conducting medium. However, the concept of the brain centers had no truly physiological meaning, and if an account had to be given of their activity and their participation in goal-directed behavior, this could be done either in the terms of idealistic introspective psychology or in physical and chemical terms.

In the scheme of the reflex outlined by Sechenov, the work of the nervous centers was defined in objective, biological terms instead of in subjective, psychological (or the associated mechanical) terms.

Taking as his starting point "the phenomena represented by the spinal cord, as being those most thoroughly studied" (*Selected Philosophical and Psychological Works*, 1935, p. 84), Sechenov sets out from the concept of reflex movements in the generally accepted meaning of the word (the so-called pure reflexes), typified by the fact that "with a gradual increase in the strength of the stimulus a gradual increase also takes place in the strength of the movement, which at the same time spreads to an increasing number of muscles . . . the same may be observed in the cranial nerves in conditions in which the brain is considered to be inactive" (ibid.). It follows that the pathway of the reflex movement may pass through the spinal cord and also through the brain. However, not every reflex whose pathway passes through the brain is a cerebral reflex. The latter arises only when, because of the inclusion of mechanisms situated in the higher levels of the nervous system, the rule is disturbed in accordance with which the intensity of movement increases with an increase in the intensity of stimulation. The disturbance is not spontaneous or voluntary, but neither can it be explained in terms of morphological connections between nerve elements, as the Bell-Magendie law applies to the spinal reflexes.

The functions of the "brain machine" can be defined only by reference to the biological meaning of the operation of its "appendages," i.e., the role of the latter in the vital encounters between the organism and the environment.

This change to a biological plane becomes evident at once in Sechenov's description of the "appendages." intensifying movements. He classifies "reflexes from fright and sensual pleasure" as involuntary movements with an intensified end. All these reflexes are goal-directed, and their goal is the "preservation of the integrity of the indivisible." "The preservation of this integrity is fully achieved, however, if the indivisible shuns harmful external influences but possesses good, i.e. useful, influences. Fear helps it with the first of these, and pleasure compels it to seek the second" (ibid., p. 93).

This wide biological approach determined the new interpretation of the physiological mechanism of the reflex. Sechenov introduces the concept of the physiological state of the center, and his "physiological state," affecting the outcome of the act as a whole, maintains a direct connection with the requirements. The mechanism of the reflex cannot be understood in isolation, without reference to the biological purpose which it serves. "Assuming, for example,"—wrote Sechenov—"that the central part of the apparatus which begins in the nose with the olfactory nerves perceiving the smell of cooking is, at that moment, in such a state that the reflexes from these nerves can pass directly to the muscles producing laughter, then excitation of the olfactory nerves will cause the person to laugh. If, on the other hand, the state of the center is such that the reflexes can pass only to the muscles depressing the angle of the mouth, then the smell of cooking will cause the person to frown. We can assume that the first state of the center we have described corresponds to the case of a hungry person, while the second corresponds to one who has eaten enough, and all becomes clear. Hence, it is perfectly reasonable to assume that involuntary movements resulting from sensual pleasure are essentially nothing more than ordinary reflexes, the complexity of which, i.e., the more or less extensive development, is dependent on the physiological state of the nervous center" (ibid., pp. 91–92).

Hence, an external stimulus is received in a definite manner by "charged" nervous centers, and depending on the "charge" the whole response reaction may differ radically. The state of the center itself—the "mechanism intensifying the reaction," reflecting the character of the relationships between the organism and environment (in the example we have cited—one of the factors of metabolism), is the nervous substrate of need.

Inhibition

The activity of the organism is expressed by the ability of the brain "machine" not only to intensify reflexes, but also to depress them. The old physiology regarded active purposeful opposition to external influences as a voluntary act. Inhibition of the reaction was explained by an effort of will, by an internal mental impulse. Sechenov's discovery of the phenomenon of central inhibition provided an objective, physiological interpretation of so important a sign of voluntary behavior as the ability to oppose stimuli and to create a barrier to unwanted impulses.

The main experimental fact underlying the hypothesis of inhibitory influence of the brain on the spinal cord was the general intensification of the spinal reflexes after decapitation of the animal. Sechenov interpreted this fact as the result of extirpation of the centers of inhibition postulated by himself. This interpretation was opposed by Schiff and his followers. They explained the intensification of reflexes after decapitation by postulating that with a decrease in the mass of nerve tissue, the process of excitation becomes more concentrated. In their opinion, inhibition must be regarded as the result of the severe shock sustained by the organism, and not as a regulatory component of nervous activity, taking place in ordinary natural conditions.

A prolonged experimental and theoretical argument followed between the schools of Sechenov and Schiff. According to Sechenov, inhibition is a unique physiological phenomenon, of great biological significance. "It is easy to understand," he wrote, "that if inhibition did not exist in the body or, on the other hand, if these inhibitory influences could not be put into operation by excitation of sensory discharges (the natural properties of the regulators of movement!) it would be absolutely impossible to carry out the plan of the 'self-mobility,' which animals possess to such a high degree" (*ibid.*, p.237).

Although, after several decades of experimental research, Sechenov continued to insist on the undoubted fact that reflex depression of movements may take place, he observed contradictions in the views held by two groups of investigators on the "vital role" of this fact.

One group—typified by the school of Schiff—limited the sphere of application of the facts described above to cases of prostration of animals after severe injury to the nervous system. The other group was inclined to ascribe to them a wider significance. Heidenhein and Bubnov, for example, were undoubtedly members of the second camp, when they carried out experiments to stimulate the cortical layer of the hemispheres and found that they could obtain, not only movements, as their predecessors had discovered, but also depression of movements. Of course, Sechenov himself belonged to the second camp, when he ascribed a wide vital significance to the phenomena of inhibition.

These divergences between Sechenov and Schiff in their understanding of inhibition rested on differences of principle in their interpretation of the physiological mechanism of the reflex, and these, in turn, rested on still more profound disagreements regarding the determination of behavior. Schiff and his followers rejected the qualitatively new type of determination characteristic of nervous phenomenon.

Hence for this reason they failed to take into account the specificity of inhibition as one of the manifestations of the activity of the organism. They saw in inhibition, not a phylogenetically developing property of the nervous system, responsible for coordinating movements and attaining the necessary "self-mobility," but a detrimental reaction interrupting the link between the organism and the environment, and exluding it from the outside world.

Sechenov did not reject the possibility that this link with the outside world may be weakened by exhaustion of nervous tissue, but he considered that this weakening was quite different in nature from the active inhibition of movements under the influence of impulses arriving from the brain.

He regarded the inhibitory apparatus of the brain as one of the formations composing the central link of the integral mechanism of the reflex act. Correspondingly, the starting up of this apparatus and the regulation of its activity invariably bore a causal relationship to external conditions, which could only exercise their influence on the brain through the channel of the afferent nerve.

Hence, the general principles of the reflex theory were extended, not only to the activity of the working organs, but also to their depression. The determining role of influences from the outside world was retained in full. Conversely, Schiff's school regarded vital phenomena, including inhibition, as entirely explicable by intraorganic conditions (construction of the path of spread of the nervous process as a factor determining the intensification of reflexes, exhaustion as a factor determining their inhibition). Sechenov associated inhibition with the idea that external influences prepare the nervous system to respond selectively to each new stimulus. Only when an impression is absolutely unexpected is a reflex reaction observed in which inhibition plays no part. "But when stimulation is expected, the activity of a new mechanism is introduced into the phenomenon, endeavoring to depress and restrain the reflex movement" (ibid., p. 81). Experience and training can develop this faculty. Inhibitory mechanisms reject when excitation of a sensory nerve is stronger than it has ever had to withstand, i.e. to experience in the past.

Hence a new and extremely important addition was made to the theory of reflexes. They were now regarded as directly related, not only to present stimuli, but also to the sum total of previous influences leaving their impression on the nervous system. Physiological data had to be found to explain this cardinal fact, and Sechenov developed the hypothesis of enduring traces in the nervous centers.

The views described above not only endowed the indefinite concept of "nervous center" with important physiological significance, but they also paved the way for the solution of Sechenov's fundamental problem: to explain mental phenomena in terms of physiological principles. Each of the physiological phenomena mentioned above bore a direct relationship to the facts of mental activity. Inertia of the nervous processes was recognized as the basis of preservation of traces in the central nervous system, and inhibition as an act responsible for the selective direction of behavior, and the work of the "amplifying mechanism" as the basis of motivation.

Monistic Approach

In modern terminology, all these functions could be called psycophysiological, for each of them, expressing a definite physiological property of the frontal nervous system, was the basis of one particular aspect of mental activity. After N. G. Chernyshevskii had put forward his anthropological theory, Sechenov declined all attempts to divide the behavior of the integrated organism "into different halves belonging to different natures." The differentiation between mental and physiological was thus surmounted in a concrete, scientific fashion, expressed by the reorganization of the actual concept of reflex, and the interpretation of the reflex as a unit of nervous activity which is at the same time physiological and mental—a point of view around which Pavlov subsequently developed his own theory.

It should be noted, however, that the logical realization of the monistic approach to vital activity required more than the discovery of the psychophysiological nature of the three functions we have mentioned above. The ontological character of the mind made it necessary to introduce a perceptual relationship, without which it would be impossible to understand the correlation between behavior and external conditions. When describing the work of the nervous apparatus, Sechenov first mentioned sensations in connection with the intensifying of reflexes. He speaks of the sensations of hunger, fear, and sensual pleasure as manifestations of the activity of this apparatus. The establishments of an irrevocable link between excitation of the center and these sensations was regarded as the first case in which a mental phenomenon was introduced into the chain of processes taking place in the manner of a machine. Here, for the first time, psychological facts were painted on a physiological canvas. "For simplicity, we may even accept that the sensation of fear and the excitation of the apparatus intensifying the end of a brain reflex are identical. At least, there is not the slightest doubt that they are extremely intimately related from the causal point of view" (*ibid.*, p. 88). The sensations with which we are dealing, it is easy to understand, are not perceptual, but impulsive in character. They may give an action its impetus, but they cannot facilitate the recognition of the objective properties of the environment or determine an adequate orientation towards it.

Meanwhile, physiological experiments have shown that the "amplifying" role of the brain may sometimes have a totally different meaning, namely the increase in sensitivity to external stimuli themselves. In the second edition of *Reflexes of the Brain*, Sechenov described Berezin's experiments to study temperature sensation in the frog. The normal animal quickly withdraws the limb from ice-cold water. After removal of the hemispheres, however, the animal remains perfectly at rest when its limb is immersed. "It is quite another matter if the area of skin exposed to cooling is now increased, for example, by immersing the whole posterior half of the trunk in the ice-cold water— the frog moves its legs. Is it not obvious that the cerebral hemispheres act in unison with the increase in the area of cooling in order to reproduce movements by cooling of the skin? Everyone knows that this last condition generally speaking intensifies the effect of cooling (the sensation of cold becomes more intolerable); hence, the hemispheres act as an amplifier in relation to the cooling—movement effect" (*ibid.*, p. 89).

Hence, the hemispheres not only evaluate the influence of the external world from the point of view of their usefulness or harmfulness for the organism, but they greatly increase sensitivity to these influences. The brain takes over from the peripheral sensory apparatus the ability to feel, i.e., to detect external impulses in the form of sensation.

But sensation, according to Sechenov, is not a side effect of stimulation of a receptor, but a determinant, an essential component of the reaction, the factor by means of which the effector mechanisms are set in motion. For this reason the development of the sensory function of the hemispheres has become an important causal factor in the structure of behavior, immeasurably widening the powers of adaptation, the "adaptive potential" of living beings, which have acquired the power of reacting to relatively weak stimuli.

Of course, as experiments have shown, in the absence of the hemispheres, before such reactions may arise it is necessary that the strength of the stimulus to be perceived and the magnitude of its threat to the existence of the organism should be increased considerably. The hemispheres perceive stimuli incapable of causing serious disturbances of the process of life, but likely to do so. Because of this property of the brain the ability of the organism to withstand harmful influences or to take early avoiding action is considerably increased. The concept of the "advance warning" role of sensation is implicitly embodied here.

Although in Sechenov's analysis of involuntary movement the idea of the receptor function of the brain is somewhat fragmentary in form, in the description of voluntary movements it is fully developed. When discussing the appearance of ideas of objects in children—elementary concrete ideas—he stresses that "these occupy the same place in the integral reflex as the sensation of fear in the involuntary movement; they correspond, therefore, to the activity of the central element of the reflex apparatus" (*ibid.*, p. 122).

In this way one further (a fourth) function—sensory—was included among the properties of the "central element of the reflex apparatus," i.e., the brain.

The concept of sensation as a specific property of nerve tissue was evolved by physiologists in the eighteenth century, and its introduction provided the scientific basis for the philosophical synthesis of the French materialists. In doctrines accepted since the time of Hall it was assumed that a movement for which sensation is not essential is truly reflex in character. Pflüger, who accepted this hypothesis unhesitatingly, once more directed attention to the sensory function. It is this, and not the reflex, he pointed out, guided by a number of theoretical and experimental considerations, that is the decisive factor in the structure of purposive behavior. Sechenov overcame the Lotze-Pflüger controversy, which had arisen out of the contrast between reflex function and sensory. He reexamined both these concepts and interpreted the reflex as an act consisting of sensation and movement, and sensation as a process of reflex type. Since sensation falls in the category of mental phenomena, this new interpretation of it, according to which it must be evaluated by its objective function in the course of activity, became a turning point in the analysis, not only of sensation, but of mental activity as a whole.

Materialistic Determinism

His book *Reflexes of the Brain* described the first variant of Sechenov's system of psychological theories. Admittedly, he did not claim to have created such a system. He emphasized that his object was merely to show psychologists "that physiological facts could be applied to the phenomena of mental life." It was essential, however, to examine these phenomena from a new aspect before this possibility could be realized.

Physiology cannot correlate its conclusions and schemes with mental facts taken at their face value, i.e., not yet rationalized in the form of definite concepts. When he declared that the introspective system of psychological concepts was unacceptable, in his book *Reflexes*, Sechenov performed in essence not one, but two tasks: While providing a physiological foundation for mental activity, at the same time he has developed a theory of this activity as such. *Reflexes of the Brain* marks an attempt, not only to introduce new physiological concepts into mental processes, but also to interpret these processes themselves from a new point of view. By regarding voluntary movement as reflex in origin, Sechenov distinguishes it from involuntary movement. The difference cannot lie in the final link of the reflex mechanism— the reaction of the muscle.

"Physiology shows us that there are no special motor nerves and no special muscles for voluntary movements. The same nerves and muscles whose activity is responsible for purely involuntary movement, also bring about voluntary movement" (*ibid.*, p. 112). No special explanation of this fact was necessary. Proof of the logical realization of the principle of materialistic determinism calls for another assumption, namely that a similarity of principle is present, not only in the effector element of the simple reflex act (muscular movement), but also at its beginning (its primary cause—the external influence), between this act and the involuntary movement. In order to make this last conclusion authentic, some method had to be found, based on the reflex theory, for explaining how this difference between involuntary and voluntary arises. The difference between them lies, not in the effector element, but in the central part of the process. In the case of the voluntary action, this is the preceding thought.

Idealism, regarding thought as a primary principle, independent of external influences, on this basis ascribes a special cause to actions regulated by thought. To Sechenov, animated with the desire to determinize "the most involuntary of the voluntary movements," it was important to show that thought itself is a creation of material conditions, that it arises as a result of the general laws of reflex activity. With this purpose in mind, he draws from a genetic viewpoint a picture of gradual conversion of sensation into thought.

If thought develops from sensation, and the latter can arise only during excitation of a receptor by an external material stimulus, then the thesis according to which the primary cause of any action, including a voluntary action, lies outside it may be considered as proven.

The justification of the deterministic view of thought-directed (will-directed) action demanded an answer to at least the following questions: (1) Why does one thought and not another appear?, and (2) if several thoughts are present, what determines the choice between them?

The recognition of the relationship between action and thought was not the abandonment of determinism, for thought itself was relegated from the dominant place of a primary cause, bestowed on it by idealistic philosophy, and had become a down-to-earth phenomenon, included in a system of concrete causal associations.

The theory that thought cannot arise in itself, without a definite cause, ultimately material, was directed towards the search for a mechanism, the links of which when joined together might account for the appearance of thought. According to Sechenov such a mechanism is associative. However, in his system of views, the theory of associations receives a new interpretation.

Thought

In the picture of the course of associative-dissociative processes given by Sechenov, several ideas developed by classical associationism can be distinguished. At the same time, elements of the new theory of association can already be found in *Reflexes of the Brain,* for it is interpreted, not as a primary psychological fact, but as a product of continuous encounters (in Sechenov's terminology,—"vital meetings") between the organism and the environment. Association is not a combination of phenomena inside consciousness, but "a successive series of reflexes, in which the end of each preceding reflex merges with the beginning of the next." For this reason association is a special form of projection of the actual course of a vital activity, of events taking place in the plane of behavioral relationships, the result of a combination of reflexes, i.e., of integrated acts. Sensations (and thought which develops from them) are regarded, therefore, not by themselves, but indissolubly connected with movement: the reality of sensation is rooted in the reality of the motor act.

This specific nature of the objectives of the book *Reflexes of the Brain* also determined the viewpoint from which perceptual processes are interpreted in this book.

Voluntary action, in contrast to impulsive, possesses an internal phase, as a result of which the completion of the action is preceded by deliberation, consideration, and selection.

Sechenov found it important to explain the origin of this phase without yielding any of the basic principles of the reflex theory. He utilizes the discovery of centers inhibiting the reflex not only to indicate the physiological basis of inhibition of the muscular reaction, but also to explain why actions may be converted from real into mental, as a result of which an "action in thought" arises, i.e., the internal plan of activity.

In *Reflexes of the Brain,* thought is assessed primarily by its function in behavior. Therefore, its absence of immediate motor culmination is put forward as its main distinguishing sign.

Sechenov's early idea of thought as an inhibited reflex was widely acclaimed; but his other, no less important views, which he subsequently developed, were by no means so popular. Yet the logical deduction from materialistic monism and determinism was that not only the possibility of the appearance (by means of inhibitory mechanisms) of the internal plan of activity and that aspect of it known as the process of thought, but also the specific peculiarities of this plan, its characteristic structure and composition, must be deduced from the principles of the reflex theory.

This problem, examined in *Reflexes of the Brain*, was solved by Sechenov in his two subsequent psychological treatises: *Who Must Investigate the Problems of Psychology and How* (1873) and *Elements of Thought* (first edition, 1878; second edition, with important revision, 1903).

Critique of the "Experimental School"

In *Reflexes of the Brain* Sechenov's object, as he himself stressed, was to point out to psychologists the possibility of a physiological and, it was hoped, not a speculative but a natural scientific analysis and investigation of mental processes. However, the subsequent development of social and scientific thought did not allow Sechenov to limit himself to this problem. A radical reform of psychology became necessary, with a fundamentally new interpretation of its subject matter, its methods, and its aims.

Sechenov developed this interpretation in the course of a sharp controversy with the idealists.

Opposition to Sechenov's system of views on mental activity was expressed at the beginning of the 1870s by the lawyer Professor K. D. Kavelin, who declared that Sechenov's achievements and discoveries were good for natural science, but did nothing to enrich psychology, for they dealt entirely with the corporeal mechanism and not at all with the internal, "mental environment."

Kavelin attempted to ridicule the whole of this vast achievement of psychophysiology in overcoming the gap between matter and consciousness created by idealism. "By means of external senses," he insisted, "we can know nothing about what is taking place in the mental environment." "Realists (i.e., materialists)," wrote Kavelin, attempting to show that a mental phenomenon is the result, the necessary consequence of material causes, "without realizing the fact themselves, jump from the material world into the mental, which is inaccessible to external senses and therefore closed to their investigation."

Kavelin's views were decisively opposed by Sechenov. Their argument stirred the whole of Russian society and filled the periodicals and even the newspapers. It was attentively followed by writers, including L. N. Tolstoi and M. E. Saltykov-Shchedrin. This is further evidence of the tremendous interest in psychological problems which has always distinguished the Russian intelligentsia.

Even the opponents of materialism were compelled to admit that Sechenov won the day. The feeling of society was entirely on his side. Without going into the intricacies of this discussion, we must examine its importance for the history of psychology.

It must be said that Kavelin was not original in his convictions. He found support in certain hypotheses put forward by the Western European "experimental school" between the 1850s and 1870s, with the object of turning psychology from speculation to experiment, and thereby converting it from a subdivision of metaphysics into an empirical science.

This school was in something of a dilemma, for it was at the meeting point of two trends:

1. the desire, derived from the natural sciences (the physiology of the nervous system and of the sense organs, and evolutionary biology) to explain ob-

jective determinate relationships, defining the structure and course of mental life;

2. the idealistic conception of consciousness as a specific principle, perceived only introspectively, and having as its ultimate cause itself.

The "experimental school" demanded that the subjective method should be supplemented by an objective method, that experiment should be introduced, and that it was necessary to go beyond the bounds of the phenomena of consciousness as such and to study their relationship to the activity of receptors (this became the dominant line for the German supporters of the experimental trend, who were influenced by the major achievements in the physiology of the sense organs, the main center of research being Germany), to the motor aspect of behavior (priority in this case belonged to Vienna), and on social-historical facts (this aspect was emphasized by French workers).

When making use of this dilemma of the "experimental school," Kavelin took support in his attack on Sechenov from its introspectionistic orientations, ignoring its achievements in the direction of the scientific investigation of mental activity.

This argument between Sechenov and Kavelin broadcast on the soil of the ideological struggle in Russia two opposing tendencies in the development of psychological thought. One tendency was associated with the spread of scientific methodology to the whole of life—activity including the activity of the mind as its integral part. This tendency was expressed in ideas of applying the objective method to the investigation of processes of consciousness, discovering their vital significance for behavior, confirming the principles of determinism and experimental control, and constructing psychological science in the image of biology. Different ideas on psychological investigation were promoted by idealistic philosophy with its teaching of the substantialness and the distinctive perceptiveness of mental acts. The new "experimental trend" was formed under the influence of both tendencies, and some aspects of its outlook were embraced by Kavelin in the hope of overthrowing the dominant conviction of the Russian intelligentsia, that Sechenov's reflex theory is the only scientific explanation of mental activity. It became increasingly evident to Sechenov during his struggle with the opponents of this theory that the demands of objectivity of investigation, the replacement of speculation by experiment, the union with physiology, the evolutionary approach, and so on acquire a different meaning depending on the ideological concepts motivating them, and that the realization of these demands acceptable to the logical naturalist presupposes a decisive rejection of the philosophical interpretations of the subject matter and aims of psychology as defined in Kavelin's program.

When criticizing the "experimental school," Sechenov showed essentially that it was just as powerless to make psychology deterministic as was the metaphysical, speculative movement. With each transformation of idealistic psychology, its hard core remained unchanged—the teaching that consciousness stands in contrast to the material world both in its nature and in its direct perceptibility.

Sechenov's argument against Kavelin became one of the turning points in the development of world psychological thought. Sechenov put forward the first uncompromising plan for the construction of an objective psychology.

It was important for Sechenov to justify the necessity for developing deterministic psychology as a science, and to defend the thesis that for a materialist, unlike Kavelin and others, psychology was the sister of physiology, possessing equal rights, and not its appendage. For this reason, immediately after his critical *Remarks on Mr. Kavelin's Book*, he gave a detailed answer to the question *Who Should Investigate the Problems of Psychology and How?*

The starting point of Sechenov's ideas on mental activity was his decisive departure from the conviction of its direct perceptibility, which had held sway for centuries. "Man has none of those special tools for perceiving mental facts such as an inner sense or psychic vision, which, merging with the thing to be perceived, can thus, in essence, perceive the products of consciousness directly (*ibid.*, p. 222). Like any natural science, psychology can investigate its objects only through an intermediary. This was where Sechenov's plan differed radically from the experimental school, which was based on the definition of psychology as the science of "direct experiment" (Wundt). Accordingly, when he said that psychology, "as an experimental science, does not elevate anything which cannot be confirmed by strict experiment to the rank of invariable truth" (*ibid.*, p. 242), Sechenov understood by experiment precisely the same as did the positivists, who regarded the indication of consciousness as the primary fact of experiment and all the rest of knowledge as delegated or deductive.

In order to become a science, psychology must become deterministic. It can only solve this problem by developing an orientation towards natural science.

Such an orientation is determined, not only by the high irrevocability of the established laws of natural science, as a result of which they acquire the meaning of an ideal and a model, but also by the fact that the phenomena forming the subject matter of psychology are related ontologically to the somatic processes studied by the natural sciences. Hence, "there is no clear distinction in any conceivable respect between phenomenon known to be somatic, i.e. bodily actions, and phenomena generally regarded as mental" (*ibid.*, p. 229).

The concept of the reflex satisfied the strict deterministic criterion, enabling it to assimilate the causal factors of phenomena, at first within narrow limits, but later over an ever-widening range of nervous actions. The great importance of the reflex to the understanding of a definite category of mental processes received the attention of many adherents of the "experimental school." It was only Sechenov, however, who saw for the first time in the reflex principle a tool for building the new objective psychology as an independent science. All the misunderstandings arising as a result of Sechenov's plan did so because of identification of the morphological and physiological scheme of the reflex arc (on which the "anatomical principle" hung heavily at this time) with the theory of the reflex nature of mental activity. The mental process is reflex in form, its structure is similar to the structure of the reflex, but Sechenov specifically emphasized that those who ascribe to it "the complete identification between mental facts and reflexes" are making a great mistake (*ibid.*, p. 192). The essence of the mistake is that "it is not the naturalists who play too much with the word explain" (*ibid.*, p. 190) "and who therefore suppose that the apparent analogy between mental and somatic implies the complete reduction of the former to the latter [as if] the whole of a mental phenomenon is reduced to its material conditions. . . . Meanwhile, there is not a single naturalist who will write such an absurdity on his psychological banner" (ibid., p. 189). Sechenov believed that to reduce a phenomenon to its material conditions implies discovering the physicochemical factors by the interaction of which it is produced. From this point of view, he stressed, not only the mental, but also the nervous process may be explained, for "the essence of nervous, i.e. of somatic activity, most closely related to mental life [but not identical with it!—M.Y.], has not been explained even to the extent that we can say which of the known physical agents plays a decisive role in the nervous act" (ibid., p. 189). When he reflected on what was meant by mental reality, Sechenov recognized that the only real feature of the nervous and the mental act is "the sum of those material processes taking place in the particular section of the nervous system" (ibid., p. 251).

However, it is impossible to establish clearly and definitely the general signs of mental realities (in contrast to fictions), when guided by the above criterion, with our existing level of knowledge of the physicochemical processes in the nervous system. Sechenov stressed that the solution of this problem belonged to the distant future. How then, do we diagnose mental reality, "which alone can and must be the object of psychological investigation?" As his initial axiom and criterion of verification, Sechenov puts forward "the idea of the mental act as a process or movement, having a definite beginning, course and end" (ibid., p. 252). Accordingly, psychology may be defined as "a series of theories on the origin of mental activities" (ibid., p. 256).

Of course, the object of psychological investigation is not a mental phenomenon as such, as the finished result, but its "origin," i.e., the process of its formation. It is therefore required of psychology that, "like its sister subject physiology, it should reply only to the question how a certain mental movement, manifested by a sensation, feeling, idea, or involuntary or voluntary movement, takes place, how the processes resulting in thought occur, and so on" (ibid., p. 252). The true meaning of Sechenov's requirements: to deduce all aspects of mental activity from the concept of a process or movement, cannot be understood without clarification of what is embodied in this concept. It must be remembered that many of the adherents of the introspective point of view also required that psychology should deal not with "things," but with processes (Wundt, James, and others).

The view that mental activity consisted of processes still does not provide a reliable criterion for discriminating between "exchanges of introspection" and real facts. It is likewise not enough to assume that the beginning and end of the mental process lie outside the bounds of consciousness. Many attempts to explain the phenomena of consciousness in terms of the dynamics of unconscious mental processes are known in the history of psychology (Leibniz, Herbart, etc.). However, not one of these cases marked a digression from idealism. The truly novel element of the idea which Sechenov placed at the basis of scientific psychology was that this idea, in its interpretation, is "only the further development of the thought that mental and nervous acts are related" (ibid., p. 252).

The nervous act is a process, the beginning of which lies outside, in the world of reality. "Physical or related influences are the executive factors of nervous acts. The completion of these acts are movements which are "desirable in the sense of serving some useful purpose to the body." Of course, the nervous act is somatic in nature; i.e., it ends in the organism at two poles (representing the cause and the result) in contact with the outside world.

Such is Sechenov's description of the architectonics of the mental act, which, like the purely nervous act, has, besides a central element, initial and terminal phases, directly connecting it with external reality. Correspondingly, the object of the psychological experiment must be a process developing in an objective system of relationship. The initial phase of this process consists of external influences determining its subsequent course in the form of sensation, the final phase consists of motor activity, regulated by sensation, and carried out for a vitally important purpose, and, in turn, directed towards the objective world. It is only by going outside the bounds of what is given in consciousness, to real objects and actions with them, that we can give a deterministic interpretation of consciousness, Sechenov suggested. His design may be described as the first plan in the history of world scientific thought for the construction of an objective psychology, if by the latter we understand, not a concept of the behavioristic type, but the investigation by means of an objective method of integral reflex-like mental processes in a system of interaction between organism and environment. This new understanding of the object and aims of psychology determined Sechenov's attitude towards its methods.

A psychology aimed at "the phenomena of consciousness" does not imply a different approach to its object from that of introspection. Sechenov distinguished between self-awareness, as "the ability of a person to analyze his thoughts and actions" (*ibid.*, p. 194) and "mental vision" (in the new terminology—introspection), claiming to play the role of "a special tool for the investigation of mental processes, as opposed to the material" (*ibid.*, p. 197). So far as the former is concerned, it is a fundamental fact of human mental life, and Sechenov suggested several variants of its explanation from the viewpoint of the general principles of the reflex theory. Introspection, on the other hand, as a special method, he not only rejected, but also blamed for the "appalling backwardness of psychology in the scientific analysis of its material."

Sechenov attached great importance, but not decisive for the transformation of psychology, to the new psychological methods which achieved widespread popularity under the influence of the "experimental school." For example, the statistical method "is unfortunately extremely difficult to apply to the study of mental phenomena in the individual person, but if it could be applied it would undoubtedly lead to far more definite results in this field than analysis by means of mental vision alone" (*ibid.*, p. 210).

The comparative method appears very promising, for "the simpler mental manifestations observed in animals, and not in man, are used as the initial material for the deduction of mental facts" (*ibid.*, p. 225). However, according to Sechenov, the study of the mental activity of animals likewise cannot be used as the starting point for the objective understanding of mental activity.

So far as the extensive historical and cultural material recommended by Wundt, Kavelin, etc. as methods of renewal of psychology are concerned, despite their importance, they do not contain, according to Sechenov, "the means for dispelling the darkness surrounding mental processes," for "the historical study of the memorials of human activity leads the investigator out of necessity to study everyday mental life" (*ibid.*, p. 209). To one who described the latter in subjective psychological terms, when turning to objective products there remained only the subjectivization of the process of their creation.

"Analytical Psychology"

The deterministic explanation of the psychological content of any living act must be based, according to Sechenov's plan, on "analytical psychology."

Whereas traditional analytical psychology concentrated its efforts on establishing the elements of consciousness, the synthesis of which was dependent on the immediate efforts of the subject, Sechenov radically modified the orientation of the analysis and considered that the analytical psychologist must adopt the same attitude towards mental activity as the physiologist adopts to physical activity. In this he assumed that the physiologist is equipped with the biologically interpreted principle of the reflex—an act which, in the vast majority of cases, is realized through sensation. The analytical psychologist constructs his work on the physiological model, comparing but not identifying the processes of development of mental acts, their combination and reproduction, with their physiological equivalents. It is for this reason that Sechenov suggested that psychological investigation should be transferred to physiologists.

His idea, so far as it concerned the problem of who should investigate this field, was interpreted tendentiously by the opponents of materialism as an attempt to deprive psychology of the right to an independent existence, and to convert it into an appendage of physiology. The true significance of Sechenov's suggestion was quite different. At that period psychology was only just beginning to make a place for itself.

The problem was, who would give psychology its independence and enable it to flourish—the philosophers, who for centuries had claimed the sole and undisputed right to solve psychological problems, or the naturalists. Of course, this was before the appearance of psychology as a profession. The man who could develop a scientific psychology had to be found somewhere. It was, in fact, from the ranks of the neurophysiologists, who, thought Sechenov, had already given evidence of their ability to investigate mechanisms of behavior and consciousness, that the investigators would be found who would give psychology a strictly scientific bias.

The old style of analytical psychology was associationism, and the adherents of this school had for a long time been engaged on the problems indicated in Sechenov's plan for the reform of psychology, as the author of the plan himself pointed out. Having stated that psychology must study: (1) the history of the development of individual elements; (2) their methods of combination, and (3) their conditions of reproduction, Sechenov writes: "phenomena belonging to all three groups have been considered for a long time in all the psychological textbooks" (*ibid.*, p. 255). He goes on as follows: "In fact, the second group of problems includes the process of association of mental activities, and the third—the process of their reproduction" (*ibid.*). The explanation of association and reproduction was the internal aim of associative psychology, and Sechenov considered that this aim must be maintained, although achieved by different methods. "Despite the similarity in outline, our objects of study are quite different" (*ibid.*). The basic material for analysis is not the elements of consciousness, but integral mental acts, carried out by the reflex principle, with "beginnings and ends." Developing the materialistic line of associationism, Sechenov transformed the concept of association and suggested interpreting it as the result of interaction between the neurophysic organization and external influences.

The psychophysiological concept of Sechenov was the third major synthesis, after Descartes and Hartley, of reflex theory and associationism. The unique feature of this synthesis was determined by its methodological basis. In all previous materialistic theories, the starting point of the causal explanation was the search for a relationship between association and intraorganic correlations or processes. According to Sechenov, who regarded the nervous system as a link in the interaction between the organism and its environmental situation, it was these conditions from the facts responsible for the development of psychophysiological associations that were converted into their determinant and modifying factor. This view was embodied in Sechenov's scheme of the organic basis of the associative processes, essentially the first attempt at a truly physiological explanation.

According to Sechenov, the nervous system continuously records the similarities and differences between objects revealed by behavior, as a result of which a specific method is available for the differentiation of their signs, distinct from analysis, which is carried out by the morphological system of the sensory apparatus. This conclusion opened up a new era in the theory and physiological mechanism of association, which had not moved a single step forward since the speculative hypothesis of Hartley. The point of issue was the distinctive type of physiological differentiation of the stream of signals reaching the higher nervous centers. Here lay the roots of Pavlov's theories of the differentiation and integration of cortical processes.

On the other hand, real objects, their associations and properties appear as a determining principle in relation, not only to the physiological mechanism of psychological associations, but to these associations themselves. This is why Sechenov attaches a dominant role to association by similarity, regarding it as the fundamental form.

Having recognized that association by similarity is important in the process of perception, Sechenov introduced several extremely important new factors into its interpretation. On materialistic grounds, he considered that this basis is the objective similarity between objects themselves, independent of the reactions of the organism. When discussing the conditions of "reproduction of impressions in accordance with the so-called law of similarity" (*ibid.*, p. 274), he gradually emphasizes that he means the similar signs of real objects. Each evaluation of a newly perceived phenomenon is carried out (as by a machine, because of the law of association by similarity) on the basis of the existing "reproduced idea of the real object which would actually have been chosen from its impression, if it had been present" (*ibid.*, p. 270).

The primary nature of external associations, and the arbitrariness of internal associations are not apparent when mental processes are viewed as starting and ending in consciousness, but they come to the fore when the sensory impression is considered in unison with the culminating motor reaction. What other meaning can be given to the latter besides that of an operation with an actual object or an orientation towards it?

Every perception of an object or direct sensory-motor contact with it, Sechenov suggested, sets in motion by association a system of movements related to a previous similar sensation. It forms the real basis of the term of comparison which, at that particular moment, is not perceived by the sense organs. Association by similarity is thus, not a simple evocation of one idea by another resembling it, but the product of an actual operation by the organism with similar objects.

Sechenov was impelled to transform the theory of associations by the demands of the physiology of the sense organs. The change from the direct sensory reaction to analytical objective perception was one of the decisive points in the campaign for the deterministic explanation of nervous and mental processes. The materialistic interpretation of the concept of association was used here as an effective weapon against "the mental isolationists." Sechenov regarded this weapon as not less important at the point of change from concrete sensory perception to abstract. He stressed that the "concrete mental underlay of intellectual acts," revealed by the study of the association and reproduction of real impressions, remains unaltered for cases of scientific, mathematical and "even mistaken philosophical thinking, in which the objects of thought are not realities but the purest fictions" (*ibid.*, p. 288).

Association, according to Sechenov, is the unity of behavior and knowledge. A perceptible objective meaning is not passively recorded by nervous tissue, but is "snapped" by a complex mechanical system, endowed with perceptual meaning as a result of muscle sensation.

When defining the concept of "neuropsychic organization," Sechenov distinguishes two groups of properties. On the one hand, it possesses the ability to become modified by external influences. This ability, long known in psychophysiology, was used as the main explanatory principle of associationism, because of the fact that, as a result of the repetition of impressions, the trace which they leave behind becomes stable, distinct and easily reproducible. However, this property is only one, the receptive aspect of organization, insufficient by itself, as Sechenov claimed, to form images and their associations (*ibid.*, p. 428). The other aspect, expressing the activity of the organism in relation to the outside world, is movement. When discussing the "advantages bestowed by movements on the development of impressions, Sechenov wrote: "There are three such advantages: by acting as a source of displacement of sensory probes in space, they enormously vary the subjective conditions of perception and hence contribute to the analytical subdivision of sensation; movement then breaks up the continuous sensations into a series of individual acts with a definite beginning and end; finally, movement acts indirectly as a connecting link between qualitatively different sensations" (*ibid.*, p.

429). Hence, the motor sphere and signals of muscle sensation proceeding from it form the initial organic background for subsequent analytico-synthetic thought patterns.

Muscle Sensations

Sechenov's theory of the role of the muscle in the formation of the sensory and mental image of objects was a completely original contribution to world psychophysiology. The fact that muscles participate in perceptual activity and, in particular, in the ability of spatial perception, had been demonstrated long before Sechenov's time. Steinbuch (1811) and, in particular, Charles Bell (1826) postulated that the perception and representation of space take place as a result of the association between purely sensory effects of stimulation of the sense organs and muscular reactions. One of the pioneers of the natural scientific investigation of muscle sensation, Bell regarded vision as an operation in which the idea of the position of an object is continuously correlated with the activity of the eye muscles. Contrary to the views of his teacher Johannes Müller, who considered the spatial image of the world to be "programmed" in inborn nervous structures, Helmholtz proclaimed that the factor determining this image is experience. In the concept of experience he included muscular activity, delegating its structure to something which, in the case of introspection, is obtained directly. Helmholtz's psychophysiology was one of the scientific sources of Sechenov's theory.

Sechenov discovered the special role of muscle sensations when developing his new deterministic approach to the reflexes of the lower divisions of the central nervous system (see above). Helmholtz's work on physiological optics had led to the recognition of the outstanding importance of sensory signals proceeding from the muscle sphere in the working of apparatus whose centers are localized in the higher division of the central nervous system—the brain. Hence, two lines of research, relating to different regions of psychophysiology —the theory of the reflex and the theory of the sense organs, reflecting the objective nature of the sensorimotor activity of the organism, came together at what was to become a turning point for both series. The category of sensation accepted in the physiology of the sense organs was applied to the initial phase of the reflex act (usually interpreted in the plane of mechanical stimulation), while the essential connection between the centripetal and centrifugal (motor) factors, accepted by the reflex theory, was transferred to the activity of the sense organ (usually regarded as effected by the passage of the centripetal process into the nerve centers).

However, by virtue of the limitations of his doctrine, Helmholtz could not extend the reflex principle to the motor activity of the eye. He postulated the existence of "innervation sensations," a special class of sensations of central, rather than peripheral origin, arising whenever an individual innervates his motor nerve by means of a volitional intention.

This hypothesis represented a hazard, not only for the causal explanation of voluntary movements. A serious threat was also presented to the scientific view of perceptual activity. There was weighty evidence to show that the muscle makes a small but significant contribution to the structure of the sensory image.

This concurs with the view that the spontaneous volitional intention directs by means of the muscles, and that the relationship between the former and the latter is established immediately after the process of perception and the process of behavior.

To the uncompromising materialist Sechenov, an external influence invariably had the meaning of a first determinant. However, in contrast to mechanistic ideas, leading to the contemplative, sensualistic interpretation of the process of perception, his theory proved that an external influence may control the process of behavior only when transformed into a sensation, and the reality of this latter, on the other hand, in accordance with the axiom of the reflex theory, is based on the reality of the motor act, associated with muscle sensations.

Consequently, the external influence does not automatically determine the sensory (and still less, the intellectual) product, but only when it has passed through the furnace of activity of the organism, of its living sensorimotor acts. Since these acts originate in the organism and do not pass through it reactively, the question of whether the world can be perceived as it is, without relation to any operation or internal adjustment, became particularly acute. Signals of muscle sensation must come from the motor system, and not from the external environment. Does this not mean in this case their invariable and continuous intervention in each sensory effect by means of its subjectivization? The danger of subjectivization became particularly great because experimental physiology revealed that muscle sensation cannot take part in sensations of individual special modalities, but only in a universal perceptual form such as the spatial image of phenomena. At the beginning of the 1890s, Sechenov published a series of articles entitled *Impressions and Reality, Objective Thought and Reality*, in which muscle sensation is evaluated as the most reliable source of information of the outside world.

When analyzing the question of what similarity exists, if any, between our impressions of the outside world and reality, he concludes that the degree of resemblance may vary. "So long as the discrimination of signs is concerned with the analysis of objects and phenomena in space and time, the indications given by the sense organs (the organs of vision, smell and hearing) will be parallel to reality. Outside these limits, the parallel will extend only to the most general features, and it will always be conditional" (Sechenov, 1942, p. 352).

So far as light or taste, for example, are concerned the correlation with the real object, according to Sechenov, is conventional in character. "In this case the relationships between the object and its sign, as a conventional mark, are the same as between the object and its name. Having become attached to the object once and for all, the name can even replace the object itself" (*ibid.*, p. 353). However, the "signs" of muscle sensation are completely different in character. The moving eye, for example, (Sechenov likened its axis to two long feelers) not only followed the object in the whole of its path, but also at its different speeds in different places. "Hence it follows that, in respect of movements that the eye is capable of performing, representation and reality coincide" (*ibid.*). The cognition of movements accessible to the sense is therefore "not conventional, but direct, leading to its root" (*ibid.*). "If, however, a movement which we can sense is always caused by a real movement—and this is an undoubted fact—and both are identical, then all the displacements of objects in space which we sense are realities and all the attributes of movement are forced upon the mind from outside" (*ibid.,* p. 348).

Since the time of Kant, the view has been widely held that mankind possesses a special organ besides internal vision for the perception of relationships of space and time, giving the consciousness direct information concerning relationships of one or the other. This idea was to some extent justified, because such an organ in fact exists and should be called "the organ of muscle sense" (p. 380). Kant's transcendental esthetics were thus seen as a gnoseological illusion, generated by the imperceptibility and the low level of awareness of muscle signals. What Kant and his followers attributed to an a-priori space-time scheme was, in fact, the product and the irreplaceable component of the most elementary manifestations of motor experience.

The spatial group and temporal series created in consciousness is the result of the work of muscle sense. However, it must not be forgotten that, according to Sechenov, in the signals of this sense, representation and reality coincide with each other. Hence the muscle, as an organ of perception, gives the most fundamental and, at the same time, the most adequate reflection of reality.

Sechenov showed, for the first time in the history of world scientific and philosophical thought, that sensory signals sent by the muscles—the organ of active and direct interaction between living beings and the surrounding world—faithfully reproduce (reflect) the main forms of existence of this world—space, time, and movement.

From Sechenov's point of view, the interpretation of muscle sense as proprioceptive, as suggested in physiology by Sherrington, was unacceptable. Sherrington divided all the sense organs into three categories—exteroceptive, interoceptive, and proprioceptive—using the last term (proprioceptive—perceiving self) to mean sensations giving information of the state of the muscles, tendons, and other components of the motor apparatus. Muscle sense, according to Sechenov, transmits information about the objective space-time properties of objects, recreating the main outlines of the world picture as perceived by the subject.

Dimness or "darkness" of this sense hides from consciousness its powerful role in perception of the outside world. So far as the physiological basis of this sense is concerned, Sechenov considered that it arose, not from any particular localized area of the body, but from "whole systems of sensory organs" (*The Physiology of Nerve Centers,* p. 37). Sechenov's theory of the reflex nature of muscle sensation was of gnoseological importance extending far beyond the bounds of purely sensory processes.

Muscle signals are not simply the impression of outside influences. They are generated by a working organ. The space-time signs which they reflect are not reproduced passively, of course, but are established by means of motor operations. These operations, according to Sechenov, form the real basis, the sensory framework, of the whole subsequent mental activity. Hence we have the theory of "the element of thought"—the basic structural components of the perceptual process at all its levels.

The muscle, according to Sechenov, "is not only a school in which the eyes are taught to evaluate spatial relationships, and hearing—temporal relationships." It is also a school in which intellectual operations such as comparison, analysis, and synthesis are taught. Concepts of all quantitative relationships, apparently extrasensory in character, are elevated to the sphere of muscle sense.

The hypothesis of the experimental, sensory origin of mathematical concepts was not an innovation. What was a novel feature was their deduction from actual operations of a muscle as a working organ and as a "detector" of information, coupled with the conviction that this information contains the most reliable—so far as is possible—information of the world itself, that it is a picture taken of reality.

The principle of unity of behavior and knowledge permeates Sechenov's reflex theory. The reflex action is accomplished purposefully, in a manner appropriate to its condition, because it is regulated by signals—by the initial elements of knowledge of these conditions arriving from outside. However, the reflex act is not a mechanical response to stimulation, but a system of actions solving a definite problem in life.

In the course of this solution (and as a basis for subsequent solutions) this system reproduces or constructs a space-time and objective image, giving knowledge "not a conventional, but a direct, radical value," which in turn regulates its behavior. This is the real meaning of Sechenov's "feedback."

The concept of muscle sensation was extensively developed in nineteenth-century psychophysiology. However, no investigator before Sechenov saw in the muscle a tool connecting the subject with an object, enabling the reproduction of the space-time properties of objects, and of forming a system of real operations, by means of which sensations, in Sechenov's words, are idealized, i.e., are converted into thought.

Association is not lacking in internal meaning, a purely external connection, but an intellectual operation. In essence, it is thought. The mechanistic view of association subsequently led, with the development of experimental psychological research, to its comparison and subordination, like second-grade connections, to connections of a higher order—apperceptive, intellectual, and so on. From the very outset, Sechenov's interpretation of association rejected this type of comparison. He took as his initial model of association, not the simultaneous appearance of two or several of its elements in consciousness (or their appearance in succession) but the structure of a judgement, crystallized into a proposition, consisting of subject, predicate, and copula.

Every encounter between the organism and an object in the outside world, according to Sechenov, contains all the elements of the proposition, for such an encounter evokes a comparison, by means of a reflex (by association), composed of at least two objective contents (for example, during the recognition of an object, the comparison between a new image and the old).

In the act of comparison motor factors are again involved, and may be regarded as the equivalent of the copula. Hence, thought must be regarded as "consisting of at least three separate perception reactions. The two extreme correspond usually to the objects of thought, while the intermediate reaction is the relationship joining them" (*ibid.*, p. 480).

Since the simplest connections between the organism and the environment are intellectual in character, in the strict sense of the word, there is no need to have recourse to the idea of a special source converting a mechanical and random association between mental elements into an orderly and logical relationship. The grounds for this conclusion drawn by Sechenov were the conviction that objects, processes, and their relationships themselves possess a definite order or "logic" to which living beings must subordinate their behavior.

Associations are represented primarily at the phase of sensory automatic thinking in concrete motor acts. Having been developed in relation to concrete behavior, they are then "interiorized"—carried out inside the central nervous system and without external expression. When thought "is born directly form concrete impression, the acts of thought correspond to a physiological series of separate reactions of a practiced sense to an external influence. When, on the other hand, thought occurs in the form of reminiscence, its physiological basis consists of the repetition of a previous nervous process, but now exclusively in the central nervous system (*ibid.*, p. 384).

The entire area of problems, called the "flow of consciousness"—images, thoughts, feelings—which the old associationism took as its starting point, must be interpreted, according to Sechenov, as the projection of a stream of "living encounters," i.e., of the concrete course of the activity of life.

This course, with the need for adaptation to the environment, leads to conversion of sensory-objective thought into symbolic. Speech, according to Sechenov, is not the demiurge of the latter, but its handmaiden. Like preceding associationists, Sechenov struck course on the unity of the whole perceptual process—from its source to its completion. Movement from one grade to another inside this unity, especially from figurative association to abstract, he tried to explain in terms of "multiplication of the number of living encounters." This was at once the strength and weakness of his theory of the associative structure of mental activity: the strength—because the real process of life took place on the basis of mental evolution, the weakness—because he did not know that at the level of man this process has acquired qualitatively new features, which alone can determine the creation of new forms of cognition.

Sechenov's theory of associations abolished one of the most vulnerable links of the old associationism—the "atomistic" approach to consciousness. In the conclusion that the most primary association is similar in its structure to a logical proposition, the idea of the separate and independent existence of mental elements was rejected.

With the discovery of the system-based and integral character of the formation of associations, Sechenov laid the foundations for the subsequent experimental investigations in Pavlov's laboratories.

When he planned the future system of objective psychology, Sechenov called it analytical. At the same time, insisting that the analytical investigation of mental phenomena should be placed in the hands of physiologists (*ibid.*, p. 241), he proposed new principles for the analysis of mental activity into elementary units and a new method of synthesis of what takes place and of how increasingly complex forms of behavior develop.

The Consciousness

The subsequent course of development of psychological science revealed the true meaning of the "Copernican" revolution carried out by Sechenov. It consisted of the radical displacement of the starting point of psychological thought from the directly received phenomena of consciousness, for centuries regarded as the primary reality for the understanding mind, to objective behavior.

This had in mind, not the fact that externally observed reactions serve as a channel for the penetration of mental phenomena perceived by introspection into the internal world, but that the position of these phenomena in the only scientific objective psychology must be occupied by integral acts, reflex in mechanism and recognizable, like all other objects in science, only indirectly.

Sechenov's plan of objective investigation of mental phenomena was opposed, one the one hand, to introspectionism and, on the other hand, to mechanism. Introspectionism lay at the basis of Wundt's system, which developed at the same time as Sechenov's and which claimed as the single object of psychological science—"direct experience"—the sum total of the subject's experiences, taken from its "prototype," i.e., what Sechenov claimed was a "psychological function," generated by the illusions of introspectionism. The subsequent collapse of introspectionism showed how futile were the attempts to construct psychological science on the indications of consciousness alone. As a counter to this, the demand arose for a radical reconstruction of psychology in accordance with objective principles. An attempt was made by behaviorism to meet this demand, but, as we now well know, this school banished mentalistic terms, because it lay under the hypnosis of a false idea of the mind (that created by introspectionism).

The subsequent evolution of "strict behaviorism" also proved unable to construct a scientific psychology based on ideas of behavior as the sum total of bodily reactions, without mental content, to external and internal stimuli. Sechenov followed another path.

The new idea of mental activity, as a special form of organization of signals reproducing an object with its main structural features, and providing for the self-regulation of action on this basis, opened the way to the transformation of subjective psychological ideas into an objective language, a science, having for its subject matter not phenomena received in introspection and not the mechanics of bodily reactions, but objective behavior regulated by the mind.

Thus a new chapter was started in the evolution of psychological thought, made up of modern objective psychology in collaboration with neurophysiology and cybernetics.

R E F E R E N C E S

BELL, C. Idea of a new anatomy of the brain. *J. Anat. Physiol.*, 1869, 3, 153–166.
BORING, E. G. A *history of the experimental psychology.* (2nd ed.) New York: Appleton-Century-Crofts, 1950.

CARPENTER, W. B. *Principles of Human Physiology.* (9th ed.) London: J & A Churchill, 1881.

MÜLLER, J. Der Handbuch der Physiologie des Menschen. Colblenz: J. Hölscher, 1838–1840.

PFLÜGER, E. F. W. *Die sensorischen Funktionen des Rückenmarks der Wirbelthiere nebst einer neuen Lehre uber die Leitungsgesetze der Reflexionen.* Berlin: A. Hirschwald, 1853.

PROCHASKA, G. *De functionibus systematis nervosi commentatio.* Prague: Academia Scientiarum Bohemslovenica, 1784.

SECHENOV, I. M. *Reflexes of the brain.* Moscow: Uchpedgiz, 1942. (First published 1863.)

SECHENOV, I. M. *Physiology of the nervous system.* St. Petersburg: 1866.

SECHENOV, I. M. *The elements of thought.* St. Petersburg: 1878. (2nd ed., with important revision, 1903.)

SECHENOV, I. M. *The physiology of nerve centers.* Moscow: Uchpedgiz, 1952. (First published 1891.)

SECHENOV, I. M. *Selected philosophical and psychological works.* (Russian.) Moscow: The All-Union Institute for Experimental Medicine, 1935.

SECHENOV, I. M. *Selected physiological and psychological works.* Moscow: Foreign Publishing House, 1952–1956.

WOLMAN, B. B. *Contemporary theories and systems in psychology.* New York: Harper & Row, 1960.

CHAPTER 6

WILLIAM McDOUGALL

Harold G. McCurdy

"PURPOSIVE action," wrote William McDougall in his *Outline of Psychology*, "is the most fundamental category of psychology" (1923, p. 51). The sentence, if properly understood, is an epitome of his system. It allies him at a certain level with Freud; it sets him at all levels against the strict behaviorists. For McDougall's purposive psychology agrees with Freud's in being psychodynamic and instinctive, but it gives less scope to nineteenth-century associationism and much greater scope to consciousness and so offends more against the externalized S-R associationism of the behaviorists and against their model of the living organism as an unconscious reflex machine. McDougall detected evidences of purpose throughout the natural order, first of all in himself and his human fellows, but likewise in the animals he loved to observe, down to the lowliest protozoon; and where he found purposive action he thought he found consciousness also, vague and glimmering though it might be. It was entirely consistent with this position that he defended animism in his *Body and Mind* (1911) and that he deemed the Lamarckian hypothesis of the transmission of acquired characteristics worthy of laborious experimental investigation.

Behavior Defined

Early in his career McDougall brought behavior explicitly into the province of psychology. His first book, the *Physiological Psychology* of 1905, begins: "Psychology may be best and most comprehensively defined as the positive science of the conduct of living creatures" (1921, p. 1). "Behaviour" accompanies "conduct" as a near synonym in his *Introduction to Social Psychology* of 1908, and in 1912 enters the title of his most popular book, *Psychology: The Study of Behavior*. McDougall's behaviorism was not, however, the later American kind; he did not define psychology as the study of behavior for the purpose of eliminating purpose and mind, but rather to accent the fact that mental processes issue in action and can be studied by other methods than those of introspection.

It is necessary to be sharply aware of McDougall's sense of continuity in nature, which is both Leibnizian and Darwinian. Within himself he recognized grades of consciousness and grades of definiteness of purpose. "From our own experience," he wrote in a 1912 appendix to his *Social Psychology,* "we are familiar with actions in which anticipation of the end varies from that of the most clear and detailed nature through all degrees of completeness down to the most vague and shadowy, a mere anticipation of change of some undefined kind" (1960, p. 309). If we add to this subjective knowledge the outlook of a Darwinian convinced that man has descended by minute steps of difference from more primitive biological forms, we pass without strain from this sentence to the next, which is about the experience of animals: "We are therefore able to form some notion of the inner or subjective side of the action of animals, even those lowest in the scale of organisation" (1960, p. 309). The same allegiance to the principle of continuity distinguishes McDougall's remarks in a 1919 symposium on instinct and the unconscious when he takes exception to the disposition of Rivers and Jung to attribute an all-or-nothing character to instinct; he objects that such a conception violates the rule of gradation of intensity in mental functions, as illustrated by the observable degrees of anger and fear in animals and men (1919). For McDougall there was no leap from unconsciousness to consciousness, from one level of behavioral intensity to another, or from the behavior of an amoeba to the behavior of a man, but many intermediate grades by transitions so slight that the inferential steps could reasonably be taken from what was well known in oneself to what was less well known both in oneself and in other organisms. He was thus able to apply in psychology the rule of method applied by Newton in physics, namely, that, starting with the familiar, "to the same natural effects we must, as far as possible, assign the same causes." McDougall found purpose consciously at work in himself and achieving expression in certain kinds of action, and he inferred similar mental processes, if of different intensity and clarity, when he observed comparable action in other living beings.

Behavior, as defined by McDougall, is not simply an observable movement. A stone may fall, and so may an animal: this is not behavior. A reflex, in the sense of an isolated partial movement of fixed pattern, is marginal behavior at the best—perhaps a relic of past behavior in the individual or his ancestors.

MARKS OF BEHAVIOR

Behavior in the full sense involves the organism as a totality. This total involvement of the organism is the seventh of the marks of behavior listed by McDougall in his *Outline of Psychology,* and of course gains its true meaning in conjunction with the other six marks, which are: (1) spontaneity; (2) persistence beyond the initiating moment and conditions; (3) variation of direction; (4) cessation upon achievement of some particular change in the situation; (5) preparatory character in advance of the concluding phase (e.g., an animal stalking its prey); and (6) learning, i.e., improvement in the effectiveness of an action when it is repeated under similar conditions. McDougall brings these marks of behavior into contact with his own self-knowledge and clarifies what he means by purpose in the following commentary:

Now, when the movements of a human being exhibit the first five marks of behavior, we do not hesitate to infer that they are purposive; by which we mean that they are made for the sake of attaining their natural end, and that this end is more or less clearly anticipated or foreseen. For any one of us, when he acts in this way and reflects upon his behavior, may observe introspectively that he himself foresees, however vaguely, the kind of end his actions will attain. In the typical case of purposive active, we foresee or imagine the end very clearly and definitely, and we desire or resolve to attain it; and we may also foresee and deliberately adopt the various steps of action which are the means to the attainment of the desired or resolved end. The natural end of a train of action foreseen and desired, or consciously chosen or intended, is properly called the goal of action or endeavor. We are said to strive toward the goal. The attainment of the goal is said to be the purpose of our action or our striving (McDougall, 1923, p. 47).

It is through this line of reasoning and with this meaning that McDougall regards objectively observed animal action, when it carries the marks of behavior he has specified, as signifying purpose and some degree of conscious foresight.

Learning

McDougall was not disposed to let a principle enjoy a purely theoretical existence. He characteristically put it to work in empirical and experimental studies. Thus, for example, learning (the sixth mark of behavior as listed above) was viewed by him as a consequence of purposive striving; and in a brief but masterly study with May Smith, to mention a single instance, he demonstrated the relative importance of the degree of this attitude in the learner (Smith & McDougall, 1919). In this study, in which he experimentally separated memory as the retention of unique experiences (Bergson's "pure memory") from memory as mechanical habit, he further experimentally separated conative learning from mechanical association as a means of acquiring mechanical habits. In the latter experiment the two subjects memorized lists of nonsense syllables under two subjective conditions: (1) they consciously strove to learn the lists, or (2) they passively exposed themselves to the successive visual stimulations. The former attitude (of conscious striving) resulted in much quicker learning than the attitude of passive exposure—an average of 13 trials as against 89 for one subject, 9 as against 100 for the other.

If the effect of purpose is demonstrable in so seemingly mechanical a task as memorizing nonsense syllables, it can scarcely be ignored in more inquiring and creative activities. McDougall's "model" of a man, the natural man Mowgli, is able to imagine distant goals and work toward them mentally without stirring a finger, forming plans to be put into execution later by bodily movements and material tools. Even words are not essential. The essence of thought is purposive striving, whatever adjunctive means it uses; it is not, according to the behavioristic prescription, the agitation of muscles, either in wild gesturing or in laryngeal tensions, nor is it, neobehavioristically, primarily a matter of verbalization, either vocal or subvocal. Natural man can think in a concrete imaginative way, he can solve problems and plan for the future without language. So can sophisticated, civilized man, though in single cases he may have become so verbal as to deny the possibility; and so can animals. Thus the Darwinian continuity of life is preserved; and purpose, which is obviously present in human thinking, can be traced down into lower biological forms—into Köhler's ape meditating on the means for reaching a banana, into a dog hunting (perhaps even in his sleep), into a wasp building her nest and at times altering her usual pattern of behavior to bring the work to completion in spite of mishaps, into a microscopic *Stentor* adjusting by various movements to an annoying rain of nonnutritive particles released upon it by an inquiring scientist. The inference of mind, to use the title of Adams's important paper *(1)*, carries McDougall far outward from the human reference point. His conclusions, however, are not the result of naive anthropomorphism or animistic "superstition." They flow rationally from the application of Newton's rule of method to a graded series of biological forms seen in Darwinian perspective.

The Role of Consciousness

From the beginning McDougall was a biologist. His first papers were on muscle contraction and the nervous system. But he was a biologist conscious of himself. He was soon deep in the problem of the relation between consciousness and the body. In a paper of 1898 he asks: "What are the conditions of occurrence of consciousness in terms of neural process? What are its immediate physiological correlates, antecedents and sequences?" *(14,* p. 159). His preliminary answer is that consciousness is no inevitable accompaniment of neural process and cannot be said to vary systematically with any assignable location or property of neural process, except possibly with novelty of the neural combination. Most of what goes on in the nervous system is unconscious process; only the *new* process is conscious, and, as the novelty wears off, so does the consciousness, and the originally conscious act becomes habit or reflex. What then is consciousness? At this stage of McDougall's thinking it is simply one of the forms of energy, which "has its heat equivalent that may some day be determined with more or less accuracy" (McDougall, 1898, p. 386). And further, "just as matter is but 'a group of various forms of energy co-ordinated in space,' so mind is still more complex group of various forms of energy of which consciousness is one. We shall then regard mental activity, not as a mixed chain of neural and psychical events, but as a flowing network of cause and effect, consciousness forming a part of the strands, a part that is of a very different importance in different kinds of mental activity" *(ibid.,* p. 387). Mental activity is thus neural activity, and consciousness is a special variant of it, typically the variant which occurs when a new functional connection is established between neurones.

Later, McDougall focused even more precisely on the synapse as the place where conscious mental activity occurs, and proposed the name "neurin" for a hypothetical fluid secreted at synapses by activated neurones, the different quantities and rates of secretion constituting the energy changes needed to account for consciousness (1901). He speculated in this 1901 paper that the difference between a sensation and an idea or memory image consists in the shortening of the cortical neurone chain for the latter. Thus sensation and idea have overlapping but not identical neural locus, the idea being deficient on the afferent side. The same explanatory scheme appears long afterwards in his *Encyclopaedia Britannica* article on hallucination (1929), where he argues that hallucinations differ from ideas and memory images by their quite peculiar sensory vividness (which he distinguishes from sensory *intensity*), and that this sensory vividness implies that extensive tracts on the afferent side of the sensorimotor arcs of the cortex have become excited, though without appropriate sense-organ stimulation.

A major difficulty recognized by McDougall in the conception of neural process advocated in his early papers is that the conception requires a unitary consciousness to arise from numerous punctuate events at widely scattered synapses. He was unwilling to surrender either the known structure of the nervous system with its separate neurones and synapses or the introspectively known unity of consciousness. Since the unity of consciousness cannot be explained by any single element in the brain (such as the pineal gland of Descartes or some master-cell), McDougall was driven by the time of his *Physiological Psychology* of 1905 to postulate a unitary psychic entity, in these words:

We are compelled to admit, or so it seems to the writer and many others, that the so-called psychical elements are not independent entities, but are partial affections of a single substance or being; and since, as we have seen, this is not any part of the brain, is not a material substance, but differs from all material substance in that, while it is unitary, it is yet present, or can act and be acted upon, at many points in space simultaneously (namely the various parts of the brain in which psycho-physical processes are at any moment occurring), we must regard it as an immaterial substance or being. And this being, thus necessarily postulated as the ground of the unity of individual consciousness, we may call the *soul* of the individual (McDougall, 1921, pp. 78 f.).

Dualism

As a result of patient analysis of consciousness and the nervous system in a series of careful studies, then, we find McDougall moving from a position very close to material monism (identifying or blending mind and brain) to a position of frank soul-body dualism of the interactionist kind. Some years later, in 1911, his *Body and Mind* concludes by arguing the advantages as well as the necessity of the soul doctrine.

We may well devote a few pages to examining the properties which McDougall assigns to the soul in *Body and Mind*. The summary statement is this:

We may then describe the soul as a being that possesses, or is, the sum of definite capacities for psychical activity and psycho-physical interaction, of which the most fundamental are (1) the capacity of producing, in response to certain physical stimuli (the sensory processes of the brain), the whole range of sensation qualities in their whole range of intensities; (2) the capacity of responding to certain sensation-complexes with the production of meanings, as, for example, spatial meanings; (3) the capacity of responding to the sensations and these meanings with feeling and conation or effort, under the spur of which further meanings may be brought to consciousness in accordance with the laws of reproduction of similars and of reasoning; (4) the capacity of reacting upon the brain-processes to modify their course in a way which we cannot clearly define, but which we may provisionally conceive as a process of guidance by which streams of nervous energy may be concentrated in a way that antagonizes the tendency of all physical energy to dissipation and degradation (McDougall, 1961, p. 365).

Point 1 in the above statement scarcely needs comment. Points 2 and 3 refer to the fact that our experience is not confined to a given set of sensations but reaches through and beyond them to structures and significances both concrete and abstract. For example, when we turn from dealing practically with some object to dealing with the idea of it, we discover that the same sensory pattern no longer seems the same. Again, a reversible cube, i.e., a fixed pattern of lines on paper, undergoes changes of meaning without change of stimulus properties. "That is to say, the system of retinal stimuli and of visual sensations evoked by them may remain unchanged, while the meaning of the whole and of all its parts is changed by the volition or intention of the observer" (*ibid.*, p. 309).

Points 1, 2, and 3 may be said to be supported by direct examination of experience. Point 4 is more speculative. And yet it is but an extension of the case of the reversible cube. Here in perception (see Figure 1) we get a spatial

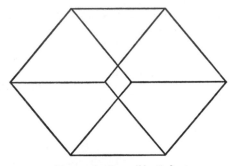

FIGURE 1. *Reversible Cube.*

reordering, with the side of a cube abruptly becoming its bottom, as if a gambler had thrown his die. Yet this spatial reordering, this tumbling of the perceptual die, occurs without any obvious expenditure of physical energy. It is a kinesis that seems to be purely psychical. What is it that we do when we will such a change? McDougall supposes that we produce a neural reordering. "If mind has such power, it may influence the processes whose phenomena we conceive as brain-processes in a way which would appear to us as a spatial redistribution of energy or a transference of energy from one part of the brain to another, without intervening phenomenal medium, and without alteration of the quantity of energy" (*ibid.*, p. 215). Just as with respect to the reversible cube we seem to be able to redistribute intentionally a perceived pattern of physical energy, so we may be able to do with respect to neural energy—for example, reverse or turn aside its direction of flow as we alter the *meant* direction of the lines and planes of the cube. I go beyond McDougall's words here, but I believe that I am faithful to his reasoning.

Volition

Now, of course, we might think of the reversals of meaning in the cube as corresponding to endogenous reversals of direction in neural processes, without volitional intervention, and such in part they may be. But McDougall, in a series of papers on the physiological factors in attention written before *Body and Mind,* had gone to some pains to show that such "spontaneous" fluctuations can be controlled to some degree by an act of will, partly but not wholly assisted by muscular adjustments. He is therefore able to bring forward evidence that, when the effort is made to hold one aspect of a reversible figure constant or to favor one of a pair of rival colors (as viewed through a stereoscope, for instance), the partial success achieved is the result of a volitional alteration of the rhythm of fatigue and recovery within the brain. To enter into more detail, McDougall agrees with Fechner that in the case of binocular rivalry between two colored fields the willed predominance of one field over the other is aided by the stronger innervation of the intrinsic muscles of the favored eye, and indeed he was able to verify the truth of this hypothesis by paralyzing the muscles of one of his own eyes with atropine and then comparing the duration of the colored field presented to the paralyzed eye with the duration of the colored field presented to the rival normal eye; under which conditions, if neither eye is volitionally favored, it is the normal eye whose field predominates. Yet, under these conditions, if the paralyzed eye is volitionally favored, its colored field can be made to endure longer than in the passive condition and, in fact, to predominate over the field of the normal eye. McDougall is ready to admit that much fluctuation of attention is involuntary. For example, the alternation of directional phases of the imitation windmill (a metal rod rotating in a vertical plane) occurred in his experiments, after the warm-up period, at the rate of once every 2 to 3 seconds for monocular vision and could be influenced only slightly by voluntary effort. Indeed, it was just such observations which led McDougall to his hypothesis of cerebral fatigue and recovery, i.e., a neural process by which the flow of energy along one sensorimotor pathway was switched periodically to another pathway and then back again. Nevertheless, he was so impressed by the power of volition that at the conclusion of much painstaking work with these and other experiments he could write:

I suggest then that, while all attention involves concentration or convergence of free nervous energy from all or many parts of the brain into some one neural system, voluntary effort results in a further degree of this concentration of energy. I have tried to show how the concentration of energy of non-voluntary attention may be explained by purely physical principles, but I am not sure that my explanation completely accounts for it or that it can be completely accounted for on physical principles, and this is I think still more doubtful in the case of the higher degree of concentration that results from voluntary effort. It is here, if anywhere, that the interactionist must seek in the insufficiency of physical causes evidence of psychical efficiency; here possibly we have a residual effect which . . . may be evidence of psychical guidance of physical process. If such power of guidance of energy by psychical effort in however small degree be granted to the interactionist, he has all that is needed for his purposes. The world is then not purely mechanical, and biological evolution may be regarded as increasingly teleological, as swayed in an ever-increasing degree by final causes, and we may hopefully look forward to the time when man will control by voluntary effort the further evolution of his species (McDougall, 1906, p. 359).

This expression of hope for mankind contains two terms, both of which, separately or in combination, have seemed unacceptable to McDougall's critics. The one term is psychical, the other biological. Jerome Bruner, in a preface to a 1961 edition of *Body and Mind*, has evidently thought it a service to his old teacher, a diplomatic maneuver to ingratiate McDougall with the Harvard of "easy answers" (McDougall, 1961, p. xiii) which nudged him out in six uneasy years, to put the psychical term in modern dress and have it pose as "the program that determines how the machine will process its data" (*ibid.*, p xv). But this will not do. For McDougall the psychical term was an active being, a conscious energy, a soul—a programmer perhaps, but not a program. Neither was the body a machine, fundamentally. It was a living organism endowed with inherited powers. A vitalistic biology, with heavy emphasis on heredity, may have been as unwelcome at Harvard in 1920 when McDougall arrived as a belief in the soul. At any rate, McDougall refers ruefully in his autobiography to his incautious lectures on "national eugenics" in 1921 which, by touching on the racial question, he supposes, aroused "much of the hostility of the American press that has continued to greet my successive publications" (28, p. 213).

The Doctrine of Instincts

An essential part of McDougall's biology is his doctrine of instincts. Nothing about him is better known than that. The details of this doctrine, however, are not so well known, and it will be the purpose of this section to remove some of the misconceptions and expose a problem or two. And first it must be noticed that, for McDougall, an instinct is a perceptual disposition, a readiness to perceive certain things in certain ways native to the organism. In the *Physiological Psychology*, where instincts are first seriously dealt with by McDougall, he defines them quite simply as "congenital perceptual systems" (1921, p. 106).

Secondly, McDougall stresses the emotional side of instinct. There is a note of triumph in the *Physiological Psychology* first published in 1905, when he recognizes the connection between the instinctive actions of animals and the emotional experiences of men. The chapter on emotion begins with this pregnant statement:

The possession of congenital nervous dispositions renders possible the perception of certain classes of things without previous experience of similar things, and determines their possessor to act in reference to these things in a manner more or less roughly adapted to promote his own welfare or that of his species. Such inherited perceptual dispositions are instincts. The only effects of the excitement of instincts that we can observe in the animals are those bodily movements which we call instinctive actions. But when such a disposition is excited in ourselves by an appropriate object, we not only perceive the object and experience an impulse to a certain kind of action, but we experience also what we call an emotion, or emotional state of consciousness, *i.e.*, the background of consciousness, on which our percepts and ideas stand out as the most prominent features, and which is ordinarily dim and vague, becomes more prominent and takes on a characteristic quality in the case of each of the primary instincts. In ourselves the bodily movements characteristic of each instinct, instead of having free play as in the case of the animals, are frequently suppressed or modified by the retained effects of previous experience and by the will. Hence of the two results of excitement of instincts in ourselves, we commonly attach more importance to the peculiar state of consciousness than to the bodily movements, whereas in the case of the animals the resulting bodily activities are alone open to our observation. So it has come about that in the past psychologists have commonly treated of the instinctive actions of animals and of the emotions of man, failing to realize that instinctive actions and emotions are but two different manifestations of the one process, the objective and subjective efforts of the excitement of inherited perceptual dispositions (McDougall, 1921, pp 108 f.).

In this early statement of 1905 we see McDougall describing instincts as he continued to describe them, in cognitive, affective, and conative terms; in short, as complete mental acts. But the discussion is not so elaborate and distinctive as it becomes in later publications, and it is necessary to read more than one passage to appreciate the full scope of McDougall's instinct doctrine, which underwent certain changes in the course of time. In particular, emotion came to be more emphasized. In the *Physiological Psychology* much of the discussion of emotion revolves around William James's theory. Though favorable to that theory insofar as it connects bodily changes with emotional experience, McDougall suggests that it should be modified to allow for the occurrence of "revived or reproduced organic sensations, without the intervention of actual visceral changes" (17, p. 114), and thus for the occurrence of emotion preceding or in the entire absence of visceral disturbance at a particular time. The modification would restore the commonsense sequence which James's theory violates—first perception of the emotion-inspiring object, then the emotional experience, and afterwards the visceral and skeletal adjustments appropriate to the experience. McDougall by no means wishes to minimize the importance of visceral involvement; he suggests indeed that the prolongation of emotional states beyond the exciting moment is evidence for a circular nervous process by which the afferent output from the viscera tends to keep up the efferent input to them. Still, he inclines to the view that there is something intrinsically emotional in the exciting perception itself—"that special kind of perception in which the synthesis includes a large proportion of organic images and sensations and feelings, and which we call emotional perception" (McDougall, 1921, p. 115). It is thus a legitimate question for him whether the emotion, as psychical fact, can *cause* bodily changes. Indeed, he concludes that emotional perception has a strong influence on nervous events and behavior.

THE ENERGY OF INSTINCTS

It appears, then, that emotion is not simply a quality of experience attached to instinctive action. It is also energy. By the time McDougall wrote his *Introduction to Social Psychology* it was clear to him that emotional energy is at the center of instinct. According to his autobiography, it was in 1906 that this idea struck him forcibly (McDougall, 1928, p. 208). From then on emotion always figures prominently in his definition of instinct and in his taxonomy of the different instincts. But it remains a problem, too. What is the exact nature of emotional energy? Is there a common source on which all the instincts draw or does each instinct have its own energy pool? How exactly is perception of external objects related to the emotional energy? These are some of the questions which McDougall never quite settled. For example, in his 1933 textbook, *The Energies of Men,* he asks: "Does mental activity involve some form or forms of energy other than those recognized by the physical sciences?" and answers: "In view of the purposive nature of human activity, the positive answer to this question seems inevitable. We must postulate some energy which conforms to laws not wholly identical with the laws of energy stated by the physical sciences. We have at present no sufficient ground for postulating more than one such form of energy" (McDougall, 1933, p. 10). And he suggests as alternative names for this one postulated form, *mental energy,* or *psychophysical energy,* or *hormic energy.* Yet, as the title of the book implies, it is possible to think of the several instincts as each endowed with a separate energy; and the possibility is discussed within the book itself. The question is taken up in an Appendix to Chapter XXII in connection with recent physiological research. McDougall here points out that certain results obtained by W. B. Cannon and other workers harmonize with his contention in 1908 that the instincts, and more specifically the emotions, have their neural base in the region of the thalamus. But in what sense is the thalamic region their base? One possibility (which he himself has previously argued for as strongly as he could and yet thought unsatisfactory) is that the thalamic centers merely collect and concentrate streams of nervous energy from the afferent nerves leading into them. Another possibility (which he thinks more probable) is that "the neurone groups constituting the affective centres of the thalamus are endowed to a much higher degree than other neurones with the potentiality of liberating and transmitting to other neurones quantities of nervous energy" (*ibid.,* p. 334), and he quotes phrases of Cannon's such as "stormy processes of the thalamus" to support this view.

THE AUTONOMY OF INSTINCT

Here we have one of McDougall's major puzzles. Is an instinct autonomous (or nearly so)? Or does the external environment through the sense organs and afferent nerves supply some of the energy and much of the direction? In McDougall's thinking, this is a question, an uncertainty. Lundholm, in his attempt to purify and extend McDougall's system, treats the uncertainty as a contradiction and tries to eliminate it by deciding for the autonomy of instinct (Lundholm, 1949).

Before coming to Lundholm, let us sharpen up the problem a bit. In the *Social Psychology* McDougall's definition of instinct runs as follows: "We may, then, define an instinct as an inherited or innate psycho-physical disposition which determines its possessor to perceive, and to pay attention to, objects of a certain class, to experience an emotional excitement of a particular quality upon perceiving such an object, and to act in regard to it in a particular manner, or, at least, to experience an impulse to such action" (McDougall, 1960, p. 25). Here the perceptual, emotional, and conative-motor aspects of the instinct are put on something like an equal footing. But in other contexts the emphasis may be more unequal, as in this from *The Energies of Men:*

In our study of instinctive behaviour we saw that the typically instinctive action expresses two distinguishable features of the native endowment; on the one hand, a special ability, simple or complex (as the ability of the wasp to recognize and master the prey natural to her species); on the other hand, a propensity, which, on being roused from its dormant state, generates an active tendency: and the tendency is, in some sense, an energy; and not merely energy in general or a special kind of energy, but an energy which is directed to a goal, which works towards that goal and is brought to rest only on attainment of it; an nergy which activates the ability and brings it into the service of the tendency as a means towards its end or goal" (McDougall, 1933, pp. 86 f.).

Here the perceptual and executive abilities, the afferent and efferent sides of the nervous system, are set apart from the driving and directing energy of the instinctive propensity. The instinct is broken in two, and we see that the perceptual part might act in relative independence of the propensity and itself furnish direction and energy—at least the energy needed to trigger the energy of the propensity. Lundholm objects to McDougall's ambiguity. He puts the problem and the solution thus: The three expressions of a conative disposition (an instinct) are the affective act, the cognitive act, and the locomotive act. These three expressions emerge simultaneously, though not necessarily in equal strength, every time the potential energy of the disposition is activated. It is a contradiction to say, as McDougall sometimes does, that a perception *precedes* the activation of the instinct, because perception is itself an instinctive function; for McDougall has argued that all perception is meaningful and that all meaning depends on conation, and hence is debarred from saying that a perception evokes the conation which gives it meaning. To be consistent, Lundholm argues, we must say that the activating event excites the instinct before it is perceived and that the aroused instinct, by the cognitive subact of conation, *creates* the object of perception (Lundholm, 1949, pp. 187–191). Strong as the logic is, McDougall evidently preferred to muddle through by allowing a low level of meaning to the simple perception that awakes an instinct.

THE PRIMARY EMOTIONS

Once he had settled on emotional energy as the essential feature of instinct, McDougall proceeded to draw up a list of the primary emotions as a guide to distinguishing the instincts. He called an emotion primary if it was displayed by the higher animals and if it occurred with morbidly exaggerated intensity in human beings in pathological states. In the *Social Psychology* the result is a list of seven major instincts: the instinct of flight marked by the emotion of fear, repulsion marked by disgust, curiosity marked by wonder, pugnacity marked by anger, self-abasement marked by subjection or negative self-feeling, self-assertion marked by elation or positive self-feeling, and the parental instinct marked by tender emotion. He states: "The seven instincts we have now reviewed are those whose excitement yields the most definite of the primary emotions; from these seven primary emotions together with feelings of pleasure and pain (and perhaps also feelings of excitement and depression) are compounded all, or almost all, the affective states that are popularly recognised as emotions, and for which common speech has definite names" (McDougall, 1960, pp. 69 f.). The list was revised several times in the course of the years, but it is not necessary here to follow the variations. It will suffice to examine the case of the sex instinct, omitted from the original list of major instincts with distinct primary emotions, but, under the designation "instinct of reproduction," included with several instincts alleged to play a great role in social life but a minor one in the genesis of emotions—namely, hunger, the gregarious instinct, the instinct of acquisition, and the instinct of construction. The brevity of his discussion in the original edition of the *Social Psychology*, and his categorization, of the sex instinct imply no insensitivity to its importance. He is explicit about its importance, but he notes: "From the point of view of this section the chief importance of this instinct is that it illustrates, in a manner that must convince the most obtuse, the continuity and the essential similarity of nature and function between the human and animal instincts" (*ibid.*, p. 70). He also points out a special connection between sex and pugnacity in males, and between sex and self-assertion (self-display) and self-abasement (coyness) in females. Beyond this he has little to say in 1908 about the one instinct which, through the Freudian literature, has dominated psychological theorizing and the popular imagination in the twentieth century.

THE SEX INSTINCT

But the lacuna is filled in the 1914 edition by a supplementary chapter. After some preliminary remarks on the brevity of his previous treatment of the theme and his reasons for taking it up now, he devotes about thirty pages to a thorough discussion of the sex instinct. He begins with the biology of fertilization, which he divides into two stages—first, the approach of two individuals of opposite sex, and, second, the effective discharge of the reproductive cells. He emphasizes, in regard to the first stage, the perceptual side of the instinct: "The sex instinct, then, illustrates very clearly a much-neglected fact of instinct on which I have insisted in the earlier chapters of this volume, the fact, namely, that an instinct is not only an innate disposition to act and to feel in a more or less specific manner, but is also an innate disposition to perceive or perceptually discriminate those things towards which such reactions are demanded by the welfare of the species" (McDougall, 1960, p. 334). He rejects the view of Moll and Ellis that there are two separate impulses, "contrectation" and "detumescence," though he himself has designated two stages; his reason being that "the quality of the emotional conative excitement that accompanies the activities is recognisably the same throughout both stages" (*ibid.*, p. 338). He adopts the name "lust" for this emotional excitement, and comments: "We must frankly recognise that, in spite of all the hard things that have been said about lust, it is an essential element in the emotional conative attitude of human lovers towards one another; and that, no matter how much the attitude and the feeling of refined lovers may be modified and complicated by other tendencies, lust nevertheless strikes the ground tone and supplies the chief part of the mental and bodily energy which is put forth so recklessly and copiously in the service of sex love" (*ibid.*, p. 338).

As to Freud's sexual theory, McDougall has two major criticisms. In the first place, he considers that Freud has overlooked the contribution of various other instincts to the development of sexual love (a more complex thing than lust), particularly the contribution of the parental instinct which leads to a tender nurturing of the partner, the woman mothering the man, the man

gently protecting the woman (part of whose natural appeal is the fact that
she has some of the traits of a child); and has consequently given too much
scope to the sex instinct. Secondly, he thinks Freud mistaken in attributing
the direction of sexual choice to such factors as sucking at the breast, McDougall preferring to assume, not without evidence, that the direction of choice
is mainly inherent in the instinct, even in some cases of homosexuality. He
does not deny, however, that the sexual impulse pervades a wide range of
social, artistic, and intellectual activities, and he is glad to accept Freud's
concept of sublimation in recognition of the fact. Nor does he deny that in
the period of immaturity when the sex instinct has become vaguely active (he
sets the normal age at about eight) its natural direction may be perverted by
seduction, and he therefore urges a policy of moderation in the rearing of
children aimed at keeping the natural heterosexual direction undisturbed and
providing some opportunity for sublimation. He advises against forcing
detailed sexual enlightenment on the very young. He especially urges the
importance of a boy's developing respect for women as personalities before
he discovers the power of feminine sexual attraction. He believes that the full
awakening of the sex instinct in adolescence increases self-awareness, both
through arousal of new bodily functions and cravings and through a heighten-
ing of interest in other persons; and that, if this process is held in bounds by
such social and moral restraints as are customary in civilized societies, the
resulting sublimation raises the intellectual life to a higher intensity. McDougall does not regard the moral code as primarily a punitive denial of sexual
pleasure, as Freud does, but as a cumulative effort of society to reconcile the
conflicting demands of self-development and propagation of the race—an
effort by no means entirely to the disadvantage of the individual.

It is curious what antagonism McDougall's instinct doctrine once aroused
in American academic circles. Instinct was sometimes treated as a crude
superstition, and the evidence in favor of it was attacked or suppressed. Even
a careful experimental study, like Schoolland's demonstration of innate
preferences in chicks and ducklings, could go virtually unnoticed (Schoolland, 1942). The situation is now different. Genetics has been rediscovered,
ethology has reminded us of species differences and the fascinating behavior
of animals in the field, and there has been some tempering of dogmatic
environmentalism by calm reflection on the realities. One begins to see
McDougall's name again and some mention of his ideas with a tinge of
respect. Instincts seem to be coming back into favor.

The Sentiment Concept

But there is an aspect of McDougall's thought of equal or greater importance which, while arousing less antagonism, has suffered more neglect. I
refer to his sentiment concept. One reason for its neglect is doubtless its
eclipse by the more glamorous complex of the psychoanalysts; but, as
McDougall pointed out, the pathological complex is only a special variety of
sentiment, which, being broadly generic, applies equally to normal and
abnormal minds. A profounder reason for neglect is that the concept of
sentiment requires a kind of theoretical thinking which is in conflict with the
old, entrenched associationism of which S-R behaviorism is the present heir.

The old associationism and modern S-R psychology both, when reduced to bare essentials, are concerned with the accidental linkage of event with event by the ancient "Law of Contiguity." Accidents and mechanical series, contingencies and habits, are the coin of the realm in this type of psychology. Creative organization, though it looks like gold, is suspect. But when one adopts the concept of sentiment one is accepting creative organization.

It was Alexander Shand who made the discovery of the sentiments, according to McDougall, and he praises Shand for introducing a principle so astonishingly important and novel, and yet so obvious and necessary when grasped (McDougall, 1960, p. 105). The essence of the principle, as phrased by Shand, is found in what he calls "the fundamental law underlying all other laws of character," namely: *Mental activity tends, at first unconsciously, afterwards consciously, to produce and to sustain system and organisation*" (Shand, 1914, p. 21). Shand means particularly the system and organization of emotional-conative dispositions.

To get the history of the matter straight we must realize that Shand's full statement on sentiments appeared in his *The Foundations of Character* (from which I have just quoted) in 1914, many years after the initial statement—an article in *Mind* in 1896 (Shand, 1896)—on which McDougall was relying when he wrote his *Social Psychology* of 1908. There McDougall states: "Mr. Shand points out that our emotions, or, more strictly speaking, our emotional dispositions, tend to become organised in systems about the various objects and classes of objects that excite them" (McDougall, 1960, p. 105). He discovered later that he had not accurately rendered Shand's idea. The concept of sentiment as developed by Shand has some kinship with the "mental chemistry" of J. S. Mill, except that it is emotional forces rather than ideational elements which are blended. Love and hate, for example, are sentiments: they are (1) innate and (2) compounded out of the four fundamental emotions of joy, sorrow, anger, and fear. What is conspicuously lacking from this formulation is any reference to *objects*; and, also, the sentiments are characterized as innate. McDougall, in the preface to the fourteenth edition of his *Social Psychology* in 1919, distinguishes his concept from Shand's in the following words: "In my view the sentiments are acquired through individual experience, and where two or more emotional dispositions become conjoined in the structure of one sentiment, as when fear and anger are combined in the sentiment of hate, we have to regard these two dispositions as connected, not directly with one another, but only indirectly through the association of each with the particular object of this particular sentiment of hatred" (McDougall, 1960, p. xi). Objects are the knots which tie the emotions together, and the emotions all derive from instinctive sources; but the objects are supplied by the environment with which the instinctively moved organism has commerce.

PERSONALITY THEORY

We have seen how McDougall and Shand disagree. We must notice that they agree in regarding sentiments as dynamic emotional organizations and in regarding them as the fundamental organizational units of character—or, to use the broader term, personality. But here again McDougall goes farther than Shand. He sees the need for a hierarchy of sentiments. The emotional and intellectual richness of a personality is in proportion to the number and complexity of the sentiments, but the multiplication of sentiments (the potential nuclear objects are very numerous) entails the possibility of confusion, discord, conflict, even outright division into part-systems. McDougall was much impressed with the phenomena of multiple personalities and with Janet's principle of dissociation as applied to the problem. How, then, account for the normal, undivided personality? McDougall answers that in the normal personality the sentiments are arranged in a hierarchy of power ruled over by a master-sentiment, and that the ideal master-sentiment is the sentiment of self-regard.

It is perfectly clear what McDougall means by a sentiment of self-regard. He means a sentiment exactly like all other sentiments, except that the object of the sentiment is the self. But the self is a peculiar object. It is not only more constantly present than any other object; it is always more than an object, it is also and simultaneously a subject. What is it that regards the self in the sentiment of self-regard? It is the self that regards the self. The circularity of the relationship differentiates it sharply from the case of the self regarding other objects. It may be true, as McDougall asserts, that "whatever mystery is involved in thinking of oneself is the mystery of thinking in general, of consciousness or awareness of anything" (McDougall, 1926, p. 426). Still, the mystery obtrudes itself forcefully in this case. We may be conscious of other objects without being conscious that we are conscious of them; but we can hardly be conscious of the self without being conscious that we are conscious of it, because the self is virtually the same as being conscious and to be conscious of the self is to be conscious of being conscious. McDougall was not disposed to indulge in such phraseology or to make use of Kierkegaard's definition of the self as a relationship which relates itself to itself. He relied on blunt common sense. But in the end he was caught between two rather different theories of personality—the sentiment theory, and the monad theory. The two theories are alike in regarding personality as composed of elements which can be bound together or broken apart, but they differ in their accent on consciousness and the role assigned to the conscious self.

The two rival theories are set down side by side in 1926 in the *Outline of Abnormal Psychology*. Chapter XXXIII is devoted to the sentiment theory, Chapter XXXIV to the monad theory. Both theories are presented in the context of the problem of personality integration and disintegration, and the exposition is controlled to a considerable extent by the reflection that, biologically speaking, man is a colonial organism composed of a vast number of cells each one of which is a vital unit, potentially independent. McDougall concentrates particularly on the cells composing the nervous system, insisting of course that certain organizations of cells, comprising the instinctive dispositions, are innately present. But these primitive integrations threaten the unity of the organism unless they are bound together in the higher-order integrations of the sentiments and, ultimately, of the master-sentiment of self-regard. That is one way of stating the sentiment theory. So stated, it seems to identify personality with the biological organism, the colony of cells. But it is to be observed that at every level of organization the cells are required by the sentiment theory to point beyond themselves to their objects, clearly to extraorganismic objects in most cases (but back to themselves in the case of self-regard?), so that from the beginning the organism gets vitally related to the rest of the world; and it appears that personality must include these objects and relations as well as the bodily cells which point to the objects and establish the relations. Even with this important object-orientation included, we can manage the sentiment theory of personality in a perfectly behavioristic manner, as McDougall tells us at the beginning of Chapter XXXIV, provided we are *purposive* behaviorists.

There remains, however, the problem of consciousness, especially the problem of coconsciousness in certain cases of multiple personality. Consideration of all the facts seems to compel us to accept two views of human personality which have been held to be irreconcilable. "According to the one view, human personality is the expression of a unitary indivisible agent capable of self-conscious thinking and striving and of true memory. According to the other view, human personality is essentially a product of an integrative process by which a multitude of activities are co-ordinated in one harmonious system of activity" (McDougall, 1926, p. 545). It is the second of these views with which the sentiment theory corresponds. The first view, which postulates a unitary soul, has been excluded as far as possible by the sentiment theory. But McDougall cannot deny the validity of the first view. He seeks to reconcile the two opposed views through the monad theory.

THE MONAD THEORY

That theory was first propounded by McDougall in his 1920 presidential address before the Society for Psychical Research. In a footnote to the version printed in the Proceedings of the Society, he explained that the basic idea comes from Leibnitz and has been developed in recent decades by James Ward, C. A. Richardson, and Gerald Balfour, the latter in a presidential address before the Society in 1906; previously, in the middle of the nineteenth century, by R. H. Lotze. The Earl of Balfour has succinctly described his own version of the theory, thirty years after he first enunciated it, as "the idea that the human individual is an ordered association of psychic units, or centres of consciousness, telepathically interconnected" (Balfour, 1935, p. 47). McDougall's version is in close agreement.

In his address, McDougall begins his exposition of the theory by reminding his audience that in *Body and Mind* he had reached the conclusion that our conscious knowing, feeling, and striving seem to require the activity of a unitary being, an ego, soul, or self. His experience in the intervening years as a medical officer in the British Army occupied with the treatment of functional nervous disorders had impressed him with the facts of dissociation, facts inclining one to believe "that sometimes, and not infrequently, a single human organism or person is the seat of more than one stream of conscious knowing, feeling and striving, more than one train of mental activity; and that these trains may be not only distinct, but may be in acute opposition and conflict one with another, just as really as I may be in conflict with you, a conflict of purposes, of efforts towards different ends" (McDougall, 1921b, p. 111). But if this is a true belief, he argues, and if the former conclusion is true, then it is logically necessary to postulate at least as many selves as there are distinct streams of purposive effort. He continues, in a passage which he later quotes in the *Outline of Abnormal Psychology,* as follows.

Are we then to fly to the ancient theory of possession, whenever we observe evidence of such multiplicity of distinct mental activities within a single organism? By no means. The obvious and, I believe, inevitable inference from the facts is that I who consciously address you am only one among several selves or egos which my organism, my person, comprises. I am only the dominant member of a society, an association of similar members. There are many purposive activities within my organism of which I am not aware, I am conscious at any moment only of those processes within the organism, and of those impressions from without, which it is most necessary that I should take cognisance of. And I consciously control and adjust only a few of the executive processes of my organism, those only which are of primary importance for my purposes. But I and my associates are all members of one body; and, so long as the whole organism is healthy, we work harmoniously together, for we are a well-organised society, the members of which strive for the common good, the good of the whole society. My subordinates serve me faithfully in the main, provided always that I continue to be resolute and strong. But, when I relax my control, in states of sleep, hypnosis, relaxation and abstraction, my subordinates, or some of them, continue to work and then are apt to manifest their activities in the forms we have learnt to call sensory and motor automatisms. And if I am weak and irresolute, if I do not face the problems of life and take the necessary decisions for dealing with them, then conflict arises within our system, one or more of my subordinates gets out of hand, I lose my control, and division of the personality into conflicting systems replaces the normal and harmonious co-operation of all members in one system. And in extreme cases such a revolted subordinate, escaped from the control of the dominant member or monad, may continue his career of insubordination indefinitely, acquiring increased influence over other members of the society and becoming a serious rival to the normal ruler or dominant. Such a rebellious member was the famous Sally Beauchamp, and such was, I suggest, the childish phase of the Doris Fischer case. All such automatisms imply literally a dis-association of the society or association" (*ibid.*, pp. 111 f.).

McDougall works out some further details by way of analogy with the organization of an army in the field, but we need notice here only the difference that, whereas in the army the general's contact with the other members is by material means, in the monadic organism communication seems to have the nature of reciprocal telepathic rapport.

Now, in all this monadic scheme it is evident that McDougall has the body in view, as a colony of cells. The great, obvious difference is that the monads are units of consciousness and the cells spatial and physiological units. But at times McDougall brings them very close together. In the *Outline of Abnormal Psychology* he ventures to write: "I do not see that we make any very greatly extended demand upon our imaginations if we assume that a cerebral cell is the manifestation in the perceptual order of a monad endowed with true memory. Whether such memory is represented by, or in any sense correlated with, the electronic or minute spatial structure of the cell must remain for the present an open question" (McDougall, 1926, p. 555). We can be sure that if McDougall was alive today he would be intensely interested in the current research on DNA and RNA. Such identity as he suggests, however, poses all the psychophysical problems with which he himself wrestled so frequently, and there remains that special problem to which I have previously referred, namely, the role of *objects* in this as well as the other variant of McDougall's personality theory. In spite of his customary attention to the object-oriented character of thought and behavior, even his insistence upon it, and in spite of his awareness of the importance of the social group for the life and development of the individual, his formal personality theory seems a little truncated on the side of objects and the relation to objects. The society of monads is ambiguous. Is it identical with the body (or something equally restricted), or does it extend beyond those limits? Granted that there is a complex limited organism consisting of monads or cells and ruled over in some way by a supreme monad or integration of cells so as to constitute a unified organism, do we stop there? Or do we, in our personality theory, take serious account of the similar organisms or organizations, things and people, to which we are so prone to become attached that the form of our action and even our organismic life seem to depend on them? The conclusion of McDougall's address to the Society for Psychical Research almost answers these questions, but not quite. He is speculating on the possibility of life after death, according to his monadic hypothesis, and saying that if he survives the dissolution of his body he will retain only functions he has not delegated and memories of his own activities. Then he adds:

Further, it would seem to follow that, just as in this life I live effectively and fully only by actively participating in the life of an intimately organised society of like members, so hereafter can I hope to live richly and satisfactorily only by entering into and playing an active part as a member of some other society which will demand my faithful co-operation and service. For we are essentially social beings; outside of and apart from such intimate communion, our selves would have no meaning and no value, and perhaps could not be said to live or be conscious in any intelligible sense of those words (McDougall, 1921b, p. 120).

Read out of context and in the obvious way, the passage clearly asserts the supreme importance of other persons and the dependence of the individual life on the life of all who comprise the social milieu; but read strictly in context, *it* could signify only the necessity for a bodily organism if the conscious monad is to carry on its functions. Perhaps it should be read in both ways.

McDougall's Influence

It may surprise some readers that I have not treated McDougall as a social psychologist. It was *An Introduction to Social Psychology* which made his fame, was it not? True, but as Flugel has perceptively noted, the crucial word in this title is "Introduction," and here it means "Preparation" or "Prolegomena" rather than "Outline" (Flugel, 1939). The book can be more profitably read for its bearing on personality than for its bearing on society. There is for McDougall, of course, a significant relation between personality and society. The analogy between the individual and the group which forms the framework of Plato's *Republic* is also continually present in McDougall's writings, and it often becomes a virtual identity. Yet this analogy or identity in his case (as in Plato's) seems to me to be used more to illuminate personality than to illuminate society.

There is no space, and it would break the unity of this paper, to take up

other aspects of McDougall's multifarious work, for which there is fortunately an adequate bibliography (31). Suffice it to say that reason and courage
and love of the truth are everywhere in evidence. Some of the things he had
to say were unpalatable and perhaps a little deficient in tact, as in *Is America
Safe for Democracy?* (McDougall, 1921a) but they were said with his eye on
the facts and out of a genuine if ruthless good will. His interest in psychical
research was thoroughly rational and critical, the interest of a scientist devoted to the study of every phase of human life, normal and abnormal, ordinary and extraordinary, and in this case with the example of his admired
model William James before him. His famous and maligned Lamarckian
experiment was a heroic, able, and necessary labor on an extremely important topic; and his results (though not his inferences in favor of Lamarck)
were confirmed in the equally remarkable experiment by Agar and his associates, who (partly because McDougall had discovered unexpected irregu-
larities in the Wistar stock on which he had counted as controls) had the
foresight to provide their own control animals raised concurrently with their
experimental animals (Agar et al., 1954; McDougall, 1938). In these and
other phases of his work McDougall was masterful and sometimes polemical,
but thoroughly conscientious and humble before the facts. Whatever he
wrote was and is worth reading. But it is his personality theory which is the
culmination of his thought and which particularly invites further development.

It is gratifying to note that a few contemporary writers have consciously
benefited from McDougall's personality theory and deliberately worked along
the lines he laid down. In particular, Adams (1928; 1953; 1954a; 1954b),
Cattell (1950), and Leighton (1959) have made contributions to the development and application of the sentiment theory. The monad theory has
affected some of my work (McCurdy 1953; 1961; 1964). To attempt to assess
the general influence of McDougall in the development of modern psychology would far exceed the scope of this paper, but, as some of the histories
are beginning to say, it has been much greater than one might judge from
the sparse and grudging references to his name in the American psychological
literature, or from his own melancholy self-appraisal (McDougall, 1930). As
a corrective, Cyril Burt's appreciative introduction to a recent edition of
Psychology: The Study of Behaviour (McDougall, 1959) can be recommended.

REFERENCES

ADAMS, D. K. The inference of mind. *Psychol. Rev.*, 1928, 35, 235–252.
ADAMS, D. K. The organs of perception: sentiments. *J. Pers.*, 1953, 22, 52–59.
ADAMS, D. K. *The anatomy of personality.* Garden City, N. Y.: Doubleday,
    1954, (a).
ADAMS, D. K. Conflict and integration. *J. Pers.*, 1954, 22, 548–556, (b).
AGAR, W. E., DRUMMOND, F. H. O. W. Tiegs, & M. M. Gunson. Fourth (final)
    report on a test of McDougall's Lamarckian experiment on the training of
    rats. *J. exp. Biol.*, 1954, 31, 307–321.
BALFOUR, EARL G. W. A study of the psychological aspects of Mrs. Willett's
    mediumship, and of the statements of the communicators concerning the
    process. *Proc. Soc. psych. Res.*, 1935, 43, 43–318.

CATTELL, R. B. *Personality: a systematic theoretical and factual study.* New York: McGraw-Hill, 1950.

FLUGEL, J. C. Professor William McDougall, 1871–1938. *Brit. J. Psychol.*, 1939, 29, 321–328.

LEIGHTON, A. *My name is legion.* New York: Basic Books, 1959.

LUNDHOLM, H. *God's failure or man's folly? A challenge to the physicalistic interpretation of man.* Cambridge, Mass.: Sci-Art, 1949.

McCURDY, H. G. *The personality of Shakespeare: a venture in psychological method.* New Haven: Yale University Press, 1953.

McCURDY, H. G. *The personal world: an introduction to the study of personality.* New York: Harcourt, Brace & World, 1961.

McCURDY, H. G. *Personality and science: a search for self-awareness.* Princeton: Van Nostrand, 1964.

McDOUGALL, W. A contribution towards an improvement in psychological method. II. *Mind,* 1898, N.S., 7, 159–178.

McDOUGALL, W. A contribution towards an improvment in psychological method. III. *Mind,* 1898, N.S., 7, 364–387.

McDOUGALL, W. On the seat of the psycho-physical processes. *Brain,* 1901, 24, 577–630.

McDOUGALL, W. *Physiological psychology.* (First published 1905, London: Dent.) London: Dent, 1921.

McDOUGALL, W. Physiological factors of the attention-process. IV. *Mind,* 1906. N.S., 15, 329–359.

McDOUGALL, W. *An introduction to social psychology.* (First published 1908, London: Methuen.) New York: Barnes & Noble, 1960.

McDOUGALL, W. *Body and mind: a history and defense of animism.* (First published 1911, London: Methuen.) Boston: Beacon Press, 1961.

McDOUGALL, W. *Psychology: the study of behaviour.* (First published 1912, London: Williams & Norgate.) London: Oxford University Press, 1959.

McDOUGALL, W. Instinct and the unconscious. VI. *Brit. J. Psychol.,* 1919–1920, 10, 35–42.

McDOUGALL, W. Presidential address. *Proc. Soc. psych. Res.,* 1921, 31, 105–123(b).

McDOUGALL, W. *Is America safe for democracy?* New York: Scribner, 1921(a).

McDOUGALL, W. *Outline of psychology.* New York: Scribner, 1923.

McDOUGALL, W. *Outline of abnormal psychology.* New York: Scribner, 1926.

McDOUGALL, W. Hallucination. *Encycl. Britannica.* 14th ed., 1929, 11, 105–109.

McDOUGALL, W. (Autobiography.) In C. Murchison (Ed.), *A history of psychology in autobiography.* Vol. I. Worchester, Mass.: Clark University Press, 1930.

McDOUGALL, W. *The energies of men: a study of the fundamentals of dynamic psychology.* New York: Scribner, 1933.

McDOUGALL, W. Fourth report on a Lamarckian experiment. Pts. I–IV. *Brit. J. Psychol.,* 1938, 28, 321–345, 365–395.

ROBINSON, A. L. *William McDougall, M. B., D.Sc., F.R.S.: a bibliography.* Durham, N. C.: Duke University Press, 1943.

SCHOOLLAND, J. B. Are there any innate behavior tendencies? *Genet. Psychol. Monogr.,* 1942, 25, 219–287.

SHAND, A. F. Character and the emotions. *Mind,* 1896, N.S., 5, 203–226.

SHAND, A. F. *The foundations of character: being a study of the tendencies of the emotions and sentiments.* London: Macmillan, 1914.

SMITH, MAY, & McDOUGALL, W. Some experiments in learning and retention. *Brit. J. Psychol.,* 1919–1920, 10, 199–209.

CHAPTER 7

IVAN P. PAVLOV AND PSYCHOLOGY[1]

Peter K. Anokhin

Introductory Remarks

THE VIEW is widely held that Pavlov was "at war" with psychology and penalized any member of his staff using psychological terms even though they had been generally accepted for centuries. For this reason some investigators have concluded that Pavlov was in fact opposed to psychology as the science of mental states and therefore, ruled out completely any possibility of collaboration with psychologists.

This, of course, is very far from the truth, Pavlov's refusal to use psychological terminology was nothing more than the act of a man of genius, a brilliant discoverer who clearly saw that the law of the conditioned reflex is the law governing objectively developed nervous processes in the human and animal brain.

Pavlov's attitude to psychology during the first years after the discovery of the conditioned reflex is best described as the *strategy of a grand creative plan*. The essence of this strategy was to make, as far as possible the most rational use of what psychology had accumulated in the course of the centuries, without, however, losing the basic principle of the objective-scientific, physiological understanding of experimentally obtained facts. It is true, also, that in the transitional period of his laboratory career, when Pavlov was teaching the objectivization of the processes of adaptive animal behavior, he did impose a ban on the use of psychological terminology. However, this does not mean, as some writers imagine, that Pavlov thereby rejected the values which were already well established in psychology. In 1934, i.e., two years before his death, he stated quite categorically: "A mixture of subjective with objective in research ruins the work" (Pavlov, 1949b). This statement shows that the rejection of psychology, as of a subjective approach to the evaluation of the facts of higher nervous activity, was only a tactical move for Pavlov. On the other hand, in his strategic plan of investigation, Pavlov never gave the impression that the final aim of his scientific, physiological approach to the study of higher nervous activity was the objective understanding of the manifestations of the human mind, or as he expressed it, "the fusion of the physiological with the psychological" (Pavlov, 1949b).

[1] Translated from Russian by Basil Haigh.

131

Pavlov's most demonstrative declaration on this question was perhaps his address at one of his traditional "Wednesdays" in his laboratory. Directing his remarks at some of his pupils who exhibited extreme radicalism in this matter, he said: "It would be stupid to reject the subjective world. Of course it exists. It is on this basis that we act, mix with other people, and direct all our life.

"Formerly I was a little carried away when I rejected psychology. Of course it has the right to exist, for our subjective world is a definite reality for us. The important thing, therefore, is not to reject the subjective world, but to study it by means of scientifically based methods" (Pavlov, 1949a).

The remarks made by Pavlov which we have quoted clearly show that his personal point of view was not to reject completely the usefulness of the psychological approach. Recognizing the subjective as a reliable fact of nature, Pavlov felt that no purpose could be served by studying it purely introspectively and, therefore, he stressed the objective, scientific investigation of subjective mental processes.

It is important to remember that human subjective states and mental activity are undoubted facts of nature, the natural results of evolution, so that any indiscriminate rejection of the psychological from the sphere of investigation can hardly be progressive. This is the meaning of the quotations we have given above.

The complete rejection of the psychological from the investigation of the working of the brain would be tantamount to throwing the compass overboard and steering the ship on a long and hazardous course through uncharted seas.

The psychological literature of the world shows that Pavlov's theory of conditioned reflexes is a contribution of the utmost importance to psychology, and it is therefore interesting to analyze in some detail the genesis of Pavlov's views on this subject. In the first place I shall try to describe the historical situation in which this break with psychological ideas took place in Pavlov's laboratory and gave way to the scientific, objective approach to the study of higher nervous activity.

The History of the Discovery of the Conditioned Reflex

This period begins when Pavlov's approach to the explanation of adaptive phenomena in the digestive apparatus was still based on the acceptance of the "psychic" factor as the regulator of these phenomena in the body. It was not until 1903 that Pavlov radically changed his earlier view and came over completely to the physiological interpretation of the fine adaptive function of the salivary glands which he was studying at this period.

What happened at this time? How was it that Ivan Petrovich developed his new idea of the adaptive properties of the secretory processes in the body as a whole? These are questions which will for a long time continue to interest all who are concerned with the historical significance of the revolution in physiology resulting from the discovery of the new type of reflexes—conditioned reflexes.

With Pavlov a new epoch of the reflex began, bringing with it discoveries of exceptional importance. During the almost 300 years of the history of the reflex every possible attempt had been made to reconcile the contradictions between the accurate, but rigid scheme of the isolating experiment and the eternally varying natural activity of the brain, as manifested by the true behavior of animals and man. The investigators of the nineteenth century were much better equipped than those of previous centuries, but they were unable to overcome the hypnosis of vivisection. They multiplied time and time again information on the finest processes of the nervous system, but left the most complex forms of its activity for the future.

If we examine the historical development of the concept of the reflex from this point of view, we can see that all the additional principles enunciated by countless investigators, such as, for example, "the passions of the heart," "the sensitive principle," "the intellect," and so on are merely attempts to widen the mechanistic ideas of the reflex act.

However, not one of these attempts proved so obvious, so precise, and so consistent as the reflex response itself. Furthermore, it was historically inevitable that a subjective character was imprinted upon all these additional principles. They were all derived from man's internal sensations, from his subjective experiences and his ideas of the external world.

These views had a thousand years of history behind them. Yet, they had not justified themselves in the past, they had established no fundamental laws which could stand on the same level as the laws of the other naturalistic disciplines. This approach was no more successful in its attempts to supplement the conception of the reflex. Nevertheless, it played a considerable role in the history of the reflex. It clarified its conditions and marked the limit beyond which the application of the reflex as a universal principle lost its logical quality characteristic of the accurate sciences.

In just the same way Sechenov's theory of the reflexes of the brain, which played a vital role in the development of the materialistic philosophy of his contemporaries, remained for a long time a "flight of fancy," unprotected by the granite bastions of accurate laboratory investigation. It lacked the laboratory method, which by the accuracy and breadth of its response could have competed with the psychological theories put forward to explain the working of the brain.

Pavlov's main contribution lay in the discovery of such a method. After three centuries of unsuccessful attempts to broaden the application of the reflex concept into the complex adaptive behavior of animals and man, he perfected the concept, and reinforced it with a precise method of investigation which preserved the basic principle of the reflex but at the same time defined the distinctive features which it acquired in the higher levels of nervous activity.

Pavlov was well aware that he was verging on the world of phenomena which for many years has been regarded as mental. At the same time, he rated very highly the fact that he was entering this field without making any change in his methodological strategy, i.e., preserving the physiological interpretation of every manifestation of the organism without exception. It was this which gave the theory of the conditioned reflex its tremendous strength at the moment of its birth. In order to understand the enormous influence which it had on the entire historical course of the science of man, it is essential to imagine the peculiar atmosphere which surrounded the problem of the "mind" as the antithesis of the "body." It is true to say that the psychological investigations of the earlier twentieth century were dominated by the idea of the psychophysical parallel, according to which everything which could not be reduced to material processes could be regarded as governed by mental principles. In 1932, Pavlov wrote the following: "I shall not be very wide of the mark if I submit that this conviction is still held even today by some psychologists, masked by the conviction of the peculiarity of mental phenomena, by which they imply, despite all their scientific and worthy reservations, that same dualism with animism which is directly shared by a mass of thinking people, not to mention believers" (Pavlov, 1932, p. 470).

The Study of the Digestive Glands

In order to reveal the decisive steps in the development of Pavlov's scientific thought at this period, the sources of the theory of higher nervous activity must be explained.

From the very outset I must reject the assertion which I have often heard and read, especially in the Western literature, that Pavlov stumbled accidentally from the digestion to the study of the brain.

It is possible to trace step by step how the laws of adaptation of the organism to external conditions began to occupy an increasingly important place in Pavlov's consciousness. It is, indeed, unimportant by what example these laws were first discovered—all that matters is that every particular fact observed during the working of an individual organ or whole series of organs is bound by invisible threads to the general laws controlling the life of the organism and its relationships with the external environment.

There is every reason to state that, having discovered the high adaptability of the gastric and pancreatic juices to the character of the food eaten in the early stage of his researches, Pavlov then throughout his life displayed the greatest interest in this remarkable phenomenon. It could not fail to amaze the physiologist, accustomed to operate with electrodes and to take the organism to pieces in order to observe directly the result of his manipulations.

In 1894 Pavlov wrote: "We are now aware of an indisputable fact, namely that the alimentary canal can adapt itself to the nature of the food, and we can distinguish certain definite types. . . . Clearly the gland adapts itself to the conditions of working and conforms to some sort of pattern.

". . . It is easy to imagine that a wide range of what may be called digestive moods or characters may develop" (Pavlov, 1946, II, p. 48).

To conclude these highly categorical statements, Pavlov asks the question: "What is there in modern physiology to explain this adaptability of the digestive glands to the nature of the food, which we have discovered?"

By the depth of its thought, this must rightly be regarded as the basic question, and along the path towards its solution a new field of physiology has developed—the physiology of higher nervous activity.

Pavlov could reply unhesitatingly that the physiology of his time indeed had nothing with which to answer this question. Worse still, it could not even indicate the factors which might help towards answering it.

At this stage the search for a higher level of synthesis of physiological processes inevitably took place. Acutely conscious of the need to go beyond the bounds of organic factors, in the narrow meaning of laboratory physiology, Pavlov introduced the universal factor of the organism—the mental factor, responsible for all the processes of adaptation of the digestive glands to the quality of the food which he had observed.

Subsequently, in 1917, in the preface to the second edition of his book *Lectures on the Work of the Main Digestive Glands*, as a correction to his original views, Pavlov wrote: "The first point concerns what we call the psychic excitation of the glands, which in the first edition of this book I contrasted with reflex excitation, speaking with great enthusiasm and familiarity of the thoughts, desires and feelings of the experimental animals" (Pavlov, 1946, II, p. 18 ff.).

However, before making this remark, Pavlov had travelled along the complex path of vacillation and doubt concerning the choice of this fundamental psychological line. He reached the conclusion of the physiological nature of the phenomena he had observed only when, after "a difficult mental battle" he had realized the complete unsuitability of this allusion to the inner mental state of the animals for physiology.

But it is here that the instructiveness of this change of attitude lies. The factual content of the subject and the formulation of the problem remained unchanged from 1894–1895, at which stage he had decided to reject completely any allusion to the mental state of the animal.

What had brought about this revolution in Pavlo's thought? What factors, conscious or unconscious, had impelled him along the new and progressive path of study of mental phenomena.

I do not know of any statements made by Pavlov during this period that would describe to some extent his quest for a new point of view or his doubts about the correctness of his earlier explanations of the adaptability of this secretory apparatus. The revolution in the interpretation of the processes of adaptation of the digestive glands took place unnoticed by all who have tried to find evidence of it in his writings.

His last printed address on the theme "The modern unity in the experimental study of the main aspects of medicine exemplified by digestion" was published in 1899. It is completely permeated with the spirit of acceptance of the psychic factor as the guiding factor of the investigation and as the decisive factor in determining the animal's attitude towards the external environment. We also know that by the word "psychic" Pavlov implied the completely material processes of the brain. After a gap of four years, the important speech which he made in Madrid on the theme of "Experimental psychology and psychopathology in animals" expresses his views on the physiological unity of what are in fact the same phenomena, views which are now fully thought out and developed down to the last detail.

In this speech, not only does he give a new and physiological interpretation of the phenomena which he discovered throughout the period of the 1890s, but he also gives the first declaration of a new classification of the phenomena under investigation. This was the first subdivision of reflex phenomena into unconditioned and conditioned reflexes. Consequently, in 1903, not only had Pavlov developed a completely new idea of his subject, but it had acquired a definite methodological significance, paving the way to new investigations on fundamentally different lines.

What was this process which had taken place in Pavlov's thinking? What was responsible for the radically new course of this thinking? We may conclude from many signs that at this period he was in a state of "creative internal searching." During this period he was torn by doubts, which he subsequently mentioned to his pupils at home, away from his laboratory.

There are a number clues to his moods at this period. For example, when Doctor Vulfson had defended his dissertation on "The work of the salivary glands" and it was in an advanced stage of preparation for publication (about 1900), Pavlov carefully edited it at all places where it seemed to deviate towards the psychic. Sometimes he deleted the material completely, at other times he altered it. This dissertation, with the editor's own corrections marked on it, is now preserved as a document in the Pavlov Museum. It shows indirectly that at the beginning of the 1900s Pavlov's mood in relation to the widespread resorting to psychological factors to explain the adaptive behavior of the salivary glands had now moderated. However, he made other remarks at a later period (January, 1902) when he still speaks of psychic juice.

For example, when Doctor A. I. Bulavintsev addressed the Society of Russian Physicians on the subject of "The psychic gastric juice in man," during discussion on the speech Pavlov said: "So far as the discovery of the psychic juice in man is concerned, this is undoubtedly of tremendous importance. I have always been surprised by the fact that, before the physiological investigation of this problem, clinicians spoke of 'appetite juice,' but as soon as this fact was demonstrated experimentally, for some reason or other most of them became opposed to it. This accounts for the importance of these findings" (Pavlov, 1946, II, p. 613).

This revolution in Pavlov's thinking showed itself in particular in his relationships with his pupils. The episodes with Doctor Snarskii and Doctor Tolochinov are particularly revealing of this critical period in Pavlov's mood. However, we shall discuss this later. At this stage we are comparing his remarks at this period, which to some extent characterize the early history of the conditioned reflex and, consequently, help us to discover the genealogy of Pavlov's ideas concerning conditioned reflexes. This early history is an instructive example of the fact that the path of genius is not strewn with roses and does not go straight, without digressions and turnings, as is often imagined by the unenlightened. On the contrary, we can see clearly that this turning point for Pavlov was very worrying and difficult as regards both his attitudes to contemporary science as a whole and his relationships with his closest pupils. In 1894, Pavlov had sharply contrasted reflexes from the oral cavity and psychic factors. Reflexes from the oral cavity, as he then said, cannot account for the delicate adaptive power of the digestive glands to the quality of the food, i.e., ultimately for the adaptation to the influences of the external environment.

When analyzing the high adaptability of the activity of the gastric glands to the physical properties of the food, he wrote:

Everybody thinks, of course, that this is a simple reflex originating from the oral cavity. If we test this hypothesis with an experiment, we have to reject it . . . however much we vary the experiments and think how to change or imitate the properties of the food as a result of which the juice flows, we shall **not** be successful. What is it in the food which we cannot reproduce artificially? It is clear that there is nothing special in the food and indeed that there cannot be, but that something else is concerned in this process: *this is the psychic factor—the pleasure of eating . . . it is clear now that the pleasure of eating is the first and a very strong stimulus of the secretory nerves of the stomach . . .* an essential factor during the passage of food through the oral cavity is the psychic element, which is the true, real stimulus of the secretory nerves of the stomach." (Pavlov, 1946, II, pp. 312–313) (Underlining mine. P.A.)

In his famous lecture given in memory of Botkin, on the eve of the birth of the theory of higher nervous activity, he summarized all the material obtained by means of the method of the Pavlov-Glinskii fistula of the salivary duct.

Since this was the eve of the revolution which took place in his idea of the subject as a whole, these statements are of particular interest to us. He wrote:

And so, above our expectation, besides the physiology of the salivary glands they were found to have a psychology; we can go further, psychology was found to have taken the place of physiology, because all that is psychological is undoubtedly psychological, while much that is physiological must now be proved to be physiological by special expriments, in order to exclude the interference of the psychological. In what we have discovered of the psychology of the salivary glands we can see all the elements of what is called mental acitivity: feeling, desire, and indifference, ideas of the properties of what is entering the mouth. . . . It is clear that not only desires and feelings, but also ideas related to the activity of such an apparently unimportant organ in the body as the salivary glands must invariably be components of our daily mental routine. There is no logical basis for not accepting this in regard to other organs of the body. These desires, feelings and ideas, however little they are recognized, nevertheless require at least minimal attention, and thus determine the permanent physiological order in our body." (Pavlov, 1946, II, p. 340)

Physiological Interpretation

I consider it absolutely essential to stress that this was the path of a conscious materialist. During these years Pavlov sought anxiously for a way out of his theoretical difficulty and having sought the aid of psychology as a method of explanation, he was now able to argue that he cannot imagine it separately from the body. He felt that without a radical break with the customary dogmas in the study of the mind, dogmas established for centuries, he could not find the correct path. Accordingly, even when he was rejecting most ardently the explanations of the adaptive phenomena by "ordinary reflexes from the oral cavity," even then he felt that the phenomena he had discovered were unusual, he steadfastly maintained his materialistic outlook. He wrote: "All that is necessary is to find the cause of this phenomenon; we suggest that its cause should be sought in psychic excitation, while others, on the other hand, think it is a reflex from the oral cavity. The misfortune is that in all of us the dualism according to which mind and body are something separate from each other is still too firmly entrenched, while in the eyes of science subdivision is impossible" (Pavlov, 1946, II, pp. 592–593).

In this speech Pavlov displayed an obvious internal conflict. On the one hand, he was well aware of the unusualness of the phenomena he had discovered which did not fit in with contemporary physiological ideas, and on the other hand he experienced an internal protest against the chance that he may thereby lose the possibility of the materialistic approach to its explanation, on the basis of which all his investigations in the preceding stages of their development had been undertaken so successfully.

It is not surprising that later, when he summarized his twenty years of experience of the study of conditioned reflexes, he said: "After persistent contemplation of the subject, after a difficult mental conflict, I finally decided that faced with this so-called psychic excitation, I should remain in the role of a pure physiologist, i.e., an objective external observer and experimenter, dealing exclusively with external phenomena and their relationships" (Pavlov, 1932, p. 12).

This period when Pavlov turned from obvious sympathy with psychological interpretations of the many facts of adaptation of the digestive glands which he had observed to the objective physiological explanation of these phenomena was one of the most interesting and complex stages in his entire creative path. A further complication for him during this period was the moral break with some of his pupils. The creator of a science, the founder of a school, after a long internal conflict unobserved by his pupils, radically broke with the past and set out decisively on new paths of investigation, while his pupils continued to remain in the sphere of traditional thought.

It was not coincidental that this first conflict with his pupils took place during this period in connection with the dissertation of Doctor Snarskii, one of the pupils of the first period of the development of the study of conditioned reflexes. Snarskii's dissertation must be regarded as the pinnacle of the psychologization of physiological phenomena. Whereas Pavlov himself, taking the psychic factor as simply the "enjoyment of eating," left everything else in the plane of physiological discussion, Snarskii almost completely excluded the physiological aspect of the phenomena and so presented his material as if the experiments had been conducted in a psychological laboratory. A rupture here became absolutely unavoidable.

Subsequently, remembering this difficult period in the life of his laboratory, Pavlov said:

Let me describe its history briefly. It all began with Snarskii's dissertation. We found new facts concerned with the excitation of the work of the salivary glands by the action of food at a distance, from merely the sight and the smell of the food. We analyzed these facts and could not understand them. He presented the matter one way, I another. I began to rebel against the psychological interpretation, while he steadfastly adhered to it. Ultimately it ended when I told him: "Anton Teofilovich, write your dissertation as you think, I cannot be a despot." He wrote his dissertation with his own explanations, and I had to criticise the psychological interpretation. (Pavlov, 1932)

A still more serious moral event of the same character for Pavlov was his quarrel with Doctor Tolochinov, particularly because he and Pavlov were great friends. Pavlov himself said: "Ivan Filippovich caused me considerable anguish. He had become a very close friend." Tolochinov deviated from the true evolution of Pavlov's views and continued to explain all the phenomena of extinction of the conditioned reflex purely on the basis of psychological concepts. This naturally destroyed the harmonious activity in the laboratory and compelled Pavlov publicly to declare his unwillingness to continue with the work.

Recollecting this painful episode, Pavlov said with bitterness: "This was such a strange thing to have to write, and I was so upset—not without forcing myself I had to write a letter against Ivan Filippovich and to say that these recollections confuse the imaginary with the real and I cannot bear the slightest responsibility for them. It was one of the most unhappy episodes. Later the whole thing settled itself" (Pavlov, 1926).

The two difficult episodes described above show the suffering which surrounded the birth of the new philosophy, which offered such tremendous scope for the precise physiological investigation of the human mind. It is understandable why Pavlov emphasized so acutely his negative attitude towards the psychological interpretation. From his own personal experience he was convinced that to explain a phenomenon by psychological causes meant to recognize a phenomenon which arose from "neither one thing nor the other."

Determinism

As a physiologist, Ivan Petrovich Pavlov was guided throughout his creative life by the law of determinism. It was only because of this that, as an investigator, he found confidence in the way he chose and assurance in the reliability of his newly discovered facts. A psychological explanation, on the other hand, would have translated the facts he observed into the plane of other laws, not immediately determinable from external, analyzable manifestations. Ivan Petrovich Pavlov, after some vacillation, stood steadfastly on the path of physiological explanation of the fact that the external signs of the food corresponded accurately with the qualitative composition of the "psychic saliva." At the same time, this explanation was not a claim by Ivan Petrovich that the whole of mental activity could be explained physiologically, but such an attempt must inevitably have arisen later with the increase in factual material and the extension of the fields of investigation.

For example, having radically broken with his previous attitudes towards the "psychic," Pavlov wrote: "At the present time the course of development of my physiological thought has led me to a completely different idea of the subject. Psychic excitation now appears to me also as a reflex, only this time a reflex formed during the individual lifetime of the animal and readily varying in its stability (to use our own terminology, conditioned). Discussion of the internal state of the animal I now consider to be scientifically useless" (Pavlov, 1946, II, p. 18).

Hence, we see that Pavlov did not find it so easy to put into words his attitude to the psychological approach to the explanation of the delicate adaptation of the secretion of saliva to the quality of the food and to the temporary conditions of feeding. He did not crystallize his ideas without agonizing conflicts and doubts, or without quarrels with his closest colleagues.

Many investigators are unaware of this eventful early history of the development of the physiology of higher nervous activity, and they therefore incorrectly evaluate Pavlov's apparent denial of the subjective, psychic components in nervous activity in general.

We have already seen from the introductory remarks that this in fact was not true, and the episodes of the quarrel with his closest pupils demonstrate his negative attitude to the confusion of physiological and psychological terminology. Having adopted the strictly physiological interpretation of the phenomena of the conditioned-reflex activity of animals, Pavlov nevertheless did not abandon the idea that eventually the whole range of reliable objective knowledge would be utilized for the explanation of human mental subjective states.

It is impossible to discuss in any further detail this period in the development of the physiology of higher nervous activity here, and I refer the reader of this article to the more detailed book in which Pavlov's creative evolution is examined (Anokhin, 1949).

The Historical and Philosophical Importance of the Discovery of Conditioned Reflexes

Little attention has been paid to the wider historical evaluation of the discovery of conditioned reflexes. The description of their properties is mainly confined to their ability to be formed de novo, or to be made by a temporary and variable connection in the animal or human brain. Pavlov himself, however, rated very highly the ability of the conditioned reaction to act as a "signal" reaction or, as he expressed it many times, a reaction of "warning character." It is this "warning" character which accounts for the profound historical significance of the conditioned reflex. It enables the animal to adapt itself to events which are not taking place at that particular moment but which will follow in the future.

In the pre-Pavlov period physiologists could work with only two categories of time—the present and the past. When some form of stimulus is applied to an animal, it reacts immediately to this stimulus, i.e., it adapts itself to an action developing in the present. This type of adaptive reaction was a constant object of investigation by physiologists and it was this type of reaction which formed the basis of the reflex theory developed originally by Descartes.

No adaptive reactions were known in physiology which would develop in connection with events about to happen. Physiologists also knew, however, that the adaptive reactions which they studied, associated with the action of stimulating agents at the present time had been evolved over many thousands of years, i.e., they incorporated the past experience of many generations. In this way the past, as a category of time, was naturally included in the form of fixation of the past experience of the species in its structures.

Consequently, before Pavlov's work, these two categories of time—the past and the present—were both incorporated in the subject matter for its investigation in a manner which was relatively well understood. However, to use philosophical terms, the development of events in the world is continuous and consecutive in character and, consequently, any subsequent event in relation to a past event becomes future provided that the particular sequence is repeated.

In psychology the forecasting of the future as one form of human mental activity has been a subject for attention for many years. However, the forecasting of the future developed entirely as an empirical matter, without any concrete mechanism and without any attempt to assess the history of development of any of the nervous structures responsible for this function of foreseeing the future.

With the discovery and development of knowledge of the conditioned reflex, it became possible to investigate the universal function of the brain. Prediction by scientific, physiological methods and the concept of the future then ceased to be purely philosophical issues.

The "Signal" Activity

This factor became decisive in establishing the role of the conditioned reflex in the development of mental functions. The "signal" activity of the central nervous system, implying in the wide sense of the term the extension of the brain processes to cover future events (foreseeing, prediction) became a subject of experimental investigation without the loss of those specific techniques peculiar to physiological investigations.

In the subsequent years (1933–1965) we have demonstrated in our laboratory the physiological basis in the central nervous system of the mechanism which can "predict" the course of future events. We have shown that when any behavioral act is formed as a result of the wide integration of all afferent information available at that moment, a highly ramified system of afferent processes is formed, integrating all properties or parameters, and taking into account results not yet obtained.

Components of this system may be found in the optic, tactile, and auditory cortex, or in brief, in any specific sensory region of the cerebral cortex, provided that this corresponds to the parameters of the future results.

This apparatus is dynamic, changing its composition with the adoption of each decision to act and with each change in the results obtained. Since, in the scale of integrated and continuous behavior the number of results is limitless, there are just as many apparatuses for predicting these results. Since this apparatus not only predicts the parameters of future results, but also compares, by means of feedbacks, the actual results of an action with those which were predicted, in our laboratory we have called it the acceptor of the results of action (or in brief, "the action acceptor").

Hence, this problem of the "signal" or "warning" function, which Pavlov raised on theoretical grounds, remains a subject for investigation in the laboratories of his pupils, and still on a purely physiological basis. More and more doubts are now being expressed: can any psychic event in general exist without elements of prediction of future results and without the rapid comparison of results actually obtained with their predicted parameters?

This leads to a very important question, largely determining our approach to all mental phenomena, in which the element of prediction of future events is of decisive significance. This question is as follows: when does this ability to prepare for future events by the formation of signals develop for the first time in the process of evolution of living organisms? In other words, when did the ability to form temporary connections first appear in evolution?

Analysis of this problem showed that the answer depends on which parameter is regarded as most important in the conditioned reflex and most characteristic of the conditioned reflex. From our point of view, it is the prediction of future events and the preparation of the organism for meeting these events.

If we adopt this approach to the living organism and do not associate the process as a whole with the presence or absence of a central nervous system, a quite definite answer will be obtained: the first manifestations of life and the earliest primitive living organisms must have possessed this faculty.

In fact, any stable structure of an organism could only be formed on the basis of numerous repetitions of the same time sequence of the same chemical reactions, associated, of course, with the influence of repeated external factors.

However, the course of these processes with a structure stabilized in this manner may develop only with the prediction of the subsequent stages of interaction between the organism and the external environment (Anokhin, 1963).

I cannot dwell here in any greater detail on this question and I therefore refer the reader to my monograph on conditioned reflexes which will shortly be published in English translation (Anokhin, in press).

All that matters at the present time is to show that the prediction of the results of a future action is a universal property of all organisms and that it appeared as the inevitable result of the reflection of successively developing events in the external world by the protoplasm of primitive organisms. A small piece of protoplasm with its extaordinary range of chemical bonds became a special form of chemical accelerator of slowly developing events in the external world after these repetitions. That is why the last link of this fixed chemical series acts before the external event corresponding to it has taken place.

By his discovery of the conditioned reflex, as a special case of this prediction of the future by the organism, Pavlov gave a powerful impetus to the objective scientific analysis of one of the most characteristic features of human mental activity. Prediction, the anticipation of future events, is positively imprinted on all forms of mental activity. In this connection we have only to remember the mechanism of speech, the correction of mistakes, recollections of something lost, and so on.

The usual idea that speech is a chain reflex is derived from the fact that, starting with the first word, every word that is pronounced acts as a stimulus for the next until the whole phrase is finished. However, with this explanation, each subsequent word of the phrase is the inevitable consequence of the preceding word, and the logical interrelationship between the individual words of the phrase loses its concrete nature. For example, in the phrase: It is a book, the relationships between "book" and "a" are completely paradoxical from the point of view of a chain reflex. In fact, the prefix "a" obtained its meaning entirely from which book is being discussed and consequently, in a chain reflex, it cannot be the afferent cause of the pronunciation of the word "book." Conversely, the word "book," although pronounced later, determines whether the word preceding it will be "a" or "the."

We could give thousands of equally logical examples showing that the relationship between words is logical in character and that the nervous connection between them was organized before the first word began to be pronounced, actually these connections predict the pronunciation.

Later, however, every word that is pronounced, because of its afferent properties (acoustic, articulatory, logical, and so on) as specific parameters, acts from the central nervous system in the form of an afferent feedback and is compared with the extensive complex of afferent elements of the action acceptor, formed as a logical whole long before the first word of the phrase is pronounced.

In brief, verification of the agreement between what is said and what it was intended to say takes place, just as in the case of other behavioral acts, on the basis of the prediction of future results, i.e., the agreement between the logical situation at a given moment and the verbal expression.

Hence, the problem of the future, solved in its general features in the conditioned reflex, extends very widely as far as the most detailed mental processes.

I wanted to stress this aspect of the conditioned reflex because it always escapes the investigator evaluating the role of higher nervous activity in the study of purely mental phenomena.

The Dynamic Stereotype

As an antithesis to the conditioned reflex, as an adaptive reaction of the organism in response to an isolated stimulus, Pavlov postulated a "dynamic stereotype," an extensive and integrated structure including not only the particular conditioned stimulus, but the situation as a whole in which the conditioned stimulus acts. The particular interest of the dynamic stereotype in psychology is that in these conditions the determinate role belongs to the dynamic stereotype and not to the conditioned reflex.

This idea put forward by Pavlov also deserves special attention because it is closely associated with such integrative concepts in psychology as the "image," "Gestalt," and so on. At the same time it introduces physiological lucidity into the mechanism of the formation and performance of integrated acts of the nervous system.

The experimental procedure by means of which the dynamic stereotype is formed is as follows. In an experiment with conditioned reflexes a series of conditioned stimuli is chosen which vary, not in composition nor in order of presentation, but in the length of the intervals between the individual stimuli. In short, the whole experimental procedure on a particular day becomes standardized or stereotyped.

A criterion used to determine that a dynamic stereotype has been produced is the result of a special test. In this test, instead of different conditioned stimuli which required a considerable time for the production of the dynamic stereotype, any one of the stimuli composing the stereotype is used throughout the experiment.

With this experimental approach, an interesting feature of the confirmed stereotyped experiment was discovered. Despite the fact that only one stimulus was used throughout the experimental day, its conditioned secretory effect was inconsistent in a quantitative respect and was directly dependent on which stimulus has been applied at this point throughout the period of formation of the dynamic stereotype. Consequently, physiological conditions were created in which a decisive influence on the magnitude of the conditioned secretory effect was exerted by the stimulus previously applied at this stage, and not the specific properties of the particular conditioned stimulus.

It was clear that, because of the stereotyped experimental conditions, usually remaining unchanged over a long period of time, some form of integrated complex was produced in the central nervous system, a distinctive type of integrated experimental model, to which Pavlov gave the name of "dynamic stereotype."

Pavlov's idea has many equivalents in psychological and clinical planes of thought. For example, the widely used concept of "body scheme," lying at the basis of the formation of many phantom phenomena, from the point of view of the concept developed above is a typical dynamic stereotype.

The numerous receptors of the body, always occupying a constant place in the organs of the body, in conformity with its constant inherited organization, always give the same pattern of signals regarding the state of a given point of the body. The position and the relative significance of these numerous receptors remains unchanged throughout the lifetime of the organism and ultimately creates something equivalent to a sensory model of the body as a whole, which has been called the "body scheme."

Pavlov considers that all the behavioral acts of animals and man, developed on the basis of conditioned reflex, must inevitably obey the law of the dynamic stereotype provided that they are repeated frequently as stereotyped copies without any change in the situation and in the stimuli evoking these behavioral acts.

The law of the dynamic stereotype is one of the cardinal laws regulating man's relations with the external environment. It is an expression of the purposive economy of energy during the formation of behavioral acts with the continuous transfer of the leading link from one afferent stimulus to another, depending on which complex of stimuli begins to undergo stereotyped repetition. In practice, the order and composition of the stimuli may serve as a stereotyped stimulus of this form.

The psychological and physiological equivalents of the dynamic stereotype are the processes of gradual transfer of conscious acts, performed with an obvious effort of consciousness, into unconscious or automatic. In his important monograph *Reflexes of the Brain*, Sechenov analyzes these forms of mental activity and distinguishes them in a special category of "involuntary movement" (Sechenov, 1863).

Neurophysiological and psychological investigations have shown conclusively that the inclusion of consciousness takes place at the moment when the maximally dynamic, and not the stereotyped, mobilization and integration of afferent impulses reaching the nervous system at that given moment is required. This integration with the participation of consciousness is, as a rule, essential either for the adoption of a decision to achieve some maximally useful result or in the case of a sudden disturbance of a given stereotyped order of action.

Conversely, the volume of integrative activity, in the sense of grasping external afferent signals, increases significantly. The process which we have called "the constriction of afferentiation" takes place here and what arises inevitably as a behavioral act becomes automatic and capable of frequent repetition. Together with this diminution of the range of afferent synthesis, consciousness is removed, so that consciousness is a natural result of the broadening of afferent synthesis.

At this point special emphasis should be laid on one important factor, which has not been emphasized in the past, as a result of which the intimate neurophysiological mechanism of the dynamic stereotype itself has been insufficiently understood. I refer to the fact that in the dynamic stereotype, for the first time in the history of Pavlov's school, the absolute role of the conditioned stimulus in determining the quality of the conditioned reaction was shaken. To give a concrete physiological example, how is it possible to imagine that an actual stimulus—let us say a light—can produce a conditioned effect characteristic, not of itself, but, for example, of the sound of a bell, if we know that the light, as a stimulus, in accordance with analytical laws can have as its destination only the optic area of the cortex, and evoke there a process of cortical excitation? This critical question was not asked when the dynamic stereotype first appeared on the scene as a new concept.

Because of this great importance of the phenomenon of the dynamic stereotype, it was very tempting to analyze this mechanism in greater detail by the adoption of modern methods of investigation. For reasons such as these, we have conducted detailed neurophysiological investigations of the mechanisms of the dynamic stereotype.

The first question which we asked was—in what state must the cortical end of an analyzer (the projection zone of the cortex), which must be stimulated at a particular moment in accordance with an established stereotype (for example, by means of a flash of light), be if instead of a flash, a testing stimulus is applied in the form of the sound of a bell, having as its destination another analyzer—the auditory. We chose the electroencephalogram as the criterion for assessment of the state of the corresponding projection zones of the cortex.

In order to obtain more precise results, the experiment was designed as follows: a subject received many times over three consecutive stimuli: a bell, a siren, and a light; and it was assumed that the depression of the alpha-rhythm produced usually by the light was a specific indicator of the state of the optic projection zone of the cortex.

After training with this trio of stimuli had been continued long enough to establish a stereotype, in one of the routine experiments the light was replaced unexpectedly by the sound of the bell. From the point of view of actual neurophysiological relationship, the bell should have evoked a reaction of excitation in its own projection zone, i.e., in the temporal region of the cortex. However, contrary to this general physiological rule, the bell applied instead of the light evoked a typical depression of the alpha-rhythm, i.e., it acted in the same way as the light.

This physiological paradox was explained by another type of experiment. After the experiment with the stereotype described above had been completed and the application of all the stimuli of the dynamic stereotype had ceased, the subject continued to remain as before in the room under electroencephalographic observation. Despite the absence of actual stimuli, it was found that at the precise moment when a corresponding stimulus should have been applied, the electroencephalogram showed changes characteristic of this stimulus. In other words, the cells of the cerebral cortex behaved just as if actual stimuli had continued to be applied. Characteristically, at the place at which the light was usually applied, even though absent at that particular moment, typical depression of the alpha-rhythm took place in the optic region of the cortex (Anokhin, 1956.).

It became clear from these experiments that during the formation of a dynamic stereotype, the changes in the cortical and subcortical processes follow a definitive rhythm and are to some extent independent of the stimulus actually applied, following strictly only the order of the stimuli previously applied. In turn, this means that the paradoxical response to the sound of the bell in the form of depression of the alpha-rhythm in fact is not paradoxical, for the bell, as a stimulus, does not produce depression of the alpha-rhythm; it merely fails to overcome the rhythmically developing process of excitation corresponding in its nature to the excitation of the next stimulus in order in the dynamic stereotype. In this way the remarkable ability of the brain to anticipate the events of the outside world, simply on the basis of a strict, constant sequence of stimuli, was discovered.

It follows from the facts described above that the ability of the brain to exhibit its own intrinsic principles created by past experience and, to some extent, independent of stimuli acting at the precise moment has been demonstrated in the dynamic stereotype. The dynamic stereotype has shown that all forms of associations in nervous and mental activity may form the elementary basis for complex psychological principles.

Since neurophysiological principles form the basis of psychological phenomena they constitute together with them an integrative whole. Pavlov's dynamic stereotype raises the question of psychological correlations in the dynamic stereotype.

Here, in the first place, it is important to consider the relationship between consciousness and the stereotyped and plastic activity of our brain.

Cortical Inhibition: Its Importance for Boundary Problems Between Highway Nervous Activity and Psychology

One of the central points of the physiology of higher nervous activity is Pavlov's discovery of "cortical inhibition." The role of this process in the formation of the mechanisms of higher nervous activity has proved to be so great that all forms of application of the conditioned reflex to the study of man and to clinical practice have been found to depend on the theory of cortical inhibition.

Recently a very outstanding monograph discussing the problem of inhibition and choice has been published in America (Diamond, Balwin, & Diamond, 1963). In this book the wide influence of the concept of internal inhibition on problems of higher nervous activity is properly reflected.

Sometime ago I published a monograph under the general title of "Internal Inhibition as a Problem in Physiology," in which I gave a close analysis of all types of cortical inhibition described in Pavlov's laboratory (Anokhin, 1958). I have now prepared for publication in English a monograph entitled

"The Biology and Neurophysiology of the Conditioned Reflex." In this book I also analyze in detail the problem of cortical inhibition.

The first and foremost feature of this type of inhibition is its consistency of formation, i.e., its acquisition of temporary inhibitory connections in accordance with the same laws as those governing the conditioned reflex. In Pavlov's laboratory this inhibition as a rule was based on the failure to reinforce with food either a previously developed extinctive inhibition or a newly applied stimulus close in nature to a conditioned reflex already established (differential inhibition).

Pavlov distinguished several types of internal inhibition which, although possessing common neurophysiological mechanisms, differed from one another, however, in the methods by which they were obtained or, as Pavlov himself stated, "by the conditions of their appearance": extinctive, differential, conditioned-inhibitory, and delayed. All these types of internal inhibition, forming as it were the negative, compensatory aspect of behavioral acts, combine with positive conditions to create harmoniously integrated general behavior.

The significance of internal inhibition for psychology is that, depending on the difficulty of its production, various states of conflict are created in animals and man, and in particular, neurotic conditions may develop.

Pavlov's subdivision of inhibitory reactions into internal and external is interesting. The criterion for this subdivision is the mechanism of development of the inhibitory process itself. It formed as a result of influences arising outside the conditioned reflex arc itself, this inhibition is called "external." Conversely, if the cause of the inhibition of the conditioned secretory defect lies within the conditioned reflex arc itself, the inhibition will be called "internal." An example of external inhibition is the inhibition of the conditioned secretion of saliva taking place as a result of some sudden application of an irrelevant stimulus, an example, the sudden experience of a noise or of new objects. An example of internal inhibition is the inhibition of conditioned food secretion as a result of a series of absences of food reinforcement.

From the point of view of the energetics of the central nervous system, the mechanisms of these two forms of inhibition differ very considerably. Whereas the first type of inhibition arises without any effort or conflict, the second type of inhibition, i.e., internal inhibition, arises, as a rule, as a result of states of conflict and requires a considerable effort by the organism.

For example, the suppression of external manifestations of human emotions, as a result of the dispatch of impulses from the cerebral cortex to the muscles of facial expression, requires a high expenditure of energy, for in this case the positive activity is suppressed by means of the cortex. The discovery of internal inhibition led to the deciphering and understanding of many mechanisms of behavior. This applies particularly to education, to the understanding of neuroses, to the understanding of hysteria, and to the explanation of many other forms of human behavior. Experience of the interpretation of these states was described some years ago by Pavlov in a series of psychiatric articles (Pavlov, 1949b).

From the psychological point of view it is important to note that Pavlov based all forms of behavioral reaction, whether normal or pathological, on the principle of the interaction, or even the "conflict," between two opposing processes—excitation and inhibition. In his opinion these two processes, which he called the "fundamental processes" of the nervous system, are in a state of constant interaction with each other, and proper harmonious behavior is ultimately achieved only by their mutual limitation.

In recent years this idea put forward by Pavlov has been somewhat modified as a result of further development and comparison with views expressed by I. M. Sechenov and N. E. Vvedenskii. This has led to a still deeper understanding of certain forms of human behavior and mental functions. This new understanding consists essentially as follows: the process of excitation and the process of inhibition in the cerebral cortex do not, in any circumstances, take sides in a "conflict." It is always two completely positive activities of the organism or, more broadly speaking, two impulses to action, each of which must be regarded as an independent and complex formation, composed of a system of excitations and inhibitions, which face each other in conflict.

In these circumstances the role of inhibition is that of an instrument by means of which one activity inhibits the other activity because of its more powerful excitation. The transformation of the formula "the conflict between excitation and inhibition" into the formula "the conflict between two impulses by means of inhibition" considerably modifies our approach to the various facts of behavior.

For example, the familiar exhortation to the teacher—"teach the child inhibition" changes its meaning considerably in the light of this new concept. Now, it has become increasingly clear that what must be taught is a more powerful impulse which can inhibit activity not required at that particular moment. In practice, in all forms of conflicting behavior, there is in fact a conflicting interaction between two positive activities, and only if one of these activities considerably outweighs the other because of its component impulses, will it inhibit the other activity and form the corresponding behavioral act. Hence, the formula: "teach inhibition" should now be replaced by a different formula: "teach stronger impulses or motives" in order that these can inhibit other, unnecessary activities. At this point it is interesting to ask two questions relating to inhibition. What is the nature of the process of inhibition at the point of direct inhibition of the unnecessary activity, and what complexes of excitation take part in these conflicting states?

So far as the first question is concerned, after the brilliant work of Eccles, Hodgkin, de Robertis, and others we can confidently conclude that it is formed ultimately by a process of hyperpolarization of the subsynaptic membranes. This hyperpolarization blocks the spread of excitation and thereby inhibits an activity which is unnecessary at the particular moment.

The second question is more complex, because every conflicting interaction in the integrative activity of the organism may arise only on the basis of two perfectly obvious emotional states. In other words, a conflict may arise if two emotionally charged impulses are present in conjunction with definite conditions of motivation. In practice, it is emotion which, because of its generalizing and ascending action on the cerebral cortex, involves a vast number of neural elements and broadens their participation with every new difficulty in the formation of a particular behavioral act (Magoun, 1958; Lindsley, 1951;

Miller, Murphy, & Mirsky, 1959). Hence, the theory of cortical or conditioned inhibition, in Pavlov's system of ideas and in the psychological aspect is inevitably bound up with activation of emotional complexes capable of making the corresponding subjective imprint on the various difficulties and conflicts arising during the formation of behavioral acts.

Experimental Neuroses

The study of experimental neuroses was founded in Pavlov's laboratory on the basis of the universal conception of the relationship and conflict between excitation and inhibition during the formation of the mechanisms of higher nervous activity. It was this idea that the relationships between excitation and inhibition may acquire the form of a conflict between two antagonistic processes that became the starting point for the development of experimental methods of obtaining neuroses in the laboratory.

Since Pavlov's ideas of experimental neurosis were widely introduced into various fields of practice, and acted as points of contact between psychology and pathophysiology, this problem deserves special attention.

The technical aspect of the production of an experimental neurosis is simple enough. If an experimenter has positive conditioned reflexes and negative conditioned reflexes in an animal, then in Pavlov's words, the production of the experimental neurosis is achieved by putting one against the other artificially.

From the technical point of view, a "conflict" must be obtained between these two processes for a very short interval of time. For example, a conditioned positive stimulus may be given, followed immediately (after 1–2 seconds) by a conditioned inhibitory stimulus, such as, for example, a differential stimulus. In these conditions, according to Pavlov's idea, for a short interval of time the two opposing processes must alternate in certain cells of the cerebral cortex (Pavlov, 1927).

However, this process of alternation must presuppose high mobility in the working of the nerve cells, for the process of inhibition in the cerebral cortex must reverse the activity of excitation previously present. Experiments showed that as a result of this technique the nervous system of the animal is unable to cope with the situation, so that the coordinated interactions in the cerebral cortex are disturbed and a generalized preponderance of either the positive or the inhibitory process results.

This method is interesting because, as a result of such a "conflict," victory falls either to the positive or to the inhibitory process depending on the type of nervous activity inherent in the animal, or the history of this nervous system before these experiments. In any case, some animals become unable to differentiate between external conditioned stimuli, i.e., they lose their ability to perform fine inhibitory processes and their nervous system develops a state of generalized excitation.

Usually in Pavlov's laboratory this type of "conflict" of nervous activity is regarded as a conflict leading towards generalized excitation, produced by highly excited and active behavior. In each case the animal loses all its precise coordination and its behavior becomes "irrepressibly excited."

In the opposite case, the victory in the "conflict" between excitation and inhibition falls to the process of inhibition, in which the animal's general behavior begins to bear all the signs of generalized inhibition. In this case we may speak of an inhibitory type of neurotic "conflict."

The development of experimental methods of obtaining neuroses served in Pavlov's laboratory as the basis for the formulation of a series of interesting clinical and behavioral correlations. For example, Pavlov's work in neurological and psychiatric clinics with patients took place for many years under this influence, i.e., from the aspect of the conflict between excitation and inhibition as two opposing processes. In many psychological situations of this type, conflicting interactions are particularly striking, so that the formula of "the conflict between excitation and inhibition" gradually becomes the basis for the understanding of emotional conflicts in the wide sense of human behavior.

We know from psychopathology that almost any vacillation during the selection of a type of behavior is accompanied by a negative emotional state, the intensity of which is the greater, the more important the objects of choice for the subject. Hence, on the broad psychological plane, the conflict between inhibition and excitation as Pavlov understood it is always correlated with agonizing efforts of the type of negative emotions. Pavlov often used the expression "difficult state" to describe this condition. Bearing in mind that Pavlov considered that the emotions are "the source of strength" for the cortical cell, the general character of neurotic states as phenomena of higher nervous activity becomes clear.

It must be remembered here, however, that in the case of neurotic conflicts, advances in neurophysiology during recent years compel us to regard such conflicts as the "collision between two impulses, i.e., between two widely ramified activities, endeavoring to destroy each other by means of the process of inhibition (see the preceding section). Consequently, in the case of the development of an experimental neurosis also, the conflict is the result of the impossibility for two mutually exclusive activities to coexist, while inhibition serves as the instrument for the suppression of one of the competing activities (Anokhin, 1958).

As an illustration of Pavlov's conception of conflicting neurotic states of the nervous system, we may cite one of his numerous characteristic statements on this subject. For example, when wishing to describe the role of inhibition in human behavior, he gives this as an illustration; ". . . you experience a strong process of stimulation, while the circumstances insist on its inhibition. . . . Someone insulted me very deeply and for some reason or other I could not find a suitable word or, still more, a suitable action with which to reply, and I had to repress this conflict." In giving these illustrative examples from life, with which Pavlov usually enlivened his lectures, we do not by any means wish to say that the idea of the collision between two systems of excitation was put forward by him in a succinct form or that he was guided by this idea when he created his working hypotheses. Any of Pavlov's pupils will know that neither was the case. Pavlov never associated the genesis of internal inhibition with the collision between two forms of excitation.

At the same time, we cannot ignore that vital fact that when Pavlov needed examples of inhibition from natural situations in life, he always cited relationships containing a perfectly obvious conflict between two activities highly ramified and developed in the nervous system.

We are thus forced to the conclusion, which is important from our point of view, that the natural activity of the whole brain compels us to widen our initial laboratory idea of the mechanisms of development of internal inhibition in the cerebral cortex.

Analysis of our second example clearly shows the correctness of our conclusion. How otherwise could we understand Pavlov's expression that "circumstances insist (!) that we inhibit" the existing nervous activity in the form of the "powerful process of stimulation"?

There can be no doubt that the "inhibitory excitation" in this particular case is the "powerful process of stimulation which is experienced," whereas the "inhibiting excitation" is undoubtedly formed in the cerebral cortex by "circumstances."

These "circumstances" are always the sum total of the external factors, and in the case of man, nearly always the sum total of social factors. On the whole they create in the human central nervous system an impelling motive towards a higher form of behavior, i.e., in the physiological sense the "circumstances" invariably act as the source of a highly ramified system of excitation, which ultimately acts as the "inhibitory excitation."

In the social sense, any inhibitory action of any circumstances as a rule presupposes prolonged training of extensive complexes of excitation, continually receiving added growth from new stimuli throughout human life. By acquiring frequently unbelievable complexity and embracing everything which is customarily called the human "personality," these systems of excitation thus make it possible for any external stimulus, to use Pavlov's words, "to excite inhibition in the central nervous system" (Pavlov, 1949a).

Types of Higher Nervous Activity

Pavlov's concepts of the types of higher nervous activity is a bridge connecting the study of the typological signs of higher nervous activity in the laboratory and the description of individual variations in human behavior. When comparing the specific features of the higher nervous activity of dogs, which he studied in great detail by the conditioned-reflex method, Pavlov saw that the wide range of signs of conditioned-reflex behavior of the animals coincided strikingly in their main features with the classical scheme of human temperaments suggested ages ago by Hippocrates. This coincidence was the more striking because investigations of conditioned reflexes were carried out in the light of recent achievements in neurophysiology, so that this coincidence was a shining illustration of the universal applicability of Hippocrates's classification, based entirely on his fine powers of observation.

The stimulus leading to the creation of this classification of the types of higher nervous activity was the extraordinarily varied attitude of different animals to the same experimental procedure—"the conflict" of excitation and inhibition described in the previous section. As we saw, some animals become extremely excitable after such a "conflict" and for practical purposes are in a state ruling out any possibility whatever of inhibition, while others, on the other hand, pass into a state of continuous inhibition, and express by their external behavior extreme depression and abject timidity.

Differences of this type were bound to strike the experimental, and must inevitably have led to attempts to classify the typological features of the different experimental animals. It was in this way that the analysis of typological features began, and these first observations led to the recognition of the presence of two extreme types of higher nervous activity: excited and inhibited. Further investigations showed that a certain type of animal exhibits other additional signs of behavior, and as a result of this, two further intermediate groups were introduced into the classification. Hence, Pavlov's complete classification of types, irrespective of the existing psychological classification of temperments, coincided very closely with Hippocrates's classification of temperaments.

In the table given below Pavlov's classification of types of higher nervous activity is compared with Hippocrates' classification of temperaments.

HIPPOCRATES	PAVLOV
Sanguinic	Excitable, compensated
Choleric	Excitable, uncompensated
Phlegmatic	Compensated
Melancholic	Inhibited, unbalanced

This aspect of Pavlov's ideas is of great interest in psychology, because it is an example of the interweaving of psychological and neurophysiological components.

The first question which arises is that of the physiological criteria of the types of higher nervous activity. What properties of the nervous system are most important for placing a given animal in the appropriate category? As his criterion, Pavlov took four neurophysiological characteristics, and by means of combinations of these signs he was able to place the animals in their correct categories. These signs were as follows:

1. The strength of the process of excitation or inhibition.
2. The equilibrium between the processes of inhibition and excitation.
3. The mobility of the nervous processes of excitation and inhibition.
4. A more integrated property—the limit of working capacity of the nervous formations.

By means of appropriate experimental tests, demonstrating the above-mentioned properties of the nervous system, Pavlov defined the broad characteristics of experimental animals in accordance with the reactions of their nervous system to these experimental tests.

For example, he found that some animals (dogs), coped very successfully with experimental difficulties during investigation of elementary processes of excitation and inhibition, yet at the same time they displayed extreme weakness and disorganization of their behavior as soon as tests were applied to study the mobility of the nervous system. As a test of this type in his laboratory, Pavlov used the so-called "modification" of conditioned stimuli. This modification could be of various degrees of difficulty. For example, a firmly established positive conditioned reflex may have to be modified into a negative conditioned reflex, i.e., from a certain moment this stimulus, hitherto always reinforced, begins not to be reinforced by food. Because of this change in the experimental conditions the animal is faced with a demand—to modify the habitual positive conditioned reaction (excitation) into a negative (inhibition). This relatively simple task sometimes meets considerable difficulties in its solution, especially if the animal concerned is one constantly dominated by excitation, i.e., one which belongs to the excited type. Depending on the overall results of the tests and the signs revealed by them, the "modification" test enables the animal to be regarded as of "compensated" type or as "irrepressibly excitable."

Tests of the types of higher nervous activity are very difficult, varied in character, and prolonged, and they always require considerable time, although after tests of all the components of higher nervous activity the experimenter can be fully confident that a particular animal corresponds to a particular type of nervous activity.

In the last years of Pavlov's work on this problem, results were obtained enabling the further subdivision of this original classification by the differentiation of certain minor variants of types of higher nervous activity.

This strict division into types of higher nervous activity is of the greatest convenience for laboratory work and also has proved useful for the development of methods of clinical treatment. For example, the same experimental procedure by no means always gives the same result, but this will always depend on the typological features of the particular experimental animal. Hence, knowledge of the type of higher nervous activity became in Pavlov's laboratory an indispensable condition of the correct evaluation of the results of every experiment.

In the same way, in clinical practice, as Pavlov's observations showed, the typological features of a person not only determines the character of therapeutic measures, but may also reveal the specific mechanisms distinguishing the reaction of a particular patient to various drugs.

Recent psychopharmacological findings show that certain types of nervous system are associated with differences in the neurochemical properties of the blood in the brain. For example, a person in a state of reactive stupor has a higher level of adrenalin and noradrenalin in the blood than normal. This is a factor which modifies the person's reaction to drugs very considerably (Anokhina, 1961).

Special emphasis must be laid on the value of the autonomic makeup of a man or animal, i.e., his ability to incorporate autonomic components in his reaction, when describing the type of higher nervous activity. Systematic investigations by my collaborators have shown that the autonomic components of the conditioned reaction (vascular, cardiac, respiratory, intestinal, hormonal, and so on) play an important diagnostic role in the assessment of the quality of the whole conditioned reaction and whether it may be classified among the positive or negative emotions. It is this emotional excitability and the ability to suppress emotions which is one of the characteristic signs both of the autonomic makeup of the individual and the strength of his cortical processes (Anokhin, 1935; Balakin, 1935).

It is pertinent to mention at this point that for many years this problem has been the subject of intensive analysis in Professor H. Gennt's laboratory (Johns Hopkins Hospital, Baltimore) and in Professor Liddle's laboratory. In our laboratory this problem is being currently examined by Professor V. A. Shidlovskii.

It has been shown that the autonomic components of the conditioned reaction are very closely connected with the character, or, more correctly, the biological modality of the emotions. As Balakin's (1935) experiment originally showed, this modality may evoke relationships of the opposite kind between the autonomic components of the conditioned reaction. For example, the application of a conditioned stimulus, reinforced by a nociceptive stimulus, evokes an extremely active autonomic reaction involving a large number of components. Conversely, a conditioned stimulus, reinforced by food, may actually lead to some diminution in the participation of autonomic components. However, if unexpected failure to reinforce the conditioned stimulus is used, a sharp difference immediately is found in the reaction of the autonomic components to failure to reinforce with food and with the electric current. Whereas failure to reinforce with food causes a sharp increase in the amplitude of the respiratory excursions of the thorax, sometimes amounting to convulsive respirations at a high inspiratory level; failure to reinforce with pain, on the other hand, causes a rapid change from active autonomic reactions to slow and weak respiration, with a fall in vascular tone and slowing of the cardiac activity.

Hence, removal of the reinforcing factor may be used as a characteristic test for determining the biological modality of the emotional state. Moreover, this fact also demonstrates that in order to obtain a more complete description of the types of higher nervous activity, it is also especially important to introduce the component of autonomic mobility, describing the energy level and the mobility of the emotional reactions of the particular man or animal.

Pavlov's views of the types of higher nervous activity are still undergoing development. It would be of the greatest importance if these developments could be matched by a corresponding flow of research from the psychologists. However, so far as I know, little is being undertaken in psychology to study the typological characteristics of man, from the standpoint of the emotional components of his reactions and of modern advances in neurophysiology, apart from systematic investigations by leading Soviet psychologists such as B. M. Teplov, A. R. Luria, and O. S. Vinogradova.

Pavlov's Views on the Second Signal System

The concepts created by Pavlov, which we have discussed above, are directly connected with corresponding fields of psychological research. They undoubtedly help in the physiological interpretation of psychological phenomena and thus contribute towards the progress of neurophysiological investigation. However, there is one field in the study of higher nervous activity which was developed in Pavlov's laboratory as a direct continuation of his theory of higher nervous activity in the direction of psychology. This field is represented by the concept of the second signal system.

By the second signal system Pavlov meant all the specifically human forms of relationships associated with the use of speech, as the most perfect form of signal activity between individuals in human society. This field of investigation, if we understand Pavlov correctly, is somewhat wider than mere speech. It includes all the processes of abstraction, which are the highest point of development of speech relationships, up to and including intellectual processes. In this concept we see a brave attempt to apply neurophysiological interpretations of higher nervous activity already developed in animals to specifically human functions. From this point of view it is most important to describe briefly the facts upon which the present development of this concept is based.

Pavlov's general view of the structure of higher nervous activity was that the whole superstructure acquired by the organism in the course of its individual development, and especially in human development, is based on inborn activity. This consists of a stock of adaptive reactions formed in the process of embryogenesis, and it represents the sum total of the phylogenetic experience of the particular species of animal. Such is the nature of inborn activity. The second stage in the formation of behavior is that this inborn activity gradually expands in the course of the postnatal life of animals and man on account of stimuli bearing the character of signals. On this basis conditioned reflexes are formed. This field of newly acquired "signal" stimuli, associated with inborn activity, Pavlov calls the first signal system or, as he expressed it, it forms the first signals of reality. These first signals of reality are very closely connected with reality itself, and are apparently substitutes for it. Whenever the need for inborn activity arises, a signal must be present and it must directly precede this inborn activity.

It is on this basis that in man, in the conditions determined by the first attempts at learning work skills and in the rudiments of society, the speech apparatus begins to develop, an apparatus for the translation of a relationship in the first signal system into a specific method of verbal symbolization.

Speech became an additional complex stimulus containing a meaning, a sum of features inherent both in phenomena of an inborn character and in phenomena of the first signal system. By associating the properties of sound, in the form of words, through the intermediary of man's vital experience with the properties of objects and phenomena already perceived in the first signal system, speech becomes an arbitrary instrument for reproducing at a given moment everything which was associated with it in the process of man's vital experience.

The sum total of these relationships, or as Pavlov called them, "signals of signals," constitutes the second signal system.

The extent to which speech, as a symbol of all the relationships laid down in the first signal system, is intimately connected neurophysiologically with all the phenomena in this system is clear from the fact that it is possible to suggest to a person the presence of fire without any real fire, and on a selected point of the skin a real burn will develop. A burn from the suggestion of fire!

From observations such as these it is possible to draw conclusions concerning the neurophysiological composition of the second signal system. It is a distinctive symbolic widening of the relationships of vital experience already fixed in the nervous system in the direction of acoustico-verbal combinations. The system of interaction between the individual components with the appearance of speech makes the whole complex of inborn first-signal processes and of second-signal processes a unified structure. In turn, this means that the ultimate effect of the system, for example, the autonomic reaction to contact with a flame, may be achieved in certain conditions from any starting point of the system. For example, this could be the site of a fire, as a stimulus of the first signal system, or it might even be the word "fire," organically woven into the previous experience of the brain.

Hence, the second signal system or the field of verbal signalization possesses a definite neurological material basis and, consequently, if they are applied strictly enough, it may be studied by objective physiological methods.

Pavlov's progressive idea, although admittedly one which he developed little himself, thus appears as a true bridge between concrete neurophysiological principles and broad psychological concepts.

The next stage of increasing complexity between the relationships in the second signal system in fact contain the generalization of signals uniting the whole group of natural phenomena with certain common qualitative signs. For example, the word "table" at a high level of generalization ceases to be the symbol of some particular table, but defines all types of tables in accordance with their common signs. Hence, abstraction inevitably arises as the result of the neurophysiological unification of the symbols of the second signal system.

Many new lines of research have arisen as a result of the characteristics of the second signal system as described above. They embody the organic unification of the physiological and psychological approaches to the same phenomena. For example, speech as a psychological and conceptual formation begins to be studied with the same technique as higher nervous activity, i.e., by the method of conditioned-reflex connections.

During Pavlov's life only the general concept of the second signal system was in fact formulated (Pavlov, 1928), and this idea received its main experimental development only after his death.

On these foundations have grown up whole schools and trends in the study of the second signal system by the methods of conditioned reflexes. We may mention, for example, work undertaken in the laboratories of A. G. Ivanov-Smolenskii, N. I. Kasatkin, M. Kol'tsova, Korotkin, and many others. In the field of clinical neurology, the second signal system has been analyzed by A. R. Luria, N. P. Bekhtereva, and other authors.

We may therefore conclude that the comprehensive development of Pavlov's idea of the second signal system is a sign of the tremendous interest shown by investigators in this borderline and specifically human problem.

Of course the study of speech as the "signal of signals" would be still more successful if a parallel study were made of the purely neurophysiological architecture of the speech function, for this would provide the canvas for the analysis of the psychological composition of judgments and concepts.

As we saw above, man's power to express in words any idea is established neurophysiologically down to its last detail before the expression begins. Every phrase is an integrated entity before it begins to be pronounced, with precise coordination of the interaction between the neural substrata of the individual words. As we have seen, this relationship between the words is by no means a linear, chain process. In the forefront of the speech complex words may be found whose meaning is determined by the last words in the phrase (see page 142). This fact emphasizes that the neurophysiological basis of speech is characterized by the same physiological architecture as any other behavioral act embodying the making of a decision.

It is hardly necessary to mention that the study of speech from the point of view of Pavlov's statements is an extremely important point of contact between conditioned reflexes and psychology. Without claiming to give an exhaustive explanation of the nature of the subjective or of the mind, Pavlov so constructed his investigations that the subjective in the second signal system is an organic component of the complex physiological interactions established during the formation of verbal reactions.

Conclusion

It cannot be said that the psychological content of the conditioned reflex, which Pavlov regarded as the elementary psychological act, has yet been fully discovered. If the conditioned reflex connection is regarded as a form of achitectural relationship in the nervous system, associated with the acquisition of experience, the psychological meaning of the conditioned reflex grows as the result of the integrative character of its neurological basis during the period of its formation. As we have seen, it is during the time of maximal activation of the nervous system, when the conditioned reflex has just been established, that consciousness is an essential participator in the activity. Conversely, when this activity becomes maximally automatized, when it is freed from superfluous afferent impulses, and hence, when its level of integration is considerably lowered, the components of the conscious or the mental in the conditioned reflex may be totally eliminated. Hence it follows that one of the current problems on the borderline between psychology and the physiology of higher nervous activity is the change from conscious to unconscious action and the mechanism of the sudden inclusion of consciousness in the case of a disturbance of automatized behavioral and specially automatized speech reactions.

The second important point of contact between the physiology of higher nervous activity and psychology is that during the physiological analysis of conditioned reflexes, psychological acts are ascribed with a neurophysiological structure and with the continuity of objective, determined interactions. This accounts for the importance of the movement of objectivization which at the present time is becoming increasingly widely adopted by psychologists, clear evidence of which is given by the appearance of the specialized journal *Neuropsychology*.

In the Soviet Union I. S. Beritashvili has long been engaged on the joint examination of processes of a neurophysiological and neuropsychological character, as is clearly visible in his monograph entitled "Psychoneurological Activity" (Beritashvili, 1947).

It is a matter of regret that the psychologist and physiologist, when attempting to create useful contacts with each other, should pay so little attention to those fields of medicine where the psychological and physiological are combined and are mutually interchangeable in a demonstrative form. For example, very few investigations have been made of such a critical state as the gradual loss of consciousness arising during the induction of general anesthesia, with the exception of a communication by Feldberg on the importance of the narcotic state for the study of consciousness (Feldberg, 1954).

Possibly the most demonstrative example of this intermingling between psychological and physiological phenomena is to be found in the case of the action of psychotropic drugs on the brain. The action of psychotropic drugs has now received detailed study in respect of its neurophysiological mechanisms, but at the same time correlative changes and transformations take place in psychological activity. Consequently, attention may be centered on both physiological and psychological phenomena. Unfortunately the theoretical analysis of this field is also undeveloped, so that its importance for the solution of the problem of the relationship between physiological and psychological has not yet been adequately realized.

As a result of the work of Penfield and Rasmussen much neurosurgical material is available in respect of the role of the material structure of the nervous system in the development of mental states.

Investigations have also shown that mental activity is the result of integrative formations embracing vast territories of nervous interaction.

The coordination of all these advances in the study of the neurological basis of consciousness is absolutely essential. I consider that Pavlov's ideas and achievements in this field could form a useful basis for such coordination.

REFERENCES

ANOKHIN, P. K. *The problem of the center and periphery in the physiology of nervous activity.* Gorky: State Publishing House, 1935.

ANOKHIN, P. K. *From Descartes to Pavlov: Three hundred years of reflex theory.* Moscow: Medgiz, 1945.

ANOKHIN, P. K. *Ivan Petrovich Pavlov: His life, work, and scientific school.* Moscow: Akad. Nauk USSR, 1949.

ANOKHIN, P. K. La Découverte par Ivan Petróvich Pavlov de la fonction de signalisation du cerveau, phase nouvelle de l'histoire de la physiologie. *In Actes du VIII Congrés International d'histoire des sciences.* Florence, September, 1956a. Pp. 758–761.

ANOKHIN, P. K. The physiological substratum of signal reactions. *J. of higher nervous activity of USSR,* 1956b, 7(1), 39–48.

ANOKHIN, P. K. *Internal inhibition as a problem of physiology.* Moscow: Medgiz, 1958.

ANOKHIN, P. K. A methodological analysis of key problems of the conditioned reflex. In P. K. Anokhin, et al. (Eds.), *Philosophical problems of the physiology of higher nervous activity and of psychology.* Moscow: Akad. Nauk USSR, 1963. Pp. 156–214.

ANOKHIN, P. K. *Biology and neurophysiology of conditioned reflex.* In press.

ANOKHINA, I. P. Physiological peculiarities of adrenergic substratum of the reticular formation. *J. Physiol. USSR,* 1961. 47(2), 154–159.

BALAKIN, S. Experimental dissociation of the integral response of animals to conditioned stimuli. In P. K. Anokhin, *The problem of the center and periphery in the physiology of nervous activity.* Gorky: State Publishing House. 1935. Pp. 379–413.

BERITASCHVILI, I. S. *Basic forms of nervous and psychonervous activity.* Moscow-Leningrad: U.S.S.R. Academy of Sciences, 1947.

DIAMOND, S., BALWIN, R., & DIAMOND, F. *Inhibition and choice.* New York: Harper & Row. 1963.

LINDSLEY, D. B. Emotion. In S. S. Stevens (Ed.), *Handbook of experimental psychology*. New York: Wiley, 1951.

LURIA, A. R. *The highest function of the cortex of man*. Moscow: Moscow University, 1962.

MAGOUN, H .W. *Waking brain*. Springfield, Ill.: Charles C. Thomas, 1963.

MILLER, R. E., MURPHY, J. V., & MIRSKY, J. A. Relevance of facial expression and posture as cues in communication of affect between monkeys. *Arch. gen. Psychiat.*, 1959, *I*, 480–488.

PAVLOV, I. P. *Conditioned reflexes*. London: Oxford University Press, 1927.

PAVLOV, I. P. Speech at the banquet on the occasion of the appearance of *Twenty years of experience* (duplicated by P. S. Kupalov), 1926. Museum of Pavlov, Inst. of Exper. Med., Leningrad, 1926.

PAVLOV, I. P. *Lectures on conditioned reflexes*. New York: Liveright, 1928.

PAVLOV, I. P. *Pavlovian Wednesdays*. Moscow-Leningrad: Akad. of Sci. of the USSR, 1949a.

PAVLOV, I. P. *Complete collected works*. Vols. 2, 3. Moscow-Leningrad: Akad. Nauk, 1946, 1949b.

SECHENOV, I. M. *Reflexes of the brain*. Petersburg: Medizinsky Vestnik, 1963. Pp. 17–48.

TEPLOV, B. M. *Typological peculiarities of higher nervous activity of man*. Moscow: Acad. Ped. Nauk Publ., 1959.

VINOGRADOVA, O. S. *Investigation of orientive reflex in children by method of pletismography*. Moscow: Adac. Ped. Nauk Publ., 1959.

PART TWO

FREE ASSOCIATION AND PSYCHOANALYSIS

INTRODUCTORY NOTE

At the crossroads of centuries a good deal of research went in the direction of human emotions and motivation. William James was the man who broke the ground for a variety of psychological schools.

Part Two of the present volume deals with free association and psychoanalysis. Chapter 8 discusses William James and the Stream of Thought from the standpoint of the evolution of the free-association method. The anticipations of Freud's use of free association serve to highlight James in both his similarities to and differences from Freud.

Freud's contemporary, Pierre Janet, and his contribution to the theory of the unconscious and his clinical works were discussed in Chapter 9. The tenth chapter, entitled Beyond Vitalism and Mechanism, analyzes Freud's Concept of Psychic Energy against the background of the history of modern science. It starts with a historical review of the vitalism-mechanism controversy.

CHAPTER 8

WILLIAM JAMES AND THE STREAM OF THOUGHT[1]

Saul Rosenzweig

THE SIMILARITY of the free-association method in psychology, on the one hand, and the stream-of-consciousness technique in literature, on the other, is evident at a glance; and students of the literary mode (e.g., Friedman, 1955) have not failed to note the influence of both William James and Sigmund Freud on such writers as James Joyce. Still largely unexplored, however, is the interrelationship of the stream of thought (James) and of free association (Freud) in the evolution of psychology itself. In this direction lies the goal of the present excursion.

Fountainhead

One is confronted at the outset by all the Jameses—not William alone—as contributing to this current of nineteenth-century thought. For any account of William in this context must embrace his equally famous brother Henry, a leading exponent of stream-of-consciousness literature, and the father of them both, Henry James, Sr., who pioneered the course. The work and influence of the sire has been described elsewhere (Grattan, 1932; Warren, 1934; Rosenzweig, 1943; Young, 1951; Anderson, 1957); here note will be taken primarily of his passing and his legacy. Henry James, Sr. died in December 1882 and his *Literary Remains*, edited with a "Memoir" by his son William, appeared soon afterward (H. James, Sr., 1885). Among the *Remains* is an Autobiography starting with the following passage:

I will not attempt to state the year in which I was born, because it is not a fact embraced in my own knowledge, but content myself with saying instead, that the earliest event of my biographic consciousness is that of my having been carried out into the streets one night, in the arms of my negro nurse, to witness a grand illumination in honor of the treaty of peace then just signed with Great Britain. From this circumstance I infer of course that I was born before

1 "William James and the Stream of Thought" copyright © 1968 by Saul Rosenzweig, St. Louis, Missouri. Aspects of this essay are derived, with permission, from a collective review published in *Contemporary Psychology*, September, 1958. The present essay is printed here for the first time.

the year 1815, but it gives me no warrant to say just how long before. The net fact is that my historic consciousness, or my earliest self-recognition, dates from this municipal illumination in honor of peace. So far, however, as my share in that spectacle is concerned, I am free to say it was a failure. That is, the only impression left by the illumination upon my imagination was the contrast of the awful dark of the sky with the feeble glitter of the streets; as if the animus of the display had been not to eclipse the darkness, but to make it visible. You, of course, may put what interpretation you choose upon the incident, but it seems to me rather emblematic of the intellect, that its earliest sensible foundations should thus be laid in 'a horror of great darkness.' (H. James, Sr., 1885, pp. 145–146)

The Jamesian phenomenological approach was thus ushered in at the opening of the nineteenth century. The manner and the imagery afford a striking demonstration of the heritage of the two sons who together did more than all others combined to give the stream of consciousness a habitation and a name.

Effluence

It is further noteworthy that the above-mentioned book, edited by William James, appeared almost simultaneously with an article of his own, "On Some Omissions of Introspective Psychology." Under this title, in the January 1884 issue of *Mind*, WJ (1884a) set forth for the first time his views about "the stream of consciousness" or "the stream of thought." It is clear that he was deeply involved in the preparation of his father's manuscripts for posthumous publication when he crystallized one of his own most influential concepts; and it may be inferred with some degree of confidence that his father's thought had some generative impact upon his own in this formulation.

But it was evidently not *thought* alone which came down to him at this time of his father's death; for in the April 1884 issue of *Mind* William James (1884b) published his now famous theory of emotion—three months after the paper on the stream of thought. This temporal conjunction highlights the phenomenological nature of James's doctrine of emotion. This paradoxical view defines emotion as what would today be called a sensory feedback from the somatic state of affairs which certain releasers (again in modern parlance) instinctively and unconsciously induce in the organism.

Common sense says, we lose our fortune, are sorry and weep; we meet a bear, are frightened and run; we are insulted by a rival, are angry and strike. The hypothesis here to be defended says that this order of sequence is incorrect, that the one mental state is not immediately induced by the other, that the bodily manifestations must first be interposed between, and that the more rational statement is that we feel sorry because we cry, angry because we strike, afraid because we tremble, and not that we cry, strike, or tremble, because we are sorry, angry, or fearful as the case may be. Without the bodily states following on the perception, the latter would be purely cognitive in form, pale, colourless, destitute of emotional warmth. (W. James, 1884b, p. 190)

That the proximity of the father's death contributed to this hypothesis when the event flooded the son's own stream of consciousness with poignant emotion is a natural surmise. The inference becomes more than plausible when a second biographical fact is coupled with the first: in 1881, ten months before he lost his father, William James was bereaved of his mother. That the father survived his wife for so short a time is not without significance as a token of his own deep bereavement—a surmise substantiated by the extant evidence. But the son was left to bear the brunt of both losses. If one rereads "What is an Emotion?" with this context in mind, the inference of a determinative relationship is inevitable.

The purpose of the following pages [James writes] is to show that . . . the emotional brain-processes not only resemble the ordinary sensorial brain-processes, but in very truth *are* nothing but such processes variously combined. . . . But although this seems to be the chief result of the arguments I am to urge, I should say that they were not originally framed for the sake of any such result. They grew out of fragmentary introspective observations, and it was only when these had already combined into a theory that the thought of the simplification the theory might bring to cerebral physiology occurred to me, and made it seem more important than before. (*ibid.*, pp. 188–189)

Similarly noteworthy is the pragmatic or therapeutic application which the author underscores. "Whistling to keep up courage is no mere figure of speech. On the other hand, sit still all day in a moping posture, sigh, and reply to everything with a dismal voice, and your melancholy lingers. There is no more valuable precept in moral education than this, as all who have experience know: if we wish to conquer undesirable emotional tendencies in ourselves, we must assiduously, and in the first instance coldbloodedly, go through the *outward motions* of those contrary dispositions we prefer to cultivate. The reward of persistency will infallibly come, in the fading out of the sullenness or depression, and the advent of real cheerfulness and kindliness in their stead" (p. 198). The writing of the article may thus have been in part an effort in self-discipline at this critical moment of his life—an exercise of the "will to believe." In this light one notes with fresh understanding its closing sentence: "The best thing I can say for it is, that in writing it, I have almost persuaded *myself* it may be true" (p. 205).[2]

If, persevering, one turns to the definitive statement of the theory six years later, in the chapter on Emotion in the *Principles* (1890), one finds WJ (at this safer distance from the precipitating personal events) *opening* his argument with an exposition of grief. At the top of his second page is found: ". . . we melt more over a mother who is dead than we ever did when she was living" (II, p. 113). Then, having discovered since 1884 the almost simultaneously published similar views of Lange, James proceeds at once to quote from that author a two-page description of *grief*, introducing thus the *James-Lange* theory.

It may be concluded that the theory of emotion and the formulation of the stream of consciousness, the two best known of WJ's psychological doctrines, not only appeared in the same year, but were in part a heritage from the

---

[2] One source of the currently popular "behavior therapies" is present here in the 1884 paper on emotion and, for that matter, in the entire functional-behavioral psychology of which it was an early expression. James's divergence from Freudian psychodynamics, to be commented upon later, is anticipated at this point.

father's thought and were, moreover, fathered by the son's introspective ruminations over the death of both his parents.

Like father, like brother. When Henry James the novelist lost his older brother William in 1910, he resolved soon thereafter to memorialize him and in 1913 published *A Small Boy and Others*. Written in the typical stream-of-consciousness manner of the later HJ, its opening paragraph affords a vivid parallel (however much intensified) to the above-quoted passage from HJ, Sr., edited by WJ. Since few psychologists will have indulged themselves in the luxurious subjectivity of this book, its opening words, at least, should have for them both an intrinsic, and in the present context, a historic interest.

In the attempt to place together some patriculars of the early life of William James and present him in his setting, his immediate native and domestic air, so that any future gathered memorials of him might become the more intelligible and interesting, I found one of the consequences of my interrogation of the past assert itself a good deal at the expense of some of the others. For it was to memory in the first place that my main appeal for particulars had to be made; I had been too near a witness of my brother's beginnings of life, and too close a participant, by affection, admiration and sympathy, in whatever touched and moved him, not to feel myself in possession even of a greater quantity of significant truth, a larger handful of the fine substance of history, than I could hope to express or apply. To recover anything like the full treasure of scattered, wasted circumstance was at the same time to live over the spent experience itself, so deep and rich and rare, with whatever sadder and sorer intensities, even with whatever poorer and thinner passages, after the manner of every one's experience; and the effect of this in turn was to find discrimination among the parts of my subject again and again difficult—so inseparably and beautifully they seemed to hang together and the comprehensive case to decline mutilation or refuse to be treated otherwise than handsomely. This meant that aspects began to multiply and images to swarm, so far at least as they showed, to appreciation, as true terms and happy values; and that I might positively and exceedingly rejoice in my relation to most of them, using it for all that, as the phrase is, it should be worth. To knock at the door of the past was in a word to see it open to me quite wide—to see the world within begin to "compose" with a grace of its own round the primary figure, see it people itself vividly and insistently. Such then is the circle of my commemoration and so much these free and copious notes a labour of love and loyalty. We were, to my sense, the blest group of us, such a company of characters and such a picture of differences, and withal so fused and united and interlocked, that each of us, to that fond fancy, pleads for preservation, and that in respect to what I speak of myself as possessing I think I shall be ashamed, as of a cold impiety, to find any element altogether negligible. To which I may add perhaps that I struggle under the drawback, innate and inbred, of seeing the whole content of memory and affection in each enacted and recovered moment, as who should say, in the vivid image and the very scene; the light of the only terms in which life has treated me to experience. And I cherish the moment and evoke the image and repaint the scene; though meanwhile indeed scarce able to convey how prevailingly and almost exclusively, during years and years, the field was animated and the adventure conditioned for me by my brother's nearness and that play of genius in him of which I had never had a doubt from the first. (H. James, 1913, pp. 1–3)

That both brothers derived this mode of experience in large measure from their uncommon father is self-evident; that they exerted a mutual influence on each other is equally clear. Comparison of the brothers has therefore often been made. Of all such attempts the most notorious states that Henry was a novelist who wrote like a psychologist while William was a psychologist who wrote like a novelist. With the contemporary broader concept of psychology in its various origins and applications, and with fuller knowledge of both Henry and William than was previously available, it would be less sententious but more sensible to say that Henry was a psychologist who expressed himself professionally as an artist while William was by choice a philosopher who worked for a time professionally as a psychologist.

The later style of the novelist is, however, full of interest for both the artist and the psychologist. For Henry James, however molded, was a master born to his obsessional art method. Though it is beyond the scope of this discussion to enter into an analysis of this method as related to his personality, an appreciative understanding of the technique is germane here. The reader is accordingly invited to scan the two following early characterizations of HJ's style.

The first is from the pen of the psychiatrist-novelist S. Weir Mitchell, found in a letter to Dr. J. William White in 1905. It runs: "I have read his [HJ's] last book with bewildered amazement. Since I played cat's cradle as a child, I have seen no tangle like it. To get the threads of his thought off his mind onto mine with the intermediation of his too exasperating style has been too much for me. A friend of mine says his 'Wings of a Dove' are unlike any dove she ever saw for it has neither head nor tail. However, I am too old to learn a new language and still struggle to write my own with clearness" (Burr, 1930, p. 322).

The second characterization likewise involves Weir Mitchell. He is now at the receiving end of a letter, again dated 1905, from his kinsman and brother-novelist Owen Wister. The layman is administering a healing balm to the distinguished psychiatrist:

Henry James is in essence inscrutable; but one thing of him I know: our language has no artist more serious or austere at this moment. I explain to myself his bewildering style thus: he is attempting the impossible with it—a certain very particular form of the impossible, namely, to produce upon the reader, as a painting produces upon the gazer, a number of superimposed, simultaneous impressions. He would like to put several sentences on top of each other so that you could read them all at once, and get all at once the various shadings and complexities, instead of getting them consecutively as the mechanical nature of his medium compels. This I am sure is the secret of his involved parenthesis, his strangely injected adverbs, the whole structure, in short, of his twisted syntax. One grows used to it by persisting. I read "The Ambassadors" twice, and like it amazingly as a prodigy of skill. One other thing of signal importance is a key to his later books. He does not undertake to tell a story but to deal with a situation, a single situation. Beginning (in his scheme) at the center of this situation, he works outward, intricately and exhaustively, spinning his web around every part of the situation, every little necessary part no matter how slight, until he gradually presents to you the organic whole, worked out. You don't get the organic whole until he wishes you to and that is at the very end. But he never lets the situation go, never digresses for a single instant; and no matter how slow or long his pages may seem as you first read them, when you have at the end grasped the total thing, if you then look back you find that the voluminous

texture is woven closely and that every touch bears upon the main issue. . . .
if you want a concrete demonstration of the method and the perfected art that
I have been speaking of, then by all means read "The Turn of the Screw" some
evening in your study, alone. (Burr, 1930, pp. 322–324)

A better description of the stream-of-consciousness technique is not likely
to be found or written. Its impact on the creative art of James Thurber, a
lifelong admirer of HJ, is a testimonial to its excellence; and after the reader
has taken the above advice (if any longer needed at this late date) anent
"The Turn of the Screw," he may wish to peruse "The Wings of Henry
James" (Thurber, 1961).

Confluence

It was in France, chiefly Paris, that Henry James found the companionship
that nurtured his talent and helped evoke his final and characteristic mode of
thought and expression (cf. Pacey, 1941–1942). And it was also there that
literary stream-of-consciousness eventually had its most complete development—in Gertrude Stein, James Joyce, and Marcel Proust. Gertrude Stein
was in her early days a student of William James at Harvard and her first
publications were based on experiments in "automatic writing" (cf. Solomons
and Stein, 1896; Stein, 1898; Reid, 1958). Joyce was manifestly influenced by
Freud and Jung, while Proust gave artistic concreteness to Henri Bergson's
concern with "durée réele" the unbroken flow of time—a concept that has
much in common with WJ's stream-of-thought (cf. Capek, 1950). But in the
1880s when James was active in psychopathology, this interest brought him to
France—just as HJ's literary dedication took him to that country. Hence the
news of their father's last illness reached WJ in Paris where, as Perry (1935,
II, p. 5) mentions, William was at the time listening to Charcot's lectures.
The year was 1882—three years before Freud was entranced by the same
Parisian master.

This common tuition makes it less surprising that James was the first
psychologist in America to call attention in print to the work of Breuer and
Freud. In a contribution which appeared in the 1894 volume of the *Psychological Review* he referred to the first pronouncement by these authors—the
Preliminary Communication (1893) on the mechanism of hysteria. As be-
speaking the broad apperceptive mass with which he read that paper on its
appearance is the circumstance that WJ's abstract of Breuer and Freud forms
part of a collective review on the general topic of hysteria. Of the other two
contributions one was by Pierre Janet—the book, *The Mental State of Hystericals* (1892, 1894)—and the other, L. E. Whipple's *Philosophy of Mental
Healing*, a pioneering recognition, despite its religious context, of what today
is known as psychosomatic medicine. As James interweaves the three works,
no doubt remains but that his preference is for Janet whose book is the first
one he considers; but his inclusion of the religious "mind-curers" [*sic*],
which antedated Janet, and of the psychoanalytic school, just burgeoning,
make this triptych a unique historical exhibit. In relation to the reviewer himself it epitomizes both his early exposure to his father's therapeutic Sweden-
borgianism and his own incipient awareness of psychoanalysis. The latter

interest culminated in the walk that WJ took with Sigmund Freud in 1909, the year in which Freud made his one visit to America. Commenting on that visit in one of his letters, James noted the intellectual tenacity of his companion—"a man obsessed with fixed ideas" (W. James, 1926, II, p. 328)—but he insisted, characteristically, that no impediment be placed in the way of Freud's working out his ideas. Freud (1959, 1925, p. 52) in a reciprocal comment recalled James's remarkable courage in the face of an attack of angina pectoris suffered during that walk: the victim asked his companion to walk ahead and leave him to his recovery. James did recover and continued the walk, but the following year he was dead.

Had Freud met James previously—on the printed page? Was the method of free association, described and developed in or about 1899 by Freud, indebted in any measure to the Jamesian formulation of the stream of consciousness or, for that matter, to the very dynamic treatment of association in the *Principles?* There, as in psychoanalysis, the keynote is that not abstract ideas but only things thought of (objects) are associated in thought. But a much stronger and more specific indication favoring an affirmative reply to the question emerges from a critical examination of what is Freud's earliest explicit description of his treatment method—his technique of the free-association interview. This statement occurs in the introduction to his first detailed psychoanalytic case history, "Fragment of an Analysis of a Case of Hysteria," published in 1905 but actually written, as the author has made clear, in the early days of 1901 (Freud, 1953, 1905). Describing how he begins the treatment, Freud says that he asks the patient to give the whole story of his life and illness. He then continues: "This first account may be compared to an unnavigable river whose stream is at one moment choked by masses of rock and at another divided and lost among shallows and sandbanks" (p. 16). He wonders how it is that most authorities can provide such smooth case histories of hysteria when, in fact, the patients are never able to provide such reports. Characteristically these patients give coherent information for certain periods of their lives "to be followed by another period . . . as to which their communications run dry, leaving gaps unfilled, and riddles unanswered. . . . The connections . . . are for the most part incoherent, and the sequence of different events is uncertain" (p. 16). Attempting to account for these gaps, Freud points out that patients intentionally hold back parts of what they ought to tell, i.e., they are consciously disingenuous; but that, in addition, some of these gaps are created during the oral anamnesis without any deliberate act of suppression: "the share taken by *unconscious* disingenuousness. In the third place, there are invariably true amnesias—gaps in the memory into which not only old recollections but even quite recent ones have fallen—and paramnesias, formed secondarily so as to fill in those gaps" (p. 17). In this light he described one of the aims of therapy: "In the further course of the treatment the patient supplies the facts which, though he had known them all along, had been kept back by him or had not occurred to his mind. The paramnesias prove untenable, and the gaps in his memory are filled in. It is only towards the end of the treatment that we have before us an intelligible, consistent, and unbroken case history. Whereas the practical aim of the treatment is to remove all possible symptoms and to replace them by conscious thoughts, we may regard it as a second and theoretical aim to repair all the damages to the patient's memory. These two aims are coincident. When one is reached, so is the other; and the same path leads to them both" (p. 18).

If now one turns to the famous Chapter IX of James's *Principles* (which superseded the 1884 article in *Mind* already mentioned), one reads: "Consciousness . . . flows. A 'river' or a 'stream' are the metaphors by which it is most naturally described. *In talking of it hereafter, let us call it the stream of thought, of consciousness, or of subjective life.* . . . But now there appears. . . between [the] thoughts . . . a kind of jointing and separateness among the parts, of which this statement seems to take no account. I refer to the breaks that are produced by sudden *contrasts in the quality* of the successive segments of the stream of thought" (1890, I, p. 239). Twelve pages later, still dealing with the same topic, he undertakes to analyze what happens when "we try to recall a forgotten name. The state of our consciousness is peculiar. There is a gap therein; but no mere gap. It is a gap that is intensely active. A sort of wraith of the name is in it, beckoning us in a given direction, making us at moments tingle with the sense of our closeness, and then letting us sink back without the longed-for term. If wrong names are proposed to us, this singularly definite gap acts immediately so as to negate them. They do not fit into its mould. And the gap of one word does not feel like the gap of another, all empty of content as both might seem necessarily to be when described as gaps" (p. 251).

Later in the chapter WJ briefly considers "mistakes of speech or writing." He gives what is essentially a physiological explanation, adding: "In the chapter on Association of Ideas, numerous instances will come before us of the actual effect on consciousness of neuroses not yet maximally aroused" (p. 258). (This now quaint use of the term "neuroses" to mean *state of the neurones* is noteworthy. Could it have constituted a "verbal bridge" for Freud?) Developing the argument, he speaks of overtones in music that blend with the fundamental note—just as "the waxing and waning brain-processes at every moment blend with and suffuse and alter the psychic effect of the processes which are at their culminating point" (p. 258). And now James proposes that the term "psychic overtone" be employed to designate the influence of a faint brain-process upon thought and, in a footnote, he cites none other than the Viennese experimental pathologist Salomon Stricker—one of Sigmund Freud's medical school teachers! This prolific professor was chief of the laboratory in which Freud did his ill-fated investigations on the effects of cocaine; "cheated by Fate," the future psychoanalyst painfully saw the palm awarded to one of his colleagues, Karl Koller, the discoverer of local anesthesia. The name of Stricker accordingly created uncomfortable gaps in Freud's stream of consciousness; various examples are prominent in his personal free association in the *Interpretation of Dreams.* One quite literal gap obtrudes itself in the Reference List of the first edition of *Traumdeutung* (1900) where the publications of this mentor (Stricker, 1879, 1883) are found tacked on, out of alphabetical order, at the end. But James, having no such conflicts, was impressed with and cited several of the Professor's investigations on "inner speech"—an equivalent of Freud's construct of the unconscious—in the heart of his chapter on the stream of thought. Later in his book WJ (II, pp. 62–65) described at greater length Stricker's work, largely self-analytic, on the thought processes as these are experienced in somatic-motor terms involving lips, tongue, throat, larynx, etc., but which escape the awareness of most individuals (Stricker, 1880, 1886). James in like manner tried to explain errors of speech and writing by reference to the (usually) nonconscious psychophysical or physiological undercurrents that mechanically interrupt the flow of conscious thought—an obvious contrast to Freud's dynamic constructions. Recognizing this difference, one may say that while James was fully cognizant of the dynamics of consciousness, it was left for Freud to add the dynamic unconscious.

For the present purposes the culmination of WJ's view comes in these words: "In all our voluntary thinking there is some topic or subject about which all the members of the thought revolve. Half the time this topic is a problem, a gap we cannot yet fill with a definite picture, word, or phrase, but which, in the manner described some time back, influences us in an intensely active and determinate psychic way. Whatever may be the images and phrases that pass before us, we feel their relation to this aching gap. To fill it up is our thoughts' destiny. Some bring us nearer to that consummation. Some the gap negates as quite irrelevant. Each swims in a felt fringe of relations of which the aforesaid gap is the term" (W. James, 1890, I, p. 259).

The common metaphor of the river, in Freud and in James, might, of course, pass as coincidence, but the further commonality of the "gaps" in the subjective life begins to rule out this possibility. When, further, one observes, more intrinsically, the dynamic quality of James's discussion both in Chapter IX and in other parts of his widely acclaimed work, published in 1890, the likelihood of some exposure of Freud to James increases. There are, moreover, the facts that Freud during the 1890s was reading voraciously in the psychological literature of Germany, France, England, and America (the Fliess letters amply substantiate this point, mentioning, among other things, James Mark Baldwin's *Mental Development*) and that in 1895 he wrote the Project which attempted, exactly as James did, a bridge between neurophysiology and psychology (Freud, 1954, 1887–1902). A fairly strong case can thus be made for the probability of some direct influence of James on Freud.

It is incidentally further noteworthy that Freud's concept of instinct, cited by Shakow and Rapaport (1964, p. 114 and *passim*) as highly characteristic of him, derived in part from James's *Principles* (1890, esp. Chap. XXIV). Shakow and Rapaport (pp. 38–39) emphasize the likeness of James's functionalism to Freud's psychoanalytic theory. They omit, however, to bring out the close similarity of the two concepts of instinct. Both concepts are rooted in evolutionary theory and construe these drives as originating in the biological organism but as being triggered into action by objects specific to them through an innate coordination. This marked resemblance was indicated indirectly when, on the one hand, attention was called (cf. Gray, 1958) to WJ's anticipation of ethology while, on the other, the findings of recent ethology were interpreted as supporting Freud's theory of instinct (Fletcher, 1957). Shakow and Rapaport are of the opinion that, as concerns the anticipations of psychoanalysis by WJ, ". . . Freud did not know about them either before or after he developed his theories" (p. 39); a different position has, of course, been taken in the present discussion.

No claim is, however, made for any far-reaching or consistent influence. For one thing, Freud's (unavowed) indebtedness to Galton (1883) in the matter of free association is now well recognized (Zilboorg, 1952). For another, there is a great deal in the general approach of James that, despite its over-all voluntarism, runs counter to the Freudian position, e.g., WJ's recommendation that to overcome undesirable emotions one should "repress" [*sic*] them by cultivating the physical expression of contrary ones! It is also evident that whereas James was thinking of gaps in recall that interrupt the naturally continuous flow of the *conscious* stream of thought, Freud, recognizing these same gaps, attempted to explain them by invoking *unconscious* dynamic factors. In this sense Freud was concerned not only with the conscious stream itself but with the unconscious bed of the stream on which obstructing psychological debris might lie to produce the gaps in consciousness. If Freud had indeed read James, he had, at any rate, added to his predecessor in a peculiarly Freudian fashion.

Caput Nili

That any debt he owed to James was not acknowledged by Freud will come as no surprise to those familiar with Freud's repeatedly avowed lack of interest in issues of priority. There is also a cognate precedent for such omission which can be cited. In 1917 Havelock Ellis published a paper (Ellis, 1917 *a* and *b*) in which he called attention to a predecessor of Freud in the matter of free association. A Dr. J. J. Garth Wilkinson in 1857 published a sheaf of verse, entitled *Improvisations from the Spirit*, all of which had been composed by a new "Method of Impression"—a method applicable to drawing, speaking, or writing. The author described it in detail in a Note at the end of his little book.

A theme is chosen, and written down. So soon as this is done, the first impression upon the mind which suceeds the act of writing the title, is the beginning of the evolution of that theme; no matter how strange or alien the word or phrase may seem. That impression is written down: and then another, and another, until the piece is concluded. An Act of Faith is signalized in accepting the first mental movement, the first word that comes, as the response to the mind's desire for the unfolding of the subject.
However odd the introduction may be, I have always found it lead by an infallible instinct into the subject. (Wilkinson, 1857, pp. 397–398)

The new book is therefore given to the reader exactly as written by this method, "without the correction of one word from beginning to end." Wilkinson then uses this production as a testimony of *faith* in (not psychic *determinism* but) spiritual guidance by a divine Providence. Still, Ellis quite rightly pointed out that the method was, in essence, that of free association and that free association was closely allied to the creative manner of the artist.
Ellis's essay was reprinted two years later in collective book form (1919) and was then answered by Freud (1950, 1920).[3] For some undisclosed reason this

---

[3] Ellis had actually first pointed out the Wilkinson anticipation six years earlier (Ellis, 1911) but the context was then a neutral or pro-Freudian one. This first account was in German, was in a psychoanalytic journal, and—most important—was much less qualified in its acceptance of Freud's point of view. But in 1917 Ellis offered the same fragment

reply was published anonymously; it was written as if from the pen of one of Freud's admirers who referred to him as the "Professor." In the course of what thus became a very private interview, Freud disclaimed all relationship to the mentioned British physician-poet. But then, as if to make some concession, the anonymous writer explained how the attention of Professor Freud had recently been called to another anticipation. Ludwig Börne, the satirist, in 1823 published an essay entitled "The Art of Becoming an Original Writer in Three Days" (Börne, 1862) in which he offered a recipe that strikingly resembled Wilkinson's Method of Impression or Improvisation. And to *this* reminder Freud's answer was more assenting. In his early youth he had, in fact, been presented with the whole set of Börne's works—he still owned it—and he had presumably read the essay in question. But Freud pleaded "cryptamnesia": he had never recalled that skit until the reminder came from the outside source.[4]

It will by now be evident that Börne, Galton, Stricker, Wilkinson, and the Jameses contributed to "free association," and that, like everything else creative, this discovery is firmly imbedded in the cultural stream of thought. Wilkinson has, however, a further interest in the present context. Though Ellis indicates no awareness of the point (he is concerned in his essay only with Freud's psychoanalysis), his observations would have been even more apposite had he cited the author of *Improvisations from the Spirit* not as an anticipator of "free association" but of the "stream of consciousness."

For, as some acquaintance with the early James menage reveals, Dr. J. J. Garth Wilkinson, who published the book of impromptu verse over a century ago, was an intimate friend of Henry James, Sr., and, even before him, a Swedenborgian. The learned British physician owed something of his impressionistic method to his interest in William Blake, but Henry, Sr. owed Wilkinson much more during the troubled forties when he was recovering via the theology of Swedenborg from a disrupting "vastation." That the elder James knew the *Improvisations* is an inevitable conclusion since during the decade of its appearance he was on the closest of terms with the author by personal visit and by continuous correspondence. To testify to this intimacy, and to the inference made from it, is the fact that Henry, Sr. named his third son, born in 1845, Garth Wilkinson ("Wilky")—and the friend returned the compliment by naming a daughter *Mary* for James's wife. Perry (1935) has published correspondence between the two men dating from 1848 to 1879.

---

of history as incidental support for the thesis that Freud was essentially an artist, not a scientist; Wilkinson's method—and the method of Freud—was an artistic, not a scientific, one. Freud's 1920 reply began with a repudiation of this "charge," which Freud interpreted as a new and very subtle form of "resistance" to psychoanalysis. The shift in attitude toward psychoanalysis in the six intervening years was, of course, clear to Freud, and he was right in sensing it. The "countercharge" was, however, more in the nature of a recrimination than an analysis. The details which would constitute such an analysis, explaining why Ellis advanced his thesis when he did and why Freud replied anonymously, etc., reveal much about both men in their respective contributions to the history of medical psychology; but such a departure would involve exploring a new tributary of the stream of thought and so must be postponed.

[4] Ellis may also have been guilty of "crytamnesia": the title of one of his chief books (Ellis, 1923) *The Dance of Life,* which was published shortly after the paper on Freud (Ellis, 1917, 1919), appears to derive from the identical title and theme of a three-page poem in Wilkinson's 1857 volume!

At this point one is, of course, reminded of the first paragraph of the *Auto-biography* of Henry, Sr. previously quoted, but whereas then it was cited in order to indicate its progenitive relationship to William's concept of the stream of thought, it now returns as itself possibly influenced by Garth Wilkinson's Method of Impression or Improvisation (and all that went into *its* provenance).[5] That the mehtod was well known in the James family is shown by the use which Henry, Jr. made of it in writing *The Bostonians* (1886)—only a year or so after WJ may have used it for his purposes in *Mind*. In HJ's novel one encounters Dr. Tarrant, the father of the heroine, a mesmerist healer and lecturer—on the prototype of Dr. Wilkinson—coaching his eloquent Trilby-like daughter Verena. She speaks publicly by "Improvisation" [*sic*], as the spirit moves her, in accordance with her training by the Doctor.

On this evidence Wilkinson would become the predecessor of Henry James, Sr. and thus a remote, if not an immediate, predecessor of Freud. Freud himself recognized such detours of association when he pointed out the principle of the Adige—a river which at Verona makes a loop that brings it back almost to the point at which it enters the city. There thus appears a continuous current as follows: from Wilkinson's improvisations to HJ, Sr.'s phenomenology, to WJ and HJ, Jr.'s stream-of-consciousness—which, from WJ, meanders, with other tributaries, into the Freudian river-of-free-association. If Ellis was wrong on the surface, he was right in the undercurrent.

> For into that beginless zone
> What man hath cast the firstling stone?
> And out of that unending stream
> What man hath seined the primal dream?[6]

REFERENCES

ANDERSON, QUENTIN. *The American Henry James.* New Brunswick: Rutgers, 1957.
BÖRNE, LUDWIG. *Gesammelte Schriften.* Vols. 1–2. Hamburg: Hoffmann & Campe, 1862.
BREUER, JOSEF, & FREUD, SIGMUND. The psychic mechanism of hysterical phenomena: preliminary communication. In *Standard edition of the complete psychological works of Sigmund Freud*, Vol. II, London: Hogarth, 1955. Pp. 3–17. (First published in *Neurol. Centralbl.*, 1893, 12, 4–10, 43–47.)
BURR, ANNA R. *Weir Mitchell. His life and letters.* New York: Duffield, 1930.
CAPEK, MILIC. Stream of consciousness and "durée réele." *Philosophy and Phenomenological Research*, 1950, 10, 331–353.
ELLIS, HAVELOCK. Die Lehre der Freud-Schule. *Zentralbl. Psychoanal.*, 1911, 2, 61–66.
ELLIS, HAVELOCK. The psychoanalysts. *Bookman*, 1917a, 46, 49–60.
ELLIS, HAVELOCK. Psycho-analysis in relation to sex. *J. ment. Sci.*, 1917b, 63, 537–555.

[5] There is a considerable likelihood that Wilkinson was reflecting a now forgotten but once very popular novel by the ugly duckling Hans Christian Andersen—*The Improvisatore* (first published 1835; English translation 1845, 1847, and 1857). The relationship of that romance to the history of psychoanalysis is, again, germane but lies beyond the scope of the present mission.

[6] E. G. Boring has attributed this quatrain to the Romanesque poet Rameau de Rose.

ELLIS, HAVELOCK. *The philosophy of conflict*. Boston: Houghton, Mifflin, 1919.

ELLIS, HAVELOCK. *The dance of life*. Boston: Houghton, Mifflin, 1923.

FLETCHER, RONALD. *Instinct in man in the light of recent work in comparative psychology*. New York: International Universities, 1957.

FREUD, SIGMUND. *The interpretation of dreams*. In *Standard edition of the complete psychological works of Sigmund Freud*, Vols. IV–V. London: Hogarth, 1953. (First published: *Traumdeutung*. Vienna: Deuticke, 1900.)

FREUD, SIGMUND. Fragment of an analysis of a case of hysteria. In *Standard edition of the complete psychological works of Sigmund Freud*, Vol. VII. London: Hogarth, 1953. Pp. 7–122. (First published in *Monatschr. Psychiat. u. Neurol.*, 1905, 18, 285–309, 408–467.)

FREUD, SIGMUND. A note on the pre-history of the technique of analysis. *Collected papers*. Vol. V. London: Hogarth, 1950. Pp. 101–104. (First published anonymously over the signature "F" in *Int. Z. Psychoanal.*, 1920, 6, 79–81.)

FREUD, SIGMUND. An autobiographical study. In *Standard edition of the complete psychological works of Sigmund Freud*, Vol. XX. London: Hogarth, 1959. Pp. 7–74. (First published in Grote's *Die Medizin der Gegenwart in Selbstdarstellungen*, 1925, 4, 1–52. [Leipzig: Meiner].)

FREUD, SIGMUND. *The origins of psycho-analysis. Letters to Wilhelm Fliess, drafts and notes: 1887–1902*. New York: Basic Books, 1954.

FRIEDMAN, M. J. *Stream of consciousness. A study in literary method*. New Haven: Yale, 1955.

GALTON, FRANCIS. *Inquiries into human faculty*. London: Macmillan, 1883.

GRATTAN, C. H. *The three Jameses. A family of minds*. New York: Longmans, Green, 1932.

GRAY, PHILIP H. Theory and evidence of imprinting in human infants. *J. Psychol.*, 1958, 46, 155–166.

JAMES, HENRY, Sr. *Literary remains*. Edited with an introduction by William James. Boston: Osgood, 1885.

JAMES, HENRY. *The Bostonians*. New York: Macmillan, 1886.

JAMES, HENRY. *A small boy and others*. New York: Scribner, 1913.

JAMES, WILLIAM. On some omissions of introspective psychology. *Mind*, 1884a, 9, 1–26.

JAMES, WILLIAM. What is an emotion? *Mind*, 1884b, 9, 188–205.

JAMES, WILLIAM. *The principles of psychology*. 2 vols. New York: Holt, 1890.

JAMES, WILLIAM. Review of Janet, Breuer and Freud, and Whipple. *Psychol. Rev.*, 1894, 1, 195–200.

JAMES WILLIAM. *Letters*. Edited by Henry James. 2 vols. in 1. Boston: Little, Brown, 1926.

PACEY, W. C. D. Henry James and his French contemporaries. *Amer. Lit.*, 1941–1942, 13, 240–256.

PERRY, R. B. *The thought and character of William James*. 2 vols. Boston: Little, Brown, 1935.

REID, BENJAMIN L. *Art by subtraction; a dissenting opinion of Gertrude Stein*. Norman, Okla.: University of Oklahoma, 1958.

ROSENZWEIG, SAUL. The ghost of Henry James: a study in thematic apperception. *Character & Personality*, 1943, 12, 79–100.

SHAKOW, DAVID & RAPAPORT, DAVID. *Freud's influence on American psychology*. New York: International Universities, 1964. (*Psychological Issues*, Vol. IV, No. 1, Monogr. 13).

SOLOMONS, LEON M., and STEIN, GERTRUDE. Normal motor automatism. *Psychol. Rev.* 1896, 3, 492–512.

STEIN, GERTRUDE. Cultivated motor automatism. *Psychol. Rev.*, 1898, 5, 295–306.

STRICKER, SALOMON. *Studien über das Bewusstsein*. Vienna: Braumüller, 1879.
STRICKER, SALOMON. *Studien über die Sprachvorstellungen*. Vienna: Braumüller, 1880.
STRICKER, SALOMON. *Studien über die Association der Vorstellungen*. Vienna: Braumüller, 1883.
STRICKER, SALOMON. De la parole et des sons intérieurs. *Revue Phil.*, 1886, 22, 1-29.
THURBER, JAMES. *Lanterns and lances*. New York: Harper, 1961.
WARREN, AUSTIN. *The elder Henry James*. New York: Macmillan, 1934.
WILKINSON, J. J. G. *Improvisations from the spirit*. London: White, 1857.
YOUNG, F. H. *The philosophy of Henry James, Sr.* New York: Bookman, 1951.
ZILBOORG, GREGORY. Some sidelights on free association. *Int., J. Psychoanal.*, 1952, 33, 489–495.

CHAPTER 9

PIERRE JANET:
THE MAN AND THE WORK

Henri Ey

PIERRE JANET [1859–1947] and his work are characteristic of French culture at the end of the nineteenth century.[1] To understand their importance one must relocate them in the medico philosophic context of this period. On the one hand, with the school of La Salpetriére and Nancy, studies of hysteria discovered the *automatic and unconscious infrastructure* of psychic life. On the other, the idea of *evolution* linked psychology and sociology in the history of human development. French university and particularly philosophical *milieux* were saturated with these ideas. One need only recall all the studies on hypnotism (Bernheim), on dynamic psychology (Maine de Biran) and genetics (Ribot).[2] This was also the period when French psychosociology was gathering impetus (Durckheim, Levy-Brühl), and when research on physiological and experimental psychology (G. Dumas, Pieron) was preeminent in the Sorbonne curriculum. Finally, the thinking of the great neurologists or the great Anglo-Saxon philosophers continued to penetrate France coming from Great Britain (H. Jackson) or from the United States (William James). It is at the crossroads of all these streams of thought that the philosophy and psychopathology of Pierre Janet are located, and it is at this intersection of ideas that they are situated as a "comparative psychology."

It should also be noted that as the inheritor of a long French philosophical tradition greatly influenced by English and American ideas and work, Janet— like all Frenchmen of that period—would not think of letting himself be influenced by anything coming from Germany or from the German-speaking countries. Neither Wundt, nor Brentano, nor Dilthey had held his attention. This is particularly true of Freud's work, which he knew only very late and never more than very partially. Janet's systematic and rather suspicious misappreciation of Freud was, moreover, largely mutual on Freud's part. Let us

---

[1] To complete the study presented here, the reader should refer to the special issue that *Evolution Psychiatrrque* devoted to Janet (No. 3–1950); to the series of articles on Janet published by the *Bulletin de Psychologie* (XIV, 184, November 5, 1960), and to the book by Leonard Schwartz *Die Neurosen und die dynamische Psychologie von Pierre Janet*, Schwabe, Basel, 1950, Fr. translation P.U.F.

[2] We use the words "genetics" or "geneticist" here to describe any psychology of *development*.

add, in order to dispel any misunderstanding, that Freud owes no more to Janet than Janet to Freud. Basically, they always disregarded each other.

Pierre Janet

Pierre Janet's father was the brother of a French philosopher of some renown, Paul Janet. His mother was Alsatian. He was born in 1859 in Paris, where he spent his childhood with his brother Jules in the district of Val-de-Grâce. It was here that the whole family was gathered at the time of the siege of the capital during the Franco-Prussian war. After his studies in the Collège Sainte-Barbe in Paris he entered that great breeding ground of the French "intelligentsia,' 'the Ecole Normale Supérieure, in 1879. There he was a schoolfellow of James, Bergson, and Durckheim. As a graduate in philosophy, he first taught at the Lycée de Châteauroux, then for seven years at the Lycée du Havre. He was admitted to the hospital of that city (in the departments of Dr. Gilbert and Dr. Powlewicz), took an interest in cases of hysteria, and it was there that he studied the case of Léonie. This gave him a taste for medicine and particularly for psychiatry. So much so that, appointed to Rollin College in Paris and later to the Lycée Condorcet, he undertook his studies in medicine which he completed in 1893. It was at this period that he frequented Charcot's department. He was included by the Director of Salpetriére in the sumptuous hospitality he offered his students. Janet also frequented Jules Falret at his Vanves sanitarium. He married in 1894 and had three children, two girls and a boy. One of his daughters married a hospital physician, Dr. Edmond Pichon, one of the first and most eminent French psychoanalysts (died in 1940).

From 1895 Janet taught at the Collège de France, a post he held until 1934. I attended his classes long enough to permit me to admire the extraordinary and sober eloquence of this Master who spoke as he wrote. His language was simple and marvellously clear. He had the gift of making a statement both familiar and profound, and those who heard him harbored the same admiration for him that the pupils of Socrates felt for their master, such was his simplicity in the art of irony, of maieutics, and of persuasion.

His life, then, was that of an "academic," of a "professor" who loved to learn through teaching. His life was spent entirely in the bosom of his family, among his doctor and philosopher friends, and in the company of the "old men" of La Salpétrière, of the Collège de France and of the Académie des Sciences morales. He freqeuntly travelled to North America where he gave many lectures, notably at Harvard University (he was very close to his friend Morton Prince). At the instigation of his other close friend, George Dumas, he made trips to Mexico and South America. Pierre Janet, because of his renown, had patients who often came from great distances in order to consult him. He treated them either at his office or in the sanitarium of Paris. Charcot had established a psychology laboratory for him at La Salpétrière, entrusting its direction to him. After Charcot's death in 1893, his successor, Raymond, continued the laboratory, and remained its director. When Raymond died in 1910, the laboratory was transferred, still at La Salpétrière, to Nageotte's department. During the Second World War, Janet took refuge with his family at the home of G. Dumas in the South of France, at

Ledignan. At the end of the war, he returned to Paris, giving several lectures. He was working on a book *Les Formes de la Croyance,* when he died in 1947 in his home in the Faubourg Saint-Germain at the age of 87. Free of any infirmity, he had seen a patient on the previous day and chatted with his friends as though, right to the end, this prodigiously intelligent, simple, and active man had not wanted to change a life entirely devoted to work among his own people, surrounded by his books and his plants.

The Work

HIS PRINCIPAL WORKS

Pierre Janet, after having written an essay on *Malebranche et les esprits animaux* in 1886, presented his doctoral thesis in philosophy at the Sorbonne in 1889. This thesis is the essence of his famous work *L'automatisme psychologique* which contains the seeds of the whole development of his psychopathology. He applied himself during this period at La Salpétrière to the study of neuroses, of hypnotism, and of hysteria. He devoted his medical thesis to the *Etat mental des hystériques* (1893; English translation, *Mental State of Hystericals,* 1907), then in 1898 published a large work in two volumes *Nevroses et Idées Fixes.* Five years later, having devoted himself especially to obsessional neuroses, he set forth his ideas on "neurasthenia" in his book *Les obsessions et la psychasthénie.* In 1908 he published a remarkable little volume in which he focussed the essentials of the studies he had untiringly pursued for 20 years, *Les Névroses.* For several years—during the 1914–1918 war—he prepared another work, *Les Médications psychologiques* (English translation, *Psychological Healing,* 1925), which appeared in 1919. Finally, in 1923, he finished his last great work, *De l'angoisse à l'extase.*

At the end of his academic life, he took great pains with the preparation of the publication of his Collège de France lectures. Thus his lectures formed a series of important books: *L'évolution de la personnalité,* 1929; *La force et la Failblesse psychologique,* 1930; *Les débuts de l'intelligence,* 1935; *L'intelligence avant le langage,* 1936; *L'amour et la Haine,* 1937. Finally, we may note two important articles which he published in the *Revue Philosophique* and the *Journal de Psychologie* in 1932, on hallucinations and persecution deliriums.

We shall discuss very briefly the most important of his works:

In *L'automatisme psychologique* (1889), Janet first studied what occurs in catalepsy (in the patients Léonie, Rose, Lucie, whom he had observed at Le Havre), which involves a state of degradation of thought. This manifests itself, in the early stages, as a form of elementary consciousness, characterized by *isolated* attitudes and movements. Everything occurs as though, by their isolation, the systems of images, feelings and of movements developed with particular intensity. The same holds true for the memory lapses or the amnesia involved in somnambulism. All these phenomena are due to suggestion, and this only possible by the *narrowing of the field of consciousness.* All hysterical symptoms, (paralysis, amnesia, split personality) are the manifestations of psychological automatisms (feelings, movements, behavior patterns), that is, the results of *psychical disaggregation* (loss of the power of psychical synthesis), as a result of which the subconscious elements free themselves. Hysterical sickness is a field which is conducive to the development of automatic and hypnotic phenomena. Essential, Janet says (p. 269), is the existence of *subconscious thought* which the post-hypnotic suggestions reveal to us, for they cannot be understood without it; but it is to the idea of *psychical disaggregation* that Janet attributes the greatest importance, thus demonstrating a fundamental divergence from the thinking elaborated by Freud in Vienna during the same period.

In *Névroses et Idées fixes* (1898), Janet offers numerous observations which illustrate the point of view sustained in his first work. One of the most typical is that of the famous "idée fixe of choléra" of Justine. Here he shows the development of what, after Breuer and Freud, was to be known as a "complex," but which for him is a system of images, of ideas which draw their strength only from the weakness of the field of consciousness. The fixity, the isolation, and the strength of these systems of images are for him characteristics of all neurotic symptoms, and the book is full of picturesque, delicately analyzed cases of somnambulistic deliriums, of possession; a very interesting chapter is devoted to modern exorcism as a therapeutic procedure, and another to a penetrating study of divination by mirrors (subconscious hallucinations). The second volume of this work marks the appearance and the systematization of what will henceforth be the principal object of Janet's studies: the phenomena, symptoms, and crises which constitute the other side of neuroses, the obsessions (impulses, abulias, tics, etc.).

In *Obsessions et la psychathénie* (1903), it is precisely the basis, the context of obsessions which is emphasized. No doubt Janet's conception here does not yet completely separate hysteria from psychasthenia when he describes hysterical obsessions (notably when he enumerates the symptoms of constriction of the field of consciousness), or when he speaks of th emotional agitations which the French authors (Maurel, Legrand du Saule, Pitres and Regis) termed "phobias" and which were to constitute Freud's anxiety hysteria. But the interest of this major work lies; obviously in the unbelievable richness of the clinical analysis of the "obsessional basis," a kind of phenomenology of compulsive thinking, exposed here in the clear style and with the concern for rigorous, detailed descriptions characteristic of this great physician. Whether it be a question of *obsessive ideas* seen from the viewpoint of their content (sacrileges, crimes, shame, hypochondria) or of their form (permanent, ideative character of the obsession), whether it be a question of *forced agitations* (manias, *i.e.*, behavior patterns and ritual amongst which he describes those of fluctuation, interrogation, hesitation, foreboding, precision, symbol, precaution, repetition, perfection, reparation, atonement, pacts, conspiracy, mental rumination), whether it be a question of *tics* (either systematized, as those that have a meaning of perfection or of defense, or diffused, as those that manifest effort or excitation)—all these fundamental symptoms constitute a clinical unity characterized by the conservation of consciousness and by incoercibility. So that it is a fundamental disorder of psychological tension which must now be described and which Janet describes as *psychasthenia*. Whence a meticulous analysis of the neurasthenic "scars" which determine the obsessional personality. There are first of all *sentiments of incompleteness* which the subject experiences as fatigue, uneasiness, automatic parasitism, domination. These are actually impressions rather than feelings, but Janet's analysis tends precisely to combine with the experience of these insufficiencies the complex feelings which animate them (shame, revolt, anxiety). At this point of Janet's masterly description, his clinical analysis attains the depth of affective life, its movement, the very temporality of experience. Under modest or abstract labels such as disorders of "perception," of "memory," of "will," he penetrates into the intimate depths of obsessional disorders, arriving at the idea that psychasthenia is a *disorder of the function of reality*. Whence his well-known table of the hierarchy of symptoms in relation to the hierarchy of the functions of reality (of which we shall speak again later). And it is here that the idea of *reduction of psychological tension* appears in the very process of this clinical work.

The book on *Les Névroses* (1908) constitutes Janet's most concentrated and synthetic work, summarizing the fundamental psychopathological work of the Master of La Salpétrière and of the Collège de France. Here he describes the neuropathic syndromes which have already been the subject of his long and meticulous clinical analyses. First of all the *idées fixes* (in somnambulistic form, in mediumistic form) and the obsessions, the latter not developing completely in psychasthenics as in the case of the obsessive hysteric. He goes on to describe *amnesias* and *doubts, language disorders* (verbal agitation, inhibition and speechlessness), *hysterical choreas* and *neurasthenic tics, paralyses and phobias, disorders of perception and disorders of the instincts and of the muscular functions*. All these descriptions are set forth with a view to making the distinction, in the symptomatology of the neuroses, between fits of hysteria and neuropathic scars, two major types of neuroses: *Hysteria* characterized by the narrowing of consciousness, the dissociation of the psychical functions and the emancipation of the systems of ideas and of the functions which by their system constitute the personality; *Psychasthenia* (or obsessional neurosis) which is a form of mental depression characterized by the reduction of psychological tension, by the diminution of the subject's ability to act on and to perceive reality, by the substitution of inferior and exaggerated operations in the form of doubts, agitations, anxieties, and by obsessional ideas which express these disorders. More generally, the neuroses are then defined as illnesses affecting the various functions of the organism. But these functions are impaired only in their superior part, arrested in their evolution, in their adaptation to the present moment, to the present state of the outside world and of the individual. On the other hand, the neuroses are characterized by the absence of deterioration of the former parts of these same functions. The neuroses are, in short, *disorders of the various functions of the organism characterized by arrested development without deterioration of the function itself*.

Les Médications psychologiques (1919) comprises three volumes. The book starts by an extraordinarily interesting history of the therapeutics which appeal to "moral action." Interesting chapters are devoted to "*Christian Science*," to the "*therapeutic philosophy*" of Dubois (of Berne), and above all to *hypnotism* and to all *methods of suggestion*. As for the author's own therapeutic methods, which constitute the practical corollaries of his conception of the neuroses, they are stated with the help of numerous observations. Janet distinguishes in this respect between "psychological economies" likely to release—as we would say, to "relax"—abnormal or anarchical psychical tensions (treatments by the various modalities of *rest*, of fatigue, of exhausting actions, and of the psychical expenditures they entail; treatments by social isolation; treatments by moral liquidation).

As far as this psychotherapeutic modality is concerned, Janet explains and criticizes the theory of psychoanalytical therapy (II, pp. 204–268). For him, the effectivness of the liquidation of traumatic memories consists in the restructuring of dispersed memories, in combating the dissociation of memory by its synthesis. It is therefore a question of pursuing analysis to a point of assimilation and reconstruction. Here Pierre Janet joins Freud with regard to the importance of achieving consciousness of subconscious memories, and with regard to the healing role of catharsis (pp. 292–303). This is highly suggestive, for we may wonder whether, if their "techniques" are related, their doctrinal differences do not lose their importance. In the third part of the work the "psychological acquisitions" are set forth as methods of treatment (methods of rehabilitation; recourse to stimulation through various euphoric or tonic drugs capable of producing it; and finally "moral direction"). On these points Janet anticipates both the psychopharmacological discoveries and the "directive" methods. We may add that in his book (mentioned above), L. Schwartz discusses and completes Janet's psychotherapeutic techniques.

De l'angoisse à l'extase (1923) is a book in which Janet's clinical genius pursues its researches and discoveries in the realm of the "feelings" which underlie action. The general thesis, on the whole a very "pragmatic" one, is that feelings (love, hate, suspicion, joy, sadness) are regulators of action, and that the abnormal or pathological affective states manifest a disorganization of these regulations. The work abounds in profound observations, subtle analyses, and original insights on all the nuances of the affective spectrum. The first volume starts with an extraordinarily detailed and profound observation of the case of Madeleine (which Janet followed from 1896 until her death in 1918). This was a case of "religious delirium" interspersed with ecstatic periods, states of euphoria and anxiety (a neurosis apparently related to a psychosis of the manic-depressive type, as the evolution schema seems to indicate, p. 199). So much so that the periods of consolation and of ecstasy, the *feelings of joy* and their relation in the system of *beliefs* with periods of abatement or equilibrium, give rise to innumerable commentaries on the primitive neuropathic state, its fluctuations and the constitution of religious delirium. In this first part of the work, devoted to mystical and esthetical joy, Janet offers further observations, particularly on Martial (p. 132–136), who is no other, under this pseudonym, than Raymond Roussell, the poet whose extraordinary *oeuvre* of fantastic invention is at present the subject of a sort of cult in certain French literary circles. The second volume (there are two thick volumes, the first of 526 pages, the second of 694 pages) is full of accounts of depressive states: feelings of emptiness, feelings of pressure, states of morose inaction, states of fatigue and melancholy. And, once again, these sad or depressive experiences and emotions alternate at the end of the work with the states of elation and beatitude to complete this imposing fresco of human misery and happiness, of the feelings in which the power of action is traced or obliterated. This psychopathology of affective life, the lack of balance of the feelings, can be clarified for the author only by a theory of the *evolution of the feelings.* Pathological feelings, in effect, cannot be confused with anxiety, hope, feelings of normal life, for the manifest a regression of behavior and of action. Perhaps no psychiatrist has more profoundly analyzed the very idea of lack of balance in affective life, that is, the vertigo which is sometimes that of the dance, of happiness, and sometimes that of collapse and of anxiety.

L'évolution de la mémoire et de la notion de temps (1928) has been profoundly studied in this series of lectures at the Collège de France. It is a book entirely characteristic of Janet's teaching, of his simple and "Socratic" manner of grasping the most profound psychological and moral problems. In it he considers duration as it is experienced in feelings which underlie the beginning and the end of action, and he analyzes in particular the phenomena of expectation *(attente)*, and the behavior patterns of "presence" and "absence" connected to them. Elementary memory coincides with the capacity to tell a story, and Janet examines the methods of narration, plotting, projection of an occurrence in the past, the interference of the present and the past *(déjà vu* and *jamais vu)* in amnesias. But what matters for him is the degree of reality of the stories, their *position in the hierarchy of reality.* Three curious chapters are devoted to the *epoch of the philosophers,* the *epoch of the scholars,* and the *epoch of the historians.* One can only admire Janet's profound reflections on time which destroys, and on space which conserves. The work ends with some penetrating analyses of the idea of evolution.

L'évolution de la personnalité (1929) belongs to the same series and is in the same vein. Personality cannot be reduced to physical experience and cenesthesia, nor to kinesthetic feelings. For Janet, the object of psychology is above all the whole of man's actions, the behavior of the living person. But the problem of consciousness cannot be eliminated, for consciousness "is what we add to ourselves to direct our actions, to reorganize the whole organism" with a view to action. To consciousness is connected the feeling of ownership which indexes, so to speak, the internal organization necessary for the direction of our actions. To consciousness must also be linked all the social feelings of love and hate, egoism, the experience of individualization and possession, all the powers which constitute our character. Thus from the possibility of being conscious to the possibility of experiencing the feelings of our ownership and of our own power, the personality appears in its temporal development as a possibility drawn from the past (biography) and open to the future.

La force et la faiblesse psychologiques (1932) constitutes first of all a study of the dynamic symptoms of mental diseases (deliriums and feelings which manifest the variations of psychological tension). Psychological strength is defined by the perfection of action and involves modalities peculiar to the strength of that action (movements, duration, psychical complexity). On the other hand, psychological weakness is defined by the mediocrity of movements, the narrowing of the mind, the exaggerated simplicity of action, the lack of initiative and of persistence. It is to these various modalities of weakness that the discharges, the agitations and the disorders of pathological actions and feelings correspond. The sources of psychological strength (Part II) are natural and restored by sleep. Their economy is in relation to the benefits and expenditures required by social life. From their reciprocal communication result the *psychological balances* (Part III). In conclusion, Janet distinguishes the *strength of actions* from the *tension of actions*. There is much more *strength* in a lofty action than in an inferior one. The *tension* measures the "contained" character of actions. There cannot be a lofty action with strong tension if there are no psychological reserves, if the subject does not have realized economies at his disposal. In this way, as I pointed out in my study on the concept of psychological strength and tension[3] and, moreover, as he himself clearly states (p. 320), Janet employs this concept less in an energy theory than, by anticipation, he refers to a level of organization with which we are today familiar by information theory.

In *Les débuts de l'intelligence* (1935), Janet studies the elementary intellectual actions which he had already analyzed in his lectures at the London Academy of Medicine in 1919 (published in the *British Journal of Psychology*, October 1920, January and July 1921). Intelligence consists in inventing behavior patterns which correspond to the "notions of grandeur, of succession, of production which fulfill the sciences." This possibility is located between the reflex and perceptive functions and the realm of reflexion, at a level which is precisely that of a nonverbal thought. From this nonverbal intelligence, various elementary forms of behavior in the child and in the animal are demonstrative (direction, orientation, change of direction, reversal of situation, notion of position, use of tools, behavior dictated by resemblance, and reproduction by imagery, for example). Janet in conclusion acknowledges *gestalt* psychology and quotes Baldwin. It is curious to note that he very rarely quotes J. Piaget in this work.

L'intelligence avant le langage (1936) takes up the same theme. It is here that we find his famous analysis of the behavior pattern of gathering objects (the "filling up of a basket of apples") and the ideas of quantity which this action requires and develops. From here Janet goes to symbols and signs and to the importance of language as intellectual action, the reflection of social behavior. Such behavior is incorporated in language and its categories, and gradually appears through the use of narrative and the behavior patterns of conversation, the organization of memory. The beginnings of time are lastly set forth in its relation with the acts of memorization, the construction of images, the behavior patterns of writing and reading; for it is in all these situations and operations that the periods of time are defined and articulated. Thus language is caught in the very movements of the construction of intelligence, but intelligence is not reduced to the capacity to verbalize.

Having reached this final point of his work, we must also point out some of Janet's very important works which are, in fact, concerned with the "interior language" (*La pensée intérieure et ses troubles* 1924), *L'hallucination dans les délires de persécution* (*Journal de Psychologie*, 1932.) In these studies Janet endeavors to apply his psychosociology of behavior to the problem of persecution feelings and illusions. "The delirious person is an individual who finds it difficult to situate his language in the hierarchy of the degrees of reality." (*La force et la faiblesse psychologiques*, p. 15). That is

---

[3] *Bulletin de Psychologie*, 1960, XIV, 184

Janet's fundamental thesis. It consists of locating delirium and hallucination in the perspective of his psychology of behavior, of feelings and of degrees of reality. What defines delirium is in fact the belief attached to the imagination, it means taking for reality what is only imaginary (a particular case of this general formula corresponds to hallucination). Consequently, the disorder to which delirium corresponds is a disorder similar to that of the neuroses; a disorder in the psychological functions whose hierarchy consists of a series of acts tending to believe in reality and to adapt to it. Every irregularity of this psychical mechanism results in an irregularity of the functions, that is, in the production of abnormal feelings (cf. what has been said on the conception of action's regulatory feelings). It is in this perspective that Janet considers persecution deliriums, which express feelings of anxiety and automatism corresponding to an imperfection of the psychical activity of adaptation to reality, (Janet has notably analyzed with great profundity a mystical *"psychasthenic"* delirium with its corollary themes of persecution and influence in his two large volumes *De l'angoisse à l'extase*.)

It is also in terms of this theory that he examines the problem of hallucinations and especially that of "voices" in deliriums which are the clinical expression of "intentional objectivation" behavior, by which the victim of hallucinations projects and personalizes the deep and lower layers of his psychical life.

HIS PRINCIPAL PSYCHOLOGICAL CONCEPTS

We shall now extract from all these works the fundamental concepts of Janet's psychology. Let us first remember that this is essentially a *psychology of behavior patterns* and that the action is envisaged in the *evolutionist* perspective and its relation with the *social milieu*. In this sense, Janet's psychology takes its place in the group of comparative psychologies by its constant reference to archaic or primitive levels of human conduct. Janet's psychology is closely allied to the psychology which, with that of William James, Baldwin, and in a certain sense the American Behaviorists, is so well known in the United States. But this does not prevent it from being a very personal conception of human behavior.

The Psychology of Behavior. Janet's philosophical tendencies are, indeed, quite original. This "psychologist" was not overfond of what is generally called psychology. He was especially removed from the psychology of the subconscious and from the phenomenological movement. His essential psychology, that of "forms of behavior (*conduites*) is even at the opposite pole of these two modern psychological movements. Rather it is allied with the *Gestaltpsychologie* of Koffka, Kohler, etc., to which Janet sometimes refers. His psychological dynamism could not remain indifferent to Bergson's philosophy; but when he speaks of psychological tension, even while noting that it is a concept identical to Bergson's "attention to the present life" (*Obsession et Psychasthénie*, I, p. 477), Janet is not at all concerned to identify psychological tension with "spiritual energy." Nevertheless, despite his obvious tendencies and preferences, Janet must be classified amongst the dynamist philosophers and the vitalist physicians. His whole system, in fact, depends on the energy which underlies it: *psychological tension*, the strength of mind, ideas which link Janet to Maine de Biran and to William James. In this respect, Janet's psychology of behavior patterns is closer to Tolman's molar behaviorism than to Watson's objectivist behaviorism.

This is how Janet conceives this *psychology of behavior pattern*, according to a passage from *De l'angoisse à l'extase* (Vol. I) where he sets forth the essential ideas he discussed in the lectures delivered in London in 1920 and 1921:

We are obliged to conceive a psychology in which the externally visible action in the fundamental phenomenon, and interior thought is only the reproduction, the combination of these exterior actions in reduced and particular forms [p. 203]. . . . This psychology of behavior is possible only under two conditions. First, a place must be found in this psychology of action for consciousness which one can, if necessary, abolish when speaking of the lower animals but which must not be ignored in men or even in higher animals. But one must deal with the phenomenon of consciousness as a particular behavior pattern, as a complication of action which is superimposed on elementary actions. One can arrive at this conclusion by studying the elementary social behavior patterns and above all the feelings which are, as we shall see, regulations of action, reactions of the individual to his own actions. A second condition is that one must be concerned with the higher behavior patterns, beliefs, reflexions, reasonings, experiences. These facts have ordinarily been expressed in terms of thoughts and to preserve the same language in all psychological science, they must be expressed in terms of action. . . . Language is a particular action, proper to man, which at the beginning is a truly external action. . . . But [which] can very easily become an internal action, that is, an action of the subject who determines reactions only in himself. I have tried to consider exterior behavior patterns and thoughts. One can call this psychology a *psychology of behavior* (pp. 204–205).

This crucial passage perfectly summarizes the antisubjectivist character of Janet's psychology. For him, all is action in psychism, all is internal or external behavior. The various modes of thought are forms of behavior. The dynamic character of such a conception will be reasserted in the *hierarchy of psychical functions* in which all these behavior patterns are classified according to their complexity, their difficulty, and their fragility.

Hierarchy of Psychical Functions. In 1903, in *Les Obsessions et la Psychasthénie* (I, pp. 477–488), Janet discussed the essentials of his theory of the hierarchy of functions. This is how he describes matters: "The most difficult mental operation, since it is the one which disappears the most quickly and the mose frequently, is the *function of reality*. . . . It is the apprehension of reality in all its forms" (p. 477). The first form of this function of reality is the action which permits us to act on exterior objects and to transform reality. This action is more difficult when it is social, professional, "interested," and new. "The thing which convinces us," he says, "to assign first rank in this hierarchy to *voluntary action*, which really modifies the given world, is that we have seen this action constantly and from the outset disturbed in the sick. Indolence, sloth, indecision, slowness of action, delays, weakness of efforts, disorder, awkwardness, incompleteness, opposition to change, indefinite continuation, characterize these psychasthenics" (p. 478). *Attention* is another operation ranked very high among the "functions of reality." It is attention which allows us to perceive actual things. Its highest degree, and consequently the most fragile, is the operation which gives us the notion of reality, that is, which determines certitude and belief. "To grasp a perception or an idea with the feeling that it is in fact reality, that is, to coordinate around this perception all our tendencies, all our activities, is the ideal enterprise of attention" (p. 478). "Under this operation of belief in the actual existence of objects, attention still finds difficulties, less serious ones, perhaps, in the intelligent perception of reading, of listening, simply in the intelligent perception of a given situation" (pp. 479–480). "The function of reality is again encountered in the consciousness of our interior states and in the perception of our own person. We must be able to perceive ourselves as we actually are. Here again we encounter the principal difficulty: perception with certitude being accompanied by a feeling of reality. We also find another which here assumes more importance and which is the perception of our unity, the feeling that the mind has really attained a unique mental synthesis" (p. 280). "These two operations, voluntary action and attention, converge by their own activity to form a synthetic operation which probably sums up all the preceding ones—the *formation in the mind of the present moment*. There is a mental faculty which one might call "*presentification*" (p. 481).

It is then one of the original features of Janet's psychology to have brought to light this group of operations by which we experience a present moment, the extreme form of our capacity to grasp reality in its most actual aspect, nothing being psychologically more real than the instant which we experience.

Below these operations which correspond to the function of reality, there exist others which can be grouped under the heading "*disinterested activity*." "These are the same psychological operations, simply stripped of what constituted their perception, that is, the acuteness of the feeling of reality. It is what is often designated as "distracted" actions or perceptions. Disinterested activity is in appearance a life identical to a complete life, but with indifference to reality. . ." (p. 482). "No doubt this group contains the automatic phenomena as one of its most interesting varieties, but it extends beyond, for it contains many forms and degrees. Between the functions of reality and entirely subconscious actions, there a thousand degrees, a thousand nuances of more or less interested action (p. 483).

Further below these disinterested behavior patterns are found modes of thought (and consequently internal behavior patterns) which constitute the *representative operations*. "Popular opinion assigns to a high level in the hierarchy of mental operations, strictly speaking, the operations which deal with ideas and not actual objects; but moralists have already frequently felt that this opinion is erroneous. To understand it one must fight the old childhood prejudice: that the abstract seems more difficut to us than the concrete" (p. 483). And so Janet reassigns to their true place the images, dreams, and empty reasonings which encumber human activity and enjoy the most flattering and false reputation.

Finally, on the level below this one are found even lower mental operations: the *empty emotions* and the *useless muscular movements*.

Janet himself summarizes this *hierarchy of the functions of reality* in this table (p. 488).

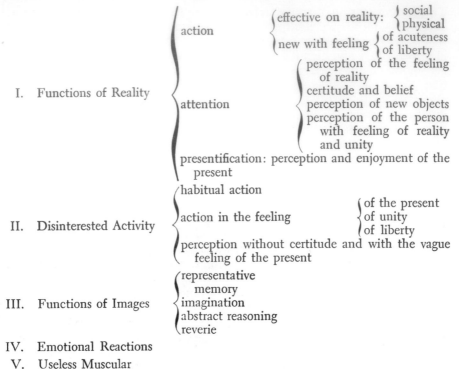

I. Functions of Reality

   action
     effective on reality: social / physical
     new with feeling of acuteness / of liberty

   attention
     perception of the feeling of reality
     certitude and belief
     perception of new objects
     perception of the person with feeling of reality and unity

   presentification: perception and enjoyment of the present

II. Disinterested Activity

   habitual action
   action in the feeling of the present / of unity / of liberty
   perception without certitude and with the vague feeling of the present

III. Functions of Images

   representative
   memory
   imagination
   abstract reasoning
   reverie

IV. Emotional Reactions

V. Useless Muscular Movements

Thus, all the mind's operations can be endowed with a *coefficient of reality*, and here is what Janet writes on this subject: "*If one considers the order of frequency and the speed with which the psychical functions are lost in the sick, one observes that they disappear more quickly when their coefficient of reality is higher, and that they persist longer when their coefficient of reality is lower. I conclude from this that these operations form a series of decreasing difficulties and complexities, that their relation to reality from the point of view of action, of understanding, tends to diminish*" (p. 487).

These operations thus hierarchized result in *beliefs* of various degrees. Belief, according to Janet, is again a certain behavior pattern which accompanies and produces the cofficient of reality attributed to the various operations (actions, perception, images, etc.). In *De l'angoisse à l'extase* (I, p. 303), he shows how the products of our psychical operations are located on a *scale of objectivity*: they are, successively (from the most to the least objective), the body, the mind, the present, actions, thoughts considered as internal occurrences, the near future, the recent past, the ideal, the distant future, the dead past, the imaginary, and finally the simple idea. More recently (*La Force et la Faiblesse psychologiques*, p. 24) he gives a more complex classification of the *degrees of objectivity* which we can describe as follows:

The first degree—the least objective—is the one at which we feel more or less confusedly that we are thinking; it is, one might say, the level of *thought*, the first Cartesian term of knowledge.

The second degree is that of *ideas*, the subjective psychical combinations which surge toward reality and already detach themselves from pure subjectivity.

The third degree is that of the *imaginary*, on which we construct, in the form of fictions, realities to which our behavior patterns of play correspond.

The fourth degree is that of the *dead past* which is already a "more real" reality: these are memories of real things to which our retrogressive behavior patterns of memory correspond.

The fifth is the degree of the *distant future*, which rules our behavior patterns of anticipation and preparation.

The sixth is the degree of the *ideal* which corresponds to our behavior patterns of direction.

The seventh is the degree of the *recent past* which is almost "still experienced" as the present.

The eighth is the degree of the *near future* ruled by behavior patterns of waiting and preparation.

The ninth degree is that of our *psychical present*.

The tenth degree is that of our *present actions* corresponding to the various present feelings regulating our actions.

The eleventh degree is that of *present happenings*, an even more synthetic construction of the present.

The twelfth degree is that of *spiritual and social reality*, grouping all the behavior patterns which represent the activation of our rational and "energetic" tendencies.

Finally, the thirteenth degree is that of the *reality of objects* detached from our mind by the perceptive action which is the most "objectivizing" operation.

As one can see, the hierarchy of psychical functions can be considered from two perspectives. Sometimes Janet describes the hierarchy of functions according to their degree of complexity and effort. Sometimes he presents the degrees of the coefficient of reality which are attached to the states of consciousness. The difficulty of picturing clearly the intersection of these two perspectives is inherent in the psychology of behavior patterns, in Janet's "behaviorism." We do not need to enter here into the disputes to which it has given rise. It is enough to have shown that the "Janctian" psychology demands as its most essential premise this dynamic architectonics of the mind's operations, always reaching, but to varying degrees, towards objectivity and reality. Thought, for Janet, is an aspect of action. The psychological behavior patterns constitute cycles of behavior of which each circle envelops and engenders a particular state of consciousness—whose "reality value" depends on the psychological tension which underlies it. Psychical life is a system of balanced forces, it is the variable and ceaselessly renewed expression of the fluctuations of psychological tension.

Psychological Tension. It is again from his long and minute clinical studies—one must not forget this, above all when reproaching Janet for being a "pure psychologist"—that Janet arrived at the notion of *psychological tension*. It was in studying mental synthesis in the course of hypnosis, the agglutination of images in the course of psychological automatism (*Psychological automatism,* pp. 444–470), and above all the reduction of the psychical functions in neurasthenic states (*Obessions et Psychasthénie,* 1903, I, pp. 488–496), that he conceived his theory of psychological tension: "In the psychasthenic, thought is always occupied by the simplest, least rich phenomena. They have memories and above all distant memories, but these memories are simplified, discolored; they are not so complex as the spectacle of a real event. They are above all abstract reasonings, ramblings in which thinking is done by means of substitutes." Therefore complexity and the richness of psychial phenomena which will constitute psychological "tension" must be made to play a part. This psychological tension must not be confused with the modalities of physical forces (*Medications psychologiques,* II, p. 94, p. 301—*De l'angoisse à l'extase,* I, p. 206–207). "If one analyzes the functions of reality in their operational capacity, it appears," Janet says, that "they are characterized by two essential phenomena: (1) unification, concentration chiefly significant when it is new and constitutes mental synthesis; (2) the number, the mass of psychological phenomena which must be a part of this synthesis. The fusion of these phenomena in a new synthesis, a strong concentration and multiplicity composed of acts of consciousness, constitute a cohesive force which must be essential in psychology and which can be called *"psychological tension"* (*ibid.,* p. 495). "The degree of psychological tension or the elevation of the mental level is manifested by the degree occupied in the hierarchy by the highest phenomena to which the subject is able to attain" (p. 426).

The tension of reality with action and belief (demanding the highest degree of tension) is a phenomenon of high tension; reverie, motor or visceral agitation can be considered as the phenomena of low tension. *This psychological tension obviously depends on certain physiological phenomena, on certain modifications in the circulation and the nutrition of the brain. Some of our experiments with vision make me inclined to think that what is involved is a reduction in the speed of certain elementary phenomena, perhaps of certain vibrations of the nervous system.* Some of M. Leduc's remarkable experiments on the electrification of the brain, it seems to me, can be interpreted in the same manner. Actually, the physiological mechanism of these phenomena is still unknown and we can determine only their psychological aspect with some precision" (*Les Névroses,* 1909, p. 363).[4]

With the help of the established scale of psychical operations, one can therefore measure, so to speak, the degree of the psychological tension.

This tension undergoes physiological *fluctuations* in effort, in the various forms of behavior patterns in which the subject is involved, also in conditions of fatigue, of sleep and drowsiness. In *Obsessions et Psychasthénies* (I, p. 428), Janet writes on this subject: "In my 1901 lectures on sleep and hypnoid states, I elaborated this idea that sleep and waking afford one of the best examples of the fluctuations of the mental level. . . . We find in dreams all the disorders characteristic of the lowering of psychological tension. One can easily observe, in the dream, automatism, indefinite repetition, declamation, illusions in the

---

[4] Our italics emphasize the organic and physiological character of Janet's theory. He relates this psychological tension to an electric phenomenon. Having discussed chronaxy in his own period, he could have written today of EEG traces in waking, or of the activation of reverberation circuits, or neuronic potentials, or even of neg-entropy.

evaluation of time, the sense of the comical, of the *déjà-vu*, of doubt, of split-ting, etc." Hence, of course, the great importance of this comparison (implied, moreover, in all dynamist psychopathology): the physiological fluctuations of psychological tension will make psychopathic states directly intelligible. For naturally, the importance of states of *psycholepsy* (lowering of psychological tension) will be considerable for the interpretation of pathological phe-nomena. Thus next to the theory of the hierarchy of functions, that of psy-chological tension constitutes an essentially *economical* aspect of Janet's psychology (cf. what has been said above about his anticipated reference to information theory).

The Genetic Development of Psychological Behavior Patterns. Here we come to the strictly genetic aspect of Janet's psychology. No doubt this evolu-tional character is implied in the very notion of the hierarchy of functions, but it is made explicit in a series of specific psychological theories upon which we shall not dwell. It is nevertheless essential, in order to understand Janet's psychopathology, to realize that the psychical functions represent, in his sys-tem, the personality's mode of organization (ontogenetic development) and that they are also the expression of an historical evolution of the species (phylogenetic development). This doubly "genetic" character is constantly apparent in Janet's analyses of a host of psychological behavior patterns.

THEORY OF TENDENCIES. This theory is inspired by a psychology of the devel-opment of instinctive activities on the various levels of behavior patterns. The point of departure of the evolution of tendencies is the reflex or explosive actions. These are actions which preserve the individual. In relation to the body itself, these tendencies create a form of activity whose object is the body (corporal tendencies). It is by the extension of this object to other similar objects that the social tendencies are born. "The essential character of per-sonal social behavior patterns seems to me to be the collaboration of tenden-cies. . . . The social animal not only collaborates with others, he collaborates with himself; he observes, arrests, completes his own actions" (*De l'angoisse à l'extase*, I, p. 215). On this level, personal and social tendencies intersect.

Above this level (equivalent to that of Wallon's genetic analysis in *L'Enfant turbulent*, the projective state), Janet places the tendencies "which constitute elementary intelligence, the first intellectual tendencies" (p. 215). He has studied these primary intellectual actions at length, in the form of be-havior patterns which conform to the same schema. He has for example analyzed the simplest behavior pattern, that of the "basket of apples" (filling and emptying a basket of apples).

This behavior pattern comprises two kinds of actions which pertain neither to the apples nor to the basket: the two actions (filling and emptying) contain parts pertaining sometimes to the one object and sometimes to the other, but these actions are merged, combined in varying degrees. We can make the same observa-tion for the behavior patterns relative to the image, the statue or the portrait. In-cidental to such objects there is always a combination of two perceptual behavior patterns, and according to the predominance of one or the other, there are always two characteristic actions: to make the tool or to use it, to blaze or follow the trail. . . . This combination of two perceptual behavior patterns into a single synthetic action shows us the character peculiar to the first intellectual behavior patterns. It is in the center of this group of combined tendencies, and concurrent with them, that language was formed, which is a behavior pattern of the same kind. (*De l'angoisse à l'extase*, p. 216)

Despite the necessarily fragmentary character of the theory as set forth here, it is evident that for Janet the tendencies to act and the necessities of action produce the first intellectual actions, the first fundamental problems (to divide into two series, to share, to follow, to fill, etc.), those that are found in intellectual processes in the form of ideas or fundamental principles of knowledge.

Above this "layer" of inferior and primitive tendencies are found the tendencies whose activity constitutes *language*. "Not only did man make use of language to communicate with his kind, but also, always obeying the fundamental law of behaving toward himself as toward others, he began to speak to himself. Man began to speak very softly—thought was born. In this way, interior or exterior words henceforth accompanied all or nearly all actions. This is what characterizes the beginning of a strictly human behavior pattern, for man is above all a garrulous animal who speaks his actions and acts his words" (*ibid.*, pp. 218–219). "In the beginning, word and action were inseparable, the word was only the beginning of the action, the cry uttered by the chief at the beginning of actions to make imitation easier" (p. 220). This notion was developed later in the 1933–1934 lectures and in several works of psychopathological application, notably on the subject of deliriums of influence and hallucinations. Janet thus pursues this genetic (evolutionist) study of the stages of language in humanity:

Men felt the need to perform special acts in order to reestablish intentionally this union between language and action (a union compromised by the practice of the 'unconscious' language). New operations attempted to give language a certain consistency: the promise became an action which transforms a word into a deed and once again into an order for ourselves . . . This union of actions and language was achieved in two ways which gave birth to the will and to beliefs. This will is an affirmation whose execution is immediate: I want to walk and I walk; I want to go out and I go out. In belief, immediate execution is impossible . . . I am alluding to certain actions, but I cannot execute them immediately. I am restricting myself to uniting language and action *conditionally*. These varieties of thought and belief are born of numerous psychological phenomena (acceptances, refusal, negation, affirmations relative to memories, etc.), but at this moment are formed the very important phenomena of desires inseparable from beliefs . . . In the same way that the perceptual behavior pattern had created objects, the affirmative behavior pattern created beings.

At this moment of development, affirmation occurs almost by chance. It depends on the momentary force which accompanies such and such a formula. We are at the stage where one believes what one desires or fears and where beliefs founded on such accidental motives assert themselves with an energy, a tenacity that will not occur again. (*Ibid.*, p. 223)

This is the phase of "*assertive belief*," that is, of form of belief which adheres to everything which presents itself to the mind. But the "defects of such a behavior pattern are too evident: all the degrees of belief are ignored and the belief is brutally applied at random. Hence there gradually developed, if not another will and another belief, at least another method of localization of will and belief. This transformation was effected by the evolution of an extremely important social phenomenon which was to have a greater place in the studies of psychology: I refer to the operation of *discussion*. It finally extended to a large number of affirmations, even when man found himself alone. *Reflection* is a behavior pattern which reproduces within ourselves the discussion of an assembly" (*ibid.*, p. 224).

Finally, at the termination of his evolution, man's mind succeeds in forming and activating the superior rational and energetic tendencies. "These operations are characterized by a particular distribution of strength: they do not limit themselves to the use of accumulated strength in the inferior tendencies, they draw their strength from a special reserve in order to add it to the ideas which are not strong enough in themselves. A man of character is capable of executing his decisions, his promises, his commitments, even if this decision affords him no actual satisfaction. Morality consists of doing one's duty. There must be a reserve of special strength to make a man capable of executing an action in this manner" (*ibid.*, p. 230).

In his book *La force et la faiblesse psychologiques*, Janet followed the entire circuit of this capital of strength which the economy of superior moral and social life achieves.

Such is the "theory of tendencies." We have explained it in some detail, as it shows the originality of the psychology Janet was able to construct between "behaviorism" and "psychosociology." But this theory particularly illustrates the genetic and pragmatic character of his conception of psychical life.

THEORY OF FEELINGS. This theory takes its inspiration from American "pragmatism." It is also set forth in all its details in the second volume of *De l'angoisse à l'extase*, and is also based on psychopathological observation. The analysis of pathological feelings is very rich and very suggestive in Janet's work (in *Névroses et idées fixes*, in *Obsessions et psychasthénie*, in *De l'angoisse à l'extase*, in his later studies on delirium and hallucinations). Feelings too are for Janet behavior patterns whose own finality is to regulate actions. It is to the functions of *regulation of actions* that their psychology is linked.

The actions of living beings present an infinite diversity in which psychological science tries to discern a certain regularity. The conception of tendencies offers a first solution to the problem . . . The actions of a single tendency determined by a single stimulation present numerous varieties. This is what we have observed in studying the problem of the feelings . . . The preceding actions determined by a peripheral stimulation should be considered as primary actions which can be complicated and diversified by other secondary acts. These secondary actions appear as reactions to the primary act, analogous to the proprioceptive reflexes. (*De l'angoisse à l'extase*, p. 589)

Thus, all feelings of effort, joy, sadness, moroseness, etc., are only the expression of this "background" of regulating behavior patterns. Despite the artificial and formal character of this conception of the feelings, it has such a precise place in the ensemble of Janet's psychology and is the cause of such fine analyses of life and of emotional attitudes that we have chosen to remark on it here, although it is only an aspect of the fundamental theory of tendencies.

The architectonic construction of the functions of *memory* also conforms to the same evolutionary schema. The same holds true of the gradual construction of the notions of time. Here again the operations of memory are decomposed into a series of behavior patterns (narrative and its varieties, plotting, illusion of the *déjàvu*, presentification) which diversify the various degrees of reality as they are displayed in time. Readers who wish documentation on this point should refer to the books *L'evolution de la mémoire, La pensée intérieure et ses troubles*, and *Les stades de la personnalité*.

HIS PSYCHOPATHOLOGY

The fundamental concepts of Janet's psychology are the *evolution* and the *hierarchy* of the psychical functions and the *psychological tension* which is the force responsible for their unity and their efficacy. These concepts have been drawn by Janet from the clinical study of mental patients and particularly from neurotic patients.

In closing this discussion, a word is in order about Janet's conception of psychopathology. We can make it all the more brief in that Janet's psychopathology is the exact opposite of his psychology, and since we have already given an account of the latter, his psychopathological conceptions easily ensue from it.

The Nature of Mental Diseases and the Organo-Dynamic Conception of Psychiatry. For Janet, mental disease is essentially a "weakness," an impotence; it implies a lowering of psychological tension. Now, this tension is the product of all the somatic and nervous forces which organize life and keep it at a level of normality or of sufficient reality. Thus is affirmed, contrary to the misunderstanding of many authors, notably in France, the organic nature of mental disease, *i.e.*, its conditioning by biodynamic factors. In this regard, Janet's conception must be related to all those which I call "*organo-dynamic*," for they are based on the hypothesis that disease is the effect of a disorganization of the dynamic infrastructures of psychical activity. The conceptions of Bleuler, Kretschmer, Goldstein, Masserman, etc., are linked to this movement (sometimes also called "organismic"). But it is of course the principles of Hughlings Jackson that inspire this doctrine movement, through the fundamental idea of a dissolution of the processes of evolution or organization, and through the primordial importance attributed to the negative process of functional deficiency. I myself, in working on the extension of this theory, have continued to show how all these great works are interdependent.

Neurosis and the Notion of Psychological Evolution. Constantly recurring in Janet's work are the terms regression, arrested development, disorganization, retrogression toward inferior psychical forms; this is because the model to which he refers in order to describe and explain mental sickness is an *evolutionist* (or geneticist) model implied in all *comparative psychology*. He often quotes Spencer, and he was familiar with the thinking of Darwin. He very rarely refers to Huglings Jackson, but he was very interested by the works of J. Piaget and the earlier work of the French sociological school. His entire psychopathology is based on the idea of a *development*, of a psychosocial *ontogenesis* of the psychic being. It is the alteration of this functional structure which, by not attaining maturity or maintaining itself at a normal level, produces a collapse of the behavior patterns and of the feelings which constitute the neurotic symptoms. We have set forth in some detail Janet's clinical work, for it constitutes the genuinely vital part of his work. It is by carefully studying the neurotic symptoms that he has demonstrated their negative structure, their deficient aspect, by assigning them a more or less inferior place in the levels of the functions of reality. Thus, hysterical and obsessive behavior patterns, anxieties and *idées fixes*, appear as manifestations of the automatic and unconscious sphere, as is the case in primitives, children, and crowds. If we thus emphasize the importance of the prehistoric and the archaic in the symptomatology of the neuroses, it is in order to arrive at the last points of the comparison of Janet's work, its confrontation with that of Freud.

The Fall into Automatism and the Unconscious—Janet and Freud. As I stressed above, Janet and Freud never, so to speak, knew each other. Each worked in ignorance of the other; this is because each followed a radically different line. Janet, careful to note weakness, states of inferiority, collapse of behavior patterns, reached the conclusion that the infrastructure of the psychical being is doomed to disorder and chance. So much so that this conception of the subconscious or the unconscious assigns to these inferior forms of psychical life a minimum of meaning and, on the whole, of importance. Freud, on the other hand, having really discovered the forces and the meaning of the unconscious sphere, applied himself to understanding the unconscious in its production and to deciphering its meaning through the symbolism which hides it from consciousness. Henceforth, the unconscious became in his eyes the essential of psychic life inasmuch as it represents the buds of instinct. There is nothing more systematically opposed than these two systems, one might also say than these two temperaments. Janet, as a rationalist, envisioned the psychopathological fact as a logical and moral scandal. Freud, more sensitive to the tumults of the feelings, has, so to speak, sided with the instincts in the discovery of their power. For Janet, the essential thing about neuroses is a loss of information; for Freud, neurosis gives us information which one must know how to decode. Thus seen in their oppositions, the concepts of Freud and Janet constitute the two poles of attraction of contemporary psychiatric thought. But in this partition, psychiatry risks its existence. A better knowledge of human ontology should be able to resolve this antinomy precisely by apprehending it as the very structure of the human being which can be reduced neither to a psychology of consciousness nor to a psychology of the unconscious.[5]

If there is no consciousness without something escaping and resisting it (the id and its unconscious connections with the ego and the unconscious superego of Freud's argument), *i.e.*, without an unconscious which is not only a "negative"—if there is also no unconscious without an order, an organization which censures or represses it, it then becomes evident that we need not choose between Janet's psychosociology of the functions of reality (or of consciousness) and Freud's psychoanalysis of pulsions (or of the unconscious). We should rather complete one by the other. For this reason, Janet's work, despite its "superficial" character, does not merely disappear before Freud's "depth psychology," for the surface and the depth of the psychic being cannot be separated.

The work of Pierre Janet does not belong only to the past.

[5] This is what I have attempted to explain in my recent book, *La Conscience*, Paris: Presses Universitaires de France, 1963.

CHAPTER 10

BEYOND VITALISM AND MECHANISM: FREUD'S CONCEPT OF PSYCHIC ENERGY[1]

Robert R. Holt[2]

THE CONCEPT of psychic energy is central to Freud's metapsychology, and was in fact the principal means he called upon to help him explain the events of clinical observation. In its development during the past 40 years, the concept has steadily ramified into a conceptual thicket that baffles some, impresses many, and at the least greatly complicates the task of anyone who tries to form a clear idea of what the basic theory of psychoanalysis is (cf. Rapaport, 1959; Holt, 1962; Modell, 1963). Up to a point, one can get a good deal of clarification by tracing its place in the development of Freud's ideas; but the thoughts of no man are a closed system. The search for historical understanding leads us past Freud's immediate intellectual ancestors, past the bounds of psychology, and into one of the major themes in the history of biology, the opposing views of vitalism and mechanism. Before considering the present methodological status of psychic energy, therefore, let us review the history of the theoretical antitheses out of which it grew.

The History of the Vitalist-Mechanist Controversy

One of the most impressive great trends in the development of science is its differentiation into separate specialties. By this token, the further back we go in tracing any one theme, the more we find it embedded in science as a whole, and the more necessary for its understanding is a grasp of the changing status of the entire scientific enterprise. A short essay can hope to sketch

[1] Preparation of this paper was supported by a Public Health Service research career program award (No. MH-K6-12,455) from the National Institute of Mental Health. Copyright © 1967 by Robert R. Holt.
[2] The basic idea for this paper, the comparison of psychic energy and vitalistic concepts, I owe to my friend Benjamin B. Rubinstein, M.D., with whom I have had a number of valuable conversations on these issues to which various other ideas could be traced. The interested reader can find a number of original and powerful arguments against the concept of psychic energy in two important theoretical articles by him (Rubinstein, 1967). Since completing the MS, I have read another valuable contribution that shows the weaknesses of the doctrine of psychic energy from yet another standpoint (Peterfreund, 1965).—The first draft of this paper was presented as part of a panel on psychic energy at the December, 1962, meetings of the American Psychoanalytic Association (cf. Modell, 1963).

only some of the most outstanding lineaments of the vitalist-mechanist controversy; for a fuller understanding, there is no substitute for a general history of science, such as that of Singer (1959) to which the following account is much indebted.

As is true of so much of the rest of the history of ideas, this theme begins with the ancient Greeks. Before either vitalism or mechanism, yet intertwined with them, are the opposed concepts of *being* and *becoming*, which became so engrained in Western thought as to create difficulties from unexamined assumptions even today. Around 500 B.C., Heraclitus promulgated the idea that "all is flux"—everything is so constantly changing that becoming was the true reality and fire the ultimate substance. Democritus, 70 years his junior, is the famous opposing atomist of antiquity. Far from admitting any reality to process, he taught that "Only the atoms and the void are real." The qualities we perceive are produced by motion of the hard, indestructible bits of substance he conceived atoms to be, and all motion originates in previous movement of atoms.

Plato was enough influenced by Heraclitus to believe that the direct objects of observation were but transitory appearances; what persisted and was ultimately real, he thought, was the *idea*. In more modern times, he rejected concrete particulars as of only passing and accidental importance and was much more impressed by the enduring abstract concept. It is easy to see how this point of view was favorable to the development of mathematics. Yet Plato's doctrine of ideas gives these abstractions a metaphysical status of a higher reality than that of sensory presentations—perhaps the first great example of the fallacy of misplaced concreteness, the reification of what are only constructs. Moreover, "The Platonic Idea contained in it the conception of form, for only in the Idea was the form separated from matter" (Singer, 1959, p. 39). This association of form with the transempirical Idea may have been a subtle obstacle hindering empirical scientists of many later centuries from tackling structure and organization analytically.

As philosophy is often taught, Plato is contrasted with Aristotle; and surely the latter's empiricism is in refreshing contrast to his teacher's lack of interest in phenomena. Yet many of the differences between them were matters of emphasis; for our purposes, the continuities are more impressive. Plato's view of the way the soul is intertwined with the body closely resembles Aristotle's monistic vitalism: though the latter postulated a soul *(psyche)* as the life-principle, he did not conceive it as existentially separate from matter. Most writers (e.g., Nagel, 1953; Rapaport, 1962; Schlick, 1953) stress the *similarity* with which Aristotle treated the physical and biological worlds. He viewed the motions of smoke and birds alike as a seeking after their "natural positions" in the sky; it was a thoroughgoing teleology, applied to all of nature.

Moreover, he modified and qualified Plato's doctrine of ideas without rejecting what was fallacious in it, which Popper (1957) calls essentialism: taking universal or generalized terms as real. Indeed, Popper says that Aristotle founded the school of *methodological essentialism,* which "taught that scientific research must penetrate to the essence of things in order to explain them. Methodological essentialists are inclined to formulate scientific questions in such terms as 'what is matter?'. . . and they believe that a penetrating answer to such questions, revealing the real or essential meaning of . . . terms and thereby the real or true nature of the essence denoted by them, is at least a necessary prerequisite of scientific research, if not its main task" (Popper, 1957, p. 10). "*Methodological nominalists*, as opposed to this, . . . hold that the task of science is only to describe how things behave . . . they regard *words* merely as *useful instruments of description*. Most people, Popper concludes, "will admit that methodological nominalism has been victorious in the natural sciences," but that is jumping far ahead in the story. For the moment, I wish only to point out how essentialism characterized all of Greek thought, and how such a doctrine as vitalism—the postulation of some kind of vital force, entelechy, etc. as the ultimate explanation of the difference between living and nonliving things—is an excellent example of essentialism.

Around 400 A.D., St. Augustine brought a good deal of Plato into Christianity, and about 850 dark years later St. Thomas Aquinas integrated Aristotle with Christian theology. It did not prove difficult to fit the immortal and transmaterial soul, the interventions of a personal God in a material world, and other supernatural dogmas into the great Greek philosophies, making a unified world-view of enormous prestige and authority. It dominated the entire intellectual world for many centuries, and still controls more of it than many of us like to admit.

Under the sway of Thomist scholasticism, vitalism and mechanism could not very well emerge as opposing ideas; not until Galileo had promulgated modern mechanics in the early part of the seventeenth century and put to rout the anthropomorphic view of force in the physical world. But not only there: "His conception of a mechanical universe swiftly reacted even on the biological sciences," Singer notes. Rejecting the Aristotelean view, "biologists sought to explain the animal body as a machine. The first important biological works of the seventeenth century—for example, those of Santorio (1600), of Harvey (1628), or Descartes (1664)—all sought thus to explain the body" (Singer, 1959, pp. 250 f.).

The first post-Galilean proponent of a widely influential unified theory of the universe, René Descartes [1596–1650], did not break with religion but kept God and the soul in a mechanical world of bodies by means of a metaphysical dualism. As so many vitalists were to do, after his example, he conceived of man's body as a machine animated by a rational soul, a nonmaterial spirit that interacted with the world of matter in only one locality, the pineal gland. It is particularly worthy of our note that for Descartes, "the special prerogative of the soul is to originate action" (Singer, p. 277). Since it was not part of the material world, it did not obey natural laws, but was *free*. Lacking this free will, lower animals were capable only of automatic actions. To him they were machines, like the impressive hydromechanical[3] automata at the Austrian palace of Hellbrunn (dating from 1615) with which he was familiar (Culbertson, 1963). Though Descartes did not originate the concept of the reflex, he focused attention on it and gave it wide currency.

Was Descartes a mechanist, then, or a vitalist? The answer must be, both; his influence stimulated and supported both tendencies. Even though he did

---

[3] It is interesting to note that Descartes is probably the father of the "hydrodynamic" metaphors of metapsychological energy theory, since he conceived of the nerves as tubes filled with a special fluid and operating essentially like a modern hydraulic brake system.

not himself focus on a gap between the living and the nonliving, his dualistic philosophy laid down a general model for the vitalist contention and helped provide a truce between religion—which could concern itself with the soul and spiritual matters—and science, to which was left the entire physical world. This Solomon's judgment split the previously prevailing unity of knowledge, however, into two great departments—natural philosophy and moral philosophy—a division that still survives.

With Newton [1642–1727], science proceeded to move in and take command over the material universe. One of the reasons Newton was so honored in his lifetime was that his elegant formulation of the laws of mechanics synthesized elements that were already familiar. Galileo had broken ground and made the rough sketches; Newton built a logically unassailable theoretical structure which was moreover completely hospitable to empirical research. But even a mansion is not a lofty enough metaphor for his achievement; here was one of those grand syntheses, which so capture the imagination that they are easy to overextend. "The full extent and revolutionary character of the change that Newton was working in men's minds was not at first recognized even by himself, but it became apparent in the course of the eighteenth century. The essential revolutionary element was that Newton had conceived a working universe wholly independent of the spiritual order.[4] This was the profoundest break that had yet been made with all for which the Middle Ages stood. With Newton there set in an age of scientific determinism" (Singer, 1959, p. 294).

The course of the new science, as a progression from the observation of a few phenomena to a world-outlook, was transmuted into a world-outlook imposed on those phenomena. . . . It had been the habit of philosophers to see all detailed things *sub specie aeternitatis* [that is, in terms of Platonic essentialism]. Hence, no sooner was the conception of inert bodies passively following the dictates of blind forces seen to be applicable to the motion of mass-points, than it was immediately generalized into a world-philosophy. Instead of being accepted as what it was—a generalized statement of certain particularly simple motions—it became a principle of universal determinism or materialism and to that principle phenomena and experiences quite unrelated to such motions were held to be subject. (Singer, 1959, pp. 419 f.)

The central elements of this concept of the world were *forces* acting on material *bodies*. But as Singer points out, "There was still much vagueness as to the limits of the two. Thus, 'phlogiston,' which was supposed to go forth from a body on combustion, and 'ether' which was at once agent and medium of light, no less than the electric and magnetic 'fluids,' remained ambiguous conceptions to the very end of the eighteenth century and even into the nineteenth" (Singer, 1959, p. 347). Some of them, like heat ("caloric") and

---

[4] It became so in the work of his followers; Newton himself remained a devout Christian to the end. See also Koryé (1956), as paraphrased below. In connection with Freud's treatment of quantity and quality in the Project, quoted below, it is interesting to read Bergson's remarks about the impact of Newtonian physics on philosophy: "the first result of the new science was to cut the real into two halves, quantity and quality, the former being credited to the account of *bodies* and the latter of the account of *souls*. The ancients had raised no such barriers either between quantity and quality or between soul and body." (Bergson, 1911, p. 349).

electricity, were thought to be weightless substances, the "imponderables."

One result of the Newtonian revolution was a great impetus to a mechanistic conception of biology. It took such extreme forms as the following:

> Given the least principle of motion, animated bodies will have all that is necessary for moving, feeling, thinking, repenting, and in a word for conducting themselves in the physical realm, and in the moral realm which depends upon it. Let us then conclude boldly that man is a machine, and that in the whole universe there is but a single substance variously modified. (From *L'homme machine*, 1748, by J. C. de la Mettrie)

Note that phrase, "but a single substance"; it implies the contemporaneous vitalistic doctrine that living things contained unique substances, or at least a special chemistry with compounds that required life to come into being. In the unitary world of Aristotle, there was no such dichotomy of substance; indeed, it was assumed that complex living beings could arise by spontaneous generation from dead matter. With the rise of microscopy in the second half of the seventeenth century it was possible to trace the life cycle of insects and to see their previously invisible eggs, and thus to prove that it was not the sun that bred maggots in dead animals. Further technical advances made the microbiologists of the eighteenth century increasingly skeptical that spontaneous generation occurred even in the wholly microscopic world of the Infusoria, but the doctrine was not laid to rest until the conclusive demonstrations of Pasteur and Tyndall in the second half of the nineteenth century. Long before, in 1828, Wöhler had struck a decisive blow at the vitalist conclusion that there must be special life-substances, by his synthesis of the organic compound urea. Thus the decisive evidence for a basic split between living and nonliving matter came after an impressive demonstration of continuity on the level of substance.

But to go back to the 18th century: there was no dearth of vitalists to combat those biologists who adopted the prevailing mechanistic philosophy. The chemist G. E. Stahl [1660–1734], who gave the notion of phlogiston wide currency, was one spokesman for the biological vitalists of his day. In "obscure and mystical language" (Singer, p. 281), he taught that the "sensitive soul" follows its own laws, which govern life. But even such men as Hoffman [1660–1742], Boerhaave [1668–1738] and von Haller [1708–1777], who also held dualistic beliefs about the influence on the body of the mind or soul as a living principle or vital spirit, made their important contributions by applying the principles of mechanics to the physiological study of the body, treated essentially as a machine.

THE "NATURPHILOSOPHIE"

Not nearly so half-hearted was the reaction against universal mechanism of a new, largely philosophical school, which arose around the middle of the eighteenth century, attained an enormous vogue in Germany particularly, and subsided slowly a hundred years later: *Naturphilosophie*, or nature-philosophy. Not a tightly knit school, it included many thinkers from the logical rationalist Kant to many wild and fantastic speculators such as Oken. In large part, it was a return to Aristotle. Dualism is an unstable equilibrium, which had been denied by a radical mechanism via the reduction of life and mind to

atoms and their motions. Naturphilosophie also proclaimed a unity, but more
by a blurring of distinctions than by a consistent idealistic monism in which
mind might be the one true reality. All of Nature (capital N) was viewed as
an organic, evolving unity by Schelling [1775–1854], perhaps the central figure.
His philosophy, says Schlick (1953, p. 523), "makes organic processes into fundamental explanatory principles, thus attempts to reduce nonliving nature to
the living." Kant [1724–1804] was of course a great deal more sophisticated;
it was an abstract unity that he postulated in nature uniting the mechanical
and teleological. Yet he taught that the parts of living organisms could be
understood only in terms of their functions for the whole. As Singer summarizes and paraphrases: "The very existence of the whole implies an end.
True, says Kant, Nature exhibits to us nothing in the way of purpose. Nevertheless we can only understand an organism if we regard it as though produced under the guidance of thought for the end" (Singer, 1959, p. 385).

Under Kant's influence, Goethe developed the Platonic implication of this
guiding thought into the conception of "ideas" in the mind of God, which
were manifested as a limited number of patterns for the structure of organisms.
Oken [1779–1851] took up this notion and applied it with a combination of
shrewd observation of animals' structure and rank speculation, developing
such hypotheses as the essential similarity of the human head and trunk, or
that of the vertebrae and the skull. To quote Singer once again, "For these
Nature Philosophers the repetition of organs, 'segmentation,' in many plant
and animal types [for example, as in the earthworm] was a plan or 'idea' (in
the Platonic sense) in the mind of God. . . . Whence comes the continued
fascination of thoughts so little related to the daily task of the scientific observer? The essence of the thought of such men is that the processes of the
mind reflect the processes of Nature" (Singer, 1959, p. 389)—a well-known
Kantian doctrine, with roots in Plato's conception of the macrocosm of nature as reflecting the microcosm of man.

By one of the choicest ironies in the history of psychology, one of its most
suffocatingly scientific branches is a direct offshoot of nature-philosophy. For
Fechner [1801–1887] invented psychophysics as the great link between mind
and matter that would prove their underlying unity. Taken ill in middle life,
he turned from physics to religious philosophy. With his deepening interest
in the immortal soul, "he was troubled by materialism" and in 1848 published
a book arguing for the mental life of plants. "His philosophical solution of
the spiritual problem lay in his affirmation of the identity of mind and matter
and in his assurance that the entire universe can be regarded as readily from
the point of view of its consciousness . . . as it can be viewed as inert matter. . . . Consciousness, Fechner argued, is in all and through all. The earth,
'our mother,' is a being like ourselves" (Boring, 1929, p. 269). This scant
selection of his views, which were set forth in a series of seven philosophical
volumes, will I hope suffice to show that the founding father of psychology,
Fechner, was a true Naturphilosoph.

Nature-philosophy was, by its attempt at monism, not quite a vitalism,
but it kept alive many of the same ancient ways of thought—both have the
Heraclitean emphasis on becoming—and its influence is strongly felt in the
thought of such a vitalist as Lamarck [1744–1829]. "In living nature," as
Gillispie (1958) summarizes Lamarck's thought, "inheres a plastic force—

indeed living nature *is* a plastic force—forever producing all varieties of animals. . . . The dead hand of inorganic nature causes discontinuities in what the organic drive toward perfection would alone achieve . . . in Lamarck, only life can act, for life and activity are ultimately one . . . it was rather as a consequence than as a statement of his view of nature that Lamarck laid down two corollaries which he described as laws: that of the development or decay of organs through use or disuse, and that of the inheritance of the characteristics acquired by organisms in reacting to the environment."—In reacting *purposively*, that is, for Lamarck stresses the role of goal-striving in the development of adaptive changes that are passed on to an organism's descendants. He was very much the teleologist, searching for ultimate causes rather than being content to observe contingencies between phenomena.

The next great name among vitalists was Johannes Müller [1801–1858], who worked at the height of the German nature-philosophical rage. "It is significant," Singer remarks, that Müller, "the most effective critic of mid-nineteenth-century mechanism . . . was himself an experimental physiologist of genius who is largely responsible for the picture of the body as a machine" (Singer, 1959, p. 491). He rejected what many thought the convincing antivitalistic evidence that urea could be synthesized, pointing out that it was after all only an excretory breakdown product of living tissue, not in itself a part of life.[5] Convinced that there was something about life that could not be measured physically and explained mechanically, he said in print that the velocity of the nervous impulse could not be determined—and in a few years, Helmholtz had measured it! Müller's respect for life did not keep him from studying it as objectively as possible; he achieved fame for his great and exhaustive *Handbook of human physiology*, and is remembered today for his doctrine of the specific energies of nerves. A measure of his greatness is that most of the leading physiologists of the next generation were his pupils, notably Helmholtz, du Bois-Reymond, and Brücke. These young men together with Ludwig, formed a club which later became the Berlin Physical Society. The purpose of their association, Bernfeld (1944) tells us, was "to destroy, once and for all, vitalism, the fundamental belief of their admired master."

THE MECHANISTIC APPROACH

In 1842, du Bois-Reymond had written the following rather melodramatic manifesto: "Brücke and I pledged a solemn oath to put into effect this truth: 'No other forces than the common physical-chemical ones are active within the organism. In those cases which cannot at the time be explained by these forces one has either to find the specific way or form of their action by means of the physical-mathematical method, or to assume new forces equal in dignity to the chemical-physical forces inherent in matter, reducible to the force of attraction and repulsion'" (Bernfeld, 1944).

In his brief text, notice first, the great emphasis on forces; it is surely a

[5] A century later, Bergson was repeating essentially the same argument: "science has reconstructed hitherto nothing but waste products of vital activity; the peculiarly active plastic substances obstinately defy synthesis" (Bergson, 1911, pp. 34 f.). Also favoring Müller's position was the fact that the substance Wöhler had begun his synthesis with, ammonium cyanate, was not for some years to be synthesizable from inorganic elemental sources.

dynamic commitment! Second, it is clearly an oath of fidelity to mechanism, the kind of prohibition law that is necessary only in the face of temptation—to invoke some kind of special nonphysical, vital energy. Third, take careful note of the strategy proposed for the difficult times the swearers saw ahead: if physical-chemical forces should prove insufficient, "new ones equal in dignity" might be assumed but only as a temporary expedient and with the understanding that they should ultimately be *reducible*. Finally, it is an oath of loyalty to the scientific, or "physical-mathematical" *method*, which as A. Rapoport (1962) points out, was always the most effective weapon of the antivitalists.

One wonders what must have been the excitement of a group so committed when at one of its meetings in 1847 Helmholtz presented his paper on the conservation of energy—interestingly enough, according to Bernfeld (1944), as a contribution to physiology. "There are certain seminal scientific ideas," writes Singer "the appearance of which makes it possible for the historian to establish time boundaries. . . . Such a one is the doctrine that any form of measurable physical activity is convertible into any other form, and that the total amount of such activity in the world is limited and remains the same." Thus, "the fundamental doctrine of the nineteenth century, that of energy, was long in gestation but was developed in the decade before 1850" (Singer, 1959, pp. 375, 417 f.). The first of the two principal points of the doctrine was mainly the work of Joule, who discovered the mechanical equivalent of heat and made the bold generalization (also in 1847) that "Heat, living force and attraction through space (to which I might also add *light* . . .) are mutually convertible." For all its vitalistic ring, Joule meant by "living force (vis viva)" nothing other than energy; there was also an ambiguity in the German, for Helmholtz, like du Bois-Reymond, had used the word Kraft (now usually translated as force). Thomson (Lord Kelvin) supplied the clarifying term *energy* in 1852, besides making important substantive contributions to the theory and the precise measurement of energy.

Several of the great physicists of the seventeenth century, from Galileo to Huygens, had suggested that "all basic physical phenomena—heat, light, chemical action, electricity, and magnetism—were susceptible of mechanical explanation. It was believed that all were due to the movements on the part of small particles of the affected bodies" (Singer, 1959, p. 247)—a theory that led to many important advances, even before the mutual convertibility of these forms of energy had been demonstrated. In 1831, Faraday had done extensive work on fields of electomagnetic force, and Maxwell's mathematization of Faraday's keen intuitions was published in 1856. These "phenomena which appeared to involve action at a distance, such as gravitational attractions and electrical and magnetic attractions and repulsions, must, if everything had a mechanical explanation, be regarded as actions through a medium connecting the bodies concerned . . . this could be no other than the luminiferous ether" (Singer, 1959, p. 428). Accordingly, the resulting mechanical conceptions of the ether had an extraordinary complexity, which by the end of the century was approaching that of the cycles and epicycles needed by the Ptolemaic theory to account for the movements of the planets before the Copernican revolution.

But the time did not become ripe for Einstein's new synthesis until after

1900; we are still back in the middle of the preceding century, when Helmholtz was confidently writing:[6]

> We discover the problem of physical material science to be to refer natural phenomena back to unchangeable attractive and repulsive forces whose intensity depends wholly upon distance. The solubility of this problem is the condition of the complete comprehensibility of nature. (Quoted in Einstein & Infeld, 1938, p. 58)

Despite this mechanistic imperialism, there were still undaunted vitalists. The purposiveness of organisms was the key to their belief that living organisms were different in kind from anything nonliving. A well-known botanist of the next generation, Reinke [1849–1931], put it thus:

> Every biological process is determined by preceding events: this is causality. But such processes can also be determined by later conditions inasmuch as the preceding ones are indispensable preliminary stages for them; this is finalism.— While causal necessity characterizes all natural sciences alike, finalism prevails exclusively in the field of biology.—In the case of teleological phenomena, the essential conditions lie not in the past but in the future. (Quoted in Schlick, 1953, p. 530)

Darwin's theory of natural selection, the other great scientific event of the century, was like the theory of energy a major contribution to the ideal of a completely mechanical world. Heraclitean concepts of flux in the organic world were central to nature-philosophy, as we have seen, and to Lamarck (Loevinger, 1963). With Darwin, it became possible to explain the origin of species and their transformations without any guiding divine purpose, Platonic ideas, or life-force "striving for perfection." Random inherited variations, the struggle for existence, and the resulting survival of the fittest could account for it all. Therefore, among Darwin's stubbornest opponents were the last of the nature-philosophers, Owen, Agassiz, and von Baer. And yet Darwin unintentionally contributed to the survival of teleology! Perhaps it was too much in the air; anyway, he did not succeed in getting it out of his masterpiece, *The origin of species by means of natural selection, or the preservation of favored races in the struggle for life.* As the title itself shows, he treated "natural selection as though it were an active and directive agent" (Singer, 1959, p. 510). Thus, though he repudiated teleology, he constantly reverted to teleological metaphors, and surely many of his readers took his work as a confirmation of the earlier, purposive view of evolution.

"The teaching of Darwin," Singer (p. 395) notes, "gave the effective stimulus" to comparative anatomy. "The alliance of comparative studies with evolutionary doctrine focused attention on structure as distinct from func-

---

[6] Compare the parallel statement by du Bois-Reymond: "We can imagine the knowledge of nature arrived at a point where the universal process of the world might be represented by a single mathematical formula, by one immense system of simultaneous differential equations from which could be deduced, for each moment, the position, direction, and velocity of every atom of the world" (du Bois-Reymond, 1892). Einstein and Infeld comment on the quotation from Helmholtz: "This view appears dull and naive to a twentieth-century physicist. It would frighten him to think that the great adventure of research could be so soon finished, and an unexciting if infallible picture of the universe established for all time" (Einstein & Infeld, 1938, p. 58).

tion. Comparative anatomy in its turn became largely a study of developmental stages, and embryology became the comparative study *par excellence*." These closely related developmental disciplines became the last strongholds of vitalists like von Baer (who around 1830 first compared slits that appear on the chick embryo to a fish's gill-slits) and Driesch [1867–1941], the last major spokesman for vitalism within science. But in the 1890's, vitalism had many highly capable proponents. For example, E. B. Wilson (1897): "The study of the cell has, on the whole, seemed to widen rather than to narrow the enormous gap that separates even the lowest forms of life from the inorganic world" (p. 330, quoted by Bergson). And "One of the most notable naturalists of our time has insisted on the opposition of two orders of phenomena observed in living tissues, anagenesis and katagenesis. The role of the anagenic energies is to raise the inferior energies to their own level by assimilating inorganic substances. . . . It is only with . . . facts of katagenetic order that physico-chemistry deals—that is, in short, with the dead and not with the living" (Bergson, 1911, p. 35).[7]

The "Project"

This has been a long pre-Freudian introduction for a paper that purports to deal with an important psychoanalytic concept. In it, however, I hope to have demonstrated (1) that the issue of vitalism vs. mechanism was a major focus of controversy in the development of science, which entailed many kinds of differences in approach to and use of concepts; (2) that Freud's teachers and many of his intellectual heroes (e.g., Goethe, Helmholtz, Fechner) were and had been deeply involved in this controversy, so that he must have been thoroughly exposed to both sides of it; (3) that vitalism was an active and respectable doctrine throughout the years when Freud was getting his education and forming his basic theoretical ideas—i.e., up to the turn of the century; and (4) that the only recently differentiated concepts of force and energy were so important to the mechanistic world-view that to use them was almost the hallmark of science. Let us look next at some of the evidences of direct impact of these issues on Freud's work.

We know from the brilliant researches of Bernfeld (1944, 1951) that the medical school Freud attended and the Physiological Institute of Brücke where he obtained his scientific training were centers of a mechanistic biology that had successfully revolted against vitalism with its mystical and nature-philosophical taint. Bernfeld has also shown that Freud came to medicine because of an attraction to Naturphilosophie, especially as espoused by Goethe, and that he did his apprenticeship working on comparative anatomy with an evolutionary aim and at times using embryological techniques, which exposed him further to vitalism as the ever-waiting alternative against whose siren songs Brücke, as one of the adherents of the famous oath, must have warned him. In another paper (Holt, 1963) I have tried to trace some of the ramifications in Freud's thought of an antithetical set of ideas that partly

[7] Bergson is referring to E. D. Cope, a well-known American paleontologist and evolutionist (cf. Cope, 1896).
The parallel between Cope's concepts and Freud's life and death instincts (Freud, 1920) is particularly striking.

overlap vitalism and mechanism: nature-philosophy and physicalistic physiology. Let me add here that he became an ardent convert to the latter discipline and worked within the framework of such ideas until the late 1890s, afterwards gradually swinging back in the direction of the speculative, philosophical leanings of his youth.

The high point of Freud's commitment to mechanism is the Project of 1895, written under the influence of Fliess, another disciple of that Helmholtz whom Freud once described as "one of my idols." Yet even here, there are occasional passages in which Freud faltered a bit in his aim to explain normal and abnormal thought and behavior in a strictly mechanistic way. He had taken over from his teachers the assumption that the nervous system had no energies of its own, but was simply a conductor of some kind of physical energy, the exact nature of which was unknown, entering it either from the external world or from endosomatic sources such as the distended seminal vesicles (Freud, 1895a). I owe this fundamentally important point to the historical researches of Amacher (1965), who has read and summarized the major works of Freud's teachers, Brücke, Meynert, and Exner, and has showed that many concepts we think of as Freud's or Breuer's were actually common property of contemporary neurology and physiology. It is almost a necessary consequence of the attempt to apply thermodynamics to man, to assume that the nervous system is passive, with the fundamental function of getting rid of the energies that feed into it. (For further discussion of the theoretical ramifications of Freud's adoption of his teacher's views about the structure and functioning of the nervous system, see Holt, 1965a.)

In the Project (Freud, 1895b), Freud assumed that the nervous impulse is *mechanical* in nature: it is the motion of material particles, the same *kind* of energy that exists in the environment.[8] If it was hard to see how particles in such a limp and soggy thing as a nerve fiber could vibrate, it was equally difficult to conceive that the neural impulse was electrical in nature: Müller himself had shown experimentally, or so it seemed, that the nerve does not conduct electricity. We know today that he was right, in a way: nervous tissue *is* a poor conductor, too poorly insulated to be a passive channel for electrical energy. Instead, the nerve impulse is generated anew everywhere along the fiber, which transmits electricity only in the sense that a train of gunpowder transmits heat—by propagating a train of energy transformations.

At several places in the Project (e.g., Freud, 1895b, p. 417), Freud complains of an inability to give a "mechanical (automatic) explanation," indicating that his goal was a mechanical model like an automaton which would not require the postulation of any psychic concepts (such as attention) except as *results* of its operation. Thus, he had described the process of primary defense as one in which the partial release of unpleasure resulting from the cathecting of a traumatic memory would serve as a signal, attracting the ego's attention so that it would institute a lateral cathexis and divert the current in

[8] Hartley, in 1749, seems to have been the first to apply Newton's laws of motion to such a hypothesis about vibrations and "vibratiuncles" of particles in the nerves; but he was not the only believer in this doctrine in the intervening century and a half (Boring, 1929). Note that Freud did not assert that the neural impulse was *not* electrical; indeed, it was part of the mechanist world-view that the electric current—like any other form of energy—was basically a kind of motion of particles.

question from the neurones embodying the memory, thus preventing the full release of unpleasure. Yet a few pages later, he indicates that this explanation, with its assumption of a homuncular ego capable of attending and acting, was not what he was after: "The question of how we are to give a mechanical explanation of primary defence . . . is, I must confess, one to which I can offer no answer" (p. 428). His attempts to cope with the problem of consciousness via the nonphysio-chemical concept of *quality* involve a similar uncomfortable regress, and an apparent necessity to leave the realm of science: "our consciousness furnishes only *qualities* whereas science recognizes *quantities*" (p. 370). It was in this context that he gave his first definition of reality: "Where do qualities originate? Not in the external world; for out there (according to the views of natural science, to which, in this discussion, psychology too must submit) there are only masses in motion and nothing else" (p. 369).[9] Ideally, then, quality should have been explained away or at least not used as a causal variable; yet despite a couple of efforts to show it redundant, he was unable to proceed without giving quality a central explanatory role.

In these important respects, the Project failed in its central aim: "to furnish us with a psychology which shall be a natural science . . . [by representing] psychical processes as quantitatively determined states of specifiable material particles" (p. 355). Note well that, accordingly, the only energies considered in it were physical ones, *not* psychic energy.

TURNING TOWARD PSYCHOLOGY

The usual account is that after recognizing the failure of the Project, Freud rejected the mechanistic doctrine of physicalistic physiology, turned resolutely to a pure psychology, and created an abstract, hypothetical psychic apparatus in place of the nervous system, in which the operative quantity was psychic, not physical energy. "Pure psychologies" are quite familiar to us, of course; in Freud's day, the vast majority of academic psychologies (whether predominantly philosophical or physiological) were of that sort: theories that focus on a narrow range of largely cognitive problems, such as sensation and perception, thinking, learning and memory. Such pure psychologies need to bring in *some* treatment of motivation and action, in which context they sometimes invoke hypothetical forces or energies. For example, the tension of quasineeds in Lewin's topological and vector psychology is a concept of energy in a model that is explicitly abstract and psychic, and says nothing about the body. But the price of such purity is poverty; these theories, for all their clarity and internal consistency, are of no value outside a severely limited range of problems dealing with matters in the "conflict-free ego sphere" and in carefully controlled laboratory situations.

Academic pure psychologies have avoided a commitment to dualistic interactionism, and have been able to maintain that their dynamic concepts

---

[9] Compare Democritus on quality, almost twenty-three centuries earlier: "By convention sweet is sweet, by convention bitter is bitter, by convention hot is hot, by convention cold is cold, by convention color is color. But in reality there are atoms and the void. That is, the objects of sense are supposed to be real and it is customary to regard them as such, but in truth they are not. Only the atoms and the void are real." (Quoted by Einstein & Infeld, 1938, p. 56.) See also footnote 4.

were "abstract" and not to be taken as having any reference to physically measurable forces, by neglecting a detailed consideration of the powerful emotions and drives of real life, especially as seen in psychopathology. True, Skinnerians may use schizophrenics as convenient laboratory animals for operant conditioning, but they have yet to try to conceptualize psychosomatic problems! For just these reasons, pure psychologies have been worthless to the clinician, who must remain true to his commitment to the physicochemical structure we call the body. Such fidelity is particularly necessary for psychoanalysis, if it is to develop in the way Freud always wanted it to: as a theory of the whole organism.

Obviously, Freud did *not* create a pure psychology in this sense. What he did was in the spirit of the physicalistic oath, whether deliberately or not: he made a temporary retreat from the attempt to talk about the nervous system, creating instead the convenient fiction of a psychic apparatus that was modeled on the brain as he understood it and was intended eventually to be reunited with anatomy and physiology; meanwhile, it could proceed with greater freedom:

Our psychical topography has *for the present* nothing to do with anatomy; it has reference not to anatomical localities, but to regions in the mental apparatus, wherever they may be situated in the body.

In this respect, then, our work is untrammelled and may proceed according to its own requirements. (Freud, 1915b, p. 175; emphasis Freud's)

The year before, he had written:

We must recollect that all our provisional ideas in psychology will presumably some day be based on an organic substructure. (Freud, 1914, p. 78)

And at the end, in the *Outline of psychoanalysis*, he made a number of similar statements; for example:

The phenomena we have to deal with [in psychoanalysis] do not belong only to psychology; they have also an organic and biological aspect. (Freud, 1940, pp. 103 f.)

It is easy to get the impression that Freud gave up neurologizing and turned to pure psychology because, with characteristic overstatement, he said as much. Many writers (including Rapaport, 1959) have been more impressed with Freud's announcement that "I shall remain upon psychological ground" (Freud, 1900, p. 536) than with his many slips in the same work back into neurological terminology. The change may have had the important effect of making Freud *feel* free and thus of releasing his creativity, but he did not in fact abandon a single one of the major errors of assumption that his medical and neurological training had built into his thinking, despite his effort to give up reference to the brain (Holt, 1965a). Indeed, this change had the paradoxical effect of *preserving* these assumptions by hiding their original nature, and by transferring the operations of the apparatus into a conceptual realm where they were insulated from correction by progress in neurophysiology and brain anatomy. Thus, the strategy that seemed to succeed in freeing him from the dead hand of Meynert and Brücke actually guaranteed the continued commitment of psychoanalytic theory to a set of postulates that became more anachronistic with every advance in Freud's original but abandoned discipline. But through his years of theory construc tion, whenever it was necessary to consider somatic events such as conversion symptoms, Freud unhesitatingly spoke as if cathectic energy was *not* psychic but physical-neural. It is to his everlasting credit, and to the huge benefit of psychoanalysis, that whenever the facts demanded it, even grubby facts in volving the connection of the abstract mind with a heavy, smelly, affect-shaken, unruly body, Freud reverted to a psychosomatic view of the organism as a whole. If he had been consistent, if he had insisted on a pure psychology in which there *could* have been a consistent concept of psychic energy, psychoanalysis would have lost its principal claim to scientific interest: that it alone really takes into account all the facts about human beings, their secret desires, their somatic aches and lusts, the pervasively psychosomatic nature of behavior and thought.

Despite this historical justification, it is a valid criticism of the psychoanalytic energy concept that it fluctuates, depending on the context, at one point being a survival of Freud's original concept of a physical cathectic quantity traversing the fibers of a somatic nervous system, and then being a purely psychological, nonphysicochemical concept. In this inconsistency, it reflects Freud's inability to reach a satisfactory position in relation to the mind-body problem: for the most part, as Rubinstein (1965) has shown, he held to interactionism, which today is generally considered fallacious.

Interactionism is the prevailing conception of the common-sense psychology that talks about willpower as "mind over matter." It assumes causal chains such as this: a physical event (e.g., a pattern of light) causes another physical event (a neural current from retina to brain), which then causes a psychological event (visual perception), that in turn causes a further psychological event (an intention to act), which causes a physical event (movement of the body). Sounds reasonable enough doesn't it? Reflect, however, that if one were to follow this chain of events on the purely physical-physiological level, there would have to be puzzling and inexplicable lacunae. At the point where the ontological gap was jumped, and physical energy was transformed into psychic energy as Freud assumed (1895a, p. 108), there would be a deficit, and at the corresponding point when the psychic was transformed into the physical there would be a surplus. Presumably these two would cancel one another out, and thus might be hard to detect, though not when there is extensive "delay of discharge." But the fact is that no hint of any such gap in the application of the first law of thermodynamics has ever appeared, no matter how the precision of measurement has been refined; the physical causal sequences flow without a ripple and with complete conservation of physical energy.[10] If you ask why psychoanalysts are not troubled by

[10] As Lashley put it: "Neural activity has been sufficiently well explored to rule out such broad assumptions as of the energy of the libido or of the id. Summation, potentiation, irradiation, and inhibition are fairly well, though not completely, understood. The energy of the nervous system is that of transmitted excitations, with its implied limitations and specificities. Energy dissociated from this, as postulated by field theories, is ruled out by definite experimental evidence. In particular, the derivation of psychic energy from one or a few 'instincts' finds no support in the nature of neural activity. . . . Where instinctive activities have been analyzed experimentally, as in our studies of hunger, mating and

this glaring incompatibility with facts of their theory's dualistic stand on the mind-body problem, I can only answer that so far as I know, they are almost all of them totally unaware of it. Yet it is a necessary consequence of the doctrine of psychic energy.

To summarize so far: Freud began his scientific work under the influence of physicalistic physiology; the Project is clearly and explicitly an attempt to sketch out a "psychology for neurologists" in the mechanistic tradition. Recognizing its failure, he tried to work instead in psychological terms, retaining energy but using an abstract model without any explicit relation to the body and nervous system. He always insisted that it should eventually become a neurological model, however, and being from the beginning faced with psychosomatic problems he was confronted by a theoretical dilemma (though he does not seem to have realized it). A consistent theory employing psychic energy would have had to remain severely limited in scope, avoiding all issues that involve the body, or else it would have had to become explicitly dualistic and interactionistic. The first of these possibilities was and remains impossible for psychoanalysis; Freud flirted with interactionism, but did not espouse it definitively, and in fact did not adopt any one clear-cut and consistent stance on the mind-body problem (see Rubinstein, 1965).

Psychic Energy and Vital Force

When Freud turned away from mechanism, did he opt for vitalism? Before attempting an answer to that question, I shall discuss the parallels between psychic energy and the active principles postulated by vitalism. First, it will be necessary to review the major characteristics of vital force; in doing so, I shall make principal reference to the two vitalistic theorists who were most nearly Freud's contemporaries, the embryologist Driesch (1929) and the philosopher Bergson (1911).

1. Vitalistic theories are dualistic, and the vital principle is accordingly something ontologically quite unlike and even antithetical to the world of matter.

    The fundamental dualism Bergson sees between life and "inert matter" is evident throughout his work, but it is difficult to find a succinct avowal of metaphysical dualism. He makes many such statements as

    In reality, life is no more made of physico-chemical elements than a curve is composed of straight lines. (Bergson, p. 31)

    Absolute Reality has also a dualistic structure. There is a permanent struggle between wholeness and non-wholeness in Reality, a struggle between *form* and *matter*. . . . Life . . . is not a specialized arrangement of inorganic events: life is something apart; and biology is an independent science. (Driesch, p. 327, p. 105)

2. The vital principle is therefore not localized in space.

---

maternal behavior, there is nothing that suggests free or transferable energy . . . behavior can be explained without assumption of any energy other than the interaction of specific neural elements" (Lashley & Colby, 1957).

In reality, life is of the psychological order, and it is of the essence of the psychical to enfold a confused plurality of interpenetrating terms. . . . what is of psychical nature cannot entirely correspond with space. (Bergson, p. 257).

An agent which is of a non-spatial nature cannot be said to have a definite localization in space. Entelechy therefore cannot possess a "seat." (Driesch, p. 299)

3. The vital principle is like, and at times is described as, energy, but it is not physical energy.

Our philosophy represents the organized world as a harmonious whole. But . . . it admits of much discord, because each species, each individual even, retains only a certain impetus from the universal vital impulsion and tends to use *this energy* in its own interest. (Bergson, p. 50, my emphasis. Note the Lamarckian, nature-philosophical tone. This vital impulsion is the translation of Bergson's famous *élan vital.*)

Ostwald, and many others following him, have admitted that, in cases of morphogenesis, and probably in nervous phenomena too, some unkown potential forms of energy may be at work, and that the specificity of vital phenomena and their autonomy is due to the peculiarities which that unknown energy possesses. . . . In other words: that entelechy is *itself* a peculiar form of energy. . . . *But entelechy lacks all the characteristics of quantity:* . . . Thus I decline most decidedly any kind of "energetical" vitalism whatever. (Driesch, p. 256 f.)

Note, however, that in Driesch's view entelechy causes animal movements and has the dynamic if not the quantitative property of energy.
4. It is directional: it steers and organizes, impels towards goals.

An original impetus of life . . . is the fundamental cause of variations . . . that accumulate and create new species. The force which is evolving throughout the organized world . . . is always seeking to transcend itself and always remains inadequate to the work it would fain produce (Bergson, p. 87, p. 126)

Why then occurs all that folding . . . and all the other [embryological] processes we have described? There must be something that drives them out, so to say. We have shown that there is at work a something in life phenomena "which bears the end in itself," the entelechy. (Driesch, p. 32, p. 106)

5. It is treated anthropomorphically: it has powers of decision, *does* things.

The profound cause [of evolution] is the impulse which thrust life into the world, which made it divide into vegetables and animals, which shunted the animal on to suppleness of form, and which . . . secured that . . . it should rouse itself up and move forward. (Bergson, p. 132)

There was a natural factor at work, *autonomous* and *not* resulting from a combination of other agents, but elemental in itself; this factor, then, may be called a factor of dynamical teleology—on analogy. There is something teleological *within* its acting. If . . . we allow ourselves still a little more of it [analogy], we may say that it is *as if* our entelechy is endowed with *knowing* and *willing.* Super-entelechy, bound into matter, *wants to know* what it has done . . . suffering from its own products. (Driesch, p. 244, p. 328)

6. It is closely related to the psychic.

Life, that is to say, consciousness launched into matter. . . . (Bergson, p. 181) [See also quotation above under point No. 2.]

The "acting something" . . . which *directs* the body [he calls] the psychoid. . . . It is only to men, according to Aristotle, that the highest soul . . . is given, that is, the faculty of reasoning, corresponding to what we have called the "psychoid" as regulating action. (Driesch, pp. 221–222)

Later (e.g., p. 229), he uses "our psychoid or Entelechy" interchangeably.
7. What the life-force operates in, however, is depicted as a mechanism.

That life is a kind of mechanism I cordially agree. (Bergson, p. 31)

Every part of these organic systems has been placed by entelechy where it must be placed to act well in the service of the whole, but the part itself acts like a part of a machine. (Driesch, p. 248)

Freud's doctrine of psychic energy shows striking similarity to vitalism on each of these particulars. First, it is generally a dualistic doctrine, as Rubinstein (1965) has pointed out in detail and as I have just reviewed. Second to the extent that Freud says that his model is *not* a physiological-anatomical one, he removes the possibility that psychic energy operates in space, as in Chapter VII when he says: "Strictly speaking, there is no need for the hypothesis that the psychical systems are actually arranged in a spatial order. It would be sufficient if a fixed order were established by the fact that in a given psychical process the excitation passes through the systems in a particular temporal sequence" (Freud, 1900, p. 537). The result must either be a metaphysical mentalism or a nonexistential interpretation of psychic energy (Rubinstein, 1967).[11] Third, the central concept of cathexis is repeatedly called an energy, analogous to but not identical with the energy of physics.

[11] Freud never explicitly said, so far as I know, that psychic energy does not operate in space. To be sure, the issue does not come up in a pure psychology any more than in mathematics: the theoretical terms are simply not interpreted existentially (as referring to anything real). Some of the time (e.g., 1900), Freud took this stance; and at others (e.g., 1915a), he wrote as if the nervous system were virtually identical with the psychic apparatus. Often, however, he either indicated that at some point in the body (physical) neural energy is converted into psychic energy (e.g., 1895a) or else he simply implied an interactionism. This last doctrine must imply an existential interpretation of psychic energy, but since there is no room in the head for a psychic apparatus in addition to the brain, the former must not exist in the same spatial world. Freud does not seem to have been as loath to make such an assumption as his early radical materialism and many explicit rejections of mysticism and the supernatural would imply. Perhaps one reason Freud did not explicitly embrace vitalism was the fact that its adherents so often have been religious mystics. Yet he did believe in telepathy and other "psychical phenomena." Just as vitalism opens the door to such concepts as ESP—Driesch was once president of the Society for Psychical Research in England—so too does a teleological, nonspatial, anthropomorphic psychic energy: if a mentalistic entity can affect the body operating from outside of three-dimensional physical space, why cannot the psychic energy from one person directly affect the mind and behavior of another without being disadvantaged in any way by the intervening gap in physical space? None of these implications proves that there is anything intrinsically invalid about psychic energy, and in the minds of some they may constitute arguments for it; my intention is not to try to induce any theoretical "guilt by association" either, but simply to note that scientists usually choose not to use concepts having these properties once they are pointed out. As long as the facts do not positively require the assumption of real but nonspatial entities, it is more parsimonious to try to get along with the realities we are accustomed to.

Fourth, it is directional in the same way as vitalistic forces are: it exists in sexual and aggressive forms, qualitative differences which amount to the assumption that the energy bears a certain kind of end in itself—destructive, or one of uniting and binding all things together. Moreover, each of these is further subdivisible into energies of varying degrees of neutralization, a concept which in turn hinges on the immanent direction or goal, whether the energy is directed towards some form of crude and immediate gratification, or is "*aim*-inhibited," directed towards socially acceptable and neutral ends. Libido in particular is often differentiated into specific kinds according to the object it is directed towards: the self (narcissistic), persons of the same sex (homosexual), or normal and appropriate partners of opposite sex (when it is usually just called object-libido). Thus, psychic energy is a teleological concept. It might appear that these are all shorthand expressions and that it is actually assumed that the energy itself does not contain its goal; David Rapaport (1959) maintained as much. Yet one examines in vain the texts of Freud and also those of most of his followers as well for any explicit statement that the direction is given by structures or by some informational concept; the assumption clearly is that each form of energy itself is intrinsically directional, and the particular direction can be gotten out of it only with difficulty, as by neutralization (cf. Rubinstein, 1965).[12]

Fifth, it should hardly need demonstration that the standard procedure in psychoanalysis has been to follow Freud's habit of speaking about psychic energy anthropomorphically. It "struggles," "presses for discharge," is "ever on the alert for opportunities," and so on and on. I hope that the dangers and fallacies of this practice are self-evident. The sixth point I quoted about vitalism was that its proponents frequently tended to equate the essence of life with that of the mind, so that the living-nonliving dualism was asssimilated to that of mind vs. matter, and the life energy was also a psychic energy. This constitutes a bridge to psychic energy rather than a point of possible similarity.

Finally, Freud's theory is surely like the recent vitalists' in that it postulates a mechanistic structure within which the energy operates. Most of the time he called it the "psychic apparatus"; as I have demonstrated elsewhere (Holt, 1965a), it remained a passive, reflex model that required an input of a disturbing energy to make it work. Without the cybernetic features of the Project, it had to rely for its control on an ego interpreted as a homunculus. In this sense, it was at best the same kind of mixed model as the combined mechanistic vitalistic systems of such neovitalists as Reinke, Pflueger, and Driesch. "Driesch called himself, not without justice, a 'consistent mechanist' because his theory presupposes a machine model of the organism and an extreme preformationist view, in which the entelechy 'is the engineer who sets this machine in motion'" (Mainx, 1955).

The above demonstration amounts to nothing more than circumstantial

---

[12] As we have seen above, the concept of energy antedated the word, and for quite awhile even the physicists were not consistent in distinguishing sharply between force (which is directional) and energy (which is not). Freud's teachers did not clearly differentiate these terms, therefore, and there can be little wonder that he often lost sight of the necessary nondirectionality of energy. There can be no excuse for us today, however, if we perpetuate this error.

evidence for the proposition that Freud was probably influenced by the vitalistic concepts that were then widely used and defended by reputable scientists, when he came to frame his own concept of cathexis, the "excitation" that operated his psychic apparatus. He did not directly discuss the matter; I have not found any reference to vitalism nor to any well-known vitalist in anything of his I have read; nor do the authors he refers to in the volumes of the Standard Edition available to date include any vitalists (if one leaves out of consideration such nature-philosophers as Lamarck, Goethe, and Fechner). Doubtless he would have rejected any attempt to identify cathectic energy with *élan vital* or entelechy. It is therefore not my intention to maintain that he knowingly turned from mechanism to vitalism. I do submit, however, that psychic energy is a vitalistic concept in the sense of being similar to and influenced by vital force, and being to a large extent functionally equivalent to it. They are at the least historically and methodologically homologous, buds from the same branch.

Critique of Vitalism

My intention so far has been to write within the tradition of the history of science rather than that of its philosophy: not so much to argue against the concept of psychic energy as to contribute to an understanding of how Freud came to use it and of the connotations it had in the scientific world of half to three-quarters of a century ago. But let us now turn to methodological critique, and examine the various properties of psychic energy in relation to its utility for a scientific discipline.

The facts that vitalism has been effectively refuted and that its adherents are a vanishing breed do not constitute an effective or sufficient argument against psychic energy. Biology and psychology are separate disciplines, and what is fallacious for one *may* not be for the other. Nevertheless, my impression is that doctrines resembling vitalism as much as Freud's have been advanced by a number of prominent figures in psychology in recent years. McDougall, who violently rejected psychoanalysis as a whole, nevertheless had his own properly named dynamic (or hormic—that is, purposive) psychology, an instinct theory complete with a doctrine of energies. On the mind-body problem he was an avowed interactionist; like many vitalists, he was a believer in the spontaneity of life, in human free will, and in Lamarckian inheritance of acquired characteristics; and by making purpose the central fact of behavior he links up with a major theme of vitalism. But he is dead and without heirs. Very much alive and still influential, however, is the author of the following words: "Whether one calls it a growth tendency, a drive toward self-actualization, or a forward-moving *directional* tendency, it is the mainspring of life. . . . It is the urge which is evident in *all organic and human life*—to expand, extend, become autonomous, develop, mature—the tendency to express and activate all the capacities of the organism. . . . [emphasis added]" The author is Carl Rogers (1961, p. 35); similar words are being written by a good many other contemporary psychotherapists who have been influenced by existentialism.

Let us take a brief look at the major objections to vitalism, and see to what extent they may be applicable to corresponding aspects of psychic energy. First, a few telling points against vitalists are clearly specific to them. Schneirla, for example, points out how the vitalists, in arguing for a monolithic explanatory life-force, obscure "the fact that somewhat similar effectiveness in adaptive behavior may exist on rather different biological and psychological levels of organization. . . . Although orthodox teleologists generously endow all animals with . . . [the capacity to project themselves] into an organized sequence of specialized adjustments of representational character dominated by the expected development of a given outcome—a 'goal' . . . its presence has been demonstrated adequately only in the mammals" (Schneirla, 1949, p. 281, p. 275). Likewise, he demonstrates the weakness of the attempt made by many vitalists to prove their theory through eliminating mechanistic alternatives; the trouble, of course, is that it is impossible to eliminate the possibility that someone will develop an adequate theory that is neither mechanistic nor vitalistic.

Another favorite, but dangerous form of argument on which vitalists rely is analogy. As Schneirla notes, "A common feature of Vitalism . . . and other procedures featuring the use of analogy is that the organization of processes underlying behavioral systems is not subjected to very close study" (Schneirla, 1949, p. 250). This becomes part of a larger point that, with a few notable exceptions like Driesch in his early years, vitalists have not been led by their theory into fruitful experimentation or new types of observation; their methods of seeking truth have been sterile. "If vitalistic precepts were generally followed, scientific procedure in studying animal capacities would be reduced to a mere general description of events under the label presumed to apply" (Schneirla, 1949, p. 249).

Hempel and Oppenheim (quoted by Nagel, 1953) make a similar point even more forcefully: all statements about entelechy are inaccessible to empirical test, because there is no provision for any means of testing assertions about it. For similar reason, Frank (1955, p. 434) called the concept of vital energy "useless" since "we have no 'practical' operation to define the energy of life."

This is a serious charge, even if one adopts the generally permissive and moderate versions of operationism that philosophers of science advocate today (e.g., Kaplan, 1964, pp. 36 ff). Not all terms—particularly theoretical terms, which get their meaning from the network of propositions in which they are embedded—need have operational definitions; but ultimately, "it must be possible to deduce determinate consequences from the assumptions of the theory," and "at least some theoretical notions must be tied down to fairly definite and unambiguously specified observable material" (Nagel, 1960, p. 40). But not only does the dualism of vitalism doom its central concept to unmeasurability, "it has no explanatory import, because it does not function in a set of general laws" (Hempel & Oppenheim, quoted by Nagel, 1953).

And how is it with psychic energy—is it vulnerable to the same charges? They have surely been leveled against it. In the NYU symposium on psychoanalysis and philosophy of science, Nagel said that he had no objection to metaphor as such, but "in Freudian theory metaphors are employed without even half-way definite rules for expanding them, and that in consequence admitted metaphors such as 'energy' or 'level of excitation' have no specific

content and can be filled in to suit one's fancy" (Nagel, 1960, p. 41). Moreover, the theory lacks the tightness of structure that would give its theoretical
terms what Kaplan (1964) calls "systemic meaning." For, to quote Nagel
again, it is "formulated in such a manner that it can always be construed and
manipulated so as to explain whatever the actual facts are." Twenty years ago,
Kubie (1947) attacked psychic energy as an unmeasurable, metaphysical
concept. Psychic energy has been criticized by Kardiner, Karush, and Ovesey
(1959) and by Rubinstein (1967) as tautologous: the only data by means of
which it can be assessed are the very ones it is invoked to explain.

I believe that Professor Nagel is unduly harsh in his strictures, and that
the picture is not so wholly black. The doctrine of psychic energy has not
been quite as sterile as he implies; a number of experimenters (e.g. Silverman,
in press) have obtained researchable ideas from it, and shortly before his
death David Rapaport had started on a broad program of laboratory research
explicitly devoted to measuring psychic energy, which has given rise to a fair
amount of published research (e.g., Schwartz & Rouse, 1961). Preceding on
quite a different, more clinical tack, Ostow (1962) has launched himself on
a program of drug research in which psychic energy is a central variable. So
long as there is investigative mileage in a concept, it has some claim to scientific usefulness. But the same thing was once true of phlogiston, caloric, and
the other "imponderables" of physics, which does not blind us to the fact that
in the end they proved empty and useless.

Despite their otherwise considerable differences of approach, the attempts
of both Rapaport and Ostow (and their coworkers) to measure psychic
energy have in common a noteworthy indirectness. Libido or hypercathexis
can only be rated or estimated from behavioral signs that are coordinated to
psychic energy by fiat, and the nomological net in which the theoretical
statements using such energy are woven is far too loose-meshed to permit a
crucial test of basic assumptions like a conservation law. I find it difficult to
believe that psychic energy and related concepts play an essential role in the
generation of empirical studies in either of these programs. Rather, they
appear to serve as a language in which to discuss cases and experiments, much
as K. Lewin's topological-vector theory served him in relation to his investigative work. Though Lewin was as fertile a source of experimental ideas as
any psychologist of his time, the theory lost its vogue quickly after his death
because it seemed intrinsically not well suited to generating new questions to
put to nature. The same fate can be predicted for the economic theory of
psychoanalysis, however long it may linger in the less exacting atmosphere of
the clinic.

To return to vitalism: it is generally conceded that the strongest argument
for it is the adaptiveness of organisms with its strong implication of purpose.
The apparent goal of many metabolic and adaptive processes, writes Schlick
(1953, p. 527), "is the preservation and development . . . both of the individual and of the species . . . reference to the teleology of organic life constituted throughout the ages the strongest argument in favor of the autonomy
of organic life." The facts of purposiveness are undeniable in biology as well
as in psychoanalysis; what is questionable is whether they require the
assumption of some finalistic, teleological concept of purpose, or whether
they can be explained by means of the causal concepts of natural science.

"Modern science . . . regards final causes to be vestal virgins which bear no fruit in the study of physical and chemical phenomena" (Nagel, 1953, p. 540). A final cause is the answer to the question *why*; it is the kind of ultimate explanation that essentialism fosters.[13] By contrast, the way of a modern scientist is to ask *how*, to describe what happens as precisely as possible, and to determine its contingency on as many conditions as he can. Newton accounted for the movements of physical objects by his interlocking, mathematical yet operational laws of motion; interestingly, he was still enough a child of his time that he did not feel satisfied by his own explanation of planetary movement, but turned to religious and metaphysical speculation about supernatural spirits, in search of the "real causes" of motion (Koryé, 1956, p. 21).

Nagel's most impressive refutation of teleology is his detailed demonstration that it is possible to construct causal, nonteleological explanations such that "the former can be replaced by the latter without loss in asserted content" (Nagel, 1953, p. 541). He shows that "The structure or character of so-called 'teleological' systems is . . . expressed by the . . . conditions for a directively organized system; and [that] these conditions can be stated . . . in a manner not requiring the adoption of teleology as a fundamental or unanalyzable category" (*ibid.*, p. 549). And without the use of any energy concept, it should be added; direction is a matter of structure and information, not force. (See also Nagel, 1961.)

Such analysis of goal-directed behavior into nonteleological elements has enabled physicists to build servomechanisms, using negative feedback, which are to an increasing extent self-regulating, self-maintaining, and goal-directed. A few cyberneticists have been tempted to attribute purpose to such machines, but even if one wants to do so, it is not as an explanatory concept and it has no metaphysical dualistic implications.

Thus, the last stronghold of vitalism has fallen. But note well that the death of vitalism has not been a victory of mechanism; that is just as dead a duck. Indeed, in the end mechanism and vitalism turn out to have had a good deal in common—a common heritage of Greek philosophy, of silent and fallacious assumptions about causality. In the realm of animal behavior, Schneirla writes, mechanism and vitalism alike went astray, "the former by endeavoring to fit all adaptive capacities directly under physico-chemical rubrics, the latter by setting out to bring all cases under a universal supernatural causal principle" (Schneirla, 1949, p. 244). As Mainx has written: "Regarded from the empiricist standpoint, the mechanistic and vitalistic systems [of theoretical biology] show a fundamental affinity, while the contrasts between them seem to lie more in the formulation. Common to both systems, in the first place, is the view of causality in the sense of an executive causality, while in the empirical science of the present day the causal connection is usually conceived only in the sense of a consecutive causality. Both systems seek for an 'explanation' of the organic event by reducing it to a 'principle' or 'category' which is 'at work' in it, which 'causes' it" (Mainx,

---

[13] One could hardly find a clearer example of Platonic essentialism than the following statement by Driesch (1929, p. 6): "It is the final object of all biology to tell us what it ultimately means to say that a body is 'living,' and in what sorts of relation body and life stand one to the other."

1955). In psychoanalysis, this type of explanation takes the form of the pleasure principle and reality principle, and the executive ego, superego, and id, as well as an energy that is defined as being directed.

"A further common feature of mechanistic and vitalistic systems," Mainx continues, "is the tautological character of their general statements. . . . In the statements in which the concept of entelechy . . . occurs these concepts are, for the most part, defined only by their connection with the processes which they are to cause. In this way such statements escape empirical testing either by experiment or by observation. It is for this reason that the formulations of mechanism and vitalism [in biology] have been discussed for many decades on the purely speculative plane, without the great progress meanwhile reached in research having permitted a decision in this controversy" (Mainx, 1955, pp. 628–629).

In physics, mechanism died near the turn of the present century. Field theory, the special and general theories of relativity, quantum theory, and related developments destroyed any hope that all science could be unified around Newtonian dynamics. Today, laymen like ourselves find it difficult to grasp the nonintuitive picture of reality implied in the physics of elementary particles, which have properties both of energy and of matter in the old sense, a physics that postulates antimatter as well as matter, time that is conceived in certain laws as flowing in either direction, not one fundamental force of attraction and repulsion but at least four and possibly five basic and apparently irreducible types of physical force. It is surely easy to long for the comfortable and intelligible world of mechanism, and the mysteriousness and disembodied quality of some physical concepts tempt some nonphysicists (e.g., Teilhard de Chardin, 1959) to revive mystical concepts like the "life-principle," which seems no more intangible than a field of force.

But there is a major, critical difference. However esoteric the new physical terms, they are given precise mathematical formulation; they are embedded in a tight system of laws; they generate testable consequences, and lead directly to research and new empirical discoveries. There may be a Heraclitean cast to a world-view in which the elemental starting points are fields and processes in them rather than substantial, Democritean atoms, but the resemblance is quite superficial. From Heraclitus to Koffka, the emphasis on process and Gestalt was opposed to analysis, empirical or mathematical. We have learned, however, that structure *is* analyzable, that one can be precise about the impalpable, and that mathematics does not destroy.

Some of the most scientifically sophisticated among psychoanalysts are not satisfied with the argument to this point. They are perfectly willing to abandon the mystical implications, argument by analogy, reification, and anthropomorphism that have characterized the treatment of psychic energy in much of the psychoanalytic literature, and which are so reminiscent of vitalism. All of that may have been true in the past, they argue, but none of it is a necessary aspect of psychic energy, and we have given it up long ago. What is wrong with psychic energy interpreted nondirectionally and nonexistentially as an abstract, quantitative construct with qualities and direction contributed by structures? True, it is not directly measurable, but not every concept needs to be operational in any simple sense, and even in physics energy is only indirectly measurable. Such is the concept of psychic energy as used by Rapaport (1959) and by his students (e.g., Schwartz and Rouse, 1961).

In this version, the concept is of course more nearly acceptable. But let us consider first the issue of measurability. The only *directly* measurable concepts in physics are the basic dimensions of time, space and mass. A great many other concepts may be quite precisely and determinately measured by means of these three, however, because of the network of laws that define concepts and relationships among them. As Rapaport himself pointed out (1959), psychology lacks dimensional quantification; psychological measurement is possible, but there is as yet no known way of tightly and systematically relating the resulting quantities to one another or to higher-order constructs. As a result, there is no true analogy in the situations of the two sciences; the indirectness of measurement in physics has never raised the suspicion that energy is a tautologous concept. In psychoanalysis and psychology, however, the burden of proof is on anyone who defends psychic energy to show that it can be measured in a useful way, so that it is estimated independently of the very phenomena it is to explain.

And then it is not so easy to escape the necessity of accepting a rather extreme metaphysical position if you want to retain psychic energy. To be both consistent and comprehensive, you must adopt interactionism and postulate a break in the chain of physical causality, which will expose you to the constant temptation to avoid any theoretical embarrassment by escaping into the second world of metaphysical mentalism. This will make it increasingly difficult for the theory to be tested in any definitive way. Psychoanalysis is already much too invulnerable to the refutation of its theoretical statements—a purely illusory safety, since philosophers of science agree that the usefulness of a theory is a function of its capacity to generate testable consequences, which means to stick its neck out and suffer the possibility of becoming extinct. But a testable theory is the only true phoenix; for a better theory usually arises from the ashes of the one that expires.

What is needed in place of psychic energy is not simply a better concept, but an entirely new theoretical model. That is a less drastic and sweeping prescription than it may sound at first, since I am using the term "model" to refer only to basic assumptions about the nature of the behaving organism and how it operates. In psychoanalysis, such propositions are contained for the most part in metapsychology, on a level of theory that is considerably removed from clinical observation. What Rapaport (1959) called the clinical theory is the distillation of actual work with patients; it is known to and is used daily not only by every analyst but by most clinical psychologists, psychiatrists, and psychiatric social workers as well. This was Freud's most original and lasting contribution, and for the most part it will stand unaffected by changes in the basic model. As Freud recognized, "basic concepts . . . are not the foundation of science, upon which everything rests: that foundation is observation alone. They are not the bottom but the top of the whole structure, and they can be replaced and discarded without damaging it" (Freud, 1914, p. 77).

I cannot undertake here a critique of metapsychology as a whole; let me make only two points. To the extent that the dynamic and structural points of view involve existentially interpreted *psychic* forces and *psychic* structures, they are subject to the same criticism that has been made above with respect to psychic energy and the mind-body problem. Partly because of the necessary ambiguities and vaguenesses that therefore exist in the metapsychological model, it is at best (e.g., as stated by Rapaport, 1959; Rapaport & Gill, 1959) only a sketch and a program, not a developed and elaborated model which can thoroughly explain a complete behavioral process. And as I have tried to demonstrate elsewhere (Holt, 1965a), many of its basic assumptions were taken from currently accepted neurological and physiological doctrine during Freud's student days. Many of these assumptions have subsequently been proved erroneous, and need to be replaced.

Theories are not dragons to be dispatched by a single stroke of a methodological sword; they are much more like social systems, which can be overthrown only by being replaced by another, no matter how creaking and inadequate the old may be. It would be naive to expect psychoanalysts to drop all reference to psychic energy as soon as they understand the fallacies and basic untenability of the term. With the best will in the world, the working analyst still needs a conceptual system in terms of which to organize his data and his thoughts about them.[14] Even though I believe that the clinical theory could be rewritten without reference to energy, and still not lose its recognizable character and its explanatory power, the fact is that economic considerations have been written into it quite extensively. As long as a new and roadworthy model is not actually competing with it, the old one will have to serve, patched up as best it can be.

Toward an Alternative Model

It will be a major job, requiring many hands for many years, for a new model to become elaborated enough to compete successfully with the old. In the remainder of this paper, all I can do is to refer to some scientific developments of the years since Freud's death, which have made many of the assumptions in Freud's model anachronistic, and which suggest some of the features of the kind of alternative model that seems to me most likely to develop, transcending the old alternatives of vitalism and mechanism.

To begin with, thermodynamics has been generalized to take into account not only the closed systems Helmholtz usually assumed, but open systems— systems like living organisms, characterized not by equilibria but by steady states, a dynamic balance of inputs and outputs (Bertalanffy, 1950). An

---

[14] In the first draft of this paper, presented in a panel discussion on psychic energy (see Modell, 1963), I made statements to the effect that the concept had clinical usefulness, and I have been so quoted (Apfelbaum, 1965). I still believe that Freud may have been aided in a number of ways by his economic concepts, which probably helped him make certain types of observations, and I was impressed by the claim of a number of psychoanalytic clinicians that they found the concept useful in their work. On further reflection, however, I have become more fully aware of the numerous ways in which emphasis on economic considerations may be clinically deleterious: it fits certain kinds of facts better than others, so creates a bias to consider observations that fit as more basic, important or valid. In another paper (Holt, 1965a) I have cited a number of examples, and Apfelbaum (1965) contributes several others. It would be difficult to strike a balance and to say whether the economic point of view has been more helpful clinically or more misleading.

organism is an energy *user*; not a closed system within which a fixed quantity of energy reverberates, is conserved, and is stored in reservoirs. Of course, Freud always realized that there were inputs (principally from the instinctual drives) and outputs (which he called discharge); what he did not realize was that this state of affairs destroyed the assumption of a closed system, and that only within a closed system did his *economic* conceptions make sense.[15] The fundamental working assumption of the economic point of view is that there is a fixed quantity of libido, and so if one object or system is cathected, there are lawful and necessary consequences: it must be withdrawn from elsewhere. This is an elegant and appealing conception, with the one major flaw that its quantitative precision is illusory because cathectic energy cannot be measured. Since the work of Bertalanffy and his associates, however, we can see that it is also based on the untenable basic assumption of a closed system.

The thermodynamics of open systems has the great advantage that it can account for the otherwise paradoxical observation of negative entropy in living systems of which Bergson made so much: that they do in fact tend towards greater complexity rather than the simplicity that classical or closed system thermodynamics would necessitate.[16] But, since we can now conceptualize negative entropy along with positive in a precise mathematical way, the facts of creativity and growth do not necessitate any Bergsonian, mystical forces or energies of a nonphysical kind.

I have already referred to another recent great development in hard science of fundamental relevance to any consideration of energies in psychoanalysis: cybernetics, the theory of self-regulating systems (living or nonliving) which control themselves by use of informational feedback. It is fascinating to go back to the Project after reading Wiener (1948), for this 1895 work is an astonishingly sophisticated, virtually cybernetic model, containing no less than five feedback loops! By contrast, at the time of Freud's death the behavioristic model had only one such loop—as indeed any model based on an uncomplicated reflex arc must have, and that includes the topographic model. Yet Freud was too many decades ahead of his time to make full use of his own insights; and so he thought that he had to supplement his self-regulating device of defense by a deus ex machina, the ego—not this time an ego in the model's overt sense, as the total of cathected neurones, but in the old philosophical sense contemporaneously described by William James (1890) as

---

[15] As Amacher (in a personal communication) has pointed out, classical thermodynamics does not *necessarily* assume a closed system, so long as it is a completely determined one with known quantities of input and output. Likewise, Freud would not have needed to assume a closed system if he had been able to determine quantitatively the status of all the energies in the psychic apparatus at any moment. Since that is completely out of the question, the general principle of conservation—if energy is used for one purpose, less is available for another—which is the essence of the economic point of view, becomes usable only on the assumption of a closed system. Though it is true that Freud never explicitly stated that assumption, it is obviously implied in such concepts as a "pool" or "reservoir of libido" or the proposition that the total amount of cathexis is a fixed quantity.

[16] "All life, animal and vegetable, seems in its essence like an effort to accumulate energy and then to let it flow into flexible channels, changeable in shape, at the end of which it will accomplish infinitely varied kinds of work" (Bergson, 1911, p. 253 f.). He contrasts this to the world of inorganic nature, in which the second law of thermodynamics holds sway.

"the pure ego or self of selves," an ultimate prime mover and knower. Quite a voluntaristic and teleological concept for the man who made the fundamental contribution of exceptionless physic determinism! And also, an unnecessary one.[17] If he were alive, I am sure Freud would be delighted to know that there are now servomechanisms that regulate themselves via negative feedback loops and can even respond defensively to signals of danger, without requiring any homunculus or any hypercathectic energies of attention.

Today, we can measure the quantities of energy propagated through the nervous system; we can even measure the slight variations of potential in various parts of single nerve cells. Psychoanalysts are not much interested in such measurements, and no doubt properly so; for the kinds of motivational phenomena they have in mind when they talk about energies have little to do with these microvolt discharges. They observe people who have violent, importunate impulses; people who strive to attain their goals for long periods of time against tremendous odds and despite physical exhaustion; people who differ strikingly in the amount of pep, initiative, and zest they have, as against depression, lethargy, inertia, or fatigue. All of these observations seem to cry out for some kind of energy concept—not just the energy that is released by the metabolism of food, but some kind of directly experienced, *psychological*, energy.[18] So, too, does the fact that thinking is hard work; if you try to make that into a quantitative statement, however, you end up with the assumption that thinking must use a great deal of psychic energy—quite the contrary of what Freud postulated.

Is his psychic energy, then, not the same thing as the energy we feel full of sometimes, drained of at others? No, it is not; it is something a good deal more abstract, a construct in a theoretical system and not *directly* detectable or measurable in any way. Where does that leave us with our conscious experience that *feels* like energy? Psychoanalysis long ago discovered that conscious experience is a poor and unreliable indicator of the most important events that go on in the psychic apparatus. The conscious feeling of energy is an epiphenomenon, a clinical observation that is to be regarded seriously and used for its behavorial import, but no more to be taken literally than the subjective sense of free will. The inner feeling of freedom and choice is a

---

[17] "In this [cybernetic] analysis afferent impulses are not in any way regarded as 'messages' to the brain. Only in a far fetched and misleading sense could we call them messages, or regard them as such. This term, and its equivalents, would presumably imply a 'receiver' of these messages. The basic perception problem would then begin over again, at the alleged boundaries of this 'receiver' " (Culbertson, 1963, p. 107).

[18] In a recent paper, Apfelbaum (1965) has shown the fallacies of the assumption that such clinical phenomena as fatigue demand an explanation in terms of psychic energy. He goes too far, however, in rejecting all use of quantitative concepts. My own belief is that psychoanalysis needs much more quantification, but that there is little point in measurement for its own sake: we need to develop quantitative concepts, not simply to try to measure whatever we have. In this sense, then, I do not mean to argue against the economic point of view in any blanket fashion, nor do I deny that in a protoneurophysiological model there will be a place for measurements of physical energy. I am persuaded that the neural impulse is on the whole more usefully considered from the standpoint of information engineering rather than that of power engineering, but it would be rashly premature indeed to assert that quantities of neural energy can be of no interest to psychoanalysis.

valuable indicator of good functioning and by no means to be disregarded, but it cannot serve as an argument against determinism nor be directly coordinated to ego autonomy (cf. Holt, 1965b).

What is loosely called the psychoanalytic theory of instinctual drives covers a great deal, from observed clinical correlations and generalizations about the unconscious goals for which people strive, to a poorly integrated set of assumptions about psychic energy and its sources in excitatory processes in various bodily zones. Again, I want to emphasize that my objection is to the latter part of the theory, not the former. Psychoanalysis must have a motivational theory that will account for unconscious striving, for the importunacy of many kinds of driven behavior, and for the phenomena of indirect or symbolic substitute-gratification. The basic outlines of a revised and more tenable psychoanalytic theory of motivation may be seen in two papers, by Klein (in press) and Rubinstein (in press). The directional aspect of motivation is given by cognitive and structural concepts, like Klein's ideo-motor system. The general activation and impulsion of the model may be provided by making use of discoveries about cortical activating systems, notably the reticular formation. Pleasure and unpleasure can now be viewed as affective feedback from the consequences of behavior without commitment to a tension-reduction theory (for critiques of tension-reduction, see Holt, 1965a; White, 1963; Cofer & Appley, 1964). Beginning with the work of Olds and Milner (1954), a great deal has been learned about "rewarding" and "aversive" centers in the midbrain, which apparently mediate pleasure and unpleasure. While these discoveries do not as yet make wholly untenable a quantitative explanation of pleasure and unpleasure in terms of changes in levels of some hypothetical tension, the facts to date are at least as consistent with a more structural theory: pleasure and unpleasure would result, not from quantitative changes, but from the nature of the circuiting of a process—whether it proceeded through one or the other of these septal centers.

Psychoanalysis cannot afford to ignore such major discoveries from the general area of neurophysiology as those just mentioned, yet it cannot take account of them with a model that relies on a *psychic* apparatus operating with *psychic* energy. With Rubinstein (1967) I believe that we must turn to a protoneurophysiological model of the operating system; that is, our concepts will be based primarily on clinical and other behavorial observations and need only be reducible in principle and ultimately to neurophysiology. To postulate a basic model that is not incompatible with the findings of the relevant biological disciplines will facilitate more fruitful dialogue across the boundaries of the sciences, and will enable psychoanalysis to conceptualize psychosomatic matters without inconsistency or metaphysical embarrassment. In clinical discussions, we shall surely not be talking about commisures and dendritic potentials instead of impulse and defense; it will be enough to clarify and redefine our clinical terminology, making sure to keep it consistent with our basic model, which will be testable from several independent directions and thus may more rapidly approximate truth. Growing by contributions from both clinic and laboratory, it will take a rightful and unquestioned place among the sciences. So long as it tries to hold on to an anachronism like psychic energy, however, psychoanalysis will have great difficulty in progressing beyond Freud's monumental contribution.

REFERENCES

AMACHER, P. Freud's neurological education and its influence on psychoanalytic theory. *Psychol. Issues*, 1965, 4, No. 4 (Monogr. No. 16).

APFELBAUM, B. Ego psychology, psychic energy, and the hazards of quantitative explanation in psycho-analytic theory. *Int. J. Psycho-Analysis*, 1965, 46, 168–182.

BERGSON, H. *Creative evolution*. Trans. by A. Mitchell. New York: Holt, 1911.

BERNFELD, S. Freud's earliest theories and the school of Helmholtz. *Psychoanal. Quart.*, 1944, 13, 341–362.

BERNFELD, S. Sigmund Freud, M. D. 1882–1885. *Int. J. Psycho-Analysis*, 1951. 32, 204–217.

BERTALANFFY, L. VON. The theory of open systems in physics and psychology. *Science*, 1950, 111, 23–29.

BORING, E. G. *A history of experimental psychology*. New York: Appleton-Century, 1929.

COFER, C. & APPLEY, M. *Motivation: theory and research*. New York: Wiley, 1964.

COPE, E. D. *The primary factors of evolution*. Chicago: Open Court, 1896.

CULBERTSON, J. T. *The minds of robots*. Urbana: University of Illinois Press, 1963.

DRIESCH, H. *The science and philosophy of the organism*, 2nd ed. London: Black, 1929.

DU BOIS-REYMOND, E. *Ueber die Grenzen des Naturerkennens*. Leipzig, 1892.

EINSTEIN, A., & INFELD, L. *The evolution of physics*. New York: Simon & Schuster, 1938.

FRANK, P. Foundations of physics. In O. Neurath, R. Carnap, and C. Morris (Eds.), *International encyclopedia of unified science*. Vol. 1, Part 2. Chicago: University of Chicago Press, 1955.

FREUD, S. (1895a) On the grounds for detaching a particular syndrome from neurasthenia under the description "anxiety neurosis." *Standard Edition*, Vol. 3. London: Hogarth, 1962.

FREUD, S. (1895b) Project for a scientific psychology. In *The origins of psychoanalysis*. New York: Basic Books, 1954.

FREUD, S. (1900) The interpretation of dreams. *Standard Edition*, Vols. 4–5. London: Hogarth, 1953.

FREUD, S. (1914) On narcissism: an introduction. *Standard Edition*, Vol. 14. London: Hogarth, 1957.

FREUD, S. (1915a) Instincts and their vicissitudes. *Standard Edition*, Vol. 14. London: Hogarth, 1957.

FREUD, S. (1915b) The unconscious. *Standard Edition*, Vol. 14. London: Hogarth, 1957.

FREUD, S. (1920) Beyond the pleasure principle. *Standard Edition*, Vol. 18. London: Hogarth, 1955.

FREUD, S. (1923) The ego and the id. *Standard Edition*, Vol. 19. London: Hogarth, 1961.

FREUD, S. (1940) *An outline of psychoanalysis*. New York: Norton, 1949.

GILLISPIE, C. C. Lamarck and Darwin in the history of science. *Amer. Scientist*, 1958, 46, 388–409.

HOLT, R. R. A critical examination of Freud's concept of bound vs. free cathexis. *J. Amer. Psychoanal. Ass.*, 1962, 10, 475–525.

HOLT, R. R. Two influences on Freud's scientific thought: A fragment of intellectual biography. In R. W. White (Ed.), *The study of lives, essays on personality in honor of Henry A. Murray*. New York: Atherton, 1963.

HOLT, R. R. A review of some of Freud's biological assumptions and their influence on his theories. In N. Greenfield and W. Lewis (Eds.), *Psychoanalysis and current biological thought*. Madison: University of Wisconsin Press, 1965a.

HOLT, R. R. Ego autonomy re-evaluated. *Int. J. Psycho-Analysis*, 1965b, 46, 151–167.

HOLT, R. R. (Ed.) *Motives and thought: Psychoanalytic essays in memory of David Rapaport*. New York: International Universities Press, 1967. Also in *Psychol. Issues*, 1967, 5, No. 2–3 (Monograph No. 18–19)

JAMES, W. *Principles of psychology*. New York: Holt, 1890.

JONES, E. *The life and work of Sigmund Freud*. Vol. 1, New York: Basic Books, 1953.

KAPLAN, A. *The conduct of inquiry*. San Francisco: Chandler, 1964.

KARDINER, A., KARUSH, A., & OVESEY, L. A methodological study of Freudian theory: I. Basic concepts; II. The libido theory. *J. nerv. ment. Dis.*, 1959, 129, 11–19, 133–143.

KLEIN, G. S. Peremptory ideation: a theory of structure and force in motivated ideas. In R. R. Holt (Ed.), *Motives and thought: Psychoanalytic essays in memory of David Rapaport*. New York: International Universities Press, 1967. Also in *Psychol. Issues*, 1967, 5, No. 2–3 (Monogr. No. 18–19).

KORYÉ, A. The origins of modern science: A new interpretation. *Diogenes*, 1956, No. 16, 1–22.

KUBIE, L. S. The fallacious use of quantitative concepts in dynamic psychology. *Psychoanal. Quart.*, 1947, 16, 507–518.

LASHLEY, K. S., & COLBY, K. M. An exchange of views on psychic energy and psychoanalysis. *Behav. Sci.*, 1957, 2, 231–240.

LOEVINGER, JANE. Conflict of commitment in clinical research. *Amer. Psychologist*, 1963, 18, 241–251.

MAINX, F. Foundations of biology. In O. Neurath, R. Carnap, and C. Morris (Eds.), *International encyclopedia of unified science*. Vol. 1, Part 2. Chicago: University of Chicago Press, 1955.

MODELL, A. H. The concept of psychic energy. *J. Amer. psychoanal. Ass.*, 1963, 11, 605–618.

NAGEL, E. Teleological explanation and teleological systems. In H. Feigl and May Brodbeck (Eds.), *Readings in the philosophy of science*. New York: Appleton-Century-Crofts, 1953.

NAGEL, E. Methodological issues in psychoanalytic theory. In S. Hook (Ed.), *Psychoanalysis, scientific method and philosophy*. New York: Grove Press, 1960.

NAGEL, E. *The structure of science*. New York: Harcourt, Brace & World, 1961.

OLDS, J., & MILNER, P. Positive reinforcement produced by electrical stimulation of septal area and other regions of rat brain. *J. comp. physiol., Psychol.*, 1954, 47, 419–427.

OSTOW, M. *Drugs in psychoanalysis and psychotherapy*. New York: Basic Books, 1962.

PETERFREUND, E. Psychoanalysis—An evolutionary biological approach. Part I. Some fundamental difficulties in current psychoanalytic theory. Unpublished paper presented at meeting of the New York Psychoanalytic Society, Dec. 14, 1965.

POPPER, K. R. *The poverty of historicism*. Boston: Beacon Press, 1957.

RAPAPORT, D. The structure of psychoanalytic theory—A systemizing attempt. In

S. Koch (Ed.), *Psychology: A study of a science. Study I: Conceptual and systematic. Vol. 3: Formulations of the person and the social context.* New York: McGraw Hill, 1959. Pp. 55–183. Also in *Psychol. Issues,* 1960, 2, No. 2 (Monogr. No. 6).

RAPAPORT, D., & GILL, M. M. The points of view and assumptions of metapsychology. *Int. J. Psycho-Analysis,* 1959, 40, 153–162.

RAPOPORT, A. An essay on mind. In J. M. Scher (Ed.), *Theories of the mind.* Glencoe, Ill.: Free Press, 1962.

ROGERS, C. R. *On becoming a person.* Boston: Houghton-Mifflin, 1961.

RUBINSTEIN, B. B. Psychoanalytic theory and the mind-body problem. In N. Greenfield and W. Lewis (Eds.), *Psychoanalysis and current biological thought.* Madison: University of Wisconsin Press, 1965.

RUBINSTEIN, B. B. Explanation and mere description: A metascientific examination of certain aspects of the psychoanalytic theory of motivation. In R. R. Holt (Ed.), *Motives and thought: Psychoanalytic essays in memory of David Rapaport.* New York: International Universities Press, 1967. Also in *Psychol. Issues,* 1967, 5, No. 2–3 (Monogr. No. 18–19.)

SCHLICK, M. Philosophy of organic life. In H. Feigl and May Brodbeck (Eds.), *Readings in the philosophy of science.* New York: Appleton-Century-Crofts, 1953.

SCHNEIRLA, T. C. Levels in the psychological capacities of animals. In R. W. Sellars, V. J. McGill, and M. Farber (Eds.), *Philosophy for the future, the quest of modern materialism.* New York: Macmillan, 1949.

SCHWARTZ, F. & ROUSE, R. O. The activation and recovery of associations. *Psychol. Issues,* 1961, 3, No. 1 (Monogr. 9).

SILVERMAN, L. H. An experimental approach to the study of dynamic propositions in psychoanalysis: The relationship between the aggressive drive and ego regression. *J. Amer. Psychoanal. Ass.,* 1967 (in press).

SINGER, C. *A short history of scientific ideas to 1900.* New York and London: Oxford University Press, 1959.

TEILHARD DE CHARDIN, P. *The phenomenon of man.* New York: Harper & Row, 1959.

WHITE, R. W. Ego and reality in psychoanalytic theory. *Psychol. Issues,* 1963, 3, No. 3 (Monogr. 11).

WIENER, N. *Cybernetics.* New York: Wiley, 1948.

WILSON, E. B. *The cell in development and inheritance.* New York: Macmillan, 1897.

PART THREE

KANT, PERSONALISM, AND THE CULTURAL APPROACH

INTRODUCTORY NOTE

The third part of the present volume starts with Kant and analyzes several culturally and philosophically oriented systems. Chapter 11 describes Kant's point of view and his impact on psychology. Chapter 12 introduces Franz Brentano and the Problems of Intentionality, and discusses his contribution to psychology and philosophy.

Chapter 13 is devoted to Wilhelm Wundt, the great psychologist philosopher, who started experimental psychology and shifted the emphasis to physiological factors. Chapter 14 describes the works of Bradley, Ward, and Stout, the three great British philosopher-psychologists. All three of them were opposed to atomistic associationism.

Chapters 15 and 16 lead into personalistic and cultural psychologies. Stern's personalistic-philosophical psychology and the cultural-historical theory of Vygotski, that bridged between explanation of actual sciences and description of cultural sciences conclude the volume.

CHAPTER 11

IMMANUEL KANT AND HIS IMPACT ON PSYCHOLOGY

Benjamin B. Wolman

SEVERAL armchairs played an important role in the history of human thoughts, but hardly any one of them could compete with the one occupied by Immanuel Kant. For Kant led an uneventful life: no change, no travel, no reaching out for the unusual, not much interest outside his study-room and university classroom. Kant's life was a life of thought. His pen was his scepter, desk his kingdom, and armchair his throne.

Kant was more punctual and more precise than the town clocks of Königsberg. His habits were steadfast and unchangeable. Passersby in Königsberg regulated their watches whenever they saw Herr Professor Doktor Immanuel Kant on his daily stroll. Rain or shine, peace or war, revolution or counter-revolution had less affect on his life than a new book he read, and certainly counted less than a new idea that grew in his own mind. Kant's thoughts were to him the center of the universe, even more sa than Descartes's *Cogito* was to Descartes.

Kant put human mind above universe and saw in perceiving the starting point of being. Yet he did not follow Berkeley, nor did he say after Descartes, "*cogito ergo sum.*" Kant was not too sure of the existence of the outer world. A priori judgments of his mind were infallible, but the existence of the outer world, of things-in-themselves, could not be proven. The empirical world of phenomena was a product of the transcendental mind whose existence could not be doubted. Kant's mind *prescribed* laws to nature, but the nature of nature was, and had to stay, unknown and uncertain forever.

It was said that Kant's life was as regular as the most regular verbs in German grammar. Yet there was something disquieting in his peculiar regularity, for Kant's times [1724–1804] were not regular at all.

Wer den Dichter will verstehen, muss in Dichter's Land gehen [he who wants to understand the poet, must go to the poet's country], wrote Heinrich Heine. So let us go to Königsberg in East Prussia, the eastern part of the buoyant, militaristic, and brutal little Prussian kingdom, established by Frederick Wilhelm [1713–1740] and aggrandized by Frederick the Great [1740–1786].

The "Age of Reason"

Kant's times were those of Enlightened Absolutism in Europe, of the French Revolution, and of the Napoleonic Wars. In his lifetime, Prussia defeated Austria in the War of Succession (1740–1747), again defeated Austria in the Seven Years' War (1756–1763), swallowed large parts of Poland (1772, 1793, and 1795), and participated in Revolutionary and Napoleonic Wars. The times were not peaceful at all, nor particularly uneventful and dull. Enlightened Absolutism was at its height, prehaps as bright as a candle before it goes out. Most rulers of that time, whether Frederick the Great of Prussia, Joseph the Second of Austria, Katherine the Second and Alexander of Russia, the British Pitt, or the great Napoleon, were enlightened rulers who favored science and education.

The Age of Reason was the age of great scientific discoveries. Isaac Newton's [1642–1727] *Principia*, published in 1687, marked the turning point in the history of science and his three laws of dynamics became the cornerstone of physical studies. Newton's concepts of force and matter remained unchallenged for two centuries, until Ernest Mach, in 1883, raised doubts regarding their validity.

Newton and Leibniz [1646–1716] invented new mathematical tools. Newton's *Optiks* was published in 1704. Euler [1707–1783], Lagrange [1736–1813], and de Laplace [1749–1827] had developed mathematical skills far beyond the systems of Newton and Leibniz, enabling scientists to introduce high-power mathematics into the study of physical phenomena on earth and in the cosmos.

Spectacular developments also took place in chemistry. Priestley [1773–1804] discovered the role of oxygen in combustion and Cavendish [1731–1810] discovered the chemical composition of water. Lavoisier's [1743–1794] research disproved the erroneous theory of phlogiston, explained the relationship between man and weight, and elaborated upon the theory of oxidation.

In biological sciences, Linné [Linnaeus, 1707–1778] introduced new classification systems of species and Haller [1708–1777], in his voluminous work in physiology, greatly advanced neurological research.

Kant's philosophy belongs to the Age of Reason and it represents, to a certain extent, a crowning effort of that age. The Age of Reason hoped to find rational solutions to scientific issues and to all problems that perplexed humanity. Social systems, legal codifications, methods of government and economic institutions were all scrutinized by reason. Although reason was at odds with emotions and religious beliefs, it was believed that all problems, whether they belonged to science, ethics, politics, or religion, could be solved through reason.

Both man and the universe were the subject matter of study. The world, divided into mind and matter since unknown times, was undoubtedly more accessible at the side of matter. Descartes [1596–1650] tried to prove that mind and matter are separate entities. "The nature of matter or of body in its universal aspect does not consist in its being hard or heavy or coloured, or one that affects our senses in some other way, but solely in the fact that it is a substance extended in length, breadth, and depth. . . ." (Descartes, 1931, I,

p. 255). Mind, on the contrary, is not a spatial term.[1] Mind is ourselves and it "consists in the operation of the understanding, and the other in volition, or the operation of the will" *(ibid.*, p. 233). "Body is, by nature, always divisible, and the mind is entirely indivisible" *(ibid.*, p. 192).

Rationalistic philosophy took a new turn in the works of Spinoza [1632–1677]. Spinoza had no use for empirical evidence. He applied the deductive method of geometry toward the solution of metaphysical problems. He started with a set of definitions and axioms, followed by an intricate system of propositions proven by logical implication or inference. The resulting picture of the world was monistic, deterministic, and wholly consistent. Sensory perception was declared inadequate, the only adequate ideas being those which were logically derived from a set of definitions and axioms.

Spinoza's picture of the world was rejected by Leibniz. A great mathematician, he divided the world into a manifold of indivisible units, monads. Leibniz [1646–1716] could not escape the prevalent notion that nature was composed of matter and motion. His *Monadologie*, 1714, bears a definite resemblance to Newton's atomistic physics, however, in Leibniz's system, materialism was replaced by metaphysical idealism. "Material atoms" were substituted by "intellectual individuals," and instead of Newton's "physical points" Leibniz introduced "metaphysical points" (Zeller, 1873, p. 107). His immaterial, active units, monads, were endowed with cognitive ("perception") and conative ("appetition") functions. All that exists is composed of these spiritual monads. Plants are composed of "low" monads, thus, their mental condition resembles sleep. Animals are endowed with higher monads capable of memory. The human soul is composed of all types of monads, from the lowest to the highest ones, capable of all functions including the "apperception" or "reflexive knowledge of the inner state." To Leibniz, perception meant cognizance of the external world, whereas apperception meant consciousness of oneself.

Christian Wolff [1679–1754] was influenced by Spinoza and Descartes, but most of all, by Leibniz. Wolff reestablished the theory of mental faculties. Analogous to the organs of the body, Wolff saw in mental faculties organs of the soul. Following Leibniz, Wolff distinguished two faculties: the cognitive "perception" and conative "appetition," the latter including feelings. Each of the two faculties was subdivided into high and low perceptions and appetitions.

Similarly, Wolff divided all sciences into theoretical (perception) and practical (appetition); furthermore, he distinguished between rational sciences, based on reason, and empirical sciences, based on experiences. Logic was supposed to serve as prolegomena (introduction) to all sciences. Wolff proposed two psychologies: rational (metaphysical) and empirical.

Knutzen [1713–1781], professor at Königsberg, was Wolff's disciple and Kant's teacher. Knutzen, in his book published in 1774, went to great pains to prove that matter cannot think. He also advocated the unity of self-consciousness or self-awareness.

Tetens [1736–1805] accepted Wolff's faculty psychology, but believed in the importance of empiricism. "Where the empirical knowledge of the funda-

[1] Pavlov (1928, p. 219) almost literally repeated this statement.

mental faculties is still absent," he wrote, "There is no use to try to explain them with the help of the obscure concept as the 'soul'. No matter how far we progress in metaphysical psychology, the validity of its propositions must be examined by empirical knowledge" (Tetens, 1777, p. xiii).

While German philosophy was mostly rationalistic and metaphysical, the British and French Enlightenment moved in the direction of empiricism, sensualism, and materialism. This movement originated perhaps with Locke [1632–1704] who was highly critical of speculative philosophers that "amuse our understanding with fine and useless speculations" (Quoted after Fox Bourne, 1876, I, p. 224). Locke preferred "rational experiment and observation." Speculative ideas were not the way "the admired Mr. Newton" proceeded in research. There are no "innate ideas"; the human mind is a "tabula rasa," therefore experience is the only source of knowledge. "*All ideas come from sensation or reflection.* . . . Our observation employed either about external sensible objects, or about the internal operations of our minds perceived and reflected on by ourselves, is that which supplies our understandings with all the *materials* of thinking" (Locke, 1894, vol. 2, p. 2).

David Hume [1711–1776] followed in the footsteps of Locke's sensualism, and propagated radical empiricism. Thus, Hume rejected the ideas of *power, force, energy,* and *necessary connection* as obscure and metaphysical. "When we look about us towards external objects and consider the operation of causes, we are never able in a single distance to discover any power of necessary connection; any quality which binds the effect to the cause. . . . We only find that the one does actually in fact, follow the other . . ." (Hume, 1894, p. 7).

Hume also delivered a blow to the idea of soul or self.

There are some philosophers, [wrote Hume in his *Treatise of Human Nature*] who imagine we are every moment intimately conscious of what we call our *self*; that we feel its existence and its continuance in existence; and are certain beyond the evidence of a demonstration, both of its perfect identity and simplicity. . . . Unluckily all these positive assertions are contrary to that very experience which is pleaded for them; nor have we any idea of *self*. . . . For my part when I enter most intimately into what I call *myself*, I always stumble on some particular perception or other, of hot or cold, light or shade, love or hatred, pain or pleasure. I never can catch *myself* at any time without a perception, and never can observe any thing but the perception. . . . Setting aside some metaphysicians . . . , I may venture to affirm of the rest of mankind, that they are nothing but a bundle or collection of different perceptions. . . . They are successive perceptions only that constitute the mind. . . . (Hume, 1826, p. 318 ff.)

Instead of Locke's sensation and reflection, Hume introduced *impressions* and *ideas.* Impressions are "more lively perceptions, when we hear, or see, or feel, or love, or hate, or desire, or will." "Ideas or more feeble perceptions are copies of our impressions or more lively ones. . . . A blind man can form no notion of colours."

In the same *Treatise of Human Nature* (originally published in 1739–1740), Hume elaborated three laws of association, namely (1) similarity, (2) spatial-temporal contiguity, and (3) cause and effect.

Associationism was further developed by David Hartley [1705–1757].

According to Hartley, external stimuli affect the nervous system and cause *vibrations*. Vibrations are "motions backward and forward of the small particles, of the same kind as the oscillation of the pendulum and the trembling of particles of sounding bodies" (Hartley, 1801). These vibrations result in sensation. Associations of the "vibrations in the aether residing in the pores of these nerves" result in associations of ideas.

Condillac [1715–1780] went even further in stressing that all knowledge "comes from the sense organs" and one's self is merely the "collection of sensations one experiences" (Condillac, 1798, III, p. 119).

Seventeen volumes of *The Great Encyclopedia* edited by Diderot and D'Alembert were published in the years 1751–1772. The Encyclopedists were all but in favor of religion Laplace had developed the nebular theory of the origin of the universe leaving no room for the good Lord or the Six Days of Creation. The ardent Jesuits were expelled from most countries and finally suppressed in 1773 Clement's Fourteenth Papal Brief. The *Zeitgeist* was predominantly one of skepticism, deism, and atheism.

Yet the Age of Reason was not wholly dominated by the Encyclopedists. Religious wars were over, but not religious fanaticism or discussions. Kant's parents belonged to the Pietist movement. Thus the Age of Reason was not entirely an age of reason. Not all thinkers participate in speculative rationalism or empirical sensualism. Romanticism and sentimentalism were at an upsurge in literature and the arts. Rousseau's *Nouvelle Héloïse* was the forerunner of the great German romantic works of Schiller and Goethe, and music was dominated by the masterpieces of Bach, Beethoven, and Mozart.

Kant read not only the learned essays of German and foreign contemporaries but also the passionate confessions of Rousseau and the mystical writings of Swedenborg. His parents were pietists, his teacher Knutzen. His abstract intellectual inclinations drew him to metaphysical system formation, but his logical mind demanded criticism and loyalty to empiricism.

Kant tried to answer almost all the problems of his times. Epistemology and psychology, mind and body, empiricism and rationalism, reason and emotions, ethics and politics, geography and history, natural sciences and art, and history and government, all fascinated Kant. His active mind was alert to the totality of European culture.

Life and Work

Kant was born on April 22, 1724 in Königsberg. In 1732 he was admitted to the Collegium Fridericianum where the major subject matter was Latin. The school was pedantic, the school days full of prayers, and the syllabus underpinned with sermons, preachings, and fanaticism. In 1776 Kant wrote a letter to Wolke: "*Denn dass die Religion nicht als eine Art von Gunstbewerbung und Einschmeichelung bei dem höchsten Wesen sei . . . ist ein Wahn.*" [It is madness to believe that religion is but the art of winning favors from and flattering of the superior Being.] Quoted after Cassirer, 1923, p. 16.)

But that was how Kant was taught religion. Schiller, in a letter to Goethe, remarked that Kant could not get rid of the dark impression of his younger years (Cassirer, *ibid.*); hence his critical attitude to religion.

Rigid discipline was also prevalent at the Königsberg University. Kant registered there on September 24, 1740 in the Department of Theology. The other two "practical" departments were law and medicine. Kant's main areas of study were however, physics, geography, and philosophy. Science and philosophy had captured Kant's interest and continued to do so throughout his life.

Kant spent several years in the houses of Prussian nobles as a private tutor of their children. In 1755 the 31-year-old Kant was appointed Privat Dozent at the University of Königsberg and remained in that position for 15 years. He taught logic, mathematics, and metaphysics, and later physical geography and natural science. A few years afterwards, he also taught ethics and physics (cf. Cassirer, 1923).

Newton's scientific system had a profound impact on Kant's philosophy. As Newton put it, he did not "define Time, Space, and Motion, as being well known to all." But it was Newton who distinguished between the absolute concepts of time and space, and the empirical, measurable corresponding concepts. Undoubtedly, this distinction considerably influenced Kant's thinking.

However, Kant was more influenced by Newton's mathematics. Newton wrote: "We give an example of this in the explication of the System of the World; for by the propositions mathematically demonstrated in the first book, we there derived from the celestial phenomena the forces of gravity. . . . Then from these forces, by other propositions which are also mathematical, we deduce the motions of the planets, the comets, the moon, and the sun. I wish we could derive the rest of the phenomena of nature by the same kind of reasoning from mechanical principles" (Newton, 1803, II, p. x).

Yet Kant proved his intellectual independence by introducing, in opposition to Newton, his own nebular theory of the origin of the universe (1755). Kant's contemporary, Laplace, came out almost simultaneously with a similar theory, believing that his nebular theory would replace the religious cosmogony. Kant, however, related his theory to an omniscient, absolute, superior Being.

Kant's early works reflect the heterogenous influence of Hume, Rousseau, Newton, Wolff, and Spinoza. Kant was, at the time, in search of himself.

In 1770, at the age of 46, Kant was appointed professor of philosophy. In the same year, his Latin work, *De mundi sensibilis intelligibilis forma et principis* appeared. This work, often referred to as the *Dissertation*, represents the first major breakthrough in Kant's new way of thinking. In this work, Kant expressed his main ideas on perceiving and being perceived, and on mind and the universe. Kant was coming of age.

Eleven years later, in 1781, the 57-year-old Kant published his *opus magnum*, the famous *Kritik der reinen Vernunft (Critique of Pure Reason)*. With this work Kant became what he has remained since—the creator of perhaps the most influential philosophical system in modern times.

Kant's system of thought as espoused in the famous *Kritik* and several other works, was basically a combination of epistemology and psychology. Kant's system was mainly concerned with what went on in the minds of men when they grasped the universe.

Apparently, this problem can be dealt with in two ways. One, is the empirical psychological study of the cognitive processes, which, for example, Köhler, Piaget, Bruner, Allport, and other contemporaries pursue. The other is the formal analysis of propositions reporting empirical data.

However, Kant's work was done in neither manner. Kant faced the heritage of Hume, Spinoza, Locke, and Wolff; the questions he tried to answer were given to him by his predecessors and contemporaries. In Kant's times there was no clear-cut distinction between the study of human behavior and the formal-logical analysis of propositions. Logic and psychology were indistinguishable. Kant was, as it were, a product of the Age of Reason and believed in the rationality of human actions. Therefore, he prescribed laws of reason to nature. His disciple, Hegel, went even further, assuming that the whole universe is governed by one particular law of logic, the dialectic law.

Philosophical Principles

Kant's starting point was his critique of both metaphysical and empirical philosophies. "Time was," wrote Kant in the *Kritik*, "when metaphysics was entitled the Queen of all the sciences. . . . Now, however, the changed fashion of the time brings her only scorn; a matron outcast and forsaken, she mourns like Hecuba . . . (Kant, 1829, p. viii). But, stated Kant, "though all our knowledge begins with experience, it does not follow that it all arises out of experience. For it may well be that even our empirical knowledge is made up of what we receive through impressions and of what our own faculty of knowledge (sensible impressions serving merely as the occasion) supplies itself. . . . This, then, is the question which at least calls for a closer examination, and does not allow of any offhand answer;—whether there is any knowledge that is thus independent of experience and even of all impressions of the senses. Such knowledge is entitled *a priori,* and distinguished from the *empirical,* which has its sources *a posteriori,* that is, in experience" (*ibid.,* pp. i–ii).

Is such *a priori* knowledge possible? Kant's answer was affirmative.

Hitherto it has been assumed [wrote Kant in *Kritik*] that all our knowledge must conform to objects. But all attempts to attend our knowledge of objects by establishing something in regard to them *a priori,* by means of concepts, have, on this assumption, ended in failure. We must therefore make trial whether we may not have more success in the tasks of metaphysics, if we suppose that objects must conform to our knowledge. This would agree better with what is desired, namely that it should be possible to have knowledge of objects *a priori,* determining something in regard to them prior to their being given. We should then be proceeding precisely on the lines of Copernicus' primary hypothesis. Failing of satisfactory progress in explaining the movements of the heavenly bodies on the supposition that they all revolved round the spectator, he tried whether he might not have better success if he made the spectator revolve and the stars remain at rest. (Kant, 1929, pp. xvii–xviii.)

Kant believed that his was a Copernican revolution, but actually it was rather anti-Copernican, for Kant put the perceiving mind into the center of universe. Time and space, quantity and quality, causation, dependence, and so on were in human minds, not in nature. Wrote Kant: "We can know *a priori* of things only what we ourselves put into them" (*ibid.,* p. xviii). Kant has assumed that time, space, quantity, and quality, causation, reciprocity, possibility, necessity, and so on were *a priori* ideas of the human mind. The world of things as they are, called by Kant *noumenon* or *Ding-an-sich* (thing-in-itself) is unknowable. What men see are mere phenomena, seen in space, time, causation, and other categories of men's minds. The true nature of things-in-themselves is unknowable.

Space, wrote Kant, "does not represent any property of things." "Space is not an empirical concept which has been derived from outer experiences. . . . The representation of space cannot, therefore, be empirically obtained from the relations of outer appearance. . . . Space is a necessary *a priori* representation, which underlies all outer intuitions. We can never represent to ourselves the absence of space, though we can quite well think it is as empty of objects. It must therefore be regarded as the condition of the possibility of appearances . . ." (Kant, 1929, p. 38).

The same applies to time. Time is not experienced. It is a prerequisite of experience. It is a "pure form of intuition," a form through which we perceive. All perceived phenomena are spatial and temporal. The other conditions of perception are called categories. The twelve categories (among them causation) are not related to empirical facts, but are a priori forms of perception.

The evidence for a priori knowledge was given by Kant in a peculiar way. It was borrowed from mathematics. All mathematical judgments, Kant maintained, are synthetic. In synthetic propositions, the predicate is not contained in the subject. They contain knowledge based on experience. For instance, this tree has flowers. This proposition or judgment conveys an empirical truth.

Kant maintained that synthetic propositions can be a priori. They are so in arithmetic. Five plus seven, wrote Kant, is a synthetic proposition, yet it also is an a priori proposition.[2]

The fact that the validity of empirical perception is limited by the very nature of our sensory apparatus and by our ability to reason was not Kant's invention. Hume said it earlier in a most convincing manner.

The novelty of Kant's assumptions in epistemology lies in his theory of a priori forms of perception. It is, in a way, a continuation of Spinoza's "adequate ideas." Kant has accepted both: Hume's skepticism and Spinoza's axiomatic way of thinking.

Kant's revolution was rather an anti-Copernican one. He maintained that "physical science will never discover to us the internal constitution of things." Thus any future empirical science was to be confined to the study of phenomena, things-in-themselves being excluded from empirical research. The cognitive process was to become a process of finding what the transcendental mind puts into it. Time, space, quantity, quality, modality, relation, and so on were not facts of nature. They were a priori forms of the transcendental mind, which shapes one's picture of the world accordingly.

Scores of thinkers had to cope with the problems Kant presented. In psychology this heritage has been exceedingly complex. (cf. Brett, 1951; Wolman, 1965.)

Since Kant's mind was dictating its laws to the universe, one could ex-

---

[2] Russell has proved that mathematical propositions are analytic (Russell, 1947, p. 245).

pect Kant's system to have been a sort of pan-psychologism. But this was not the real, empirical mind of average human beings. Kant, as it were, developed two psychological systems. One was the study of the superb, transcendental, mind that operates with time and space and views the universe through the glasses of its categories. The study of this mind was immediate, given in a direct, introspective answer. The validity or introspection of the introspecting mind was never questioned by Kant. It was, however questioned by Herbart. (See Chapter three in this volume.)

Then came "anthropology," the "empirical" psychology. It is empirical if one may call empirical what doctor Kant thought of the minds of average people. In addition to his philosophical courses, Kant taught two "worldly" courses, anthropology and physical geography at Königsberg. The course in anthropology was given largely for pedagogical reasons. "I am trying," wrote Kant in 1773, "to furnish by means of these very interesting facts of observation, as they appear to me, a training of the academic youth in address and readiness, and also in wisdom" (Paulsen, 1902, p. 62).

Anthropology: The "Empirical" Psychology

Wolff and Knutzen have discerned rational from empirical psychology. Rational psychology was a metaphysical speculation concerning the nature of the soul, while empirical psychology dealt with introspective data.

Kant has refuted rational psychology and intended to develop an empirical psychology. However, Kant's empirical psychology dealt with phenomena only. The true functions of the mind, and its categories remained outside the scope of empirical psychology. Today one would classify Kant's *Kritik der reinen Vernunft* as an epistemological monograph. In Kant's times there was no sharp distinction between epistemology and psychology. Kant's disciples and followers treated the two as if they were one, drawing psychological conclusions from epistemological theories.[3] Kant himself clearly distinguished between mind as a transcendental phenomenon or thing-in-itself and mind as a phenomenon. Kant's psychology dealt with mental phenomena.

Kant rejected Locke's sensualistic notion that said: "*Nihil est in intellectu quod in sensibus non fuerat*" [There is nothing in mind that was not in the senses]. Kant also rejected Wolff's rationalism that maintained that sensations are merely "confused ideas." Sensation, believed Kant, supplied the material, to be formed by the ideas of the mind. Cognitive processes require both passive sensation and active reasoning.

Kant accepted Tetens's division into cognition, feeling, and will. Kant has distinguished between understanding, reason, and judgment, corresponding to the three logical terms of cognition.

While Kant rejected rationalistic psychology, he did not reject its main idea of separate mental faculties. In fact, Kant stressed the irreducibility of the faculties to each other. The cognitive faculty is based on sensation. There are two main senses. The senses internus (inner sense) provides the perception of time, while the external sense involves spatial perception of sight, touch, smell, taste, and hearing.

[3] Piaget (1965) has reversed the order of research; he has tried epistemological theories from psychological studies.

Kant's attitude toward feelings and emotions was typical of the Age of Reason. Kant assigned a secondary and rather negative role to emotions. "Pleasure is the idea of the agreement of the object or the action with the subjective condition of life." Desires cause the "realization of ideas." Normal human behavior is controlled by reason ("practical" reason) and not by emotions. Emotions inhibit the normal functioning of reason; Kant, however, made an exception for the esthetic feelings.

Will, in Kant's theory, became a highly important part of personality. Descartes's "I think," has been replaced by Kantians with "I will."

Kant also wrote about mental disorders. His ideas on this subject were largely a repetition of the widespread concepts of his times. (Kant, 1964).

Kant rejected the traditional ideas of a soul as a substantive entity. Instead of dealing with the metaphysical concept of soul, Kant has introduced the concept of ego or self *(Ich)*, representing the unity of consciousness. Self-knowledge substituted the old concept of soul; it was obviously a phenomenal and not a noumenal concept.

Kant's concept of self represented the unity of consciousness or the *transcendental unity of apperception*. This self counterposed to the rest of the world was a prerequisite for any knowledge. "There can be in us no modes of knowledge, no connection or unity of one mode of knowledge with another, without the unity of consciousness which precedes all data of intuitions, and by relation to which representation of objects is alone possible. This pure, original, unchangeable consciousness I shall name 'transcendental apperception' " wrote Kant (1929, p. 164).

The true ego, the transcendental mind, was inaccessible to knowledge, but its counterpart, the self or the empirical ego, was accessible to introspection. While Hume questioned such a central force, and James saw in consciousness a continuum (see the chapter on James), Kant invented the concept of "unity of consciousness" or "transcendental apperception" and saw in it the core of human mind. Introspection became therefore the main if not the only method of psychological study.

Kant had some misgivings about empirical psychology. The foremost objections stemmed from his conviction that science must be based on mathematics, for mathematical propositions were a priori and synthetic. Kant doubted whether psychology could ever use mathematics and become a true science. Herbart, Fechner, Weber, Wundt, Ebbinghaus, Brentano, and a great many other thinkers influenced by Kant, believed that psychology could not be scientific unless it was mathematized. Yet Pavlov, Freud, and Piaget, the three greatest contemporary psychologists, have made little if any use of mathematics.

Kant's Heritage

Kant left another heritage besides empirical psychology. It was not meant to be psychology, but it was. It was a description of the mind as a thing-in-itself. How can the observing mind observe itself? protested Herbart. According to Kant, the transcendental mind armed in the a priori cognitive forms, was a prerequisite of knowledge.

Certainly Kant expressed here a circular notion. The prolegomena of knowledge was the prolegomena of itself, and the knowing mind knew the knowings of the knowing mind. Thus Kant's transcendental psychology was an a priori absolute science about a cluster of logical concepts called by Kant "mind," and was saying a lot about nothing while his empirical psychology was saying practically nothing about human action and mental life (cf. Wolman, 1960, pp. 394 ff.).

It was Kant's theory of the absolute mind that fired the imagination of philosophers and scholars. Volume after volume discussed, admired, or criticized the Emperor's New Clothes, while the Emperor had none. Kant's absolute mind was never more than a set of logical concepts arbitrarily set by the great philosopher, yet generations of scientists and philosophers have argued back and forth about the nature of the nonexisting transcendental mind.

Kant, in a truly anti-Copernican fashion, put man and his perceiving mind in the center of the universe. Copernicus "made the spectator revolve and the stars remain at rest." Kant made the "objects conform to our knowledge." According to Kant, the objects had to revolve around the spectator. Certainly the history of science hardly knows of more self-centered a man and more man-centered a philosophy.

Kant's epistemology was, in a way, a theory of the organization of the "transcendental" human mind. This human mind was, according to Kant, endowed with some a priori knowledge, independent of any experience. According to Kant, the human mind had an a priori knowledge that $5 + 7 = 12$. No empirical proof was needed. The mind was autonomous. Accordingly, "pure" thought was based on intuition. Thought was active, sensory perception passive. Kant assumed in a Platonian fashion that sensation yielded the "matter" of phenomena, but their "form" came from within, from the human mind.

This intuitive function of the pure or transcendental mind was a priori. The ideas of time and space were forms that the human mind attached or prescribed to the external world. Cognition of the outer world required both the a priori forms and the aposteriori sensory perception. Knowledge of phenomena was a combination of empirical, sensory perception and the a priori, transcendental forms of cognition, built-in, as it were, in the human mind.

Kant has tried to solve several crucial issues, such as (1) empiricism versus rationalism, (2) materialistic monism that denied the existence of a soul versus metaphysical idealism and dualism, (3) associationism versus faculty theories, and (4) epistemological realism versus epistemological idealism.

One can, perhaps, see in these controversies various aspects of a more general problem, the problem of *man's place in nature*. This problem, as old as human thought, was stated dramatically in the *Book of Genesis*. What is man? "Dust thou art," was the first answer. Dust, a small, infinitesimal particle in the infinite universe. But it was also said that man was created after the Lord's image. What is man? A speck of dust or a godlike creature?

Kant did not solve any of these problems; he merely complicated them by creating additional questions, and ultimately confusing the entire issue. Empiricists influenced by Kant had to give up the empirical approach, for no matter how hard they tried to see the true world, they could see only phenomena or appearances shaped by time, space, and categories imposed by man's mind upon nature.

Kant's critical idealism rendered the solution of the mind-body dichotomy impossible; for both mind and body became sheer appearances. The true nature of man and the universe had to remain unknown forever.

Kant introduced into psychology a radical split between man as a cognizant subject and man as an object of cognition. Man as a subject was called "transcendental mind" and taken out of the context of empirical discipline. True, also the traditional "soul" of Judaism, Christianity, and scholastic philosophy became a useless concept, but Kant's "mind" was not any more useful or comprehensible than the traditional "soul" was.

The budding associationism (see Chapter two on Early Associationists) was adversely affected by Kant. Kant's philosophy was certainly more sophisticated than the theories of the early associationists. Small wonder that Ward (1886) sought to adjust associationism to Kant's philosophy. Ward, being under Kant's influence, assumed that the "material" for experience comes from without through the sensory apparatus, but the perceiving subject "synthesizes" the material along principles corresponding to Kant's categories.

A great many profound issues were introduced by Kant into epistemology and the methodology of science. Since things accessible to human knowledge were products of human mind, why bother to study them? What is the purpose of the scientific search for truth, if the true things are not accessible to human cognition, and what is accessible is determined by the allegedly self-evident forms of human thought?

Kant, as it were, took mankind out of the context of the universe. Not the man as a living organism, but man's cognitive apparatus, his mind. Kant analyzed not the true "mind," of real living men, but the transcendental mind of men in general. The existence of such a mind could not be proven, yet, according to Kant, the existence of such a mind was self-evident. It was as evident as the rules of Euclidean geometry, traditional arithmetic and algebra.

It took a long time to prove that mathematical propositions are neither synthetic nor true in the empirical sense. They are mere definitions, it is analytic a priori propositions that could be erected and destroyed at will (Russell & Whitehead, 1925–1927).

But Kant did not know this; nor could he, for Lobatchevski, Riemann, Boyle, Poincaré, Whitehead, Russell, and Goedel were to come later. History of science hardly has any logic; if there is any logic there, it must have a very peculiar one.

Kant was firmly convinced that he had discovered a great truth. The transcendental mind was hovering above the universe and outside of it, like the Lord's spirit in *Genesis* before Creation. Kant was sure that he had laid safe foundations for any future metaphysics and perhaps for any future philosophy.

Kant's Influence on Psychology

Kant's "empirical" psychology had a modest following. Freis [1773–1843] has added three developmental stages of the three faculties, namely sense, habit, and understanding. This distinction has, in turn, influenced Karl Bühler, Külpe's disciple. Kant's version of faculty psychology found its way into Hegel's and Schelling's systems.

Fortunately, wrote Klemm, "Kant did not adhere to the schematism of the three *Critiques* in his principal psychological work, *Anthropologie,* but presented instead a body of practical psychology which he had inherited from the Enlightenment and which is still worthy of study today" (Klemm, 1914, p. 63).

But while Kant's "practical" or "empirical" psychology soon became obsolete and forgotten, Kant's schematic ideas have had a lasting impact on psychology. Beneke (1833), for instance, was opposed to Kant's faculty psychology, but maintained that knowledge of one's own mind must serve as the foundation for historical sciences and metaphysics.

The man who tried to fight off Kant's influence could not see another way but to set the clock back. Herbart [1826–1827] see chapter three, was not as sophisticated nor as brilliant a thinker as was Kant. Herbart sought inspiration in the British and French empiricism and materialism of the Eighteenth century but, in defense against Kant's critical idealism, Herbart withdrew into the barren land of a dogmatic and cumbersome metaphysical materialism. And even this system was, to a great extent, an effort to continue and develop Kant's ideas.

The great German philosophers that followed Kant have developed a sort of pan-psychologism. The transcendental mind, firmly entrenched in Kant's armchair empire, has assumed dictatorial powers over man and nature. In Fichte's [1762–1814] philosophy, the pure and infinite transcendental ego became the center of the universe. Another disciple of Kant, Schelling [1775–1854] ascribed spiritual and creative powers to nature.

Hegel [1770–1831] and Schopenhauer [1788–1860] were probably more Kantian than any other Kantians. To Hegel the *Absoluter Geist* and the dialectic laws of reasoning became the absolute and undisputable lord and master over the physical world and human history.

Arthur Schopenhauer was perhaps the most consistent of all Kantians. In his classic work *Die Welt als Wille und Vorstellung,* first published in 1819, the world, as a system of phenomena, was viewed as merely an idea of the perceiving mind. The world is my idea, wrote Schopenhauer, but I, as a thing-in-itself, am my will. "Will is the thing-in-itself, the inner content, the essence of the world. Life, the visible world, the phenomenon, is only the mirror of the will" (Schopenhauer, 1923, Bk. 4, § 54). Schopenhauer's radical solipsism was the most logical conclusion that could be drawn from Kant's epistemological revolution.

Neither philosophy nor science could thrive on Herbart's metaphysical system, nor could they accept Kant's *Critique* or his idealistic-solipsistic disciples. The change in cultural climate was brought about not in armchairs but in laboratories and scientific expeditions.

The rapid progress of natural sciences forced Kant's followers and disciples to reconsider their position. Mayer [1814–1874], Darwin [1809–1882], Spencer [1820–1903], and others were not Kantians. Some of them were anti-Kantian, but most did not bother to take a stand in regard to Kant's system. Natural sciences forged ahead irrespective of Kant's philosophy. Psychology was less fortunate than other sciences.

The gulf between man and nature created by Kant's critical idealism has induced Kant's disciples to distinguish between cultural or historical sciences (Kultur or Geisteswissenschaften) on one hand, and natural sciences (Naturwissenschaften) on the other. Accordingly, natural sciences seek general laws; they are nomothetic. The historical or cultural sciences, however, are concerned with the individual case, for every human action is an unrepeatable and unique phenomenon. Cultural sciences study these unique idiophenomena; thus they are idiographic (Windelband, 1921). This problem has played a significant role in the works of two outstanding psychologists, Allport (1937) and Lewin (1936).

One may say that all that happens is unrepeatable and unique. Not only the battle of Tobruk and D-Day are idiophenomena, but also the desert wind that blew in Tobruk and the Atlantic wind that blew at the Channel crossing are unrepeatable events. Yet, although science starts with idiophenomena, all sciences group idiophenomena together on the basis of at least one common denominator, and seek regularities. Facts are idiophenomena, but science is nomothetic (Wolman, 1960, ch. 14).

Kant's distinction between noumena and phenomena perplexed Stern. His solution was to counterpose the experiencing person to the world of things. The person, wrote Stern, is "a living whole, individual, unique . . . capable of having experience" (Stern, 1938, p. 70).

Lewin went even further. He assumed that Galileo had rebelled against Aristotle's principles and suggested the study of individual cases. Therefore, Lewin believed that scientific laws "are nothing more than principles according to which the actual event may be derived from the dynamic factors of the concrete situation. . . . The application of the laws presupposes the comprehension of the individual cases" (Lewin, 1936, p. 11).

Psychology took another turn under the influence of Dilthey. Dilthey deviated from Kant and maintained that perception of the outer world is a perception of phenomena, while perception of one's own self is a perception of the thing-in-itself, thus it is a true perception. Dilthey wrote: "In contrast to external perception, inner perception rests upon an awareness (Innewerden) a lived experience (Erleben), it is immediately given. . . ." This lived experience "bears no resemblance to the processes of nature. Here we continually experience combinations and connections in ourselves" (quoted after Hodges, 1949, p. 13).

Dilthey believed psychology should serve as the fundamental discipline for sociology, education, law, ethics, and other humanistic sciences the way mathematics serves the natural sciences. Natural sciences must "explain" (erklären) the phenomena perceived from without, but nothing of this kind is needed in psychology. Psychology does not deal with phenomena, but with the totality and continuity of the mind. The mind is obvious, for it is the "innermost, immediate experience," a "living reality."

Dilthey's solution was not entirely Kantian, but it was an effort to solve the problem posed by Kant. According to Dilthey, all sciences should be divided into Naturwissenschaften (natural) and Geisteswissenschaften (humanities). Kant's gulf between man and universe was deepened by Dilthey. Natural phenomena were to be observed, studied, and explained, but there was no need to do this in regard to man. Mental processes were obvious, self-evident, immediately given; they were no longer phenomena in the sense that Kant used the term. They were real, true, things-in-themselves; accordingly, it was enough to "describe" and to "understand" them.

Spranger undertook the job of "understanding," Lewin that of "describing." Were they aware that they struggled with a dichotomy created by the lonely man from Königsberg? Spranger (1929) doubted whether psychology could ever become an objective science. Psychological propositions had to remain value judgments, depending upon the cultural and philosophical preferences of psychologists. Lewin tried to solve this problem in a highly original and complex manner. For him, theory was not a generalization of empirical data but a formalization of scientific propositions.

Although Dilthey himself must not be considered as a leading figure in European psychology, his ideas influenced Spranger, Stern, Gestalt psychologists, and Lewin (cf. Wolman, 1960, chs. 10–13). Dilthey accepted Kant's ideas that causation was a form of the human mind: "The causal relation itself again arises through a synthesis which springs from within us" (Hodges, 1949, p. 133). Dilthey further elaborated Brentano's and Husserl's distinction between mental act and its content. Mental act is awareness (Bewusstsein) of something; what one is aware of is the content of awareness.

Dilthey's ideas of "understanding" have had a profound impact on psychologists and other behavioral scientists. While natural sciences "explain" facts (erklaren), psychology must "understand" (verstehen) human life as a whole. Holism, purposivism, and counterposing man to nature, so prominent in the works of Spranger, Stern (see Chapter 15), Lewin, Adler, Fromm, and many others originated in Dilthey's neo-Kantian ideas.

Another solution to the problems posed by Kant was offered by Brentano (1874). While the external world is observed and innerly perceived, one's own psychological experiences are externally perceived. Brentano, in search for a line dividing physical and mental phenomena, stressed (1) introspection as a method of cognition of mental phenomena, and (2) their intentionality. Only mental phenomena are perceived innerly, and only they are "intentional acts" (Brentano, 1874, pp. 131 ff.).

Some of Brentano's ideas were further developed by Husserl. Husserl's phenomenology grew out of Kant's distinction between the experiencing (perceiving) subject and the perceived world of phenomena. Human experience (Erlebnis) is the fundamental fact underlying all science. Thus science must start with the study of these experiences. The world is a world of phenomena experienced by the experiencing subject, and phenomenology is the science of those cognitive processes.

Husserl's Logische Untersuchungen (1900–1901) was an effort to save psychology and all other science from the inevitable Kantian solipsism and Brentano's dualism. Husserl rebelled against Kant's idea of things-in-themselves. We do perceive the true world, but we must study our perceptions before we study anything else, maintained Husserl. Psychology, as an empirical science, has to analyze the subjective experience of the experiencing subjects. Thus, although phenomenology was opposed to Kant's critical idealism, it, implicitly, preserved Kant's idea that the perceiving man was the center of the universe.

Gestalt psychology is, in a way, another solution to the problems posed by

Kant. Certainly it is not a mere offshoot of Kantianism, but it is not sheer coincidence that Köhler has praised Kant's epistemological revolution. Gestalt psychologists did not accept the idea that the human mind perceives the world as it is. Wrote Köhler: "Sensory data do not appear as such to the observer" (1933, p. 11). Some cognitive elements had to stem from within. "The form, the weight, and the movement of things had to be given the same interpretation as colors and sounds; they, too, depended upon the experiencing organism and were merely end results of complicated processes in its interior" (Köhler, 1947, p. 6).

Köhler and Gestalt psychologists went even further than Kant, ascribing *Gestalt* qualities to physical bodies and believed that the Gestalt law of *Prägnanz* was applicable to both cognitive processes and to the physical world. Apparently, the gestalt psychologists tried hard to resolve Kant's "man versus nature" dichotomy, and their idea of isomorphism is certainly related to these efforts.

Kant's influence also extended to neurological studies. Johannes Müller maintained that no one can be a psychologist without being a physiologist *(Nemo psychologus nisi physiologus)*. Yet he believed that time and space were terms of the perceiving mind and not of the perceived reality. The concept of space originates in the feeling of expansion experienced by the retina. The images of the spreading out retina are two-dimensional; the third dimension comes from viewing objects from various distances and viewpoints (Müller, 1826).

Also, Helmholtz [1821–1894] in his work *Über die Natur der menschlichen Sinnesempfindungen*, 1852, stressed the gulf between the perceived world and the perceiving subject. In a truly Kantian fashion, Helmholtz maintained that sensory impression was merely a sign of the outer world but not a direct cognition of it.

The relationship between the content of sensory perception and the thus-perceived world continued to perplex scientists and philosophers. For instance, Ernst Mach [1838–1916], who certainly was not a loyal Kantian, represented Kant's pan-psychologism at its best. Mach had been influenced by Berkeley's [1685–1753] *esse est percipi* [to be is to be perceived].

> The table I write on I say exists; that is, I see and feel it: and if I were out of my study I should say it existed; meaning thereby that if I were in my study I might perceive it, or that some other spirit actually does perceive it. . . . For as to what is said of the absolute existence of unthinking things, without any relation to their being perceived, that is to me perfectly unintelligible. Their *esse* is *percipi*; nor is it possible they should have any existence out of the minds or thinking things which perceive them. (Berkeley, 1901, Part 1, §3)

Mach followed Kant's ideas as expressed in *Prolegomena*. Mach suggested expelling "mental artifices" from science and sticking to experiences. "Nature," wrote Mach, "is composed of sensations as its elements. . . . The thing is an abstraction, the name of a symbol. . . . The reason we assign a single word to a whole compound is that we need to suggest all the constituent sensations at once. . . . Properly speaking, the world is not composed of 'things' as its elements, but of colors, tones, pressures, spaces, times, in short what we ordinarily call individual sensations" (Mach, 1907, p. 483).

Operationism is another offshoot of Kantianism and Machism. Wrote Mach: "The world consists of colors, sounds, temperatures, pressures, spaces, times and so forth, which now we shall not call sensations nor phenomena, because in either term an arbitrary, one sided theory is embodied, but simply elements" (Mach, 1943, p. 208). For, Mach believed, "Nature is composed of sensations as its elements. . . . Properly speaking, the world is not composed of 'things' as its elements but of . . . individual sensations" (Mach, 1960, p. 482).

Bridgman substituted human sensations with human operations. "We mean by any concept," wrote Bridgman, "nothing more than a set of operations: the concept is synonymous with the corresponding set of operations" (1927, p. 5).

Kant suggested looking on man's inner, transcendental mind. Mach turned the light on man's sensations, and then Bridgman recommended to watch man's actions. In a truly Kantian tradition, Bridgman assumed that the observations of the observing man were more valid than the observation of anything else.

In conclusion, one may ask whether Kant's influence on psychology was or was not beneficial. Brett, in his classic *History of Psychology*, wrote: "Many would regard the legacy of Kant as a disaster for psychology. It perpetuated the rigid distinction between what we know of our own minds and what others know of them, and that overt behavior alone can be scientifically described" (Brett, 1951, p. 508).

REFERENCES

ADICKES, E. *Kants Lehre von der doppelten Affektionen unseres Ich als Schlussel zu seiner Erkenntnis theorie.* Tubingen: Mohr, 1929.

ALLPORT, G. W. *Personality: A psychological interpretation.* New York: Holt, 1937.

BENEKE, F. E. *Lehrbuch der Psychologie als Naturwissenschaff.* 1833.

BERKELEY, G. *Principles of human knowledge.* Oxford: Oxford University Press, 1901.

BRENTANO, F. *Psychologie vom empirischen Standpunkte.* 1874.

BRETT, G. S. *History of psychology.* Ed. by R. S. Peters. London: Allen & Unwin, 1951.

BRIDGMAN, P. W. *The logic of modern physics.* New York: Macmillan, 1927.

CASSIRER, E. Kant's Leben und Lehre. In *Immanuel Kant's Werke.* Vol. XI. Berlin: Cassirer, 1923.

COHEN, H. *Kant's Theorie der Erfahrung.* Berlin: 1871.

COHEN, H. *Kant's Begründung der Ethik.* Berlin: 1877.

CONDILLAC, E. B. DE *Oevres.* Paris: Honel, 1798.

DESCARTES, R. *Principles of philosophy.* In E. S. Haldane and G. R. T. Ross (Trans.), *The philosophical works of Descartes,* Cambridge: Cambridge University Press, 1931, 2 vols.

FOX BOURNE, H. R. *The life of John Locke.* New York: Harper, 1876. 2 vols.

FRIES, J. F. *Handbuch der psychischen Anthropologie.* 1820.

HARTLEY, D. *Observations on man, his frame, his duty, and his expectations.* London: 1801.

HODGES, H. A. *Wilhelm Dilthey, an introduction.* London: Routledge & Kegan Paul, 1949.

HUME, D. *Philosophical works.* Edinburgh: Clark, 1826.
HUME, D. *An enquiry concerning the human understanding.* Oxford: Clarendon, 1894.
HUME, D. *A treatise of human nature.* Oxford: Clarendon, 1896.
KANT, I. *Prolegomena zu jeder künftigen Metaphysik.* Riga: 1783.
KANT, I. *Anthropologie in pragmatischen Hinsicht.* 1798.
KANT, I. *Principles of politics.* Ed. and Trans. by W. Hastie. Edinburgh: Clark, 1891.
KANT, I. *Gesammelte-Schriften.* Berlin: G. Reimer & Königlich Preussische Akademie der Wissenschaften, 1902.
KANT, I. *Fundamental principles of the metaphysics of morals.* Trans. by T. K. Abbott. London: Longmans Green, 1927.
KANT, I. Critique of pure reason. 2nd ed. Trans. by N. Kemp Smith. London: Macmillan, 1929.
KANT, I. *Prolegomena to any future metaphysics.* Trans. by L. U. Beck. New York: Liberal Arts Press, 1950.
KANT, I. *The critique of judgement.* Trans. by J. C. Meredith. Oxford: Clarendon, 1952.
KANT, I. *The classification of mental disorders.* Ed. and Trans. by C. T. Sullivan. Doleystown, Pa.: *Dobystown Fundation,* 1964.
KNUTZEN, M. *Philosophische Abhandlungen.* Jena: 1774.
KÖHLER, W. *Psychologische Probleme.* Berlin: Springer, 1933.
KÖHLER, W. *Gestalt psychology.* New York: Liveright, 1947.
LANGE, F. A. *The history of materialism.* 3rd ed. London: Routledge & Kegan Paul, 1950.
LEWIN, K. *Principles of topological psychology.* New York: McGraw-Hill, 1936.
LIEBMANN, O. *Kant und die Epigonen.* Leipzig: 1805.
LOCKE, J. *An essay concerning human understanding.* Oxford: Clarendon Press, 1894.
MACH, E. *Popular scientific lectures.* Trans. by T. J. McCormack. LaSalle, Ill: Open Court, 1907.
MACH, E. *The science of mechanics.* 6th ed. Trans. by T. J. McCormack. La Salle, Ill.: Open Court, 1960.
MILLER, J. *Zur vergleichenden Physiologie der Gesichtsinns des Menschen und der Tiere.* Jena: 1826.
NEWTON, I. *Principia mathematica* (A. Mothe transl.). 1803.
PATON, H. J. *Kant's metaphysics of experience.* London: Allen & Unwin, 1951. 2 vols.
PAULSEN, F. *Immanuel Kant. His life and doctrine.* New York: Scribner, 1902.
PAVLOV, I. P. *Lectures on conditioned reflexes.* New York: Liveright, 1928.
PIAGET, J. *Early growth of logic in the child.* New York: Harper & Row, 1964.
PIAGET, J. Psychology and philosophy. In B. B. Wolman and E. Nagel (Eds.), *Scientific psychology: Principles and approaches.* New York: Basic Books, 1965.
RUSSELL, B. Philosophy of the twentieth century. In D. D. Runes (Ed.) *Twentieth century philosophy.* New York: Philosophical library, 1947.
RUSSELL, B., & WHITEHEAD, A. N. *Principia Mathematica.* 2nd ed. Oxford: Oxford University Press, 1925–1927. 2 vols.
SCHOPENHAUER, A. *The world as will and idea.* Trans. by E. S. Haldane and Kemp Smith, New York: Scribner, 1923.
SMITH, N. K. *A commentary to Kant's "Critique of Pure Reason."* 2nd ed. New York: Humanities Press, 1950.
SPINOZA, B. *Ethics.* Trans. by R. H. M. Eleves. London: Bell, 1919.

SPRANGER, E. Der Sinn der Voraussetzungslosigkeit in der Geisteswissenschaften. *Preussische Akad. d. Wissenschaften*, 1929.

STERN, W. *General psychology from the personalistic standpoint.* New York: Macmillan, 1938.

TETENS, J. N. *Philosophische Versuche über die menschliche Natur und ihre Entwickelung.* Leipzig: 1777.

WARD, J. Psychology. *Encycl. Britannica*, 1886.

WINDELBAND, W. *An introduction to philosophy.* London: Allen & Unwin. 1921.

WOLMAN, B. B. The chance: A philosophical study. *Tarbitz, Hebrew Univ. Quart.* (Hebrew), 1938, 10, 56–80.

WOLMAN, B. B. *Contemporary theories and systems in psychology.* New York: Harper & Row, 1960.

WOLMAN, B. B. Toward a science of psychological science. In B. B. Wolman and E. Nagel (Eds.) *Scientific psychology: Principles and approaches.* New York: Basic Books, 1965.

WOLMAN, B. B. Immanuel Kant. In *Encyclopedia of Social Sciences.* New York: in press.

ZELLER, E. *Geschichte der deutschen Philosophie.* Munchen: 1873.

CHAPTER 12

FRANZ BRENTANO AND THE PROBLEMS OF INTENTIONALITY

John J. Sullivan[1]

Mein Standpunkt in der Psychologie ist der empirische: die Erfahrung allein gilt mir als Lehrmeisterin: aber. . . .

FRANZ BRENTANO

FRANZ CLEMENS BRENTANO [1838–1917] wrote on many topics but I shall discuss here only his conception of mind as it appeared in *Psychologie vom empirischen Standpunkt*.[2] When compared with physical phenomena, mental phenomena, Brentano thought, could be distinguished by the intentional inexistence of an object in a mental act. The doctrine of intentionality was not clear in Brentano's formulation in PES. The relation between an act and its object was stated as: (1) inexistence, (2) reference, (3) direction, (4) immanence, and (5) containment. I shall distinguish three formulations of the nature of intentionality: (1) a nonrelational inexistence, an Aristotelian-Thomistic view; (2) a descriptive, synthetic relation, a classical phenomenological view; and (3) intentionality as a logical tie, Bergmann's recent formulation. To serve as foils in the assessment of the nature and significance of Brentano's formulation, I shall present a brief review of Bergmann's schematization of intentionality, but only mention Husserl's conception. Brentano is at least historically important because he represents an attempt to conceptualize an act theory of mind consistent with nineteenth-century philosophical thought. Through his emphasis and his personal example and influence, he was an important catalyst for the development of the thought of his students, among whom were Stumpf, Freud, Husserl, v. Ehrenfels, Meinong, Marty, and Hillebrand. His work also influenced Stout, Moore, Russell, and Bergmann.

No satisfactory designation exists to indicate the unique field in which a discussion of intentional relations occurs. The topic of the relation of a

---

[1] This article has been discussed many times with Fritz Fluckiger and, in addition, owes much to my understanding of Gustav Bergmann's thought.

[2] Hereafter referred to as PES. All references are to the Felix Meiner edition published in Hamburg in 1955.

mental act to its content is one that appears in both the field of psychology, in philosophically oriented discussions of the conceptual foundations of the field; and in philosophy, in discussions of the philosophy of mind. Clearly "philosophical psychology," although a name for an area of study acceptable to a small group of psychologists, is looked upon with justifiable suspicion by a large group of both philosophers and psychologists who have stressed the differences between their respective fields. In the latter half of the nineteenth century, discussions in philosophy were strongly infused with assumptions of a psychological nature. At the same time, discussions in psychology contained philosophical issues to such an extent that the period has been called "prescientific."

The separation of the two fields was achieved in philosophy at the turn of the century by the elimination of psychologism from logic. The principles of logic were seen as being independent of the way a person thinks. This achievement set Anglo-American philosophy on a course that resulted first in an analysis of philosophical problems by linguistic methods and then in the analysis of language itself. In psychology the definition of the scientific problems was achieved by the elimination of philosophical issues as sources of research. By this separation, the traditional dialectics on the topic of mind were simultaneously eliminated from each field. The philosophers claimed that the nature of mind was a factual problem of the science of psychology; the psychologists claimed that it was a problem for philosophical analysis.

The claim that all problems of describing the world are either factual or linguistic has the merit of stressing both the empirical grounds for and the need for clarity in any particular statement about the world. In this study of Brentano's work, however, there is a blend of psychological and philosophical issues in which arise problems of schematization, of metaphysical imagination, and of decisions of an ontological nature.

Philosophical Foundations

One notion of explanations involves the concept of entailment. This implies that to explain, even in a loose sense, any particular set of ideas, recourse must be had to the metadiscipline that entails them. Brentano's conceptions of mental acts and their contents, for instance, are entailed by his decisions about the subdivisions of psychology. His definition of psychology is derivative from the epistemological emphasis in his philosophy; the epistemological emphasis is derived from his perception of the history of philosophy. A direct logical connection cannot be shown between these different aspects of his thought. Brentano, however, was an unusually rigorous thinker and his consistency is a measure of his intellectual rank.

Brentano's perception of the history of philosophy is developed in his doctrine of Four Phases, which is presented more fully in Note A (p. 266). Briefly, it can be summarized as a cyclic progression of philosophical thought that repeated itself in ancient, medieval, and modern philosophy. The first phase is characterized by emphasis on fundamental philosophical issues in both an empirical and rational way. In the second phase primary attention is directed to practical matters; such a period is characterized by philosophical skepticism. The third phase is a reaction from skepticism which results in dogmatism. In the fourth phase the dogmatism, now out from under empirical and rational controls, transmutes into mysticism. Brentano reacted against Hegelian Idealism, although he saw it as essentially correct in its emphasis on the analysis of consciousness and the activity of mind. However, he thought that when it lost its empirical base it became philosophical mysticism.[3] His own task within the framework of this perception of history was to start anew the analysis of experience, an activity which had characterized the beginnings of great philosophical periods in the time of Aristotle, of Aquinas, and of Descartes, Leibniz, and Locke.

Brentano has stated his philosophic position succinctly in the following quotation:[4]

Mein Standpunkt in der Psychologie ist der empirische: die Erfahrung allein gilt mir als Lehrmeisterin: aber mit anderen teile ich dieÜberzeugung, dass eine gewisse ideale Anschauung mit einem solchen Standpunkte wohl vereinbar ist.

<PES, p. 1>

My position in psychology is that of empiricism: experience alone is my teacher: but along with others I am of the opinion that such a position is quite compatible with a certain idealistic viewpoint.

*The interaction between the idealistic and realistic tendencies in philosophy resulted in an emphasis on epistemology. The idealists stressed the existence of the knower; the realists, the existence of the known. Brentano's statement is an attempt to fuse both. Such a task led to the problem of the relation between the knower and the known; with the primary focus on this relation, he took the epistemological approach to philosophical problems.

To understand the sense in which Brentano is an empiricist, and a realist, but not a naive one, and how the epistemological issues became central in modern philosophy, consider the following dialogue.[5] A Realist philosopher points to a chair and says, "This is a chair." The Idealist asks him for grounds for the statement. If the Realist replies, he can be asked for grounds for the grounds. The argument is endless unless both can agree on a rule for breaking off the justifications for grounds of knowledge. Historically speaking, both contestants agreed to stop the justification of knowledge claims with a rule called the*Principle of Acquaintance (hereafter referred to as PA). PA is, "Every statement must be analyzed down to what we are acquainted with." The broad interpretation the Realist of our discussion holds is that if

---

[3] Hegel emphasized activity of mind at the expense of suppressing the object of the mental act. Brentano's famous dictum was: *Nur Reales ist vorstellbar!* [There is always a reference to real entities in acts of mind!] Marx (Die heilige Familie, *Marx and Engels, Werke,* II, p. 138), for instance, stressed in his early philosophical papers a similar point of view: "If man constructs all of his knowledge, sensation, etc. from the world of the senses and from experience in the world of the senses, the sensory world must be so arranged that in it man experiences and habituates himself to what is really human with a result that he experiences himself (becomes aware of himself) as a man" (my translation —J.J.S.).

[4] The translation from one language to another sometimes requires a shift in idiom to preserve the meanings of the original. Both the German originals and the English translations will be presented here so that questions about the original quotations can be checked.

[5] This dialogue and the Principle of Acquaintance are from Bergmann (1964).

one thoroughly inspects a physical object, say a chair, he can be said to be acquainted with it. The Idealist narrowly interprets PA as meaning that we are directly acquainted only with phenomenal things. In the example asserting the existence of a chair, he would hold that we are only acquainted with a chair percept. Some Idealists would hold that what is seen as a chair percept is only a property of the mind. Others hold that phenomenal things, like chair percepts, exist as components of consciousness and that reference to these is the distinguishing characteristic of empiricism. To classify Brentano's philosophical position is not easy. He was an Idealist in his restriction of philosophic thought to the analysis of consciousness; he was a Realist in the sense that he denied that only acts of mind, or a mind that acts, exists; and an Empiricist in his consistent reference to the objects of consciousness, which he conceptualized as having a special form of existence in mental acts.

A variation in the conclusions of the epistemological dialogue indicates another characteristic of Brentano's thought: the simplicity pattern. Brentano's position is that phenomenal things exist and that phenomenal data can be analyzed into introspective simple reports (called "introspective simples") of the type, "This green exists." There is a dispute about whether he could have held this position consistently in view of his belief in the substantial nature of the soul and the denial of the existence of properties and relations. However, the chair percept is said not to have primary existence but to consist of introspective simples. To emphasize the significance of this position, it will be recalled that it is similar to that of Wundt, James, and John Stuart Mill, although the latter's notion of chemism is an important qualification. The simplicity pattern of analysis was rejected by Mach, v. Ehrenfels, Husserl, and the Gestalt psychologists. Brentano's notion of acts is compatible with the British empirists' Laws of Association of Ideas. His act is not the associating of ideas, but how a sensation is to be conceived.

Brentano's basic problem as a philosopher was to construct a scheme in which elementary experience could be talked about consistently. A preliminary consideration for this task was the definition of the field of psychology, its divisions, and within one of the divisions, the concept of mental activity.

He says that the name "psychology" (PES, p. 6) signifies *Wissenschaft von der Seele*. Science[6] of the soul.[7]

By the name "soul" Brentano refers to the substantial carrier (*Träger*) of presentations *(Vorstellungen)*, which through inner experience are directly perceived. This is a doctrine of (1) a substantial theory of mind and (2) immediate experience, or as in our previous discussion of PA, direct acquaintance.

Brentano's position was decisive in the conceptualization of an act psychology. It is one which places Brentano between the Aristotelian-Thomistic

[6] *Wissenschaf* from the German is not correctly translated into English as "science," for in English the term refers exclusively to what the Germans call *Naturwissenschaft*. There are other divisions of *Wissenschaft*, such as *Geisteswissenschaft*, a term originally introduced into German as a translation of John Stuart Mill's phrase, "moral science."

[7] The notion of soul makes many of those who have unresolved theological tensions slightly suspicious. Sharp distinctions were not made between soul and mind in the discussions that developed out of the Scholastic tradition. Freud used the term *Seele* frequently in his early work; later this was supplanted by the term "Ego." The same is true of Husserl.

and the Husserlian idea of intentionality. Brentano held that to conceive of an act and its relation to an object, it was not necessary to raise metaphysical issues about either the substantial nature of the soul or its immortality, important as these were for a person of his religious beliefs. By refusing to introduce the substantial nature of the soul into his definition of psychology, he was forced to consider the relation of the act to its object as the special problem of the nature of mind, rather than the relationship between a substantial soul and an object. Husserl, by contrast, distinguished between *Ego*, *Cogito*, and *Cogitatum*. He held that the failure of Descartes, and by implication also that of Brentano, was the failure to develop the notion of a transcendental ego. Husserl's classical phenomenological position was that intentionality is a relation between a substantial Ego and a phenomenal object. The Aristotelian-Thomistic position was based on the idea that what is perceived in the external world exists as a form in the substance of the mind. Hence, the object exists in a special state in the mental substance.

To state the formulations in another way: (1) The Aristotelian-Thomistic point of view was that the substance of the mind takes the form of an object. Brentano held that an object inexists in an act and that mind does not have to be conceptualized in substance terms; later he preferred to talk about intentionality as a reference to an object. Husserl thought of intentionality as a relation between a Transcendental Ego and a *Cogitatum*. Bergmann, to anticipate, holds that intentionality is an analytical, logical, and specific tie between an act and its intention.

Brentano thought that a substance theory of soul makes sense, but that it is not necessary to introduce it in discussing mental acts and their contents (see PES, note 10, p. 257). For him it was not the assumption of a substance that was fiction, but rather the assumption of a property, like a mental act, without a substance, that was an absurd fiction. According to Kraus (see PES, note 12, p. 258, a later opinion of Brentano was that the assumption of the substantial nature of the soul was not a metaphysical, that is, a transcendental, assumption. However, in PES Brentano put aside the question of the nature of the soul as irrelevant to the conceptualizing of mental acts. He held that the elimination of irrelevant problems meant the strengthening of a science.

Brentano stated then:

Wir erklären also in dem oben angegebenen Sinne die Psychologie für die Wissenschaft von den psychischen Erscheinungen.

<PES, p. 27>

With the above considerations in mind we define psychology as the science of psychical appearances.

Brentano said, in accord with the opinion of John Stuart Mill, that the task of psychology is the investigation of laws of psychical phenomena (in Mill's terminology, the Laws of the Association of Ideas). Brentano's definition of psychology is further specified in the following quotation presented by Kraus:

Meine Schule unterscheidet eine *Psychognosie* und eine *genetische Psychologie* (in entfernter Analogie zur Geognosie und Geologie). Die eine weist die sämtlichen letzten psychischen Bestandteile auf, aus deren Kombination die Gesamtheit der psychischen Erscheinungen wie die Gesamtheit der Worte aus den Buchstaben sich ergibt. Ihre Durchführung könnte als Unterlage für eine characteristica universalis, wie *Leibniz* und vor ihm *Descartes*, sie ins Auge gefasst haben, dienen. Die andere belehrt uns über die Gesetze, nach welchen die Erscheinungen kommen und schwinden.

<PES, p. xvii>

My school makes a distinction between Descriptive Psychology and Genetic Psychology. The first shows forth the totality of psychic elements, the combination of which makes up all the psychic phenomena, in the same sense in which the letters of the alphabet make up all the words. Its completion might serve as a foundation for a *characteristica universalis* (as conceived by Leibniz and, before him, Descartes). The second informs us about the laws according to which the phenomena come and go.

Brentano's primary interest, as was Husserl's and after him the Gestalters', was in the formulation of a descriptive psychology. Descriptive psychology is more basic than genetic psychology. In the Freudian system there is a theory of mind (a descriptive psychology) and a theory of psychosexual development (a genetic psychology). The presupposition of Freud's theory of psychosexual development, which is explicitly recognized by Erikson in his theory of psychosocial development, is that development takes place if mind has certain properties such as defenses against anxiety, identification with parents, projection of infantile wishes, and so forth.[8] Of the classical systems of psychology, only Freud's system has an explicit descriptive and genetic psychology, and within the genetic psychology, a personality typology. His descriptive psychology consists of act psychological schemes which went through various developments: (1) *Cs-Ucs*, (2) *Cs-Pcs-Ucs*, and (3) Id-Superego-Ego-Reality. Psychoanalytic genetic psychology is a *Naturwissenschaft* in which the primary problem is the establishment of links in the events of the history of the individual which constitute causal chains associated with particular symptoms. Freud's formulation is similar to what Brentano conceived genetic psychology to be in distinction to descriptive psychology.

The next step in the delineation of Brentano's conception of mind is to define psychical phenomena. Distinction between psychical phenomena and

---

[8] The psychophysical doctrine of stimulus reception depends, as Dewey (1896) noted in his criticism of the reflex arc concept, upon some prior properties of mind. Furthermore, the foundation of the doctrines of association of ideas is laid in the conception of how an idea or sensation is experienced. Marx's theory (cf. Deutsche Ideologie, *Marx and Engels, Werke*, III, p. 31.) can be reconstructed as positing that there exist active minds, nature, other people, and productive relations. The structure of nature, social class relations, modes of gratification of basic needs, and the nature of man's self-consciousness (relation to himself) determine the content of mental activity. The precondition for response to nature, others, or self-activity is a mind that acts. This doctrine and idea of the dialectic are the Hegelian heritage in Marx. An act theory of mind and a concern with self-consciousness are the core notions that in Sartre's thought are the links to Husserl, Marx, Hegel, and Freud.

psychical appearances here and in Brentano's work is blurred.[9] Brentano
differentiated between psychical and physical phenomena as follows:

Ein Beispiel für die psychischen Phänomene bietet jede Vorstellung durch
Empfindung oder Phantasie; und ich verstehe hier unter Vorstellung nicht das,
was vorgestellt wird, sondern den Akt des Vorstellens. Also das Hören eines
Tones, das Sehen eines farbigen Gegenstandes, das Empfinden von warm oder
kalt, sowie die ähnlichen Phantasiezustände sind Beispiele, wie ich sie meine;
ebenso aber auch das Denken eines allgemeinen Begriffes, wenn anders ein solches
wirklich vorkommt. Ferner jedes Urteil, jede Erinnerung, jede Erwartung, jede
Folgerung, jede Überzeugung oder Meinung, jeder Zweifel—ist ein psychisches
Phänomen. Und wiederum ist ein solches jede Gemütsbewegung, Freude, Traurig-
keit, Furcht, Hoffnung, Mut, Versagen, Zorn, Liebe, Hass, Begierde, Willen,
Absicht, Staunen, Bewunderung, Verachtung, usw.
    Beispiele von physischen Phänomenen dagegen sind eine Farbe, eine Figur,
eine Landschaft, die ich sehe; ein Akkord, den ich höre; Wärme, Kälte, Geruch,
die ich empfinde; sowie ähnliche Gebilde, welche mir in der Phantasie erscheinen.

<PES, p. 111–112>

An example of a psychic phenomenon is given by every presentation in sensation or imagination; and by presentation I do not mean that which is presented,
but the act of presenting. That is, the hearing of a sound, the seeing of a colored
object, the sensing of warm or cold, and comparable states of imagination are
examples of what I mean; but the thinking of a general concept (if such a thing
actually does occur) is an example as well. Furthermore, every judgment, memory, expectation, inference, conviction or opinion, every doubt is a psychological
phenomenon. And so is every emotion, joy, sadness, fear, hope, courage, despair,
anger, love, hate, desire, will, intention, astonishment, admiration, contempt, and
so on.
    By contrast, the following are examples of physical phenomena: a color, a con-
figuration, a landscape that I see; a chord that I hear; heat, cold, or odor that I
sense; as well as similar images which appear to me in my imagination.

The above quotation provides the occasion for four comments:

1. The quotation exhibits the simplicity pattern to which previous reference has been made. There are both simple sensa, such as a color or a tone;
and simple acts, such as the seeing of a color or the hearing of a sound. In
Brentano's inventory there are, in addition to simple sensings, simple psychical acts of the species judging and remembering, and also a group that are
emotions, such as joy, sadness, fear, hope, despair, love, hate, and so forth.
From this inventory of acts, three general classes were developed: the presenting (Vorstellungen), the judging (Urteile), and the emoting (Gemütsbe-
wegungen). Attention is called to the fact that the inventory corresponds
to commonsense notions and linguistic distinctions of ordinary language, and
is also a list of faculties in the ancient philosophical tradition. Yet a precise
explication of these terms would be a useful enlargement of descriptive terms

---

[9] Kraus (see PES, note 15, p. 259) maintained that Brentano held that existence is
not an attribute of physical phenomena, in opposition to Mach. Kraus insisted that the
Brentano doctrine gives existence only to the person who sees colors, hears tones, etc. If
Kraus is correct, Brentano's system is only about the properties of mind. If Kraus is correct, what is reconstructed in this paper as Brentano's system is, then, only a Brentano-
like system that assumes the existence of psychical and physical phenomena.

in psychology. These terms refer to mental activities that appear only in existential novels and in psychoanalytic case studies.

2. Kraus, who carefully studied the relations of Husserl to Brentano, indicated (see PES, note 2, p. 266) that Brentano in this quotation made a mistake that was taken up and developed by Husserl. The mistake was in referring to an instance of a physical phenomenon as, "a landscape that I see." This was a departure from the simplicity pattern of Brentano's work. Kraus (PES, p. 267) said: "Husserl cites (*Logische Untersuchungen*, 1901, II, in a note on page 243) Brentano as *Eine Figur, Landschaft, die ich sehe*. . . . Husserl omitted the example of the color and printed the word 'landscape' without noticing that this was his and not Brentano's blocking." Kraus added that it would have been better if Husserl had left in "color" and left out "landscape."

3. The significance of Brentano's proposals can be made clear by a brief comparison of the ontological inventories of Wundt, Külpe, Stumpf, and the Gestalters. Wundt's program was to analyze the contents of consciousness provided by the introspective reports of subjects. The difficulty with this program is that in addition to reports of sensa, which were the only objects in his ontology, subjects would also give reports like "seeing green," "feeling tired," etc. His program was to translate these "act" terms from the introspective reports into a language that contained only reports of contents. The program was a failure. Wundt abandoned this type of research and began the study of a social-cultural-anthropological psychology in which mind develops as a national or historical characteristic as a response to cultural institutions. Külpe and his school, in analyzing the same type of introspective reports, identified "impalpable (*unanschaulich*) contents" in addition to phenomenal contents. To avoid a mental act terminology, these faint awarenesses were later referred to as *Funktionen* (see Boring, 1950, pp. 405–408). Stumpf's ontology had everything: sensa, relations, acts, and formations.[10] As is well known, Köhler and Koffka were students of Stumpf, and Wertheimer was a student of Külpe. They discarded acts, *Gebilde*, and relations, and held that there are only wholes and parts; the nature of the wholes and the location of the parts within them determine the properties of the parts.

4. The proliferation of such varieties of models of mind occurs when there is release from controls of scientific methodology. This period in the history of psychology, which was focussed exclusively on the analysis of consciousness, has been the despair of students, with the result that the simple clarities and easy confirmations of the Behaviorist doctrines have been studied with relief.

Brentano defines the doctrine of intentional inexistence as follows:

Jedes psychische Phänomen ist durch das charakterisiert, was die Scholastiker

---

[10] These formations, called *Gebilde*, referred to the status of the term "green" in the sentence "I like green." In this report, "green" was clearly not a sensum, yet Stumpf thought of it as an existent of some kind. In logic a distinction is made between the use of a term and the talking about it. In this case, in which there is a lack of distinction between the experiencing of and the talking about the sensum, a confusion was elevated into an ontological category. The term "green" could have been referred to as the content of an act of liking that had as its content another act, the awareness of green.

des Mittelalters die intentionale (auch wohl mentale)* Inexistenz eines Gegenstandes genaunt haben, und was wir, obwohl mit nicht ganz unzweideutigen Ausdrücken, die Beziehung auf einen Inhalt, die Richtung, auf ein Objekt (worunter hier nicht eine Realität zu verstehen ist), oder die immanente Gegenständlichkeit nennen würden. Jedes enthält etwas als Objekt in sich, obwohl nicht jedes in gleicher Weise. In der Vorstellung ist etwas vorgestellt, in dem Urteile ist etwas anerkannt oder verworfen, in der Liebe geliebt, in dem Hasse gehasst, in dem Begehren begehrt usw.†

Diese intentionale Inexistenz ist den psychischen Phänomenen ausschliesslich eigentümlich. Kein physisches Phänomen zeigt etwas Ähnliches. Und somit können wir die psychischen Phänomene definieren, indem wir sagen, sie seien solche Phänomene, welche intentional einen Gegenstand in sich enthalten.

<PES, pp. 124–125>

Every psychic phenomenon is characterized by that which the Scholastics of the Middle Ages have called the intentional (or mental*) inexistence of an object, and which we, in somewhat ambiguous terms would call the reference to a content, the direction toward an object (which need not be a real thing), or an immanent objectivity. Every (psychic phenomenon) contains something as its object, but not every psychic phenomenon does so in the same manner. In presentation, something is presented; in judgment, something is affirmed or denied; in love, something is loved; in hate, something is hated; in desire, something is desired and so on.†

* Sie gebrauchen auch den Ausdruck "gegenständlich (objektive) in etwas sein," der, wenn man sich jetzt seiner bedienen wollte, umgekehrt als Bezeichnung einer wirklichen Existenz ausserhalb des Geistes genommen werden dürfte. Doch erinnert daran der Ausdruck "immanent gegenständlich sein," den man zuweilen in ähnlichem Sinne gebraucht, und bei welchem offenbar das "immanent" das zu fürchtende Missverständnis ausschliessen soll.

† Schon Aristoteles hat von dieser psychischen Einwohnung gesprochen. In seinen Büchern von der Seele sagt er, das Empfundene als Empfundenes sei in dem Empfindenden, der Sinn nehm das Empfundene ohne die Materie auf, das Gedachte dei in dem denkenden Verstande. Bei *Philo* finden wir ebenfalls die Lehre von der mentalen Existenz und Inexistenz. Indem er aber diese mit der Existenz im eigentlichen Sinne confundiert, kommt er zu seiner widerspruchsvollen Logos und Ideenlehre. Ähnliches gilt von den Neuplatonikern. *Augustinus* in seiner Lehre vom Verbum mentis und dessen inner lichem Ausgange berührt dieselbe Tatsache. *Anselmus* tut es in seinem berühmten ontologischen Argumente; und dass er die mentale wie eine wirkliche Existenz betrachteete, wurde von manchen also Grundlage seines Paralogismus Hevorgehoben (vgl. Uberweg, *Gesch. der Phil.* II). *Thomas von Aquin* lehrt, das Gedachte sei intentional in dem Denkenden, der Gegenstand der Liebe in dem Liebenden, das Begehrte in dem Begehrendn, und benützt dies zu theologischen Zwecken. Wenn die Schrift von einer Einwohnung des hl. Geistes spricht, so erklärt er diese als eine intentionale Einwohnung durch die Liebe. Und in der intentionalen Inexistenz beim Denken und Lieben sucht er auch für das Beheimnis der Trinität und den Hevorgang des Wortes und Geistes ad intra eine gewisse Analogie zu finden.

* They also use the expression, "to be in something as an object." If this expression were used today, it might well be taken in the opposite sense, that is, as the designation of a real existent outside of the mind. But one is reminded of the expression, "to be immanent objective" which is sometimes used in a similar sense, and in which the word, "immanently" is clearly meant to avoid the misunderstanding that was to be feared.

† Aristotle has already mentioned this psychic inherence. In his treatise on the soul he says that that which is sensed, as such, is in him who senses; that the sense (mind, psyche) registers that which is sensed without (its underlying) matter, that that which is thought is in the thinking intellect. In Philo, too, we find the doctrine of mental existence and inexistence. But by confounding this with existence in the proper sense of

This intentional inexistence is exclusively characteristic of mental phenomena. No physical phenomenon manifests anything similar. Thus, we can define mental phenomena by saying that they are such phenomena as include an object intentionally within themselves.

The above is the famous quotation from PES. At the risk of expanding on the obvious, mention will be made of its methodological significance. The fundamental idea of Brentano's system has been indicated to be the doctrine of "intentional inexistence," because this is the distinctive formula of the system. The components of any logical system are: (1) terms; (2) definitions that either collect the terms or define some additional terms by others; and (3) formulae, which specify the rules of manipulation of the elements and definitions. The definitions give the abbreviations allowable in the system; what is abbreviated gives the explicit properties of what is defined. The formulae, however, by specifying the relations of the terms defined, give implicit properties to the terms.

For example, the Freudian system at a quick glance might be said to have a massive list of terms that occur in reports of the observations of a patient over a long period. These terms may be put into groups, the members of which are referred to by general names such as libidinal impulses, aggressive impulses, socially-learned inhibitions, socially-learned expectancies, acts of sensing the external world, acts of judging, and so forth. These general names may then be grouped into Id, Ego, Superego, Reality categories. So far, this is not a system but only a collection of classified terms which refer to observations made of a patient. The formulae of the system are revealed when the relations and transformations of these terms are specified.

In the above quotation from Brentano, the formulae are two: (1) an object intentionally inexists in an act and (2) one act may intentionally inexist in another. The second formula raises two further questions: (a) Are Judging and emoting second-order acts of a different kind than presenting? and (b) If all acts have the same properties, what is the status of objects like "Pegasus" in reports such as "thinking of Pegasus"? These questions have been important historically in the discussion of Brentano's doctrines. Three comments can be made with regard to the quotation:

1. The general distinction between an act and its object is similar to, but is not identical with, the classical distinction between form and matter. In a two-level world composed of physical phenomena and mental phenomena, the form-matter distinction applies to the physical and not to the mental phenomena. The act-intention distinction applies to mental phe-

---

the term, he arrives at his contradictory doctrine of logos and ideas. More or less the same is true of the Neo-Platonists. Augustine refers to the same facts in his doctrine of the *Verbum mentis* and its internal origin. Anselmus does the same in his famous ontological argument; and the fact that he thought of mental existence as real existence has been pointed out by many as the foundation of his paralogism (cf. Ueberweg, *Geschichte der Philosophie*, II). Thomas Aquinas teaches that that which is thought exists intentionally in him who thinks, that which is loved in him who loves, that which is desired in him who desires; and he uses this for theological purposes. When the Scriptures speak of an indwelling of the Holy Ghost, he explains this as an intentional indwelling by way of love. And he seeks to use intentional inexistence in thinking and loving as an analogy for the mystery of trinity and the emergence of the Word and the Spirit.

nomena and not to physical phenomena. Any mixing, such as act-physical or matter-mental, results in a philosophic disaster. The form-content distinction applies to logical and linguistic domains and not to phenomenal and physical domains. The act-content (better, in terms of these distinctions, the "act-object") as well as the form-matter distinctions are widely used in psychology. Consider the fundamental relation in the psychoanalytic theory of dreams, that between the wish (a species of act) and its so-called content. There may be either one wish with two contents, latent and manifest contents, or different wishes that are acceptable to the ego or unacceptable to the ego. One of Freud's formulae is, "The non-fulfillment of one wish signifies the fulfillment of another." In this sense, in addition to wishes and contents, we have acts in special relations to other acts. In Rorschach theory there are acts of selection of parts of the inkblot (W, d, dd), and there are form-attributing (F), movement-attributing (M), and color-organizing (C) acts, each of which has distinctive "contents." Two formulae of the system are: (a) selection acts fuse with the determinants and (b) the latter may further fuse with each other. The relation of Gestalt wholes to their parts, however, is in the Platonic tradition and applies to the physical world. This distinction is not in the act tradition until some Gestalter, who does not know his own theory, attributes the notion of the whole to a perceptual process instead of to the structure of the outside world. The outside world, as far as mind is concerned, includes anything that is sensed, such as physiological events. The relations of laws of reinforcement are not of an act type, nor are they about mental phenomena. The reinforcement laws are relations between classes of experimental operations, which modify the physical world, and classes of responses of an organism. The law is widely applicable in many instances because the situations are members of the behavior classes and reinforcement operations which are related by the law. This is not an act-content (object) relationship.

2. In Brentano's system it is important to have second-order acts with the same simple properties that first-order acts have, with the exception that one act can inexist in or be the object of another act. Brentano's analysis of judgment (See Note C, p. 000, for his contribution to logic) is that judgings are acts similar to *Vorstellungen*. This position is possible because he was a thing ontologist who did not believe in the existence of properties and relations. Mind, in this sense, is not judging and comparing by a process of giving structure to an amorphous object, or relating subjects to predicates such as, "Some man is sick." Brentano would formulate this sentence as a judgment that, "A sick man exists."

One may report a state of "thinking of X," but may or may not be directly presented with X. To an empiricist of Brentano's type, terms of existence apply only to what has been in consciousness as the contents of *Vorstellungen*. This is a condition in order for anything to be discriminated, judged, or identified. Brentano accounts for the thinking of objects which have no existence, such as a past event, a golden mountain, or a round square, by considering them to be existent in the imagination or thought of a person. The issue raised about nonexistent objects of acts has not been settled. There is an issue of this type in current psychological literature.

The analysis of a statement is (a) sometimes given by reference to antecedent events in the history of the speaker (physical phenomena), (b) some-

times given by reference to thought processes of the speaker (mental phenomena), and (c) sometimes given by reference to what the statement refers (syntactical and semantical rules). Analyses (a) and (b) are psychological accounts and differ only in choice of what events are considered relevant, either behavioral or mental. Analysis (c), however, is a view of language as a picture or mirror of the world. Questions with this idea of language are requests either for a logical analysis of structure or for an interpretation of what the statement refers to. With these distinctions is mind, recall
the request to Skinner by Whitehead to account for his behavior while saying, "No black scorpion is falling on this table" (Skinner, 1957, p. 45).
Skinner's reply is in terms of (a); Brentano's, as well as a psychoanalyst's
reply would be in terms of (b); a philosopher would want an answer in
terms of (c). The dialogue of philosophers with psychologists often has the
form of asking questions of this type. When the psychologist attempts to answer, questions are raised not about psychological states or antecedent verbal
behavior, but about employment of terms and reference of statements. Such
questions are not about pragmatics but about sematics and syntax. Brentano
and Skinner were caught by this type of predicament; Brentano's answer is
still being discussed in philopsophical literature (Grossmann, 1963; Kamitz,
1962).

3. There are acts, there are objects, and there is a condition called intentional inexistence, according to Brentano. In the report, "direct acquaintance
with green," the act is a sensing; green is its intentional object. The green
sensum, it is to be noted, is only in consciousness and if one is a consistent
empiricist it cannot be said to be a reflection of an external world. We only
know the green that is sensed and not a thing that corresponds to it in the
transcendental world. Brentano makes a similar point with Locke's example
of dipping one hand into lukewarm water and then dipping the other into
the same water after having had it previously in cold water. The sensory reports are different but that is all we know. This argument by Brentano is
weak, for by specifying other additional circumstances, these sensory events
can be intrasubjectively related to each other. That which is intrasubjectively
stable then refers to the physical world.

Act and Content

The principal difficulty with Brentano's doctrine is not the notion of the
acts, for these are simple processes not of the Idealist type; or their objects,
for these are, in commonsense terms, existents. The notion of "inexistence"
and how to conceive the nexus between acts and objects is the core and the
difficult part of his doctrine. To explicate "inexist," brief reference will be
made to Aristotle, Anselmus, Aquinas, and Brentano.

ARISTOTLE

As Brentano notes in the second footnote of the above quotation, the Aristotelian formulation was that what is sensed is in he who senses. Mind or
soul was thought to consist of special matter, a particularly mobile set of
atoms that took on the form of whatever was sensed. In Aristotle's scheme
there is an external object that is perceived by a person. By analogy, we can

consider a chair being televised; it exists in the television camera, not by any transfer of its own substance but in terms of (we now know) the possible reflected energy that determines rearrangement of some substance in the camera due to properties of the camera itself. The camera, in the Aristotelian scheme, in which the physics of energy propagation were not known, reports its own properties, and the chair form, since it is a property of the camera, has only an existence status. This doctrine is familiar to psychologists as Köhler's notion of isomorphism, which is fundamentally a physiological account of inexistence.

ANSELMUS

Anselmus's contribution to the history of philosophy is a "proof" of the existence of God based upon an equivocation on the word "existence." The argument is as follows: Some things are more perfect than others. The chain is endless. Can we conceive of a most Perfect Being? His answer was in the affirmative and he then added that the existence in thought of this Perfect Being is proof of His existence. The equivocation, Brentano notes, is based upon two uses of the term, "existence," which results from not making the distinction between existence and inexistence in thought. Frege's distinction between direct and indirect reference applies here.

AQUINAS

Thoughts and acts of loving, according to Aquinas, are recognized as acts that have contents. Aquinas increased the number of mental acts of interest to the psychologist. The utility of act and content distinction to the Scholastic was that the doctrine led to accounts of special existence for the Holy Ghost. It also provided a rationale for the idea that faith, love, and charity were acts. Christian virtue inexisted in these acts. By expanding the inventory of acts, he weakened the substance theory of mind, but did not abandon the notion of inexisting form in the mental substance.

BRENTANO

In Brentano's scheme the Scholastic doctrine is generalized to psychological activities; there is only consciousness and no external object. In his early thought there is no relation between the act and its content; there is a special existence in the act that makes a relational tie unnecessary. There is no relation between the object of an act and the external world. There is no relation between an "I" and the phenomenal sensum that would permit such sentences as "I see green." There is only "seeing green." It is not necessary to have "I" as a subject in a sentence as our Indo-European ancestors thought; it is enough to have something predicated.

Intentionality

The idea of intentionality of Bergmann can be distinguished from that of Brentano by (1) an incorporation of 50 years of discussion of the difficulties in the latter's doctrine, (2) a different philosophical climate and style, and (3) the separation of logic from psychology. Brentano's work raised two possibilities for the development of the nature of the intentional relation.

Husserl took one, Bergmann the other. For Husserl, "reference" became a synthetic, descriptive relation between an Ego and a phenomenal object. For Bergmann, it became an analytical and logical tie between an act and its intention. Bergmann's thought (1964) may be schematized briefly in the following way:

The greatest weakness of contemporary philosophy is the lack of an adequate philosophy of mind. By "adequate" is meant a philosophy of mind which will provide answers to perennial questions. Bergmann is committed to discuss philosophical issues in commonsense terms. He refuses to use philosophic terms because they lead to absurdity and paradox. He accepts PA, that "every statement must be analyzed down to what we are acquainted with." Along with this principle, another called "K" has been conjoined in philosophical discussions: "We cannot know anything to exist, what it is like unless we are acquainted either with it or with part of it, wholly or in part with a thing of its sort." Accepting PA and K leads to classical phenomenology. Bergmann accepts PA and holds that in commonsense language, K is false. Logically, K is a tautology (to know is to be acquainted with). Bergmann can say that in commonsense terms, we live in a two level world. His rejection of K is based upon the claim that he can know that a physical object exists (Moore's commonsense argument is an influence here). Philosophically, he can also state that the acceptance of PA and the perception of K as a tautology puts him in a position to hold that we live in a two-level world, one of phenomenal things and one of physical things. The acceptance of PA allows him to say that for every sentence written about a physical object, another sentence can in principle be written in a phenomenal language such that they are both simultaneously true or false.

The phenomenal-physical dualism, called dualism$_1$, he holds along with an act-intention dualism, called dualism$_2$. Dualism is justified on the grounds that in the doctrine of scientific parallelism the nexus between brain function and mental activity is not strong enough. The characteristics of the act, the relation, and the intention depend upon Bergmann's ontology. He holds that things exist and facts do not. He further believes that individuals, properties, and relations exist, but quasi-characters do not.

To illustrate Bergmann's analysis of the act-intention issue, consider the following two sentences:

> A. "The proposition this is green means this is green."
> B. "The proposition this is a chair means this is a chair."

1. The act is a character indicated by (a), "The proposition this is green."
2. The intention is a fact expressed by (b) "This is green."
3. The intentional relation is expressed by (c) "means."
4. The sentence (A) is *analytic*. This is why the nexus, "means," is analytic.
5. The sentence (A) expresses a quasi-relation between a character (a) and a fact (b).
6. The subsisting *logical* feature is expressed by "means."
7. This logical feature occurs only in a world in which there are minds. Thus the intentional tie is called *specific*.
8. Sentence (B) has the same form as (A). Its intention is a fact about a physical object. The act is a thought or proposition "this is a chair."

From this position he holds that (1) Acts are facts, not things, and therefore cannot be said to exist. (2) The ingredients of acts, however, exist and constitute "mental" phenomena. (3) The logical constituent "means" is the intentional relation, is a quasi-character, and does not exist, but subsists as a logical form. (4) The intention is a fact and not a thing .(5) The constituents of the intention exist and may be either phenomenal or physical objects. (6) The intention that is a physical object like a chair, rather than being constructed in the simplicity pattern, is a recognition of a commonsense Gestalt notion that the chair as a unit is knowable. (7) Mental things, instead of being substances or continuants, are momentary things.

Compared with Brentano's formulation, it can be noted that Bergmann's: (1) accounts for objects that are both phenomenal and physical without calling physical objects congeries of phenomenal objects; (2) separates the act and its mental ingredients by an external logical relation from physical objects by a tie that is analytic, thus close; logical, thus having a special existence status; and specific, in that it occurs in a world with minds; (3) holds that mental phenomena are momentary things, as distinguished from mind as either a substance or a continuant; (4) admits one core of idealist thought, the closeness of the act to its intention, without denying the existence of matter; and admits the reality of matter, without denying mind and elementary acts.

To give a final estimate of Brentano's significance at this time is premature. Clearly, though, his doctrine is between that of Aristotle and Bergmann, and a source of that of Husserl. Brentano started with a *substance theory* of mind in which the act-object relation was that of "inexistence." He (1) put aside the problem of mental substance in developing his theory of mind in terms of consciousness, (2) extended the species of acts to cover a wide domain of consciousness, (3) developed by this extension a *psychological theory* of mind, (4) the fundamental component of which shifted from a special existence in an act into a relation of *reference* between a mental act and an object (the nature of the reference, however, he did not specify). A sophisticated reference theory of intentionality has been proposed by Bergmann. Brentano's work was an assessment of the nature of mind in a world, the existence of which was defined by consciousness. The limitations of his philosophical commitments to the analysis of consciousness and the stage of philosophical thought of late German Idealism of his period reflect in the characteristics of his doctrine of the relation of acts to objects.

SELECTED BIBLIOGRAPHY

THIS selected bibliography contains three parts: (1) Brentano's works, (2) books and articles primarily on Brentano, and (3) books and articles in which Brentano's conceptions are discussed.

Anyone today wishing to study the works of Brentano has the great advantage of the results of the previous scholarly labors of Kastil, Kraus, and Franziska Mayer-Hillebrand. With the addition of a few scattered contributions selected from my general reading in philosophy and psychology, the following bibliography leans heavily on their works. On May 25, 1961, the "Franz Brentano Foundation" was established under the management of the Boston Trust Company, 100 Franklin Street, Boston 6, Mass.

The entire scientfic works of Franz Brentano have been put on microfilm and deposited in the following libraries:

1. In Austria: in the library of the University, of Innsbruck.
2. In Germany: in the Staatsbibliothek of Munich, in the Goethe Museum in Frankfurt.
3. In the United States: in the university libraries of Harvard, California at Berkeley, Northwestern, and Minnesota; in the Library of Congress in Washington, D.C.; microfilm of some typewritten manuscript is in the library of Brown University, Providence, Rhode Island.
4. In Mexico: in the library of the University of Mexico.
5. In Argentina: in the library of the Philosophy of Law in Buenos Aires.
6. In Australia: in the library of the University of Melbourne.

Brentano's Works

A complete bibliography of Brentano's works will be found in Kraus's Introduction to the 1955 Felix Meiner edition of *Psychologie vom empirischen Standpunkt.*

Von der mannigfachen Bedeutung des Seienden nach Aristoteles. Fierburg: Herder, 1862.
Geschichte der mittelalterlichen Philosophie. In Möhler's *Kirchengeschichte,* 2. Mainz: Regensberg, 1917, pp. 328–484.
Die Psychologie des Aristotles, insbesondere seine Lehre vom Nus poietikos Mainz: Kirchheim, 1867.
Psychologie vom empirischen Standpunkt. Vol 1, Leipzig: Meiner, 1874. New ed. Leipzig Meiner, 1955.
Über die Gründe der Entmutigung auf philosophischem Gebiete. Vienna: Braümuller, 1874.
Vom Ursprung sittlicher Erkenntnis. Leipzig: Duncker & Humblot, 1889. (Published in English under the title: *The Origin of the Knowledge of Right and Wrong.* Westminster: Constable, 1902.)
Das Schlechte als Gegenstand dichterischer Darstellung. Leipzig: Duncker & Humblot, 1892.
Über die Zukunft der Philosophie. Vienna: Alfred Hölder, 1893.
Die vier Phasen der Philosophie und ihr augenblicklicher Stand. Stuttgart: Cotta, 1895.
Meine letzten Wünsche für Österreich. Stuttgart: Cotta, 1895.
Über Individuation, multiple Qualität und Intensität sinnlicher Erscheinungen. (Proceedings Third National Congress for Psychology. Munich, 4–7 Aug., 1896). München: Lehmann, 1897.
Untersuchungen zur Sinnespsychologie. Leipzig: Duncker & Humblot, 1907.
Thomas von Aquin (Written in memory of Thomas on the anniversary of the day of his death 7 March.) *Neue Freie Presse,* Vienna, 18 April, 1908.
Aristoteles' Lehre vom Ursprung des menschlichen Geistes. Leipzig: Veit & Comp., 1911.
Aristoteles und seine Weltanschauung. Leipzig: Quelle & Mayer, 1911.
Von der Klassifikation der psychischen Phänomene. Leipzig: Duncker & Humblot, 1911. (Simultaneously published in an Italian edition with an introduction by M. Puglisi. Lanciano: Carabba, 1913.)
Zur Lehre von Raum und Zeit. *Kantstudien* 25, 1920.
Die Lehre Jesu und ihre bleibende Bedeutung. Leipzig: Meiner, 1921.
Versuch über die Erkenntnis. Der Phil. Bibl. 194, Leipzig: Meiner, 1925.

Die vier Phasen der Philosophie und ihr augenblicklicher Stand. Der Phil. Bibl. 195. Leipzig: Meiner, 1926.
Wahrheit und Evidenz. Der Phil. Bibl. 201. Leipzig: Meiner, 1930.
Kategorienlehre. Der Phil. Bibl. 203, Leipzig: Meiner, 1933.
Religion und Philosophie. Edited by Franziska Mayer-Hillebrand. Bern: Francke, 1954.
Die Lehre vom Richtigen Urteil. Edited by Franziska Mayer-Hillebrand. Bern: Francke, 1956.
Grundzüge der Asthetik. Edited by Franziska Mayer-Hillebrand. Bern: Francke, 1959.

Books and Articles Primarily on Brentano

BARCLAY, J. *Brentano and Freud, A comparative study in the evolution of psychological thought.* Dissertation. University of Michigan, Ann Arbor, 1959.
BARCLAY, J. Themes of Brentano's psychological thought and philosophical overtones. *New Scholasticism,* 1959, 33.
BARCLAY. J. BRENTANO, F., & FREUD, S. J. *Existentialism,* 1964, 5, 1–36.
BEAR, H. *The Theoretical Ethics of the Brentano-school. A psycho-epistemological approach.* Dissertation. University of Michigan, Ann Arbor, 1955.
DEL.–NEGRO, W. *Von Brentano Über Husserl zu Heidegger.* Zeitschr. *f. Philos. Forschung,* 1953, 7.
FELS, B. Besprechung von über die Zukunft der Philosophie. *Philos. Jahrb,* 1930, 43.
GILSON, E. Franz Brentano's interpretation of mediaeval philosophy. *Mediaeval Studies* I., New York and London: Sheed and Ward, 1939.
GILSON, LUCIE, *La Psychologie descriptive selon Franz Brentano.* Librairie Philosophique. Paris: J. Vrin, 1955.
GILSON, LUCIE *Méthode et Métaphysik selon Franz Brentano.* Libraire Philosophique. Paris: J. Vrin, 1955.
GROSSMANN, R. Acts and relations in Brentano. *Analysis,* 1960, 21.
GROSSMANN, R. Brentano's ontology: A reply to Mr. Kamitz. *Analysis,* 1963. 23.
KAMITZ, R. *Franz Brentano's Lehre vom wahren Urteil.* Dissertation. University of Innsbruck: Innsbruck, 1961.
KAMITZ, R. Acts and relations in Brentano. A reply to Prof. Grossman. *Analysis,* 1962, 22.
KASTIL, A. Franz Brentano und der Positivismus. *Wissenschaft u. Weltbild Jahrg.,* 1949, 2 (Heft 4).
KASTIL, A. Brentano's Stellung zur Phänomenologie. *Zeitschr. f. Philos. Forschug,* 1951, 5.
KASTIL, A. *Die Philosophie Franz Brentanos.* Bern: A. Francke, 1951.
KRAUS, O. (With contribution by C. Stumpf and E. Husserl), *Franz Brentano, Zur Kenntnis seines Lebens und seiner Lehre.* Munich: Beck, 1919. (The remembrances of Stumpf here are the best description anywhere of Brentano's life and personality.)
KRAUS, O. Franz Brentano, *Neue österreichische Biographien* 1815–1918, 1, Vienna: Amalthea-Verlag, 1926.
KRAUS, O. Franz Brentanos Stellung in phil. Leben der Gegenwart, *Philos. Weltanzeiger,* 1928, 2.
KUBAT, D. Franz Brentanos Axiology.—A revised conception. *Rev. Metaphysics,* 1958, *12.* 133–141.
LINKE, P. Intentionalität und Transzendenz. *Wissenschaftl. Zeitschr. d. Friedrich-Schiller-Universität.* Jena, 1955, 12, 133–147.

MAYER-HILLEBRAND, FRANZISKA. Franz Brentanos ursprüngliche und spätere Sein-slehre und ihre Beziehungen zu Husserls Phänomenologie. *Zeitschr. f. Philos. Forschung*, 1959, 13.

MAYER-HILLEBRAND, FRANZISKA. Remarks concerning the interpretation of the philosophy of Franz Brentano. A reply to Prof. Srzednicki. *Philos. and Phenom. Res.* 1963, 23.

MERLAN, P. Brentano and Freud, *J. Hist. Ideas*, 1945, 6. No. 3.

MERLAN, P. Brentano and Freud, A sequel. *J. Hist. Ideas*, 1949, 10. No. 3.

PUGLISI, M. Franz Brentano. *Amer. J. Psychol.*, 1924, 35, 414–419.

SELLARS, W. & Chisholm, R. M. Intentionality and the mental. *Minnesota Studies in the Philosophy of Science*, Vol. 2. Minneapolis: University of Minnesota Press, 1958.

SPIEGELBERG, H. *The phenomenological movement.* Vol. 1 The Hague: Martinus Nijhoff, 1960.

SRZEDNICKI, JAN T. J. Remarks concerning the interpretation of the philosophy of Franz Brentano. *Philos. Phenom. Res.*, 1962, 22.

STUMPF, C. Franz Brentano. *Deutsches biographisches Jahrbuch II* (1917–1920).

STUMPF, C. Franz Brentano. *Lebensläufe aus Franken*, 2, Würzburg, 1918.

TERRELL, D. B. *Ethics, Language and Ontology: A Study of the Implications of Franz Brentano's "Sprachkritik" for ethical theory.* Dissertation. University of Michigan, Ann Arbor, 1956.

TERRELL, D. B. Franz Brentano's axiology. Some corrections to D. Kubat's *Rev. Metaphysics*, 1959, 12, 639–648.

WINDISCHER, H. Franz Brentano und die Scholastik. *Phil. und Geisteswissenschaften*, 6, Innsbruck: F. Rauch, 1936.

WURZBURGER, WALTER S. *Brentano's theory of a priori judgments.* Dissertation. Harvard University, 1951.

Books and Articles in Which Brentano's Conceptions of the Issues Raised by His Work Are Discussed

BERGMANN, G. *Meaning and existence.* Madison: University of Wisconsin Press, 1960.

BERGMANN, G. *Logic and reality.* Madison: University of Wisconsin Press, 1964.

BORING, G. *History of experimental psychology.* 2nd ed. New York: Appleton-Century-Crofts, 1950.

CHISHOLM, M. *Realism and the background of phenomenology.* New York: Free Press, 1960.

DEWEY, JOHN. The reflex arc concept in psychology. *Psychol. Rev.*, 1896, 3, 357–370.

FARBER, M. *The foundation of phenomenology.* New York. Paine-Whitman, 1962.

FINDLAY, J. N. *Meinong's theory of objects and values.* Oxford: Clarendon, 1960.

FLUCKIGER, F., and SULLIVAN, J. J. Husserl's concept of a pure psychology. *J. Hist. Behav. Sciences*, (in press).

HEGEL, G. W. F. *The phenomenology of mind.* Fifth Impression. Baillie trans. London: Allen & Unwin, 1961.

HINSLEY, F. H. (Ed.) *New Cambridge modern history.* Material Progress and World-Wide Problems, 1870–1898, 11, Cambridge: University Press, 1962.

HUSSERL, E. *Cartesian meditations.* Trans. by Dorion Cairns. The Hague: Martinus Nijhoff, 1960.

JAMES, W. *The principles of psychology.* Vol. 1. New York: Holt, 1890.

Marx K. and Engels F. *Werke* (Planned 40 volumes, Vols. 1–30 published by 1965.) Berlin: Dietz, 1961.

Mayer-Hillebrand, Franziska. Rückblick auf die bisherigen Bestrebungen zur Erhaltung und Verbreitung von Franz Brentanos philosophischen Lehren und kurze Darstellungen dieser Lehren. *Ztschr. f. philos. Forsch.*, 17, 146–169.

Quine, W. *Word and object*. Cambridge: M.I.T. Press, 1960.

Russell, B. *The analysis of mind*. London: Allen & Unwin, 1921.

Ryle, G. *The concept of mind*. New York: Barnes & Noble, 1949.

Skinner, B. F. *Verbal behavior*. New York: Appleton-Century-Crofts, 1957.

Sykes, N. *Cambridge modern history*. Cambridge University Press, 1960. Vol. X.

NOTE A
BRENTANO'S DOCTRINE OF THE FOUR PHASES OF PHILOSOPHY

Brentano's doctrine of the four phases of philosophy can be looked upon in some senses as an analogue in reverse with cycles within the history of philosophy to Comte's conception of the development of theories of causation (to which, we note, Piaget also owes much.) Comte's theory is that there were three states in the development of conceptions of causality: theological, metaphysical, and positivistic or scientific. The theological explanation is a superstitious projection into the relations of the physical world of relations of social experience. The progression of religious thought goes through three substages: fetishism, polythesism, to monothesism. The development from monotheistic religious explanations is achieved by the translation of the purposes of a hypothetical deity into abstractions of reason. The construction of metaphysical systems follow. The final stage is the scientific one in which rational relations are displaced by concepts of force and are studied on the basis of empirical grounds and with scientific procedure. Comte's insights had been previously formulated without the detail and supporting evidence by Turgot and Saint-Simon.

Brentano's doctrine, whether or not it was influenced by his study of Comte, has the complication of a psychological process that has repeated itself in ancient, medieval, and modern philosophy. It has the character of *Weltgeschichte* explanation that accounts for history as a dialectical development of an idea (freedom, social class exchanges of political power, economic structural determination of political power). The Brentano doctrine is that we can observe in the history of philosophy an *Aufstieg* and *Abstieg* that consists of three phases. The Aufstieg, the ascent, is characterized by attention to fundamental problems in a rational way but grounded in experience. The Abstieg, the descent, is characterized by the three successive phases of skepticism, dogmatism, and finally, mysticism. Table 12.1 gives the main personages whose thought is related in this scheme.

Three comments can be made about Brentano from the view of this conception of the historical movement of philosophical thought.

1. Brentano was a deeply religious man who wanted religion to be rational and grounded in the experience. His religious metaphysical efforts were an attempt to construct a system that was deistic and which had a place for a substance theory of soul and for the immortality of the soul. On rational and empirical grounds, he was forced by his belief in religion to oppose the doctrine of the infallibility of the Pope.

2. Brentano was sharply critical of the tradition of German idealism. One suspects that Brentano's suspicion of the German Idealists was derived from his preferences for Aristotle, Thomas, Descartes, Locke, and Leibniz. From Aristotle and Thomas he took the act theory of mind and the distinction between act and

TABLE 12.1. BRENTANO'S DOCTRINE OF FOUR PHASES

AUFSTIEG

PHASE I: Empirical philosophers engaged in rational reconstruction of philosophical issues.
Ancient philosophy (600–300 B.C.)
   Apogee: Plato (429–347 B.C.)
            Aristotle (384–322 B.C.)
Medieval philosophy (Thirteenth Century)
        Thomas Aquinas (1225–1274)
        Duns Scotus (1270–1308)
Modern philosophy (Seventeenth Century)
        Descartes (1596–1650)
        Locke (1632–1704)
        Leibniz (1646–1716)

ABSTIEG

PHASE II: Philosophers engaged in popularization and practical activity that leads to loss of conviction of basic insight and into skepticism.
Ancient philosophy (325 B.C.–200 A.D.)
        Stoics
        Epicureans
Medieval philosophy
        William of Occam (1270–1347)
Modern philosophy
        Hume (1711–1776)

PHASE III: Skepticism combatted by dogmatism.
Ancient philosophy
        Schoolmen of Plato's and
        Aristotles' academies.
Medieval philosophy
        Minor religious thinkers
Modern philosophy
        Kant (1724–1804)

PHASE IV: Dogmatism transmutes into mysticism.
Ancient philosophy
        Neoplatonists
        Neopythagoreans
        Plotinus (204–270)
Medieval philosophy
        Meister Ekhardt (1260–1327)
        Cardinal de Cusa (1401–1464)
Modern philosophy
        Fichte (1762–1814)
        Schelling (1775–1854)
        Hegel (1770–1831)

content. From Descartes, he took the distinction of mental and physical, and from Leibniz the rationality, interest in logic of language, and the possibility of a *lingua characteristica universalis*. His formulations were closest to those of Locke. It has been said (by Bergmann) that it took Brentano to point out how such in the Aristotelean tradition was Locke. Considering the differences and similarities between Brentano, Husserl, and Russell, it is interesting to note that the major early preoccupation of each was respectively Locke, Descartes, and Leibniz.

3. Brentano has been said (by Husserl) to have seen himself in the historic role of bringing philosophy back to its empirical and rational roots, a task Husserl saw himself later as his primary mission. In combating Idealism, Brentano avoided falling into either a sterile materialism or abandoning philosophy for science or an empirically groundless metaphysic. He attempted a theoretical reconstruction of the nature of mind and thus hoped for a renewal of philosophical interests based upon empirical grounds. This Viennese empiricism in philosophy, exemplified by Brentano in philosophy, in science by his contemporary Mach, and in psychology by Freud, was distinguished by its rational acuity. Viennese empiricism was not a "mindless empiricism" and out of this tradition of antimetaphysical empiricism controlled by rational thought came the Logical Positivism of the 1920s and 1930s.

NOTE B
BRENTANO AND THE DOCTRINE OF PAPAL INFALLIBILITY

In ancient classical times philosophers often were forced to flee for their lives because of the opinions they held. In the nineteenth century more than a few doctrines of literary and philosophical import were written while the author was either in jail or in exile; this was true not only of the Marxist writers. By contrast, it is not an uncommon fate of our contemporary philosophers that they are social conformists and apologists for any civil or religious powers. Notable exceptions in philosophy are Bertrand Russell and Jean-Paul Sartre; in psychology, Edward Chase Tolman. Franz Clemens Brentano is another such individual. How much of this defiance of local social, political, and religious mores is cultural heroism and how much is unresolved Oedipal complex, we shall not judge. For whatever reasons, Brentano's stand on religious issues took courage and he reached an inner calm conviction of the rightness of his action. The story is a complete one that can be summarized briefly as follows:

There were conservative groups and liberal groups in the Roman Catholic hierarchy at the beginning of the nineteenth century. Two principal issues at stake were: (1) the control of certain civil rights, marriage, etc, and education by the church or by the state and (2) whether religious belief should be based on faith or on reason. The liberals were in favor of religion based upon rational grounds, more recognition of the rights of the individual, and tended to align themselves with the restriction of temporal powers of the Church by the state. The conservatives took the opposite alternatives. Whatever were the liberal hopes for both political and religious reforms, they were defeated by nationalism in politics and a recoil from science into faith in religion. The revolutions of 1848 were a threat not only to the Church but also to church-supported conservative monarchial political systems. The response of the Papacy in this situation was, after appropriate councils in the Church, to publish on 8 December, 1864, the *Syllabus Erorum*, and on the same day an encyclical, *Quanta Cura*. This Syllabus, or Collection of Modern Errors, contained eighty propositions.

According to Sykes,

The first two sections condemned pantheism, naturalism, and absolute rationalism in seven propositions, followed by a further seven in condemnation of moderate rationalism. . . . A single comprehensive condemnation sufficed for socialism, communism, and secret societies, including Bible societies and free church societies. Twenty propositions relating to the nature, rights, and authority of the church were arraigned, specifically denials that the church is a perfect society, that the Catholic Religion is the only true religion, and that the church has any temporary power, either direct or indirect. Seventeen erroneous propositions concerning civil society were reproved; including the opinions that the civil power had the right to concern itself with religion and morals; that the state should control education, and that church and state ought to be separated. (Sykes, 1960, X, pp. 90–91).

The Encyclical was directed against modern theological errors; the Syllabus was a compendium of these errors. The shock of these two documents in the liberal catholic world was considerable and in no place more so than in Bavaria, particularly Munich. Meanwhile there were rumors circulating that a dogma of the infallibility of the Pope was also being considered. On the 18th of July, 1870, the dogma was promulgated. The wording of the doctrine translated by Sykes was as follows: ". . . that the pope, when he speaks *ex cathedra* to define a doctrine regarding faith or morals to be held by the universal church, is possessed of that infallibility bestowed by Christ on his church, and therefore such definitions of the Roman Pontiff are irreformable of themselves and not from the consent of the church." Sykes notes that the doctrine gained acceptance in ecclesiastical circles, although not the recognition of the temporal powers. He further notes: "A few prelates east of the Rhine, notably Hefele, Schwarzenverg, Haynald and Strossmayer, held out for varying periods before publishing the decrees and requiring their acceptance; but the most determined resistance came from the German universities of Munich, Bonn and Prague, culminating in the excommunication of professors Döllinger and Friedrich." (*ibid.*)

Brentano, when in Munich, had been a student of Döllinger and knew him personally. Under the direction of Bishop Kettler of Mainz, Brentano prepared a memorandum of the history of errors of papal pronouncements, so was placed in a difficult position of conscience. This was his inner break with the church. He was allowed to resign his vows. Since he had been appointed to the professorship at Würzburg as a priest, he felt obliged to resign. There was, in addition, considerable pressure within the university for him to resign that was due to university politics and not entirely due to this ecclesiastical affair. It is detailed by Stumpf in Kraus (1919).

After his resignation, Brentano visited England for a short time. In the fall of 1873, following a short stay in Paris, he returned to Vienna and started the writing of *Psychologie vom empirischen Standpunkt*. It was finished in a few months! Of course, it was based on eight years of lecturing on the general topics. The book had not appeared yet when, on the recommendation of Hermann Lotze, he was appointed a lay professor of philosophy at the University of Vienna. The appointment was made by the liberal Austrian Minister of Education, Stremayer, over the objections of Emperor Franz Jospeh and Cardinal Rasucher. Brentano's inaugural address was given in an atmosphere made tense by assertions in some of the Viennese newspapers that he was a "disguised Jesuit." The title of his address was "On the Grounds for Discouragement in Philosophy." The lecture ended in a storm of applause.

In 1879 Brentano decided he would like to establish a home. It is reported that in 1879 he was converted to Protestantism. However, he was always in metaphysics a deist. He married a sister of one of his faculty colleagues. This step was not against the letter and spirit of Austrian law, according to Kastil (1951), who states that the law prohibits priests from marrying, but allows the marriage contract to noncatholics. Puglisi (1924), however, interpreted the law as not applying to Franz, but as a prohibition that Ida could not marry an ex-priest. The result of the situation was that Brentano wished to get married, but was not allowed the marriage contract. He, therefore, gave up his citizenship in Vienna and took up a nominal citizenship in Leipzig in order to get married there. Giving up the citizenship in Vienna automatically required him to renounce his professorship. He returned, but from 1880 taught only as *Privatdozent*. The faculty of the university more than once petitioned the Ministry of Education for his reinstatement as a professor, but by then the German-oriented liberals were no longer in power. The petitions of the faculty were refused.

The "Affäre Brentano" reached great public proportions. It is remarked by Kastil to have been a forerunner of that "poison of nationalism" that hounded all independent intellectuals 40 years later.

NOTE C
IMPORTANT DATES IN BRENTANO'S LIFE

These dates were collected primarily from Kraus (1919) and Kastil (1951).

16 January, 1838.   Born in Marienberg, Boppard, Rhineland, one of a family of five children of Christian and Emilie Genger Brentano. In the same year the family moved to Aschaffenburg, Bavaria. Franz's middle name was Clemens, named after his uncle, a poet and writer of the "Jüngere Romantik" Heidelberg School. His mother, born Emilie Genger, was a very religious Catholic noted for her piety and regular attendance at 6:00 A.M. mass. She was a strong influence in his early life. Stumpf says that Franz was "the hope and pride of her strong belief." The Brentano family was descended from an old Italian family who left Italy in the seventeenth century for the Rhenish provinces. His uncle was the noted jurist Savigny, with whom he lived while a student in Berlin. Sophia Laroche, famed in German letters for her correspondence with Goethe, was his grandmother. His grandfather, who married Mamimiliane Laroche, was widely held to be the original of Maxe in Goethe's *Werther*. Bettina von Arneim (nee Elizabeth Brentano) was his aunt.

26 October, 1851.   Death of his father.

Fall, 1856.   Matriculated in the philosophy faculty of University of Munich.

17 July, 1862.   Graduation from Tübingen.

6 August, 1864.   Ordained a priest as a member of the Dominican Order.

Winter, 1866.   Habilitated at Würzburg. Examination on 14 July, 1866.

13 May, 1872.   Appointment as extraordinarius professor at Würzburg.

March, 1873.   Resigned professorship and travelled to England. Visited H. Spencer, Cardinal Newman, and others. Had been in correspondence with John Stuart Mill on theory of judgment, but Mill died before they could meet.

11 April, 1873.   Formal separation from the Catholic Church.

22 January, 1874.   Appointed lay professor at University of Vienna, upon the recommendation of H. Lotze.

1879.   Converted to Protestantism.

16 September, 1880.   Marriage with Ida v. Lieben, a sister of a colleague at the University of Vienna. He was denied the marriage contract in Austria and became, in order to get married, a nominal citizen of Leipzig. In giving up his citizenship of Vienna, he had to resign from his professorship at the University. When he came back to Vienna after his marriage, he taught as a *Privatdozent* at the University of Vienna.

30 September, 1882.   Death of his mother.

1887.   Purchase of his summerhouse in Schönbühel on the Danube. He was often visited while here by his students. Stumpf was an especially frequent visitor and in later years on occasion was accompanied by Husserl.

1888.   Birth of his son, Michael Johannes. Michael Johannes became a professor (physics, chemistry) in England and later in the United States. He recently retired from Northwestern University.

18 March, 1894.   Death of his wife, Ida.

8 April, 1895.   Departure from Vienna and travel from Zürich to Lausanne, and finally to Italy (to Palermo, Rome, and finally settling in Florence) in 1896.

30 December, 1897. Married to Emile Rueprecht.

1903.   Operation of both eyes in Vienna. The operation was not too successful and he could not read for the last ten years of his life.

May, 1915.   Moved to Zürich. Hostilities between Austria and Italy resulted in considerable local propaganda against the Austrians. Since he was by this time a citizen of Florence, he was in no actual danger. As a pacifist, he did not like living in such an atmosphere, so he left.

17 March, 1917.   He died in Zürich. According to Mario Puglisi, a close friend who wrote the Forward to the Italian edition of *Von der Klassification der psychischen Phänome* and as an Italian philosopher, the death was caused by appendicitis. Kastil (1951) says of Brentano's death that it was very painful and that in the moment of deepest pain instead of complaining he commented, "*Es ist so schwer, die Sinne zu überwinden.*" [To overcome the senses is difficult.] When he was in spasms from repeated vomiting, he is quoted as saying, "*Was Gott schickt, muss uns willkommen sein; es geht nur manchmal über der schwache Kraft.*" [What God sends must be welcomed; it happens sometimes to be stronger than our weak strength.]

NOTE D

BRENTANO'S CONTRIBUTION TO LOGIC

Brentano's contribution to logic, which was not only characteristic of his intellect and intellectual style, was also a clear anticipation of an important development in the field. In the analysis of the Aristotelean conceptions of logical forms, it can be shown that every categorical proposition can be translated into an existential one without a change of meaning. (Chisholm, 1960, pp. 66–67.) I will prove this with some examples.

1. The categorical proposition, "Some man is sick," has the same meaning as the existential proposition, "A sick man exists," or "There is a sick man."
2. The categorical proposition, "No stone is living," has the same meaning as the existential proposition, "A living stone does not exist," or "There is no living stone."
3. The categorical proposition, "All men are mortal," has the same meaning as the existential proposition, "An immortal man does not exist," or, "There is no immortal man."
4. The categorical proposition, "Some man is not learned," has the same meaning as the existential proposition, "A nonlearned man exists," or "There is a nonlearned man."

Since all of our four classes of categorical judgments which logicians are accustomed to distinguish are represented in the four examples I chose,[1] the possi-

[1] The particular affirmative, the universal negative, and the so-called (mistakenly) universal affirmative and particular negative. The truth, as the above reduction to the existen-

bility of the linguistic transformation of categorical propositions into existential propositions has thus been demonstrated; and it is clear that the "is" and the "is not" of the existential proposition are nothing but equivalents of the copula and so they are not predicates and are entirely meaningless taken all by themselves.

This serves in two ways to confuse the mistaken opinion that judgment is distinguished from presentation by the fact that judgment has a conjunction of attributes as its content . . . the being of the existential proposition replaces the copula and so lets it be known that it no more involves a predicate term than the latter. Further, it is seen quite plainly now the compounding of several elements which was believed to be so essential for the general and the specific nature of judgments, the combination of subject and predicate, is in fact nothing but a matter of linguistic expression.

Although Brentano was adverse to the formulation of an algebra of logic, but very interested in *Sprachkritik*, he arrived independently at a modern statement of the form of existential propositions. He did not, however, have the perception that his proposals were fundamentally only proposals of logical conventions. Brentano's proposals were similar in form to those constructed by Pierce with a symbolism and which later developed into an important convention in modern symbolic logic.

Logic, it will be recalled, was the ruler of judgment for Brentano. Leibniz held that categorical propositions A, E, I, and O were to hold for non-empty classes and thus were given existential import. Brentano's contribution, important for his theory of judgment and rejection of statements like the "existence of a golden mountain" or the "nonexistence of Pegasus," needed this doctrine for consistency in his system. Acts of judgment may have *Vorstellungen* as contents, but do not differ in kind from first-order acts in relation to predicates of existence.

NOTE E

THE RELATIONS OF STUMPF, FREUD, AND HUSSERL
AS STUDENTS TO BRENTANO

From the comments of Stumpf, Freud, and Husserl, and research about them, we are able to reconstruct Brentano's interests over a twenty-year period: (1) Würzburg, 1866–1870, from Stumpf, (2) Vienna, 1875–1876, from work on Freud, and (3) Vienna, 1884–1886, from work on Husserl's life.

Stumpf as a student and friend of Brentano. Of all Brentano's students, Stumpf was the closest and remained so during his life. Thus, it is to Stumpf, in O. Kraus's *Franz Brentano, Zur Kenntnis seines Lebens und seiner Lehre* (München, 1919), that we owe our most revealing insights into Brentano's life and character. Stumpf writes, "Was ich aber in erster Linie zum Ausdruck zu bringen wünsche. das is die Liebe and Dankbarkeit, die ich meinem grossen Lehrer shulde." [In the first line I want to express the love and gratitude that I owe my great teacher.] After Brentano had received his Ph.D. at Tübingen in 1864, he spent two years studying as a noviate and then habilitated himself at Würtzburg. At the beginning of this period a series of theses are presented by the candidate for habilitation and he is publicly examined by the faculty. The students and town people may, if they wish, attend the examination. Stumpf and his older brother, although

---

tial formula reveals clearly, is that no affirmative judgment is universal (in general it must then be called a judgment with individual content [*Materie*]), and no negative judgment is particular.

they had not known of Brentano previously, attended the examination. Stumpf was so impressed with Brentano's defense of his theses and the clarity and care with which he answered his examiners that he decided to take Brentano's course in the Winter of 1866.

In the Fall Stumpf heard Brentano lecture on the history of philosophy. These lectures consisted of a long introduction on the concept and method of philosophy. At this time (1866) Brentano lectured on his doctrine of four phases which, according to Stumpf, were formulated by Brentano while recovering from an illness during his Easter vacation in 1860. In these lectures the presentation of Greek philosophy was very detailed. Stumpf says that the friendly relation to his students on the basis of a mutual and unqualified dedication to the highest goals was one of the strongest needs of his life.[2]

Stumpf says that psychology was Brentano's starting point, but that metaphysics was the beginning and end of his thought. In 1886 he wrote to Stumpf from Vienna, "*Ich bin augenblicklich ganz Metaphysiker. Ich muss gestehen nachdehm ich ein paar Jahre ganz Psychologe gewesen bin, freut mich der Wechsel.*" [I am at the moment a pure metaphysician. I must admit after having been a psychologist for a couple of years, I am pleased with the change.]

Freud as a Student of Brentano. Philip Merlan, in two notes (*J. Hist. Ideas,* June, 1945, 6, No. 3; June, 1949, 10, No. 3) provides the following data on Freud and Brentano:

Freud was enrolled in the following courses given by Brentano: in Freud's third, fourth, and fifth semesters (Winter 1874–75), Summer 1875 and Winter 1875–76, respectively), "Readings of philosophic writings"; in addition, in his fourth semester (Summer 1875), "Logic"; in his sixth semester (Summer 1876), "The philosophy of Aristotle."

These were the only nonmedical courses taken by Freud during his whole course of studies (eight semesters).

In reading Maria Dorer's *Historische Grundlagen der Psychoanalyse,* (1932), in which she suggests that the assertion of a direct relation between Freud and Brentano cannot be proved unless they were purely personal in character, Merlan recalled a conversation with his former teacher, Heinrich Gomperz. To quote Merlan:

When Gomperz was preparing the second volume of the biography of his father, Theodor Gomperz, (the first volume of this biography was published under the title: *Theodor Gomperz, Briefe und aufzeichnungen ausgewalt,* erläutert und zu einer Darstellung seines Lebens verknüpft, von Heinrich Gomperz; 1. Bd. (1832–68) (Wien, 1936) he had to consider the German translation of John Stuart Mill's works, which Theodor Gomperz edited. The translation of the twelfth volume of this edition is the work of Freud (*John Stuart Mill's Gesammelte Werke,* Autorisierte Übersetzung unter der Redaction von Professor Dr. Theodor Gomperz. Zwölfter Band. Vermischte Schriften III. "Über Frauenemancipation." "Plato." "Arbeiterfrage." "Socialismus." Übersetzt von Siegmund Freud [Leipzig, 1880]); therefore, Heinrich Gomperz became interested in the question of how Freud came into contact with Theodor Gomperz. He wrote a letter to Freud asking for information and received the following reply, dated Vienna IX, June 9, 1932.

"Ich weiss dass ich Ihren Vater durch Franz Brentano empfohlen worden war. Er hatte in einer Gesselschaft . . . geäussert, dass or einen Übersetzer suche, und Br., *dessen Hörer ich damals oder noch vorher gewesen war,* nannte meinen Namen."

---

[2] We note below, Brentano's relationship to Freud on which we have very little data because of Freud's unfortunate destruction of his private diaries of that time. Freud's relationship with his young colleagues and his personal needs were very similar to those attributed to Brentano by Stumpf. We further note, in considering Freud's psychological acuity before he developed the psychoanalytic apparatus, that in his description of Charcot he was especially sensitive to this type of warmth and collaborative relationship with students, which was so rare in German universities.

In translation: "I know that I was recommended to your father by Franz Brentano. Your father, at a party . . . mentioned that he was looking for a translator, and Brentano, *whose student I then was or had been at an earlier time*, named my name." (Italics in the original and in translation mine [Merlan's].)

Husserl as a Student of Brentano. Marvin Farber in *The Foundation of Phenomenology* (2nd ed. New York: Paine-Whitman, 1962, pp. 8–9) says the following:

"My teacher Brentano" was an expression frequently heard in Husserl's classroom. His intellectual debt to Brentano was considerable in the early period; but it was the moral element and the personal example of Brentano which led him to choose philosophy as a life work, and which consituted a lasting influence on him. Husserl was a grateful student of Brentano, whom he accompanied, along with Stumpf on occasion, during vacation trips. He was not at the time prepared, however, to profit fully by such contact. The effectiveness of Brentano as a teacher is sufficiently shown by a number of noted scholars owing their start to him, a group including Stumpf, Husserl, Meinong, Höfler, and Marty.

He (Husserl) attended Brentano's lectures for two years, from 1884 to 1886, after having completed his formal university studies, in which philosophy had been a minor subject. Brentano lectured on practical philosophy, elementary logic, and its necessary reforms, and also on selected psychological and aesthetic questions. . . . He was impressed from the beginning by the slender form with the mighty head. The expressive facial lines seemed not only to bespeak mental labor, but also deep mental struggles. Brentano impressed him as one who was always conscious of having a great mission. The language of the lectures was free from all artificiality and display of wit. The peculiar, soft, veiled tone of voice and the priestly gestures made him appear to be a seer of eternal truths and an announcer of another world.

Brentano was most effective in the seminars, in which the following works were studied: Hume's *Enquiry Concerning Human Understanding* and *Principles of Morals,* Helmholtz's speech on "The Facts of Perception," DuBois-Reymond's "Limits of Natural Knowledge." He was at that time especially interested in questions of descriptive psychology, which he discussed with Husserl. In the lectures on elementary logic he treated Bolzano's *Paradoxes of the Infinite,* and also the differences between "intuitive and non-intuitive," "clear and unclear," "distinct and indistinct," "real and unreal," and "concrete and abstract" ideas. Other topics included the investigation of judgment and descriptive problems of phantasy.

It remains to note that Husserl dedicated his book *The Philosophy of Arithmetic* to Brentano, but as Husserl (and Farber) note, it was 14 years later that Brentano noticed this, and then "heartily" expressed his thanks.

CHAPTER 13

WILHELM WUNDT: THE GREAT MASTER

George Humphrey

Experience teaches slowly and at the cost of
mistakes

Wundt (1832–1920)

"'THE HISTORY of experimental psychology seems . . . to have been so intensely personal. Men have mattered much. Authority has again and again
carried the day." This characteristic dictum of Boring's (1950) is in effect an
epitome of Wundt's life and psychological influence. Wilhelm Wundt, of
Leipzig [1832–1920] was the Master. Other people had performed what were
and indeed are today regarded as psychological experiments. Bessel and Helmholtz had busied themselves with reaction time, soon seen as involving an
obviously psychological problem. Weber and later Fechner had related meas
urable stimuli with what had seemed to be nonmeasurable mental events;
Müller had related sensation and nerve. These men were physiologists or
physicists. Wundt, himself originally medical, took the great and what now
seems the obvious step. He founded a psychological laboratory and thus became the first experimental psychologist, the teacher of many German, other
European, and of American experimentalists and in consequence the instruc-
tor of two continents. Thus developed the grand master of the psychological
ipse dixit. The editor of this book has forbidden anecdotes. More than an
anecdote but rather a symptom of a great man is the fact that this writer was
once approached by Dodge, his then chief, with a letter saying that Titchener's forthcoming lecture would be "On the structure of the Physiological
Psychology." What did it mean? An Englishman should know! But he did
not. The lecture was given to a packed and applauding audience. The sub-
pect was the structure of Wundt's *Foundations of Physiological Psychology!*
There was no other "physiological psychology," at least none that would be
mentioned in the same breath! Carpenter's *Mental Physiology* had been published in 1874, 13 years before Ladd's *Psychology, Descriptive and Explanatory* in 1887, and 2 years before Maudsley's *Physiology of Mind* in 1876. But
in 1923 *The Physiological Psychology* had been written by Wundt, at least
in the Cornell laboratory and its offshoots!

The effect of Wundt's work was roughly to change psychology from the concern of a number of nonexperimental, somewhat philosophically minded systematists, and a kind of side interest of a numbr of experimentalists in other subjects, into an experimental science.

It is almost always the case that when one makes a statement about this man an immediate qualification comes from somebody. Someone may then say: but he was really a philosopher! Of course he was. His book on *Logic* ran into four editions, as did that on *Ethics*. The writer was privileged to hear him lecture on the latter subject, as well as on others. His general treatise on philosophy ran into four editions, the last in 1919. But yet he was the Great Man of psychology, the international Shouter Down. On at least two continents his pronoucements provoked disagreement, and investigation by his own method, experiment. For, at times, although he shouted he did not by any means silence every opponent. And of course an experimenter who provokes experiment is performing his own service, which is what Wundt did.

It has been said also that he borrowed from the work of others. Of course he did. For over two thousand years a string of great names had been associated with the subject. In many cases their influence lingers today, for good or for bad. There was Aristotle, "the master of those that know," many of whose chapters may still be read with profit; there was the great Aquinas [1225–1274], not so far from Aristotle's track, with his penetrating discussion of association, and what we must now regretfully dismiss as his "faculty psychology" (e.g., "is the nature of Reason superior to that of Will? This appears not to be the case." Rand's Tr.); Hartley [1705–1757], who wrote in the shadow of the great Newton and greatly developed the doctrine of association; Hume [1711–1776], "Here is a kind of Attraction" (referring again to association!); and Herbart, the antiexperimentalist [1776–1841], certain of whose principles were regarded by many, and well into this century, as fundamental for the theory of classroom instruction. It is important that these names be remembered today, but it is still more important to remember that none of them had used the powerful method of experiment, which Wundt was the first to turn systematically to the purposes of psychology.

For like other subjects, psychology has always tried to keep in the intellectual fashion. When the way to acquire knowledge was to sit in the armchair and think, thinkers, who were then philosophers, sat in the psychological armchair, or perhaps walked under the trees. When, a little later the *observation* of nature began to seem the proper method, Aristotle developed the first functionalism, maintaining that the subject of the science is the working body. ("If the eye were an animal, vision would be its mind [soul]".) When the philosopher was a theologian, we find a penetrating analysis of the problem of "faculties" in Augustine's [354–430] book on the *Trinity*. And when some of the more enterprising philosophers, finding that ordinary observation was not enough, began to live off the method of experiment, not that long afterwards psychology became experimental, and a science in the modern sense. And thus the curtain rolled up to disclose Wundt in his psychological laboratory, the first to make systematic observation of the "chainless mind," the man who in 1918, two years before his death, wondered at the certainty with which "imperfectly it is true," he saw matters fundamentally correctly (*Vorlesungen über die Menschen und Tiersele*, 1920, 1922). He was then 86 years old, and the first professional experimental psychologist.

It comes about inevitably and to some rather surprisingly, perhaps, that this account of the founding father of experimental psychology must begin and for a while continue with a catalogue of mistakes. For there is no doubt that Wundt, the originator of the first psychological Institute, and the earliest experimental psychologist, the teacher of two continents, was our founding father. And yet while he did use the new experimental method he made mistakes on such a colossal scale that one almost feels that the opponents of his Movement, such as the Oxford Philosophers, had a good deal in their favor.[1]

The Learned Establishment which opposes a new science for reasons that seem to spring from common sense is of course much older than psychology. It is in fact as old as the ancient Greeks, who thought it funny that people were interested in mosquitoes. Nor, as we shall see, is it unique to our science that its first laboratory should make mistakes as egregious as those of the inventor of phlogiston, as those of the Greek comedian; or of the nineteenth-century physicists, all of whom used the concept of the "ether." Phlogiston (1733), "A hypothetical substance or principle formerly supposed to exist in combination in all other combustible bodies, and to be disengaged in the process of combustion; the principle of inflammability': the matter of fire, conceived as fixed in inflammable substances" (S.O.E.D.) lasted at least to the end of the century. It did not hinder the great chemical discoveries of Lavoisier [1743–1794] and Priestley [1733–1804]. And yet it was such nonsense chemically that the first-year student of today if he knows the word at all would mention it only with a smile. The same thing may be said about the "ether" of space. It existed from Newton to Einstein. The properties of light were many of them accurately demonstrated by its use. But not until Einstein's theory of relativity did it disappear as supererogatory or more. It would be possible to find many more examples. But enough has been said to establish the fact that science, and for that matter other knowledge, has progressed on the shifting shoulders of falsehood. It will be remembered that in the fable, dwarfs can see farther than the giants on whose shoulders they stand.

The same is true even inside the experimental method itself. We of today are so much accustomed to regard experiment as the universal solvent that we fail to realize that even the best and greatest experimenters may fail dismally, both in their conclusions and their general attack on their subject. And yet in spite of this they may be great men, great physicists, great chemists, great psychologists. And it must be remembered that it was some worker or other working in a laboratory who saw through the mistakes. *Somebody* had to see that phlogiston was superfluous, and he had to do this through many inspired hours of ceaseless experiment and thought. Progress in science

---

[1] Many years ago the writer took at Oxford what is known as the "Greats" course, a compound of Roman and Greek history, philosophy, and modern philosophy. At the late Professor Pritchard's request he handed in his last essay proving that experimental psychology is impossible, Wundt being still alive. It was his last contact with philosophy, except for the occasion noted.

has often proved to involve the correction of old, obvious, and false ways of looking at things in order to see them in a new and better way. All this will be illustrated in what follows. It must form part of any account of Wundt's contribution to psychology.

The general outline of Wundt's work and teaching is dealt with at length and fairly exhaustively in Brett's *History of Psychology* (edited and abridged by R. S. Peters, 1953, pp. 479–490), in Murphy's first-class *History* (1929), and of course by the inimitable Boring. Here are set forth the main facts of Wundt's psychological life. They contain succinct and at the same time comprehensive accounts of the place of this great man. For, at the risk of repetition, great man he was. Since these volumes are so easily available, the writer does not feel it incumbent to repeat what has been so admirably stated elsewhere. A few paragraphs will suffice. In very brief summary one may say that *Wundt's psychology was subjective and analytic.*

Physics, chemistry, biology, and other experimental branches of knowledge properly called sciences all have their data, which constitute the foundations upon which the structure of their knowledge must be built. There were the atoms (we are now at the end of the last century), molecules, energy, motion, heavenly bodies. In the same way experimental psychology must start from its own data which broadly speaking are comprised in experience and the succession of experiences. There are many things which though they may seem, at first sight, directly given experiences, are not so on examination. One might instance any written or spoken word, which seems to be given in experience as directly as anything can be. But this is not so, since on looking at the printed word we see not the immediate fact of black marks on paper but something else as well, namely the *meaning* of the marks. If a rifleman is psychologizing he must describe only the movement of a patch of brown which he sees, not the enemy soldier which he knows it means. Thus "meaning" is not the final product of psychological analysis, just as the molecule is not the final product of chemical analysis. It is a kind of adjunct of direct experience, belonging not to the subjective world of consciousness but to the objective world outside. It is "context" of experience. To describe the enemy soldier, that is, the meaning of the moving patch of brown, is to commit the "stimulus error," which is one of the cardinal sins when one is introspecting. The "mistake" of describing "meaning" does not give the *final* product of psychological analysis, just as the molecule is not the final product of chemical analysis. This mistake is still sometimes important in experiments of the psychophysical kind. A subject with eyes bandaged is given a weight in each hand and asked which feels the heavier. There are two ways in which he can do this. He can honestly "heft" the two, and then, from what he "feels," make his decision. Or knowing somehow that the right hand one *is* indeed the heavier, he may so judge. That is, his decision may be based not on his immediate experience, but on what he knows or thinks to be there. Thus in point of fact, the fallacy of judging by "meaning," is in many cases at least closely related to the stimulus error.

The other notable part of Wundt's experimental method was *analysis*. For, once again, keeping in the intellectual fashion, psychology must have its elementary data out of which the complex, shifting mass of experience can be built, and into which it can be analyzed. The psychological element is of course the sensation, which has its own attributes such as intensity and clearness. The sensation is of course not an isolable fact of psychic life, any more than is the atom of physical matter but "a necessary assumption following the necessities of psychic analysis" (Wundt, 1893, vol. 1, p. 280), though, he thought, most chemical elements can be isolated.

Now consider some of the headings in the classic *Principles of Physiological Psychology*. The writer here makes use of the 3rd edition of 1893, since his personal copy of the last (6th) edition has disappeared in the way known to all teachers. For the present purpose no injustice is done. We have first of all twenty pages of Introduction, including ten of "Psychological Presuppositions: soul and mind. . . ." The latter distinction he finds it necessary to dismiss, as existing, together with Reason and Understanding, "in pre-scientific days." Here, for example, it is Wundt himself we see as the innovator, casting away distinctions and terms that had seemed indispensable to earlier workers. Early science always raises its own difficulties. Existing terms must often be not only discarded but firmly suppressed. Conventional language has frequently led science astray because of the implications it carries, rather than the "facts" it describes. (Salt *does* have the property of melting ice!). And yet, without the use of existing language and terms description is of course difficult or impossible, so that recourse is often had to neologisms which even then sometimes carry false implications. Will the "strange particles" of today's physicists sound ludicrous in a hundred years' time?

After the introduction there follows Wundt's first section "Concerning the bodily substrata (*Grundlagen*) of the inner life," comprising 200 pages of anatomy and physiology, and thereafter 300 more concerning "The Sensations." The next volume has a 100 pages on "Apperception." Of course, to a psychologist of today, these terms date strongly even though "sensation" is still in use. In the last edition of the *Handbook of Experimental Psychology* (Stevens, 1951) neither *soul* nor *mind* are indexed, even as historical curiosities, and psychologists hardly need to be reminded that the book comprises 1,300 pages. There is no chapter on sensation; "Sensory Processes" (an ingenious body-mind alternative) is substituted. Sensation appears twice in the index, each time referring to a footnote, though there is one appearance in a diagram. How many of today's generation of psychologists know what apperception is, in contradistinction from perception? It will appear later that the word is a legacy from the philosophers.

The point need not be labored. Summarized: it is that every pioneer in science has necessarily to stand on experience accumulated from the past. This accumulation is both of facts and of the description of facts. What seem to be facts often turn out not to be so; what seem to be descriptions are often found to be erroneous or misleading. Sometimes an observation is half true, which is obstructive. Does not the sun clearly move around the world? It is the business of science and of the scientist to examine these "observed" facts, and these descriptions, to subject them to analysis and experiment, using whatever techniques they may invent, or indeed that other disciplines may have bequeathed. All this was, to repeat, very much the case with early psychology and with the first "experimental psychologist."

Apperception

Common observation and common knowledge being available, but not necessarily or ultimately correct, how does this apply to Wundt? Dodge, who died between the wars and was one of the foremost experimental technicians of his day, explained the different impression made by a landscape seen by day and by moonlight as due to the difference in the "apperceptive masses." When, about 1924, Dodge was asked to explain this, he was referred to Erdmann's book *Apperception;* it was a mode of description of certain psychological processes which every young psychologist should be familiar with. In spite of the authority of the *Oxford English Dictionary* which dates it from 1839 (perhaps as an English word) quoting the Scottish philosopher Reid, the word will be found in Kant's *Critique of Pure Reason* (1781), who speaks of the synthetic unity of apperception; in Herbart [1776–1841], who makes the process into the basis of his still influential educational psychology; and, perhaps first of all in Leibniz [1646–1716], who says of it: "Therefore it is well to make a distinction between the *perception* which is the internal condition of the monad [perceptual entity, to paraphrase the *Oxford Dictionary*] representing external things, and *apperception* which is *consciousness* or the reflective knowledge of this internal state; the latter not being given to all souls, nor at all times to the same soul" (1695: Duncan's translation, of Leibniz's *Works* 1890). Now according to Titchener, apperception had in Wundt's developing system, that is, in the successive editions of the *Physiological Psychology,* an "overpowering influence." What then is this process as *Wundt and his contemporaries* saw it?

A concise statement is to be found in the 5th edition of the *Grundzüge der Physiologische Psychologie* (1902). Titchener's translation is used. Titchener was Wundt's pupil and his translation is in part paraphrased. Associations, says Wundt, in all their forms are regarded by us as *passive experiences,* because the feeling of activity, which is characteristic of all processes of volition and attention, never arises except as it is added to the already completed association process in a kind of apperception of the *resultant, given content* [Titchener's italics]. Associations . . . can arouse volitions . . . but are not directly influenced by volitions. . . . They are thus a *passive* process. The *apperceptive combinations* are different. The feeling of activity, with accompanying sensations of tension, precedes these, and the combinations [i.e., mental syntheses, G. H.] are *immediately recognized as formed with the aid of attention.* So that these are *active* experiences [Titchener's italics throughout].

Wundt goes on to enlarge on the notion, and we find that thinking, reflection, imagination, and understanding (to use popular terms), are considered to belong to a higher type of mental process, and involve apperception. The apperceptive combinations are based on association but their essential attributes cannot be found in association.

So far, so good. Apperception is seen to be something over and above the automatic, associative processes and thus constitutes a higher class of mental function.

Here it is worth mentioning that during classroom experiments on the conditioned reflex the writer found something like the kind of thing indicated. In this experiment which has for many years been used by the writer for class demonstration and has invariably been successful, a metal Xylophone running over two octaves, low G_1 to G^1, is used as the conditioned stimulus, a 6 v. car battery through a carefully adjusted Harvard Porter inductorium, as the unconditioned one. See Humphrey and Coxon (1963, page 25) and Humphrey (1927) for fuller descriptions, with instructions to subjects and so on. All classroom subjects learned without exception to lift the (shocked) hand when the preceding tone was heard, i.e., before the shock (20 to 30 stimulations). All who were asked stated that the hand "lifted itself," or some such phrase, ultimately, i.e., when the CR had been learned. These same subjects said, again with personal variations, that *at first*, when hearing the tone they "knew" the shock would come, but did not lift the hand until the shock came (Until I got a good shock! etc.). This gave way to the "automatic" phase. One may suppose Wundt would claim that "apperception" was at first at work (Query, with Volition?) and that it gradually faded as the passive association appeared. Of course the fact that skilled action at first involves complex "conscious process" which gradually disappear during learning was well known in Wundt's time as it is today; he himself mentioned this as a special property of the human mind.

In accordance with Wundt's interest in physiology it is not surprising to find that he assigned "an extensive region of the brain" (cortex), namely the frontal lobes, to the process of apperception, which, he says, the work of a number of eminent investigators has connected with the "functions of the intelligence." But intelligence is a complex affair, and all in all "These processes must be such as can be connected with a clear and simple psychological idea. We find what we want in the elementary idea of the *apperception* of a mental contents (sic) e.g., of a sensation . . . we understand by it a psychological process in which . . . a certain contents becomes clear in consciousness and . . . certain *feelings* arise which . . . we ordinarily term the state of 'attention'." (Titchener's translation, which is throughout adopted where available.)

In effect we now have apperception, the process by which a content of consciousness becomes clear, plus the state of "attention." Physiologically "the substrate of the simple apperception process may be sought in *inhibitory processes* which by the very fact that they arrest other concomitant excitations secure advantage for the particular excitations not inhibited. . . . We thus regard apperception as the one elementary process indispensable to any sort of 'manifestation of intelligence, and indeed to the higher functions at large. The considerations with respect to its physiological substrate are of course hypothetical." The general theory is of course not far removed from that of Pavlov (1927, Lecture 22. *Passim.*)

Throughout this discussion, which to a modern reader may seem to involve a good many "nonfunctional" words, it must be remembered that we are dealing with an experimentalist, one who maintains that the experimental method must employ physiological techniques to examine the body-mind complex that comprises a human being. We may think today that the term physiological has been somewhat stretched, especially when dealing with apperception, the subject of the present discussion. Physiological considerations seem to be dragged in by the hair. Rejecting intelligence as complex and indefinite (how right he was!), we still find that apperception is the one elementary process indispensable to any sort of "manifestation of intelligence" and indeed to the higher mental functions at large. For all to see, there follows an elaborate discussion of the neurology involved, including a very elaborate diagram, a "hypothetical schema"; here is shown an "apperceptive organ" with inhibitory and excitatory paths to and from it, centrifugal-sensory and centrifugal-motor. Thus Wundt listed himself among the "diagram makers" later castigated by Head. But Wundt's was the age of cerebral diagrams, and it needed a Head to shake them out, and even so they are perhaps due to return. It may be noted, however, that the whole schema rests on the notion of "inter-connection" between the separate cortical areas, "Physiologically, the principle of the connection of elements implies that every physiological activity which is open to our observation and analysis is composed of a large number of elementary functions the nature of which we may be able to infer but which we can never completely isolate. Our discussions of the act of vision and of the function of speech bear witness in both directions to this physiological significance of the principle of elementary connexions" (Wundt, 1893, p. 321). We seem to come out of the fog. "Every conscious contents, though it be . . . quite simple, conceived of in isolation from its connexions, and therefore insusceptible of further analysis, is always, physiologically considered, a complicated formation made up of various nerve processes spread over a large number of elementary parts" (Wundt, 1893, p. 322). Here one should remember that this was written before Sherrington delivered his lectures on *The Integrative Function of the Nervous System* (published in 1906). Had the master found the right road by now discarded paths? And should we equate Wundt's apperception with the conscious side of Sherrington's integration—remembering of course that Sherrington's work was with spinal animals—or at least make integration a necessary, perhaps indeed a complete prerequisite of the former?

These questions indicate the sort of turmoil which agitated the psychological world before Watson's revolution. The whole history of the doctrine of apperception shows able men feeling somehow that there was something there, something that had to be explained, but without the real techniques to explain it. The "Association centres" . . . centralize the functions of the body by "bringing into connexion all the different partial functions, sensations, movements, reflexes, synergies of sensations and sensations and movements that work together in the functional whole, . . . the connexions still admitting of continual adaptation to external conditions." One can see the almost inevitable confusion that Wundt found himself in before behaviorism had scoured the deck. Partial functions, yes. The *connections* admit of *continual adaptation to external conditions* (present writer's italics); of course. This is all consonant with modern physiological thought, and was, e.g., a generation ago emphasized by Bancroft in his account of human acclimatization at high altitudes. Bancroft showed that certain bodily "constants" change *en masse* with change of external conditions, the oxygen content of the blood, CO_2 pressure in alveolar air, the pH of the blood: "If artificially one is altered the rest alter in unison" (Bancroft, 1925, p. 178). Bancroft quotes St. Paul, who died about 64 A.D., who in turn might have quoted Hip-

pocrates [460–359 B.C.] whose oath of Medical Service is still used by graduating doctors, and in whose writings occurs a nearly identical passage. So that
this insight of Wundt, himself to some extent a classical scholar, had been
"in the literature" for a long time, and will long stay in it, and has been and
will be expressed in the technical terms of the day, whatever they may be.
It was a valuable thing to point out. But how can one *unify* sensations and
their groupings? How can a facet of "consciousness" with no mass or chemical constitution change a reflex, which is physically constituted and controlled?

Wundt and the Body-Mind Problem: Watson

Wundt has put his finger on a very important spot, and one which present-
day psychologists try not to see, like a Victorian lady "cutting" an out-of-
favor friend. It is the problem of "consciousness" and "will" in relation to
the human body of the physiologist. Present-day psychology has no reason
to be proud of its treatment of this enigma. The "explosion" brought about
by J. B. Watson's revolution of course liquidated, or attempted to do so,
one side of the uneasy couple. Henceforward psychologists were to take into
consideration only those processes which were amenable to scientific treatment, namely the bodily ones, their movements, and so on; the "objective"
processes. It is worth noting that this meant processes of the kind which
physical science had already found itself competent to deal with, and this was
perhaps not a very glorious program for a newish science, although it did
seem to be a real beginning. And so it was, of course, and *is*. It did also do
away with many morasses from which introspective psychology had been trying to free its feet. Watson stated in a lecture that one of the introspective
psychologists had claimed that nine degrees of clearness could be distinguished within attention, while another maintained just as stoutly that there
were only seven. Who could decide between them? "Clearness" said Ladd
and Woodworth in 1911 (p. 597) "has here a special meaning, which can
only be defined by referral back to attention. A vague or obscure impression
may be clear in this sense since it can be the object of attention!" Could
scientific psychology put up with this kind of thing? (It is fairly certain that
it was Ladd who was responsible for the statement, since there is a footnote
here referring to attention as one of the "most general forms of all mental
life" and explaining that such treatment is available in the previous edition
of the book by Ladd alone. (See Ladd & Woodworth, 1911, p. 597; Ladd,
1887, ch. III.)
Returning to Wundt we read further that "Consciousness is regarded as a
field of vision; objects enter it and are at first only obscurely and indefinitely
perceived, as are those visual objects whose images enter the field of the eye
at the sides of the retina. Time is required for the objects to arrive at the
spot of clear vision . . . where discerning attention is bestowed on them and
they are *apperceived*" (Ladd & Woodworth, p. 483, slightly paraphrasing
Wundt, 1896, Vol. 3, p. 384; and also 1893, p. 267. In (Wundt, 1922) one
reads of the motive of the will! One can sympathize thoroughly with Watson, and with the reviewer who wrote: come, come, THIS WILL NEVER
DO! In this chaos, confusion seems worse confounded!

A modern psychologist with the fury of the iconoclast in his typewriter may ask at this point whether time is not wasted in recording such things. This is of course the question Watson did ask. But we are dealing here with the historical antecedents of the revolution, and are trying to show that these able people had a reason for what they did and thought. For without exception everybody, lay philosophic and ecclesiastic, savant and man or woman in the street, *knew* at that time that his will enabled him to move his arm or to walk down the street, so that those who were interested and educated enough to bother with such an obvious fact would be glad to find in the great Wundt's writings (1893) a scientific treatment of it all. The headings read: "Fifth Section. Concerning the Will and the External Actions of the Will" (*äusseren Willenshandlungen*) A selection of the subheadings follows. "Inner and outer activity of the will" . . . "The will not an unconscious power" (*Vermögen*); while the next chapter, ch. 28, is called; "Influence of the Will on the Bodily Movements."

It is true that Wundt himself apparently modified these statements later at least to some extent. And it must be remembered that it takes a great man to reject such apparently obvious conceptions, and that in any case the fact that he made this change himself is part of the history of psychology. *Somebody* had to reject the old and ring in the new, and one must honor the man who did it. We of today, standing on great men's shoulders, are so much accustomed to regard experiment as the invincible method, perhaps as the universal scientific solvent that we are in danger of forgetting that powerful though it is, all experiment is not good experiment, and that without the adequate theory on which it must stand and which it slowly breeds the most meticulous laboratory technique may be entirely worthless, except as happened to some extent here, for the purpose of getting rid of apparently obvious but false "facts."

Once again many experiments were done on the hypothesis of phlogiston; the experimentors were able men, and their experiments, though we can see in many cases worthless, ably performed. Able men had to build on their work (there was no other) and, what is more important, the mistakes, the absurdities, did advance the cause of science. For knowledge must proceed and always has proceeded by trial and error, and in the process the errors are often as important as the true steps. There are "obvious" things which must be cleared out of the way before progress can be made. This was exactly the case with the "apperception" of Wundt and others of his day. Countless experiments were done in the Leipzig laboratory showing that association was not enough of itself to explain the facts of introspective experience, and which found that the additional experienced process of apperception was present. (Something like the same point was made by St. Thomas Aquinas [1225–1274]. We of today think the factor of appercertion unnecessary, and scientifically superfluous. Titchener himself, in his *Textbook of Psychology* (1915, p. 366–367) states, in 1915 (during Wundt's lifetime), "It is a question . . . whether there is any real gain in the introduction of the term." And it must be remembered that this remark was made by a great psychologist who both fully accepted, and was himself a distinguished expert in the practice and theory of introspection. But it would be entirely wrong to condem the work and the thought that went into the idea of apperception as a waste of time, "when there were so many other real problems crying for examination" (said to the writer by a distinguished experimentalist). For according to Titchener (1915, p. 286), Wundt's *Lectures on Human and Animal Psychology* (1896, p. 270) "began the *series of researches* that have culminated in his doctrine of apperception," and these researchers, have many of them enlarged our knowledge of association. Many features of Wundt's description of apperception (I quote Murphy, 1929, p. 166) are still current under the caption of attention. This the psychologist of the 1960s may accept, but he must add the restriction that present-day psychology has not yet really come to terms with what the introspectionists called attention; though physiological research on the reticular formation seems as though it may perhaps help!

Timing Mental Processes

Here was again a conception taken over by Wundt with attempted classification. He states that the figures show that the duration of mental processes is by no means so brief as has often been assumed. The phrase "quick as thought" does not refer so much to the actual rapidity with which idea succeeds idea in consciousness, as to our undoubted ability to drop out the intermediate terms in a train of thought, and so pass at one jump from the first to the last link in the chain of ideas. Apart from this, it is obvious, according to Wundt, that the absolute times of the various mental processes are of no importance whatever in themselves; they become important only when they help to throw light upon the nature and interconnection of our "states of mind." And for this reason the quantitative examination of the temporal course of ideas must always go hand in hand with the qualitative investigation of their relations. If it pays heed to these facts, the psychological chronometry of the future may be looked to for the solution of many an important problem. (Wundt, *Lectures on Human and Animal Psychology* 1896.)

To a modern psychologist this is a new world, almost like the world at the sea bottom. It introduces a famous chapter in psychology, one which, at least to the writer's knowledge, has been turned and never looked at since. If a subject whose reaction time is being taken, is asked to "pay attention" to the stimulus, such as the light which is to appear or the click he is to hear, recorded reaction times are different. "The attention may be principally directed upon the expected sense-impression. Or the attention may be mainly turned to the movement which is to be made. We may therefore designate the first kind of reaction where the sense organ is attended to the *sensorial* form; the second where the attention is directed upon the organs of movement, the *muscular*." These are the well-known *sensorial* and *muscular* reaction times, which, in view of the fact that the distinction is made by many athletic trainers, it is surprising to find omitted from the index of Stevens's *Handbook*. The distinction is not regarded as being so important as it was, but there is no question that it corresponds to a real time difference. There is now evidence of increase of muscular tension during the waiting and the reacting period, and it is possible that the distinction later made by Wundt in his *Lectures* (the 7th and 8th ed., 1922, p. 315) between instruction to react when the stimulus is as clear as possible (the final form of instruction) or as quickly as possible corresponds to differences in muscular tension. In fact, Wundt himself seems later to have had an inkling of this later experimental finding (1922, p. 318).[2]

But if Wundt's explanation, again, is examined, it will be seen how the introspective technique and aim of his time led him astray. First of all, Wundt claimed that a third kind of reaction was possible, where the two instructions ("when the stimulus-impression is apprehended as clearly as possible, and when the request is to react as quickly as possible,") which, as

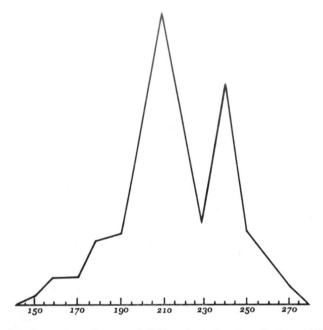

FIGURE 2. *Wundt's figure shows the natural division of reactions into the "sensorial" and "muscular" types. Reactions are from one subject and to a visual stimulus. They were of the so-called "natural" type, where no special instruction is given except to react when the light came. Wundt says: Such a curve does not show a single maximum but two maxima, "right and left of the center (Mitte) of which one is usually a little higher than the other. The time-values of the two most frequent do not completely coincide, but approximate rather closely to the sensorial and muscular reactions, taken in average, as these have been determined by methods previously described" (not intended as a literal translation but rather as a paraphrase). Wundt does not give the number of subjects whose reactions were thus plotted, but he does state that the maximum more often corresponds to the muscular time, though the contrary is sometimes the case; nor does he give the values for the ordinates. Time in minutes along the abscissa. (Wundt, 1922, p. 319).*

already noted, was an elaboration of the original instruction involving "attention to" the stimulus or to the movement and called by Wundt complete (*völlständig*) and abbreviated reactions respectively, admits of an intermediate, "when these special instructions are omitted or are only approximately

2 For an excellent discussion of the role of muscular tension, based on the work of Kennedy and Travis, see Woodworth & Schlosberg, 1954, p. 30, ff. Jacobson (1958) perhaps did the anticipatory work.

followed" (Wundt, Ibid., p. 315). He believes, however, that the two principal forms are more interesting psychologically, since they more clearly
exhibit the distinction between certain psychic states and processes (ibid).
In the present account and in what follows the last published opinion of
Wundt, now 86 years old (1918), is paraphrased. (As to chronology, the
publication date of the "seventh and eighth" edition of the Lectures on Human and Animal Psychology was 1922, two years after Wundt's death, while
the preface to the sixth edition was dated 1918. This was the last preface
Wundt wrote.) To continue his argument, he says that the direction to "apprehend the impression as clearly as possible involves an Apperception of
the impression [i.e. of the stimulus, G. H.], of its entry into the point of
regard (Blickpunkt) of Attention." The instruction, "React as quickly as
possible," just as necessarily entails the result that an apperception does not
take place until afterwards, since during the stage of pure perception, indeed
possibly simultaneously with it the reaction movement is not released until
the stimulus (sic) rises above the threshold of consciousness. From this difference of conditions says Wundt, it is easy to see the special attributes
which distinguish the two forms of reaction. Conversely when all these attributes are present in combination we can deduce the class of reaction in
an individual case. The distinguishing characteristics are in part objective,
in part subjective. The time taken over a full (Sensory, see Figure 2) reaction
is 210 290 ms. (Wundt of course used the older sigma for what is now
known as a milli-second. He also recognized, apparently with reluctance, the
terms sensorial and muscular), for a shortened one 110–180 ms., these times
including visual auditory and gustatory stimuli. Using at least 25 subjects,
the duration of a "full" reaction time is 210–290 ms., of a shortened one
110–180 ms. The mean deviation of at least 25 individual observations is
20–40 ms. (full reaction) and 10–20 ms., respectively. The longer time belonging to the visual sense. There are more "false starts" (Fehlreaktionen)
among the shortened form, none among the others.

It will be noticed that Wundt's psychological preoccupation with "subjective," "mental" events prompted him to use the terms full and shortened,
where later usage employed "sensorial" and "muscular" to which he himself
seems to have been driven. For, seeing that to him psychology concerned itself with conscious events, with "experience subjectively regarded," in the
total sensory reaction the relevant states of consciousness involving the stimulus (and the response) are clearly under observation, while in the muscular
type the series of conscious events is foreshortened. After all, he seems to
have argued, the stimuli must have been perceived, or reaction to it could
not have taken place. For it will be remembered that an important characteristic of the mind is its ability to cut out the intervening terms of a series of
mental events. In the case in question, of the series perception-apperception-
will-movement, the intervening terms apperception and will have been
skipped, and movement immediately follows perception. This skipping makes
a "shortened" form of reaction—the logic of which seems to the present
writer to need an examination which is not in place here. It may be noted
that Wundt's observation that in the shortened form there are more false
starts, i.e., in Wundt's own terms more reactions to chance stimuli from
other senses, reminds one of the effect of "extraneous stimuli" in Pavlov's

laboratory, the major investigation into which seems to have been done by Vassiliev in 1906, 16 years before Wundt gave his final statement. Of course the phenomenon of the false start as Wundt seems to have recognized, is transitory only, disappearing with practice. All this is easily verifiable in classroom experiment, either on the conditioned reflex or on reaction time. (Wundt 1922, p. 316, bottom; Pavlov, 1927, Vol. 3, p. 413, under Vassiliev). It may be noted that Vollborth's German translation of Pavlov's Lectures, *Die höchste Nerventätigkeit (das Verhalten) von Tieren* containing an account of "external inhibition" did not appear until 1926. So that one can hardly blame Wundt for not seeing this parallel.

Wundt elaborates: one may require a subject to choose between two stimuli and not to react until he has chosen. Then by subtracting the time for straight discrimination from that of *discrimination with choice*, we get *simple choice* time. By continuing in this direction we get the following table:

Cognition of a colour	30 ms.
Cognition of a short word	50 ms.
Choice between 2 movements	80 ms.
Choice between 10 movements	400 ms.
Association	300–800 ms.

Thus, he says (1922) *time of reaction is not in any way to be considered as a natural constant, but clearly affords a means of measuring the special conditions under which the mental events take place, rather than of measuring these events themselves.*

Thus Wundt, in his old age, seems to have cut loose from the notion that mental events of various kinds, such as apperception, perception, discrimination, etc., may or should be timed. This whole business of timing mental events which was at one time fashionable, must have been close to Wundt's heart. For in 1888 in the Leipzig laboratory Donders had invented (or was it Wundt?), what became known as the subtractive method, by which subtraction of one kind of complication time from another, it was thought possible to measure the actual time taken for mental events. The matter has been dealt with notably and clearly by Boring, (1950, p. 148). For example, by subtracting the simple sensorial reaction, as above indicated, from the simple muscular reaction, the time of apperception was obtained. This timing of mental events must have seemed to Wundt the beginning of an entirely new era in psychology, one in which the subject came onto the same plane, at least, as the older and better established sciences. It is indeed an earnest of this man's stature that in spite of the fact that the apparent advance had been made in his own laboratory, and in spite of the further fact that the death blow was administered by another pupil with whom he had desperately quarrelled (Külpe) Wundt nevertheless, finding the evidence gradually accumulate against this apparently brilliant step, abandoned it altogether. Wundt, one has to repeat was an experimentalist, the first real experimental psychologist.

What is wrong with the subtractive method? The process by which time taken by one "mental event" is subtracted from time taken from another more complicated one seems at first sight a reasonable method of estimating the extra time involved in the more complex process. And so of course it

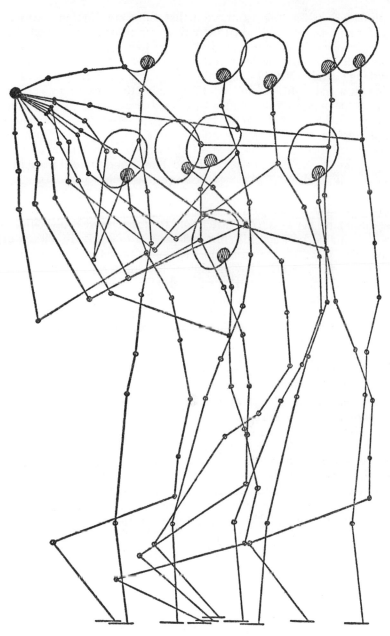

FIGURE 3. *Rosett's diagram of the manner in which a point in space can be reached by any one of a number of movements and postures. To say that a* person *has* chosen *any one of these to the exclusion of the others is to do violence to language, and does not correspond to psychological fact. There are, for instance, no organic processes corresponding to the postures not taken, processes either subjective or objective (behavioristic). (By permission of the publishers,* The Mechanism of Thought, *Rosett, 1939, p. 196).*

is. The false step was the assumption that the time difference was that required for an assumed additional mental operation or function. That is, that the time involved in paying careful attention to a red light (when it comes) may be added to the time for reacting to a light without regard to its color or anything else about it. One may say that reacting carefully to a red light is reacting to a red light. As indeed Külpe said, that reacting to a red light means not paying careful attention to a red light, and, thereafter reacting to the red light to which one has just paid attention. The subtractive method implies a kind of phrenology, as though "paying special attention to" were located in one part of the brain, from which a specialized message goes to some other part of the brain, and indeed this is exactly what Wundt said when he assigned apperception to the frontal lobes. To take another instance, a boxer hits his opponent on the chin. It would be absurd to fractionate this activity into separate processes, e.g., I see this man, I pay special attention to (apperceive) his chin, having first discriminated between his chin and the rest of his body. I then call the will into play, discriminating the most favorable movement out of the multitude possible for the arm, having chosen the most favorable of all stances for that special movement, but as we, with all students of the biological sciences, realize today, the body acts as a unity and the neurophysiological processes act as a unity, nor are there separate "mental processes" which must be undergone—or even skipped—for organic reaction. It is easy to see that Wundt's "out," i.e., of claiming that the mind skips part of the normal series of mental events, will not pass. For, in the case of the boxer described, let us say that there are ten "movements and postures" (see Figure 3) by which the chin of the opposing boxer can be reached. It is preposterous to say that there was a *choice* of *one of ten* possibles. The boxer does not choose, nor does he "skip" intermediate processes of perception, apperception, etc. He hits the other fellow's chin; the "skipped" mental processes are purely hypothetical. And in any case the reaction time for one stimulus and one movement chosen out of ten is given as 0.588 ms!

In view of the hypothesis of "skipping" mental processes this is perhaps not entirely a fair criticism, though one does seem justified in asking the purpose of an analysis that sometimes applies, sometimes not!

The fact is, of course, that the body is not a slot machine, with separate functions for each coin slot, nor can its total function be added or subtracted as such. This, I believe is what Wundt at the end of his life forced himself rather reluctantly to see.

Imageless Thought

It has been mentioned that Külpe, one of Wundt's many eminent pupils, took a part in destroying the subtractive theory by showing that introspection itself did not reveal the postulated subjective processes occuring during a complex reaction. It was, further, Külpe who by introspective methods disapproved Wundt's doctrine of the thought process, and with it certain of the dogmatic props of Wundt's whole theoretical structure.

It will be remembered that Wundt started with the assumption that just as physical science had analyzed physical matter into irreducible units, the

atoms, so must psychological science analyze conscious experience into its irreducible units, such as sensations and feelings.

Now Külpe, a progressive and highly experimentally minded pupil of
Wundt's, who had been appointed Professor of Philosophy and Psychology
at Würzburg in North Germany, had set some of his pupils to examine
experimentally the whole problem of thought. Aristotle had laid it down
that imagery was essential for thought. "We cannot think without imagery"
(*de Memoria*, 11, 453a). It is important however to notice that he did not
claim that imagery *constituted* thought. Images are necessary if thought is to
take place, which is a different thing. One may perhaps say that scaffolding
is necessary for building but is not a building.

What first interested Külpe was the nature of the judgement, which was
stated by the logicians to be the unit of thought (see Humphrey, 1951 p.
34). This obviously posed a problem for the New Psychology. A very elabo
rate series of introspective experiments however, as Külpe later remarked
(1922, p. 309), failed to find any distinguishing mark of this fundamental
constituent of experience. Everybody knew what it was to make a judgement;
nobody, least of all the philosophers, could say what the difference was between it and any other mental experience. This will hardly do for a science
that has broken down all possible experience into irreducible units which can
be recognized by qualified observers. It was as though a modern chemist had
discovered that certain chemical compounds could not be analyzed into any
known or any possible elements.

But the worst was yet to come. Marbe, one of Külpe's "young men" did
actually find experiences that broke all the rules of conventional psychological analysis, in that science could not describe them at all. These experiences
were called by the forbidding name of *Bewusstseinslage*, a name which has
frightened many psychologists but which is no more formidable than many
technical terms used by professional psychologists today. But the trouble with
this particular term is that, being in German, it has usually to be translated
for English speakers, and almost always in translation it has been distorted
according to the presuppositions of the translator. The chief sinner was Titchener, who translates the word as "conscious attitude" (1909–1910).

But anyone reading the papers (Marbe, 1901; Mayer & Orth, 1901) in
which the term was first employed must recognize that the word was used to
indicate that there were conscious data which could not be fitted into the
conventional scheme of analysis. If one may quote: "Certain events of consciousness which they could quite clearly designate neither as definite images
nor yet as volitions." That is to say, the term was *invented*, because there
was no other ready to hand. Actually the necessity of making such a new
term showed clearly that the conventional analytical framework had broken
down, not in its technique or its theory, but in its presuppositions concerning
the ultimate products of analysis. One may say that granting the introspective
method, Wundt was quite justified in adopting the hypothesis that conscious
experience might be analyzed down to final terms; but that he, with the
conventional theorists of the time, had failed to recognize and enumerate
these ultimates.

Returning to Titchener, for whom one must always retain the highest possible respect, this great psychologist claimed that the conventional analysis

could perfectly well be applied to these newly observed conscious events. They were "conscious attitudes" and the work was based on experiment for two faulty reasons. First, because the conscious events in question actually had contained imagery, kinaesthetic imagery which had not been detected by the experimenters. For Titchener "the kinaesthetic contents [he is speaking of conscious experience during reaction time experiments] are in the main sensations of intended movement" (1909, p. 448) and so the translation of *Bsl* is again *conscious attitude* implying that movement is going to take place, looking one may say, to the future, carrying the notion of anticipation, and consisting of kinaesthetic sensations, as Wundt had said. But this, it has been seen, is exactly what the Würzburg psychologists *did not imply*; rather they intended an entirely new and neutral term; both the translation and its implication are illegitimate. Secondly, the Würzburg experiments were spurious because what was reported was not solely events in consciousness but the meaning of those events. Now it is not difficult to show that the elaborate series of experiments carried out in the Cornell laboratories in support of Wundt's massive condemnation failed to prove this, just as they failed to prove the first point. When an observer was describing his experience we find in the introspective report "*Visual image of adult and then of child*; reference to my own experience. That was a line representing the time from the present to the past; there was nothing more that I can tell. . . . Memory of child was very plain but scattered and disarranged; a visual pattern made up of bits which were very clear, and which I could see very plainly; clear-cut and separate from one another. Memory of adult was like a spider's web, all united. All this fitted in, in some way, with the reference to past experience; . . . the two things fitted together; but I can't say whether at this stage there was any representation of past experience" (Okabe, 1910, p. 584). It should be remembered that this was professedly a pure description of a conscious experience, with no reference to the external conditions calling out the experience, either now or in the past. No "*Affekt*" is mentioned. That is to say, it was the description of what happened in somebody's consciousness, not of anything objective calling out that experience, such as meaning.

The example, one of very many possible ones, is taken from others in the writer's *Thinking* (Humphrey, 1951, p. 123). If he is not acquainted with that book, nor the original, the reader is challenged to answer the question: *What kind of experience was being described?* Nothing is omitted from the report save references to the instructions, which give the answer to the question (Okabe, 1910).

Other examples are given in the book quoted; here again only a selection is possible.

Before discussing this in the context of its surprisingly close relation to present-day thought the dramatic sequel of these very meticulously conducted experiments must be mentioned.

The new, hitherto unkown "element" of conscious experience had been examined by the conventional techniques, and had emerged triumphantly from the perennial accusation: "It is absurd" and "We knew it all the time!" But as often happens, when closely examined it actually yielded, not long after, to experimental classification or perhaps better description. The outcome was the doctrine of "imageless thought," a word of much controversy. This was in effect the doctrine that thought itself, or rather the process of thinking, was independent of sensation, perception, or imagery; that is, independent of immediate or immediately derived products of the senses, the receptors. According to the experimental results, thought was not even "sense-like," though it probably could not exist in a person with no receptors at all.[3] The ultimate form of the doctrine was that thinking is a separate species of experimental organic activity, with its experimental component falling within none of the sensory modalities. There is of course generally imagery during thinking, but it does not constitute thinking.

This then is the much debated doctrine of "imageless thought." For some time, until perhaps after World War I, it was almost a term of abuse among Wundt and his followers. A former President of the American Psychological Association once said to the writer, "You surely don't believe in that nonsense!" Titchener claimed that the dilemma was avoided by the notion that the image "carried" the meaning, possibly in a "purely physiological way" though what the difference was between the image that carried a meaning and one that did not, he never explained. Woodworth, when asked by the writer if he could get over this difficulty in Wundt-Titchenerian terms, said that, under these conditions, the question was unanswerable. One was left with Titchener's claim that recognition of a shade of grey might consist in a "quiver of the stomach." And the writer hopes that this treatment of a careful, meticulous, and learned experimenter, hard-headed disciple of his master, Wundt, may not seem derogatory to a modern generation. In 1951 the present writer wrote: "One who has in early days fallen under his [Titchener's] spell feels uneasy at thus criticizing him when he cannot reply!" (1951, p. 131). May the apology still hold!

These postulates and controversies of the beginning of this century seem a little ridiculous as the century begins to draw to its close. But it must be remembered that it was 1400 years before Galileo could correct Ptolemy, 200 before Newton could put order into Copernicus' work, while Einstein came three centuries after Newton. Külpe born 30 years after Wundt, the first systematizer of experimental psychology, showed by Wundt's own methods that Wundt was wrong; and Külpe died 5 years before his master. A psychologist may justly pride himself on the fact that the advance in his subject during 60 years has been unprecedented.

It must be added that the work of the great physical scientists was largely assisted from the outside, that is, by the use of mathematical or other techniques not before available, and in many cases invented *ad hoc* by the innovator. But the doctrine that thinking is of a fundamentally sensory nature was displaced by more exact psychological experiment, performed in a psychological laboratory by psychologists. Nobody pretends that the step which psychology took at Würzburg was as great as those taken by the great physical scientists. (Although it may be asked, how great is thinking?)

---

[3] Condillac's *Treatise on Sensations,* Paris and London 1754, has an interesting account of the possibility of thought with minimal sensory intake. He suffered of course, quite unwittingly, from the sin of being a philosopher, and is popularly termed the Founder of Sensationalism.

Equally it cannot be denied that the correction of this plausible piece of apparent common sense came from psychologists themselves as a normal part of the development of their own subject.

It may be asked what difference all this makes in present-day psychology. Actually the whole thing is mainly a matter of coordinates. We now say receptors instead of sense organs, though, for the sake of conscience, perhaps, we sometimes think and speak of sensory processes. We speak of reaction, instead of conscious state, and of motor performance, avoiding as far as we can any reference to conscious experience. The reason is of course that modern psychologists have found, just as the Würzburgers, and just as Wundt and Titchener did, the extreme difficulty of dealing with subjective facts in any scientific way. Though there are perhaps signs of a certain reaction as evidenced, among others, in the volume entitled *Cognition* (Scheerer, 1964). The classic example is of course to be found in Watson's statement already quoted that some psychologists distinguished seven, some nine degrees of clearness in attention.[4] If the question at issue between Wundt and Külpe is translated into modern terms, we should say: Can organic response be reduced without remainder to response strictly correlated with individual receptors? (Humphrey 1951, p. vii). That is, considering the organism which is being played on by multiple stimuli from the environment, is response relatively unaltered by the fact that the whole *organism* has made the response? For example, this has been thought to be approximately so in the case of the conditioned reflex, where bell-sound is originally followed by the "orientation reflex," *food* by salivation. By this way of thinking the organism's contribution then is merely to drop out (inhibit) orientation and to respond by salivatoin. to the bell alone. This function of the organism may therefore be regarded as mainly one of elementary integration, something in the classical Sherringtonian manner where a reaction is inhibited. On the other hand, ought the conditioned reflex to be regarded as a response of the whole organism to the totality of the surrounding organic conditions, thus profoundly changing to a response-of-the-organism what might have been thought of as a simple reaction to an elementary stimulus? That is, as the followers of the Gestalt school maintain, is the organism continually creative? In support of the latter possibility it may be remembered that the experimental evidence of the last 30 years does seem to show that the conditioned response is only as an almost unique case identical with the unconditioned one, that the chemical composition of what may be called conditioned saliva is not identical with that of non-conditioned saliva. The question is not yet settled, since psychologists of the highest standing are ranged on the side of either hypothesis. But it is obvious that the problem is at least a parallel one to that in issue between Wundt and his critics, always remembering that "images" are of sensory modality.

The General Contribution of Wundt

What then has this man done for psychology as it has developed until today? Certainly he has taken the subject out of the hands of philosophers,

---

[4] The writer does not know to which workers he was referring.

and put it into the laboratory. There were indeed, those who performed psychological experiments. There was Helmholtz [1821–1894], whose unparalleled work on the sense organs, and whose equally remarkable volumes on *Hearing* and *Vision* are still standard. It is even true that Helmholtz is reported (the writer heard it said) to have remarked that some of Wundt's experiments were a bit "sloppy" *(schlampig)*. Perhaps by his standards some of the work done in the Leipzig laboratory was indeed "schlampig." Perhaps even then the new science was beginning to annoy the Establishment, as in many countries it has continued to do ever since. Also there were as forerunners the reaction-time workers, such as the astronomer, for whom it was a professional problem. Their results were adopted by Wundt and upon them he used, perhaps unfortunately, his own psychological methods of analysis, however wrong in theory, yet refined in detail of timing to a degree such as has never since been demanded. There was the inimitable Fechner; and his predecessor Weber, from whom stem the "psychophysical methods"; Hering, authority on color. There was Ebbinghaus, whose methods are still in use, and so on. These were great men, and they have contributed greatly to experimental psychology as it is today. And as for Wundt himself, he recognized the problem of visual size constancy, and could not understand why the retinal image was "inverted." (When the eye turns up the muscles pull down, he said.) But the credit and the insight of establishing for the first time a laboratory, work in which was to be nothing but experimental psychology, this is due to Wundt. He cleared the ground for modern experiment, by making mistakes, as earlier indicated. They were the right and inevitable mistakes presupposing as they did the adoption of beliefs and "common sense," inherited from many years of speculation, and "obviousness" on the part both of the man in the street and of the philosopher in his study. Somebody had to put his head down and charge at this clear and distinct fact, that is, to take the theological and philosophical presuppositions of the day and show where they led. And if they occasionally led to what a generation of later workers can recognize as absurdity, so what? It will be remembered that the common sense of today is often the speculation of yesterday, and this was certainly so in the case of early psychology. It must also be remembered that Wundt did what he did against great opposition, personal and official. Many of his opponents were sure that the study of the mind would cause an epidemic of insanity at the University because the students would be forced to examine their own minds too much! One should realize that in addition to the direction of a large department his days were spent, according to Boring, writing over two pages a day throughout his professional life; editing— the *Philosophische Studien* was started in 1883, and continued off and on for most of his life; discussing at great length Social Psychology—his *Völkerpsychologie* ran to ten volumes; revising his massive *Physiological Psychology* to the sixth edition (three volumes), a work which has indeed been described as comprising mostly anatomy and less physiology. There were works on Human and Animal Psychology, Hypnotism, Spiritualism, and many more. In addition to all this, he was highly and fluently productive in philosophy, of which subject he actually held the chair, despite his early training in anatomy and medicine. In the library of Cambridge University the writer counted well over thirty book titles under his name, and the list is certainly by no means complete. He sent out his young men to spread through two continents the notion that the mind itself was to be the subject of experiment, and founded for that purpose the first of all psychological laboratories. Could the number of psychological laboratories be counted today in three figures? The inexhaustible energy of his pen smote those who dared oppose him, and sometimes his own previous writings, even though, one feels, a number of his own young men, with others, refused to be smitten! This was the man who, through his pupils and his own labors, and starting with the traditional mistakes of his time and making them his own, and who by many thousands of hours of experiment and controversy showed current presuppositions, for what they really were. He prepared the way for the experimental psychology we have today.

REFERENCES

BANCROFT, J. *The respiratory function of the blood.* Cambridge: Cambridge University Press, 1925.

BORING, E. G. *A history of experimental psychology.* New York: Appleton-Century, 1950.

BORING, E. G., LANGFELD, H. S. & WELD, H. P. *Foundations of modern psychology.* New York: Wiley, 1948.

BRETT, G. S. *History of psychology.* R. S. Peters (Ed.) New York: Macmillan, 1953.

CARPENTER, W. B. *Principles of human physiology.* London: Churchill, 1874.

HUMPHREY, G. Effect of sequences of indifferent stimuli on a response of the conditioned reflex type. *J. abnorm. soc. Psychol.,* 1927, 22.

HUMPHREY, G. *Thinking.* New York: Wiley, 1951.

HUMPHREY, G., & COXEN, R. V. *The chemistry of thinking.* Springfield, Ill.: Thomas, 1963.

JACOBSON, E. *Progressive relaxation.* Chicago: University of Chicago Press, 1958.

KULPE, O. *Vorlesungen über Psychologie.* Leipzig: Hirzel, 1922.

LADD, G. T. *Psychology, descriptive and explanatory.* New York: Macmillan 1887.

LADD, G. T., & WOODWORTH, R. S. *Elements of physiological psychology.* New York: Scribner, 1911.

LEIBNIZ, G. W. *Philosophical works.* (Trans. Duncan.) New Haven: Tuttle, Morehouse, & Taylor, 1890.

MARBE, K. *Experimentell-psychologische Untersuchungen über das Urteil: Eine Einlietung in die Logik.* Leipzig: Engelmann, 1901.

MAUDSLEY, H. *Physiology of mind.* New York: Macmillan, 1876.

MAYER, A., & ORTH, J. Zur qualitativen Untersuchung der Associationen. *Ztschr. f. Psychol.,* 1901, 26, 1–13.

MURPHY, G. *Historical introduction to modern psychology.* New York: Harcourt, Brace, 1929.

OKABE, T. An experimental study of belief. *Amer. J. Psychol.,* 1910, 21, 563–596.

PAVLOV, I. P. *Lectures on conditioned reflexes.* New York: Liveright, 1927.

ROSETT, J. *The mechanism of thought.* New York: Columbia University Press, 1939.

SCHEERER, CONSTANCE. *Cognition.* New York: Harper & Row, 1964.

STEVENS, S. S. *Handbook of experimental psychology.* New York: Wiley, 1951.

TITCHENER, E. B. *Lectures on the experimental psychology of the thought processes.* New York: Macmillan, 1909.

TITCHENER, E. B. *Textbook of psychology.* New York: Macmillan, 1915.

WOODWORTH, R. S., & SCHLOSBERG, H. *Experimental psychology.* New York: Holt, 1954.

WUNDT, W. *Lectures on human and animal psychology.* 2nd ed. London: (Trans. by E. B. Titchener.) Allen, 1896.

WUNDT, W. *Principles of physiological psychology.* 3rd ed. (Trans. by E. B. Titchener) London: Macmillan, 1893. 2 vols.

WUNDT, W. *Elements of folk-psychology.* London: Allen, 1916.

WUNDT, W. *Erlebtes und Erkanntes.* Stuttgart: Kröner, 1920.

CHAPTER 14

BRADLEY, WARD, AND STOUT

D. W. Hamlyn

THE THREE men to be considered in this chapter were as much philosophers as psychologists. None of them occupied a post in psychology as such; but this is understandable, since, in their heyday no such post existed. James Ward, however, was Professor of Mental Philosophy at Cambridge; and G. F. Stout, while Professor of Logic and Metaphysics at St. Andrews, was at some time Wilde Reader in Mental Philosophy at Oxford. Hence, they were professional psychologists to the extent that it was possible to be in Great Britain at their time. F. H. Bradley was always officially a philosopher—Fellow of Merton College, Oxford; but he was as interested as the others in many of the same problems—the nature of feeling and perception, of the thought processes, and the paraphernalia of cognitive psychology generally. There was much argument and discussion among all three of them in journals such as *Mind* during the years about the turn of the century. It is impossible to consider these men as psychologists without also considering them as philosophers, since behind their thought on psychological matters lay a whole mass of philosophical and metaphysical thought arising out of related but nevertheless differing traditions. They had this much in common—an opposition to the principles of empiricism, both in the form which that movement took among the British empiricists of the eighteenth century, and more particularly in the form which it took at the hands of James Mill, J. S. Mill, and Alexander Bain in the nineteenth century. In this respect they form part of a general reaction which took place at the end of the nineteenth century against the sensationalist and associationist psychologies which were an essential part of nineteenth-century empiricism. In particular, they were uniformly opposed to the view that what goes on in the mind can be analyzed and broken down into a number of elements of an atomic kind—sensations and their corresponding ideas—which might subsequently be compounded together by the processes of the association of ideas. They were opposed to this in two main ways, firstly in denying that experience could be so analyzed into atomic elements, and secondly in emphasizing the point that the mental life is a far more active business than the sensationalists and associationists allowed for.

Their common opposition to sensationalism and associationism had, nevertheless, somewhat different roots. Ward and Stout were closest together, a fact which they acknowledged in their publications. They both admitted a particular debt to Herbart and Brentano, although the influence of the latter was perhaps stronger and more obvious in the case of Stout. They were both agreed on the importance of William James, as was also Bradley, however much he was opposed to James in his general metaphysics. All three were metaphysicians in their own right, but in an important sense the thinking of Ward and Stout on the philosophy of mind stemmed from a long acquaintance with the associationist tradition, especially perhaps Bain. They were soaked in that tradition, however much they reacted against it. Bradley, on the other hand, was first and foremost a philosopher of the idealist school; he was, indeed, the leading English idealist. The roots of his philosophy were in Hegel. He was, in consequence, profoundly opposed to the very principles upon which associationism rested. His was not just an opposition to associationism as such, but an opposition to the philosophical standpoint from which associationism stemmed.

F. H. Bradley

Hegel maintained in his *Phenomenology of Mind* that what is presented to the mind in experience is merely the bare fact of experience, without distinctions or relations. Experience as we are ordinarily aware of it is what the understanding makes of this bare "given" by means of judgment, by the attachment of universals or ideas to experience. Bradley also maintained this point of view, asserting that as far as what is "given" is concerned there is not even a distinction between self and not-self; this too is something that the understanding brings with it. There is nothing such as the self or an ego to be found directly in experience. In emphasizing the passiveness of bare experience, Bradley, following Hegel, was no doubt at one with the empiricists; but in this alone. For the lack of relations or distinctions within "given" experience means that it is impossible for it to be broken up into basic sensations or ideas. Furthermore, Bradley maintained that the whole notion that thought could be built up out of ideas, particular mental occurrences, by means of association, was wrong; for this notion leaves out of account the essential role played by universals. In Bradley's view, an idea was not, as it was for the nineteenth-century associationists, a particular mental item; it was something strictly universal. Association, he said, marries only universals.

Bradley's conception of an idea, however, was not without its own ambiguities. The term has suggestions of the tradition to which he was so much opposed. It *suggests* the notion of individual mental items, whatever the role which they play in thought. There is, moreover, in ordinary discourse the distinction between "my idea" and "the idea," the latter being an objective conception of something, not some particular person's thought. Bradley's failure to distinguish these completely was criticized by G. E. Moore at the beginning of his revolt against idealism in favour of realism. In spite of Bradley's attempt to keep psychologism out of logic, he failed to do so completely. In another but connected respect Bradley himself became conscious of an inadequacy in his thought, largely due to the prompting of his fellow idealist, Bernard Bosanquet. This was that by speaking with too much emphasis about ideas he was giving the impression that he thought the existence of separate ideas a possibility in some sense. This view was too close to the associationist tradition with its emphasis on separately existing ideas as the constituents of the mental life. For, in one respect at least Bradley was certainly at one with logicians such as Frege and Russell who developed the new formal logic at the end of the nineteenth century; that is that the basic unit of thought was not the idea but the judgment (or, in more logical terms, the proposition). The whole empiricist tradition had thought of ideas as the building blocks out of which were to be constructed different mental processes. According to Bradley, ideas had no existence apart from judgment, a fact which he insisted on by saying that there were no "floating ideas." In effect, ideas were merely the universal, predicative part of judgment, the latter consisting of an attribution to something, to some part of reality, of a universal content. This view did not, of course, free him from objections of the kind which Moore made against the ambiguity of the term "idea." For, similar objections can be made, and were made, against the notion of judgment.

What, then, Bradley substituted for the earlier conception that the whole of the mental life is built up from a number of atomic building blocks, sensations and their corresponding ideas, was the conception that the basic unit of the mental life is judgment. This last is the work of the understanding. Apart from the understanding itself, there is at the one end reason and at the other end bare experience, featureless and without differentiation, the only "given." But what is the relation between this bare, featureless experience and judgment? If it were the case that judgment merely organizes experience, imposing ideas upon it, this would be an entirely arbitrary matter, and would for that reason lack all objectivity. To be objective, judgment must somehow be rooted in experience. This was no problem for the sensationalists, since, in their view, all relevant distinctions were already given in experience. The Hegelian doctrine, on the other hand, is that each level of the mental life is unstable, even contradictory, and points the way towards its resolution or transcendence at the next higher level. Hence, experience, while featureless, has to point the way to the distinctions which will emerge from it. There are other difficulties here also which derive from similar points in the sensationalist predecessors. Their "sensations" were supposed to be both sensations in the sense in which a pain is one, and also something having perceptual content, i.e., something that tells us of a world quite separate from us, as pains do not necessarily do. Similarly Bradley views experience both as feeling and as something that constitutes an awareness of something else. Some sensationalists, for example, James Mill, had spoken as if things, material objects, were just collections of sensations, and had thus carried on a tradition of idealism which goes back to Berkeley. Bradley's thinking is in this respect too in much the same vein. On his view, experience is feeling and yet is also an awareness of an object. If all that is "given" is experience, then what one is aware of can only be experience. Hence, experience must be both "given" and aware of itself. How this can be so is a problem for Bradley, and one which he really finds unanswerable.

The featureless mass of experience has, then, a tendency to differentiate itself. There is first the differentiation between the permanent conditions of sensation and what is variable, and this leads to a differentiation between what is the self and what is not. Similarly, between parts of the not-self groupings tend to occur in relation to their content. Indeed Bradley maintains that every mental element tends "by means of fusion and reintegration to give itself a context through identity of content" (Bradley 1935, I, p. 212). This he calls the Law of Individuation. The whole process remains obscure, and there is indeed an essential obscurity here in the attempt to say how what is originally quite featureless can acquire characteristics, without this being in any way an arbitrary matter. Reality has to fit the ideas under which it is subsumed, even if there is originally no distinction within to make this possible. In one sense we impose universal features on reality when we attribute ideas to it in judgment; in another sense these are already based on experience itself and thus somehow already in what is "given." This apparent contradiction has, however, no terrors for the Hegelian, since on this view such contradictions appear at every level of experience or thought, and are resolved at the next higher level.

The issues so far discussed are on Bradley's view, however, the subject of philosophy, not psychology. The correct approach to adopt in psychology, he argued, was what he called phenomenalism, it is the study of events, considered only in terms of coexistence and succession—the study of sensations, feelings, images, etc., without regard to their logical role. The significance of mental events is not a matter for psychology at all. This view makes psychology a very trivial business, and so it is perhaps for idealist philosophers in general. (R. G. Collingwood, for example, maintained that psychology was just the study of feeling; it could have no concern with the thought processes.) According to Bradley, as we have seen, the original featureless experience tends to organize itself into groupings having identity of content. These groupings are fundamentally mere abstractions from the whole "given." There is merely an inevitable tendency for experience to form wholes in this way in cooperation with the understanding. Psychology can study these features of experience as they develop. Given this view, it may appear that the most important thing which Bradley offered to psychology is what he thought was no part of it—the part which judgment plays in perception and experience in general.

His immediate historical influence was of a more negative kind, in his rejection of the earlier view concerning the atomistic elements of experience. For, Bradley repeatedly maintains that there are no such elements. We are not given atomic sensations, particular mental elements, which bring with them a certain content or information. In the first place, Bradley maintains, there are no such elements to be found in experience; and in the second place, the content which the sensationalists asserted was provided by sensations must be universal in nature and cannot for that reason be provided by mere particulars. For similar reasons, association cannot be a process which links particulars of this sort. Whether the association be one of contiguity or similarity, it depends on the particular mental events having an identity which can only be determined by content. When it is said, for example, that mental event X becomes associated with mental event Y because X and Y are contiguous in experience, this presumes that we can speak of mental events occurring at different times as the same event, the same X and the same Y. But are we entitled to do this unless the identity of the mental events is determined by their content? For, events which occur at different times may not be numerically the same. Hence identity of mental events reduces itself to identity of content, of the universal features which they possess, or of their signification. But in this case our knowledge of the identity of mental events presupposes knowledge of universals, and hence, what we associate, properly speaking, are the universal or general features of mental events. It is for this reason that association, Bradley claims, marries only universals.

In this way Bradley undermines the whole foundation on which sensationalism and its accompanying associationism were built. Furthermore, what he says brings out the point that we cannot understand perception, for example, without appreciating the part which judgment, or at least the ascription of general features to things, plays. Perception is not just passively receiving sensations, and the sensationalist attempt to make what they called sensations more then sensations in the ordinary sense (i.e., feelings like pains), and so to analyze perception, exhibits a radical incoherence. In this respect Bradley was surely right, whatever one may think of his general idealist apparatus. Yet, as we have already seen, Bradley was at one with the sensationalists in one respect—in supposing that there was a "given" at all. The attempt to square the view that the "given" has fundamentally no content, being featureless, with the view that it provides a basis or ground for judgment has the paradoxical consequences already noted (even if for an idealist they are not paradoxical at all). Behind the view that there is a "given" lies an epistemological view that knowledge must have certain and sure foundations. This view is, at least on one traditional interpretation, mistaken even in epistemology. It has certainly no place in psychology, and perception must be understood without it.

It can be said in sum that Bradley's contribution to an understanding of psychological principles is an indirect one. What was perhaps the chief positive contribution—the emphasis on the part played by judgment in mental processes like perception, and all that this entails—was, in his view, not a psychological matter at all. From a negative point of view, the application of idealist philosophical principles was one contributory factor in the rejection of sensationalism, the belief in atomic sensations as the building blocks out of which was to be constructed all other mental processes and our knowledge of the world. In Bradley's case, the general framework was the all-important thing; what details there are follow from it. We shall, nevertheless return to him on some points in dealing with the other two men with whom we are concerned.

James Ward

Ward was as much a metaphysician in his own way as Bradley was, but he was much more obviously concerned with psychological matters for their own sake. His initial and chief claim to fame in this respect rested upon an article on *Psychology* which he wrote for the 9th edition of the *Encyclopaedia Britannica* published in 1886. This article was revised for the 10th and 11th editions. In 1913 Ward gained permission to publish the substance of the article in book form provided that it was somewhat longer. This appeared as his *Psychological Principles* in 1918, a book which, as Ward admits in the preface, he expected to be described as "a belated patchwork, mostly of antiquated rags." The criticism that it was old fashioned even for 1918 has perhaps a certain justice. Of the then new, experimental psychology, Ward could only say, "New it undoubtedly is, and there are signs that in its present form it will not long survive!" Yet, Ward's ideas had been in the air for some years, and they had clearly been influential, as the demand for the book showed. Ward defined psychology as "the science of individual experience— understanding by experience not merely, not primarily, cognition, but also, and above all, conative activity or behaviour" (Ward 1920, p. 28).[1] The emphasis on conation here, as also in Stout, is in some ways an anticipation of McDougall. Yet the general impression, in Ward's case, is of a cognitive psychology, all the same.

Ward was opposed to the atomism of the earlier sensationalism as much as was Bradley, but the character of that opposition was somewhat different from Bradley's. It stemmed from his rejection of what he called "presentationism." His use of this term can be somewhat confusing, since he himself relied heavily upon the notion of "presentations." To understand his attack on presentationism, we need first to understand the framework of his own ideas. Ward adopted the term "presentation" as a translation of the German "*Vorstellung*"; it was meant to cover all that was presented to the mind— sensations, percepts, images, concepts—all that Locke meant by an "idea." A presentation is an object of consciousness and so stands in a relation to the subject. Presentations constitute the "given"; they are in a certain sense objective. They are thus from the point of view of the individual subject objects. In this sense, feelings like pain are not objects; they are purely subjective. Hence feelings must be distinguished from presentations. Insofar as we treat feelings as objects of which we can be aware, it is, Ward maintains, because we know of them by the changes which they bring about in our presentations. We have, then, presentations (objects of consciousness) and feelings (subjective modifications of consciousness); but we need also the act of consciousness itself. This Ward calls "attention," and hence the three constituents or features of the mental life are presentation, feeling, and attention. To be more precise, they are inseparable components of states of mind. Of these it is possible to distinguish two main classes, (1) the sensory or receptive attitude in which attention to presentations of sensory objects is nonvoluntarily determined, and where feeling follows the act of attention; and (2) the motor or active attitude in which attention to presentations of motor objects (i.e., movements) is voluntarily determined and is for that reason preceded by feeling. These three factors are all indispensable, and Ward's distinction of presentation from feeling was important and unusual for the time. (Bradley had called the basic experience "feeling" and William James tended to use the term similarly.) It is to be noted on the other hand that presentations are not only objects of consciousness in themselves; they are also *of* things or objects. In this respect, they might be said to be both forms of awareness and objects of such awareness—a difficult and dubious notion. They were in this respect like the sensationalists' sensations and

[1] References to the *Psychological Principles* are throughout to the 2nd edition of 1920.

Bradley's feeling. It was difficult for thinkers of this time to get away from the tradition which they were opposing.

The thesis which Ward calls "presentationism" is in effect the thesis that only presentations are required in an account of the mental life; it is thus as it stands in effect the sensationalist doctrine. Ward's opposition to it chiefly turns on the point that it fails to take into account the part played by the active subject. One consequence of the view that it is necessary, apart from feeling, to distinguish presentation from the act of attention directed voluntarily or involuntarily toward it is that it was necessary also to maintain the existence of a subject which so acts. Ward's analysis, therefore, implied the existence of an ego to be aware of presentations, and he claimed that this was an indispensable part of any account of experience. This last view was one of which Bradley was very critical; for, he maintained, it is impossible to detect in experience any such thing as an ego. According to Bradley, as we have seen, experience is originally featureless, and the differentiation between self and not-self is something that tends to occur in conformity with the working of the understanding. Ward, on the other hand, claimed that the distinction was immediately apparent in experience itself.

In another respect Ward was in agreement with Bradley—in maintaining that the field of consciousness is continuous. It is initially undifferentiated; any differentiation within it is the result of experience, and hence develops in time. This applies both to the presentations of passive consciousness and those of active consciousness, i.e., to those of movements which we make. This field of consciousness Ward calls the "presentational continuum." Once again there is an explicit rejection of sensationalism with its atomic, point-like sensations given immediately to the mind. Ward is even willing to admit the possibility, and indeed likelihood, of subconscious presentations, where these are necessary to fill up gaps and make the continuum complete. But the continuum is the original datum, and the individual presentations are really an abstraction from it. On the other hand, no such differentiation of individual presentations would be possible without the active role played by the subject; and this role is constituted by attention. This emphasis on attention is the central feature of Ward's scheme of things. While it undoubtedly has to do duty in perhaps a number of different roles, Ward's emphasis upon it marks him off from other thinkers of the period (although Stout also employed the notion). Ward indeed expressed a preference for the term "attention" in place of the more common term "consciousness" on the grounds that "consciousness" does not always possess a sufficiently active connotation.

The differentiation of presentations from the presentational continuum is a process of progressive modification of the original whole. Ward says, "At any given moment we have a certain whole of presentations, a 'field of consciousness,' psychologically one and continuous; at the next we have not an entirely new field but a partial change within the old" (Ward, 1920, p. 77). No presentation, therefore, is entirely new; it is always a modification of what has preceded it. Such modifications may persist, and there may be fusion or blending of presentations into wholes. These last two processes Ward calls retentiveness and assimilation respectively, and the whole combination of assimilation, retentiveness, and differentiation he refers to as the "plasticity" of the presentational continuum. He admits that in the normal individual the processes have gone on so far that we are never aware of an undifferentiated continuum as such. The existence of a presentational continuum must, therefore, be set down as a demand of analysis, not as an introspectible fact. On the other hand, Ward maintains that the existence of pure, individual sensations is a myth; so that it is not really open to the sensationalist to reply that the presentational continuum is just an erroneous piece of analysis. For, Ward could and did counter that move by saying that this was even more true of discrete sensations. What then is the foundation of the view that experience constitutes a continuum? It must be the fact that it seems natural to speak of, for example, a field of vision, and to suppose that the same notion can be applied to the other senses. This is perhaps questionable, although it must be admitted that the different sense modalities are concerned with features of things which are often continuously variable, so that the incidence of any one feature may be thought of as set against a field. This, however, is perhaps not quite the point, since what Ward seems to have in mind is a more obviously spatial kind of field; he seems to have in mind that what we are presented with in vision is something that has spatial properties. It is less obvious how *this* idea is to be extended to all the other senses.

The same issue or an analogous one arises over what Ward calls the "extensity" of sensations. Sensations as such, he maintains, bring nothing along with them, although the possibility that any should exist in a pure state, apart from other forms of consciousness, is a psychological myth. We can, nevertheless, consider sensations by themselves in the course of analysis. They can then be seen to have three types of property or characteristic—intensity, duration or protensity, and extensity. There is little problem over the first two, but what about extensity? Most authorities, Ward claims, would restrict this property to sensations of sight and touch, and not admit it to sensations of the other senses. Yet, he goes on, the existence of extensity is confirmed by our ability to localize the relevant sensations, i.e., to locate their origin, although the reverse does not hold. Since Ward does not admit that localization is impossible even with senses like smell, he maintains that extensity is a universal property of sensations.

What is at stake here can be seen by considering what Ward is reacting against. The sensationalists had maintained that sensations as such were atomic and point-like; they had no spatial properties. Given this, it was necessary to explain our perception of the spatial properties of things in terms of the temporal succession of sensations. That is to say that it was supposed that in the case, for example, of visual perception the movement of the eyes over a thing produced a temporal series of visual sensations, each differing from the preceding. How, nevertheless, it was possible to distinguish between a merely temporal series and one which was also representative of spatial characteristics, and how, in any case, knowledge of spatial characteristics could be obtained from what was nonspatial, was always a problem. Ward maintains in opposition to this point of view that a necessary condition of spatial perception is that the sensations themselves must have spatial characteristics. This, of course, is entirely dependent on the presumption that perception consists in having sensations which are representative of their cause, i.e., that they are what Ward calls presentations. On the other hand, sensations cannot literally be extended in space, since they are not themselves material things. Hence they can only be *as it were spatial*; they can possess properties which are analogous only to spatial ones. For this reason they may be said to have extensity, but not extension. Moreover, Ward takes it, as we have seen, that a sufficient indication of extensity being a property of the sensations of a given sense is that it is possible to localize those sensations, i.e., that it is possible to locate things by their means.

This was not a view which was found generally acceptable by Ward's contemporaries, although Stout seems to have accepted it. Bradley, for example, wrote a paper entitled "In what sense are psychical states extended?" (Bradley 1935, II, p. 349 ff.), in which while agreeing that the perceived spatial world cannot arise "from what is quite nonspatial," he says that "spatial perception, however it arises, cannot have at first the relational character of developed space." To some extent he might be taken in this to be agreeing with Ward, but Bradley hesitates to accept what Ward says about extensity, because, as he says, (1) when he observes he seems either to get something which implies space outright or to be presented with mere volume, and (2) volume is not identical with space. Ward's *extensity*, in other words, is neither one thing nor the other. Ward wishes to suggest by it more than mere volume or voluminousness, since extensity is meant to provide the grounds for the perception of space. Yet, on the other hand, extensity is not itself extension; for the latter implies the whole concept of space. In other words, we cannot be said to perceive objects as spatial without having a concept of a space in which they are set. Without this we merely have sensations which may be voluminous; the latter gives, as we might say, the "feel" of the sensation, but does not constitute spatiality as such. Ward's *extensity* will not do the trick. There is some justice in these criticisms. What they mean in effect is that Ward is still too close to the empiricist tradition, trying to derive our knowledge of the spatial characteristics of things, and, more important, the concept of space itself, entirely from experience (and this despite Ward's Kantian leanings). A further fundamental error, although Bradley in effect saw this too, is the whole doctrine that sense-perception is a matter of receiving presentations.

Ward did not, however, think that perception is simply and purely a matter of having sensations. Far from it. In the first place, as we have already seen, all experience consists of a modification of the presentational continuum, so that no presentation, no sensation, is literally repeated. Through the process of assimilation in experience, presentations or groups of presentations acquire a familiarity. They become so that they are recognized as such. This is the first stage in perception. "Thus," Ward says, "we receive together, *e.g.*, those impressions we now recognise as severally the scent, colour, and 'feel' of the rose we pluck and handle" (Ward, 1920, p. 142). But there is more to the perception of a rose than the sum of these separate perceptions. There is, first, spatial reference; we "refer" the impressions to a certain point of space. Secondly, we interpret the impressions as impressions of a thing. This implies what Ward calls the "intuition" of things. Thus the whole process involves the recognition and localization of impressions and the intuition of things. None of this, of course, would be possible without that form of consciousness which Ward calls "attention."

The localization of impressions is made possible, Ward thinks, by the fact that sensations have local signs, although he hastens to add that such local signs are merely the ground of spatial distinctions, and do not, as Lotze supposed, provide an immediate awareness of the location of things. By "local sign" Ward means that each sensation has certain relations to the others which make up the presentational continuum. These relations are invariable because they correspond to the relations that exist between distinguishable parts of the sensitive surface of the body. Thus we are aware of every sensation as in a certain relational context. Indeed it is not clear why, apart from the existence of a tradition, Ward did not just say this; for, in his account the notion of a local sign becomes so enervated that it is doubtful whether it does any real work. It certainly has the wrong suggestions, which Ward has to repudiate in his remark about Lotze. In any event, the existence of "local signs" in Ward's sense, is not sufficient to constitute perception of space, however much it is necessary. It gives us, Ward says, a *plenum*, but not *occupied space*. The latter is provided only when the presentational continuum's "several local signs have been complicated in an orderly way with *active* touches; when, that is, we have frequently experienced the contrast of movements with contact and movements without, or *in vacuo*" (Ward, 1920, p. 149). He goes on to say that the difference between the two might be expressed by saying that "extension implies the distinction of here and there, while extensity suggests rather a certain ubiquity." Perception of space depends on movement. This provides us with a succession of kinaesthetic presentations, which he calls "positional signs." These yield "potential position without place," while local signs yield "potential place without position." Together they provide spatial perception.

Ward expresses surprise that the importance of extensity (as the precondition of local signs) had not been recognized before; but the part played by movement in spatial perception is just as important for him, even if his views are in this case not so original (they go back in fact to Berkeley). His theory concerning this applies as much to visual space perception as to tactual space perception. In the case of vision, the existence of retinal differentiations provides local signs, and for the perception of distance there are the signs provided by binocular disparity and the accommodation of the eye. But the final ability to see spatial characteristics of things depends ultimately on movements of the body, especially movements of the eyes. This is all in the Berkeleian tradition. But it must be admitted that Ward has little idea of the complexities of the subject and does not go into any great detail. He appears in particular to have no knowledge of any of the so-called constancy phenomena. He maintains, for example, that "in vision the apparent size of an object is relative to its distance from the eye" (Ward, 1920, pp. 153–154).

The perception of things as things depends, in Ward's view, on our attribution to objects of solidity, unity, permanence, and substantiality; and its reality in turn depends upon these. These characteristics are attributed to objects in the light of feelings of effort, of the groupings of presentations, of the comparative fixity which we attach to our own body and thereby to other things, and of the fact that the objects in question fill space. Perception is, finally, partly re-presentative, in that it involves not only present experience but also experiences of the past. This, Ward maintains, does not involve memory in the strict sense, nor, for that matter, association; for, the latter is strictly a process of passing from one representation to another, while this is a matter of a presentation involving a representation. "Though the percept is complex, it is but a single whole, and the act of perception is single too" (Ward, 1920, p. 168). The phenomenon which Ward has in mind is that which Aristotle referred to by means of the example of seeing that sugar is sweet as well as white. Ward himself refers to it by the Herbartian term "complication."

Association proper Ward thinks occurs only by contiguity. Thus he says, "Any primary presentations whatever, occurring (1) together or (2) in close succession, tend to grow together or to cohere, in such a way that when any one recurs it tends to revive the rest as secondary presentations—such tendency increasing with the frequency of the conjunction" (Ward, 1920, p. 192). This, he maintains, is the only "law of association." Images are secondary presentations of the kind mentioned, depending for their character on primary presentations. So-called association by similarity and redintegration (the tendency of the occurrence of one mental item to revive the whole of which it has been a member) are second-order processes dependent on ordinary association. The succession of presentations in time, which this presupposes, has as a secondary effect the succession of representations in memory. In consequence, Ward makes use of the notion of a memory continuum, and, more generally, an ideational continuum. In order to explain the fact that items may be located within the continuum, i.e., that we may be said to remember events as occurring relatively at a certain time or in a certain position in the series, Ward invokes the notion of temporal signs, parallel to the positional signs mentioned earlier. These temporal signs are provided by movements of attention from one representation to another. Apart from the fact that memory involves images which are more fixed than those of the imagination, it may in general be distinguished from imagination by its reliance upon temporal signs.

The conclusion is almost inescapable that Ward's analysis has run riot here. The notion that it is plausible to speak of a continuum in this context, on the analogy of the presentational continuum, is certainly not derived from experience, but is the product of a certain way of thinking about the phenomena under consideration. Ward's inclination is to think of memory, like perception, as a selection of items out of a continuum which exists for the purpose. This makes a certain sense in the case of perception, whether or not it is ultimately valid; but the so-called memory continuum is one in time, and how then can memory consist of a selection from it. Granted that what we remember is remembered in a context, and is positioned relatively by this means, there is no reason why memory need be thought of as a selection of an item from a continuum; for the items which are supposed to make up the continuum do not exist until picked out, even if some basis for them exists physiologically. Stout is on firmer ground in using the notion of a disposition for similar purposes, instead of supposing that mental items exist even when we are not aware of them. It seems that Ward's tendency to adopt the same approach to his subject matter consistently throughout is not very happy.

So much for presentation and representation. Of the triad, attention, presentation, and feeling, there remains to be discussed feeling and the part which it plays in action. As we have already seen, feeling differs from presentation in being a subjective state of mind only, ranging between the opposites of pleasure and pain. (Ward appears to have no doubt that these *are* opposites.) As such, feeling provides a bridge between receptive states and active states, between perception and action. It is, Ward says, "at once the effect of a change in receptive consciousness and the cause of a change in motor consciousness" (Ward, 1920, p. 245). To the objection that we are not always conscious of feeling when we perform actions, he replies that this is because voluntary actions "originally initiated by feeling" tend to become "secondarily automatic." That is to say that all action, even that which is habitual, must at one time have been a response to feeling of pleasure or pain, which was itself set up by some condition of presentation. Furthermore, at the higher levels of mental life, presentations which are in themselves indifferent may have an indirect effect upon action, by being signs of presentations which do arouse feeling. Once again, this view is a product of Ward's analysis; it is the result of an attempt to view the phenomena in a simple light, by reference to a simple and consistent theory. It is very doubtful whether it really conforms to the complexity of the facts. The same is true of Ward's general theory of pleasure and pain, which is, as he himself admits, the theory of Aristotle and Hamilton (given, he insists, "a more accurately psychological expression"). It is the theory that "there is pleasure in proportion as a maximum of subjective activity or attention is effectively exercised, and pain in proportion as such effective attention is frustrated by restraints, distractions, shocks, or incomplete and faulty adaptations, or fails of exercise, owing to the narrowness of the field of consciousness or the slowness and smallness of its changes" (Ward, 1920, p. 262). Such a theory has well-known obstacles to overcome. It is not clear how it copes with simple bodily pains on the one hand and bodily thrills on the other; and its terms of reference are in any case extremely vague.

Pain and pleasure, Ward thinks, tend to lead to action or movement; but this is especially true of pain. Indeed, pleasure, by concentrating attention on its object, tends to repress movement, except where the object is a pleasureable movement itself. Pain, on the other hand, tends to set up movements which may remove the source of the pain. Hence, it is in this in particular that the source of action is to be found, *via* emotional expression. Ward rejects the James-Lange theory of the emotions as "psychologically and biologically absurd." In his view, the expression of emotion must be regarded as active, not passive, even if called out by feeling in association with presentation (or, in the case of desire, in association with an idea). It is so called out because the subjective feeling produces changes in active consciousness. There is clearly an implication here that the expression of feeling is at bottom or initially voluntary, however much it may become habitual. For, conation in general is for Ward, as we have already seen, a matter of active attention. There is something in the view that voluntary or intentional action presupposes consciousness, and moreover consciousness of a certain sort—practical consciousness, not that which is to be found in purely sensuous awareness. Yet there is something fundamentally wrong with Ward's notion that this plays a causal role, i.e., that there is a chain of cause and effect consisting of presentation, feeling, active consciousness, movement. This is brought out, apart from other considerations, by the vagueness which is inherent in Ward's account at this stage.

The subjects considered so far exhaust what is dealt with in Ward's encyclopaedia article. In his *Psychological Principles* (1920) he goes on to consider thought and intellection, belief and faith, the self and self-awareness, value, choice and freedom, the individual, individuality and its connection with character, personality, and the like. In the last stages of this discussion Ward claims that he is making a transition from the "general psychology" so far considered to "special or individual psychology." Of the latter he says that it is "a new and almost unexplored domain, at which we shall hardly be able even 'to glance.' To make good its essential conformity with our general psychology is about all that we can attempt" (Ward, 1920, p. 409, n. 1). To this end he invokes the concept of "*anlage*," the inherited disposition or point of view of the individual (for which notion he seeks a prototype in the "point of view" of Leibniz's monads). Thus he says, "In place of the formal duality of subject and object we have now to consider the 'special point of view' of the actual subject and the world that is there confronting it in perspective" (Ward, 1920, p. 452). Ward does little more, as he admits, than sketch out the approach, but it is perhaps not too much to see in it and his general attitude to the psychology of individual differences an anticipation of Kurt Lewin's approach in his topological psychology. On Ward's view, differences between individuals are best seen as differences from a phenomenological point of view, differences in their relations to the world as it appears to them.

Much of the treatment of the other topics in the last chapters is of philosophical relevance, rather than psychological, even if Ward claims to be treating the topics from a psychological point of view. We have already seen that he asserts the existence of a pure ego as the subject that is responsible for all that is active about us. This is distinct from the empirical self—what we know about ourselves in experience. To a large extent Ward follows Kant in adopting this view, particularly in respect of Kant's doctrine of the transcendental unity of apperception; although he puts the matter differently from Kant, saying that "we know *intellectually* what we are as experients" (Ward, 1920, p. 381). In other words, the postulation of an ego is a necessary condition of thinking about ourselves and our psychological functions.

What, finally, of thought? Ward rightly refuses to make a radical distinction between thought and sensitivity. Concepts play a part even in sense-perception. Thinking in general amounts in his view to problem solving, wherever it is to be found. The development of language (which arises, he thinks, from emotional expression in the first place) makes possible, however, the development of more and more abstract forms of thinking. Language, he believes, makes possible the gradual transformation or transfiguration of the ideational continuum already referred to. This means that images too play a part in thought. Yet, of itself, thought is different from either language or images. It is different from language because, as already indicated, it is prior to language; it is different from imaging, since however much it may involve images its function or intention is more abstract and general than anything that images consist in. In other words, the essence of thinking lies in the use to which images are put rather than in the images themselves, and it is language which makes that use possible in any abstract way. Thus Ward says, "All thought, strictly speaking, is imageless; for all thought is concerned with propositions sought or found, in other words with problems, suppositions or assertions; it is 'intentional' not presentational. But on the other hand all thought is concerned, primarily or ultimately with images (or impressions), that is to say with such of their relations as are relevant to its immediate problem" (Ward, 1920, p. 301). Ward also discusses the ways in which thought may be synthesized into higher and higher forms, a discussion which owes much to Brentano and Meinong.

So much for Ward—a somewhat austere, not to say difficult thinker. His approach is in many ways Kantian, although it has a variety of origins in fact. His emphasis on the active self and that form of consciousness which he calls "attention" is clear enough, as is his general opposition to sensationalism. On the other hand, Ward's chief claim to originality perhaps rests upon his use of the notion of the presentational continuum on which attention focuses. Yet it must also be confessed that his use of this and similar notions tends sometimes to run riot and become almost obsessional. Ward had a schematic and rigid approach to the mind as much as any of those to whom he was opposed, and this sometimes gets in the way of our appreciation of him.

G. F. Stout

Apart from articles and his more philosophical writings, G. F. Stout's main contributions to psychological thinking are to be found in two books, his *Analytic Psychology* (1896) and his *Manual of Psychology* (1899). The latter went through various editions, and the fourth and fifth editions were revised by C. A. Mace in collaboration with the author. The fifth edition (1938) also included an appendix by R. H. Thouless on Gestalt Psychology, with a further note by Stout himself on his position in relation to Gestalt theory. The *Manual* is what its title suggests, a complete survey of psychology for the student, in the tradition of William James's *Principles of Psychology*. It makes reference to current work and findings in various psychological fields, though Stout, like Ward, was never very impressed by the behaviorist approach, maintaining that behaviorists limited too much the application of the notion of "behavior," as well as committing other sins. Stout also declared that any explanation of learning on mechanical principles was doomed to failure. These are both criticisms to which behaviorists might well pay attention. Apart from this, however, there is in the *Manual* a good deal of reference to empirical findings and work in psychology, and also to current physiology and biology. The *Manual* is, nevertheless, in no sense a handbook of experimental psychology. Stout's main interest was in the analysis of psychological concepts, and his concern in the *Manual* is with the development of psychological functions, once given the scheme of analysis which he had worked out. Stout also believed that the bones of psychological facts and theories should be given flesh, and for this reason he makes every attempt to bring down the discussion to the student's own experience. Once again there is a parallel with James, although it cannot be said that Stout possessed James's literary turn. Nevertheless, the *Manual* is a comparatively easy book to read, especially for one coming from Ward.

The same cannot be said of Stout's *Analytic Psychology*, which is in many senses the more fundamental work. In this Stout sets out to give his analysis of the conceptual framework of psychology as he sees it—a conceptual framework which is largely presupposed and reproduced in the *Manual*. It is far from an easy work—in this resembling Ward's. Moreover, its layout is far from perspicuous; for, it is not written so as to go through the various psychological functions in a systematic way, or at any rate not obviously so. Nevertheless, it must be on his analysis of psychological concepts that Stout's contributions to psychological thinking must be assessed. It is for this reason that the *Analytic Psychology* must be considered as fundamentally the more important work; and it is upon it that the present discussion rests most heavily.

As already indicated, Stout was more explicitly influenced by Brentano than was Ward. There are frequent references to Brentano throughout the *Analytic Psychology*. Not that Stout always agrees with Brentano or that he always accepts his arguments. But on the general principle that different forms of consciousness have their own object towards which they are directed they are in full agreement. This view had been accepted by Ward, but it is much more explicit in Stout. Indeed Stout suggests that the different psychological functions might be classified according to the objects which forms of consciousness have. Like Ward, Stout was strongly opposed to the sensationalists and associationists. This opposition emerges in perhaps three main ways—in his emphasis on the distinction between thought and sentience and his denial that sentience is ever really independent of thought, in his emphasis on mental activity, and in his use of the notion of apperception. Another important feature of Stout's thought is his use of the notion of disposition, and this often sets him in opposition to Ward. Perhaps the most noteworthy aspect of his thinking, however, is his emphasis on the conative side of the mental life—and in this he has been rightly said to anticipate McDougall. Indeed Stout proclaims that the law of mental processes is that they are directed towards ends. This notion of an *end* is, as Stout himself points out in the *Manual* (Stout, 1938, pp. 113–114),[2] ambiguous; it can mean either the aim which the person sets himself or has in mind, or the end-state which terminates the process. It is not always clear in which sense Stout is using the term, but it is probably true that when he says that mental processes are directed towards ends he means this in both senses of the word "end." That is to say that all mental functions must, if they are to be properly understood, be set in the context of aims which the person has, and they are intelligible only in terms of the idea that the person is pursuing

[2] References to the *Manual* are throughout to the 5th edition of 1938.

those aims. At the same time, the mental processes involved in the performance of those mental functions must be understood as having a tendency to continue until an end-state is reached; whereupon they are terminated.

Both of these points recur in Stout's writings, although the relationship between them is perhaps never properly explored. It is by no means obvious that they are necessarily coincident. The point about end-states terminating mental processes states a principle of what might be called the mechanics of mental life, and it is by no means clear that it makes sense to suppose that there is such a mechanics (although the underlying physiological processes may be subject to something like mechanical principles). On the other hand, it is at least an exaggeration to say that in performing every mental function a person has some end in view. Certainly the understanding of a person demands reference to his intentions, and no adequate account of men can be given without such reference; but a person can perform something intentionally and with intention, without having any further intention or aim in view. In sum, while Stout's emphasis on conation is of vital importance, to the extent that no theory which fails to make some such point will be at all adequate, his tools of analysis may be still too crude for his purposes.

If, in the employment of the concept of an end-state, there is doubt whether it should properly be applied to psychology, rather than to physiology, the same might perhaps, though with less cogency, be said of Stout's use of the concept of a disposition. Stout recognizes the existence of physiological dispositions, but asserts also the existence of psychological dispositions. There is, he thinks, a general disposition for experiences, once having occurred, to recur, a disposition which is reinforced by repetition of the experience. This lies at the root of memory, which is not to be analyzed merely in terms of ideas associated with past experiences. It is in this case literally the experience which has the disposition to recur, not some copy of it. Stout also has recourse to the notion of a disposition in criticizing Ward's use of the notion of subconscious presentations (Stout, 1909, I, pp. 24 ff.).[3] Ward had invoked subconscious presentations not only as presentations to which we are not at the moment giving our immediate attention (an idea which Stout approved), but also in order to account for the progressive modification of the presentational continuum. In the latter case, he maintained that the whole of past experience is present at any time, though subconsciously. This view Stout rightly refused to stomach. For, such subconscious presentations are not ones which we could discover if we attended to them properly; they are merely postulated in order to provide an explanation of the relevant phenomena. What Stout is maintaining is that the notion of a mental or psychophysical disposition is in the context a more adequate theoretical concept than that of subconscious dispositions. This is reasonable enough. On the other hand, it is not clear whether any actual work is done by the notion of a disposition unless it has a physiological basis. Without the latter it may (be only a shorthand device for indicating what happens under certain conditions. Stout does refer to *psychophysical* dispositions. This suggests the physiological backing, but what exactly is its nature is another matter.

Stout, as we have seen, accepts Brentano's doctrine that mental functions

---

[3] References to the *Analytical Psychology* are throughout to the 3rd edition of 1909.

always involve reference to an object. But he maintains also that consciousness, of whatever kind it is, not only has an object; it also receives a modification of itself in the process. That is why, in his view, thought always involves the having of images, and volition always involves feeling. All cognition involves, as well as reference to an object, a modification of consciousness which is the presentation. The latter performs the function of making
thought discriminative, but neither thought nor presentation is really possible without the other. This implies a general principle of the interdependence of thought and sentience. Thought presupposes sentience, and sentience in general implies some form of thought. That is to say, in the latter
case, that there are not in general bare sensations given to the mind, as the
sensationalists supposed. But Stout is not so definite about this as he is
about the dependence of thought on sentience. While he admits, in the
latter connection, the occurrence on occasion of what might be called imageless thought—the awareness of something in implicit form, what he comes
to call implicit apprehension—this is never *absolutely* independent of images.
These are required if thought is to have any discriminative content. Without
some such content the thought is nothing. In other words, the presentation
itself and what the presentation means for the subject are quite different
things, but the meaning can exist only if there is something to mean.
Whether or not presentation can exist independent of thought is another
matter, and, as already indicated, Stout is not quite so definite here. He says
on the one hand that the question whether a creature exists which is purely
sentient, or which possesses, as he puts is, a "purely anoetic consciousness,"
is one the answer to which he does "not know and dare not guess" (Stout,
1909, I, pp. 50–51). But at any rate it is impossible "to pass from mere sentience to thought by any process of differentiation or complication." Hence the
functions of thought and sentience are quite distinct. On the other hand, he
says later that "we have no sufficient ground for asserting that any experience
of a normal human being is so completely anoetic that it has no objective
reference whatever" (Stout, 1909, I, p. 180). Hence, for human beings at any
rate, experience is always related to an object and thus presupposes some kind
of thought. In fact, despite differences of emphasis, Stout's attitude to the
possibility of pure thought and pure sentience is really the same in each
case. Thought and sentience are distinguishable logically and can be relatively
independent of each other in fact; but as far as normal human experience
is concerned they are never absolutely independent of each other. Sentience
provides the vehicle, the means, by which thought can be directed to an
object, and thought gives sentience the only meaning which it has. The
consciousness of an object which is inherent in thought, Stout calls, as Ward
does, "attention."

Stout's problem here is really the fundamental one of the relationship
between the active and passive features of the mental life, between what is
given to us and what we make of it. Like Bradley, he opposes the notion
that we are "given" a series of differentiated sensations with distinct content,
as the sensationalists supposed. Sensations provide us, in his view, only with
the grounds for the distinctions and differentiations which thought or judgment makes. (While judgment is, he thinks, a distinct modification of consciousness, there is no thought without judgment of some kind; the distinc-

tion between thought or mere consciousness of an object and judgment is merely a relative one.) The content of experience is thus what the understanding makes of the sensations which we receive. Yet this remains a problem, as it was for Bradley. It is a problem which, if not the same, is very like the one which Stout deals with in the second chapter of Bk. I of *Analytic Psychology*—the problem how analysis of presentations is possible. For, does not the analysis produce new presentations? Stout's answer is that "all that is necessary is that each analytic distinction should correspond to an undistinguished difference in the original experience" (Stout, 1909, I, p. 61). But the problem still remains. What are the criteria of validity? How can we be sure that the correct distinctions have been made? The general problem of the relationship between thought and sentience, of the criteria of validity for the imposition of the one on the other (how, if you like, one can be sure that thought organizes what is given in sensation properly) remained with Stout all his life—and rightly, given the terms of reference. In the later editions of the *Manual*, he says, "The trap is that the material characters of the physical object are present only to thought; but the thought must, so to speak, have a foothold in sense-experience, and be more or less determined by the nature of present sensations in seeing, touching, hearing, etc." (Stout, 1938, p. 410). His recipe in earlier editions was that sense-experience is from the beginning apprehended as conditioned. Now he says that "present sensation originally 'means' for the percipient corresponding characters of the physical object" (Stout, 1938, p. 412). This is something like Thomas Reid's view that sensations are natural signs of perceptible qualities of things. It is doubtful whether this answer will do, as in perceiving something as such and such we are not aware of any sensations as such which could "mean" anything to us. The relationship between sensation and what we perceive cannot for this reason be one of meaning, sign-significate relation or suggestion (as he maintained earlier—Stout, 1909, II, p. 30). But the problem is a real one.

Stout agrees with Ward in thinking that presentations form a unity in experience—a field or continuum. The rest of what is presupposed in the discrimination of a physical object—spatial and temporal unity, its unity and identity as object, and its unity in respect of causation—is what thought brings to the matter. This involves attention which, as we have seen, is the general attitude of consciousness towards objects. Most of what Stout says about attention reflects what Ward says about the same notion. Attention, he says, is "the direction of thought to this or that object in preference to others" (Stout, 1909, I, p. 209). It leads to greater distinctness and is itself distinguished from interest in that the latter brings in pleasure or pain. Attention is fundamentally an active business, although this is necessarily a relative matter. This being so, and given that sentience is never independent of thought, the mental life is always active to some extent or other. Thus Stout says, "To be mentally active is identical with being mentally alive or awake. According to this view, therefore, there can be no such thing as purely passive consciousness" (Stout, 1909, I, p. 168). Conation is a form of active attention to an object, the end towards which the activity is directed, and the processes towards that end. In all this, Stout stands in complete opposition to the sensationalists.

He does so in another respect also. Stout was interested in the work of

Von Ehrenfels on *"Gestaltqualitäten"*; hence he devotes some space to a consideration of the perception of form. This emphasis on form and the perception of it sets him against the atomism of the sensationalists. Stout maintains that form may remain the same while the parts alter. While it is possible to perceive the parts without perceiving the form of their combination, there is a sense in which it is impossible to apprehend the form without apprehending the parts. On the other hand, there can be an apprehension of a whole which is implicit rather than explicit; and Stout uses the notion of implicit apprehension to deal with other phenomena, such as the understanding of the meaning of a word and the summing up of results (phenomena to which Wittgenstein was later to give so much attention). The emphasis by Stout on the implicit apprehension of wholes has prompted the view that he anticipated Gestalt psychology. It is easy enough to find such anticipations. Yet, as pointed out by C. A. Mace in the introduction to the 5th edition of the *Manual*, a more true estimate is that Stout is one of those who reacted against the sensationalist tradition, as did the gestaltists also in their own way. Common features among those who so reacted are not surprising. In any case, Stout never said, as the gestaltists did, that we are "given" wholes in perception. His view of the relationship between thought and sentience forbad this, and his theory of sense-perception was, philosophically, a good deal more sophisticated than theirs, whatever its own drawbacks.

In the last chapter of the first volume of *Analytic Psychology*, Stout discusses habit, association, and the like. Habit, he maintains, is due to tendencies or dispositions which are themselves due to repetition. Association plays some part in the tendency of a disposition to recur, and the main principle of association is that of contiguity. Stout formulates this principle in a comparatively novel form: "(1) When part of a complex disposition is excited, the whole tends to be excited in some manner and degree. (2) The whole presentational content of consciousness at any one moment, and the corresponding conations, so far as they are not realised, leave behind them, not a plurality of independent dispositions, but a single complex disposition. The union of the constituents of such a complex is more or less perfect according to the circumstances" (Stout, 1909, I, p. 270). This formulation is the reverse of atomistic and reveals Stout's antithesis to the normal associationist psychology. Like Ward, Stout discounts the possibility of association by similarity, as a fundamental principle; for, it is not a principle which could be called mechanical and is not one met with in any form in nature. But the most important point is that Stout sets severe limitations on the part played by association altogether. Identification of something, for example, does not in his view rest on association; and the same applies to phenomena such as those which he interprets in terms of the notions of conflict and coalescence of dispositions. Under that heading he discusses phenomena like those which F. C. Bartlett came to call "serial reproduction"—the progressive modification of memories in time. But many of these phenomena, and all those which cannot be dealt with by association proper, come under the heading, properly speaking, of "noetic synthesis"; and it is with this that Stout begins the next volume.

It should be noted that Stout does not discount association altogether; he merely gives it a subordinate role and asserts that it is not the whole of the truth. He agrees with Bradley that association "marries only universals," and criticizes the associationists on the grounds that (1) they laid too much emphasis on mere combination, (2) they failed to recognize the possibility of the apprehension of a *form* of combination, and (3) they failed to see that mental elements are transformed when they enter new combinations. In the case of productive thought, he adopts the idea of relative suggestion first put forward by Thomas Brown nearly a century earlier. This he formulates as follows: "If the presented content b has formed part of a presented whole bc, then the presented content β, when it recurs, will tend to call up a whole $\beta\gamma$ formally corresponding to bc" (Stout, 1909, II, p. 52). The ways in which this is possible are complicated by the variety of possible relations or analogies which exist between b and β. He claims that this plays a part in, e.g., distance perception, which is a constructive, not a reproductive, process. The details here are not easy to grasp. The main point, however, is that relative suggestion is meant to account for any new function or process of thought, as opposed to mere habit to which association proper is limited.

Perhaps a more radical innovation in respect of association is Stout's claim that there is such a thing as impressional revival and association without the intervention of ideas. This occurs, for example, as a complicating factor in perception. The way in which we perceive things, the actual impressions which we have, may be modified by past experience, without this being in any way due to the intervention of ideas. What Ward called complication, or at least what he implied when he said that "the sight of a suit of polished armour, for example, instantly reinstates and steadily maintains all that we retain of former sensations of its hardness and smoothness and coldness" (Ward, 1920, p. 168—the sentence is repeated from his *Encyclopaedia Britannica* article) is, according to Stout, something of this sort. Our actual impressions, not just associated ideas, are changed by past experience. Here indeed is a case in which mental elements are supposed to be altered by being put in new contexts. The real question is whether it ever occurs as Stout says that it does. Granted that ice may look cold, is this to say that our past experience of ice by touch modifies the visual experience (cf. Stout, 1909, II, p. 26)? The truth is that perception is a more complex matter than Stout seems to allow. He still has the tendency to think of perceiving something as having impressions of it, modified as these impressions may be by thought or associations. The phenomena, e.g., that ice may look cold, are real enough, but they cannot be explained simply in terms of having impressions. Perception in general cannot be analyzed in terms of the having of impressions, modified or not by other processes.[4] These problems have already in effect been broached in what was said earlier about Stout's account of the relation between thought and sentience. The problem for him is not just that there is such a relation, but that the one may modify the other. In passing from mere sensation to the perception of an object there is, in his view, a modification of the experience itself. (And so there may be in some sense of the word "experience," but not in that sense of the word in which a sensation is an experience; rather, if at all, in the sense of what I am aware of.) Thus,

---

[4] See my *Sensation and Perception, passim,* but especially, Ch. 11.

according to Stout, the process is one in which thought modifies the sense-impression itself. This is precisely an example of what he calls "noetic synthesis."

Noetic synthesis is first involved in simple perception, where there is an immediate identification and distinction of an object presented to the senses. Whatever is perceived, Stout rightly says, is recognized as a such and such. This implies a reference beyond the given object, and thus involves implicit apprehension. There can be grades of simple perception according to the fineness of the distinctions recognized. As opposed to simple perception there is, according to Stout, complex perception. In this the object is seen (1) as having a configuration in space and thus as having a plurality of locally distinguishable parts, (2) as having a plurality of qualities, and (3) as changing in time. In other words, complex perception is involved when an object is seen as complicated or variable in some sense. In all this, Stout maintains, thought and sentience are synthesized, and the setting up of trains of ideas involves even higher levels of noetic synthesis. The last is therefore the process by which mental items of higher and higher levels come into existence out of the lower. A parallel can be found here again with the views of the Graz school of psychology, e.g., Von Ehrenfels and Benussi, who used the notion of "production" for similar purposes, to show how higher mental elements could be produced out of lower ones by the acquisition of structure. In Stout's view, it is all a funciton of what he calls, following Herbart, "apperception." (Wundt had used a similar notion, though Stout emphasizes the differences between his own view and that of Wundt.)

Like all notions of this kind, that of apperception is puzzling. It has the air of a magical process of transformation. It is defined by Stout as "the process by which a mental system appropriates a new element, or otherwise receives a fresh determination" (Stout, 1909, II, p. 112). It is meant to cover, he says, all such processes as understanding, interpreting, identifying, subsuming, etc. Presentations or dispositions may apperceive each other. The process cannot, however, be divorced from the conative aspects of the mental life, since the principle of mental processes is that they are directed towards ends. A precondition of apperception is that there must be attention; without this there is not apperception but merely assimilation.

What is fundamentally puzzling about all this is not merely that there is an air of magic about it, but that the notion does not fit in very easily with all aspects of Stout's thought. The issue is in many ways similar to that already raised about his treatment of conation and the notion of an end. In the latter case, it was pointed out earlier, there is an ambiguity between the notion of an end as an end-state and as the aim which we have before us. Stout's treatment is such that either he does not distinguish them or he wishes to use both notions at once. But this is to combine two quite different approaches to the subject. In one we should be concerned with what people do; in the other we should be concerned with the processes, the mechanism of what happens in the mind. The first approach is an active, functional one; it is concerned with people's actions and activity, and the natural implication which it has for psychology is that the psychologist should examine the functions which people perform. The second approach is a more passive, structural one; it is concerned with what happens in the mind, and its natural implications for psychology are that the psychologist should examine the structure of the contents of the mind, and the principles of their development—if there is any such thing. Stout insists, as we have seen, on the activity of the mind, and much of his discussion presupposes this, but the emphasis on apperception implies a quite different story. Indeed, the notion of apperception was always a linchpin of structural psychology, e.g., in Herbart and Wundt. Stout himself points out, "An important distinction between attention and apperception is that, whereas attention is an attitude of consciousness towards a presented object, apperception is merely a process of interaction between presentations or dispositions. The apprehension of an object is to be regarded as a result of this process" (Stout, 1909, II, p. 114). "But *how?*" one feels like asking. Beneath our activity, both mental and physical, may lie certain physiological mechanisms or processes (although the relation between these and our activity is puzzling enough); but the suggestion that there are also certain *psychological* mechanisms is much more puzzling, and it is perhaps doubtful whether it is even intelligible.

Stout deals with other subjects in *Analytic Psychology,* and even more in the *Manual*—conception and comparison; language and thought; belief and the imagination, and feeling, especially pleasure and pain. On the last, Stout adopts a view similar to that of Ward—the Aristotelian view that pleasure goes with unimpeded progress towards an end, while pain goes with impeded progress—but he admits that there are difficulties in applying this view to bodily pain sensations. The main framework of Stout's approach to psychology is, however, that already presented, and it is in this if anywhere that his importance lies.

Conclusion

What is one to make of the three thinkers who have been under discussion? They had of course an importance for, and made contributions to, philosophy which are quite other than any which have been mentioned here. What, however, of their importance in the history of psychology? Present-day psychology shows little evidence that they exerted any long-term influence on the subject. This may be due to factors which have nothing to do with their intrinsic importance. But the conclusion cannot be avoided that they were transitional thinkers, part of a reaction against the sensationalism and associationism which had prevailed for so long in the nineteenth century. While they, for this reason, show anticipations of other reactions and developments, their thought was very much of a compromise in many ways; they were still part of the tradition from which they developed and against which they reacted. Both psychology and philosophy have moved on since their day, and to many modern thinkers in both subjects much of the writing of Bradley, Ward, and Stout on psychology and the philosophy of mind must seem dull and old fashioned. Yet as transitional thinkers, as part of a reaction, they had considerable importance. Moreover, this importance is not just an historical one. For anyone who has the patience to penetrate the fringe of background thought and accept its presuppositions there is much there which would repay examination. For, if they were nothing else, they were men who were prepared to think about the mind intelligently, if sometimes within the blinkers of a tradition. Many of the problems which they faced are still problems today. Few contemporary psychologists, perhaps, would be prepared to go through the analysis of mental concepts which Ward and Stout thought necessary. This kind of link between psychology and philosophy is no longer, regrettably, considered necessary, even if philosophers often argue to the contrary. One who wanted such analysis, however, would not get all the truth, by any means, from these thinkers, but he would do well to consider seriously many of the hints which they threw out.

REFERENCES

BRADLEY, F. H. *The principles of logic*. London: K. Paul, Trench, 1883.
BRADLEY, F. H. *Appearance and reality*. London: Sonnenschein, 1899.
BRADLEY, F. H. *Essays on truth and reality*. Oxford: Clarendon, 1914.
BRADLEY, F. H. *Collected essays*. Oxford: Clarendon, 1935.
HAMLYN, D. W. *Sensation and perception*. London: Routledge, 1961.
PASSMORE, J. A. *A hundred years of philosophy*. London: Duckworth, 1957.
STOUT, G. F. *Analytic psychology* (1896). 3rd ed. London: Sonnenschein, 1909.
STOUT, G. F. *Studies in philosophy and psychology*. London: Macmillan, 1930.
STOUT, G. F. *A manual of psychology* (1899). 5th ed. London: Clive, 1938.
WARD, J. Psychology. *Encyclopedia Britannica*. London: 1886.
WARD, J. *Psychological principles* (1918). 2nd ed. Cambridge: Cambridge University Press, 1920.
WOLLHEIM, R. *A. F. H. Bradley*. Baltimore: Penguin, 1959.

CHAPTER 15

THE PERSONALISTIC PSYCHOLOGY OF WILLIAM STERN[1]

Gordon W. Allport

WILLIAM STERN was both a pioneer and a systematizer in psychology. His mind was one of the first to range several of the special fields that are now familiar territory. He will be remembered especially for his sure-footed explorations in differential psychology, forensic psychology, psychotechnics, child psychology, and intelligence testing. But he will be remembered likewise and, I think, with increasing renown for his theoretical system of personalistic psychology wherein he ordered his manifold research, and which, in turn, he incorporated within his comprehensive philosophic doctrine of Critical Personalism.

Stern's life—in spite of his last five troubled years of exile—was remarkable for its orderliness of purpose. Already at the age of 19 he had planned the intellectual road that he would travel, and, never doubting, he pursued it to the day of his death.[2] His every act seemed an efficient expression of his dominant purpose. He worked eagerly, without lost motion, keeping throughout his lifetime a distinctive boyish zeal and optimism. His own enthusiasm made him an effective teacher, and his well-ordered life was reflected in the high morale of the two institutes that he directed.

[1] In preparing this chapter I have drawn freely upon my two previous papers: William Stern: 1871–1938, *American Journal of Psychology*, 1938, 51, 770–774; and the personalistic psychology of William Stern, *Character and Personality*, 1937, 5, 231–246.

[2] In 1926 when he had reached what he called a "provisional resting point" (after the appearance of the third and final volume of *Person und Sache*, his system of Critical Personalism) Stern wrote his intellectual autobiography which was published in both German and English (*Die Philosophie der Gegenwart in Selbstdarstellung*, ed. by Raymond Schmidt, 1927, 129–184; *A History of Psychology in Autobiography*, I, ed. by C. C. Murchison, 1930, 335–388). This source, though stressing Stern's philosophical work at the expense of his psychological, gives the best picture of Stern as man and thinker. Its bibliography, however, is by no means complete, listing only 36 selected titles up to 1926 (twelve years before his death). The *Psychological Register*, III, 1932, lists 95 titles for the same period; and 29 additional titles (1927–1931). From 1931–1937 the *Psychological Abstracts* lists 15 titles. The total thus becomes 139 published articles and books including a few translations and basic revisions.

The Man and His Accomplishments

Born on April 29, 1871, in Berlin, (Louis) William Stern lived in that city until he was 25 years of age. In his third semester in the University he began to study with Ebbinghaus, a fact which decided his training and his career. Yet the influence of Lazarus and of Paulsen, with whom he likewise studied, led him to an early decision that he must transcend the naturalistic views of Ebbinghaus and work out for himself a fuller and less limited conception of proper scope of psychological science. Even in his doctoral dissertation, *Die Analogie im volkstümlichen Denken* (1893), he attempted a synthesis of cultural and experimental science, blending, as it were, the teachings of Lazarus and of Ebbinghaus.

Before going to Breslau as Privat Dozent in 1897—at the invitation of Ebbinghaus who had moved there in 1894—Stern worked for five years upon his experimental monograph, *Psychologie der Veränderungsauffassung* (1898). In this work we find an account of his invention, the *Tonvariator*, and likewise one of the earliest discussions of the "conscious present." Treating the perception of change in many sense modalities, the work foreshadows, though none too clearly, the purely phenomenological descriptions of the Gestalt school. It begins to break with the "constancy hypothesis" and may fairly be ranked as an early expression of the *Strukturbegriff*. Yet, in this work the interpretation of the nature of structure is lacking. The author only vaguely felt the need for a substantial agent which he might designate as the cause and the carrier of perceptual change. The Person was not yet discovered. The logical completion of this early monograph was not reached until 37 years later in his paper, *Raum und Zeit als personale Dimensionen* (1935).

Before his promotion in Breslau to the post of *ausserordentlicher Professor* in 1907, Stern manifested his originality to its fullest extent. The first seven years of this century were for him a period of true genius. In rapid succession there appeared his pioneering books and monographs in five virgin fields of psychology. (1) *Über Psychologie der individuellen Differenzen* was published in 1900, and in it the author declared, fulsomely perhaps but none the less prophetically, that individuality would be the problem of the twentieth century. The book was completely rewritten in 1911 under its more familiar title, *Die differentielle Psychologie*. (2) *Zur Psychologie der Aussage* appeared in 1902, followed by two volumes of the *Beiträge zur Psychologie der Aussage*. It is interesting to note that his last public lecture delivered in New York City in December, 1937, dealt with this same problem in relation to trial procedure at law. (3) The child studies likewise began at this time. Children's interest in their school work, their manner of reporting, and the accuracy of their testimony first engaged his attention. There followed soon an account of the case of Helen Keller, and the two famous monographic studies based upon observation of his three children, written in collaboration with his wife, Clara Stern, *Die Kindersprache* (1907) and *Errinerung, Aussage und Lüge in der ersten Kindheit* (1908). (4) Applied psychology was christened and presented to the psychological public in a brochure entitled *Angewandte Psychologie* (1903). In this publication he likewise advanced the concept of *psychotechnics* (eleven years before Münsterberg appropriated it and brought it to fame). In 1906 (with the help of his student Otto Lipmann) Stern founded the *Institut für angewandte Psychologie* in Berlin and shortly thereafter the *Zeitschrift für angewandte Psychologie* (1907). Stern remained codirector of the *Institut* until 1916 and coeditor of the journal until 1933. (5) In 1900 he began to work on the foundations of his Critical Personalism, choosing definitely in that year the title for his first volume and doing much of the writing. His first philosophical publication (1903) was an article considering the second law of thermodynamics in its significance for mental science, controverting the pessimistic deductions that Von Hartmann had drawn. To the same period belongs the first publication of his system, Volume 1 of *Person und Sache: Ableitung und Grundlehre* (1906).

Thus between the ages of 29 and 35, while still a Privat Dozent, Stern fashioned with marked sureness of touch new views and new methods in four important departments of psychology—differential, forensic, child, and applied; and at the same time accomplished the initial, and therefore most creative portion of his theoretical system.

His work in child psychology, for which he is best known in America, soon grew beyond the bounds of the diary method. He became interested in more exact methods of study, and undertook to introduce into Germany the new movement of intelligence testing. His influential book, *Die psychologischen Methoden der Intelligenzprüfung und deren Anwendung an Schulkindern* (1912) was twice later rewritten. It was in this work that the concept and first formulation of the I.Q. were advanced. Soon followed another notable book, written from the normative and developmental point of view, *Psychologie der frühen Kindheit bis zum sechsten Lebensjahre* (1914). This volume found its way into several editions both in German and in English.

In 1915 Ernst Meumann died in Hamburg. Stern immediately became his successor as editor of the *Zeitschrift für pädagogische Psychologie*, and in 1916 his successor as professor of philosophy, psychology, and pedagogy at the *Kolonialinstitut* and director of the psychological laboratory that Meumann had founded. After the war the demand for new universities, caused by the return of the soldiers, led to the transformation of the colonial institute into a full-fledged university. In this transformation Stern himself played a strategic and leading part.

At Hamburg the interest in child psychology spread in a practical direction, partly to satisfy the demands of the local school system. Valuable researchers are to be found in the *Hamburger Arbeiten zur Begabungsforschung*. The Institute soon became a well-known center for research in educational and vocational psychology. All the while fruitful researches in psychotechnics, legal psychology, and experimental psychology were continuing. In 1925–1928 Stern gave considerable attention to the study of puberty and adolescence, planning to extend his treatment of child psychology through these ages. Several miscellaneous papers mark this period in addition to the monograph, *Anfänge der Reifezeit* (1925), containing a psychological analysis and commentary on the diaries of a boy from his twelfth to his fifteenth year. This work takes on special interest when the reader comes to realize that the anonymous writer of the diaries and the commentator are one and the same person. Stern as boy and Stern as man were too much alike to make complete disguise possible!

The story of the Hamburg Institute (1916–1933) is told by Stern himself in four reports.[3] The last is an ominous *Schlussbericht* (1933), hastily written under the shadow of Hitler, but as ever an orderly and workmanlike report, winding up the affairs of an active, democratic, and renowned center of psychological research.

The story of his last five years serves best of all to reveal his character. His first asylum was in Holland where he worked doggedly on his last and most comprehensive volume, *Allgemeine Psychologie auf personalistischer Grundlage*. Unable to issue it in Germany, he found for it a Dutch publisher (1935). With this writing completed, he joined the trek of exiled German scholars to America, accepting a position as lecturer and later as professor at Duke University (1934–1938). Though he had visited America twice before (once for the celebrated conference at Clark in 1909, and a second time for the IXth International Congress at New Haven in 1929), he spoke little English and was entirely unfamiliar with American educational practices. Courageously, he and his gifted wife, who was his close collaborator since their marriage in 1899, set to work to master a new language and a new way of life. Besides teaching at Duke he gave occasional lectures in Eastern colleges and taught in the Harvard summer school in 1936. He held two honorary degrees from American educational institutions (Clark, 1909; Wittenberg, 1928). America had been good to him, and so with bright prospects here he undertook the task of refashioning his personal and professional life. His chief desire was to introduce personalistic psychology into America, to counteract, as he said, the "pernicious" influence of his earlier invention, the I.Q. In February 1938 he was deeply gratified by the appearance in America of the translation (by Howard D. Spoerl) of his comprehensive text, *General Psychology from the Personalistic Standpoint*. For his next work he planned a new volume on child psychology. Suddenly, in the night of March 27, his work was ended, his prospects over. He died, without warning, of coronary occlusion.

Stern had the completest confidence in psychology, never doubting its firm position among the sciences nor its practical value for mankind. He had equal confidence in his own mission as a leader in theoretical and applied work. Consistent with this self-confidence were his ease and dignity of manner and his fluency and lucidity of expression. These qualities, combined with the vivacity and enthusiasm of which I have spoken, gave him a prominent place in public gatherings. He was a gifted conciliator. When tempers were frayed in debate, when awkward pauses followed an awkward scene, or when the occasion called for friendly remarks, it was he who could be relied upon for the right word easily spoken. Though fully conscious of his prerogatives as a German professor, and vocal about the merits of his own work, he was at

---

[3] Das Psychologische Laboratorium der Hamburgischen Universität, *Ztschr. f. Päd. Psychol.*, 23, 1922, 161–196; Aus dreijähriger Arbeit des Hamburger psychologischen Laboratoriums, *ibid.*, 26, 1925, 289–307; Das psychologische Institut der Hamburgischen Universität in seiner gegenwärtigen Gestalt, *Ztschr. f. ang. Psychol.*, 39, 1931, 181–227; Aus den letzten Arbeiten des psychologischen Instituts der Hamburgischen Universität, *ibid.*, 45, 1933, 397–418.

the same time responsive to the thought of others and patient and kind in all his personal relations.

Unlike many philosopher-psychologists, Stern held to the end of his life his interest in the detailed problems of general psychology. His philosophical work may be said to have been completed with the publication of his *Wertlehre* (1924) or perhaps with the short volume, *Studien zur Personwissenschaft* (1930). In his last years he returned (with only a slightly relaxed grasp) to the finer details of general psychological analysis. His final text covers much the same ground as any modern text. The difference, however, lies in its tireless locating of every fragment and fact within its proper personalistic niche. For him all difficulties were resolved in the Person. This concept, and this concept alone, he thought, could provide the substantiality, the causality, and the individuality required in every mature psychological analysis.

It troubled him relatively little that his formulations ran counter to the trend of the times, particularly in American thought. Intellectually he lived largely in a world of his own making, and he believed so intensely in the liberating powers of personalistic thought that he had faith in its ultimate acceptability to others. He simply could not believe that psychologists would dwell for long within the narrow cells that they had created for themselves by a prior act of freedom. Any system other than personalistic, he felt, makes a travesty of the very mind that created it. Thinking in this vein Stern became a momumental defender of an unpopular cause.—And what of that? he would ask. Are there not fashions and fashions in psychological theory? The personalistic way of thought will yet have its day, and its day will be long and bright.

The Personalistic System

Very few psychologists have succeeded in writing a comprehensive, full-bodied, and systematic interpretation of their science. To do so requires that the author find a place for all the discordant fragments of research gathered under diverse points of view; and also that he face up to and resolve the troublesome antinomies of mental life. Determinism and freedom, dualism and monism, mind-in-general and mind-in-particular—all these and other fundamental issues call for a solution (or at least for a clear statement of position) if a psychologist aspires to be a systematist. True systematists are rare; Stern was one. His ambition was to place all psychological detail under his own philosophical tent. We watch the process as we read the three volumes of *Person und Sache* whose first editions appeared in 1906, 1918, 1924 respectively. Helpful too are *Studien zur Personwissenschaft*, 1930, and *Psychology from the Personalistic Standpoint*, 1938 (Macmillan).

THE METHOD

The first thing to understand about Professor Stern's approach is that he offers a direct, straightforward analysis of mental life. In the manner of most scientists in the past he believes that by fixing one's gaze directly upon the course of nature, nature's own categories and cleavages will eventually appear.

The argument against this direct method is that it seems solipsistic; it fails

in the test of social agreement. No two people, it is said, have the same interpretative insight. Their various accounts of nature have been likened to
the slicing of a cheese. Each person slices it differently, and then declares
that everyone else's cuttings fall in the wrong place. But did Galileo, Newton, or Darwin do any differently? Their data, drawn from observation and
experiments were verifiable; so too are Stern's. Their theoretical interpretations attempted to tell something about the course of events occurring in the
depths of nature. Stern's interpretations are of the same order. All of them
undoubtedly made errors in their slicing, but so far as we can tell they are
for the most part only errors of *approximation* which subsequent scientists
can correct. The direct method, naive though it may be, is the most fruitful.

Although he is untroubled by the hypercritical methodologies of today,
Stern uses most of the common safeguards of science. Observation and experimentation are employed for the data they will yield, but to his data he
applies understanding, interpretation, and orderly arrangement; and he is
much bolder about it than most psychologists of today are willing to be.
He adopts the findings and some of the procedures of "exact" (elementaristic)
psychology but only on the basis of an entirely different theoretical assumption, namely, that *everything mental is at the same time personal, and everything personal is either a totality or a part of a totality.*

At the outset this assumption of functional wholeness creates a serious
difficulty for personalistic psychology (as it does for Gestalt and all other
modern structural theories). Stern states the difficulty as follows: "As soon
as we name anything and thus assign it to some definite psychological category, it is no longer the same thing that it was before; it acquires a peculiar
rigidity and fixity that cannot be ascribed to mind itself." And yet science (including general psychology) is possible only by virtue of abstraction which
substitutes for the complex pattern of relationships that obtain within the
personality a different, purely conceptual system of relationships that have no
organic connection with one another.

Being forced to adopt this familiar method of abstractive analysis, Stern
plunges into the use of methodological dimensions much as any other psychologist would do. In fact, he has probably more polarities, more resulting
dimensions, and makes a more intensive use of dialectic than any other
psychological author. Yet there are two *differences.* Never is the reader allowed to forget that the procedure is artificial, that it is not an end in
itself, but is merely a tool for disclosing *aspects* of personal existence. There
is constant reversion to the primary fact of the total personal organization.
The second difference is even more significant. The dimensions that are
chosen are dictated by the primary assumption that the person is the locus
of every mental event. They are for the most part utterly unlike any
dimensions ever used in psychological analysis hitherto. For example, there
are such strikingly personal dimensions as depth-surface, embeddedness-sali-
ence, reactivity-spontaneity, nearness-remoteness, genuiness-disingenuousness,
expectancy-retrospect, subjectivity-objectivity. Unlike most dimensional analyses these are not merely empirical constructs of the laboratory. They are
dimensions dictated by the datum. It is not the hobby of the experimenter
that is being located with their aid, but the personal experience of the subject
himself.

PSYCHOLOGY AS A BRANCH OF PERSONALISTICS

The person is a living whole that is individual, unique, goal-directed, self-contained, yet open to the world around him. He is capable of having experience.

Of all the properties of the person mentioned in this definition, that of experience is the least indispensable. The person is *complete*, whereas experience is *fragmentary*. And yet it is the province of psychology to deal with this very fragment. It is for this reason that psychology is not coextensive with personalistics; it is a narrower discipline, defined as the *science of the Person considered as having experience or as capable of having experience.*[4] Experience and the capacity for experience are only a portion of personal existence. Since the latter is rooted not only in experience, but in the biosphere and in the sphere of objective values as well, there is need for a more comprehensive philosophical discipline of personalistics of which psychology is only a part.

THE PERSON-WORLD DIMENSION

However unified and self-contained the person may be in the metaphysical sense, he is actually open at every moment to the surrounding world. He acts upon and is acted upon by the environment; a tension always exists. When the tension is most acute there is a resultant state of consciousness. The most important of all facts about consciousness is that it is graded; sometimes it stands out, as it were, against the diffuse background of personal life. It is *salient (abgehoben)*. Whenever we are acutely aware of objects or of our own states there is this sharpness. At other times, as in states of feeling, consciousness is embedded *(eingebettet)* more deeply; there is less clearness, less salience. Salience represents an act of pointing, a directedness of the person toward something that at the moment has special significance for him. The more salient an experience, the greater is its objective meaning; the more embedded, the greater is its subjective meaning. Complete embeddedness is of course unconsciousness. The minimal threshold represents the first degree of salience; and all the thresholds familiar to psychophysics are, when interpreted, so many boundaries of the personal significance of the world.

According to Stern, Gestalt psychology with its sharp studies of perception deals too exclusively with salient experience, neglecting the no-less-important sphere of embedded experience which by its very nature constitutes an *Ungestalt*. Embeddedness of experience is marked particularly within the province of vital processes. For instance, the experiences produced through the lower senses, viz., through smell, taste, and the organic modalities are characteristically embedded. Vision and audition on the contrary, because of their superior capacity for making contacts with the outer world, usually yield salient experiences; touch is in this respect an intermediate modality.

---

[4] A remarkable similarity exists between this definition of psychology and Titchener's. The latter wrote, "*Psychology is the study of experience considered as dependent on some person.*" How could such similar definitions lead their authors into diametrically opposed courses? The only explanation seems to be that Titchener paid no further attention to the second part of his definition after he wrote it. For him the dependence was purely rhetorical, for Stern it is the most significant fact in all of science.

Experience is embedded likewise when it is emphatic, when it is introceptive (nonsalient adoption of surrounding cultural values), or when it bears a "physiognomic" correspondence to the surrounding events in the environment.

MONISM

Psychophysical neutrality, which is Stern's solution of the body-mind problem, is, of course, not altogether original with him. Any double-aspect hypothesis in effect refers body and mind to a common underlying substratum; they are two sides to the same shield. But generally the shield itself has not been considered of any psychological significance. It is generally only the mutual conformity of the two sides of the psychophysical shield that interests the psychologist (as in isomorphism). But for Stern this conformity, though always present, is of much less importance than the shield itself. The shield is none other than the tangible, psychologically important *person*. Mental phenomena and bodily processes are properties of the person, but the person himself is not a passive theater for the play of psychophysical events, he is their true generator and carrier, and regulator. There are no specific mental or physical elements that are isolable and stable enough to form *between themselves* a direct relationship independently of the person. This is the weakness of parallelism, and of isomorphism as well.

That the person is the locus and generator of every psychophysical event is not merely a tautological proposition for science. For, with the aid of this person, new light is cast on virtually every problem. The monism is not therefore like most current monisms simply a denial of the dualism of mind and body. It is a constructive monism, increasing rather than decreasing the range of problems that can come within the field of psychology. A remarkable feature of the personalistic doctrine is the immensely broadened range of categories that it is able to offer to the psychological investigator, otherwise crippled by monisms and dualisms that place restrictions on the scope of problems admitted to good standing in psychology.

DYNAMIC, PURPOSIVE (GOAL-DIRECTED)
AND VOLUNTARISTIC EMPHASIS

Unlike most American psychologists who are critical and sparing of their motivational concepts, selecting the minimum with which to work, Stern has use for them all; instinct, impulse, motive, need, disposition, goal-striving, urge, interest, inclination, wish, will, drive, and even the more inchoate principles of entelechy and "personal energy"—all find their place in his system.

But to say that personalistic psychology is dynamic and purposive does not sufficiently characterize it, for there is at the same time an additional flavor of voluntarism. This flavor does not arise merely from the fact that the terms *Will* and *Volition* appear constantly in the book, for in German psychology they have a more generic connotation than in America. In this country these terms terrify most psychologists because they bring to mind the problem of freedom with which the psychologist finds himself utterly unable to deal. Professor Stern has no respect for the taboo on will, but rolls up his sleeves and attacks the problem from all sides. The result is the voluntarism to which I have alluded. The person is not merely a reactive creature, the product of biological adaptation to the environment. He is likewise creative; he has, besides his equipment of biological needs, for example, a need for thinking which is but one reflection of his capacity for *spontaneous* as well as *reactive* behavior. Stern cannot be classed as a mere evolutionist nor as an organismic psychologist, for these doctrines stress only the biological unity of the reactive (not the creative) organism.

The author's frank admittance of volition to good standing in his psychological domain leads him to treat a number of problems that many psychologists never recognize: problems of intention, attempt, effort, and especially that characteristically human ability of conscious planning for the future.

The tendency of the living organism to preserve and advance its own life is taken for granted in personalistics. Inorganic substance may under certain circumstances seem reactive much as living creatures are, but there remains an unbridgeable gap. All the important domains of life—vital functions, experience, and introception (the adoption, creation, and enhancement of values)—are denied to inanimate nature. These domains reflect *spontaneity* as well as *reactivity*.

But personalistics is not a biological vitalism, because the *human* person is to be distinguished from the *animal* person. The latter, to be sure, possesses vital functions and rudimentary conscious functions (experiential), but the sphere of introception is completely denied to lower animals. Human beings have two poles to their life of experience: *vitality* and *value*; animals one pole alone, *vitality*. The theory then is not a biologism. Nor does it merely reiterate, in the manner of Driesch, a somewhat hollow principle of vitalism, for each page of the entire book is in effect a documentation and definition of the distinctive vital and value properties of the human being.

Some Detailed Applications

The best way to indicate the value of personalistic theory for the problems of general psychology is to suggest a few typical applications. But, we are warned, "since all special fields of experience may be understood only with reference to the totality of the person, they are bound up with one another and interfused in such a way that any sequence of treatment remains arbitrary."

PERCEPTION

The historic category of "sensation" receives as scant treatment in personalistic psychology as it does in Gestalt theory, for "sensation" is not only an elementaristic conception but is nonpersonal as well. Both schools agree that it is only at the level of sensory perception that problems become psychological. In spite of this initial agreement personalistic psychology deviates widely from the Gestalt approach. Stern fears that if Gestalten are made the true fundamental phenomena in perception and endowed, as it were, with their own laws (e.g., "self-distribution") the danger of a new elementarism arises; for then the Gestalten themselves may be regarded as elements out of which all mental activity is composed, just as was formerly true of sensations. For Stern there can be no *Gestalt* without a person who forms *Ges-*

talten (Keine Gestalt ohne Gestalter). On occasion, of course, the *Gestalt* is dominated by features of external constraint; the objective stimulus situation determining by its very definiteness of boundaries the type of salience that arises in experience; but even here the significance of the phenomenal *Gestalt* is invariably its relevance to the person in his intricate process of adaptation to the complexity of the world. In the last analysis *Gestalten* require some active participation of the person himself; they are never self-sufficient. It depends upon *me*, for example, whether I arrange the ticking of my watch into three-part or four-part rhythm, or see the cloud in the sky as a menace or as a negligible factor on the day of a picnic.

Furthermore, not every experience is salient; the category of *Ungestalt* (embeddedness) is quite as important as is the category of *Gestalt*. Its significance is especially apparent in the domain of feeling with which Gestalt psychology is ill-equipped to deal. In various respects, then, the boundaries of personalistics are wider than those of Gestalt theory.

Both theories are much interested in the phenomena of intersensory perception. The personalistic approach holds that experience mediated by the separate modalities is "dissociated" from the nonspecific total perception that is deeply embedded in the person, and originally represented by a state of diffuse feeling. "Sharpness," for example, in smell, taste, hearing, and touch is not to be explained by the association of various specific sensations. It is a prior total experience that under certain conditions may become ascribed primarily to one modality or another. The Gestalt theory of course does not take into account the unifying substratum of the person, nor does it imply as does Stern's theory a genetic process of differentiation among modalities.

The experiences of space and time are admirable instances of intersensorial perception. There are no special "spaces" for each sensory modality, but only one personal space. The locality and volume of a tone may seem to be a spatial experience of a predominantly auditory nature, but space *in* which these impressions exist is not a sound-space, but *my* space, the same space that is the common ground of my visual and tactual experiences as well.

Without doubt the recasting of the experiences of space and time is one of the most original features of personalistic psychology, sustained and convincing in its development. What impersonalistic psychology is able, for example, to give an intelligible setting to the fact that my seat-mate in the plane is distant from me while the friend toward whom I am riding is already near me? The essence of space and time, psychologically considered, is their *personal relevance*. Events are distant when they lack such relevance; near when they possess it. The synthesis of space and time is likewise possible on the basis of personalistic theory, for there is at the center of my experience the feeling of *here-and-now*, an unanalyzable blend of space-time.

MEMORY

Memory too brings up the problem of personal time which, of course, is much more irregular than the unidimensional schema of objective time. Thus, a segment of life that is ten years behind me may be far nearer to me subjectively than the period two years ago; or vice versa, some act that I performed yesterday may today appear incomprehensible to me, a totally foreign element in an otherwise continually unfolding past.

The significance of memory is found in the midposition that it occupies in personal life between the function of instinct (the conservational factor) on the one hand and the function of intelligence (the progressive factor) on the other. Memory conserves the past, providing salient features of experience for the present in the service of future goals. It is thus not merely a matter of reactivated traces. Without memory each present state would be self-sufficient and rigid; having lost its connection with the total person, it would be meaningless. Salient experience (e.g., perception) must continually be embedded in the life of the person through the function of memory in order to acquire vital significance and utility. The image, for example, is more deeply embedded than the perception, and for that reason has a more personal content.

In most acts of memory remembrance of self and remembrance of the outer world are not differentiated; even attempts at critical analysis never give a wholly separate picture of what occurred in the world around us and what occurred in ourselves. The entire episode has become embedded in the substratum of personal existence. It is for this reason that objective recall never possesses complete fidelity. Testimony in a court of law is seldom fully trustworthy.

THOUGHT

Personalistic psychology readily finds a suitable place for all facts known concerning imagery, insight, attitude, fantasy, and intelligence. It arranges these facts, however, under teleological principles. Thought takes place whenever our personal world seems insecure, that is, whenever occasions arise that cannot be taken for granted; herein its functions differ from instinct, habit, or memory. Thought has survival value; it facilitates adjustment. But that is not all. Thought is not merely reactive; it is spontaneous and creative as well. It reaches out, as it were, *looking* for trouble. The person not only adapts in a passive sense, but having the capacity for self-development, for asserting himself against the world, he has therefore an active *need* for thought.

There is a special role assigned to precategorial thinking and to fantasy. Purely objective and rational thinking is brittle and artificial. It is so salient that it is ever in danger of becoming depersonalized. It is *too* objective; it is far from life, and lacks *understanding*. The most comprehensive and adequate products of thought, the works of art, religion, literature, and metaphysics, are a result of embedded experience that comes from feeling, from empathy, and from "physiognomic" understanding quite as much as from sharply salient, rational analysis.

Fantasy, dreams, and play fit readily into the personalistic system, for they reflect in various ways the restorative, anticipatory, creative, and symbolic functions of which the person is capable.

FEELING

Since of all types of experience feeling is "nearest to the person" one would expect personalistic psychology to be most productive in this province. And it is. The dimensions that it uses are exceedingly numerous, and more distinctions are turned up than other schools of psychology ever dreamed of. Wundt's tridimensional framework is made to look like a bony scarecrow.

Although all feelings are embedded, some are relatively more salient than others, i.e., some pertain to objects, some to self; some are near and some distant in their reference (e.g., terror vs. grief). There are feelings of expectancy and of retrospect, of alienation from the world (anxiety) and of harmony with it; there are feelings of familiarity, of unfamiliarity, of premonition and recollection; there are positive and negative feelings toward the future (hope and dread). There are feelings of success and of failure, of the expansion or of the negligibility of the self (as in various aesthetic experiences); of preparation for action or reflection after action. Some feelings are broad, some narrow, some intense or weak, some lasting or temporary. They possess depth or shallowness, genuineness or disingenuousness, seriousness or playfulness; they may pertain to cultural or to vital functions, and may lead to adaptive action or to expressive action. All these are recognized and used in addition to Wundt's dimensions, pleasure and unpleasure, strain and relaxation, and excitement and calm.

The author finds no difficulty in fitting known facts concerning affectivity into his system. Full recognition, for example, is given to the principle of "affective equilibrium," the phenomenon of the relativity of feeling. As all experimentalists now admit feelings depend very largely upon a state of contrast, and contrast is exclusively an intrapersonal relationship, and therefore a typical personalistic concept.

The category of feeling includes emotional seizure and states of passion, as well as mood, temperament and the emotional toning of objects. All feeling has a formless character; it is *Ungestalt*. It occupies a middle position between that which is perfectly embedded in the personal life (utterly habitual or instinctive) and that which is sharp and salient (clearly intellectual or volitional). It is transitional between the unconscious realm of smooth running vital activities and the state of acutely voluntary conduct. Feeling often precedes salient thought or action; it represents a period of preparation. For example, the adolescent with his turbulent emotions and moods will later develop the more salient volitional consciousness required for his sexual, vocational, and social adaptations. Feeling also exists when conduct has been completed, and the experience is subsiding through the affectively toned period of retrospect into oblivescence.

Personalities and Self Psychology

In America the closest counterpart of Stern's system of thought is the Self Psychology of Mary W. Calkins. For Calkins the Self is a *given* that cannot be defined. (Definition requires a *class* to which an object may be referred. The Self being entirely *sui generis*, belongs to no class.) The principal characteristics of the Self, however, are identifiable, and they turn out to be characteristics that Stern likewise recognizes as highly central in the Person. The Person, like the Self, is *persistent*, it *changes* as it develops; it is *unique*; it is *many-sided*; it is the *groundwork of all its own experiences*; and it is *related to its physical and social environment*.[5]

[5] Mary W. Calkins, *Psychological Review*, 1917, 24, 279–300.

Stern, however, does not share Calkin's belief that all of these characteristics are immediately experienced. An exaggeration of the role of self-awareness is a feature of Calkins' system, and springs naturally from her body-mind dualism. The Self, she says, is not made of body-mind; rather it *is* mind, and *has* a body. The Person, on the other hand, is psychophysically neutral. Human personality cannot be characterized as *mental* because mind in turn must be defined in terms of its significance within and in the service of the Person. The Person, to be sure, is sometimes sharply aware of itself, sometimes dimly (or even wrongly) aware, and sometimes totally unaware. Personal unity, however, is not endangered by this fitful course of consciousness. Calkins sought her support almost entirely from introspective evidence; for Stern the person is an inescapable postulate; not immediate experience alone, but all evidence, of whatever type it may be, points to its central position.

Critique

Let us consider the charges that are leveled against the personalistic system by its critics.

1. *It is solipsistic. Comment:* It is true that the author spent many long years weaving together his experiments and observations into a single view of the psychological universe. To an operationist, of course, it is scientifically meaningless to have a coherent view of the psychological universe, or of any other universe. One should view only such portions of it as other people may agree with him about. Hence personalistics will be regarded as solipsistic—a *Weltanschauung* of one man only. To this charge there are two possible lines of defense. One might say, the application of operational criteria to restricted parts of the system, and eventually perhaps to some of the more inclusive concepts is not impossible. In part this answer seems acceptable. But a number of the personalistic categories (e.g., those of feeling) inevitably rest upon the evidence of immediate experience. As such they become operationally weak. Then there is the conceptual unification of the system as a whole for operationism to scorn. When this point is reached, I suspect the author might have to reply "so much the worse for operationism. There are tasks of synthesis for science more significant than the piddling regress of operationism. If mine is a solipsistic view of life, so too are all *Weltanschauungen,* and whether they get agreement or not, psychologists, like all other philosophers, cannot and will not live without them."

2. *It is common sense.* There is something about the selection of the person for central emphasis that seems both self-evident and question begging. In other words, personalistics is a kind of common-sense characterized by its obviousness and by its *petito-principii. Comment:* In stressing the person, the author with remarkable directness calls psychologists back from their wanderings and confronts them with their forgotten man. Is it necessarily a deficiency in a system if it accepts the datum that everyone (excepting psychologists) would agree is the property par excellence of psychology? Personalistics takes pride in the fact that it is *lebensnah,* and therefore in a better position than other psychologies to codify and refine common sense. Furthermore, the concept of the person is more than the name of a self-evident

datum; it furnishes unexpected aid in recasting many thorny problems of a metaphysical and epistemological order, among them the relation between body and mind and between consciousness and unconscious mental activity.

The charge of question begging is more intricate. To select some one disposition or state for analysis from the total person, then to proceed with the analysis up to a point, and then to refer the disposition or state back to the person, saying that only in the light of the total personality can it be interpreted, does seem to be somewhat of a circular process. And yet if the person is the sole authentic point of reference to what other source of explanation or clarification can a state be referred? If the person is *ex hypothesi* both origin and terminus, is it truly circular to depart and arrive by the same door?

If one agrees with Stern that in a peculiar sense the person is real, and that analyses merely employ artificial constructs, one cannot consistently object to this procedure. Yet I for one confess that I wish there were less frequent emphasis upon the totality of the person. One example might be given. Stern's trenchant criticisms of intelligence testing are well known, and all the more significant because of the part he himself has played in the testing movement. Yet his frequently abrupt dismissal of the test result and his haste to embed it within the total person does, I think, blind him somewhat to the merits of a reliable test score; its significance often reaches farther than he admits. The same may be said of his impatience with any sustained attempt to explore personality at the level of traits, attitudes, and dispositions. Even though it is true that the person is not divisible, progress comes not from reiterating this fact, but from finding some level of analysis that does the least possible violence to the structure of personality (e.g., a concept of *personal disposition* that in a sense epitomizes the whole person), and following it to the bitter end before returning to the totality.

3. *It is formalistic.* In personalistics the polarities and the resulting dimensions are almost bewildering. E. G. Boring has pointed to the possibility of infinite dimensions in psychological analysis, but only in personalistics does one seem to encounter them all. *Comment:* To be sure, the author uses a great many abstractive dimensions, but he uses them only as temporary aids; they are not intended to be true divisions of the person; they simply disclose aspects under which he may be viewed. Furthermore, he tends on the whole to use dimensions of maximum personal significance (such as depth-surface, nearness-remoteness, retrospect-prospect). And yet he does not always do so. Thus his account of motivation might be improved by a logic of truly personal (characterological) traits, attitudes, interests to replace the universal dimensions of need, instinct, and drive.

The method is not merely dimensionalistic; it is dialectical, as well. There is often a thesis and antithesis; the opposition is overcome by synthesis. This characteristic of peronsalistics is more apparent in Stern's philosophy than in his psychology. But there are instances of it in the psychology as well. One example will serve. The doctrine of convergence holds that forces from within the organism and forces from without may *converge* to form new states in the person: the stimulus converges with disposition, the environment converges with heredity. Although this concept has been taken over by some American psychologists, it is not, I think, a psychological doctrine at all. The "forces" of the environment are so different in kind from the "forces" of the dispositions that true convergence is unthinkable. All that happens is that the environment furnishes stimulus-situations or provides models for conduct, which in turn provoke processes of change within the person. Although Professor Stern would no doubt agree with this interpretation of the meaning of "convergence," the fact remains that the term itself is a product of dialectic and does not (like "learning," "suggestion," "imitation," or "resolution of conflict") refer to purely psychological functions.

It is important to understand the reason for Stern's use of dialectic. It does not spring, as in Hegel, from an abstract idealism or from an a priori conception of logical necessity, but rather from the incessant flow and ebb of personal existence itself; the individual is ceaselessly striving and resting, approaching and avoiding, responding and causing others to respond. To exist at all means to struggle, and in every conflict there are contrasting poles and an eventual resolution of some sort. The formalistic use of dialectic, therefore, has its basis in the very nature of the person himself. And yet I cannot feel that every personal event requires such dramatic representation. The gradual growth of—let us say—an attitude can be characterized without stressing the ideal extremes between which it might in principle, but does not in practice, oscillate. I am not here questioning the prevalence of conflict in personal life, nor am I rejecting altogether Stern's use of contrasts and dialectic. I am suggesting merely that I think the method is on occasion overworked.

4. *Common dimensions cannot account for personal uniqueness.* Even though Stern criticizes the isolation of a single dimension (e.g., the I.Q.) from the personality as a whole, he implies that all personalities, however unique, are in fact woven from the same common threads. *Comment:* An example would be his handling of motivation. He employs the customary rubrics of instinct, drive, and need, assigning essentially the same motives uniformly to all persons. Thus, for example, he speaks of a universal drive of men to broaden their intellectual horizons. Is there in fact any such universal need, even granted that it might have myriad forms of expression? Isn't Stern here manufacturing a uniform dimension out of the behavior of a relatively small population of intellectuals?

It is an odd fact that Stern does not go to the logical conclusion of personalistic reasoning, and say that the dynamics of each life are in the last analysis unique. He does not say that we need idiographic (or morphogenic) methods that will enable us to discover where in fact the cleavages and tensions in a given life fall. While dimensions (common traits) may be useful for comparing one personality with another, they are always approximate. Stern does not perceive the need for morphogenic methods which focus on one individual alone as a population of unique events arranged in a unique pattern.[6] On one occasion when I confronted Stern with this particular criticism his eyes twinkled while he replied. "Oh no, there is such a thing as being *too* personalistic." I persist in my conviction that Stern in employing throughout his system uncritically a plethora of common dimensions, was not genuinely consistent with his own goals. Or perhaps I should say that individuality and uniqueness as a problem did not intrigue Stern as deeply as did

---

[6] Cf. G. W. Allport, The general and the unique in psychological science, *Journal of Personality*, 1962, 30, 405–422.

the simple substantive fact of personhood. The unity of the person impressed him more deeply than did his uniqueness.

Stern's Influence

Stern was an innocent victim of Hitler's blind rage against *Judentum*. After hastily writing his *Schlussbericht* for the Hamburg Institute, to which I have already referred, he and his wife fled first to Holland and then to America. A son and a daughter likewise escaped to America; another daughter, after serving in Germany as long as possible to rescue Jewish children from the wrath, settled in Israel. Two of Stern's closest professional associates (Dr. Martha Muchow and Dr. Otto Lipmann) were political suicides. Just at the time when he might be consolidating his influence in Germany (at the age of 63) every anchor was lost. His major psychological book, *Allgemeine Psychologie auf personalistischer Grundlage*, had to be printed in Holland. All his other books, if not burned, were allowed to go out of print. The new generation of students grew up without knowledge of Stern's monumental work, and after World War II there was little remaining of his influence. One of his students, Professor Curt Bondy, likewise a fugitive in America, did return to Hamburg after the war, and for more than a decade worked toward reestablishing Stern's Institute.

Yet it is questionable whether, if conditions had remained normal in Germany, Stern would have founded a school of personalistic thought. For all his alertness and boyish friendliness he lived intellectually pretty much in a world of his own making. His line of thought was *sui generis*, having the flavor of the nineteenth-century "myth in the grand style." The younger generation was about to clamor for operationism, physicalism, mathematical models. At least such was the situation in America where he lived too short a time to win disciples. In Germany the postwar fashion was stratification theory *(Schichtentheorie)* which had the merit of accounting in terms of personality layers for the appalling regressive degradation which the Hitler era had provoked.

To be sure, Stern's students were spread around the world—his Institute had an international reputation. I have mentioned Bondy who eventually returned to Hamburg. There were also Vucić (Jugoslavia), Katzenstein (Brazil), Klüver and myself (U.S.A.), and many others. Some of these have acknowledged Stern's inspiration in their work. But one cannot claim that there is today either in Germany or internationally a school of personalistic psychology. The movement known as personalistic philosophy in America, centered at Boston University and at the University of Southern California, acknowledges a limited kinship with Stern, but no causal connection.[7]

The most we can say is that Stern's many students borrowed rays from the "star." And that their students in turn have absorbed some of the same light. The influence is most evident when certain specific topics are under discussion, such as the I.Q., the psychology of testimony, early childhood, cloud pictures as a projective method.

[7] A. C. Knudson, *The philosophy of personalism.* Cincinnati: Abingdon Press, 1927, pp. 25 ff.

Today the personalistic system as a whole is nowhere intact, although I suspect its rays may increasingly have powers of penetration. The time may come when psychologists will be less afraid than they now are to delve into problems of personal emotion (lest they seem emotional), or into the study of sentiments (lest they appear sentimental), or into the riddles of personhood (lest they become personal). When this time comes Stern's influence may again grow.

CHAPTER 16

THE PSYCHOLOGICAL IDEAS OF
L. S. VYGOTSKII[1]

A. N. Leontiev and A. R. Luria

THE FLOURISHING of the short but brilliant period of creativeness of L. S. Vygotskii, an outstanding Soviet psychologist in the 1920s, coincided with the years of a most grave crisis in psychology.

It had become clear at that time that psychology was divided into two camps which were increasingly drifting apart. At one pole there were the attempts of natural scientists to *explain* the fundamental mechanisms of psychological processes. This included investigations by psychologists and psychophysiologists devoted to the analysis of thresholds of senitivity and the forming of simple forms of time relationships and elementary laws of memory.

One could not doubt the scientific nature of these investigations or fail to appreciate the contribution which they were making to the scientific analysis of the foundation of human mental activity. However, in arriving at a natural-scientific analysis of the elementary forms of psychic life (sensations and motions, associations and memory), these studies did not approximate even a tentative explanation of the *higher* forms of psychical activity, such as cogitation and volition, intellectual activity and consciousness. It is therefore not coincidental that even in the works of such eminent investigators as W. Wundt the laws of apperception and will power were not related to the natural laws of sensation or association, whilst such brilliant scientific investigators of elementary forms of organization of neural processes as Sherrington became dualists as soon as they became confronted with the need to describe complex forms of man's conscious life.

At the other pole were those philosophers and psychologists who were little interested in scientific analysis of elementary processes of sensation and motion, association and habit forming. Their interests were centered on analyzing the most complex manifestations of the human mind, such as abstract thought or active will, and on analyzing subjective personal experiences or creative manifestations thereof. This camp included all the psychologists of the Würtzburg school and the protagonists of the "noetic" line, and also

[1] This chapter will appear as an Introduction to *Selected Papers* of L. S. Vygotskii to be published by Pergamon Press London. Translated by O. M. Blunn.

philosophers occupied in describing basic human "values" such as Dilthey, Spranger, and supporters of the phenomenological description of the structure of consciousness.

The merit of these investigators was that they were concentrated on analyzing the most important higher forms of human psychical life. Their weak side was that by *describing* the phenomena as purely subjective, they rejected scientific *explanation*, and have assumed, as some did, that psychology is only descriptive, or have tried to develop it as a field of intuitive "understanding" of "values" of spiritual life.

In one respect, however, these investigators, who represented the extreme views of modern idealism, were in agreement with the representatives of the first group: they were united in the conviction that a monistic scientific approach to psychical life was impossible, and that whereas elementary psychophysiological phenomena could be *explained* in natural-science terms, the *higher* forms of psychical life could only be *described* phenomenologically.

The dualism of Henri Bergson that created an unbridgeable gulf between the "memory of the body" and the "memory of the mind," was not different from Sherrington's views. Sherrington's approach to elementary reflexes was scientific, but he has left to intuition the analysis of higher forms of human consciousness.

Vygotskii, who began his scientific work in an atmosphere of sharp clashes between these two schools of thought, set himself the task of overcoming that crisis by developing a monistic system in which also the *highest forms of psychical life* could be approached by *scientific methods*.

This was the main idea of his unpublished theoretical investigation "Historical meaning of the psychological crisis" [*Istoricheskii smysl psikhologicheskogo krizisa*], written in 1926–1928. Vygotskii was helped by the traditions of Russian materialistic science and, above all, by the theory of dialectical materialism, the exceptional value of which he not only understood from the start of his work, but which was the basis of his investigations.

By the second half of the last century I. M. Sechenov, the founder of Russian physiology and scientific psychology, had established two basic traditions of materialistic thought which have since characterized advanced Russian philosophy and science. The first postulated a single deterministic approach to all, even most complex, life phenomena and to psychical activity; the other consisted in the interpretation of these most complex natural and social processes as products of *evolution*. By defining behavior as a system of determinate reflex actions, stemming from the the organism's environment, Sechenov once and for all broke off with those whom he regarded as "isolationists," who kept psychology outside the other branches of natural science, and so he laid the foundation for a reflex interpretation of the most complex psychological processes. By defining psychology as "the Scientific study of the forming of psychological activities," he postulated the genetic approach to all psychological processes and their interpretation as the product of a complex evolutionary process. This approach has become the fundamental tenet of the contemporary Soviet psychological science.

Unlike many recent representatives of Russian physiological science, Sechenov never rejected psychology; he believed that as life becomes more complex and the nervous system reaches new levels of activity, "sensation changes into cause and purpose, and motion into effect," and that these complex psychological responses should also be explained from the same deterministic positions as the more elementary physiological phenomena.

Vygotskii, who started his career decades after Sechenov had passed away, continued where Sechenov had left off.

The start of Vygotskii's work as a psychologist coincided with the decline of the official idealistic school of Russian psychologists, headed by G. I. Chelpanov, professor of Moscow University (at the beginning of the 1920s Chelpanov lost all support and then vacated the directorship of the Research Institute), and the flourishing of materialistic physiology centered around the laboratories of I. P. Pavlov and partly around the laboratories of V. M. Bekhterev.

The works of these investigators were not, however, the starting point for Vygotskii. Though highly valuing their significance for a deterministic study of higher neural processes and for explaining the physiological mechanisms underlying relatively elementary forms of behavior, Vygotskii could not accept the tendency, then setting in, to reduce *all* psychological processes to a physiological conditioned-reflex schema and so interpret the most complex aspects of psychological activity, which he called "higher psychical functions," as composite conditioned-reflex relationships.

To reduce complex forms of psychological activity to conditioned reflexes and the forming of higher mental functions to mechanisms of conditioning, meant, in Vygotskii's view, a restriction of the scientific inquiry into common mechanisms undoubtedly present at all levels as psychological processes build up, but in no way specific for each level.

The job of scientific analysis, in Vygotskii's opinion, was to preserve the strictly deterministic approach to the phenomena of psychological life and to track the course of their origin, to discover their characteristics and then to analyze them out into specific "units" singly inherent in them.

Any attempt to arrive at such "units" from the idealistic point of view, or to regard them as independent phenomena of the spirit or the consciousness, was totally unacceptable to Vygotskii. Such an attempt would only deepen the crisis of psychology and not resolve it. Scientific psychology ought not only to conserve the specificity of higher psychical functions, but provide for a deterministic approach to their investigation.

The solution offered by Vygotskii was to go on beyond the naturalistic study of man's psychological activity and to interpret it as the product of *sociohistorical development*.

Historical Materialism

The idea that complex phenomena of man's mental life should be approached as the product of community life, was the basic idea of historical materialism. Karl Marx advanced the proposition that consciousness has from time immemorial been a historical product, and that even man's sense organs are the product of universal history. But this basic proposition, though firmly asserted in marxist philosophy, had not, prior to Vygotskii, been related to concrete psychological investigations.

Only in the works of the French sociological school were attempts made to show that even such seemingly simple manifestations as memory or "time-telling" are, in fact, the outcome of man's social life and depend on social consciousness. However, these works were far from being a systematic materialistic interpretation.

The idea of broadening the representation of the fundamental forces of psychological development by interpreting the basic mechanisms of higher psychical functions, i.e., the nature and the internal structure of man's consciousness, as the product of social history became the basis for all of Vygotskii's creative work.

Vygotskii was one of the first Soviet writers to appreciate the importance of the problem of consciousness for a systematic materialist psychology. In one of his earlier papers (1925), he wrote, "By ignoring the problems of consciousness, psychology is shutting itself off from investigating any complex problem in human behavior, and this exclusion of consciousness from the sphere of scientific psychology perpetuates to a certain extent the dualism and spiritualism of the early subjective psychology." Very soon the problem of consciousness was to become the center of his psychological inquiries based on the postulate of a historical approach to man's mind.

The task facing Vygotskii required not only the refutation of behaviorism, but also of the old idealistic theory of consciousness viewed as a special self-contained world of purely subjective phenomena. It was necessary to find in life itself, in the conditions of man's being, the real factors that have created his consciousness.

At the beginning of 1927 Vygotskii was still endeavoring to arrive historically at the process of evolution of man's psyche and to formulate the initial points for his future investigations.

Man lives his life in the process of work. Work requires tools. Man's activity differs from animal's because it is always based on material and social mediation, and use of means. "In the sphere of psychological evolution," wrote Vygotskii, "the same breakthrough occurs at the instant of bringing a new tool into use as in the sphere of biological adaptation." For this reason, the evolution of man's psyche is conditioned not by the laws of biological evolution, but by the laws of historical development of society."

But what precisely is the "humanitization" of psychical processes, and how does the sociohistorical evolution of these processes take place?

Vygotskii's hypothesis, that underlies his later works, was that man's psychological processes change according to the processes of his practical activity; in other words, they too are aided by tools and means. The psychological activity of a man is radically different from that of an animal because man uses means and tools. A work tool itself, of course, does not belong to the psychological sphere and cannot enter the structure of psychological processes. Thus special "instruments of mental production" must exist. Man uses language and mathematical symbols and applies mnemotechnic aids for remembering. The first and foremost of these socio-selected tools is language, which, using Marx's expression, is man's "real consciousness."

This implies that man's consciousness is formed not by material production, but by the personal relationships and by the porducts of cultural development of society which arise out of this development. That is why Vygotskii originally called his psychological conception the *cultural-historical theory of the psyche*, contrasting it with the idealistic interpretation of mental processes viewed as intrinsic primordial properties of the spirit and with the naturalistic concepts that saw no difference between the behavior of an animal and the mental activity of man. This theory of evolution of mental processes has serious shortcomings, related to an insufficient regard for the formative role of man's practical activity in the evolution of his own consciousness. Thus it has counterposed too sharply the various forms of conscious activity of social origin with "naturally formed" mental processes. Yet it was an important step forward and it played its positive role in forming a materialist theory of man's mental activity.

In attempting to arrive at a breakdown of the forms of mental activity that arose in man's historical development, Vygotskii paid special attention to the role of the use of auxiliary means (and above all language) in social intercourse. All these means were regarded by Vygotskii not only as aids formed in the process of social evolution for relationship with reality, and not just as complex forms of reflection of the external world, but also as main means of mastering psychological processes that have a decisive influence on the forming of man's psychological activity. These means possess the singularly special trait inherent in them that they are always a reflection of something and they always mean something. A word which means nothing is not a word at all; a mathematical symbol which means nothing or a mnemotechnic mark which means nothing, is nonsense. Consequently, whatever helps the psychological processes, is always meaningful and it is a "sign." The term "sign" is also used by Vygotskii in the sense of "having significance," for it has a psychological meaning and not only a theoretical-cognitive significance.

By using auxiliary means and signs, such as, for instance, tying knots to remember or making a nick for that purpose, man produces changes in external things, but these changes later react back on his inner mental processes. In changing the medium, man is thereby able to master his own behavior and direct his own mental processes. That is why the motto to one of Vygotskii's books was the saying "*Natura parendo vincitur*" which he interpreted as "By mastering nature we also master ourselves," attaching to this Bacon's proposition" "*Nec manus nuda, nisi intellectus sibi permissus, multum valent: instrumentis et auxilibus res perticitur.*" [Neither bare hand, nor intellect by itself, are worth much: things get done with the aid of tools and means.]

Precisely this mediated indirect nature of psychological processes enables man to change his environment and thereby master his own behavior, and makes his behavior rational and free. The use of means creates a radical difference between conscious activity and more elementary forms of psychological life. This implies that psychological exploration of the consciousness should begin with a study of the laws of evolution of mediated mental processes. The theoretical significance of this approach in psychology Vygotskii saw as an opportunity, as it then seemed, to break away from the idea of consciousness as a self-contained or a special spiritual world. The prospects arose from acknowledging that consciousness, as a specifically human form of reflection, is created by external conditions outside the sphere of consciousness itself and by complex social forms of practical activity. A word, as also a "tally" (a notched stick), or a "tamga," or a Peruvian "quipu,"[2] is not intrinsic, only psychological. It arises in the process of conflict with nature, in the process of practical social activity, i.e., it is a fact of objective reality, independent of the individual consciousness of man.

The systematic investigations undertaken by Vygotskii and his colleagues suggested some general regularities related to the evolution of man's psyche. Firstly, specifically mediated human mental functions arise in the process of people's joint activity, in the process of cooperation and social intercourse, and they cannot arise otherwise. Any psychological means was originally created by one person for another person and only subsequently was used for mastering one's own psychical processes too. Thus the track mark is first made by the original explorer to point the road to others of his kin and only afterwards as an indication to himself; man's speech itself can arise, of course, only in the form of speech addressed to another person. Only later on, these forms of social communication are used by an individual to organize his own activity. According to Vygotskii, *a function, developed in interaction between two persons, becomes an intrinsic psychological function of one person.*

In this context we have to view the general law of evolution of the human psyche; the specifically human structure of mental processes starts in man's external activity and only later it can become internalized and become the structure of his inner processes. Thus, for instance, the processes of memory first changed their structure when man, wishing not to forget, used external marks; later man acquired the capacity to mark and remember mentally, "in the mind." The processes of direct memorizing now acquired the form, as a whole, of inner psychical processes.

This leads to further proposition of important significance for genetic analysis of the main forms of mental acitivity. A two-fold functional relationship exists between the constitution of the psychological processes and their interrelation one with another, viz. on the one hand this "cross-covariance" is the result of the emergence of new mediated structures; on the other hand, in the course of interplay between individual functions, it is necessary also for the functions themselves to realign.

Perception, attention and memory, for instance, experience this facet in their development.

Perception of the outer world is immediate in intent and strength. It becomes gradually strengthened by its previous visual experience entering into close relations with its memory, and then—as speech develops—begins to reflect reality with greater depth; perception rests on the basic functions of words—abstraction and mental association—and it then enters into the closest relation with the processes of thought. The emergence of such characteristics of human perception as its orthoscopicity or constancy, cannot be conceived aside from this complicated history of the evolution of the interrelationship between perception and all other aspects of psychological activity.

The development of memory follows the same path. In its initial stages it

---

[2] Knotted cords of different colors used by ancient Mexicans and Peruvians for conveying orders or recording events (Translator).

is closely related to the child's immediate requirements and actions; here it is in the nature of an emotional and pictorial memory; then it enters into relations with object-perception and becomes concrete and pictorial; finally, increasingly relying on words, memory assumes a mediated nature and becomes semantic; it is bound up with abstract thinking, and logical memory emerges.

The same can also be said of attention. In all these cases the development of mediated mental processes implies the development of new forms of inter-relationships between the mental processes, new forms of "interfunctional relations." New forms of activity of a child, related to new forms of rapport, and also the use of new means, become the important factor in forming a *system* of psychological functions.

Clearly, all these secondary and historically arising systemic relationships between psychological functions, as opposed to the primary and organic relationships which were created in the process of biological evolution, come entirely within the ambit of external factors by virtue of the fact that persons adopt objective socially evolved ways and means of acting. In this way the process of mediated mental functions necessarily leads to the formation of new relationships and interrelations; it is these interrelations which constitute the specificity of human consciousness. "Consciousness is not simply some 'plane' in which mental processes and phenomena take their course; consciousness," wrote Vygotskii, "has a *systemic structure*." It is characterized by the relationship and interrelation of the separate mental functions. The characteristics of these relationships, in turn, determine the characteristics of the separate mental processes. Consequently, in order to understand the special characteristics of any particular mental process, it is necessary to proceed from an analysis of the system of processes, i.e., from the structure of consciousness as a whole.

All these views had a fundamental significance for psychological science of that time. Their progressive significance consisted above all in that the earlier static notion of mental processes being once-for-all given and constant "mental functions" (sensation, perception, memory, attention) was contrasted with a rather more dynamical idea according to which these functions themselves arise in the process of children's mental development and then cross-covary in transition to increasingly complex forms of mental life.

The progessive significance of these views also consisted in that they posed the problem of investigating consciousness as that of studying the *forming* of the specific structure of the mental processes of man themselves. This removed the chief obstacle which for so long had prevented the building up a proper psychological conception of consciousness: on the one hand it removed the artificial seclusion of the consciousness problem as an altogether special problem intrinsically not associated with other psychological problems whilst on the other hand it eliminated the possiblity of an artificial and also unjustifiable substitution, viz. the investigating of mental functions separately in lieu of the investigation of consciousness.

Word and Significance

The theory of the systemic structure of consciousness was only a first stage in the development of Vygotskii's ideas. When the first experimental investigations into the development of aided mental functions were nearing completion, Vigotskii persistently pointed to the narrowness of the overall conception envisaged in them. Unlike those who were inclined to criticize the investigations as supposedly overcomplicating the issues, he saw their shortcoming in that they excessively schematized the representation of the human psyche.

The oversimplification and schematism of the psychological views which were being worked out experimentally at the time, Vygotskii attributed to the fact that they were concentrating on analyzing out the structure of processes and so they were losing sight of their meaning.

If one abstracts oneself from the meaning of the mental processes, one cannot unravel the process of emergence of the relationships which characterize the "systemicity" of the structure of consciousness.

A knot in a handkerchief does not help the process of recollection because of its inherent real properties. Only by acquiring a definite significance can it play its role in memory. Consequently, for a fact to be made psychological, it must receive significance and become the bearer of this significance.

Thus the next task was psychologically to investigate meaning and the origin of meaning, and then the laws governing the construing of meaning.

In its basic classic form significance was represented as a word. Naturally the investigations were first of all along these lines.

What then, psychologically speaking, is a word's significance? Reality is reflected in the significance of a word. Therefore the significance of a word is above all a reflection. But is it a special form of reflection. It is not a psychological fact of the same kind as, for instance, the fact of sensation. A word by its significance assists the process of direct sensory reflection of the world: a person sees not only something rectangular, white, and covered with lines; and not only some wholeness is seen, some whole image; the person sees a sheet of paper, or paper generically. This happens not simply because the person has gained previous experience in direct practical activity; it happens because his experience of objects was formed philologically as a corresponding significance—"paper"; persons who do not grasp the significance "paper" and who do not know what paper is, are in fact only gazing at something white, oblong, and so on. However, when they perceive paper, they perceive the *real* paper, and generally not the significance of "paper." Significance, as such, is not usually present in consciousness: in refracting and mentally associating the visible, the significance remains unseen itself.

The significance of a word is never exhausted by its assignment to a particular thing; the significance of a word—it is always so—is the known system of relationships and relations which is designated by it; it is an idealized mental form of crystallization of social experience and social practical activity of mankind. The full range of ideas of the community, its scientific studies, its language itself—all this is a system of significances. In developing the conditions of the community mankind masters the significances already evolved; therefore one's personal consciousness is *social* in nature. Mankind perceives and apprehends the world as a concretely historical creature; a man is equipped and thereby restricted by the ideas and concepts of his era and his class. So in belonging to the range of objective social phenomena, and to the manifestations of social consciousness, significance exists as a fact of personal consciousness, and so as a psychological fact.

How is it possible to investigate significance psychologically? One needs to appreciate all the difficulty of this question that Vygotskii faced at the time.

Any significance is a generalization. Consequently, significance is characterized, firstly, by the particular range of the phenomena to which it refers and the particular range of phenomena associated with it. But this still does not constitute a psychological characterization. The question as to what is objectively associated with the significance of a "triangle," is a question of geometry and not one of psychology. One may, indeed, pose this question in a slightly different manner. One may ask what is the particular significance *for me*; what I think, understand, and know about a triangle, may not coincide exactly with the scientific concept "triangle." This, however, is not a difference in principle. The one and the other are not opposed to each other, for significances generally do not have existence other than in real human heads. Consequently, one cannot set off the scientific significance against the safe significance in a man's consciousness as a "psychological" significance. But does not a scientific concept cease to be a concept as soon as it becomes a concept for me? Not unless a "concept for nobody" can exist.

One can approach significances also from another angle. One can set oneself the task of tracing the historical development and the changing of meaning of words in a language. But also this task, obviously, is outside the scope of psychology; it is a problem in linguistics. It seems as if psychology is left with the study of passing experiences of significance. However, as already shown by several psychological investigations, significances, as such, are as a rule not experienced at all; usually a person completely fails to realize the significance and is unaware of significance of a word, but comprehends what it is to be signified by a particular word. Only in special conditions can the significance itself become the object of his consciousness and of this thought.

It is easy to show what complication this fact produces in psychological investigation.

When I see something white, rectangular, and so on, and at the same time apprehend "this is paper," I naturally have in mind not my own sensations, not the experienced image of white or rectangular and not the association "paper," but the article itself which enters into the particular association. One therefore needs to distinguish between the two. The old psychology of thought did this by introducing, on the one hand, the concept of "content," which is interpreted as sensory content of consciousness, and on the other hand the concept of "object," meaning what is thought, "what's in mind."

However, the phenomena and processes which belong to the sensory "content" of consciousness, i.e. its sensory elements, do not determine and cannot characterize the comprehension of the object itself. "Whosoever would think to characterize comprehension and thought by observing the sensations and images which they contain, would be like someone endeavoring to capture the essence of money by studying only the substance from which it was made" wrote Messer. So it was generally agreed upon that the process of understanding of an object does not boil down to the sensations and sensory images which arise, but corresponds to understanding and significance, not at all to the sensory elements of the consciousness. On the other hand it is impossible to give a psychological characterization of significances and concepts themselves. "One can assert," wrote Marbe, another representative of the Würtzburg school, "that no psychological equivalent of a concept exists." Even in those cases when it was the concept which was made the object of study, actually it all the same continued to slip away from investigation. We have in mind the known investigation of N. Ach, another representative of the same school of psychology.

Ach has shown that the forming of a concept is not the result of an action of those laws which direct the course of sensory images, and so these laws cannot explain concepts. Formation of concept requires a special mental process. Ach tried to show that this process is determined by the *task* confronting the person to be tested. Thus the initial object of investigation appeared to be forfeited and, as a result, not the concept, nor the significance, received a psychological characterization, but the task.

From these conclusions, which had been reached in numerous previous works on the psychology of thought, it was essential in psychological investigation to achieve the principle of the unity of word and significance. It was the attempt of the psychologists of the Würtzburg school to discard the "shell" of the word and penetrate straight to the concept, to the significance, which had been decisive for the success of psychological investigation. A word is not a shell; a word does not at all point to the significance like the cloak of a friend recalls the person; a word is inseparable from its significance, and the significance is inseparable from the word. To study psychological significance means to study the function of the word and its use in social intercourse. Such were the first premises of the experimental investigations which Vygotskii began on the development of concepts. This line of investigation was prompted by Vygotskii's entire train of thought.

Significances differ from one another by the objective content which is associated with them. Particular general contents require different mental processes, i.e., different mental operations. Here, depending on the structure of the appropriate system of processes, the same objective content can be realized differently and also at different levels of generalization.

Thus, for example, for forming significance of the type "fluffy" or "rough," only the simple operations of isolation and then sensory association of the particular attributes are needed. It is a different matter with abstract significances of the type "aided" or "functional"; here, obviously, complex processes of logistic treatment of the respective contents reflected in these significances are involved.

So, to study the significance of a particular word, one needs to study the system of processes which in real life is called forth by the use of the word which is mediating the objective content that is reflected in its significance.

This approach has eradicated the false contradistinction of "objects" and "contents" of consciousness, and of "functions" and "phenomena" of consciousness.

The experiments of one of Vygotskii's pupils, L. S. Sakharov, continued later by Vygotskii himself, have discovered the function of words in the process of forming of concepts. This made Vygotskii's research directly opposite to the path followed by N. Ach. For Ach the main factor determining the course of the process was the task, the purpose engendering the "determining tendency." For Vygotskii, however, the chief problem was to study the mental processes themselves which lead to the forming of the generalization.

From experimental investigations, the various processes of "functionally using words" which result in association then taking place, can be very different.

In some cases these processes consist in singling out attributes on the basis of direct sensory impressions, in others they consist in unifying objects according to their participation in an actual situation (practical situational relationships); finally, they may consist in establishing correlations between different abstracted and generalized attributes (theoretical, logical relationships).

The data of this investigation disclosed different phases of development of concepts in children. It showed that in a child's process of development the type of relationships and correlations between things which the child can single out, essentially changes and this constitutes the typical level of the concepts within his reach. Vygotskii's description of the stages of development of generalization from directly sensory and syncretic to the practical and situational and then to the logistic and conceptual, is one of the many achievements of Soviet psychology which have produced a broad response in world psychological literature.

These investigations are equaly valuable in that they point to an important psychological fact: the change of structure of the generalizations which become manifest at successive stages of a child's mental development involves a change in the mental processes (mental operations) whereby these generalizations take place. The dominating role of direct emotional impression in the first phase, the leading role of direct practical experience and memory in the second, and then the decisive role of words in the third phase of development of concepts point to different psychological processes in each phase of a child's generalizing activity. Thus, a psychologist who studies the successive changes of forms of reflection, should also study the successive changes of the psychological processes whereby this reflection goes on.

It is this which gave Vygotskii the reason to say that the study of the development of concepts leads psychologists to a rather broader aim—to the study of what he called the *semantic structure of consciousness*.

The procedure which Vygotskii employed in his investigation has been subjected more than once to a valid criticism that pointed out that the development of concepts was investigated in conditions divorced from the child's practical activity and the influence of education, and so the procedure produces only successive "media" of development. Nevertheless, Vygotskii's investigation of the development of concepts has made a major contribution to the experimental study of thought and so enabled to work out the abovementioned and other challenging issues.

Motivation and Consciousness

Human consciousness is a product of evolution of man in society; it is the product of his social life. Consciousness reflects activity, and not only of directly sensory elements. Consciousness always is the consciousness of a thinking person. Sensory impressions, restricted to the narrow limits of personal experience, do not form human consciousness. These are only its source. Consciousness is the reflection of reality refracted through general human experience and reflected in language. Consciousness is reflected more deeply and more fully in the significance of words and in thought than in direct sensations, for in it is crystallized not only the infinitesimal experience of the individual person, but also the boundless experience of generations, in the experience of all humanity.

Man perceives his environment in all its colors, in its wealth of shape and sound. He feels its resistance, its virile and violent forces, but man comprehends his environment in the relationships and the relations opened in him by the practical experience of humanity, and in the real properties of this world, i.e., as significances.

Significances are mastered in the process of mastering speech and words, the bearers of significances. Speech is not a correlate of thought alone; speech is a correlate of all consciousness. By mastering significances in the process of using words, man reflects in his consciousness objective relationships and regularities of the external world of objects and subordinates his behavior to them. Man's behavior becomes rational. To man, who lives in a society, the significances of his own actions are open; they are comprehended in their necessity and in their objective social results. Hence man's behavior acquires traits of spontaneity and volition. But man masters not only external behavior, he also comprehends the processes of his own thinking. His thinking becomes controllable.

In his inner world man finds an individual special circle of deep and frequently vague personal experiences. In comprehending them, he recognizes in them manifestations of human senses, passions, and compunctions, generalized and objectivized in language and in the productions of art. He enters into a cognitional relation to these personal experiences and he comprehends them. Not only man's reason, but also his emotional life becomes intelligible.

The assertion of wisdom and freedom of man, the heritage of immeasurable cultural wealth, accumulated from the experience of generations over thousands of years, is the kernel of Vygotskii's teaching on consciousness.

It remains, however, to consider the main question: the question of motivation in the development of consciousness.

A child relates himself to the world in a practical way. In the course of his development does the child begin to apprehend the world. How does this process take place?

The child is not alone in the world; in his development he does not follow and, of course, cannot follow the paths of evolution of human existence. Just as he finds the material conditions of human existence, he also finds capabilities that perfect him for society, representations generalized in language and in science—in the system of semantic significances. A child does not generalize the phenomena of the environment as a single solitary being. This is impossible. Were it so, the development of a child's consciousness would take place infinitely slowly, where in fact it is completed with striking rapidity. Just a few years is enough for the comprehension of the most complicated relations; it has taken humanity thousands of years to comprehend these relations and a milliard times of practice. Only extreme separation from the study of the actual process of development of a child's mind can explain the possible naive pedagogic assertion that the process of development of a child's consciousness and the process of evolution of human consciousness are fundamentally the same processes and that in both cases the same laws govern the transition from inability to ability.[3] On the contrary, the first task in studying the development of a child's consciousness is precisely that of understanding this process in its own right, thus finding the actual forces motivating it and not those that are supposed to do so.

A child does not really fill in by himself the "content" of words, for their significance is still unknown to him. He assimilates, as it were, ready-made meanings of words—significances fixed in the social usage of language. On the other hand, a word which a child meets with, cannot "grow" in significance on its own accord; words are not the demiurge of significance. Therefore the process whereby significances evolve is not reducible to the process of a child's mastering the reality which is associated with the words, nor is it reducible to the process of independent assimilation of words themselves—bearers of particular significances.

What then in that case is this process specifically?

Words as mental associations and then as means of communication become entities not by chance, but of necessity. Man enters into relationship with his environment only through other people, i.e., in social intercourse. It is in the conditions of such interrlationship that the system of significances has been created. Generalization and social intercourse are inherently inter-related processes. Vocal communication is impossible without generalization: "Any word (speech) is a generalization" (Lenin). Therefore it is in the process of social intercourse that one needs to look for the actual conditions of evolution of significances.

The very first steps in the development of a child's consciousness are already related to his evolving vocal communication. The necessity for a child to master speech is rooted in his own mode of life, in his dependent state, depending on the actions of the people about him. Even before he is one year old he begins to understand what adults say to him; when he is two, he begins to talk; in imitating the people about him in describing objects, the child singles them out from the visual and chance relationships in which they are sensorially presented to him; they become unified in his consciousness in a name-word according to their more material attributes, according to deeper relationships and relations; cognitional vocal associations are formed in the child's mind.

Word designations, however, are in general an "extraordinary act of comprehension" which does not depend on anything further. It is the natural result of the adult introducing the child into actual reality, not forsaking the child, not leaving it to the mercy of circumstances, but wisely guiding him, familiarizing him with the manifestations of reality and, contrary to Rousseau's pedagogical claim, trying to forestall its unfortunate "experiments."

In other words, the child grasps significances because the adult is instrumental in forming the child's attitudes and his everyday relationships with the world.

At first the child comes across words in their direct relevance to various objects or manifestations. The first significances are unstable and diffuse. Diaries of the development of children in their first 2–3 years are full of such descriptions : these early significances in general are not alike the philological

---

[3] Vygotskii was opposed to the biogenetic theory of recapitulation (Ed.).

significances of adult language. When a child first begins to make active use of a word, it appears to have a different significance for the child than for us.

It is therefore necessary to distinguish, on one hand, the "actual" significance, i.e., the meaning which the word actually has for the child, and on the other hand the significance of the same word at the highest stage of its development, i.e., its "ideal" significance, which more or less approximates to the language of adults. According to Vygotskii, a word can be "ideal" in the sense that it is rather more developed, or because it represents, as it were, the point towards which the actual significance of the child is gradually approximating and so, at the same time it is the yardstick that measures the level of child's development. Thus, in the process of vocal communication between a a child and an adult, "actual" and "ideal" significances meet up and interact.

How is such interaction possible? How can the mutual understanding between child and adult develop, when one and the same word has a different significance at their different levels? This is possible because for all the difference of meanings there is a real intersection between them due to the identity of that objective and "concrete" object to which the particular word-meaning is related in the process of communication between the child and the adult. Consequently, that which connects together the significances and so makes vocal communication possible, is that objective reality itself, which precisely because it exists independently of consciousness, identically influences by its properties both the child and the adult, although it is associated and apprehended by them slightly differently.

One may say that the child *learns* significances, i.e., he grasps significances in the process of intercourse with adults. But this is only a necessary condition for the development of consciousness; the rapport itself demands the presence of actual interaction between the child and his environment; such a rapport is impossible without that interaction. "At first there was a deed"—this formula retained for Vygotskii all the fullness of the thought expressed in it.

The situation, however, changes as soon as we come to the problem of teaching at school and the theory of education was the last link in Vygotskii's work, and so therefore it has a final word here.

It is meaningless to speak of education as the result of any intercourse or practice which teaches a child something. Education must be the particular systematic process which is most typically represented by the teaching of children at school.

School education is qualitatively different from education in the broad sense. At school the child is faced with a particular task: to grasp the bases of scientific studies, i.e., a system of scientific conceptions.

In the process of school education the child starts off from what have become his own complex generalizations and significances; but he does not so much proceed from them, as proceed onto a new path together with them, onto the path of intellectual analysis, comparison, unification, and establishment of logical relations. He reasons, following the explanations given to him and then reproducing new, for him, logical operations of transition from one generalization to other generalizations. The early concepts that have been built in the child in the process of living and which were assisted by rapport with his social environment (Vygotskii called them "everyday" or "spontaneous" concepts, spontaneous in the sense that they are formed aside from any process specially aimed at mastering them), are now switched to a new process, to a new specially cognitive relationship to the world, and so in this process the child's concepts are transformed and their structure changes. In the development of a child's consciousness the grasping of the bases of a science-system of concepts now takes the lead.

According to Vygotskii, this change is of decisive importance; the transition which is completed in the process of grasping the science-system of concepts is also a transition to a different structure of consciousness on a higher level. Not only does the environment now appear quite different to the child, but all the system of his relations, all his behavior and all his mental activity also change. At this stage great changes also take place in the development of the child's personality and his awareness of himself. However, all that is acquired by the child in this period while the development of his cognitive relationship to reality is particularly noticeable, was prepared in his early stages of development. So the dictum "At first there was a *deed*" now comes to be read by Vygotskii with a logical new emphasis: "At *first* there was a deed."

We have been speaking of school education: but beyond this Vygotskii saw the overall pattern of the development of consciousness. Of course, neither school education itself, nor education in its broad sense alone, attunes the original motive of development. This role of teaching must itself be based on something; something must determine it. Even a child who for one or another reason did not go to school, enters, albeit differently, upon fundamentally the same path of development and then passes on through the same higher phase. This is a result of the course of development of consciousness itself and of its intrinsic logic. The transition to the higher and properly intelligent type of structure of significances is impossible otherwise than with a changed relation to the cognizable world; the higher phase of the structure of significances is not attainable in the process of development of mental associations which goes on alone from necessity due to practical experience. School education is only the concretely historical form in which the transition to this higher phase of consciousness is accomplished. In a child who has remained away from school, cognitive and ideal interests arise in the course of development of his everyday relations, for these interests arise from his perception of the world of human ideas and abilities. A child does not remain indifferent to the thoughts and ideas of the people whom he comes across in life; he listens to them, discusses them, and ponders on them. He assumes an attitude to the socially determined ideas and concepts that reflect the real life that he already knows or that has just become known to him for the first time. He learns; he himself does not try to guess the relationships and relations of reality that are concealed from him (no human being could do this independently!), and so he tries to find out what is known about them to mankind; he now becomes confronted with the problem not only of the world, but also that of *Weltanschauung*.

In the light of these considerations the general conclusion which gradually emerges has to be reinterpreted. Vygotskii's logical reemphasis in the words of Goethe no longer seemed to him sufficient. So the last sentence immediately after them on the last page of Vygotskii's book *Thought and Speech*, once again changes their meaning: "The word crowns the effort."

Should one interpret this latter conclusion of Vygotskii's to mean that speech, vocal communication and in general the theoretical relation to reality, which had previously only seemed to be prerequisite of the development of consciousness, determine consciousness? And, conversely, that the practical everyday relations, which at first seemed to determine consciousness, turn out in the end to be only a general prerequisite for its development?

The study of the actual process of formation of a child's consciousness proves that the scope for grasping significances is not confined to the framework within which the child's practical relationship to his physical environment develops. In discussing this idea Vygotskii well remembered a child who had lain paralyzed from early childhood but who nevertheless had rapidly developed intellectually. The sphere of a child's vocal and mental grasp is usually in fact much wider than the sphere of his practical activity and sensorial experience, this disparity becoming especially great at school age—in the decisive phase of development of consciousness. One cannot shut one's eyes to this obvious fact. Yet if we accept it, one also has to accept that whatever is of major importance for the development of individual consciousness, is introduced into it through social consciousness. Do people really, in fact, create their own views in the course of their life? No, they are introduced into their consciousness. They, then, determine how in the last analysis people perceive the world about them and their own being in this world. One has to acknowledge this.

The logic of the investigation and the logic of the investigator do not directly coincide with one another in all phases of development. In Vygotskii's last works the noncoincident is especially clear and so this testifies to the fact that his investigation as a whole is unfinished.

Throughout his scientific career in psychology Vygotskii resolutely stood out precisely *against* the attempt to conceive the development of a child's individual consciousness as the direct product of the influence of social consciousness. This was the central proposition of J. Piaget's criticism of him.

Dozens of times on the pages of his works Vygotskii returned to the thought that psychology is the science of the individual and the higher form of life on which man's material life rests. "Life opens up beyond consciousness,"—this was Vygotskii's main guiding principle.

Vygotskii followed the logic of the investigation itself, endeavouring to subordinate his own theoretical tendencies to it and not at all imposing the investigation from above and so avoiding to explain the unknown by what is still less known.

The contradiction between his general purpose—to conceive consciousness as the product of interaction of man with the world around him—and the particular postulates which derived from his investigation of the development of a child's concepts, was to Vygotskii a contradition which should find its own resolution at the next stage which he already visualized. This contradiction remained in Vygotskii's works; it is even to be seen in his book *Thinking and Speech* published posthumously. The divorce of consciousness from the real life of personality, as also "intellectualistic" comprehension of consciousness itself, was to the result of incomplete elaboration of one aspect of his theory. Vygotskii saw this incompleteness in the abstraction from the problem of the relations between affect and intellect. Thus, at the very beginning of his book and also at its very end Vygotskii posed this problem with great incisiveness: "The divorce of the intellectual side of our consciousness from its volitional side is one of the fundamental defects of all traditional psychology," Vygotskii wrote. "Reason is unavoidably converted into an autonomous flow of cogitative thoughts, it has lost touch with all the fullness of animate life."

"Thought is not the highest instance. Thought itself is not born from another thought, but from the motivating sphere of our consciousness, which embraces our inclinations and needs, our interests and compunctions, our passions and emotions. Beyond reason there is an affective emotional and volitional tendency. Only it can give the answer to the last 'why' in the analysis of thought."

Vygotskii failed to develop these last propositions formulated by him. We only know that he related the problem of emotion in to the overall problem of psychological analysis of significance as a "unit of consciousness."

Socio-Cultural Determinants

The key question which arises in connection with these latter ideas of Vygotskii's, is whether the intended line of thought leads to the resolution of the stated contradiction and to the possibility of a gradual reaching of a view of consciousness as the product of man's life in the society, and thus as a reflection of his actual being?

Of course, affective manifestations, such as emotions, feelings, and attitudes, are generated by the processes which effectuate the interaction of man with reality, and so they directly express the biological sense of these processes. For this reason the study of emotions was seen by Vygotskii as the way to question whether the consciousness is determined by the conditions and evolution of man's life. But here a new and as yet hardly surmountable difficulty arises. Affective processes in turn depend on how their causes are perceived by man's mind, i.e., they depend upon the system of significances that form consciousness. Thus also in this line of thought there is the danger of psychological investigation reentering some "circle of consciousness." It is therefore impossible not to notice that, even the most complicated psychological problem investigated by Vygotskii remained incompletely elaborated. It is also impossible not to see that Vykotskii's investigations considerably advanced the theoretical study of consciousness in leaving far behind everything that had been done in this direction in older psychology. This is why we think that any psychological inquiry must become aware of its past history and the path upon which it traveled.

A quarter of a century has passed since Vygotskii's works were written. During this time in Soviet psychology, as also in all Soviet science, the greatest changes have taken place; many psychological questions have been further developed and the general theoretical level of the investigations has been sharply raised.

All this applies to the general concept of mental evolution. Though proceeding from the standpoint that the specific characteristics of man's psyche are determined by the conditions of the social life and that the development of consciousness is based on man's practical relations toward reality, Vygotskii at the same time rightly rejects simplified attempts to infer man's consciousness directly from his practical activity. But in his own psychological theory of consciousness, he illegitimately deduced the purely cognitive relationship of man to the world from man's practical activities and relations. This then found its expression in the thesis that the unit of personal consciousness is significance, the purely cognitional formation, is a product of culture. He overlooked a most important factor, i.e., that the assimilation of socially elaborated ideas, concepts and beliefs and the role they acquire in man's activity depend on what the objective conditions and sensorial content of his life, of his actual being. Man is not indifferent to the ideas and conceptions which the environment introduces into his consciousness. Some, although he may apprehend them, remain only externally perceived and so they do not acquire effective meaning; some other ideas are grasped by him with special force and play an active and effective role in his life. All this does not depend simply on man's intellectual possibilities, but on the soil onto which these humanly perceivable ideas and conceptions fall, and which is also created in his practical experience of life. It is the latter, i.e., life experience, in the broad meaning of this phrase, which is decisive.

Another important theoretical contradiction which was left unresolved in Vygotskii's works consists in the incorrect comparison as it were, of two spheres of mental processes in man, "natural" processes versus social processes.

Such, for instance, is the contrasting of "natural" memory with memory through "culture." This contradiction is less justified, for in the investigations of Vygotskii and of his pupils, there is the general idea of elementary processes realigning in the course of development into a more complicated system which results in the higher specifically human psychical functions.

Finally, the psychological terminology used by Vygotskii is under-elaborated and invites criticism. Many of his terms need clarification. Such, for instance, is the terminology which Vygotskii uses for his characterization of concepts at different stages of their development ("syncret" "complex," "preconception," and others). These terms, largely taken from other psychological schools, have an essentially different meaning in his work; they express the characteristics of the mental operations which bring children to generalization, and thus characterize the structure of a child's concept formation. Thus, for instance, Vygotskii's view that genuine concepts take shape in children at relatively late stages of their development, does not at all signify that children of earlier age groups generally do not have concepts. It is merely being said that only when they are older do the mental processes of children acquire the fully developed logical operations peculiar to theoretical thinking, and that this in turn is expressed in a more complicated structure of the generalizations which are formed as a result of these operations.

The many other terms must also be explained in which Vygotskii expresses his own concept of education and mental development of children. We have already come across the qualified meaning which he imparts to the terms "spontaneous" and "everyday" in reference to the concepts acquired by a child, albeit in the process of social relations with adults, aside from specifically teaching activity. The same applies also to the substance of other concepts, like, for instance, the concept of "cooperation," as used for designating the process of a child fulfilling a task with the aid of an adult.

Vygotskii and Pavlov

A special question is Vygotskii's relation to Pavlov's physiological teaching and his contribution towards a deterministic analysis of the mechanism of higher psychological processes.

Even in his early works Vygotskii has expressed the thought that psychology cannot successfully develop without the firm physiological base which it received in the physiological teaching of I. P. Pavlov. Reflex responses to stimulations from reality always were to Vygotskii the fundamental processes characterizing the general physiological mechanism of mental activity. That is why, as rightly pointed out in the published literature, Vygotskii, ahead of many other psychologists, turned to Pavlov's teaching.

The question arises, however, if Pavlov's reflex teaching gives the physiological basis to psychology, does this mean that all the multiformity of man's mental life can be reduced to those relatively simply physiological phenomena which Pavlov observed in studying the conditioned-reflex processes in animals? Can man's consciousness be reduced to conditioned-reflex acts?

It is generally known that whereas mechanistically minded investigators openly agreed with this standpoint, the psychologist-idealists, who stood for the "isolation of psychology," replied to this question in the negative. In man's consciousness, which they continued to regard as some primordial, inherent, subjective state of our spiritual life and as primary self-awareness, some elements remained that are not reducible to reflex processes; consciousness was always synonymous with a special inner spiritual world which natural-science investigation should not touch. Pavlov pointed this out too, mentioning that in the approach of many psychologists animism still remains; certainly this is inconsistent with genuine science.

Vygotskii's reply to the question was quite different. Though he never became attached to the animistic-idealistic approach to consciousness, or to the purely subjective inner world, inaccessible to scientific analysis, Vygotskii did not agree either with the mechanistic claims that the mechanisms of conditioned-reflex acts explain everything, even the most complex forms of activity of consciousness.

There is no doubt, he often said, that the reflex process is the most universal manifestation in the working of the brain. The conditioned reflex, as studied on animals by Pavlov, is a necessary factor in behavior of any kind. But does this mean that the laws established for this factor can exhaustively explain the concrete mechanisms of the most complex forms of human activity?

No doubts are ever roused by the fact that water consists of two particles of hydrogen and one particle of oxygen. But, by knowing the properties of these elements, can one find out the actual properties of water?

Here evolves the line of thought which leads Vygotskii to the distinction between two basic concepts—the concept of an "element" and the concept of a "unit" and which has for him a great fundamental theoretical-cognitive significance.

Science has to break down the objects of reality into its constituent parts;

every branch of science must be analytical in order to construct out of the products of this analysis that synthetic system which corresponds to the actuality under investigation. But must we always reduce our analysis to the most elementary particles? This depends on the problem under investigation and on precisely which relationships and relations we are trying to disclose.

Desiring to find elements of behavior which enter into any form of activity and the laws by which they are governed, one must break down the behavior and study the laws of the simplest conditioned nerve relationships. But these laws, which equally apply to elementary skills as to the most complicated volitional acts, to eye movements in inspecting an object and to the complex processes of writing and reading,—can they tell anything more than that to say that these forms of reality are of a different kind? The concept "means" and "methods," and in general the various forms of mediated activity, were not accidentally introduced into the physiology of higher nervous activity which makes up the mechanisms of the most basic forms of behavior and so in the same measure are peculiar to animals as well as to man. Only in later years did Pavlov arrive at the "second signal system"—that "extraordinary appendage" which "introduces a new principle of neural activity—the principle of segregation coupled with association of innumerable signals," which is what "specifically human thinking" is.

But how is one to approach the analysis of these specific characteristics of human activity without losing sight of their specificity, without replacing the operation of concrete analysis by another logical operation, the elucidation of the most general and universal laws of reflex activity, and at the same time without descending into an idealistical separation of consciousness from its neuroreflexologic mechanisms?

Vygotskii saw the resolution of this issue in analysis of the manifestations to be studied, not into simplest elements, but into specific units for this manifestation, and in reducing this analysis to the particles which in their most simple form preserve their attributes and so distinguish the particular phenomenon.

Such "analysis into units" is typical of every branch of science. A physicist who is studying the properties of liquids, will not decompose a droplet of water into its constituent elements of hydrogen and oxygen, but studies the H_2O molecule and then its properties, which vanish upon further decomposition.

Ought a psychologist to proceed otherwise than to set for himself the task of studying the specific properties of the most complex forms of activity of consciousness?

It is known that it can only be on the basis of the brain's conditioned-reflex activity that consciousness can arise and so consciousness does not go beyond those mechanisms which are studied in the physiology of higher nervous processes. However, it is known also that conscious activity arises only in social interaction, and in the use of tools and language, which acts as the main means of social intercourse, that qualitatively modify these reflex processes and create special conditions for the historical forming of that higher complicated form of reflection of reality, the consciousness. It is natural that a psychologist who sets himself the task of studying these the most complicated forms of reality should not confine himself to mere repetition, and, in analyzing these phenomena, to indicating those elementary mechanisms which are peculiar to all behavior—including also the more simple forms. He should find the most simple combinations of systems of these reflex processes which have arisen in the community's historical process and so which conserve all the characteristic features and properties of the most complicated forms of activity. In other words, he must also here follow the path of analyzing the most complicated phenomena into characteristic units, without forgetting that they can be decomposed into still simpler elements. The psychologist must be also aware of the fact that by allowing any further "analysis into elements," he may lose the specificity of the phenomenon being studied by him, and at the same time the specificity of his own branch of science.

That is why Vygotskii considered "analysis into units" to be the main road for scientific psychology. That is why even in the early stages of his work he tried to outline the theoretical tasks and then to follow this path in his own experimental research.

Simple "volitional effort" can change nothing in a psychological process; to think that a direct "effort of will" can make substantial changes in our behavior is indicative of a fundamental error leads to indeterministic thinking. Only by a reflex action directed to the external environment and then by submitting to the changes which have been caused in the external medium by our action, can we convert these reflex responses into a mechanism for mastering our own behavior. The two reflexes—the response to the newly changed medium—constitute together a single functional system—a system of a mediated act which acquires traits of spontaneity.

By tying knots in a handkerchief we introduce changes into the external medium; in perceiving this knot and returning in this way to the ideas which it should represent, we mediate the process of remembering and so master our own memory. By performing a certain act, such as placing a note in front of oneself and then submitting to the conditions of this changed medium, we begin—with the assistance of such aids—to direct our own attention. By reproducing a system of verbal relationships, assimilated by us earlier in the process of social intercourse, we can submit to their influence and then pass on to complex forms of spontaneous and conscious behavior.

In all these cases conditioned-reflex relationships are the foundation of the complex forms of activity; these relationships form a definite system in which the final link of the first reflex, as it were, returns to the subject and leads to new and correspondingly changed reflexes appearing. That is why Vygotskii says that his experiments on mediated types of activity were carried out by the "double stimulation method" which reflects the essential features of the phenomenon being studied. Like the distinguishing basic "units" (of psychological investigation) which he saw becoming a self-regulating system of reflexes leading to the mastery of one's own behavior with the assistance of known means, so also the adoption of "doublestimulation," which was expected to be an adequate method of studying these most simple units of "higher psychical functions," is the great credit of Vygotskii who resolutely repudiated both the mechanistic disregard for the specificity of human consciousness, and also the idealistic view of consciousness as a subjective condition inaccessible for objective study.

In one of his early articles devoted to the problem of consciousness,[4] Vygotskii tried to develop his idea of the reflex nature of consciousness in its most general and at the same time most intelligible form.

"The most elementary and also the fundamental and universal law of the reflex relationship," he wrote, "can be formulated so: reflexes are inter-related according to the laws of conditioned reflexes, the response of one reflex (motor or secretor) here being able to become under appropriate conditions the stimulus (or inhibitor) of the other reflex and re-entering along the sensorial path of associated peripheral stimuli into the reflex arc with a new reflex. . . ." Academician Pavlov called this mechanism a chain reflex and used it to explain instincts. "However," Vygotskii continues "if one pays attention, not to one system of reflexes, but to several different systems, and then to the possibility of transference from one system to the other, it is this which in the main will be mechanism of consciousness in its objective significance."

Later Vygotskii more than once returned to these propositions which he had put forward at the beginning of his career, viz. that psychological study of the higher forms of human behavior must proceed from an analysis into specifically human "units" representing complex functional systems which vary as psychical activity develops and become disturbed during pathological states of the brain—these always remained central to Vygotskii's psychological Weltanschauung.

Neurophysiological Factors

His study of the systemic structure of consciousness, which occupied the central position in Vygotskii's psychological concepts, did not drive him into describing psychological phenomena; the phenomenological approach to the manifestations of psychical life and rejection of the causal explanation of psychical processes and their formation and decay, were foreign to Vygotskii and were at variance with his psychological views.

That is why, having begun his work with analyzing the actual conditions of a child's reality and then finding the main factors in a child's development to be its rapport with adults and the use of external means which change the medium and so regulate its behavior, Vygotskii attempted to conceive complex forms of psychical activity in terms of a material substrate of the psyche, the brain, and then to study the basic forms of brain activity which would enable his systemic structure of psychological processes to be made more intelligible. For this purpose Vygotskii had already in the first stages of his work intensively analyzed how mental processes are disturbed during cerebral affections, and then continued to study these conditions throughout his life. In this respect Vygotskii can be regarded as one of the founders of the new branch of psychological science, the neuropsychology.

[4] L. S. Vygotskii, *Consciousness as a problem in behavioral psychology* (Soznaniye kak problema psikhologii povedeniya). In *Psychology and Marxism*, 1925.

Even in the first years Vygotskii turned to an analysis of how mental activity is disturbed at the time of affection of individual brain structures, and then in what ways the defects arising in these cases can be compensated.

In the first stages of his neuropsychological investigations Vygotskii's attention was attracted to those changes in behavior which became manifest in affection of the subcortical ganglions—in patients with Parkinson's disease —which was particularly prevalent in the neurological clinic in those years. It is generally known that affection of the subcortical motor ganglions, which leaves the cerebral cortex relatively intact, leads to gross disturbances of voluntary motion and a patient, though clearly realizing what he intends to do, quickly gets into a state of constraint which makes movement impossible; it is known also that voluntary effort produces no notable effect in these cases and a patient who meets with obstacles in his way soon abandons any attempt to master his own movements.

It was these observations which Vygotskii to an idea which at the time could not help but be strikingly bold. "Is it impossible," he asked, "to compensate these defects by the same method of aiding behavior as appeared as productive in comprehending the forming of a child's higher mental functions, and then going beyond the limits of "natural" forms of brain work, to organize its activity by relying on external means?"

The experiment which Vygotskii proposed for the purpose was exceptionally simple. Noting that a patient with Parkinson's disease, who is unable to take one step across a smooth floor, goes upstairs well, moving slowly across each step and thereby compensating the disturbed subcortical automatisms by conserved reactions of the cortex, Vygotskii suggested that a patient should himself introduce into the external medium additional stimuli which would have the reverse effect upon him and, in a mediated way, regulate his behavior. This experiment produced significant results. When Vygotskii suggested that the patient throw paper cards onto the floor and then step across each of them, he could be sure that by creating new additional stimuli in the external medium and then submitting to them, the patient could without difficulty walk across the floor performing in a mediate way the task which he was incapable of doing directly.[5]

These observations of Parkinson's disease presented themselves to Vygotskii as having a fundamental significance. In place of the naturalistic approach to the work of the brain, a new approach was coming about which used new "extracerebral" factors to regulate brain activity: the use of external means, "signs," which had evolved in man's social history, appeared to be a new and very real form of organization for behavior itself and for forming new functional systems to reconstruct the work of a sick brain, and then, with the assistance of new ways of organizing cortical processes, to compensate an existing defect. One can therefore with complete justification state that this experiment, carried out as long ago as the 1920s, even though not leading to a permanent therapeutic effect, has had great and fundamental significance; it has linked the new scientific psychology with neurology and so showed the impossibility of the conventional naturalistic approach to the analysis of the

[5] These experiments, carried out later by one of the present writers, have been described in detail elsewhere. See A. R. Luria, *The Nature of Human Conflicts*. New York: (Liveright), 1932.

activity of the brain. Vygotskii's study has been almost the first model of these "feedback" systems which have enabled new possibilities of the brain as a self-regulating system to be elucidated on the basis of that new branch of neuropsychology (the theory of adjusting functional systems that have been disturbed by local affection of the brain) which only many years later found its own application in the practice of restoring disturbed functions of the brain.

Having dwelt at the beginning of his work on analyzing those cases of local impairment of the brain when the intact cortex can compensate the defect by a functional system of external means, Vygotskii soon came to a thorough study of the functions of the cortex itself and then to an analysis of its specifically human forms of organization.

The ideas then prevailing of a narrow localization, which came into conflict with the ideas of the work of the "brain as a whole," and also the proposition of "equipotentiality" of its parts, equally could not satisfy Vygotskii. Knowing the decisive significance of speech, not only as the main means of communication but also as the instrument of a generalized reflection of reality as well well as the basis of complex functional systems and "higher psychological functions," Vygotskii had to reassess the role played by the speech zones in the system of cortical activity. This idea brought him to the study of aphasia and of those specific changes in the structure of mental processes to which affection of the speech zones of the cerebral cortex leads. Vygotskii's investigations into the problem of aphasia were cut short by his premature death before the bulk of them were completed. However, these investigations show clearly the exceptionally productive pathway which his neuropsychological works had laid.

Proceeding from the role which speech plays in building up higher mental processes in normal development, Vygotskii focused his special interests not so much on those disturbances of the processes of abstract thinking which arise in the presence of known forms of aphasia, as on the secondary systemic influence which disturbance of speech has on such processes as interpretative perception, voluntary attention, logical memory, and discriminatory and directional behavior.

These investigations, which included a wide comparative analysis of cases of affection of individual parts of the cerebral cortex at different stages of physical development of children and adults, led Vygotskii to new representations concerning the functional organization of the cerebral cortex and also the localization of psychical functions. These ideas for many years determined the lines of development of neuropsychology and it is hard to overestimate their scientific value.

The first of these representations, formulated by Vygotskii in the later years of his life, was that of the systemic structure of higher cortical processes.

If man's vocal activity enables him to isolate essential attributes in the field of perception and ensures a selective, interpretative, and mobile kind of perception, it becomes quite clear that the processes of optical (as also acoustic or tactile) perception are effectuated with the closest participation of the speech zones, and also that the ageing of the latter inevitably reflects on the course of cognitive processes. If, conversely, the vocal activity itself, related to abstraction and association of the signals reaching the person, is formed on the basis of sensorial reflections of reality, it becomes obvious that the vocal processes are also formed with the closest participation of the sensory (or gnostic) departments of the cortex and so can materially suffer by their impairment. These facts brought Vygotskii to the conclusion that each specific "function" is not related to the work of some particular isolated "center," but is the product of the entire *functional system* of jointly operating zones, each of them connected into a functional system with their own special roles, and then, introducing their own specific, contribution into the structure of the system. Therefore the affection of parts of the cerebral cortex must inevitably cause disturbance of the functional system as a whole and can lead to disturbance of the whole complex set of higher psychical functions. A lesion of the various parts of the brain cause different types of systemic disturbances and leads to different secondary (or systemic) afflictions. The central problem for neuropsychology becomes therefore not the "dropout" of individual mental functions, caused by this or some other focal lesion of the brain, but the change of the "inter-center" relations and systemic relationships due to a local cerebral lesion.[6]

Of almost still greater value is another of Vygotskii's views, formulated by him not long before his death.

If in the process of forming higher mental functions, the main interfunctional relations change, and so sensory perception or direct memorizing, having at first been fundamental for vocal thought, at a certain stage of mental development the sensory perception falls under the influence of complex forms of vocal activity, then it is clear that this cannot be a matter of indifference for analysis of those "inter-center" relations which actually occur in the cerebral cortex.

The theory of functional organization of cortical activity and localization of functions in the cerebral cortex must be based on the historical theory of higher psychical functions and be refracted through the prism of the theory of their development, and only then does this approach reveal new possibilities in the assessment of the actual corelation between the zones of the cerebral cortex and the place which each occupies in the organization of mental activity.

The usefulness of this view comes out clearly in comparative analysis of the changes of mental processes which arise if the same focus of lesion arises at different stages of a child's mental development.

It is well known that lesion of the occipital parts of the cerebral cortex in a grown adult leads to comparatively limited disturbances of visual perception, not affecting vocal processes or intellectual activity; these latter at a mature age appear to be so well formed that they can even take part in compensation of cognitive defects.

It is quite different if a similarly localized lesion of the occipital parts of the brain occurs at an early age in children. At this stage of speech and intellectual development, the focal lesion of the brain invariably destroys the sensory basis for the development of the semantics of speech and fullvalued vocal thought. That is why, so Vygotskii thought, cases of optical

---

[6] This systemic approach to the working of the brain was only outlined by L. S. Vygotskii and it was then developed by his pupils. See A. R. Luria *Higher cortical functions of man and their disturbance with local lesions of the brain.* Moscow, 1962.

agnosis at an early age had not as yet been described: children with a focal lesion of the occipital cortex invariably do not develop, and a local lesion which causes only a limited defect in a mature adult, leads to massive mental retardation in children.

The comparative-genetic approach to the localization of functions in the cerebral cortex enabled Vygotskii to formulate the fundamental law of neuropsychology which one may with qualifications call the law of chronogenic localization of functions, the value of which is still insufficiently valued: the systemic influence of a focal lesion of the brain is different in direction at different stages of mental development: with local lesion of an adult's brain the "lowest" center functionally dependent on it suffers mostly systemically, but with local lesion of the brain of a young infant the highest center formed on its base suffers mostly systemically.

Undoubtedly the ideas of this scientist whose life was cut short prematurely, were way ahead of his time and they will still have considerable influence on neuropsychology.

By showing how much one's ideas about the basic methods of the working of the brain, the material substrate of the psyche, depend on the right concept regarding the structure and development of mental processes, Vygotskii opened new vistas in this new branch of knowledge.

Developmental Psychology

Our survey of the value of Vygotskii's work would be incomplete if we did not dwell on a further topic which occupies a special place in his creative work.

Since oldest times psychology has sought to be recognized as a branch of science not confined to abstract study of the laws of mental processes, but as a province of knowledge with great practical everyday value. Stemming from the observations of doctors of ancient and mediaeval times and also pedagogic thinkers, psychology studied the laws of mental life in order to help cure sickness, educate man, and to give scientific bases to the teaching of children. The leading representatives of psychological thought not only did not digress from these tasks, they always regarded them as their major preoccupation.

However, having fallen under the influence of philosophy which divorced mental phenomena from the life of the body, psychology was inevitably separated from its practical application and has lost its practical everyday value.

That is why the different branches of applied psychology, educational psychology, medical psychology, and industrial psychology, not having the necessary soil in the general theory of mental life, inevitably had to go beyond academic psychology and create as their own basis a system of special concepts formulated afresh each time. Therefore the different branches of applied psychology were in fact without a scientific basis, and this lack of a scientific foundation inevitably brought these branches into a most grave crisis.

It was necessary to change profoundly the whole basis of psychological science and the comprehension of the essence of mental processes, in order that everyday practice of psychology should receive its own scientific justification. The works of L. S. Vygotskii did much for this task.

Rejecting right from the start the metaphysical notion of the psyche as a sum total of isolated and constant "mental functions," Vygotskii at an early stage of his investigations defined psychology as the science of mental life. This signified that in the process of development different forms of life super-cede each other and then in its higher stages life assumes a special form which is the nature of a conscious mental life related to a most complex type of reflection of reality and aided by rapport with other people at work and by vocal communication. The idea of an ontogenetic evolution of mental life was closely related by Vygotskii to the idea of children's relationship to reality. The helplessness of the infant who is physically separated from his mother but remains dependent on her biologically, his initial rapport with adults at the time when his mental life emerges, the early practical experiences that become consecutively "object" actions, games, and studies, all this became the basic material for the theory of mental development. Vygotskii gave his creative years to the formation of this theory.

Vygotskii's studies led to a radical revision of the ideas about the psyche prevalent at the time, and to the replacement of the subjectively idealistic concepts of mental phenomena by objectively determined concepts and then by basic materialistic ideas about man's mental life and its development.

By including the child's "object" activity and his rapport with adults amongst the motive forces of development, by ascribing to them the value of factors which form the child's mental life, Vygotskii decisively broke away from the idea of spontaneous maturing of mental abilities and the idea that environment merely retards or assists the manifestation of intrinsic mental properties. He revealed the fallacy of the metaphysical concepts of spontaneous mental development and then contrasted the new materialistic views on the forming of a child's mental life with the widespread views of such contemporaries of his as W. Stern regarding the spontaneous development of a child's psychical processes in which 1½-year-olds make "the most important discovery in their life—the discovery that words have significance," and of J. Piaget who regarded children's mental development as the displacement of intrinsic forms of psychical life inherent in the "child itself" by new social forms of behavior.

Vygotskii's idea that all complex forms of a child's mental life are formed in the process of social intercourse, and that a function, earlier divided between the two persons, later becomes an intrinsic mental function of the child, and finally the view that the most important factor in mental development is assimilation of the experience of humanity as a whole, all this became the starting point for resolving such important issues the relation between education and development, which Vygotskii proposed in a number of his papers, and brought him to a revision of the fundamental propositions in the practical application of psychology to infants and to education.

At the time when these works of Vygotskii's appeared (in the early 1930s) many psychologists held to the firm belief that only the maturing of a child's mental processes ensures success in further education. Teaching waits upon development; this was the practical implication of the theory.

Vygotskii decisively revised this concept. If all the development of a child's mental life takes place in the process of social intercourse, this implies that this intercourse and its most systematized form, the teaching process, forms the development of the child, creates new mental formations, and develops higher processes of mental life. Teaching, which sometimes seems to wait upon development, is in actual fact its decisive motive force. Only the forms of teaching change in the course of development, and so, by analyzing the processes of mental development at the preschool and school ages, Vygotskii established the typical forms of teaching peculiar to each of these age groups. In saying that teaching forms mental development, that the assimilation of knowledge does not leave the structure of the mental processes unchanged but creates new and special forms of voluntary and cognitive activity, Vygotskii comes right up to a new materialistic comprehension of mental development which had not previously been expressed in psychology so clearly. The assimilation of general human experience in the teaching process is the most important specifically human form of mental development in ontogenesis. This deeply significant proposition defines an essentially new approach to the most important theoretical problem of psychology, the challenge of actively developing the mind. It is in this that the main significance of this aspect of Vygotskii's enquiries lies.

It is easy to see that this new idea of mental development has yet another important aspect.

The analysis of the relations between teaching and development which are typical of different stages of mental life enables one to arrive at a scientific delineation of pedagogic influences related to preschool and school education. Vygotskii's analysis of the wealth of relevant material gives an incontestable credit to him. It is particularly in these works, starting with his early publication *Pedagogic Psychology* (1926), that education obtains much valuable material for concretization of its didactic positions. A special importance has been attached to the psychological features of teaching at the pre-school age, and also to "sensitive periods of teaching." Vygotskii raised the question of rational use of the initial teaching time and of assimilation of scientific and everyday concepts at school age.

The new concepts of mental development proposed by Vygotskii have, however, an additional value which goes far beyond the problems of teaching. We are talking of psychological methods of assessing the mental development of normal and abnormal children.

Writers who have regarded children's psychological development as spontaneous, proceeded from this also in elaborating procedures for identifying different disturbances of mental development and assessment of possibilities of the child's development. "Psychometric tests" were created and widely used in many countries. The fate of the child is often decided on their basis.

Such practices of psychology, having a false theoretical foundation, led this field of knowledge into a blind alley and have met with a profound theoretical critique in Vygotskii's works.

As Vygotskii points out, the fact that a child does solve a problem presented to him, does not tell anything else about this child's psychological possibilities. In some cases the child's inability to solve the problem is actually the result of defects in mental development and a sign of mental deficiency, but in other cases it is the result of the child having insufficient knowledge and know-how that prevents the child from finding the necessary solution independently. Does this imply that both children are "imperfect" in the same measure and the mental development of both children will be defective?

Vygotskii answers this question categorically in the negative.

Mental development, he says, goes on in the process of interaction between the child and adult, in the process of teaching. In this process new forms of mental life and new abilities are formed. For this reason, what a child cannot do by himself, he can do with an adult's assistance, and it is this which determines the child's further development: what the child can do today with assistance, tomorrow he may be able to do independently.

This view led to a radical change in psychological methods of assessing children's mental development. Hence Vygotskii's idea of the "area of next development" opened up quite new possibilities in this important field of applied psychology.

Proceeding from the foregoing representation concerning the essence of children's mental development, Vygotskii proposed a new method of investigating the characteristics of children's mental activity. He proposed to reject assessing children's mental development according to an index of the degree of success in solving independently a problem which is presented to him. Unlike what is usually done, Vygotskii introduced a procedure for assessing development from the ratio of two indices: (1) how the child solves the problem independently and then (2) how he solves the same problem with an adult's assistance. The divergence between these two indices (and by no means not the absolute valuation of success in independent solution of problems) is, according to Vygotskii's way of thinking, an index of the "area of its next development," and, consequently, it is an important component part of the general assessment of a child's potentialities.

If a child appears to be in no state to solve some problem (within the capabilities of other children in the particular age group) either independently, or with assistance; and if he cannot avail himself of the adult's assistance and, after "coaching," cannot apply it in independent solution of the problem, there are many grounds for speaking of a genuine defect in the child's mental development and then raising the question of the child's possible mental retardation. But if a child who cannot solve a particular problem independently, appears, however, to be in a state to solve it with adult assistance and assimilates the experience which it gains and applies it in independent solution of similar problems, the investigator has no grounds for a low assessment of the child's mental possibilities, and he has every ground to say that this child will in the future display good speed in the development of mental activity.

The idea of an "area of next development" and the proposals for studying it enabled Vygotskii to introduce a dynamic principle into the study of children's mental development. This enabled him to solve another most important problem, namely, to produce scientific bases for a rational pedagogic influence on children. By realizing what operations a child can perform with an adult and, consequently, what potentialities are in its "area of next development," the teacher may not only foresee his pupil's further mental growth, but also influence this growth rationally and control its development on scientific bases. It is easy to see in these views the beginning of many productive inquiries which will enable a scientifically proven theory of teaching to be arrived at, i.e., the psychological bases of control of children's mental development.

Vygotskii's constant endeavour to introduce change into applied fields of psychology ran through all his work, and not only in the foregoing cited works, and he did succeed in introducing changes in a number of branches of applied psychology. His work on the principles of defect compensation and also the teaching of [deaf-and-dumb children,] on the fundamentals of pathopsychological investigations with an assessment of primary defects and the secondary (systemic) defects arising from them, and his research into most important problems of "logopaedia" and neural and psychiatric treatment, have left a deep impression in these fields.

Vygotskii demanded that psychology become more than a scientific study of education and go beyond abstract theoretical knowledge and intervene in human life and actively help in shaping it. Psychology, he said, must cast off indifference and become "partial" (not impartial); it must not bypass either the great ethical problems of personal life, or the little day-to-day problems. A psychologist cannot but be a thinker, but he has to be a practitioner too. "I am for practicing psychologists," Vygotskii wrote, "for practical work, and so in the broad sense for boldness and the advance of our branch of science into life."

Such are the main psychological views of L. S. Vygotskii—an outstanding Soviet psychologist whose brief but brilliant work has since largely determined the lines of psychological science in the Soviet Union.

INDEX

Absorption (*Vertiefung*), 41
Abstraction, 155, 156; defined, 13
Acquaintance, Principle of, 250–251, 261
Act-object relationship, 248, 252, 257–260, 262
Action: interested and disinterested, 187–188; regulation of, 182, 186, 193; source of, 198, 309; strength of, 184; voluntary, 95, 186–187, 309
  See also Movement
Action acceptor, 141
Activity: feeling of, 280; mediated, 358, 360
  See also Mental activity
Acts: mediated, 358; mental, 243, 248, 252, 254
Adaptation, 83, 93, 108, 185, 216
  See also Conditioned reflex
Adaptive response 50
Amnesia, 169, 179, 181, 183
Analytical psychology, 101–104, 108
Animal psychology, 47–69; beginning, 50–52; contemporary research, 52–58; future, 68–69; general works on, 57–58; primates in, 62–67
  See also Comparative psychology
Animals: early reference to behavior of, 48–52; exeprimental, *see* Comparative psychology; monads in, 231; the Person of, 329
Anthropology, 237–238
Anthropomorphism, 211, 213
Anticipation, 292
Anxiety, 180, 181, 185
Apperception, 280–283, 287; attention in, 40; defined, 37, 43, 231, 318, 319; experiments, 284; locus of, 281, 296; stages, 40, 41; unity, 238, 310
Apperceptive masses, 37, 280
Appetites, 39
Appetition, 231
Applied psychology: start, 322; of Vygotskii, 338–367
Apprehension, 316, 317, 319; implicit, 314, 316, 318
Aristotle, 3, 48, 197, 200, 259–260, 276, 291
Arithmetic, association in, 23–24
Arousal, degree of, 25
Assimilation, 304–306, 318, 364
Association, 301, 308, 309, 316, 317, 330; absorption stage of, 41; in apperception,

Association, (*continued*)
280, 282; classification, 15; degrees and frequency, 25; free, 169–174; laws of, 232, 308; limitations, 316–317; role, 299, 302; sensation-movement, 82; suggestion as, 22
Associationism, 11–26, 31, 37, 81, 95, 123–124, 232–233, 300–302, defined, 11; Kant's influence on, 240; reflex theory, 101–103, 107
Associationists, 11–26, 29–44, 108; words as, 350
Associations, 280; in the dynamic sterotype, 146; interiorization of, 108; words as, 350
Atomism, 197, 300–301
Attention, 40, 137, 186–187, 280, 283, 285, 287, 303–304, 307–308, 318, 344; conation as, 309; as consciousness, 304; defined, 37, 314, 315, 319; feeling of, 281; fluctuation of, 117; on reaction time, 285; role of, 304; types, 40
Audition, 327; insect studies, 54
Automatism, 185, 195, 360; psychological, 179, 189–190
Awareness, 87, 88, 242, 243, 300, 327; forms of, 303; objects of, 303; of presentations, 304

Bacteria, psychology of, 56
Bain, Alexander, 25–27, 298–299
Behavior: conflicting, 148; control of, 238; as a datum, 57; defined, 111–113, 339; early reference to animal, 48–52; evolution of, 50–52, 112; heredity on, 55–56, 62; insect, 54; Janet's psychology of, 185–186; marks of, 112–113; maturation of, 62; meaning of, 49; predeterminism, 88; prenatal, 53, 61–62; psychosomatic nature of, 209; rational, 342, 349, 358; species-specific, 59, 62; tropistic, 56–57
Behavior patterns: gathering objects, 184, 191–192; genetic development of, 191–194
Behaviorism, 109, 186, 189, 311; purposive, 58, 111–129
Belief, 182, 187, 192–193; assertive, 192; defined, 188
Bewusstsein, 35, 37, 42, 242–243
Biogenetic law, 51–52
Biography, on history, 7–8